Contemporary Japanese Film

Contemporary Japanese Film

by Mark Schilling

Weatherhill
Boston & London

To Donald Richie, for making it all possible.

Weatherhill
An imprint of Shambhala Publications, Inc.
Horticultural Hall
300 Massachusetts Avenue
Boston, Massachusetts 02115
www.shambhala.com

Printed in the United States of America

⊗This edition is printed on acid-free paper that meets the American National Standards Institute Z39.48 Standard.

♻Shambhala Publications makes every effort to print on recycled paper. For more information please visit us at www.shambhala.com.

Distributed in the United States by Random House, Inc., and in Canada by Random House of Canada Ltd

Book and cover design by Noble & Israel Design

Library of Congress Cataloging-in-Publication Data available.

Contents

Preface

The first question I should answer is "why?" It is the question I hear most often from new acquaintances, foreign or Japanese, when I tell them I review Japanese films and write about the Japanese film industry. "Why Japanese films?" they want to know, the implication being, why bother? Weren't most of the best ones made decades ago? Isn't the Japanese film industry trundling down the slope to oblivion?

This attitude has a basis in certain unpleasant facts. In 1960 the Japanese film industry released 547 films—an all-time peak. In 1998 it released only 249. In that same period, its share of the local market declined from seventy-eight percent to thirty percent. Also, no director working today equals Yasujiro Ozu, Akira Kurosawa, or Kenji Mizoguchi as a universally acknowledged master. Takeshi Kitano may have won the Golden Lion prize at the 1997 Venice Film Festival for *Hana-Bi* (Fireworks)—an accolade that propelled him into the directorial front ranks—but his films have yet to surpass *Tokyo Monogatari* (Tokyo Story) or *Shichinin no Samurai* (Seven Samurai) on critics' all-time best ten lists. (Given the conservatism of these lists, perhaps they never will, but that's another essay.)

While containing a kernel of truth, the view that Japanese films have long since seen their best days can also be a cover for ignorance. Many classics of Japanese cinema are commercially available on subtitled videocassettes and discs, while many newer films are not, which means that, for most foreign-film scholars, critics, and fans, they simply don't exist. Overseas distribution of new Japanese films has improved in the past decade, with more film festival screenings and theatrical releases, but few foreign film-goers, even those who travel the festival circuit or live in major cities, see more than a small fraction of the total output. This is not to say that there are dozens of modern masterpieces out there waiting to be discovered, only that many recent Japanese films deserve more international attention than they are getting.

Thus my interest in Japanese films when the *Japan Times*—Japan's leading English-language daily newspaper—offered me a regular reviewing job in 1989. There wasn't a lot I could say about *Jurassic Park* that hadn't been said a hundred times before, but I could be among the first to write in English about Rokuro Mochizuki, Takashi Ishii, Takashi Miike, Jun Ichikawa or other Japanese directors doing excellent, if not always appreciated, work. Given the circulation and readership of the *Japan Times*, I couldn't do much to bring their films to the attention of the outside world, but I could do something—and that gave me reason enough to continue.

At the same time, I never considered myself a cheerleader for the Japanese film industry. My first obligation was to the newpaper's readers, not the directors or producers or PR flacks. If a director was a charming fellow who gave a terrific interview, but his latest film was a botch, then I had to say so. This may seem obvious, but among writers on Japanese films, too often it is not.

The second question I should answer is what, if anything, has changed in the ten years since I started. Structurally, the industry of 1999 resembles that of 1989. Three major distributors with their own exhibition chains—Toho, Toei and Shochiku—still dominate the industry mainstream, while independents still face an uphill struggle to get their films financed and released. Also, the majors are still largely run by graying executives who react to trends rather than set them, and prefer the tried-and-true to the new. Looking at their schedules for 1989 and 1999, one sees the same holiday animation for the kiddies, the period films for the oldsters. The directors and even the stars of the latter are often of the same generation as the executives giving the greenlight.

Yet cracks have appeared in once-impregnable industry facades. At the beginning of the decade, the majors were still block-booking their domestic films the way they had for years, while allowing their exhibition infrastructure to deteriorate. Despite the occasional renovation or construction of a downtown theater complex, the number of theaters continued to decline as more theater owners in the provinces shut their doors. The downward drift, said industry wise men, was all but inevitable. The mass audience might leave the blue tube for the *pachinko* parlor, but seldom for the movie palace. Meanwhile, In the competition for a shrinking pie, Hollywood was just too strong. How, the wise men asked, could even bigger-budgeted Japanese films compete head-to-head with Hollywood stars and effects? Better to play the demographic edges, where the local product still had an advantage. Godzilla and Tora-san forever!

By 1999, however, the multiplex building boom launched in the early 1990s by foreign-backed operators had not only stopped the slide in screens and admissions, but was transforming the moviegoing experience for millions of Japanese. Instead of trekking hours to antiquated downtown theaters, residents of suburbs and provincial cities now had a choice of eight or nine screens in one nearby location, with all the American-style comforts and high-tech trimmings.

Unfortunately for domestic filmmakers, the advent of the multiplex did not result in an increase in market share. In 1989 Japanese films claimed a 46.6 percent share of the market. By 1998, this figure had fallen to 30.2 percent. Though one may argue that *Titanic* was mostly responsible for the plunge in 1998—it smashed the all-time earnings record that year with sixteen billion yen in film rentals—the general trend was nonetheless downward.

Hit by a string of box office disappointments, Shochiku and Toei fell ever farther behind leader Toho during the decade, with Shochiku bringing up the rear. In 1989 Shochiku and its subsidiary Shochiku-Fuji accounted for four of the eight domestic films that earned one billion yen or more in film rentals, with Toho and Toei splitting the remaining four. In 1998 Toho distributed seven of the nine Japanese films that topped the one-billion-yen mark, while Toei claimed the rest. Shochiku, on the other hand, had not a one-billion-yen film since the last installment of its signature Tora-san series, in 1996.

Meanwhile, the majors were filling more of their lineups with films from outside producers. Shochiku tried to reverse this trend in 1997 with its Cinema Japanesque project for producing and distributing low-budget films, but quickly retrenched when the first Cinema Japanesque slate failed at the box office.

To improve its fortunes, Shochiku restructured its operations, beginning in January with the ouster of a father-and-son top management team. In March 1999 the company announced that it would no longer block-book domestic films in its theater chain. Toei and Toho did not follow Shochiku's lead, but by the end of the decade the block-booking system looked more likely to crumble that recover.

Despite the various troubles of the major distributors, the number of domestic releases grew over the course of the decade, from 255 in 1989 to 278 in 1998. One reason was the still strong demand for product from the video industry. In 1998 national video-shop sales rose 6.8 percent to ¥409.5 billion, with much shelf space given over to new domestic animation and action titles.

Another was the stubborn vitality, against all odds, of the independent film sector. In the first half of the decade the most active of the indie film companies was Argo Project, a consortium of six independent producers that, with the backing of beverage-maker Suntory, tried to break the near-monopoly of the majors on exhibition and distribution by producing and screening its own films in two theaters, one in Tokyo and one in Osaka. Although enjoying several critical and commercial successes, beginning with Shun Nakahara's award-winning ensemble drama *Sakura no Sono* (The Cherry Orchard) in 1990, Argo Project was handicapped by an unfavorable rental contract for its theater in the Shinjuku district of Tokyo that made it hard to turn a profit on all but the most popular films.

With the red ink in its distribution and exhibition business mounting, Argo changed its name to Argo Pictures in April 1993 and shifted its focus to film development and production, while linking with other companies to gain wider distribution for its films. Hits, however, were hard to come by and the red ink did not recede. In January 1995, after screening fifty-four films in four-and-a-half years, the Shinjuku theater closed its doors and, later that year, Argo suspended feature-film production.

Despite Argo's failure, a growing number of mini-theaters began screening independent Japanese films during the decade, and several mini-theater operators, including Tokyo's Theater Shinjuku and Eurospace, started investing in film production. Also, the rise of new-media venues, including cable and satellite channels, created more demand for independent films. One prominent investor was the Wowow satellite station, which financed the J Movie Wars series of low-budget shorts and feature films beginning in 1992, and underwrote the 1998 launch of Suncent CinemaWorks, the stand-alone production unit of J Movie Wars producer Takenori Sento.

In addition to these new trends in the business of making and distributing films, audience tastes shifted over the course of the decade. Traditional genre films, such as samurai swashbucklers and *yakuza* action pictures, declined in popularity, while formula series, which had once accounted for a high proportion of commercial product, dwindled in number. Even the few survivors, such the *Tsuri Baka Nisshi* (Free And Easy) series, tended to find more success in video shops or on television than in the theaters.

While the mainstream was growing ever more sclerotic, young directors from the worlds of advertising, television and music videos were bringing a new vitality to Japanese films, though they weren't always welcomed by the industry establishment.

Among them were Shunji Iwai, whose work was informed by everything from girls' comics to MTV, and Hirokazu Koreeda, a TV documentarian whose films used documentary methods to explore central humanistic concerns, including the role of memory and the meaning of death. Many younger filmmakers followed Iwai and Koreeda in moving toward a more contemporary and personal cinema. A series of films featuring young rebels and others on the social margins poured forth from under-forty directors, while relatively few chose to explore Japan's past or issues affecting the larger society.

One corollary to this trend was the fascination, among older and younger directors alike, with Asians and other minorities. Although some of the films based on the theme of the alien other were straight exploitation vehicles designed to jerk tears or stir outrage, many filmmakers took a more nuanced and balanced perspective—and in the process made some of the more noteworthy films of the decade.

Ironically, during this period advancement to the upper echelons of the film industry by women, gays, and other members of formerly excluded groups was spotty and slow. Several younger women directors made their feature debuts, including Naomi Sento with the 1997 Cannes Camera d'Or winner *Moe no Suzaku* (Suzaku) but their impact was small. Also, gay-themed films by openly gay directors enjoyed a brief vogue in the early 1990s, but, once the vogue ended, the gay presence in films again became marginal.

Several directors from ethnic minorities had success with films set in their communities, most notably ethnic Korean Yoichi Sai with the 1993 hit comedy *Tsuki wa Dotchi ni Deteiru* (All Under the Moon) but Sai had little interest in further exploiting his background. Likewise, younger Okinawan directors made several films about Okinawan life in early years of the decade, but a distinct Okinawan cinema was slow to emerge.

Even so, this injection of new blood and new influences has had a significant impact on the direction of Japanese cinema. Even Yoji Yamada, that most mainstream, if populist, of directors, introduced minority characters into his films, while animator Hayao Miyazaki took his heroes for *Mononoke Hime* (Princess Mononoke)—an eco-fable set in medieval Japan that became the most popular Japanese film of all time—from members of marginalized groups, including aborigines, prostitutes, and lepers.

Meanwhile, young indie filmmakers have been moving to the center of the industry. One is Hideo Nakata, who made his debut with a film for Wowow's J Movie War series, but went on to direct *Ring* (1998) and *Ring 2* (1999), linked psycho-horror films that hit with audiences both in Japan and abroad. Another is Katsuyuki Motohiro, a TV director who made the jump to feature filmmaking with *Odoru Daisosasen* (Bayside Shakedown) a comic police drama that became the highest-earning Japanese film of 1998.

Also, instead of adapting to mainstream filmmaking conventions, these younger directors have imported innovations from other media. *Odoru Daisosasen* may be television writ large, with plenty of tube-ready mugging and Hollywood-inspired pastiche, but it also has a visual excitement and narrative drive that lifts it above the common run of commercial cinema.

The third question, I suppose, is whether the Japanese film industry has any future. Given the current dire situation of the other Asian film industries, notably Hong Kong's, why should Japan's fate be any different? Despite various downward trends, my feeling is that in ten years Japanese movies will still be very much around, just as Japanese television programs and pop music will still be around.

Japan is a highly sophisticated, largely inward-looking society with a large population and an oversized appetite for entertainment. For all their surface Westernization, Japanese audiences usually prefer most of that entertainment to be Japanese. Kids here would rather see familiar animated faces in the theater than the latest Disney, while older folks would rather watch samurai swashbucklers than British costume dramas. Little of that is going to change.

The core young adult audience, however, likes the way Hollywood puts all those dollars on the screen in the form of effects and explosions. They are also lured by the glamour of the Hollywood product. There is no real local equivalent to Leonardo DiCaprio. But they are also willing to turn out for Japanese films that possess the Hollywood qualities they find attractive, while addressing purely local concerns, as the success of *Odoru Daisosasen* so abundantly proved. If the young filmmakers coming into the industry from outside can make more such films—and there little reason to believe they can't—the audience will be there. Also, even if the Masayuki Suos and Takeshi Kitanos are poached by Hollywood, there will be more to take their place. The talent pool here is broader, if not necessarily much deeper, than Hong Kong's.

The fourth and last question might be why I wrote and organized this book the way I did. Nearly all books about Japanese films, or Asian films for that matter, are written by either scholars or enthusiasts. As a working film journalist and a reviewer for an English-language newspaper, I am properly neither. Instead of graduate students or Miyazaki animation fans, I write mainly for industry professionals and general readers with an interest in film. The book is intended principally for this wider readership—thus the use of Western order for Japanese names, thus the exclusion of most jargon, academic or otherwise.

I have included as many of my *Japan Times* reviews as possible, knowing that many of the films are not yet available abroad. Why bother? In the hope that I might be able to open up the pipeline—still far too narrow—by which news of Japanese films reach the West. Someone may read these reviews, realize that Jun Ichikawa is a criminally neglected director, and organize a retrospective for him at a major festival. I have other dreams, but let this one serve as an example.

In the review section I have indicated my favorites of the decade with a star. The range is wide, from world-renowned festival winners to obscure video titles, from high art to genre entertainment. Some are in the syllabi of every course on Japanese film, while others languish in obscurity. I hope that with this book I can rescue a few of the latter.

I would like to thank Yoshie Yamaguchi of the *Japan Times* and the late Oscar Moore of *Screen International*, who first gave me the chance to write about Japanese films. I also thank Donald Richie, whose words of encouragement and advice have been a much-appreciated support over the years, and my editors at Weatherhill, Jeff Hunter and David Noble, who have been unfailingly patient and professional with a writer who is at times neither. Finally, I would like thank my wife, Yuko, for putting up with the long hours I have devoted to this project—hours I might have otherwise spent watching movies.

Notes on Nomenclature

I have tried, as much as possible, to make this book accessible to readers with a limited knowledge of Japan and the Japanese film industry. In rendering the titles of Japanese films and other genres such as TV shows and popular songs, I have left the many English words sprinkled about in them in their English spellings: thus *Perfect Blue*, not

Paafekuto Buruu. Translations of titles normally follow the Japanese title, except when the title is an English loanword, such as *Love Letter,* or a Japanese name (personal or geographic). When there is an "official" English title (given by the filmmaker or distributor) I have used it, even if it doen not reflect the Japanese title very accurately; otherwise, titles are translated literally. Japanese words that may not be familiar to Western readers are set in italic. Japanese personal names are given in the Western order, i.e., given name first, followed by the family name.

The following terms may unfamiliar, but I have used them frequently for the sake of both concision and accuracy, and so offer definitions here:

Film rentals Instead of box office gross (the total amount the public pays exhibitors to see a given film), the text makes frequent reference to film rentals, which are the share of the film's box-office earnings the exhibitor pays to the distributor. This is the preferred measure of box-office success in Japan, normally roughly equivalent to half the film's gross.

Manga Usually translated as "Japanese comic books," *manga* are far more various in content than comic books in the West, appealing to everyone from tots to middle-aged businessmen. They are quite different stylistically as well, relying more on cinematic scene-setting and atmospherics.

Anime A Janglish rendering of "animation," *anime* has also become a distinctly different popular art form in Japan. They tend to have a narrower range of themes than *manga,* with SF or fantasy predominating, and are aimed at a narrower audience segment, mainly teenage and young adult males. Accordingly, sex and violence in all their variegated forms are far more common than in mainstream Western animation.

Salaryman Often translated as "businessman" or "white-collar office worker," the salaryman has become, in the popular mind, an Everyman who regards his company as a surrogate family (or samurai clan) that he must serve loyally, while knowing that his job is the closest capitalism will ever come to a lifetime sinecure.

OL A Janglish abbreviation for "office lady," the OL is often defined as a "female office clerk." In addition to the usual clerical chores, young OLs at many companies clean desks, make tea, and otherwise serve as handmaidens to their male superiors. In recent years, however, popular representations of OLs have tended to depict them as assertive and even sassy with their male colleagues, using their youth and sex to compensate for their lack of power.

Otaku Often translated as "geek," an *otaku* is commonly viewed as a seriously obsessed, socially inept expert on subjects that mainstream culture considers trivial or obscure, from the history of sumo wrestling to the films of Yuzo Kayama.

Yakuza Japanese gangsters, with a real-life tradition that stretches well back into Japan's premodern past, and a tradition on stage and then screen that has been just as durable. *Yakuza* movies have been as prominent and popular a genre category in Japan as Mafia movies have been in Hollywood.

Essays

Mainstream JAPANESE FILM

Japanese go to the movies an average of once a year and, to hear many of them tell it, they rarely, if ever, devote that annual visit to a Japanese film. If they have recently bought a ticket to a domestic movie, they often have little good to say about it. Japanese films, goes a common refrain, are boring, silly, trite, just plain bad.

In more than two decades of listening to Japanese moviegoers complain about Japanese movies, I have often wondered how the domestic film industry has managed to survive so long, given that so many people claim to loathe its products and prefer the foreign competition, especially Hollywood. Surely the number of Japanese films released annually should, except for animation aimed at schoolchildren, be approaching the vanishing point?

Production levels have indeed fallen, from a high of 547 domestic films in 1960 to 249 in 1998, of which 65 were released by the three major domestic distributors: Toho, Shochiku, and Toei. But throughout the 1990s, the percentage of distribution revenues accounted for by Japanese films has hovered at about the one-third mark, reaching as high as 41.5 percent in 1997. (In 1998, however, with the recording-smash run of *Titanic* boosting foreign-film market share, it dropped to 30.2 percent.)

This one-third figure may represent a decline from the mid-1980s, when domestic films still accounted for half the total box office, but it is still higher than that claimed by local filmmakers in almost every other developed country. (The glaring exception, of course, is the United States, where the market share of subtitled foreign films is less than one percent.) In 1993, when the box office share held by Japanese films fell to a then all-time low of 35.8 percent, the share claimed by domestic films in Britain was 8 percent, in Germany, 7 percent, and in France, where a system of government and industry subsidies supports local production, 33 percent. Also, in this *annus horribilis* for Japanese films, five of the top ten box-office hits were Japanese. Not a bad showing for an industry whose products are apparently held in such universal contempt. Has my anecdotal sampling of Japanese filmgoers' preferences been skewed toward fans of foreign films? Or were my respondents simply not telling the truth?

The common complaint that "Japanese movies are no good" may well come from the heart, but it usually refers to the titles handled by the Big Three distributors—Toho, Shochiku, and Toei—not the dozens of independent films released every year, which often surpass the Big Three releases in quality, but seldom come to the attention of the average moviegoer. As bad as many of the Big Three's films often are, they get far more publicity, far wider releases, and account for all the domestic films in the box-office top ten, year after year, decade after decade.

The mass audience for Japanese films has long resembled an hourglass, with filmgoers under twenty and over forty occupying the ends. Thus the strange skewing, to Western eyes at least, of the Big Three's lineups, which seem to consistent largely of animation for the kiddies, idol movies for young teens, and period dramas and other cinematic strolls down memory lane for the old folks. Those who are in between—i.e., much of the core movie audience in Japan—thus often find themselves left out, or diappointed when they leave the theater.

Core Genres Decline

The Big Three have adapted this strategy out of self-defense or, alternatively, desperation. They once made a broader range of films, for a broader audience, but much of that audience—and the genre products that attracted it—have since migrated to television and video. Period dramas (*jidaigeki*) featuring sword-wielding samurai moved en masse to the small screen in the 1960s; gangster movies (*yakuza eiga*) to the video racks in the 1980s.

The studios did not abandon their core genres easily, but by the 1990s success was becoming ever more elusive. The only *yakuza* series to become a hit during the decade was Toei's *Gokudo no Onnatachi* (Gang Wives), starring Shima Iwashita and Rina Katase. Based on a best-selling book by freelance journalist Shoko Ieda, who spent more than a year living with the wives of *yakuza* gangsters and had close encounters with an ongoing gang war, the series began in 1986 and was into its tenth installment by 1997, when Iwashita decided to bow out.

Rather than slavishly obey the whims of their macho mates, the women of the *Gokudo* series, beginning with the redoubtable Iwashita, were often assertive types not adverse to shedding blood. Toei, however, did not consider the *Gokudo* films as really belonging to the *yakuza* genre. ("It's all a fantasy," Toei president Tan Takaiwa once told me. "There are no real women *yakuza*.") In 1994 Toei announced that it was making its "last *yakuza* movie," *Don o Totta Otoko* (The Man Who Killed the Don), featuring *yakuza*-movie veteran Hiroki Matsukata, adding the proviso that if the film earned more than four hundred million yen in rentals it would reconsider its decision. But instead of falling for this transparent PR ploy and pouring into the theaters to see this tired recycling of genre clichés, *yakuza* fans stayed in their six-mat rooms with their VCRs, and Toei temporarily abandoned a genre that had been its mainstay for nearly three decades.

Subsidiary Toei Video, however, was still releasing made-for-video *yakuza* films that found favor among fans, including the *Shuraba ga Yuku* (The Carnage Comes) series. In 1997, Toei attempted another theatrical revival of the genre with *Gendai Ninkyo Den*

(A Tale of Modern Chivalry), a film directed by Michio Furuhata and starring Eiji Okada that reworked classic *yakuza* film conventions, including the hero's ultimate one-against-all battle with rival gangsters, but only demonstrated why those conventions don't work anymore.

Toei tried yet again in 1999 with Ikuo Sekimoto's *Zankyo* (Remains of Chivalry), a gangster *roman fleuve* starring Takahiro Matsushima that was essentially a "best of" cliché collection from the *ninkyo eiga* ("chivalry films"), a subgenre commonly set in the early decades of the twentieth century, which typically features a climatic showdown between a stoic loner embodying the traditional *yakuza* virtues and armed with nothing but a sword, and a gang of rival baddies. But Matsushima, whose goofy grin could be seen gracing ads for the Lawson convenience-store chain, was only a pale reflection of *ninkyo eiga*'s icon, Ken Takakura.

The period-drama genre, usually set in the Edo period (1600–1868), popularly considered the most "typically Japanese" historical era, accounted for one half of the industry's output in the 1950s. The decline of the period drama was not as dramatic as that of the *yakuza* film, but despite sporadic big-budget attempts to revive the genre in the nineties, filmgoers, especially younger ones, did not turn up in the expected numbers, forcing the studios to put their long swords and topknots in storage.

One exception to this downward trend was Haruki Kadokawa's *Ten to Chi to* (Heaven and Earth), which earned ¥5.05 billion in film rentals in 1990, making it the year's number-two hit, after *Back to the Future II*. To finance the production of this epic about the clash between two rival sixteenth-century warlords, the budget for which was a record-setting five billion yen, Kadokawa recruited thirty-eight corporate backers, many of whose core businesses had little or nothing to do with film. To ensure that his magnum opus achieved its goal of becoming the biggest hit in Japanese film history, Kadokawa printed nearly five million advance tickets, yet another record. The number of ticketholders who actually turned up to see this torturously plotted, leadenly paced movie was relatively low, however. Thus the odd phenomenon of a film topping the box-office chart week after week, while playing to empty seats.

Kadokawa may have proven that he could put even the dullest of films over by brute force, but even he could not save the period-drama genre from dwindling popularity. In 1994 Toho flopped with Kon Ichikawa's *Shijushichinin no Shikaku* (Forty-Seven Ronin) and Shochiku with Kinji Fukasaku's *Chushingura Gaiden Yotsuya Kaidan* (Crest of Betrayal), both big-budget period dramas based on the classic Chushingura story about forty-seven loyal retainers who sacrifice themselves to avenge the death of their lord.

Based on a best-selling novel by Shoichiro Ikemiya, Ichikawa's *Shijushichinin no Shikaku* was a straightforward retelling that presented its samurai heroes less as romantic exemplars of the *bushido* ideal than as loyal and dedicated organization men doing their best in bad circumstances. Ichikawa filmed this quintessentially Japanese story with his usual visual flair. Even so, his pacing was ponderous and, as audiences squirmed, box office receipts suffered. The film failed to recoup its ¥900 million yen production cost.

Best known for his *Jingi Naki Tatakai* (Battles Without Honor) *yakuza*-film series of the 1970s, Kinji Fukasaku focused *Chushingura Gaiden* on a retainer of the dead Lord Asano who did not take part in the fateful mission of revenge, and afterwards became entangled in a fatal love triangle. Based on *Tokaido Yotsuya Kaidan*, a classic tale of the supernatural, the film had Fukasaku's characteristic energy and flamboyance, but failed to inspire enthusiasm among moviegoers.

Following these two expensive misses, the Japanese film industry shied away from big-budget period dramas for several years, but did not give up on the genre entirely. In November 1997, Toei and five TV *jidaigeki* production houses formed a Period Drama Contents Promotion Council with the aim of keeping period dramas alive. The products of the council members, however, found homes first in, not theaters, but the Jidaigeki Channel (Period Drama Channel) of digital satellite TV platform DirecTV.

As the end of the millennium approached, a spate of period dramas went before the cameras. Masahiro Shinoda made *Fukuro no Shiro* (The Owl's Castle) an effects-filled *ninja* drama based on a novel by Ryotaro Shiba that was to be Toho's big New Year's release for 2000. In February 1999, after many fits and starts, 83-year-old Kon Ichikawa began filming *Dora Heita*, whose script about a magistrate who cleans up an Edo-period castle town was written in 1969 by Ichikawa, Akira Kurosawa, Masaki Kobayashi, and Keisuke Kinoshita. Shooting of yet another Kurosawa script—his last—started in April 1999, with long-time Kurosawa assistant director Takashi Koizumi helming the project. Titled *Ame Agaru*, the film tells the story of a poverty-stricken swordsman whose talent won the attention of a local lord and earned the enmity of local rivals. After a long delay caused by a debilitating stroke, Nagisa Oshima began shooting his gay-themed period drama *Gohatto* in Kyoto that same April, with a premiere set for the 1999 Venice Film Festival.

Meanwhile, other producers, including Takanori Sento and Kazuyoshi Okuyama, announced their intention to make *jidaigeki*. Sento, however, insisted that he was going to make, not a period drama, but "a Japanese action movie." "That means it has to be set in the past—that's the most realistic way to do it," he explained. "Not pistols, but swords. [Pistols] don't have any reality for us. If Japanese are going to make action movies, they have to go back to the past."

Selling Japanese Films in Advance

As films featuring gun-toting gangsters and sword-wielding samurai faded from their lineups in the 1980s and 1990s, the majors financed and promoted more of their big-budget films using the advance-ticket strategy employed by Haruki Kadokawa in *Ten to Chi to*.

The hallmarks of the strategy are sales of large blocks of advance tickets by the Big Three distributors and their corporate partners, and block-booking by the Big Three in their theater chains. The aim is to eliminate competition by controlling every aspect of the pipeline from development to release, while guaranteeing a certain level of income by putting a floor under ticket sales. The only ones left out of this cozy arrangement are the filmmakers, who are basically subcontractors working for a fee.

The practice of selling advance tickets is hardly new or uniquely Japanese, but in Japan their original purpose—as a device to prime the box-office pump—became obscured as more producers used them to literally buy a film's success. With advance ticket sales covering a major share of the film's production cost before release, quality became a secondary concern. Having already largely recouped their investment before their film opened, the producers could have screened a blank reel. (Given the films many of them ended up releasing, perhaps they should have.)

Although big advance-ticket sales campaigns came to full flower in the heady boom years of the late 1980s and early 1990s, they originated in the 1960s. Among the first films to use them were Kei Kumai's *Kurobe no Taiyo* (A Tunnel to the Sun), a 1968 movie starring Yujiro Ishihara and Toshiro Mifune about the building of Kurobe Dam, then Japan's largest, and Hideo Sekigawa's *Chokoso no Akebono* (Skyscraper!), a 1969 film about the construction of the Kasumigaseki Building, then Japan's tallest. Kansai Electric backed *Kurobe*, and Kajima Construction, *Chokoso*. Not surprisingly, both companies were also involved in the construction projects the films glorified.

Having underwritten what were essentially corporate PR films, Kansai and Kajima undertook the chore of peddling advance tickets—the more the better. Kajima reportedly forced *Chokoso*'s 1.7 million advance tickets on not only its subcontractors, but even *ramen* vendors who sold lunchtime noodles to Kajima employees. To further ensure the film's success, the company used trucks to transport employees, who had thoughtfully been given the day off, to the theaters. But though Kajima showered advance tickets like confetti on one and all, *Chokoso* played to largely empty seats.

Yet another early beneficiary of an advance ticket sales campaign was Masaki Kobayashi's *Moeru Aki* (Fiery Autumn), a 1978 romantic drama set in Iran and backed by Shigeru Okada, the president of the Mitsukoshi department-store chain. This unusual choice of locale was no coincidence; Okada and his mistress, Michi Takehisa, had opened a Persian rug shop in Mitsukoshi's Nihombashi flagship store, and the film was essentially a travelogue designed to interest potential customers in Iran—and Persian rugs. Mitsukoshi pushed wads of advance tickets on its suppliers, but when the media charged that Okada and Takehisa's rugs were phonies, a firestorm of criticism erupted and the Japanese Fair Trade Commission investigated. After a long season of media bashing, climaxing in the revelation that most of the artifacts in a Persian art exhibition held at the Nihombashi store were fakes, Okada resigned in disgrace in September 1982.

Not all advance ticket sales campaigns ended in disaster, however. To promote Koreyoshi Kurahara's *Nankyoku Monogatari* (Antarctica, 1983), a film about two dogs that survive an Antarctic winter after being abandoned by a Japanese expedition, one of the film's backers, the Gakken publishing house, hawked 3.5 million advance tickets through its sales force, generating 3.3 million admissions. *Nankyoku Monogatari* earned ¥5.95 billion in film rentals—a record for domestic films that stood until Hayao Miyazaki's *Mononoke Hime* (Princess Mononoke) broke it in 1997.

Large advance ticket sales boosted several other event films of the bubble-economy era to box-office success. Until 1997, they accounted for the top five all-time domestic grossers. In addition to the aforementioned *Nankyoku Monogatari*, they were, in order of box office rank, *Koneko Monogatari* (The Adventures of Milo and Otis, 1986), *Ten to Chi to* (1990), *Tonko* (Tun-Huang, 1988) and *Burma no Tategoto* (The Harp of Burma, 1985).

For companies flush with cash in the booming 1980s, these movies were not simply money-spinning machines, but tools for boosting the corporate image and—a reason that should not be underestimated—trimming the corporate tax bill. Film investments could be depreciated within two years after the film's release and, if a movie went into the red, used as a tax write-off.

Also, large advance ticket sales were a means of reducing risk in what had become, during the long decline of the Japanese film industry, a highly risky business. Rather than promote films on their individual merits, distributors found it safer to flog them with advance ticket sales and block book them into their domestic film chains. Even if audiences stayed away, distributors could fill their lineups while limiting their losses.

This safety-first approach dictated not only a film's release strategy, but the choice of subject as well. Although market forces were certainly at work—the success of *Nankyoku Monogatari* inspired a flood of animal pictures over the next decade—a project would get the greenlight simply because a company was willing to produce it with a budget in the billions and promote it with advance ticket sales in the millions. Content—and even commercial viability—were secondary.

The studio executives with greenlight authority thus preferred the historical drama that would attract corporate sponsorship over the contemporary film that might have a better chance of pleasing the young core audience—but not the elderly executives writing the checks. The result was a procession of biopics about Japanese historical figures, whose releases dates were usually tied to a death anniversary. The title character of the 1991 *Fukuzawa Yukichi* was a renowned Meiji-era educator, the 1993 *Waga Ai no Uta: Taki Rentaro Monogatari* (My Song of Love: The Rentaro Taki Story), a beloved Meiji-era composer, while the 1992 *Toki Rakujitsu* (Faraway Sunset), featured the revered bacteriologist Hideyo Noguchi, who became the first Japanese to win a Nobel Prize, for his work on the origins of syphilis and yellow fever.

All three were heartwarming four-hanky melodramas that stylistically and thematically recalled Hollywood biopics of the 1930s about Alexander Graham Bell, Emile Zola, and Madame Curie. If MGM mogul L. B. Mayer had been reborn as Japanese producer during the early nineties, he would have found his natural home on a Shochiku or Toho sound stage, cranking out yet another costume drama about a bespectacled genius's devotion to his sainted mother.

As a corollary to this corporate preference for the tried and true, the directors hired to film these epics were inevitably graying veterans on whom the producers could rely to turn in a workmanlike job, with no unpleasant surprises. That the film would look much like the veteran's other workmanlike jobs, that the veteran, in fact, had not had a new idea in decades, didn't matter to the executives doing the hiring. If Steven Spielberg had been born in Japan, he would have either made an early escape to the more open and lucrative worlds of television and advertising, lived a hand-to-mouth existence as an independent filmmaker, or spent his twenties and probably much of his thirties working as an assistant director for these veterans before directing his first film.

Although the Japanese economy plunged into recession in 1991, producers and distributors continued to print advance tickets by the truckload. The distributors argued that they needed the tickets to maintain the stability of the block-booking system. Without a certain number of ticket sales, exhibitors would become more reluctant to commit their theaters to a distributor's lineup of films. Also, advance ticket sales occasionally did what they were intended to do: bring large numbers of regular ticket holders into the theaters.

But as Japan's recession deepened, the downside of the system also become more apparent. With the rise of discount ticket shops, bargain-hunting moviegoers could often go around the corner from the theater and buy advance tickets for giveaway prices. By issuing large number of such tickets, distributors were effectively cutting their own throats. Also, with profits tumbling, companies had less incentive to shield their earnings from the taxman by investing in films. Lastly, prospective investors had had several grisly object lessons in the dangers of taking the movie plunge.

One was Jun'ya Sato's *Oroshiya Koku Suimutan* (Dreams of Russia) a four-billion-yen epic based on the true story of an eighteenth-century Japanese fur trader's decade-long struggle to return home after being shipwrecked in Siberia. The film was expected to record seven million admissions, 3.5 million of which were to be accounted for by advance ticket sales. But though investors began selling advance tickets in December 1991, six months before the film's release, *Oroshiya* earned only ¥1.8 billion in film rentals, compared with ¥4.6 billion for Daiei's previous historical drama, the 1988 *Tonko*. All the spectacular scenes shot in Siberian snowstorms or St. Petersburg palaces could not persuade moviegoers to buy tickets to this plodding epic. During its run, discount ticket shops were selling adult tickets to the film for as little as six hundred yen, one-third of the standard price.

Another example of the dangers of discounting was the dinosaur-fantasy *Rex: Kyoryu Monogatari* (Rex). Soon after producer Haruki Kadokawa was arrested on drug-smuggling charges in August 1993, distributor Shochiku announced that it was pulling this sappy film about a girl and her cute T-Rex from its theaters. Before the ax fell, discount ticket shops slashed prices, until an adult ticket to *Rex* could be had for as little as two hundred yen.

Toho

Although the advance ticket sales strategy was under assault after the bursting of the bubble, the Big Three distributors continued to block-book Japanese films. Throughout the 1990s, the most successful has been Toho, which operates the biggest theater chain and owns many of the best downtown venues, and consequently enjoys a large advantage in securing major films. While fighting the same rearguard action against Hollywood as its rivals, Toho has been able to regularly exceed its annual target of ten billion yen in distribution revenues over the past decade. Accordingly, it has been less dependent than the other two majors on cheap advance tickets to fill seats.

After scoring in 1984 with its Godzilla-revival film, *Godzilla* (released as *Godzilla 1985* in the United States) and its followup, the 1989 *Godzilla tai Biollante* (Godzilla vs. Biollante), Toho churned out new Godzilla pics annually from 1991 to 1995 for the peak New Year's holiday season. All of these entries appeared in the annual domestic box-office top ten, and two, the 1992 *Godzilla tai Mothra* (Godzilla vs. Mothra) and the 1995 *Godzilla tai Destroyah* (Godzilla vs. Destroyah), topped the domestic box office chart, with distributor revenues of ¥2.22 billion and ¥2.0 billion, respectively.

The basic format of the new series was the same as that of decades past—Godzilla battled a bloody-minded monster, while the fate of Japan and the world hung in the balance. The films also featured a supporting cast of other lethal creatures, including one in *Godzilla tai Destroyah* that combined a praying-mantis body with a dripping, tearing mouth straight from the *Alien* series.

Most of Godzilla's opponents in these installments, however, were essentially updatings of monsters who had first appeared in earlier, "classic" films, including Mothra the giant moth, from the 1964 *Mothra tai Godzilla* (Godzilla vs. the Thing), King Ghidorah, the three-headed dragon, from the 1965 *Sandai Kaiju Chikyu Saidai no Kessen* (Ghidorah the Three-Headed Monster), and Mechagodzilla, a robotic version of Godzilla himself, from the 1974 *Godzilla tai Mechagodzilla* (Godzilla vs. the Cosmic Monster). While these well-known monsters were no doubt intended to appeal to the nostalgia of adult fans who had first seen them as children, they were also evidence that, creatively, the series was as exhausted as Godzilla himself after yet another battle to the death.

Toho wisely targeted the films at a wide demographic, from adults who could presumably follow the film's convoluted storylines and understand their absurd pseudo-science, to small children who viewed them much as they would the TV live-action shows that pitted teenage superheroes against bad space aliens. Production costs averaged a billion yen, the top of the line for the Japanese film industry, and the films' special effects, though not so special according to Hollywood's ever-escalating standards, were splashy enough to thrill younger moviegoers. Toho resisted the urge to turn its signature character into a self-kidding buffoon, even though it was well aware that, in the West, Godzilla had become a camp icon. Instead, it regarded Godzilla's destruction of yet another Japanese cityscape as serious onscreen business. He was, like so many other Japanese popular culture heroes, from Yoshitsune to Tora-san, permanently frozen into a typical attitude—in Godzilla's case, fiery rage—and that's just the way fans liked him

At the same time, Toho managed to inject contemporary concerns into the series. The 1991 *Godzilla tai King Ghidorah*, released when trade friction between Japan and the United States was at a height, tells a story of time-traveling visitors from the year 2204 who warn that Godzilla will destroy the world in the twenty-first century. The only solution, they say, is to travel back to World War II, when Godzilla was still a mere dinosaur, and teleport him away from the atomic blast that will transform him into an hell-raising monster. But once Godzilla is out of the way, the foreigners from the future unleash three cuddly-looking creatures called Dorats. They quickly mutate into a fearsome three-headed dragon known as King Ghidorah, who wreaks more havoc on Japan than Godzilla did in his worst tantrums. The lesson: beware of foreign imports.

Despite the series' success, Toho ended it in 1995 with the release of *Godzilla tai Destroyah*. Although Toho general producer Shogo Toyama insisted that the studio had made the decision because "some constraints came to be imposed on the character and the background story," a more cogent explanation was Toho's desire to avoid cannibalizing profits from Roland Emmerich's *Godzilla*, which Toho had contracted to distribute in Japan after selling the international rights to the character to Tristar Pictures. Toho officials said that they did not intend to revive the series until after the new millennium, presumably when the American Godzilla had worn out his box office welcome.

In December 1998, however, the studio announced plans to make a new Godzilla movie for release the next New Year's season. Tentatively titled *Godzilla Millennium*, the film went into production in April 1999. One reason for Godzilla's early return from hibernation was the disappointing local reception accorded his American cousin following his release in the summer of 1998. Although Toho had predicted that Tristar's *Godzilla* would clear eight billion yen in film rentals, it finished its run with only three billion—less than another Toho summer entry, an animated film based on the popular *Pokemon* (Pocket Monsters) game and TV show.

Not a few of the series' local fans were angered by what they considered a Hollywood trashing of a national icon—and regretted his departure. "We considered the Tristar movie to have been a success in Japan, but there were also many Japanese fans who wanted to see the Toho Godzilla again," said Toho publicist Shigehisa Kamikawa. "It was in response to those fans that we decided to revive the series." Another factor in the company's decision was the likelihood that a Tristar Godzilla sequel would not be ready for Japanese theatres until the end of 2000. "We thought we could fill the slot in our line-up for the 1999 New Year's holiday season with our own Godzilla film," said Kamikawa.

Other than its signature Godzilla series, Toho produced relatively few films during the decade, preferring to fill its lineup with movies by independents. The most successful was Juzo Itami, whose string of hit satirical comedies, beginning with *Ososhiki* (The Funeral) in 1984, along with his talent for self-promotion, made him a national celebrity. His formula soon became as predictable as Godzilla's: a spunky woman, played by his wife, Nobuko Miyamoto, contended with the targets du jour, be they tax cheats (*Marusa no Onna* [A Taxing Woman], 1987), lecherous men (*Ageman*, [A-Ge-Man: Tales of a Golden Geisha],1990), or *yakuza* gangsters (*Mimbo no Onna* [The Gentle Art of Japanese Extortion], 1992), and after many comic vicissitudes, triumphed.

Itami later departed from this formula with forays into serious drama, but the thumping failure of *Shizuka na Seikatsu* (A Quiet Life), a 1994 film based on the family life of Nobel Prize–winning author and Itami brother-in-law Kenzaburo Oe, forced him to return to it. Itami made a comeback in 1996 with *Super no Onna* (Supermarket Woman) a punchy, if predictable, comedy about a struggle of a spunky housewife, playe (as always) by Miyamoto, to save a failing supermarket. His 1997 follow-up, *Marutai no Onna* (Woman of the Police Protection Program), was an uninspired, uneven outing about an actress who witnesses a murder and decides to testify against the killer. A disappointment at the box office, a dartboard for the critics (one critic's poll named it "the worst film of 1997"), *Marutai* was yet another indication that Itami had reached a creative impasse. In December 1997 he leapt to his death from the roof of the Roppongi building that housed his office. Although his suicide note said that he was killing himself in response to a photomagazine story about his alleged affair with a twenty-six-year-old woman, his professional troubles had no doubt pushed him nearer the brink.

Two other outsiders making large contributions to Toho's coffers were Hayao Miyazaki and Isao Takahata, veteran animators who had co-founded the Studio Ghibli animation house in 1985. Though often compared with the products of Disney, Studio Ghibli films proved, with a metronomic regularity, that they were in a box-office class by themselves. By 1997 they had not only outgrossed their Disney rivals six straight times, but, beginning with *Majo no Takkyubin* (Kiki's Delivery Service) in 1989, topped the year's domestic chart five times. In 1997, Hayao Miyazaki's *Mononoke Hime* (Princess Mononoke), an animated eco-fable set in premodern Japan, broke the all-time box-office record set by *E.T.—The Extraterrestrial*, finishing the year with film rentals of ¥10.7 billion

Yet another steady earner for Toho was *manga* artist Hiroshi Fujimoto. Together with partner Abiko Moto, Fujimoto had created a total of forty-nine *manga* series under the collective pen name Fujio Fujiko by 1988, when the two men amicably separated. The most popular was Fujimoto's *Doraemon*, which featured Nobita, a boy who was constantly getting into scrapes with teachers, parents, and his neighborhood friends, and Doraemon, a blue robot cat from the twenty-second century who was forever extracting Nobita from said scrapes with gadgets from his magic pouch.

Paperback collections of the *Doraemon* comics have sold more than more than one hundred million copies since its debut in 1969. Also, since 1979 the TV Asahi network has regularly hit the ratings jackpot with a weekly half-hour *Doraemon* cartoon show. Not surprisingly, the *manga* and TV show spawned a series of animated film programs—a total of twenty by the spring of 1999—nearly all of which became hits.

Unlike the *manga* and TV program, which confine Nobita's misadventures to his Tokyo home, school, and neighborhood, the main features in these two- or three-film programs are boy's adventure tales of journeys to other times and worlds, with Doraemon, Nobita, and their neighborhood pals plunged into titanic, if at times silly, struggles to defeat an evil power. Aimed at children on their spring school holiday, the films are technically a cut above the TV program, several cuts below the products of Studio Ghibli. The spring 1998 entry—a program of three films—earned two billion yen in film rentals, making it the eighth-highest-earning film of the year. Though Fujimoto died in 1996 at the age of 62, the series seems likely to roll on forever.

In addition to these stalwarts, which have served as the tentpoles to Toho's lineup for a decade or more, the studio has released other animated hits, many of which have, like the *Doraemon* series, first become popular on the small screen before migrating to the big one. Among the more successful titles are the 1991 *Chibi Maruko-chan* (Little Miss Maruko), whose title character is a cute-but-willful third-grader in 1970s Shizuoka Prefecture, and the *Crayon Shin-chan* series, which features an obnoxious kindergart-ner with a preciousness interest in the opposite sex.

Hit TV dramas also supplied material for films, including the 1993 *Koko Kyoshi* (High School Teacher), which portrayed a male high-school teacher's affair with a female student; the 1994 *Hero Interview*, a love story about a pro baseball player and woman reporter whose hearts were in the right places but whose careers were on the skids; and the 1994 *Ie Naki Ko* (Sans Famille), which featured a feisty young orphan, played by the saucer-eyed Yumi Adachi, whose best-known line, repeated in countless TV ads, was "If you love me, give me money."

Also making a box-office splash in 1994 was Joji Iida's *Night Head*, which had begun life as a late-night show about the consciousness-expanding adventures of two broth-ers endowed with psychic powers. Bearing a generic resemblance to David Lynch's *Twin Peaks*—a smash on video in Japan—the original program aired on Fuji TV in 1992 and quickly attracted a cult following. It propelled its two male leads, Etsushi Toyokawa and Shinji Takeda, to stardom, while offering evidence that some of the most innovative work on television was appearing after midnight.

Transferring hit TV formulas directly to the big screen, however, has not been an infallible recipe for success. Although under-twelves never tire of seeing their favorite TV-animation characters on the big screen, women in the eighteen to thirty-four age group, the core audience for TV-derived films, have proven more fickle. In 1997 Yasuo Hasegawa's *Koi wa Maiorita* (Love Comes Floating Down), a formulaic blend of screw-ball comedy, supernatural fantasy, and sentimental romance, performed poorly at the box office despite the presence of hot TV stars Toshiaki Karasawa and Makiko Esumi.

The 1998 detective drama *Odoru Daisosasen* (Bayside Shakedown), which was based on a hit Fuji TV series, was not the usual big-screen TV special for fans, but a real stand-alone movie. Prior acquaintance with the show (which related the seriocomic adventures of a salaryman-turned-detective) was not necessary to understanding the story. Also, director Katsuyuki Motohiro and scriptwriter Ryoichi Kimizuka, both TV veterans with long lists of hit shows to their credit, may have lightened the film with TV-friendly slap-stick but they also gave it a density and gloss richer than any TV cop show could afford. Finally, despite its familiar elements, from the inevitable J-Pop theme song to the hero's Columbo-like trenchcoat, *Odoru* brought a fresh approach to a genre in desperate need of it. These elements added up to an enormous hit for Toho; *Odoru* became the highest-earning Japanese live-action film of the year, with admissions exceeding six million and film rentals reaching the five billion yen mark.

Shochiku

While Toho was moving from success to success and strengthening its grip on the local market, rival Shochiku was struggling to find its feet throughout much of second half of the decade.

For nearly a quarter century, beginning in 1969, Shochiku had a steady money-earner in its Tora-san series, whose generic title was *Otoko wa Tsurai yo* (It's Tough Being a Man). Tora-san was a wandering peddler, played in all forty-eight installments by former vaudeville and TV comedian Kiyoshi Atsumi, who was forever falling in love, but never got the girl. Despite the sameness of the films, which took Tora-san to every prefecture and one foreign country, fans never tired of them.

Yoji Yamada, who directed all but two early episodes and had, together with Atsumi, conceived the TV show on which the film series was based, often likened his labors to those of a *ramen* cook who makes good bowls of noodles the same way every time. An apt comparison: *ramen* is a national obsession in Japan and subtle variations in texture and flavor are an endless source of fascination to *ramen* gourmets. In the same way, the new elements Yamada injected into the series, including one episode with an "American Tora-san" played by comedian Herb Edelmann, provided the dash of fresh seasoning needed to bring fans back for more, without spoiling the Tora-san "taste" that had drawn them to the theater in the first place.

The series came to an end with the death of Atsumi in August 1996. Yamada, who had been preparing to shoot the forty-ninth installment that fall, instead made an homage film called *Niji o Tsukamu Otoko* (The Man Who Caught the Rainbow) that may have had the same Japanese title as *The Secret Life of Walter Mitty*, but was primarily inspired by Guiseppe Tornatore's *Cinema Paradiso*. Toshiyuki Nishida played the manager of a provincial movie theater who was, like Tora-san, an inspired monologist, a hopeless romantic, and a confirmed bachelor incapable of expressing his true feelings to the woman he loved. The cast was heavily populated by familiar faces from the Tora-san series, and Tora-san himself, played by a double, appeared for a cameo. But despite heavy doses of Yamada's characteristic sentimentalism, *Niji o Tsukamu Otoko* and a 1997 sequel did not replicate the success of the Tora-san series at the box office.

Before Atsumi's death, however, Shochiku had prudently prepared a Tora-san replacement in the *Tsuri Baka Nisshi* series about a salaryman, also played by Nishida, who would rather fish than work. The hero is constantly getting into hot water with the higher-ups for his violations of the corporate code, but finds an unlikely ally in the crusty company president (played by Rentaro Mikuni), who becomes his fishing *deshi* (disciple) and corporate protector. Based on a popular *manga* by Juzo Yamasaki, the series was launched in 1989 as the lower half of a double-bill headed by a Tora-san film, and quickly began to rival the Tora-san series in popularity. In the summer of 1994, Shochiku released the sixth installment, *Tsuri Baka Nisshi Special* (Free and Easy Special), independently, and the series subsequently became a staple of the studio's summer schedule. In 1998, Shochiku released two episodes, one for the Obon holiday in August and one, a period drama, for the New Year's season.

In 1993 Yamada launched yet another series with *Gakko* (A Class to Remember), a drama about adult students studying for their junior-high diplomas at a Tokyo night school. In 1996 Yamada released a second installment and, in 1998, a third, but though the series won critical plaudits for its examinations of students who fall through the cracks of the Japanese educational system, it did more to burnish Yamada's reputation than brighten Shochiku's bottom line.

The Tora-san series and its spin-offs remained core franchises for Shochiku throughout most of the decade, but more than its rivals, the studio made strenuous efforts to reach beyond formula fare and revitalize its lineup, with mostly disappointing results. The driving force behind this reform effort was Kazuyoshi Okuyama, the son of then Shochiku president Toru Okuyama. Raised in the movie business, Okuyama began producing films while still in his twenties. Though hardly fitting the stereotype of the big-bellied, cigar-chomping producer—Okuyama was a slight man, with a mild, soft-spoken public manner—he quickly pushed to the forefront of his profession, while demonstrating a flair for self-promotion

In addition to making mainstream entertainments, such as *Hachiko Monogatari* (A Story of the Dog Hachi), a 1987 hit film about a dog that kept loyally returning to Tokyo's Shibuya Station to greet its master for years his death, and *Toki Rakujitsu* (Faraway Sunset), a 1992 biopic of Nobel Prize–winning scientist Hideyo Noguchi, Okuyama took the studio in new and, at times, controversial, directions.

He produced the critically-acclaimed early films of comedian-turned-director Takeshi Kitano, but the two men had a public falling out when *Sonatine*, a 1993 black comedy about a gang war in Okinawa, went over budget and flopped at the box office. In an interview with a national magazine, Okuyama accused Kitano, whose improvisatory style had added days to the location shoot in Okinawa, of auteurist egotripping. In response, Kitano broke all ties with the studio and began distributing his films through his own production company, Office Kitano.

Okuyama had his revenge, albeit indirectly. In 1996, while attending the Cannes Film Festival, Kitano learned that *Sonatine* had won the Grand Prize at the 1993 Taorima Film Festival. Shochiku staff in charge of submitting the film to Taorima had not bothered to inform him and the trophy was gathering dust in Shochiku's Tokyo office.

Okuyama's most spectacular public quarrel with a director ended, ironically, in his greatest personal triumph. Late in 1992, Okuyama screened a rough cut of Rintaro Mayuzumi's *Rampo*, a period drama based on life and work of mystery writer Edogawa Rampo that Shochiku was making to commemorate the one hundredth anniversary of the birth of film, Rampo, and the studio itself. Unfortunately, Okuyama did not find *Rampo* to his liking. Accusing the director of botching the studio's biggest release of 1994, Okuyama told a reporter for a sports newspaper that he wanted to reshoot certain scenes. His remarks touched off a bitter, long-running dispute with Mayuzumi, a TV director on loan to Shochiku from NHK Enterprises.

In May, Mayuzumi agreed to a compromise; Okuyama would reshoot the disputed scenes himself and Shochiku would distribute both versions of the film. The audience would then presumably decide which was better. During principal photography, which wrapped in November 1993, Okuyama reshot nearly seventy percent of the film, using the same actors and much of the original script. Several of the changes he made, including the addition of subliminal images and the use of celebrity extras in a party scene, generated even more publicity for the film. Following its release in June, *Rampo* became the biggest domestic hit of the summer, earning ¥1.2 billion in film rentals. Distributed in the United States by the Samuel Goldwyn Co. in 1995, the film received glowing reviews from U.S. critics, with several placing it on their annual best-ten list. Okuyama could claim, with some justification, to have had the better side of the argument.

Nonetheless, his later films for the overseas market, including Masato Harada's 1994 *Painted Desert* and 1996 *Eiko to Kyuki* (Rowing Through), died at the local box office, while failing to make an impression abroad. Also, Okuyama was frustrated in his attempts to co-produce films with foreign partners. In December 1995 Shochiku concluded a deal with Universal to jointly produce and distribute a remake of *Kiroi Handkerchief* (The Yellow Handkerchief), a 1977 hit by Yoji Yamada about an ex-convict's long journey home. Okuyama wanted to cast Kevin Costner in the lead role, but the actor's fee would have been larger than the film's entire budget, and *Kiroi Handkerchief* remained in development. In March 1996 Okuyama signed an agreement with Robert De Niro's Tribeca Pictures to coproduce what was to be De Niro's next directorial effort, a remake of *Moby Dick* with De Niro starring as Ahab, but the Tribeca *Pequod* was slow to set sail.

Finding international success elusive, Okuyama turned his attention to revitalizing the stagnant domestic film industry. In April 1997 he launched Cinema Japanesque, a project for producing and distributing independent films through Shochiku's theater chain on a free-booking basis. Among the eleven films in the Cinema Japanesque line-up for 1997 were Shohei Imamura's *Unagi* (The Eel), which won the Palme d'Or at the 1997 Cannes Film Festival, and Jun Ichikawa's *Tokyo Yakyoku* (Tokyo Lullaby), which received the Best Director prize at the 1997 Montreal Film Festival.

In 1998, Okuyama planned to expand the Cinema Japanesque lineup to thirty films, while adding another circuit to accommodate the increased output. The rapid increase in production was intended to supply not only Shochiku's theater chain but its pay-per-view and premium channels for cable and satellite television, primarily Eisei Gekijo (Satellite Theater), which specialized in Japanese films. Unluckily for Okuyama, the Cinema Japanesque lineup failed to find success at the box office. Also, losses were piling up from other ventures launched by Okuyama and his father Toru, Shochiku president since 1991, including the Cinema World theme park near the company's Ofuna studio. In January 1998, Shochiku directors, led by Nobuyoshi Otani, a grandson of the company's founder, deposed the Okuyamas in a boardroom coup. Otani assumed the presidency and promptly began to dismantle the legacy of the Okuyama regime, beginning with Cinema Japanesque.

In March the ever-resourceful Kazuyoshi launched a film production unit called Team Okuyama with the corporate backing of arcade-game maker Namco. In August, he announced his first slate of films under his new Team Okuyama banner. One was *Dora Heita*, a period drama whose script had been written in 1983 by Kon Ichikawa, Keisuke Kinoshita, Masaki Kobayashi, and Akira Kurosawa. Ichikawa was to begin principal photography in September 1998, with Koji Yakusho playing the lead role of a magistrate who cleans up a corrupt Edo-period town. The death of Kurosawa shortly before shooting was to begin forced a delay, and citing differences of opinion with Ichikawa, Okuyama later turned the project over to Nikkatsu, a long-established studio that was also under the Namco umbrella. Another Okuyama project was *Sekigahara*, a period drama about the battle in 1600 between rival feudal lords that determined the course of Japanese history for the next 250 years. Once again, however, Okuyama had to first jump a high budgetary hurdle to make the film a reality.

Meanwhile, Shochiku continued to struggle at the box office. None of its releases earned more than one billion yen in film rentals in 1998, compared with seven for Toho and two for Toei. Also, its entire earnings from films for that year amounted to only

¥3.1 billion, less than Toho's take from its hit *Pokemon* (Pocket Monsters) movie alone. In fiscal 1998, the company recorded an operating loss of ¥4.4 billion.

Seeking to stem the tide of red ink, Shochiku launched a restructuring drive. In December 1998 the studio transferred its corporate headquarters to a new location in Tokyo's Ginza district and closed the Cinema World theme park. Soon after the New Year, it also shuttered the Shochiku Central theater complex that had been a Ginza landmark for nearly four decades. A commercial developer planned to tear down both the headquarters and theaters and erect a high-rise office building in their place. After selling the land to the developer, Shochiku intended to lease the building and generate income from the rent. In March 1999, the studio announced a drastic cutback in film production, with the resulting gap in the lineup to be filled by primarily by foreign films. It also said it would end the block-booking system for domestic films—the first Japanese major distributor to take such a step—and, in August 1999, close its Shochiku Fuji foreign-film distribution subsidiary.

One bright spot during this dismal period was the announcement that Shochiku would distribute *Hohokekyo Tonari no Yamada-kun* (My Neighbors the Yamadas), a Studio Ghibli animated feature set for release in the summer of 1999. The studio, however, delayed the production of *Nihon Chimbotsu* (Japan Sinks!), a big-budget remake of a 1973 hit film about a natural holocaust that devastates the Japanese archipelago. Company officials were evidently worried that the film's real damage might be to Shochiku's fragile financial health.

Toei

The third major domestic film distributor, Toei, has long been without the equivalent of a Godzilla or Tora-san franchise. The studio's *yakuza* films, a signature genre for three decades, once served this function, but as their audience migrated to video in the 1980s, they faded at the box office, and Toei, more than its rivals, filled the gap with costume dramas supported by the sales of advance tickets. Toei's conservative management preferred the relative safety of the subsidized historical epic to the riskier, but potentially more lucrative course of developing new projects for the younger core audience.

In addition to Haruki Kadokawa's *Ten to Chi to*—the ultimate example of the advance ticket-sales strategy in action—Toei distributed Toshio Goto's 1990 *Aurora no Shita de* (Aurora), a coproduction between Toei, TV Asahi, and Mosfilm about the loving relationship of an Alaskan wolf-dog and its Japanese master; Toshio Masuda's 1991 *Doten*, a feature starring period-drama veteran Kin'ya Kitaoji about a merchant in the early days of Yokohama, and Shin'ichiro Sawai's *Fukuzawa Yukichi* (Passage to Japan), a biopic of the revered Meiji-era writer and educator whose face graces the ¥10,000 note.

Though these films all earned more than one billion yen in distributor revenues with the support of masssive advance ticket sales, Toei also released some of the bubble era's more memorable flops. One was Toshio Masuda's 1991 *Edojo Tairan* (The Great Shogunate Battle), a big-budget samurai swashbuckler that Toei staffers ruefully referred to as the studio's *tainan* (great disaster). Another was Akira Tomono's *Rakuyo*, a clumsily-told drama of international intrigue set in wartime Manchuria, whose failure to recoup more than a small fraction of its five-billion-yen budget sent its production company, the eighty-year-old Nikkatsu studio, into receivership. (Unfortunately, the presence of Donald Sutherland and Diane Lane in the cast did not help sell the movie abroad, and their filmographies in English-language film reference works pass over *Rakuyo* in silence.)

Despite these disasters, Toei continued to distribute such epics long after other studios had started to phase them out. Not all its post-bubble costume dramas were flops, however: Yasuo Furuhata's 1995 *Kura*, an archetypical women's picture about a blind girl who becomes, after many tribulations, the owner and manager of a *sake* brewery in prewar Japan, earned one billion yen in film rentals.

Toei's management displayed its conservatism in political ways as well. In 1995, to commemorate the fiftieth anniversary of the end of the World War II, the Big Three all released big-budget war films. Toei's entry, *Kike, Wadatsumi no Koe* (Last Friends), was the most blatant in its exaltation of its Japanese soldier-heroes, while depicting the misdeeds of the Japanese army as the work of a rotten few. Directed by Masanobu Deme, *Kike* was a cinematic war-memorial service; not an approach designed to appeal to members of the generations born after the war's end. Promoted as Toei's big film of 1995, it was a box office disappointment.

In 1998 Toei revealed its political colors even more clearly when it released *Pride— Ummei no Toki* (Pride), a Shun'ya Ito film about the war-crimes trial of Hideki Tojo. Underwritten by Higashi Nihon House, whose chairman was a notorious rightist, and starring Juzo Itami regular Masahiko Tsugawa in a bravura performance as Tojo, *Pride* was a lavishly produced revisionist defense of Tojo and Japan's expansionism in Asia. Though it used verbatim testimony from the Tokyo war-crimes trial to bolster its case, it was highly selective in what it chose to remember about Japan's wartime deeds.

Boosted by the sale of nine hundred thousand advance tickets by Higashi Nihon House and the uproar over its treatment of its subject—even the Toei's employee union circulated a letter of protest—*Pride* was a box office success, recording film rentals of ¥1.1 billion, though negative coverage of the film by the international media hardly bolstered the studio's image abroad—not that Toei's management seemed to care.

Animation was another a mainstay of the Toei lineup throughout the decade. Toei Animation, a Toei subsidiary, has long been Asia's largest animation studio, producing dozens of animated programs for television, including the enduringly popular *Dragonball* and *Sailor Moon* series. In 1991, Toei began releasing packages of Toei Animation short features twice a year, during the spring and summer school vacations, under the collective title Toei Anime Fair. Essentially extended versions of *Dragonball* and other popular Toei TV cartoon shows, the Toei Anime Fair packages have proven popular with the under-twelve audience, which has propelled them over the one-billion-yen mark in film rentals time after time.

The studio has also long been a producer of live-action TV shows for children, most notably the so-called "five hero" shows that pit a brave band of superheroes —usually five in number—against an array of bad space aliens. The TV Asahi network has been broadcasting the shows, with an annual change of characters, since 1975. Mass merchandising of toys and other character goods have helped make them an inescapable part of growing up for a generation of Japanese boys. Repackaged by Saban Entertainment with American actors in the non-action scenes, a "five hero" show called *Kyoryu Sentai Ju Ranger* (Dinosaur Attack Force Beast Rangers) debuted on the Fox network as *Mighty Morphin' Power Rangers* in 1993 and quickly became a ratings hit and social phenomenon. Toei has repeated this success with its "five hero" shows in dozens of countries around the world.

In addition to feature-length animation, Toei was a pioneer in the production of made-for-video films. In March 1989 subsidiary Toei Video launched its V Cinema series for the video shelves—the first of its kind—with an action pic titled *Crime Hunter*. The film was a hit with video-shop customers and by the end of 1990 the company was releasing V Cinema titles at a rate of nearly two a month. Other studios, including Nikkatsu and Shochiku, weighed in with their own "original videos" or OV— the Janglish term for straight-to-video titles, but Toei remained the leader.

Following on the success of its V Cinema films, Toei Video added other live-action series to its lineup, including the V America series in 1992, whose four entries were shot in the United States using American actors and staff, and the V World series in 1993, whose two installments were set in Australia. Toei made seven more video titles with foreign locales in 1995 and 1996 but, hit by an industry-wide decline in sales of video titles, has since cut back on overseas production and concentrated on domestically-made films.

Despite the déclassé reputation of straight-to-video movies, Toei's V series entries had relatively big budgets and featured such well-known names as Toru Nakamura, Bunta Sugawara, Jimpachi Nezu, Koji Yakusho, and Masaya Kato. Several of the foreign actors in these films were also familiar faces, including Jacqueline Bisset, who starred in the first V World film, *Crime Broker*, and George Kennedy, who appeared in the first V America film, *Distant Justice*. Others, such as Mira Sorvino and Russell Crowe, were unknowns who later went on to Hollywood stardom.

Many of these films received brief theatrical releases to boost video sales, including Jun'ichi Suzuki's 1995 family drama *Sukiyaki* and Frank Cappello's 1995 male-bonding action picture *No Way Back*, which featured Russell Crowe as an FBI agent and Etsushi Toyokawa as a *yakuza* in his custody. Columbia Tristar bought worldwide English-language rights for *No Way Back* with the intention of releasing it theatrically in the United States, but later changed its mind. The film, a coproduction of Toei Video, Tohoku Shinsha, and First Look films, did find a home on U.S. cable TV, however.

In 1997, Toei finally scored a much-needed box-office success with Yoshimitsu Morita's *Shitsurakuen* (Lost Paradise), a film based on a best-selling novel by Jun'ichi Watanabe about a passionate adulterous affair between middle-aged lovers that ends in suicide. The film earned more than two billion yen in film rentals, the most for any Japanese live-action film since the 1990 *Ten to Chi to*. In addition to the book and movie, a hit TV-drama series fueled a *Shitsurakuen* boom. Though love suicide (*shinju*) had been a favorite device of Japanese drama dating back to Chikamatsu and beyond, its use in *Shitsurakuen* struck many Japanese moviegoers, especially those of the same generation as the film's couple, as less regrettably retrograde than excitingly romantic. The film's many steamy soft-focus bed scenes also added to the film's box office appeal.

That same year Toei profited from the boom generated by the *Shinseiki Evangelion* (Neo-Genesis Evangelion) television series. Broadcast on TV Tokyo from October 1995 to March 1996, the show gained a large following among *anime otaku*—fans, primarily teenage boys, seriously obsessed with Japanese animation. Set in the year 2015, the twenty-six-part show told the story of teenagers who piloted gigantic robots called Evangelions into battle against equally gigantic beings called *shito* (angels) who were attacking, for mysterious reasons of their own, a Tokyo rebuilt from the ashes of a cataclysm called the Second Impact. The focus of the show, however, was the fourteen-year-old pilots, particularly one Shinji Ikari, a troubled teen who had become estranged from his scientist father and spent much screen time in angst-filled inner struggle.

Shinseiki Evangelion director Hideaki Anno and his Gainax studio animators produced two films based on the show, one for release in March and one for release in July 1997. In reworking his TV series for Toei, Anno created an elaborate, phantasmagoric future world that may been all-but-incomprehensible to the uninitiated—the first film, especially, piled up plot points at warp speeds—but thrilled its under-twenty-five audience. Both films cleared over one billion yen in film rentals.

In 1998, however, Toei had less success, with only two films going over the one billion yen mark. Also, its video, TV, and real-estate business suffered sales slumps. In the first half of fiscal 1998, the studio recorded an operating loss of ¥1.09 billion ($9.65 million), the first such splash of red ink on its books since the company started business in 1952. In 1999 its big film for the first half of the year was *Poppoya*, a Yasuo Furuhata melodrama starring Ken Takakura as an aging Hokkaido stationmaster and hugely popular idol star Ryoko Hirosue as his daughter, who returns from the dead to his doorstep. Toei was praying for the film to work a similar miracle for its ailing bottom line—and fortunately, it became a smash hit.

New Forces Break Free

At the beginning of the 1990s, the strategies of the Big Three for countering the threat of Hollywood were little more than holding actions. Rather than nurture new talent or develop new ideas, they recycled tried-and-true formulas whose appeal was largely limited to narrow audience segments. Though their franchise series—the Tora-san, Godzilla and Toei Anime Fair films—brought steady returns, they did not usually generate breakout hits.

Once the home of serious auteur directors—the Kurosawas, Ozus, and Mizoguchis— the major studios were now hostile environments to filmmakers who could not, or would not, produce the required mass-audience fare. Even directors with outstanding talent and proven track records, such as Yoji Yamada and Juzo Itami, became tightly chained to the formulas they had first made successful. Yamada accepted these restraints, while Itami chafed under them, but neither could easily break free. It was as though Steven Spielberg, having once hit with *Raiders of the Lost Ark*, were to spend the rest of his career making Indiana Jones sequels.

The studios had the logic of the box office on their side: Japanese audiences would come again and again for Tora-san, while not nearly as many would buy tickets to Yamada's non-Tora-san films. But this logic was also self-limiting: by making only what had worked before, the studios may have controlled their risk, but they also failed to reach out to the young core audience who rarely went to a Japanese film, but eagerly lined up for *Jurassic Park*.

To further limit the risk, they largely left production to others, including television networks, video distributors, publishers, and trading houses, who viewed films as part of a multimedia business strategy, and companies with few or no media interests, who regarded film investment as a PR tool or tax write-off. Films by the latter group were often expressions of corporate politics and hubris that would have been DOA at the box office without large injections of advance ticket sales. To use another Hollywood analogy, it was if Kentucky Fried Chicken were to fund a biopic about the life of Stephen Foster, with a scene of Foster eating fried chicken while composing "My Old Kentucky Home," and forced its suppliers and franchisees to buy millions of advance tickets.

As the decade wound to its close, however, this industry power structure, which was once set in stone, was being challenged from all directions. One of the challengers was Studio Ghibli, whose animated period drama *Mononoke Hime* (Princess Mononoke) became the highest-grossing Japanese film of all time following its release in the summer of 1997. Studio co-founders Isao Takahata and Hayao Miyazaki rejected the standard industry practice of creating recyclable formulas from popular *manga* and TV shows and grinding out films based on them as cheaply and quickly as possible. Instead, they made each of their Studio Ghibli films a stand-alone, though the earnings from merchandising, books, and other spinoffs were considerable. In producing *Mononoke Hime*, Studio Ghibli spent twice the usual budget for a top-of-the-line Japanese film—nearly two billion yen—to achieve a high level of technical and artistic excellence. In pursuing this admittedly risky strategy—Studio Ghibli president Toshio Suzuki once commented, "Every time we make a film, we are betting the company"—Studio Ghibli has been able to reach a far wider audience than the typical Japanimation film, to compete successfully not with only Disney, but also with the Hollywood special-effects shows that would have otherwise dominated the Japanese market.

During the past decade, while Studio Ghibli challenged industry conventional wisdom from above, other filmmakers chipped away at it from below. Among the most successful of the upstarts was Masayuki Suo, whose *Shall We Dance?*, a comedy about a middle-aged salaryman's infatuation with a young dance instructor and his subsequent reawakening to life, earned ¥1.6 billion in film rentals in 1996 and, the following year, became the most popular Japanese film ever released in the United States, grossing more than ten million dollars. With his next project, Suo intended to hit the industry where it really counts: the wallet. Instead of going to the usual sources and signing away all his rights in exchange for financing, Suo planned to invite interested investors to publicly "bid" for stakes in his film. "Essentially, I'll borrow their money to make the movie and pay them back from the profits, while retaining all the rights." Suo explained. "Otherwise I'll just be ripped off by the film companies and TV networks."

Still another successful defier of the status quo was Shunji Iwai, a former music video and television drama director who burst onto the scene in 1995 with *Love Letter*, a debut feature about a young woman who wrote a letter to a dead lover and received a reply. Though its story was contrived in the extreme, *Love Letter*'s MTV editing rhythms and TV-drama romanticism drew the kind of audience—young, fashionable, and mostly female—that seldom paid to see Japanese films. *Love Letter* became a long-running hit and was later purchased by Fine Line for distribution in the United States. The following year, Iwai released *Swallowtail* (Swallowtail Butterfly), a film about outlaw Asians in a near-future Tokyo. Thematically and visually inspired by Ridley Scott's *Blade Runner*, *Swallowtail* had a flimsy excuse for a story, but enough of the Iwai style and attitude to make it an even bigger hit than *Love Letter*. "Iwai has made Japanese films trendy again," commented Shin'ya Kawai, the producer of both *Love Letter* and *Swallowtail*. He has also helped open the door for young filmmakers who may have, like Iwai, gotten their start outside the film industry, in TV commercials, TV dramas, or music videos, but are more in tune with the tastes of young audiences than their studio-trained elders.

By mid-decade, in response to these trends, the major studios began to give younger filmmakers more opportunities to reach a mass audience. Shochiku opened the door widest with its Cinema Japanesque project, though it was not limited to young directors. Meanwhile, in 1996 Toho and Pia, the publisher of a popular Tokyo entertainment listings magazine, launched a project called YES (Young Entertainment Square) for producing low-budget films by young directors and distributing them in Toho theaters. Both projects, however, have since bitten the dust. Cinema Japanesque was doomed by the departure of Kazuyoshi Okuyama, while YES financed only two films—Ryosuke Hashiguchi's 1996 *Nagisa no Sinbad* (Like Grains of Sand) and Shinobu Yaguchi's 1997 *Himitsu no Hanazono* (My Secret Garden)—before Toho bean counters axed it in 1998.

Nonetheless, in the closing years of the decade, production activity outside the studios picked up, with the media companies that fill most of the studios' lineups leading the way. In August 1997 video software maker Pony Canyon and advertising agency Hakuhodo announced their backing for Pony Canyon producer Shin'ya Kawai's PeacH project for making, marketing, and exhibiting films by young Japanese and Asian directors. Although Hakuhodo and Pony Canyon provided development money, they were not committed to funding production, at a cost of between three hundred and five hundred million yen per film. To make up for shortfalls, Kawai intended to recruit outside backers, both foreign and Japanese.

Kawai announced an initial slate of eight films to be made under the PeacH banner. The mission of the PeacH project, said Kawai, was to "systematize the filmmaking process" in Japan. "I believe that an instinct for filmmaking is important," he said, "but instinct needs to be backed by objective data." The development process, which was often underfunded by the domestic industry, would be given first priority. With the backing of Hakuhodo, Kawai and his PeacH associates market-tested prospective projects before giving them the greenlight. "We will continue market testing throughout the filmmaking process, beginning with scripting and casting, " Kawai said. "This is considered standard practice in Hollywood, but not yet in Japan." Unfortunately, the first film under the PeacH banner, stage director Amon Miyamoto's debut feature *Beat*, flopped following its release in September 1998.

In December 1998, Wowow (Japan Satellite Broadcasting), Japan's leading satellite entertainment channel, underwrote a new film-production unit. Called Suncent Cinema Works, the new unit is headed by Takenori Sento, the producer who was responsible for the Wowow J Movie Wars series of low-budget films since its inception in 1992. While not producing any blockbusters, Sento's J Movie Wars series generated arthouse hits and boosted several of its directors to domestic and international recognition. One was Hideo Nakata, whose success with the 1996 J Movie Wars film *Joyurei* (Actress Ghost) earned him the nod to helm the 1997 psycho-horror smash *Ring* (The Ring). Another was Naomi Sento (née Kawase), Sento's wife, who in 1997 become the first Japanese woman to win the Camera d'Or prize at the Cannes Film Festival for *Moe no Suzaku* (Suzaku)—a J Movie Wars film.

Through Suncent Cinema Works, Sento intends to work with the best of the Japanese New Wave. In April 1999, Sento launched New Project J–Cine-X, which he described as "a major project that will assemble directors who have gained strong reputations at foreign film festivals and make films with them aimed at the overseas market." Among directors anounced as participating were Naomi Sento, Hirokazu Koreeda, Makoto Shinozaki, Go Riju, and Shinji Aoyama. "The Japanese film industry is lagging behind that of Europe and the United States," added Sento at the press conference announcing the new unit. "I would like to introduce Western production methods into that industry as quickly as possible. That is one of the missions I hope to accomplish with this new company."

Although individual innovators such as Kawai and Sento are transforming the way the Japanese film industry makes and distributes movies, structural agents of change are also becoming increasingly important. One is the multiplex building boom. The Japanese exhibition sector was long in decline, with the number of theatres falling from a postwar high of 7,457 in 1960 to a low of 1,758 in 1994. In recent years, however, construction of multiplex cinemas has proceeded apace, with the number of screens growing to 1,993 by the end of 1998, the fourth straight year of increase, with a net gain of 259. With foreign-backed exhibitors such as UCI, AMC, Virgin, and Warner Mycal leading the way, and Japanese companies such as Toho, Shochiku, Sony, and Jusco entering the multiplex business, three thousand screens are expected to be in operation by 2002, creating new venues for both domestic and foreign films.

Also, by the end of July 1999, nearly 1.6 million subscribers had signed on for the DirecTV and SKY PerfecTV! digital communications satellite TV platforms, generating a larger demand for the products of Japanese filmmakers. In addition to their pay-per-view channels, the platforms were broadcasting both new and classic Japanese films on a range of premium services, including the Jidaigeki (Period Drama), Neco, Wowow Plus 2, and Eisei Gekijo (Satellite Theater) channels. These platforms will not have the digital satellite business to themselves for long, however. In December 2000 the BS-4 digital broadcast satellite is scheduled to begin beaming HDTV and SDTV channels backed by NHK, Wowow, the five commercial networks, and other broadcasters, offering yet more new markets for Japanese films.

Also, foreign markets, long largely closed to Japanese films, have started to open up. Masayuki Suo's *Shall We Dance?*, which in 1997 became the highest-grossing Japanese film ever released in United States, is perhaps the most outstanding example of this acceptance, but it is not the only one. In July 1996 the Tokuma Shoten media group (parent company of Studio Ghibli and Daiei) and Buena Vista International (worldwide distribution arm of the Walt Disney Company), agreed to distribute Hayao Miyazaki's *Mononoke Hime* and other Studio Ghibli and Daiei films worldwide. Disney distribution subsidiary Miramax plans to release *Mononoke Hime* in October 1999 in twenty major U.S. markets. Warner Brothers topped this by announcing that it would release *Pokémon the Movie: Mewtwo Strikes Back*—a feature-length animation that was the second-highest grossing Japanese film in 1998 under the title *Pokemon Mewtwo no Gyakushu*—on 1,500 to 2,000 screens in the U.S. in November 1999.

Still another sign of resurgence was the spate of film-festival awards won by Japanese films in 1997, most notably a Palme d'Or for Shohei Imamura's *Unagi* (The Eel) at the Cannes Film Festival and a Golden Lion for Takeshi Kitano's *Hana-Bi* (Fireworks) at the Venice Film Festival. *Hana-Bi* was later sold to more than thirty territories worldwide and, in March 1998, was released by independent distributor Milestone in nearly fifty U.S. cities. In addition, Kitano's follow-up film, *Kikujiro no Natsu* (Kikujiro), was purchased by Sony Classics for U.S. release.

Although the West is still a primary target of Japanese filmmakers with international ambitions, in mid-decade they also began to find more opportunities in Asia, where local audiences were eager consumers of Japanese music, TV shows, fashion, and increasingly, films. The result was a mini-boom in films made with Japanese and Asian talent and money, targeted primarily at Japanese and Chinese-language markets, including Tony

Au's 1995 *The Christ of Nanjing,* Takayoshi Watanabe's 1997 *Hong Kong Daiyasokai: Touch & Maggie* (Hong Kong Nightclub), Yim Ho's 1997 *Kitchen,* Kenki Saegusa's 1997 *Misty,* Takashi Miike's 1997 *Gokudo Kuro Shakai Rainy Dog* (Rainy Dog), and Lee Chi Ngai's 1998 *Fuyajo* (Sleepless Town). The Amuse talent agency cofinanced the first three of these films, together with Japanese and Asian partners, with the aim of promoting its contract talent to Asian audiences. *Misty,* a remake of *Rashomon* produced by Gaga Communications, and *Fuyajo,* a gang movie set in Shinjuku, made by Kadokawa Shoten and Ace Pictures, exploited the pan-Asian popularity of Takeshi Kaneshiro, a half-Taiwanese, half-Japanese actor who first rose to prominence in the films of Wong Kar-Wai. *Rainy Dog* was a Toei Video gangster film that, in its hard-eyed refusal to exoticize its Taipei setting or glamorize its ruthless Taiwanese gangsters, was the best of the lot.

In January 1999 this trend continued with the start of production on Stanley Kwan's *Tale of an Island,* the first film of the Y2K Project. Launched in mid-1998 by Pony Canyon, Nippon Herald, Omega Project, and other partners, the Y2K Project was a consortium for producing films by three leading Asian directors—Hong Kong's Stanley Kwan, Taiwan's Edward Yang, and Japan's Shunji Iwai—with Asian casts and crews, for Asian and other international audiences.

These trends, taken together, do not mean that another Golden Age is at hand. The domestic commercial success of a *Mononoke Hime* and the foreign critical acclaim for a *Hana-Bi* are bright spots in a picture that is still all too dark. Government support for Japanese filmmakers is nearly non-existent, the industry remains formula ridden and under financed, and the success of a few promising local talents is easily steamrollered at the box office by a *Titanic.* Anyone willing to bet that the Japanese films can take on the Hollywood juggernaut and win is taking a long shot indeed.

Even so, a positive synergy, driven by new talent and new markets, is in place. Industry survival, once in doubt, now seems likely, for another decade at least. Change, for long so slow, is at last accelerating, as new players and practices emerge. Block-booking is one likely casualty in the coming multiplex age, while Japanimation, which can cross national borders more easily than live-action films, is one likely winner. Also, erosion of the Big Three's dominance of distribution and exhibition is likely to continue. Studios, however, have a way of weathering even the worst of catastrophes. Once given up as a goner after its 1993 bankruptcy, Nikkatsu is making movies again under the aegis of Namco. Shochiku is a probable candidate for this kind of corporate death and resurrection.

The long-term prosperity of the industry, however, depends less on recruiting the right corporate angels than in developing the right kind of human capital. For too long the studios have been run by salarymen only interested in carving out their accustomed share of a shrinking pie. But if mainstream Japanese films are to appeal to more than cartoon-crazy kids, idol-besotted teens, or tradition-loving old folks, more filmmakers able to innovate, instead of imitate, have to get the greenlight.

The New Wave OF THE NINETIES

n the 1990s, the independent sector was a fertile breeding ground for new talent as well as new themes. The old, dark image of the Japanese movie industry—where aspiring directors could labor for years, if not decades, in the shadows before their debuts—began to change as Gen X independent filmmakers entered the industry via many routes. Some got their start making Super-8 student films, while others learned their craft filming TV commercials and music videos. Some turned out film after film while still in their early thirties or even younger. Many would-be Kurosawas still had to struggle and scrape to get their first movies made, but the light at the end of the tunnel had at least become less dim.

The director who most strikingly exemplified the new optimism was Shunji Iwai, who burst onto the scene in 1995 with *Love Letter*. An ingeniously contrived, stylishly photographed tale of a woman who writes a letter to dead lover—and gets a reply— *Love Letter* played for fourteen weeks to standing-room-only crowds at a central Tokyo theater and enjoyed similarly long runs in the rest of Japan. After the success of his first feature, Iwai was a natural for the title of Hottest Young Director of the Decade. He stood out for not only his pop-star good looks, but his eclectic background (he had made music videos, promotional films, and TV dramas before directing his first feature), techno-geek approach to filmmaking (he preferred to storyboard his films on computer before filming a single frame), and unconventional views (he called himself an *eizo sakka* [image artist] who was willing to work in any film media and had no use for the traditional industry pecking order that placed feature movies on top and other forms of film beneath).

Following *Love Letter*, Iwai released two bills of short films in quick succession, *undo* and *Uchiage Hanabi: Shita kara Miru ka Yoko kara Miru ka* (Shooting Fireworks), followed by *Picnic* and *Fried Dragon Fish*. *Uchiage Hanabi* and *Fried Dragon Fish* were originally one-hour dramas shot in video and broadcast on late-night television in 1993, while *Undo* and *Picnic* were short films shot in 1994 for theatrical release.

Taking as its theme the awakening of sexuality and the end of childhood, *Uchiage Hanabi* depicted a preteen world by turns theatrically intense, wildly giddy, and heart-piercingly romantic, but which had the feel of lived reality. It earned Iwai a Newcomers Award from the Japan Directors Guild—an unprecedented honor for a young TV director.

Picnic was a seventy-two-minute film about three young patients of a mental hospital who escape by, not going over the wall, but walking on top of it. Slated for release in the spring of 1995, it was abruptly pulled in the wake of the poison gas attacks on the Tokyo subway system by members of the Aum Shinrikyo cult. The distributor felt that the film's story—three young mental patients enjoying a last breath of freedom before the coming of Armageddon—was too close to the headlines for comfort.

Based on a photo story Iwai shot for a Japanese magazine, *Undo* was also filmed in 1994. The story is again about life on the edge, this time focusing on a couple, played by Etsushi Toyokawa and Tomoko Yamaguchi, who live in a stylishly bohemian apartment in Tokyo. The man is a deadline-pressed writer; the woman is slowing going mad because her lover doesn't pay enough attention to her. She becomes obsessed with tying food, books, the family pets, and finally herself in layer after layer of rope and twine. The ties that bind, we see, end by strangling.

In these early films Iwai was, in a way common to his generation of filmmakers, focusing more on private than public concerns, while often emphasizing visual style over narrative substance. His strengths and weaknesses were most fully on display in *Swallowtail* (Swallowtail Butterfly), set in a twenty-first-century Tokyo swarming with yen-mad foreigners from all over Asia. The film's heroes live in Yen Town, a ragtag encampment on the edge of Tokyo. Among them are a Chinese prostitute named Glico, played by popular rock diva Chara, who wears a tattoo of a swallowtail butterfly on her chest to make herself stand out from the faceless masses around her, an orphaned teenage girl (Ayumi Ito) whom Glico takes under her care, and a street-smart Chinese hustler (Hiroshi Mikami) who is crazy about Glico and will do anything for a yen.

There is a paper-thin thriller story line about the struggle between Yen Towners, including the Chinese hustler, and a rival gang over a computer code for generating phony ¥10,000 notes. There are scenes of Glico singing funky rock numbers with an ensemble called the Yen Town Band that are essentially video clips plugging the group's CDs (which became real-life hits). There are strikingly deliquescent images of a society in chaotic and creative ferment that are undoubtedly Iwai (although others are lifted from *Blade Runner*.) But for all its sexy stylistics, *Swallowtail* lacks the impact of Ridley Scott's cult classic. Iwai presents his Asians-in-Japan as more vital and sympathetic than the conformist mass of Japanese around them, but he fails to make their dilemmas either compelling or real. At the box office, however, none of these critical quibbles mattered: the film attracted the same young trendies who had made Iwai's other films box office smashes, only in greater numbers. Iwai's title as Hottest Young Director was still secure.

In 1998 Iwai released *Shigatsu Monogatari* (April Story), a simply told, lushly produced film about a college freshman's tentative steps toward adulthood and love. Though featuring idol star Takako Matsu, *Shigatsu* had too much of Iwai's directorial personality to simply be a Matsu vehicle. Filled with hypergeneric scenes of cherry blossoms blooming and spring rains falling, it was aimed at Iwai's core audience, with their *shojo manga* (girls comic) sensibility, but was only a modest success at the box office. It also marked a new, more traditional direction for Iwai, who put most of the editing tricks of his earlier films back in the box.

Another director who resembled Iwai in the brilliance of his visual imagination, the speed of his rise, and the privacy of his concerns was Shinji Aoyama, who started a rock band in high school, made 8mm films while a student at Rikkyo University, worked as an assistant director after graduation, and in 1996 released his first feature, *Helpless*.

A tale of Gen Xers who float through their lives without direction, resort to random violence, and view their deeds with a casual indifference, *Helpless* was a disturbing film, not only for what it said, but the way it said it. Aoyama was, like Iwai, fundamentally sympathetic toward his protagonists, viewing them as outsider heroes. Also, like Iwai he was at times more into stylistic attitudinizing than in creating a credible emotional universe. *Helpless* featured Tadanobu Asano as a drifter who becomes an unwilling witness to a *yakuza* murder and, after the suicide of his father, turns violent himself. Asano's explosive performance and dark charisma helped make *Helpless* an art-house hit.

In the space of little more than a year following his debut, Aoyama directed three more films: *Chimpira* (Two Punks), *Waga Mune ni Kyoki Ari* (There's a Weapon in My Heart), and *Wild Life*. This industry did not gone unnoticed abroad: both *Helpless* and *Chimpira* were screened widely at foreign film festivals.

By making four low-budget films in a year, Aoyama was able to quickly develop his considerable talents in new directions. The proof was in his fourth feature, *Wild Life*. One again there was a tall, longhaired hero, this time played by Kosuke Toyohara, lost in a sea of anomie. And once again, the hero found himself mixed up with the *yakuza*, with predictably violent results. But Aoyama's treatment of this familiar material was drier, funnier, and stronger. Despite cartoonish moments, *Wild Life* was less a genre send-up than a carefully stylized exercise in genre-stretching. While delivering the entertainment goods, including a few laughs, a few chills, and a few fresh takes on *yakuza* movie conventions, the film went beyond genre limits to explore broader themes, including the unpredictability of life and the elusiveness of truth. It wanted to be an existential black comedy, but with a thriller punch—and largely succeeded.

Many films by young directors in the latter half of the nineties featured Gen Xers living on the edge of society or even in the center of the underworld, flouting laws and convention with a blank casualness or unreasoning fury. Their heroes, including the young lovers embarked on crime sprees in Akira Nobi's *Secret Waltz* (1996) or Ataru Oikawa's *Nihonsei Shonen* (The Boy Made In Japan, 1995), exemplified the alienation of many young people, who struck not a few older Japanese as creatures from another planet.

Japanese Gen Xers' first loyalties were to themselves and a select circle of friends and lovers, rather than a clan, a company, or society as a whole. Their interests were often intensely, even bizarrely, personal, rather than being group-oriented and socially sanctioned. Their resistance to the conforming pressures of Japanese society manifested itself more in small individual gestures of defiance—dying one's hair blonde or eating fast food on commuter trains—than in organized acts of protest.

The expression of that anomie in films by young directors, however, often seemed more inspired by the films of Quentin Tarantino or Wong Kar-Wai than by Japanese realities. Not many Japanese young people, after all, mugged salarymen for kicks (*Secret*

Waltz) or wandered about the hinterlands with a Beretta 935 (*Nihonsei Shonen*). Some young directors, however, evinced a perspective that extended beyond a movie-fed imagination to encompass real Japanese social issues, in films populated by recognizable Japanese types.

Among the best was Satoshi Isaka, who debuted in 1996 with *Focus*, a film about the manipulativeness of the Japanese media, the fragmentation of Japanese society, and the rage boiling within young Japanese who were excluded from—or divorced themselves from—the mainstream. Its central characters were a slimeball TV director (Akira Shirai) who would exploit his own mother for a story, and his latest interviewee-cum-victim, a brilliant but introverted nerd (played by Tadanobu Asano, yet again) who interacted with the world through his electronic eavesdropping devices.

The director tries to wheedle his way into the nerd's good graces, while playing him on camera for a Peeping Tom creep. The nerd, though rightly suspicious of the director's motives, takes him for a drive in his car and, while they are cruising through the night streets of Tokyo, overhears a conversation about a smuggled gun. The director is frantic to follow up on this hot lead and, with the nerd's reluctant assistance, fakes a discovery scene. Soon after, this pair encounters a trio of skateboarders who want to know what they have been up to. When the director irritably shoos them away, they jump on the nerd's car. Enraged, the nerd runs over one of the skateboarders and drives the director and his terrified female assistant to his apartment for the taping of a true-life horror story, in which they are the reluctant stars. Isaka used his camera to actively express, not just passively record, filming one cut per scene, entirely from the viewpoint of an invisible cameraman. This approach gave *Focus* immediacy and intensity of front-line documentary filmmaking. Isaka, who apprenticed as an assistant director for Shoji Segawa and Yoichi Higashi, and worked as a TV director before making his feature debut with *Focus*, exposed not only the mass media's exploitation of its victims, but the complicity of its audience. We are, his camera tells us, not just innocent witnesses, but voyeurs who can't stop watching.

His follow-up film, the 1998 *Onna Keiji Riko: Seibo no Fukaki Fuchi* (Riko) was a thriller about a woman detective who investigates a baffling murder case while schlepping her baby to and from the daycare center. Despite a strong performance by Ryoko Takizawa as the title character, *Onna Keiji Riko* was a little more than a well-plotted, competently told cop-on-a-mission movie, with a few New Age twists to set it apart from similar fare on the video shelf.

Like Iwai, Aoyama and Isaka, many new directors were trying to reinvent Japanese cinema for the 1990s, not continue the tradition of the Golden Age directors. Iwai bluntly said that young Japanese audiences knew neither the films of Kurosawa or Ozu nor the society they depicted. "We have to make movies that appeal (to younger moviegoers) and reflect the world they're living in," he commented.

A few younger directors, however, incorporated elements of classical Japanese cinema into their films, while addressing contemporary concerns. One was Makoto Shinozaki, whose 1996 debut feature, *Okaeri*, described the disintegration of a marriage and a mind. Takashi (Susumu Terajima), is a cram-school teacher who, like so many other Japanese men, leaves early and comes home late. While his wife, Yuriko (Miho Uemura), is waiting for his return, with a cold dinner on the table, he is out drinking with friends. A former classical pianist who now transcribes tapes for a living, she begins to go mad with loneliness. Soon, she slips over the edge and starts patrolling the neighborhood to thwart a mysterious "organization." By the time Takashi realizes something is wrong, Yuriko is already in the grip of psychosis. He tries to free her with persuasion, professional help, and in the end, the power of love.

A film journalist and projectionist before he directed his first film, Shinozaki firmly rejected the hackneyed devices of Japanese screen melodrama. *Okaeri* had none of the usual confrontation scenes between husband and wife, with their perfervid speeches and loud lamenting, no dramatic entrances of grieved parents or angry siblings as the soundtrack swelled. Instead, Shinozaki told his story quietly but eloquently, in episodes that were carefully shaped but sprang directly from life. He employed music sparingly, making subtle use of background sound, including the bustle of neighborhood life outside Yuriko's window, to underscore her feeling of isolation. Rather than trying speed up the action with camera moves and quick cuts, he allowed his scenes to develop at a natural pace. In a crucial reconciliation scene, in which Takashi comforts a sobbing Yuriko, he held his camera in medium closeup for what seems an eternity, but instead of irritating with its length, this cut drew the audience into the raw emotional core of the scene. Without imposing an obvious style, Shinozaki impressed as a stylist of a high order.

Okaeri received an enthusiastic critical reception both in Japan and at dozens of festivals abroad, including a Best Director and a FIPRESCI international film press prize at the International Film Festival in Thessalonika, Greece, but Shinozaki did not find it easy to raise money for his next film. While recruiting backers and writing a script, he shot a video about the making of Takeshi Kitano's eighth film, *Kikujiro no Natsu* (Kikujiro) in the summer of 1998.

Shinozaki was not alone in adhering to a less-is-more aesthetic or taking a greater interest in naturalistic stories of intimate relationships than in *manga*-esque tales of feral teens indulging in ultraviolence. Hirokazu Koreeda's debut feature, *Maboroshi no Hikari* (Maborosi), which was screened in competition at the 1995 Venice Film Festival, went even farther in rejecting not only Hollywood-derived storylines and MTV-inspired editing tricks, but virtually the entire media-mad, consumption-crazed side of modern Japan. The pace was deliberate, the colors were muted, and the settings were purely Japanesque. Even the actors seemed to blend tastefully and modestly into the background, like figures in a classical landscape scroll.

A director for the TV Man Union production house, which was known for its high-quality documentaries, Koreeda ran the risk of simply creating pretty pictures that had as much relation to modern Japan as a retro-themed Ginza coffee shop, but he created a world of beauty so compelling and told a story of mortal loss so absorbing that the audience could not stand outside, looking in. It had to enter.

The heroine is a young woman, played by Makiko Esumi, whose first husband (Tadanobu Asano) steps out the door one day, and without any warning, walks under the wheels of a moving train. Five years later she marries a kindly widower in a remote seaside village. But for all her new-found happiness, she cannot escape the feeling that she is doomed to lose the ones she loves.

Though this plot summary sounds bleak, the movie is anything but. Instead, Koreeda creates a mood that is dreamlike but vibrant, suffused with a sense of life's transience, but filled with a simple human warmth. Comparisons were made with Ozu, but whereas the director of *Tokyo Monogatari* (Tokyo Story) offered a view of middle-class life that selectively reflected contemporary realities circa 1953, Koreeda constructed a cinematic refuge from the frantic hurry, blaring ugliness, and grinning vulgarity of Japan in 1995.

In his second feature, the 1999 *Wonderful Life* (After Life), Koreeda returned to a theme he first explored in *Without Memory*, a 1994 documentary about a man with a rare neurological condition that robbed him of his memory and forced him to live in an eternal present. In *Wonderful Life*, the setting is a limbo where the spirits of the recent dead come to select, with the assistance of sympathetic guides, their most precious memory to take with them to eternity. Some have no trouble choosing, while others agonize—or refuse to cooperate. Many of these stories, including several of the funniest and most touching, emerged from interviews that Koreeda and his staff conducted with nearly five hundred ordinary Japanese, several of whom appear on camera. Abjuring the use of surrealistic effects—the film seems to take place on the tree-lined campus of an abandoned school—Koreeda creates an intimate human reality that has nothing to with New Age wish-fulfillment, everything to do with the essence of who we are and the meaning of where we've been. A film about death becomes a quietly moving essay on the importance of love.

Another new director who explored the fragility of modern relationships, but with an approach more realistically here-and-now than lyrically what-if was Nobuhiro Suwa, whose 1997 debut film *2/Duo* recorded a young couple's interpersonal meltdown with the immediacy and realism of a documentary. Not surprising, actually: Suwa had worked as a documentarian and, in filming his first feature, made extensive use of documentary methods. Instead of writing a conventional script, he had lead actors Hidetoshi Nishijima and Eri Yu improvise from a brief treatment. He even interviewed their characters at crucial stops along their journey to separation. The result was a closely observed portrait of a couple—and by inference, a generation— that appear to have it all, including an unerring instinct for the right style and attitude, but find adulthood a terror and intimacy hard, if not impossible, to achieve.

It is tempting to draw a neat line between Iwai and other Gen Xers who reject the cinematic past, cross genre boundaries, and push artistic envelopes, and Shinozaki and other neoclassicists whose aesthetic invites comparisons with Golden Age masters, and whose sensibility is more identifiably Japanese. Such lines, however, have a way of getting smudged. Naomi Sento's debut feature, the 1997 *Moe no Suzaku* (Suzaku) would seem to fit nicely in the neoclassicist category. In depicting fifteen years in the life of a family in a remote Nara Prefecture village, Sento creates a seemingly idyllic world with close ties to the nature and an ancient past. In the opening scenes, which take place in the early 1970s, the Tahara family is living in a farmhouse in the mountains of Nara Prefecture, making their living from the majestic forests of Yoshino cedars that surround them, as they have for generations. Their three-generation household includes a three-year-old girl and an eleven-year-old boy—the son of the father's sister—who never seem to watch television or read comic books.

This idyll soon ends, however. The father (Jun Kunimura) is devastated when construction on a railroad tunnel, which he had hoped would revive the declining economy of the village, is suddenly abandoned. When the film flashes forward fifteen years, he has become a blanked-out shell and his wife has been forced to take a job at a local inn to make ends meet. Meanwhile, the two children, now grown, have begun to take a more than cousinly interest in each other.

While Sento's themes, including the disintegration of the family and the abandonment of traditional lifestyles, are also those of many Golden Age masters, her methods are anything but orthodox. A documentarian who won acclaim for her autobiographical

8mm films, Sento shot *Moe no Suzaku* in a mountain village that was experiencing the economic crisis described in the film. A Nara native, she researched conditions in the village for three years, and had her staff live there for three months prior to shooting. As one of their preproduction chores, they repaired an old farmhouse that was to be the Tahara family's home. Finally, Sento cast all of the parts, save for that of the father, played by Jun Kunimura, from amateurs, including several local people. *Moe no Suzaku* may not have the you-are-there feel of Suwa's *2/Duo*, but went even farther in using documentary methods to impart a sense of both inner and outer reality. As a pusher of artistic envelopes, Kawase was, in her own unobtrusive way, as bold as Aoyama and Iwai.

In her 1998 documentary, *Somaudo Monogatari* (The Weald) Sento returned to the village that was the setting for *Moe no Suzaku* to record the life stories of nine elderly villagers. Instead of describing the problems of the aged in rural Japan, she tried to capture the flavor of her interviewees' lives and the essence of their characters through not only their words, but their environment, their work, and even the images of their faces in extreme closeup, as though she were trying to read their souls from the lines on their weathered skin. As in *Moe no Suzaku*, her approach was personal, impressionistic, poetic and minimalist. There was no narrator, no soundtrack music, no designer-clothed reporter conducting interviews with talking heads. Instead, Sento addressed her subjects as a loving, inquisitive, and at times sassy daughter. They, in turn, spoke straight from their hearts, from the depths of their lives.

Given her interest in family life, her concern for broader social issues and her generation-spanning story line, Sento was also something of an exception among younger directors. Most, from either side of the aesthetic divide, focused squarely on the present lives of members of their own generation. One reason was budgetary; it was cheaper to make a Gen X coming-of-age movie that a period drama. (Though in his 1998 feature debut *Samurai Fiction* music-video wunderkind Hiroyuki Nakano tried, with a bare-bones budget, to do for samurai swashbucklers what Quentin Tarantino did for crime thrillers: reinvent a tired genre with the cheeky sensibility of a pop-culture addict.)

A more compelling reason, however, was a lack of inclination. The big issues that occupied (and, in some cases, still occupy) older directors, including the collapse of traditional values brought about by Westernization and the impact of World War II on both individuals and society as a whole, no longer engaged filmmakers born decades after the war's end into the abundance of the world's second largest economy.

Estranged from politics, alienated from their ancestral roots, flooded with information, they and their young audiences had become highly sophisticated consumers of visual software, including films, television, comics, and computer games, and seemed to be more interested in expressing their personal concerns—with an attitude detached rather than engaged, with an emotional temperature cool rather than hot. The sentimentalism that was so long a hallmark of so many mainstream Japanese dramas was hard to find in the films of younger directors. The explosive, even anarchic, energy that once characterized so many Japanese genre films—from the samurai dramas of Kurosawa to the *yakuza* action films of Kinji Fukasaku—had become less common as well, save in such parody forms as Sabu's frenetic 1997 *Postman Blues*, whose intricately constructed chase scenes were an over-the-top homage to Buster Keaton, or Shin'ya Tsukamoto's 1995 *Tokyo Fist*, which made wonderfully twisted comedy and compellingly bizarre drama from a white rage that pounded its victims to a literal pulp and whipped audiences into dazed submission.

Interestingly, the decade's biggest domestic hit, Hayao Miyazaki's 1997 animated feature *Mononoke Hime* (Princess Mononoke), went directly against these trends. Set in medieval Japan, it focused on the one-sided battle between nature and humankind, imaginatively recreated Japan's ancient mythopoetic universe and was populated with members of despised and oppressed minority groups. Many in the audience, as it happened, were the same Gen Xers who had lined up for *Swallowtail* the year before. Perhaps Japan's younger directors, at least those of them who hope to reach beyond a coterie to a wider audience, could still learn a lesson or two from their distinguished predecessor.

Asians in Japan
JAPANESE IN ASIA

apanese independent filmmakers, by default, have been at the forefront in seeking
out new themes—and new audiences. Throughout the 1990s, one of the themes
they have found most fruitful is the growing intercourse between Japan and its
Asian neighbors. During the bubble economy years of the late 1980s and early 1990s,
Asian students and workers began to flood into Japan in unprecedented numbers and
enter the popular consciousness through a variety of media, including film. Although
they may have wanted to exploit a hot topical theme, many Japanese filmmakers took
a decidedly sympathetic view of their Asian heroes, be they Bangladeshi day-laborers,
Filipino bar hostesses, or Taiwanese gangsters, and tried to dig beneath the usual
stereotypes, with varying results. Many of their films had a freshness and inventiveness
lacking in mainstream commercial product. Through their Asian characters, Japanese
directors seemed to be viewing their own work and their own society with new eyes.

By mid-decade, with Asians in Japan no longer as much in the news, the earnestness
of the early films began to give way to a more comic, less advocatory approach, as
Japanese characters not only interacted with the Asians in their midst but ventured out
to Asian countries themselves. By the end of the decade, with more film companies
seeking to exploit the Asian market, Japanese-Asian coproductions started to flourish,
with the emphasis shifting from art to entertainment.

The first in the spate of bubble-era films about Asians in Japan was Nobuhiko
Obayashi's 1989 *Pekinteki Suika* (Beijing Watermelon), a seriocomic drama inspired by
a true story about a Japanese vegetable-store owner who befriended a group of Chinese
students. A pioneer experimental filmmaker in the sixties and early seventies, Obayashi
made his feature debut with the 1977 horror-fantasy *House* but was best known for his
films about young people, often with fantasy themes, notably the 1982 hit *Tenkosei*
(Sayonara, Me). In *Pekinteki Suika*, Obayashi was again working with a youthful cast
while taking a playful, unconventional approach to his material.

In outline, the story sounds like typical feel-good fare. A vegetable-store owner who begins the film as a hard-nosed businessman with little time for the Chinese students living in a nearby dorm undergoes a change of heart when he discovers one dying of malnutrition. He becomes a Good Samaritan, selling his vegetables at a discount to the students and taking them on tours of Tokyo. When he falls into debt and collapses from exhaustion, the students rally to save their "Japanese father." The film's tone, however, is anything but maudlin. Taking a cue from Robert Altman, Obayashi allowed his cast of newcomers to improvise much of their dialogue in group scenes, giving *Pekinteki Suika* a *cinema verité* feel, with more jokes flying than tears flowing.

When the occasion demanded it, however, Obayashi abandoned the illusion of realism altogether. In the original script the vegetable-store owner and his wife, played by Bengal and Masako Motai, visited Beijing with the students. Unfortunately, the 1989 massacre of pro-democracy demonstrators at Tiananmen Square made it impossible to shoot on location. Instead, Obayashi elected to have his two principals face the camera in front of an airplane mockup, step out of character and explain why they were unable to go to China. Though unorthodox, this scene fit in well with the documentary methods Obayashi had used for the rest of the film and served to underscore the students' plight. In this case necessity truly did prove to be the mother of fertile invention.

Although Obayashi was already an established figure by the late 1980s, the directors of many of the films about Asians in Japan were industry newcomers or outsiders. Like Obayashi, they were sympathetic to their Asian heroes and innovative in their treatment of their unusual subject matter. In telling the stories of Asians living on the fringes on Japanese society, they rejected conventional humanist pieties and appeals to sentiment, while embracing less didactic, more personal approaches.

One of the newcomers was *manga* artist and animator Katsuhiro Otomo, who had become known to international audiences for *Akira* (1988), a dark fantasy set in an intricately imagined Neo Tokyo in the year 2019. In his first live-action feature, the 1989 *World Apartment Horror*, Otomo returned to the present to tell a story about Asian workers and students battling a *yakuza* manager in a rundown boarding house, audaciously combining low comedy, serious social commentary, and supernatural fantasy.

The residents of the rooming house represent the Asian spectrum, from a rotund Pakistani factory worker to four Chinese who live together in a six-mat room and seem to spend all their time either cooking or playing mah-jongg. The *yakuza* manager has been sent by his boss to clear them out in preparation for the construction of a new building—a storyline ripped from bubble-era headlines about *jiageya*, underworld characters sent to persuade, with force if necessary, owners and tenants of lucrative downtown properties to move elsewhere. The gangster, played by the lantern-jawed Yuji Nakamura, soon learns that the boarding-house residents have mysterious powers on their side: the ceiling heaves violently when he is making love to his tarty girlfriend, and even his boom box develops a mind of its own. Despite the menace implied in its title, *World Apartment Horror* is closer in spirit to *Ghostbusters* than *Friday the 13th*. In its climax, however, the film lurches from comedy to heavy-handed drama and violates its own mood. Also, despite its all-Asians-are-brothers message, the film's Asian heroes are more amusing caricatures than clearly defined individuals.

Hirotaka Tashiro's 1991 *Afureru Atsui Namida* (Swimming With Tears), a film about a young Filipina adrift in Tokyo, dug deeper beneath the surface to provide an intimate look at the conflicted relationship between Asians in Japan and their Japanese hosts. Its title, however, was misleading; instead of jerking tears, first-time director Tashiro told his story with a sympathy that was all the more powerful for its restraint.

The film's heroine is Fey (Ruby Moreno), a young Filipina who runs away from her Japanese husband (Masayuki Suzuki), a close-mouthed Tohoku farmer who regards her more as a breeder and worker than a wife. The deep snow that she stumbles through in her escape seems to symbolize the state of her marriage. Arriving in Shin Okubo—Tokyo's Mecca for Asian workers—she becomes a waitress at a Chinese restaurant and befriends a college professor (Shiro Sano) and his lover (Jun Togawa) who live next door to her flat. After escaping from her marriage and finding a measure of peace and happiness, she begins to confront her past in the person of her father, a Japanese who left her mother and returned to Japan twenty years ago. Fey arranges to meet him, more to ask questions about her identity than to claim kinship. A successful businessman who has hidden his past, the father stands for the ugly Japanese who exploit other Asians and think that money solves all problems, but Tashiro also shows us the weary face of a hardworking corporate warrior who still longs for the Philippines' tropical pleasures.

Although Tashiro is a more obviously committed filmmaker than either Otomo or Obayashi, his film's politics do not outweigh its individual human dramas. In a way very Japanese (or one might also say, very Asian), he refuses to assign blame. Everyone in the film, both Japanese and Filipino, are alike in their suffering humanity. His river of tears has many tributaries.

In the early 1990s, younger Japanese filmmakers began taking a new interest in not only Asians, but all minority groups in Japanese society, including Okinawans, *buraku-min* (outcastes), gays, and AIDS victims. The obsession of a previous generation of filmmakers with the meaning of Japanese identity in the wake of postwar cultural upheaval and spiritual malaise was giving way to a new awareness of the diversity among Japan's ostensibly homogenous masses. Their films broke new ground, with a welcome lack of the self-lacerating *Sturm und Drang* that long characterized so many Japanese problem films. One was Go Takamine's 1989 *Untama Giru*, an exercise in magic realism that satirized the exploitation of Okinawa by its Japanese and American conquerors. Another was the 1992 three-director omnibus *Pineapple Tours*, a delightfully vivacious examination of the Okinawan cultural and historical landscape. Still another was Takehiro Nakajima's 1992 *Okoge*, a frank and sympathetic view of gay life in Japan.

This new, personal, largely apolitical interest in "the Other" was epitomized by Yoichi Sai's *Tsuki wa Dotchi ni Deteiru* (All Under the Moon), a 1993 comedy about a cynical Korean cabby (Goro Kishitani) who finds himself in bed and, eventually, in love with a Filipina bartender (Ruby Moreno). A second-generation ethnic Korean, Sai skewered all sides equally and, in doing so, erased the distinction between "us" and "them" found in even the best-intentioned films about Asians in Japan. *Tsuki* enjoyed a long run and swept domestic film awards in 1993. Sai, however, said he had no interest in repeating his success and being tagged as a "Korean" filmmaker. His next two films, the 1994 murder mystery *Marks no Yama* (Marks Mountain) and the 1995 caper comedy *Tokyo Deluxe*, were non-ethnic attempts to appeal to the mainstream.

In 1998 Sai returned to the Asians-in-Japan theme with *Inu, Hashiru* (Dog Race), another black comedy whose heroes were a tough, cynical police detective (Goro Kishitani) and a timid, weak-willed Korean gangster (Ren Osugi) who shared a disregard for the rules and an affection for a lithesome Shanghainese hooker (Makoto

Togashi). The story, which Sai wrote together with long-time collaborator Chong Ui Shin, was a typical blend of down-and-dirty comedy and action, with the aim being less edification about the plight of Asians in Japan than fast-paced, taboo-free entertainment. But though *Inu*'s take on its underworld milieu was intelligently un-PC, its knockabout comedy was forced, its slam-bang action unconvincing. What remained at the end was the pathos of two outsider buddies who found that, though they could cross ethnic boundaries, could not rise above their assigned social roles. This most iconoclastic of movies was about the way society—both criminal and legitimate—crushes its outcastes with an inexorable logic that has little to do with right and wrong.

In the first half of the decade, other directors were literally crossing borders in their explorations of the Asian Other, but given the expense of location shooting and the consequent need to appeal to a mass audience their films were usually intended more as entertainments than serious social commentaries. Comedies such as Shusuke Kaneko's *Sotsugyo Ryoko* (Trip to a Strange Kingdom, 1992) and Yojiro Takita's *Bokura wa Minna Ikiteiru* (We Are Not Alone, 1993) and *Nettai Rakuen Kurabu* (The Tropical People, 1994) kidded the cluelessness of Japanese abroad, who were far more lost in Southeast Asia than they would ever have been in Waikiki, but they also presented stereotyped views of other Asian countries as cultural backwaters comically sunk in ignorance, venality, and corruption.

The most ambitious of these films was Takita's *Bokura wa Minna Ikiteiru,* whose salaryman hero, played by Hiroyuki Sanada, is sent to a fictional tropical hellhole where nothing works, the natives are cadgers and cheats, and the longtime Japanese expats are either degenerates or slowly going mad. Together with three Japanese business rivals, he has to curry favor with the country's slimeball military dictator to win a large construction contact, but while he and his compatriots are attending a garden party at the dictator's mansion, a shooting war breaks out, and they have to run for their lives through rebel territory to reach the airport and the safety of home.

Though the film has its amusing moments, including a scene of the salarymen walking though a war zone flashing toothy grins and Japanese passports, it can't quite decide whether it wants to be a knockabout farce, a male-bonding movie, or a social drama that exposes the human face of the Ugly Japanese abroad. The resulting narrative stew is rather bizarre—goofy antics reminiscent of *Duck Soup* followed by violent bloodletting more suggestive of *Apocalypse Now.* But director Takita and scriptwriter Nobuyuki Isshiki offer humorous insights into the mentality of Japanese businessmen living and working in Asia while having only the slimmest of connections to the culture around them.

More successful, at least in its internal consistency, was *Sotsugyo Ryoko,* a comedy that Shusuke Kaneko directed from a script by Isshiki. The story has all the plausibility of a Bob Hope and Bing Crosby road movie. A dweebish recent college graduate (Yuji Oda) persuades his boss-to-be to let him have one last fling before settling down life as a corporate drone. He journeys to Chitowan (yet another fictional Southeast Asian country) to explore its archaeological treasures, but when he arrives, he discovers that the people are mad about old Japanese pop music—nothing from the last decade seems to have replaced *enka* tunes and Hideki Saijo's Japanese-language cover of "YMCA" in their affections. The hero, whose own tastes are also hopelessly retro, finds himself in pop-music heaven. The next thing he knows, a sleazy Japanese acquaintance is promoting him as Chitowan's next big pop star and he is performing bad disco tunes to enthusiastic crowds.

Complications soon ensue, however. The wealthy heir to a rubber plantation fortune befriends the hero and offers him his sister in marriage. The hero falls for the sister—a Dorothy-Lamour-like dazzler— but before he can claim his exotic prize, his old girlfriend, a prim, proper representative of Japanese middle-class values, arrives in Chitowan together with his parents to bring him back to reality. Instead of the expected plane trip home, however, *Sotsugyo Ryoko* ends with the hero and his girlfriend, who has started to shed her conventional facade, lighting out for the territory together in a native boat. As bad as its taste in pop stars may be, Chitowan promises the hero a warmly human paradise infinitely preferable to the lockstep life awaiting him in Japan.

In 1995, to commemorate the fiftieth anniversary of the end of World War II, Japanese filmmakers produced movies about the war that ranged from the turgidly sentimental and blatantly jingoistic to boldly unblinkered looks at Japan's dealings with other Asians during the war and after. Among the most ambitious was Seijiro Koyama's *Mitatabi no Kaikyo* (Three Trips Across the Strait), which examined the plight of Koreans drafted into Japan's war effort. Based on a novel of the same title by Hosei Hahakigi, the film takes the side of its Korean characters and details the atrocities committed against them by their Japanese masters with a commendable straightforwardness.

Filmed partly on location in Korea—then a rare privilege for a Japanese filmmaker—*Mitatabi* used the familiar device of a modern-day framing story. Han (Rentaro Mikuni), a prosperous Pusan businessman, accepts an invitation from an old comrade to return to Kyushu, where he had worked in a mine fifty years earlier. As forced laborers, he and his fellow Koreans had been treated harshly by their masters, some of whom were Japanized Koreans. Tiring of the beatings and deaths in unsafe mines, they had presented a list of demands to their boss, the cold-blooded Yamamoto. Soon after, the miners had found their leader hanging by his neck in a dormitory—his private parts missing. Han is convinced that Yamamoto is responsible, but he must wait fifty years to get his revenge. The film takes a sudden turn toward the melodramatic when, after escaping from the mine, Han meets and marries a Japanese widow (Yoko Minamino). The marriage, however, founders on the disapproval Han's parents, who have an unshakable prejudice against the Japanese. Though narratively uneven and conventionally weepy, *Mitatabi* was an admirable attempt to come to terms with the complex reality of the Korean wartime experience.

The year 1995 also saw the release of Kei Kumai's *Fukai Kawa* (Deep River), whose Japanese tourists discovered eternal verities in modern India; Kazuki Omori's *Kinkyu Yobidashi* (Emergency Call), whose young Japanese doctor served the poor of Manila's Smoky Mountain slum; and Hiromichi Horikawa's *Asian Blue*, whose Korean slave workers struggled to survive in wartime Japan. All three were, like Koyama, veteran directors with lengthy lists of credits. Both Kumai and Omori also filmed on Asian locations, with all the attendant hardships and frustrations. It was as though the elders of the Japanese film industry were finally addressing the theme of Japan's relations with Asia, after years of leaving it to newcomers and outsiders.

In 1996, the *zeitgeist* began to shift again. Asian workers and refugees were old news, but Asian gangsters and hustlers were quickly advancing into the Japanese *yakuza*'s underworld turf and filmmakers were following close behind. One of the most successful was Shunji Iwai. His *Swallowtail* (Swallowtail Butterfly), a dark future fantasy about Asians hustling for yen in the Tokyo urban jungle, became a widely discussed box-office smash. Though Iwai had conceived *Swallowtail* in the bubble economy days of the early 1990s, he did not film it until his 1995 debut feature, *Love Letter*, became a long-running art-house hit. Set in Yen Town, a ragtag encampment of human flotsam from all over Asia, the film presents a dark, chaotic urban landscape close in look and spirit to Ridley Scott's *Blade Runner*. Unlike earlier films about Asians in Japan, which tended to depict their heroes as innocent victims of Japanese prejudice and exploitation, Iwai presents his Asian characters as engaging in every imaginable hustle, from whoring and contract-killing to puncturing the tires of passing Japanese motorists so they will have to make an unscheduled stop at the encampment's filling station.

In the 1993 *Ai ni Tsuite Tokyo* (About Love, Tokyo), Mitsuo Yanagimachi portrayed his young Chinese heroes and Japanese villains with a similar ambiguity—one of the former, a slaughterhouse worker, chucks his job of killing cattle for the lucrative scam of fixing pachinko machines at a local parlor to give bigger payoffs—but he took care to justify their actions in a name of a higher morality. Cheating the Japanese gangster who runs the parlor (and who, significantly, happens to be impotent despite his macho swagger) strikes the hero as a cleaner way to make a yen than shooting defenseless animals with a pistol.

In *Swallowtail*, however, the characters run their various hustles with little regard for moral considerations. But though the film's Asian opportunists struggle to survive by whatever means and at whatever cost, their raw vitality makes the Japanese around them look like pale drones. Instead objects of pity or butts of jokes, *Swallowtail* presents its Asians as life-force role models. But though Iwai's MTV-inspired visual and musical pyrotechnics connected with young audiences in a way that no other Asian-in-Japan film had attempted, its condemnation of a soulless, materialistic society whose yen corrupts all it touches was too pat and, in the recession-mired mid-nineties, even passé.

In the later years of decade Japan film companies took a cue from Iwai's success in crossing Asian cultures and began making co-productions with Asian partners targeted at both domestic and Asian audiences. Like *Swallowtail*, these films rejected both the idealism of the Asian-in-Japan dramas and the condescension of the Japanese-in-Asia comedies of the early nineties. Instead they tended to be carefully designed packages of Japanese and Asian—usually Hong Kong—talent, in which attitude and style counted for more than message. Iwai himself was at the forefront of these pan-Asian projects, becoming one of three Asian directors— the other two being Hong Kong's Stanley Kwan and Taiwan's Edward Yang—who signed to make films for Y2K Film Partners, a consortium led by Japan's Pony Canyon, Omega Project, and Nippon Herald that was launched in 1998 to make films for the international market with Asian casts and crews.

Among the better of the Asian co-productions was Yim Ho's stylishly intelligent 1997 version of Yoshimoto Banana 's *Kitchen*, a novel about a young woman, bereft by her beloved grandmother's death, who finds comfort in the kitchen and human connection in the person of an unusual young man and his transvestite "mother." Made by Hong Kong's Golden Harvest (known primarily for its Jackie Chan martial-arts comedies) and Japan's Amuse talent agency, *Kitchen* evinced few signs of its Japanese origins—it was set in Hong Kong and even its Japanese star, Yasuko Tomita, spoke dubbed Cantonese onscreen.

Kenki Saegusa's 1997 *Misty* took a similar approach in remaking Akira Kurosawa's *Rashomon* (1950). In casting the half-Taiwanese, half-Japanese actor Takeshi Kaneshiro (who had risen to stardom in the films of Wong Kar-Wai) as a Heian-era aristocrat, backers Amuse and Nikkatsu were less concerned about adding a new Asian angle to their film than in attracting Kaneshiro's army of Asian fans. They also tried to boost the

Japanese box office by casting local heartthrob Etsushi Toyokawa in the Toshiro Mifune role of the robber. Conceived from the start as a product for export to young Asian audiences, *Misty* did not imaginatively reinterpret the *Rashomon* story so much as take a popularizing steamroller to it, replacing Kurosawa's narrative ambiguities and rich visual sonorities with steamy looks, macho posturing, vulgar clowning, and over-wrought atmospherics.

Misty was a resounding flop, but Amuse, together with the Nippon Television Network and Hong Kong production partners, returned to the screen in 1997 with *Hong Kong Daiyasokai: Touch & Maggie* (Hong Kong Night Club) a comedy based on Billy Wilder's *Some Like It Hot*. Set in Hong Kong and starring Shingo Katori of the pop group SMAP and Hong Kong star Anita Yuen, *Hong Kong Daiyasokai* was reminiscent of the made-in-Asia comedies of the early nineties—not surprising given that scriptwriter Nobuyuki Isshiki was also responsible for writing three of them: *Sotsugyo Ryoko* (1992), *Bokura wa Minna Ikiteiru* (1993) and *Nettai Rakuen Kurabu.*(1994). Unfortunately, the film is so busy spinning out its frantic story that it has little time or inclination to do more than broadly caricature its Hong Kong setting and characters.

Hong Kong Daiyasokai gives a nineties twist to the Wilder classic: a gay reporter (Goro Kishitani) and a straight-but-naive photographer (Shingo Katori) come to Hong Kong to do a story about the local underworld. When they are caught photographing a gangland murder, they must flee for their lives from the enraged gangsters. The reporter hits on the brilliant—if devious—idea of dressing his unwitting partner as his wife, Maggie, and posing as his husband, Touch. But before he can consummate his "marriage," he and Maggie find themselves performing a magic act in a nightclub. Love, however, does not wait: Maggie falls for the club's singer (Anita Yuen), the singer's childhood friend falls for Maggie, and the singer falls for Touch, who only has eyes for his "wife." Though the film is mostly wretched excess, Kishitani and Katori's energetic and occasionally inspired clowning make *Hong Kong Daiyasokai* less than a total loss.

In 1998 veteran Ace Pictures producer Masato Hara scored the biggest box office hit among pan-Asian productions with *Fuyajo* (Sleepless Town). Once again the star was Takeshi Kaneshiro, this time playing a half-Japanese, half-Taiwanese hustler in Shinjuku's Kabukicho entertainment district who becomes mixed up in a Chinese gang war, meanwhile pursuing a passionate, volatile affair with the former lover (Mirai Yamamoto) of a man he is trying to kill. Based on a best-selling novel by Seishu Hase, a young writer who did his research while working as a bartender in Shinjuku's Golden Gai district, *Fuyajo* was directed and cowritten by Hong Kong director Lee Chi Ngai. (Hara had hired Lee after successfully releasing his 1995 *Lost and Found*, another film starring Kaneshiro, in Japan.) Filming on an open set that replicated the Kabukicho entertainment district down to its barfing salarymen, Lee created a vision of Japan's most notorious underworld that was less a realistic slice of Japanese lowlife than a journey through an exoticized borderland in which Japan was little more than a backdrop to the war of its Chinese gangsters.

While mass-audience films of the late nineties tended to use Asian actors mainly as marketing hooks and Asian settings as exotic backdrops, other directors were more successful in cultures integrating their Japanese characters into an Asian environment—or vice versa. One was Masashi Yamamoto, whose 1996 *Atlanta Boogie* and 1998 *Junk Food* celebrated life on Japan's social fringes with an anarchic energy and humor, and in places, an unbridled self-indulgence. His characters may have been international bohemian types that the mainstream regarded as scum on the Japanese social pond, but were nonetheless more vital than the gray-suited masses who surrounded them. Among them were young Asians who related to their Japanese counterparts on a basis of equality, including their acts of sex and violence.

Another director who succeeded in crossing Asian cultures was Takashi Miike. In his 1998 *Gokudo Kuro Shakai Rainy Dog* (Rainy Dog), a hard-boiled actioner set in Taiwan, Miike gave his audience a tour of the island's underside from the viewpoint of an insider, albeit one almost totally alienated from the human race, while refusing to view his Taiwanese characters as cartoon exotics. Instead he allowed them to be themselves, assuming quite rightly that his gangsters and whores needed no cross-cultural filters.

His hero is a hitman (Sho Aikawa) who works for a Taipei gang and spends his free time in a dingy apartment surfing the Internet. A loner who barely gives even his gang boss the time of day, the hitman suddenly finds himself a parent when an ex-girlfriend shows up one day and leaves him with a boy that she claims is his son. Though the hitman begins by treating the boy as little more than a stray dog, he ends by forming a family of sorts with the boy and his mother as he is being hunted by a rival gang. Drenched in monsoon rains that continue for days and weeks, the hitman can never find a shelter dry enough, safe enough. His nationality gives him no protection, no exception from the bullet that awaits him. It has, if anything, made him more vulnerable, though fear never shows on his mask of a face.

In 1998 Miike also released *Chugoku no Tojin* (The Bird People in China), whose story of an unlikely pair of Japanese discovering paradise in a remote Chinese valley made it as different from *Rainy Dog* as *Seven Years In Tibet* was from *Seven*. Based on a story by nature writer Makoto Shiina and shot entirely on location in China's Yunnan Province, the film traces the spiritual paths of an ordinary businessman (Masahiro Motoki) and a tough-guy *yakuza* (Renji Ishibashi) from earthbound pragmatism to the realization that life offers more than the usual grubbing for money, status and, power—that one can soar above the mundane to unknown, even impossible, heights.

Set in a corner of southwestern China where minority tribes still live much as their ancestors have for generations, *Chugoku* posits an earthly paradise in danger of extinction as the outside world edges closer. The businessman, who has come to oversee the export of jade from the province, and the *yakuza*, who has come to collect on a debt he says the businessman's predecessor owes his boss, are unwitting agents of that world. Guided into the remote mountain fastnesses by a Chinese guide (Mako), who loses his memory at a most inconvenient time, and bearing such poisoned gifts of civilization as electronic gadgets and guns, they stumble upon a tribe whose children wear birdlike wings. Their teacher, a blue-eyed young woman named Yan (which is written, significantly, using the character for "swallow") tells them that they are practicing how to fly. Impressed by her goodness and sincerity, as well as a book on flying she claims her grandfather—a British airman downed the war—left behind, the two Japanese start wanting to believe her.

Here we have come full circle, back to the view expressed in *Pekinteki Suika* that, in their pursuit of prosperity, Japanese have somehow lost sight of the values that made them human, and that it is up to other, poorer Asians, whose hearts are still unsullied by materialism, to remind them of what is important. By the end both the salaryman and the yakuza have begun to spread their own wings. In the land where so much of Japanese culture began, they have finally found their spiritual home.

Interviews
AND PROFILES

The following filmmaker profiles and interviews appeared over the course of the past decade in various publications—including the *Japan Times Weekly*, the *Japan Times*, *Winds*, *Screen International*, and the Japan edition of *Premiere*—and are presented in the chronological order of their appearance. Although the directors and producers featured here represent some of the most important filmmaking talent working in Japan in the 1990s, I did not choose them with any master plan in mind. There are individuals whose work I admire as much, or more, but who, for one reason or another, I have not yet cornered with a a tape recorder. The next edition, perhaps.

Masahiro SHINODA

Masahiro Shinoda and Kevin Costner have at least one thing in common: both directed films that, in 1991, earned them Best Picture and Best Director awards from their respective film academies. Shinoda's film was *Shonen Jidai* (*Takeshi: Childhood Days*), a poignant, beautifully photographed tale of a friendship between two boys in wartime Japan.

The two principals are a study in contrasts. Shinji (Tetsuya Fujita) is a slight, studious fifth-grader raised in middle-class comfort in Tokyo. Takeshi (Yuji Horioka) is the tall, raw-boned son of a poor fishing and farming family that lives in a village in Toyama Prefecture, near the Sea of Japan. He is also the boss of the local boys and the first to befriend Shinji when he is evacuated from Tokyo to a relative's house in the village.

Shonen Jidai begins with a clash of cultures: Shinji's neatly pressed school uniform and leather shoes strike the local boys as outlandish and exotic. The film, however, quickly moves beyond surface differences to examine the dynamics of boyhood friend-ship and power politics. Takeshi becomes angry at Shinji for an imagined slight and forces him to sing in front of the other boys. In reluctant revenge, Shinji joins a faction that is plotting Takeshi's overthrow. The film shows how the coup threatens and finally strengthens the bond between the two boys. *Shonen Jidai* depicts Toyama, with its spec-tacular mountains and pines, as the best of all possible Japanese worlds, but it also rejects gauzy nostalgia.

"It's not a story for children, but for adults," says the sixty-year-old Shinoda. "I wanted to make it for my generation—people who were children during the war." But though *Shonen Jidai* became a hit with middle-aged Japanese, as he had hoped it would, Shinoda was surprised to find that their children and even grandchildren also responded to the film. "I've had people my age tell me that it was about their lives, but I've also had schoolchildren—both boys and girls—say the same thing," he says.

Instead of following the example of so many other Japanese films about the period and take a stroll down memory lane, Shinoda says he wanted to make a movie about "a children's Mafia and children's politics."

"In a way, the struggle between the boys in the film is like Japan's dispute with American over rice," he adds. "It illustrates the localism so strongly rooted in the Japanese character."

The idea for *Shonen Jidai* came from an unlikely source: Fujio Fujiko A (a.k.a. Motoo Abiko), a *manga* artist who, together with partner Hiroshi Fujimoto, created dozens of popular of *manga* under the joint pen name Fujio Fujiko, including *Obake no Q-Taro* (Q-Taro the Ghost), which became a pioneering television cartoon program in the 1960s. Their actual joint productions were relatively few, however; they preferred to work independently. In 1988, Abiko and Fujimoto came to an amicable parting of the ways, with Fujimoto taking the name Fujio Fujiko B and Abiko, Fujio Fujiko A. Several years ago Fujio Fujiko A asked Shinoda if he would be interest in making a film of *Shonen Jidai*, a book-length *manga* that he had based on *Nagai Michi* (Long Road), a novel by Shozo Kashiwahara. "I had never met him and was a bit surprised when he contacted me," says Shinoda. "He told me that he had chosen me because he had liked one of my films, *Kawaita Hana* (Pale Flower, 1964)."

Once he signed on, however, Shinoda became absorbed in the project, especially the casting. "With professional actors, all you have to do is contact the agent. With non-professionals, you have to do the looking yourself," he said. "The children were fish in the sea and I was the fisherman, scooping them up. It was fascinating." It was also time-consuming. Shinoda spent three years sifting through 3,400 hopefuls and interviewing 1,200 before he selected his cast. "I watched the finalists for a year before I made up my mind," he says. "If a boy grew too big, I had to give up on him."

After choosing the boys for his cast, Shinoda had them experiment with various roles. "I made them try different combinations so that they would have more chances to observe each other's acting and understand why they were suited for a particular part," he explained. The boy who played Takeshi may have needed this practice more than most—the film was his acting debut. "He was a soccer player who didn't talk very much," Shinoda said. "He was very much like his character in the film."

Shinoda found that in working with these young, often inexperienced actors, he often had to become what he called "a mother figure." "I had to accomodate myself to their rhythm and try to respect their feelings, which are very easily hurt at that age," he said. "At the same time, I tried to treat all of them equally. Everyone lived together, staying at the same hotels and inns." This communal living experience not only brought the boys closer together and made them feel more like real classmates, but helped them better understand their director. "I got to the point where I didn't have to say very much—they could understand me from my looks and gestures," says Shinoda. "I directed them with body language."

In the process of making the film, Shinoda became what he describes as a cinematic "insect collector." "Japanese want to live abundant lives now," he says. "They've all become white-collar workers and have left the growing of rice and the tending of fields to others. As a result, they've forgotten about their agricultural past. The sights, sounds, customs, and manners of the countryside are disappearing. I wanted to capture them on film, as though I were collecting rare insects, before they vanished forever." One of the most important of those "insects," Shinoda believes, is the dialect the local boys speak in the film. "Today children all learn to speak standard Japanese by watching television. They are forgetting their local dialects—and I find that sad."

Shinoda realizes that one film, however, accurately and passionately made, does not constitute a complete "collection" and that much is being lost. "We are facing a cultural crisis in Japan," he says. "We have to find ways to preserve our traditional culture while creating a new culture."

Shinoda is facing a crisis of his own: getting his next project underway. "I want to make a film about Richard Sorge, the famous spy who was active in Japan in the 1930s and 1940s," he says. "It's an idea I've had for the past twenty years. I think that exploring the mind of a spy like Sorge is the best way to understand the political situation in Japan at that time and find an answer to the question of why we went to war with America. Sorge wasn't on either the Japanese or American side, so he could see both opponents fairly."

(*Japan Times Weekly*, May 4, 1991)

Akira KUROSAWA

"They're missing the point," says Akira Kurosawa. "*Hachigatsu no Rhapsody* (Rhapsody in August) is about much more than the bomb." Japan's most celebrated director is not in a good mood; foreign journalists have focused on his new film's references to the atomic bombing of Nagasaki and criticized it for being historically one-sided.

He is right: the heart of his twenty-eighth feature is the relationship between an eighty-year-old grandmother (Sachiko Murase) and her four grandchildren, who are spending the summer at her home in the Nagasaki countryside. The bombing of Nagasaki plays an important role in shaping that relationship, however. As the grandmother reminisces about loved ones she lost, the children learn, for the first time, how the effects of that tragedy still echo, four decades later.

Kurosawa fills the film with signature touches, including a dramatic chase through a driving rainstorm, but the film's attitude toward the bombing is one shared by many Japanese. Kurosawa, who has been accused by Japanese critics of pandering to Western tastes, has made a very Japanese film indeed, with an emotional climate familiar to anyone who has sampled the endless procession of Japanese TV shows and films about the events of August 1945.

But to many foreign, especially American, reporters who attended a pre-release press screening for *Hachigatsu no Rhapsody*, it seemed that the eighty-one-year old director had tried to portray Japan as a victim, America as a villain. They also have a point. In one scene, during the grandchildren's visit to the Nagasaki Peace Park, one boy asks why America has not, like so many other countries, erected a memorial to the dead. "Because they're the ones who dropped the bomb," an older girl replies. In another scene, Richard Gere, playing the grandmother's Japanese-American nephew, expresses regret for the bombing. The grandmother, who lost her husband in the blast, absolves him—and by extension all Americans—of blame. "It's all right," she tells him. "Don't worry about it." Why, the reporters wanted to know, did only America need to be forgiven? What about Japan's role in the war? They fired so many unfriendly questions that Kurosawa finally stopped taking them and walked out of the press conference.

Now, several days later, he is still smarting from the criticisms—and anxious to clarify his intentions. The years may have rounded his shoulders and slowed his gait, but he still speaks pointedly, forcefully and, as the conversation shifts to the subject of war, passionately. He is dressed casually in a blue denim shirt and dark blue slacks and wearing his trademark yachting cap, also blue. We are in a second-floor room in his house in the Seijo Gakuen district of Tokyo, which has been fitted out for interviews like this: comfortably apholstered brown leather sofas and chairs surround a large, rectangular coffee table. On the wall behind us is a banner for *Hachigatsu no Rhapsody*. On a corner table is a large framed photo of Kurosawa's wife, who died in 1985.

"Originally, the bombing of Nagasaki was not a major theme," he says. "But it started to grow in importance as I was writing the script. It wasn't something I consciously planned—it just happened naturally." One example of such serendipity was the scene at the Peace Park. "A member of our staff was shocked when he heard that America had no memorial in the park," Kurosawa explained. "The reason why, of course, is that America dropped the bomb. I wanted to show that feeling of astonishment in the film. I wasn't trying to say that America is bad."

He is also not trying to say that Japan—particularly the wartime regime—was good. In *Sugata Sanshiro*, his first film, Kurosawa celebrated the martial virtues, but the young director of 1943 was under pressure from a militarist government to toe the ideological line. Looking back on that period, he expresses anger at the government's reliance on lies and terror. "The Japanese people didn't know what was really happening. We were told we were winning when we were losing. If you were against the war, you were killed or imprisoned."

Now, at eighty-one, he believes that peoples of different nations must "talk with and understand each other" if new wars are to be avoided. Thus, the "reconciliation" scene between the grandmother and her American nephew—and the grandmother's gesture of absolution. "She doesn't blame the Americans, but she is saddened by the tragedy of the war. In the same way, it's wrong to blame the Germans because of Hitler. Wars are not between peoples—it's the leaders who are responsible for starting them. Hitler was terrible, but that doesn't mean we should hate the German people. The people are the real victims." He also defends the nephew's apology as a natural response to the human cost of the bombing. "I had (the nephew) say 'I'm sorry' to the grandmother because I wanted to show the importance of having a kind heart, of expressing regret for what happened. Again, I wasn't saying that the American or Japanese people were bad, but that the war itself was bad."

Despite his protestations that the film is "not anti-American," Kurosawa believes that the United States "opened a Pandora's box" by dropping the atomic bomb. "Again, I'm not blaming them. It was a very difficult decision to make. They said it was necessary for ending the war, but because they dropped it thousands of people have died of radiation sickness. A lot of people are still suffering the effects today." Kurosawa says that his message is quite simple: "I'm sad about what happened and I hope that it never happens again."

Although Kurosawa has dealt with the atomic bombings before, in *Ikimono no Kiroku* (Record of a Living Being, 1955), he had never worked with a major Hollywood star prior to Richard Gere. Gere may seem an odd choice as the grandmother's nephew: he doesn't look the part of a Japanese-American. But when Kurosawa saw him at a party in New York—it was their second chance encounter—he asked him if he would be interested in taking the role. "He immediately said that he was, but I told him to read the book first," Kurosawa said. *Hachigatsu no Rhapsody* is based on *Nabe no Naka* (Inside the Pot), a novel by Kiyoko Murata.

Although he had worried that Gere might demand special treatment, the star of *Pretty Woman* "wanted to be treated the same as everyone else—he was quite modest," says Kurosawa. Gere, however, did suggest two minor changes in the script, to which Kurosawa readily agreed, and made an unusual request: he wanted to take the grandmother's Japanese-style house, which had been built in the mountains of Chichibu especially for the film, back to the United States with him. "He finally decided that it was too big," Kurosawa remembered with a smile. Instead the actor settled for a small temple used in one of the film's key scenes. "He has a strong interest in Buddhism," Kurosawa said.

As Gere's ready acceptance of Kurosawa's offer indicates, the director has come a long way since the dark days of the 1970s, when he could not find financing in Japan, despaired of making another film and even attempted suicide. Since then, Hollywood, in the persons of George Lucas, Steven Spielberg, and other film-business luminaries, has stepped forward to support his work, financially, technically, and personally. Steven Spielberg presented and Martin Scorsese played Vincent Van Gogh in *Yume* (Dreams), Kurosawa's 1990 film about the wanderings of his nocturnal mind.

But despite his recent triumphs, including an Academy Award for Lifetime Achievement in 1990, Kurosawa believes that he is far from having directorial carte blanche, especially in Japan. "It would hard to make a film about modern-day Japan," he says. "There would be a lot of resistance to such a movie. If I wanted to make a film about the Recruit scandal [an influence-buying scandal involving many top politicians]—which would be an excellent topic, by the way—I probably couldn't get any companies here to finance it. We are supposed to have freedom of speech in Japan, but in fact there are a lot of restrictions."

The greatest taboo, however, is not the exposure of corporate misconduct, but criticism of the emperor system. "If I were to make a film about the emperor, I would probably be killed," he says. "For example, the life of Emperor Showa [the posthumous name for Emperor Hirohito] would make an entertaining movie, but if I were to make it, I would be assassinated by rightists who oppose any film about the emperor. Even if the film were highly positive, just the fact that I was using the emperor as a character would be enough to make them mad."

Despite his often-stated desire to make more films—retirement is definitely not in the works—Kurosawa has not yet decided on his next project. One candidate is said to be Gabriel Garcia Marquez's *The Autumn of the Patriarch*. Last fall, the Colombian Nobel Prize–winner came to Japan to discuss the possibility of filming the book with Kurosawa. "I won't make any decisions until after Cannes in May," he says. "First I have to forget my previous film. Also, it takes time to decide—there are so many possibilities. It's like planting seeds—you never know which one is going to come up first."

Among the seeds that have become films, Kurosawa says he has no favorites. "My movies are like my children," he explains. "I love them all, though I feel more affection for the failures. It's like they say—you love your wayward children the best. But when I'm asked which film is my favorite, I always say my next one. Potters never feel that they have made the perfect piece, no matter how good it is—they always want to make something better. I'm the same way—I'm never satisfied."

His goal he says, is a film that is a "real movie" from beginning to end. "Certain portions of my films are 'real' in that sense," he says. "I know that when I see them, but I can't explain why—it's just something I feel. It's as I said at the [1989] Academy Awards ceremony—I don't feel that I know what a film is yet."

In Japan, Kurosawa believes that fewer young filmmakers understand what "real films" are. "They need to learn more about good Japanese movies," he says. "In America and Europe, they often show the classics of Japanese cinema, but in Japan, they aren't shown in theaters anymore. It's a shame."

But though he feels that Japan once had more directorial talent than anywhere else in the world, he realizes that the glory days of the 1950s, when he and such masters as Kenji Mizoguchi and Yasujiro Ozu were winning international acclaim, are not likely to come again soon. "One reason why we had so many good directors is that Japanese studios gave talented people the freedom to make the movies they wanted. Now, however, the people in the marketing department are in charge—and all they think about is the box office," he says. The result is a steady diet of formula fare. "They keep remaking the same kinds of pictures," Kurosawa commented. "If a movie about a cat does well, they make one about a dog."

He also has harsh words for his colleagues who direct such films. "I question whether they have vision," he says. Kurosawa knows all about the difficulties of having—and selling—a vision. After *Dodeskaden* failed at the box office in 1970 and Japanese companies refused to finance him, he traveled all over the world raising money for his films. He finally returned to filmmaking with *Derzu Usala* (1975), *Kagemusha* (1980), and *Ran* (1985), films that won domestic and international awards, attracted new audiences, and reestablished his reputation as an important filmmaker. "It doesn't happen if you sit back and wait," he says.

But even young, talented hopefuls who want to make it happen have difficulty getting started in Japan: the studio apprentice system that nurtured the directors of Kurosawa's generation has largely disappeared, film schools are few, and government support virtually non-existent. ("The Japanese government's attitude is too cold," Kurosawa complains). There is, however, one way into the business that Kurosawa believes directors-in-embryo too seldom try: scriptwriting. "I have five or six assistant directors who want to make their own films, but can't find anyone to back them. I tell them that scriptwriting is a good way to learn filmmaking. It's cheap—all you need is a pencil and paper—and if you write a good script, you can get it made into a movie or TV drama. But they aren't willing to sit down and write, so there's nothing I can do for them."

When he was starting his own career as an assistant director under Kajiro Yamamoto, Kurosawa was a dedicated and successful scriptwriter himself (Yamamoto urged him to write for the same reasons that Kurosawa now uses with his own assistants). "Most people can't endure the hard, painful work involved," he says. "They claim they are too busy. But if you write one page a day, you can write 365 pages in a year. When I was an assistant director, I was busy too, but I still wrote scripts. If I had no money to go drinking, I would sell a script and use the money to drink with." He smiles broadly, but he is also in earnest: "It helped me to become known. Even a genius must show someone that he has talent."

But writing, he emphasizes, requires more than sheer persistence. "You have to read books," he says. "The more you read the better, because the more you read the more you can make of your own experience. Just your own experience is not enough to create." An avid reader since boyhood ("I read even when I was walking to school"), he has a lifelong devotion to classic literature. He has, by his own count, read Tolstoy's *War and Peace* thirty times. He has also based several of his films on works of literature: Dostoevsky's *The Idiot* (*Hakuchi* [The Idiot], 1951), Shakespeare's *Macbeth*

(*Kumonosujo* [Throne of Blood], 1957), Maxim Gorki's *The Lower Depths* (*Donzoku* [The Lower Depths], 1957) and Shakespeare's King Lear (*Ran*, 1985). But Japanese young people, including aspiring filmmakers, do not read seriously—they would rather curl up with comic books than *Macbeth*—and that bothers him. "I'm shocked by how little they read," he says. "If this continues, I worry about the future of the country. The schools ought to teach them to read instead of watch TV. Dostoevsky, Balzac, and Shakespeare are a lot more interesting than TV—if you know how interesting they are."

(*Japan Times Weekly*, May 11, 1991)

Yoji YAMADA

As the director of a series that began in 1969 and has since produced forty-three films, nearly all of them hits, Yoji Yamada would seem to be in a highly successful rut. But Tora-san, the itinerant peddler from Tokyo's Katsushika Ward who seemingly walked down every highway in Japan and into the hearts of millions of Japanese, is not Yamada's only creation. Throughout Tora-san's long run, Yamada has taken time out to make other films, including *Shiawase no Kiiroi Handkerchief* (The Yellow Handkerchief), which won the 1977 Japan Academy Award for Best Picture.

His latest non-Tora-san film, *Musuko*, focuses on the clash between modern and traditional values, youth and age, city and country. None of these themes are new in Yamada's work; even the Tora-san films explore them. His approach in *Musuko*, however, is drier-eyed, darker-edged. A tragicomedy about a farmer father and his two sons, it tries to extract both smiles and tears from its audience (it would be hard to imagine a Yamada film that doesn't), while taking a close, unblinking look at state of family relationships and society in modern Japan.

Yamada pointedly contrasts the loveliness of the father's Iwate Prefecture countryside and the urban jungle surrounding his elder son's Tokyo condo; the leisurely pace of old-fashioned family life with the rush-rush existence of modern urbanites. "Japanese have air conditioners, cars, TVs, and stereos, so their lives may seem rich, but they don't have time to eat a meal together with their families," says Yamada. "They're not really living human lives. They may not be hungry in a material sense, but they have hungry hearts."

As a child in wartime Manchuria and a junior high school student in postwar Japan, Yamada learned all about the former type of hunger. But now he is in an elegant French restaurant in the Ginza, discussing his film and the issues it examines in a soft, deep voice that conveys the conviction and quiet authority of Japan's most successful living director.

"The contrast between the city and country is very important to the film," he says. "I wanted to show how the Japanese countryside is disappearing and how Japanese are losing their sense of *kokyo* (native place). In Japan, when people think of the country-side, they imagine a green fertile valley with rice fields, a river, and mountains in the background. But I was raised in Manchuria, where there are no mountains, just an end-less plain. Maybe that why I'm in love with the Japanese countryside — it's something I never knew as a child."

For the role of the father, Yamada chose Rentaro Mikuni, a veteran actor who most recently played tea master Sen no Rikyu in Hiroshi Teshigahara's *Rikyu*. In *Musuko*, however, Mikuni portrays a stubborn, hardheaded farmer who is slowly losing ground to old age and changing times. "I couldn't imagine another actor in the part," says Yamada. "The father had to be in his late sixties or early seventies and have a big frame that would look powerful even when he was sitting quietly. Mikuni was the only one who fit that description."

The film's central character, however, is the younger son, a rebel who rejects his father's values and makes a precarious living as a waiter in a Shinjuku pub. As the film progresses, however, he changes not only his job, becoming a laborer in a metal shop, but his attitude. This self-centered, know-it-all kid discovers the meaning of love and learns to tolerate the ways of his impossible father. The son is played by Masatoshi Nagase, who starred in Jim Jarmusch's 1989 *Mystery Train*. "I auditioned several actors for the part, but Nagase was the best," says Yamada. "He had lived in New York for six months and had spent a lot of time going to European and American movies and learning about filmmaking. I think he understands how much power films have and how important a job filmmaking is."

"Also, he was born and raised in a little town in Kyushu. His father was a poor farmer. I thought he could understand the feelings of a boy who comes to Tokyo from the countryside. The character, Tetsuya, speaks with a Tohoku accent that people in Tokyo laugh at. He doesn't want people to make fun of him, so he remains silent and has a lot of problems as a result. He has a complex about where he's from and who he is. Nagase could portray that side of the character quite convincingly because he's been there himself."

Japanese, Yamada admits, also have an inferiority complex about their film industry; Japanese films have been steadily losing ground to competition from Hollywood and elsewhere for nearly three decades. The problem, he believes, is that instead of making films that are the cinematic equivalent of main courses, Japanese filmmakers have been whipping up desserts. "You might say that people aren't eating what they want to eat," he says. "They're getting films that are like shortcake and ice cream, but their real hungers aren't being satisfied. Spiritually, they're starving. "Japanese directors may think that by making these films they can catch up to America and Europe, but actually they're falling farther behind. They're going to destroy Japanese cinema."

Yamada sees this trend as symptomatic of a social failure to address deep human needs. "That's why we have these stock market scandals. People have empty hearts, but they don't notice it. They take the status quo— working from morning to night, cramming hard to pass examinations—for granted."

In *Musuko*, that status quo is represented by the elder son, who graduated from an elite university, works for a big company, and lives in a tiny Tokyo condo that he paid for with a thirty-year mortgage. Playing the dutiful son, he persuades his father to stay with him, but ends up resenting the old man's presence. "I think he knows he's being cold and that's makes it even harder for him," comments Yamada. "He wants to be kinder, but he can't. His apartment isn't big enough and his wife has to take care of her own mother—it's an insoluble problem."

Initially, the younger son is even more of a materialist. "He measures everyone by how much money they make," says Yamada. "He mocks his father for earning so little as a farmer. His father tells him that everyone needs a skill and that farming is his. The son, however, has no skill, he just carries mugs of beer in a bar."

"That's another point I was trying to make—that Japanese are losing skills that they have spent hundreds of years developing. Machines are making everything, while people are losing the joy of making things with their own hands."

Yamada, however, has not lost that joy. When he is talking about his characters, he seems to be describing members of his own family. They intrigue him with their complexity, amuse him with their unpredictability. He has stayed with Tora-san so long because he wants to see what his creation will do next.

"I haven't given up hope for Japanese movies or Japanese society," he adds. "I think that things are starting to head in a different direction. For a long time, Japanese didn't like anything serious. They just wanted light entertainment that had a quick tempo and a surface dazzle. But now people are getting tired of that. They want more seriousness, not only in films, but in music and TV dramas as well."

Does that means more films like *Musuko*, fewer Tora-san adventures? After forty-three outings, isn't Yamada tiring of his most famous character? "No, I'm not tired," he says with a smile. "Tora-san is an interesting guy. The fans don't seem to be getting tired of him either. In fact, the last few movies have done better than the previous ones. If I can, I want to keep making both kinds of films, the comic and the sad. Japanese need more films for adults and I'm one of the few people making them."

(*Japan Times Weekly*, September 1991)

Kazuyoshi OKUYAMA

Slight, boyish and affable, Kazuyoshi Okuyama is an unlikely revolutionary, but the veteran producer and Shochiku vice-president wants to change the way the Japanese movies are made—and with his latest project, *Rampo,* he intends to show everyone how to do it. "This film was born because of problems in the Japanese film business," he says. "In America and other parts of the world, filmmakers have integrated art and entertainment to make high-quality movies. In Japan, there is still a large gap between the two. Directors aiming for awards at international film festivals tend to discard entertainment and concentrate only on art, while films for the domestic audience are often poor imitations of Hollywood, made cheaply, quickly, and badly."

As a result, he believes, the public is turning away from Japanese movies. "They see Japanese art films as introverted, gloomy, and sentimental, Japanese entertainment films as trash," he says. "They've basically given up on them. I can't say that I blame them; watching this year's U.S. Academy Awards ceremony, I was keenly aware of the enormous distance we have to go. It will take us ten to twenty years to catch up."

Okuyama has spent most of his fifteen-year career trying to cover that distance, producing critically acclaimed films like Naoto Takenaka's *Muno no Hito* (Nowhere Man), and Takeshi Kitano's *Sonatine* and mass-audience hits like *Hachiko Monogatari* (A Story of the Dog Hachi) and *Toki Rakujitsu* (Faraway Sunset). He has also experimented with the way the industry makes and distributes movies. Two years ago he produced *Gekashitsu* (The Operating Room), a sixty-minute feature directed by Kabuki star Tamasaburo Bando. Shochiku priced tickets at ¥1,000, compared with the ¥1,700 standard, and screened the film seven times a day in first-run theaters. These tactics helped propel *Gekashitsu* to a long, successful run.

In the making of *Rampo,* a period film loosely based on the life and works of pioneer Japanese mystery writer Edogawa Rampo, Okuyama found himself striking out in another new direction, albeit unwillingly. When he screened rushes of the film in late 1992, he did not find them to his liking; he felt that the director, Rintaro Mayuzumi, had delivered an auteurist mishmash. When negotiations over retakes fell through, Okuyama decided to direct them himself, and ended up reshooting nearly seventy percent of the film. Okuyama says his purpose in making the film, which is set for release in June 1994, was "to combine entertainment and art."

"If it's a hit, it will set the course for the company's and the industry's future—our films will become more producer-oriented than director-centered," he adds. "If it is not a hit, then everyone will probably go back to the old ways. So box office success is absolutely crucial."

To assure that success, Okuyama says he is willing to "play dirty." "Japanese audiences are attracted to a film because it is an event, not because it's good," he explains. "So I've tried in various ways to make *Rampo* an event—something people feel they have to see because everyone else is talking about it." To create the right must-see mood, Okuyama has added subliminal images to the film, sprayed theatres with a *Rampo* perfume, and cast TV celebrities as extras in a party scene. "These things may improve the film, but I'm doing them mainly to get people's attention," says Okuyama. "I want to expose them to quality, but first I have to get them into the theatres. I don't want to sound arrogant, saying that I've made a high-quality film—that's not for me to judge—but we have to do better. I put it right on the poster: 'Films are progress.' I have to progress—and so does the Japanese film industry."

(*Screen International*, April 1994)

Yoichi SAI

Many Japanese directors have a bit of the schoolmaster in them. But though it may be easy to imagine them in classrooms, holding forth behind a lectern, not all teach at the same level. Watching Yoichi Sai on the set of his latest film, *Heisei Musekinin Ikka Tokyo Deluxe* (Tokyo Deluxe), I imagined him as a popular teacher in a tough junior high school. A pear-shaped man with short, scraggly hair and a beatnik goatee, he had the kind of loud, gravelly voice that carries to the back of a noisy classroom and the kind of gruff, frank style that wins affection and commands respect. He may have dressed down to the grunge level of his young staff, but his instructions, delivered as he sat crosslegged on the floor of his set, tapping cigarette ashes into a can, were concise, pointed, casually assured.

"Goro, your timing is a bit too fast. Watch it this time, will you?"

Goro Kishitani, who had starred in Sai's last film, *Tsuki wa Dotchi ni Deteiru* (All Under the Moon), had just entered the house of an elderly couple—built inside a ramshackle studio on the Nikkatsu lot—for the fourth time. Playing the con-artist son of an extended con-artist family, he was trying, with aid of his nefarious kin, to persuade the couple to regard him as their son-in-law, though his only relationship with their daughter was that of ex-boyfriend. The object was to con the couple out of food, lodging— and anything else not nailed down. It took Kishitani several more tries, however, before he finally made his entrance to Sai's satisfaction.

"I would be lying if I said there's no pressure," Sai said over lunch at the Nikkatsu studio commissary. "But I'm not about to make another *Tsuki wa Dotchi ni Deteiru*. I wanted to take a break from the theme of Koreans in Japan."

Tsuki, which swept major Japanese film awards in 1993 and became the year's biggest independent hit, with a gross of three hundred million yen, was a fresh, knowing look at the life and loves of an ethnic Korean cabby in Tokyo. Previously known as a director of hard-boiled TV and video actioners, Sai suddenly found himself, at age forty-four, as a hot talent and a spokesman for the Korean community. It is a position he finds uncomfortable. Rather than pontificate on the state of his career and the status of his fellow Koreans in Japan—Sai was born to first-generation Korean immigrants in Nagano Prefecture in 1949—he says that his only aim in *Tokyo Deluxe* is to make people laugh. "The main rival to this movie is Hitoshi Ueki's *Musekinin Otoko*

(Irresponsible Man) series," he says with a straight face. Launched in 1962, this popular series featured Ueki as a carefree, conniving salaryman who schemed his way up the corporate ladder. But times, Sai admits, have changed. instead of riding the rocket of GNP growth, as it did in the sixties, Japan is struggling through an endless recession. "This movie is about an 'irresponsible family' in the present-day Japan," he says. "The scams they work are rather petty. It's a story that stinks of poverty, but light-hearted poverty."

Though the stated theme of *Tokyo Deluxe*—money and family—may be a staple of Japanese melodrama, Sai and fellow Korean Chong Ui Shin (also his collaborator on *Tsuki*) have written a script that treats it in a decidedly unmelodramatic way. "We don't want the movie to be drippy," he explains. "We are also not aiming for any kind of realism." Even so, an incident similar to the story occured in Okinawa about twenty years ago. Several Okinawans stole ¥1.5 million from the U.S. military and split it among their friends and relatives. "It was a kind of Robin Hood story," said Sai. "We didn't have the budget to shoot a period film set in Okinawa, so we moved the locale to Tokyo and the date to the present."

An Okinawa native does make an appearance, however, in the form of a teenage boy who is the product of a union between the hero's mother and an Okinawa-based U.S. soldier. Unable to find a boy suitable for the part in Tokyo, Sai finally scouted Dave Kureiken, a newcomer who fits the character's ethnic profile, in Okinawa. Other cast members include *Tsuki* stars Ruby Moreno and Moeko Ezawa.

Despite his emphasis on entertainment, Sai is hardly going Hollywood. "When I made *Tsuki* I realized that I'm really an Asian, not a Westerner. Why should I make a movie that expresses a Western outlook?," he asks. "In writing the story for *Tokyo Deluxe*, I did not cut off the hero and his family from the world around them; they are in a Japanese environment. They are also partly a product of my own psyche."

Sai hopes that *Tokyo Deluxe*, scheduled for release in 1995, will be the first of a series. He also plans to return to the world of *Tsuki* at least twice for sequels. "I don't want them to be regarded as 'problem dramas' about Koreans living in Japan," he says. "I hate the term 'Koreans living in Japan' (*zainichi Kankokujin*), to begin with. I want them to be seen as Japanese films. After all, if an American appeared as the hero in a Japanese film, would you call it a *zainichi American* movie? Of course not."

Sai's next project, due to start in October, is *Marks no Yama* (Marks), a psychological thriller based on a best-selling novel by Kaoru Takamura. "It will not be a hardboiled movie," says Sai, smiling. "My rival this time will be Kurosawa's *Tengoku to Jigoku* (High and Low). I feel like saying 'Kurosawa, come on! I'm going to beat you!'"

(Japan Times, August 1994)

Isao TAKAHATA

In the summer of 1994 the biggest battle at the Japanese box office was between a pride of Disney lions and a spunky community of *tanuki* (badger-dogs), who looked, with their fat bellies and black-rimmed eyes, like overfed cousins to the raccoon, but morphed with the adroitness of Power Rangers. It turned out to be no contest: *Heisei Tanuki Gassen Pompoko* (Pompoko) not only beat *The Lion King* handily, with distributor revenues of ¥2.63 billion, but all the domestic competition as well. It also garnered several awards, including Best Animation Prize at the 1994 Mainichi Film Concours and a Special Academy Award at the 1995 Japan Academy Awards.

Isao Takahata, who scripted and directed *Pompoko*, and longtime collaborator Hayao Miyazaki, who helped develop it, have been called the Walt Disneys of Japan for the quality of their animation and the size of their box-office success. Though Takahata professes to admire Disney animation ("especially the films of the classic period"), he also sees deep differences between the American and Japanese approach to the art of animation. "In the United States, some subjects are thought suitable for animation and others are not," he says. "In Japan, we don't draw such distinctions; anything can become a *manga*. We just like looking at *manga*, without worrying about whether the genre is appropriate for *manga* treatment. The same is true of animation."

Yet another difference is the American emphasis on entertainment values over story content. "Classical Disney animation is like the American musical," Takahata explains. "It draws out the entertaining parts, even if the story stops dead in its tracks. Japanese audiences used to be too restless to sit back and enjoy that kind of long scene—they wanted things to keep moving. It's changed somewhat now, but Japanese animation tends to be rather fast paced and full of narrative complications."

Though Takahata and Miyazaki have worked together since the early 1960s, when Takahata was an assistant supervisor and Miyazaki an animator at Toei Animation, and have run their own animation studio, Studio Ghibli, since the mid-1980s, Miyazaki has spent more time in the media spotlight for such films as *Tonari no Totoro* (My Neighbor Totoro, 1988) and *Kurenai no Buta* (Porco Rosso, 1992). Even *Pompoko* and *Omoide Poro Poro* (Only Yesterday, 1991), both major hits that Takahata developed and directed, have been referred to in the press as "Miyazaki movies." If this inequality irritates the mild-mannered Takahata, he doesn't show it. "I don't feel a feel sense of rivalry with him, but at the same time I don't want to make the same kinds of films as he does. I would never be able to equal him if I tried. He has a wonderful sense of fantasy, while I'm more interested in creating a feeling of reality in my films. To use an expression from sumo, I want to fight my bouts in a different *dohyo* (sumo ring). In that way, I think we can better enrich Japanese animation and please Japanese audiences."

In fighting his animated bouts, Takahata feels that his primary task is to make his characters, including his badger-dogs, interesting to the audience. "I never think about whether a character is going to sell products," he says. "And the marketing people at Studio Ghibli would never ask me to think about it. The same goes for the international market. I would be happy if audiences in Europe and America see my films, but I don't have them in mind when I plan a project. My only concern is my audience right here in Japan." That audience, he believes, is more receptive than an older generation to the kind of adult-targeted animation he and Miyazaki produce. "Today's adults grew up in the manga and animation boom of the postwar period. Unlike an older generation, they no longer feel that animation is only 'kid's stuff.'"

In creating his *tanuki*, however, Takahata went deep into the past, back to traditional folk beliefs about the power of *tanuki* to metamorphose into anything, often with a mischievous end in mind. The *tanuki* in *Pompoko* begin the film living peacefully in a tight-knit, thatch-roofed village in the Tama Hills and practicing the ancient *tanuki* arts of transformation. In the course of the film, however, they become hardened eco-warriors, who use their powers to protect their way of life from the encroachments of modern civilization. But scriptwriter Takahata is also a realist, and his *tanuki* are only partly successful in their battle against the bulldozer; by the end they are still fighting, but in retreat. "I choose the *tanuki* as the central character because it's not an ordinary mammal; it has the power to transform itself," explained Takahata. "I thought I could build an interesting film from that premise. Also, modern Japanese no longer believe that the *tanuki* has the power of transformation, but they are all familiar with it, even if they have never seen *tanuki* in the wild."

Takahata has not decided on his next project, although he has, he says, "several ideas floating around in my head." But it is likely to come, like *Pompoko*, from traditional Japanese stories. Studio Ghibli has already announced its next film, scheduled for release this summer: *Mimi o Sumaseba* (Murmur of the Heart), a modern story of young love with written by Miyazaki and directed by Yoshifumi Kondo. Not much traditionally Japanese about that.

But whatever their differences of theme and approach, says Takahata, he and Miyazaki share one thing in common. "Whether the story leans towards fantasy, as his tend to, or realism, as mine tend to, we want the audience to feel that what they're seeing on the screen really could have happened. We want to make animation that the audience can believe in."

(*Japan Times*, April 9, 1996)

Shunji IWAI

Japanese film studios' long-time policy of relying on the tried-and-true rather than attempting the new effectively hollowed out the industry, as talented wannabes abandoned the movies for the more open, lucrative, and fashionable worlds of advertising, video, and television. Now one former wannabe has grabbed the attention of young moviegoers, while issuing a brash challenge to the filmmaking establishment.

His name is Shunji Iwai, a thirty-two-year-old director with extensive experience in music videos, TV commercials, and TV dramas. In the spring of 1995, Iwai's first feature film, *Love Letter*, was released in five Tokyo-area theaters. Usually a first film by a new Japanese director attracts only a coterie audience and enjoys only a token theatrical run. But *Love Letter*, a drama about a young woman named Hiroko who writes a letter to a dead lover in Hokkaido—and receives a reply—played fourteen weeks to standing-room-only crowds at a central Tokyo theater, and was widely publicized in the media.

In its self-consciously stylish romanticism, *Love Letter* bears a family resemblance to the dramas about the love troubles of fashionable young urbanites that have flooded the TV airwaves in recent years. But while giving his audience what it wants, Iwai stays one step ahead of it. There is much in *Love Letter* that looks familiar, little that is merely reworked or recycled. He takes influences from everywhere, including sources considered suspect by traditionalists such as music videos and television, and makes them unmistakably his own.

The Hokkaido letter-writer is not a ghost, as it turns out, but a young woman who has the same name and went to the same high school as the dead boy—and is a dead ringer for Hiroko (both roles are played super-idol Miho Nakayama). This results in complications, especially when Hiroko and a friend of the dead boy (Etsushi Toyokawa) travel to Hokkaido to solve the mystery of the letters. But rather than simply run comic changes on the identity crisis when the two women meet, Iwai focuses on their respective voyages of self-discovery, love, and loss. This may sound like old-fashioned Japanese cinematic sentimentalism, but Iwai's approach is edgier, sexier, and cooler.

In contrast to the less-is-more aesthetic of Yasujiro Ozu and other Golden Age directors, Iwai wants to show that more can be more. When the dead boy's friend tries to make love to the still-mourning Hiroko, Iwai expresses her swirling emotions of denial and desire with short cuts, extreme camera angles, and quirky editing rhythms.

Though older moviegoers used to the slower pace of mainstream Japanese films may flinch at the onrush of images, younger audiences raised on the fast pace of Japanese TV (including MTV) sense that Iwai is one of them, and understands their way of looking at the world.

In person, Iwai looks like a director as imagined by a *shojo manga* (girls' comic): a slender, long-legged, stylishly dressed man, whose youthful, delicately handsome face is partly masked by a shock of long copper-colored hair. Though initially soft-spoken and shy, Iwai soon begins to talk about his work and the state of Japanese cinema with fluency and passion.

Unlike industry traditionalists, who place theatrical films at the top of the visual media pyramid and the director at the top of the filmmaking pyramid, Iwai sees himself primarily as an *eizo sakka* (visual artist) who draws inspiration from all media and looks down at none. "You can get all kinds of practice working in video or TV drama," he says. "I had seven years of it before I made my first film, and it was extremely valuable to me."

He also actively embraces new technologies. After writing the script for *Love Letter*, he storyboarded every shot on a computer, until he had "filmed" the entire movie before touching a camera. His colleagues, he feels, are reluctant to follow his lead. "The Japanese film industry doesn't know anything about digital technology and doesn't want to know," said Iwai. "Film editors are among the worst; they are afraid that they'll lose their jobs."

Transferring Iwai's brand of expertise to films is not easy; the Japanese film industry does not easily admit newcomers from TV and other media more open to new ideas. But, as evidenced by Iwai's own success, that situation is slowly changing. As the industry opens up, Iwai believes, more new talent will pour in. "Every director on television wants to make movies," he says wryly. He also feels that, despite their lack of a filmmaking apprenticeship, considered essential in the days of the studio system, these newcomers will fit right in. "I never had that kind of apprenticeship myself; I've been a director from the beginning," he says. "But I was raised watching television; thinking in terms of images became second nature to me. From an early age I knew things that directors of an older generation had to learn from hard experience. With a little practice, I found that I was able to transfer that knowledge to films."

In contrast to many older film-industry professionals, who have seen repeated attempts to penetrate foreign markets end in failure and are pessimistic about the future, Iwai is convinced that if the industry gives enough new people a chance to succeed, it can "catch up with the rest of Asia in three years." One obstacle to overseas recognition, however, is the tendency to hold up the Golden Age films of Mizoguchi, Ozu, and Kurosawa as the model of what Japanese cinema should be—a model that Iwai has little interest in emulating. "I want to show [foreign audiences] that Japan isn't that way any more," says Iwai. "Young Japanese don't know those films or the society they depict. We have to make movies that appeal to them and reflect the world they're living in."

Iwai's next film, *Swallowtail* (Swallowtail Butterfly), which went before the cameras early in 1996, is about Asians in Japan. "I don't want to show Asians as simply suffering, the way some recent Japanese films have," he says. "I think that a lot of them see Japan as gold-rush country. They've got yen fever. I hope that some of their energy rubs off on the Japanese who see this film. Other Asians have a vitality that we lack."

(*Winds*, April 1996)

Masayuki SUO

Following the smash domestic success of his romantic comedy *Shall We Dance?*, Masayuki Suo has been presented with a dilemma that most of his Japanese colleagues would envy—deciding which of two well-known studios will do the Hollywood remake. He is also looking forward to the film's North American release next year by Miramax. "When I attended a preview screening in New York, the audience laughed at nearly the same things the Japanese audience did, but their reaction was stronger—louder laughter, more applause," Suo said. "The same was true of the preview I attended in Hong Kong. They really seemed to understand the feelings of the hero."

The film, about a straight-arrow businessman who signs up for dancing lessons to get next to a beautiful instructor, earned nearly $1.5 billion for distributor Toho following its January 1996 release. Set in present-day Japan, and offering a comic but sympathetic glimpse into the arcane world of ballroom dancing, *Shall We Dance?* is closer in tone to the feel-good romanticism of Steven Spielberg than the work of Ozu, Kurosawa, and other directors Westerners usually associate with Japanese cinema. "My aim was never to become the Japanese Spielberg," says Suo with a quick smile. "But I did see a niche that needed filling. There were very few good Japanese entertainment films that didn't target a particular audience, that could appeal to everyone from children to old people. One reason is that they are extremely difficult to make well."

Suo, whose 1992 sumo comedy *Shiko Funjatta* (Sumo Do, Sumo Don't) became a hit in Hong Kong and other Asian territories as well as in Japan, feels that his brand of well-made entertainment is becoming more exportable. "I may sound as though I'm promoting myself in saying this, but I truly believe that we no longer have to make movies about samurai warriors and other uniquely Japanese subject matter to succeed abroad," he says. "The world has become a smaller place and audience tastes are converging. That's why I feel that the U.S. release of *Shall We Dance?* is so important. If it does well there, perhaps we can overcome this idea that exoticism is the only thing that sells abroad and become more confident that Western audiences will watch films about contemporary Japan."

At home, Suo faces a different problem. Although a national celebrity—sports newspapers splashed news of his engagement to *Shall We Dance?* star Tamiyo Kusakari across their front pages—he must still deal with a distribution and exhibition system that has changed little in three decades of decline and often relegates filmmakers to the status of hired hands. "The biggest bottleneck is that the film companies own the theatres," he says. "If you want to distribute your films yourself, you would find it extremely difficult to get the right venues. The three big film companies—Toei, Toho, and Shochiku—monopolize the industry. You must distribute on their terms or not at all."

The studios, together with the TV networks, major publishing houses, and other big companies with media interests also control film financing, says Suo, resulting in a business that is deal- rather than content-driven. "Often it simply comes down to contacts," he says. "A studio executive knows a company president he can tap for money if he makes a film on a subject that will boost the company's image. The decision to make the film has nothing to do with its intrinsic worth, either artisically or commercially."

The aim of this system, says Suo, is to "eliminate competition" by controlling every aspect of the pipeline: "With block-booking, the film companies know they are going to get venues and a certain amount of revenue. With corporate support, they are guaranteed to sell a certain number of tickets—the companies investing buy large blocks and distribute them to employees and clients." The only ones left out of this cozy arrangement are the filmmakers, who are basically subcontractors working for a fee. "Almost all the profits go to the film company and other rights holders," says Suo. "We directors are little more than volunteers."

Suo hopes to change that system with his next, as yet undecided project, which he hopes to announce by the end of 1996 and finance outside the usual channels by inviting interested investors to publicly "bid" for stakes in the film. "Essentially, I'll borrow their money to make the movie and pay them back from the profits, while retaining all the rights." Suo explains. "Otherwise I'll just be ripped off by the film companies and TV networks."

The ultimate agents for change, Suo believes, are the foreign companies who are shaking up the fossilized Japanese film industry by building multiplex theatres. "They're going to bring in more competition and that's going to help filmmakers here. We're going to get a better deal than we are now. But without foreign pressure, nothing will happen. The Japanese film companies won't make the effort. There are good theatres in Japan, but too often people are paying the same prices to see movies under poor conditions. How can the [film companies] expect people to pay so much for so little? It's a strange way to run a business."

(*Screen International*, October 5, 1996)

Juzo ITAMI

Best known in the West for his social comedies of the 1980s, including *Ososhiki* (The Funeral), *Tampopo*, and *Marusa no Onna* (A Taxing Woman), Itami became a Spielberg-like brand name in Japan, turning out hit after hit. In the 1990s, however, his attempts to tackle more serious themes, including terminal cancer (*Daibyonin* [The Last Dance]) and mental disability (*Shizukana Seikatsu* [A Quiet Life]) left Japanese moviegoers cold and made the industry wonder whether he had lost his touch.

On the day of our interview, he was very much back on top—his latest film, *Super no Onna* (Supermarket Woman), had become a superhit. As we walked into his sparely but elegantly furnished Japanese-style studio, a few steps away from the throngs of the Roppongi entertainment district, he was in deep communion with his Macintosh computer. Long interested in things technological—he was the first Japanese director to use a TV monitor on the set to watch his film-in-progress—Itami had set up a Web site during the shooting of *Super no Onna* to give fans an over-the-shoulder view of the director at work, with daily updates.

Though the rich, deep voice was familiar from his many television appearances, Itami looked wearier than his vibrant public image; perhaps the thought of submitting to yet another interview did not fill him with excitement. But as we progressed into our conversation and began to touch on themes close to his heart—the role of the father in Japanese society among them—he became animated, with opinions, anecdotes, and laughter flowing freely. A self-described pessimist, who "believes in nothing," he nonetheless had strong views and was not shy about explaining them in revealing detail.

Before I saw your latest film, Super no Onna, *a PR person at the distribution company told me that with this movie your total box office would exceed ten billion yen—nearly a hundred million dollars. Among Japanese directors, perhaps only Yoji Yamada, Hayao Miyazaki, and Kon Ichikawa have achieved this level of success. Is a big box office total a major concern of yours when you make a film?*
Of course, films are entertainment. Unless a lot of people see them, they're meaningless. But in Japan few directors can make entertaining films. So in that sense, I feel strongly that I want to my movies to do well at the box office—I want as many people to enjoy them as possible.

I make films for ordinary people, not for film freaks. But understanding what ordinary people want is extremely difficult. There are various things that I want to make movies about, but I have one theme that I have long pursued through my work in television, in my essays, and in my films. That theme is "what does it mean to be a Japanese?" or *Nihonjinron*. It would nice if everyone would accept what I have to say on this theme in exactly the way I want to say it, but that's not possible. Unless I put my message in a form that people want to see, they won't accept it.

But it's very difficult to find the right melding between what I want to say and what people what to see. The level of what people expect from films is extremely high. What I'm talking about is the amount of satisfaction that people expect when they come to a movie theater and pay their money. The rivals to Japanese films are not just television and American movies, but eating good food at restaurants, shopping, foreign travel, sports— a whole range of experiences. If you can't make a film that will satisfy that very high level of expectation, people will not come to the theater. But the people who are making films in this country don't realize how high that level is. They think that the general public has a very low level of expectation.

The industry seems to think that it can get away with serving up the same kinds of films again and again. The American film industry also has series films, but if you keeping giving people the same thing there, they stop coming.
That's true in Japan as well. In general, the audience for a sequel is only seventy percent that of the original.

In your films your wife (Nobuko Miyamoto) plays similar characters, but the angle of approach is always different. For example, in Tampopo *the owner of the failing ramen shop (Miyamoto) is helped by the truck driver (Tsutomu Miyazaki) to make the perfect bowl of noodles, but in your latest film,* Super no Onna, *the housewife (Miyamoto) helps the supermarket owner (Masayuki Tsugawa) make his failing store a success. Does this indicate a change in the relationship between the sexes in Japan?*
(Laughs) No, not at all. *Tampopo* was based on a Western—Howard Hawk's *Rio Bravo*. Both had the same basic theme of several unlikely people helping the hero to achieve a goal. The heart of the film was that of a classic Western, with the episodes about food added to the mix. The characters in the film had a strong desire for both food and sex. In Super no Onna, the main female character is strong, but that was also true of *Mimbo no Onna* (The Gentle Art of Japanese Extortion), *Marusa no Onna* (A Taxing Woman)—nearly all of my films, in fact. *Tampopo* was an exception—a Western parody. It wasn't really about Japan at all.

Usually the main male characters in your films, like the owner in Super no Onna, *tend to be sophisticated and intelligent, but spiritually weak.*
That's my portrait of the typical Japanese man [*laughs*].

But how did the present-day relationship between the sexes in Japan come about? While women are making progress in various areas, men seem to getting weaker.
But Japanese men have always been weak [*laughs*]. It may have been different in the Edo period (1600–1867), but maybe not even then. Japanese culture is not one in which men are strong.

But still you have the image of the samurai.

The samurai were only a small part of the whole culture. And even though the samurai tried to act macho, it didn't come naturally. The samurai part of the culture has been exaggerated by the West, but even though I watch television nearly every day, I hardly ever see the samurai type of man.

I hardly ever see anyone on television of whom you could say "he has courage." Ministry of Health and Welfare Naoto Kan and Yoshiyuki Konno, the man who was falsely accused in the Matsumoto sarin poisoning case, are about the only two I can think of recently who have acted courageously. Much more common are the men who think only of their own self-interest or the self-interest of their organization or company. When something goes wrong, they try to cover it up and deny responsibility. That's the most common posture of Japanese men—avoiding responsibility at all costs. They can't do anything on their own initiative. The refrain is always, "I have to consult with my superiors" [*laughs*].

So when I make a movie those kinds of men always appear. I wouldn't mind making a film about a truly noble character, but I can't find the material.

Even when you look at the recent Olympics—the Japanese women seem to have out-shone the men. Arimori finished third in the marathon, while the best a Japanese man could do was nineteenth.

I don't blame him for that. Before the race he was saying that he would not break the two hour and ten minute barrier, and that we shouldn't expect too much from him. So he did about as well as he said he would.

What bothered me much more about the Olympics was the attitude of the Japanese media. All they cared about was the Japanese athletes. They lack a sense of reality. Though foreign athletes may have been stronger mentally and physically and were closely studying their Japanese rivals with the aim of beating them, the Japanese media didn't seem to take any of that into account. Instead, they thought that because a Japanese athlete had taken a medal before they would definitely take a medal again. It was as though the foreign athletes didn't even exist for them when they were making their predictions. So none of those predictions came true.

That's so typical of the Japanese. They enclose themselves in a circle and regard only what goes on inside that circle as important. What goes on outside that circle is of no concern to them. The smallest circle is mother and child, then as the child grows, the circle expands to include the family, the school and finally, the company or bureaucracy. On a larger scale there is the circle of a certain industry and, on an even larger scale, the Japanese nation. You try to get along with others inside the circle and ignore those who are outside it. That's the Japanese way. It makes for a society that is peaceful and orderly. If there are disputes, they can resolved relatively easily. The weakness of this society is that it has no real connection with the outside world.

Japanese ought to stop huddling inside that circle. Instead, they should break the circle and expand their lives into the world beyond. That, in various ways, is what I have been trying to say in my films.

It seems that, with a few exceptions, the Japanese film industry is not thinking very much about the outside world.

They're not thinking about it all all [*laughs*].

What about you?
Of course, I want people outside Japan to watch my films. And I try to make my films so that they can understand them. But the Japanese audience is my first priority. I want Japanese audiences to see my films. At the same time, I want foreign audiences to understand them. So as much as possible, I try not to use stories, jokes, and puns that only Japanese will understand.

I've been strongly influenced by American movies. I learned how to make films—how to construct stories and develop characters—by studying American films. In American films, the basic concept is clearly stated. Americans feel that unless you can quickly sum up what a movie is about, you can't really call it a movie. For example, it would hard to state in a word or two what the Tora-san series or the *Tsuri Baka Nisshi* (Free and Easy) series are really about. If someone were to ask you "what are the themes of those films?" you'd be stumped for an answer [*laughs*].

The themes of my films, however, are clearly stated. For example, in *Super no Onna*, you have the story of a woman who make a success of a poorly run supermarket. When you get right down to it, my films are like little essays. For example, *Mimbo no Onna* is a kind of essay on how to fight against the Japanese mob. Of course, it's in the form of a drama, but within that drama, the flow of ideas are very much like that of an essay. *Super no Onna* is another kind of a essay. In a democratic society, what is proper way to run a business? What is wrong with Japanese business methods? The film is an essay on those questions.

The essay approach would seem to come naturally to you. You have been an essayist as well as a film director.
That's right, but my weak point as a director is that I use too many words [*laughs*]. That's a major weak point, but I just can't seem to help myself [*laughs*]. When I take my films abroad, I always have a big problem with subtitles. In *Super no Onna*, the characters are speaking a huge amount of dialogue very quickly.

Until recently I thought that the best subtitles were as faithful as possible to the original script, to avoid losing the nuances, but I suddenly realized that that was a big mistake. When you translate the original dialogue faithfully, the audience spends all its time reading the subtitles and doesn't watch the movie.

The tempo of my movies is very fast, but Americans who saw them complained that the tempo was too slow. The reason was that they were just reading the subtitles—and getting bored with the film [*laughs*]. So for *Super no Onna* I'm trying to make the subtitles as simple as possible. I'm thinking of rewriting the script in a kind of telegraphic Japanese and then having it translated into English.

Backtracking a bit, you said that you were strongly influenced by American films. Which American director do you feel the closest to as a filmmaker?
People have said that I resemble various directors—Preston Sturges for one—but I really don't know which one I feel the closest to. What I do feel, though, is that Americans are the best in the world at writing scripts. The worst are the Japanese [*laughs*]. They write stories that only they themselves can understand. Also, there's no structure. I use the three-act structure of Western drama. In the first act you develop the incidents that bring the hero into the drama. At the end of each act you have a climax and, in the third act, the climax for the entire film.

One characteristic of American films is that, before the final climax, the hero is confronted with a moral dilemma and has to make a choice between two courses of action, with no easy or safe way out. He's put on the spot, as it were. He makes his choice and, on the basis of that choice, the film moves toward its climax. That structure can be found in ninety-nine percent of all American films— it might be called the very definition of American film. Events move in a straight line toward a climax.

In Japanese films, instead of a straight line, you have a circle. The time frame in Christian societies and Japanese society is totally different. In the Christian world view, time is moving toward a conclusion—the Last Judgment— and cannot be reversed. That's the time frame within which Westerners live.

But in Japanese society, time moves in circles. In Japan the year is basically formatted (laughs), beginning with New Year's. You start off with a clean slate at the beginning of the year and over the months that follow the slate gradually gets dirty. Then, at the end of the year you have *bonenkai* (literally, "forgetting-the-year parties") at which you wipe the slate clean and start out fresh again. And so it goes, around and around in a never-ending circle. So I don't know whether it's right to try to make Japanese films in the Western straight-line time frame. Do you have the game of *jan-ken-pon* (scissors-paper-stone) in America?

Yes, we do, but we usually play it as a game, not as a way of making decisions—who is to go first and so on. Also, we don't play it nearly as often as the Japanese do.
In *jan-ken-pon* you keep going around and around—there's no right or wrong, black or white.

In America it's more common to toss a coin—heads or tails, win or lose.
Exactly. It's matter of plus or minus, yes or no. But in *jan-ken-pon*, there are three possible choices, with none better than all the others. Scissors beats paper beats stone beats scissors. It just keeps going around and around. That's a cultural difference; one way is not better than the other. But it illustrates that, even at an everyday level, Japanese and American cultures are quite dissimilar.

So by looking in the American cultural mirror, Japanese can find out a lot of things about themselves. For example, the supermarket came from America and is completely American. In *Super no Onna* I wanted to show how the proper way to run a supermarket differed from the typical Japanese business methods. Also, I wanted to ask Japanese businessmen whether the Japanese way of doing business was the best.

Before seeing the film I thought that a supermarket was a supermarket [laughs]. But in the film you show that what goes on in what you called the "backyard" of a Japanese supermarket is quite different. In Japan you have shokunin—*craftsmen—doing the skilled work and behaving like a race apart from the lowly part-timers—mainly housewives—who perform the more menial tasks.*
Shokunin are extremely secretive. They don't teach other people their skills. Traditionally, *shokunin* have learned their craft by apprenticing to an *oyakata*, or master craftsman, and learning what he does on the sly, what we call *shigoto o nusumu* ("stealing a skill"). That's the way these skilled crafts and trades are passed on: the *oyakata* doesn't teach, but expects his apprentices to "steal" his skill. If he would teach them they would get it right away. After all, how much skill does it take to cut *sashimi*? (laughs).

Also, they love to establish hierarchies, to make it clear who is superior and who is inferior. Japanese don't really like the mass-production method of dividing a job up into discrete parts, with all the workers on more or less on the same level. Instead, they like to make a hierarchy.

American businessmen are always complaining that the Japanese market is hard to enter, that there are various barriers to doing business here. Seeing the movie, I realized that, in some ways, they are more right than they imagine.
The biggest barrier is the Japanese practice of making a circle and huddling inside it. Japanese companies in the same industry form this kind of circle. They basically agree to get along with each other. This is much more important to them than competing. As much as possible they want to create an environment in which there is no competition. So they do things like conspire to fix prices, or agree not to lower them. Or when a new company from America threatens to enter the market, they will get together to shut it out. This works out well for those inside the circle, but of course those outside the circle don't like it.

What I was trying to say in *Super no Onna* is that business should be conducted from the viewpoint of the consumer. In a story about one small supermarket, I wanted to show that the real basis of capitalism is competition.

You were saying that the basic theme of all your films is Nihonjinron—*the search for Japanese identity. But what about the younger generation—the kids who dye their hair brown and go on overseas trips? Are they in any significant way different from Japanese of your generation?*
There are a lot of wonderful young people in Japan. Living in an information society, they absorb so much more information than members of my generation at their age that there's no comparison. Also, now that it has become so much easier to travel abroad, they are much more knowledgeable about foreign countries than we were.

The major problem with the younger generation, as I see it, is that the role of the father has become extremely weak. In the relationship between mother and baby, it's enough to make the baby feel good. When the baby is hungry, the mother gives it her breast, when it wets its diaper she changes it, and when it cries, she comforts it. In the world of mother and baby, the pleasure principal rules.

But the pleasure principal alone is not enough to build a society. The role of the father is also necessary. To put it simply, the role of the father is to teach the child that life is more than feeling good, that in order to become an adults and live in society, human beings need rules, laws, principles and, in the final analysis, God. To show the child, in short, that there is another, higher level of life than simple pleasure and that, to function on that level, one must develop self-control. That's the role of the father— to teach their children that they need *gaman*, or perseverance and fortitude, that they cannot live simply according to their own desires, that there are morals and laws that human beings must follow.

But in Japanese society that role has become extremely weak, particularly in the postwar period. Because Japanese men fought the war and lost it, their value as role models has really declined [*laughs*]. Japan has become a society in which women and children don't pay much attention to what Dad says. The result is that children have no way of learning to control their desires, and it's been that way for some time. So now we have a generation of young people who cannot control their desires, or rather, who have no underlying principles for controlling their desires.

One example is the ease with which junior and senior high school girls engage in prostitution. They get pleasure out of it, make people happy, and even earn money—so what's wrong with it? There are no rules saying that this is something you shouldn't do. Japan has become a country in which only the pleasure principle matters. My feeling is that Japan has come to a very dangerous pass.

I have that feeling as well, that Japan is becoming a country without a sense of values. Japanese values are all about human relations—getting along well with others. They just try to get along with the person in front of them. They don't want to get on that person's bad side or start an argument.

That has its good side. The bad side is that when A and B and C and D try to get along, but have different values, you get a very strange situation as, for example, when gangsters and cops try to get along (laughs). You have a contradiction there.

But that kind of thing often happens in Japanese society. What A, B, C, and D say to members of their group is quite different from what they say to outsiders. Japanese find it very easy to make this kind of shift. In trying to get along with the person in front of them, they will say what that person wants to hear, even though they may say something entirely different to someone else. Outsiders can't help thinking that, because Japanese change their story depending on whom they are speaking with, they are liars.

This decline of the father, as you say, is a postwar development. What was it like before? Well, all I know personally is the postwar period, but from the Meiji period (1868–1912) until just before the war Japan had the *ie* ("house" or family) system. It played a very important role in society, as did the village and the local neighborhood. Within those social bodies, rules and traditions were very strong forces for governing human behavior. Also, people were very poor and had to work hard. They had to be careful about following the rules if they wanted to survive.

These social structures kept people from indulging in their desires. But now the *ie* system has been destroyed, the local community has been destroyed and all we have left is the nuclear family. The brakes that used to be applied from the outside have disappeared. Instead, we have built a society in which people live only according to their desires. That worries me a great deal.

What about the relationship between you and your own father, who was also a film director? How were you influenced by him? Well, he died when I was about twelve years old. So I was not influenced by him as an adult. When he died I was still at an age when my father was at his most frightening [*laughs*] and that's regrettable. But he did leave me books that he had written. I read them again and again while I was in elementary school—he wrote in a way that was very easy to understand. From those books I learned about his way of thinking and how he found material for his films from everyday life and used that material to address social major issues. In that sense, I was strongly influenced by him. I was also influenced by his use of humor.

My father made a very fine period drama called *Akanishi Kakita* in 1935. That was a time when Japan was going down the dark road toward militarism and becoming a fascist country. Seeing what was happening, my father wanted to express his opposition in a film. But at that time people were being arrested for stating their opinions, and forums for free expression were disappearing. Directors who wanted to criticize the powers-that-be made samurai-period dramas, where they could better hide their messages.

The story concerned a stupid lord who was surrounded by evil retainers. But a group of good-hearted samurai get together to sacrifice their own lives and defeat the bad guys. Within the film was a criticism of the Japanese authorities who were using the emperor system to impose a militaristic dictatorship on the country. So back then there was a reason for making period dramas, because it was the only way that filmmakers could criticize society. But now I don't think there's any reason to go back to the Edo period in movies [*laughs*]. At least I don't see any reason to do it. There are so many contemporary topics that deserve to be filmed.

Period dramas don't seem to be doing very well at the box office either.
I can't think of any that have become hits recently. Maybe the last was Kurosawa's *Kagemusha* [in 1980].

In America, though, everyone in the industry thought that Westerns were dead. Then Dances with Wolves *became a hit.*
After that American movies started getting longer [*laughs*]. I'm not sure I like that trend. I'm a two-hour director. Most of my films seem to last two hours and several minutes. That length is the best for saying all I want to say. But in America there are really good directors who can do it in one hour and forty minutes—one hundred minutes. But I can't do it.

The element of comedy in your films has always been a strong one, but looking back on your films since the beginning of the 1990s, it seems that your have become more serious, as in Daibyonin (The Last Dance) *and* Shizuka na Seikatsu (A Quiet Life). *Do you intend to make films of different genres in the future as well?*
I don't know what you mean by "serious" [*laughs*], but in general pessimists make comedies, optimists make tragedies. In other words, people who believe strongly in something can make films about human tragedy and misfortune, but people who don't believe in anything make comedies. I don't believe in anything, because I'm a pessimist. I tend to look at things in a pessimistic way, so my films naturally become comedies.

As much as possible I want to extend the range of what my audiences will accept, but I haven't been very successful so far. *Tampopo* didn't do well at the Japanese box office. *Daibyonin* was a half-flop and *Shizuka na Seikatsu* was a complete flop. So it's very difficult. On the other hand, if you keep making the same thing again and again, people get bored. Also, I would get sick of it. So I want to extend myself as much as possible within the limits that the audience is willing to accept. That's extremely difficult.

Once the Japanese audience finds something it likes, it tends to want it the same way, again and again.
That may be true. *Sazae-san* [the long-running animated television series] is one example.

They never get tired of it, do they?
Japanese like getting what you call in English "reinforcement." They like to be told that

Japanese are wonderful people and that things are just fine the way they are. I'm the opposite. I want to make movies that destroy existing values. My movies have a dose of poison in them—they say that Japanese are no good [*laughs*]. So I have to make them as comedies, or the dose of poison would be too strong.

I've always thought of your movies as something unique. Though you take the position of an outsider, your films do extremely well at the box office. There seems to be a contradiction somewhere.
Within the movie industry I'm an outsider—that's all. I'm really closer to the world of television. That's where my roots are.

You had a long career as an actor before you started directing films. How has that career influenced your work?
It's been a great help to me when I shoot a film. I know how the actors are feeling and how to best bring out their talents. And when things aren't going well, I can play out the scene myself to show them what I want [*laughs*].

Also, when I write a script, I can develop the part so that it will be believable and the actors will be enjoy playing it. I try to write so that even actors in minor roles will be satisfied with what they are doing and give a good performance.

Like Woody Allen, you tend to use the same actors again and again. Do you do that to make your job easier?
No, I do it because there are few Japanese actors who can perform at the level I demand. I wouldn't mind using a lot of different actors in my films, but the level of acting in Japan is low. I would say that the majority of actors do little more than say their lines. That makes casting extremely difficult. It's especially hard in the case of male actors in their forties and fifties—there are very few who are any good. The only ones I can think of are Masahiko Tsugawa, Tsutomu Yamazaki, and Ken Ogata.

Why is that?
The main reason is that there hasn't been much of a need for father-figures in TV dramas. There have been few TV dramas in which men of that age group played major roles. On the other hand, male actors in their twenties are interesting. There are a relatively large number who have talent and vitality. I'm thinking of making a film with actors in that age group.

What about the films of younger directors?
I'm embarrassed to say that I haven't seen their films. I also haven't seen many recent American films.

You can't really call him young, but I like the work of Masayuki Suo, director of *Shall We Dance?* I like his personality and I think his films are well made. He is very smart about selecting material that is easily filmable—as in the film he made about a rock singer who becomes a Buddhist priest (*Fancy Dancer*, 1989) and his latest, about a salaryman who takes up ballroom dancing. Both themes lent themselves well to cinematic action. His approach to filmmaking is both correct and intelligent.

As for me, I only pick material that is hard to film. I don't think anyone else makes it as hard on himself as I do [*laughs*].

I'm sure you are asked this a lot, but after you made your anti-gang film, Mimbo no Onna *in 1993, you were attacked by gangsters and nearly killed. What effect did that attack that have on your way of thinking?*

I don't know if could say that my way of thinking has changed, but when I was in the hospital I received letters and telegrams from people all over Japan. Also, in newspapers and on television a lot people expressed anger on my behalf. That support made me very happy—it heartened me and gave me courage. So I had the experience of feeling how wonderful it can be when people stand behind you in a time of hardship. It's been important to me to have had that experience. At that time, I realized what a great thing it can be to make films that give people courage or energy to go on. And that whatever happens, I have to say what I have to say. No matter how dangerous or frightening it might be, I have to say what I have to say. In Japan there are still a lot of movies to be made about things that have to be said [*laughs*].

But in Japan, even if you manage to make a film on a taboo topic, you often have a problem finding a distributor.

That's true. If I were to make another film about gangs, it wouldn't be impossible to find a distributor, but it would be difficult.

After the release of Daibyonin, *your next film after* Mimbo no Onna, *a rightist slashed that screen at a theater in the Ginza and the distributor, Toho, temporarily withdrew the film.*

Toho's response to that was very weak. They should have struck back right away. Instead they didn't try to fight at all. They didn't even bring charges against the perpetrator.

Unfortunately, you can't make and distribute movies on your own. You need producers and distributors with the courage of their convictions.

That's why I want Warner-Mycal, UCI, and other foreign exhibition companies to quickly build a lot of new cineplexes [*laughs*]. If we had five hundred new screens, the whole situation in Japan would be very different. We could get rid of the stupid block-booking system for domestic films that we have now and have free booking, so that the best films could be seen on as many screens as possible. That would be ideal. Right now we only have three major distributors and exhibitors of domestic films. If more foreign companies came in, it would be a great thing.

(*Winds*, January 1997)

Naomi
SENTO

Japanese films have been in decline for as long as many Japanese have been alive. As admissions fell, theaters closed, and the 1950s Golden Age of Kurosawa, Ozu, and other masters faded ever farther into the past, fans, critics and industry insiders issued a never-ending stream of laments about the state of Japanese movies. Then came 1997—the miracle year. A beautifully crafted period film by master animator Hayao Miyazaki titled *Mononoke Hime* (Princess Mononoke) broke the all-time box-office record set by *E.T.— The Extra-Terrestrial* and Masayuki Suo's romantic comedy *Shall We Dance?* became the highest-earning Japanese film ever released in the United States. On the festival front, Shohei Imamura's *Unagi* (The Eel), a seriocomic study of a wife-murderer's search for redemption, won the Palme d'Or at the Cannes Film Festival and Takeshi Kitano's *Hana-Bi* (Fireworks), a violent drama about a rogue cop on an existential mission, took the Golden Lion at the Venice Film Festival.

The most surprising festival winner of all, however, was a twenty-seven-year-old director named Naomi Kawase, who was awarded the Camera d'Or prize at the 1997 Cannes festival for her first feature film, *Moe no Suzaku* (Suzaku), a compellingly told, visually stunning drama about the dissolution of a family and the decline of a way of life in the mountains of Nara Prefecture. The youngest-ever winner of the festival's prize for new directors, Kawase found herself, on her return to Japan, an instant celebrity, with her pleasantly smiling face in every major newspaper and magazine. In October 1997 a press conference to announce her marriage to *Moe no Suzaku* producer Takenori Sento was splashed across the entertainment pages of the nation's daily sport papers, who usually cover independent filmmakers the way they cover semioticians.

Though a newcomer to the world of feature filmmaking, Kawase—who now prefers to use her husband's surname, Sento—had made sixteen documentary films prior to *Moe no Suzaku*, beginning in 1988 while she was still a student at the Visual Arts College of Osaka. Several won prizes at festivals in Japan and had been screened widely abroad, thrusting her into the forefront of the local documentary scene. She had also become a figure of controversy.

Many of the previous generation of Japanese documentarians, led by Noriaki Tsuchimoto, with his series of films about the victims of Minamata disease, and Shinsuke Ogawa, with another acclaimed series about the farmers and radical students opposed to the construction of Narita Airport, were social activists who regarded documentary filmmaking as a political act and worked as members of filmmaking collectives.

Sento, however, represented a new generation of documentarians less committed to politics, more interested in expressing a personal vision. *Ni Tsutsumarete* (Embracing), which won the Award for Excellence at the 1993 Image Forum Festival, was an impressionistic record of her search for her long-missing father, who had left her family while she was still a child. *Katatsumori*, which received the Award for Excellence at the 1995 Yamagata International Documentary Film Festival, portrayed her relationship with her grandmother, who had raised her following her father's departure.

But together with the prizes and praise, Sento attracted the scorn of leftist critics for what they described as her political naiveté and artistic conservatism, and from feminists for what they perceived as her indifference to women's issues. She was attacked with particular ferocity for her decision to take her husband's name—a still nearly universal convention now being sharply challenged by women who regard it a symbol of Japanese society's suppression of their independence and individuality.

Sento, who in person projects a puckish humor and quietly stubborn determination not apparent in her sweetly smiling public persona, firmly rejects what she calls the "heavy baggage" that her feminist critics would have her carry. "I've had members of women's groups tell me I should make this type or that type of film, but I think it's strange—it becomes a kind of reverse discrimination," she said. "I just ignore them." She also opposes what she sees as the tendency of feminists to view the problems women face in Japanese society through a rigid ideological filter. "I find that attitude scary," she says. "For me, being a woman is like having a certain shoe size—it's a natural condition, not something I think about."

Sento is hardly alone today in preferring a personal, non-ideological style of filmmaking. She has organized a group of like-minded filmmakers called Kumie that has screened films all around Japan. Also, a growing number of talented young documentarians, such as Hirokazu Koreeda, whose debut feature film *Maboroshi no Hikari* (Maborosi) was screened in the competitive section of the 1995 Venice Film Festival, and Nobuhiro Suwa, whose first film, *2/Duo*, won the NETPAC Award at the 1997 Rotterdam Film Festival, are making fiction films that focus on intimate personal relationships, while excluding the media-saturated, technology-obsessed world outside. Some, such as Suwa and Sento, use documentary techniques to give their films an added immediacy and verisimilitude.

Sento, however, sets herself apart from other young independent filmmakers, whose imagination is often more informed by the movies they have seen than the lives they have lived. "I got into filmmaking by a different route," she explains. "I grew up seeing almost no movies or television. I'm more like filmmakers of sixty years ago—I make films based on what I've actually seen and felt in my life—the sadness and the happiness and all the rest—in my own way. I haven't followed any filmmaking trend. Instead, my films have been formed by the environment in which I grew up." That environment was a residential neighborhood on the outskirts of Nara. Sento spent her childhood exploring the nearby fields, woods, rivers. She grew up with a love of nature and rural people who have often been left behind in Japan's postwar rush to modernize and urbanize.

Prior to making *Moe no Suzaku*, which traces fifteen years in the life of a family in Nishi Yoshino Mura, a mountain village in Nara Prefecture, Sento spent more than three years researching conditions in the village and getting to know the villagers, many of whom were facing poverty and loneliness in their old age, while their children were leaving to search for a better life in the cities. Three months before the start of shooting, her crew joined her in the village to rebuild the old farmhouse in which the film's fictional family was to live and even plant the field where they were to farm.

Also taking part in these preparations were the film's actors, all but one of whom were locally recruited amateurs. Sento's aim to make them to feel that they were not acting, but actually living in the world of the film. "Instead of forcing them to act in a certain way, I tried to create an environment in which they could perform," she explained. "I didn't tell them to 'do this' or 'do that.' Instead everyone worked together in the field, harvested the crop, and built the house. So when the son came home from school in the film, he could enter the farmhouse as though it were his real home."

The film's significant events—the father's fall into a long depression after the cancellation of a railway line he was hoping would boost the village economy, the collapse of the mother's delicate health caused by overwork, the growing love of the daughter for her shy but handsome cousin—are implied by looks and gestures, not the usual connect-the-dots dialogue. The result is a drama absorbing in its emotional honesty and its depiction of a world in which human beings are still vitally connected to the natural world, living in harmony with natural rhythms. "When people are sad or lonely there are things that they can't put into words," Sento says. "After the father dies [in the film], I didn't want to the characters to explain why they felt sad. I thought they could better express that sadness by their expressions. I wanted to do the explaining with images, not words."

Her object was not to create another didactic semidocumentary on the depopulation and decline of mountain villages, but to make the audience participate in the drama of her family's life, using their own imagination and originality—qualities she feels are in short supply in today's Japan. "People nowadays can get information from a variety of sources," she says. "You can get along without finding out things yourself. Everything is served up for you on television. But I feel that human beings are animals that naturally have to experience things themselves, whether it is beauty or sadness."

Sento has released a new feature-length documentary, *Somaudo Monogatari* (The Weald) about elderly people living in the same Nara mountains she depicted in *Moe no Suzaku*. Once again she creates the impression of having entered deeply into her subjects' lives, but as a sympathetic if inquisitive daughter, not an intrusive reporter. Once again, she reaches beyond the usual talking heads interviews to evoke, with poetic imagery, the soul of their living world.

Sento's next movie will to be a love story set in Nara. She plans to spend a year shooting it, finishing by the summer of 1999. The seasons play an important part in the story, she says, and she wants to film them in real time. Celebrity and success may drive others to hurry and cash in, but Sento is determined to keep working in her own way, in her own time. "I don't want to be thought of as a one-film wonder," she says. "I want to keep making films as long as I can... so I can't just coast. I can't assume that, because I can make a film more easily that I could before, everything is going to be all right. The world doesn't work that way."

(*Winds*, May 1998)

Makoto SHINOZAKI

A Tokyo native, Makoto Shinozaki began making 8mm films while still in junior high school. After graduating from Rikkyo University with a degree in psychology, he began working at a Tokyo movie theater and, later, as a projectionist at the Athené Française French cultural center. He also became a widely published film writer, known for his lengthy interviews with Takeshi Kitano, Abbas Kiarostomi, Quentin Tarrantino, Alex Cox, and other directors.

Beginning in 1977 with *Jugeki* (Gunshot) and *Anchi Daisakusen* (The Anti Big Operation), he made a series of 8mm films, leading to his debut as a feature filmmaker with *Okaeri* in 1996. Winner of the Best Director prize and FIPRESCI prize at the 1996 Thessalonika Film Festival and screened at many other film festivals around the world, including Berlin, London, Turin, Hong Kong, and Sao Paulo, *Okaeri* catapulted Shinozaki into the front ranks of Japan's younger directors.

Meeting Shinozaki for this interview at a Tokyo coffee shop, I was impressed by his enthusiasm, his lack of pretense, and his deep knowledge of films and the film world.

You're writing a new film?

Yes, I plan to have the script finished by the end of 1999. A college friend of mine named Ryo Yamamura is going over it now. We're working on it together.

What's it about?

Life in postwar Japan. The main characters were born in the 1920s and lived though the important events of the postwar era. We're getting Tomio Aoki—the famous child actor Tokkan Kozo of the thirties who also appeared in *Okaeri*—to star.

During World War II the hero fought on Peleliu, an island in the South Pacific. One of his friends said that, after the war, he wanted to become a musician. He was always carrying a harmonica around, but ended up dying in the war. The hero, who is now an old man, has treasured this harmonica for more than fifty years.

I want to insert documentary elements into this film. I want people who were in the war to come on camera and talk about their experiences. Everything else is a secret!

What are your influences? Watching Okaeri *I couldn't help thinking that you lean more toward European than American cinema.*
Not entirely. I love American noir films—that's what I was raised on. I learned a lot from European films, but I also learned a lot from Hollywood B movies, especially gang films until about the 1970s.

Modern Hollywood films put a great emphasis on story, but do the characters represent real people? No. I want to make films that are realistic fictions. Not like the *Die Hard* movies, in which the only reality is in the explosions. I also hated *Independence Day*, which was about special effects, not people.

My next film will have violence in it—but no explosions. What interests me more is mental violence. I don't think the distinction between entertainment and art films has much meaning. If a film has emotional reality, that's all that matters.

I love the films of Nicholas Ray, Humphrey Bogart, Robert Aldrich. I like genre films in which the characters are morally ambiguous, and have their own way of living. I wouldn't want to make a simple gang movie with stereotyped characters—that kind of thing is too phony. I want to make films in which the emotions are grounded in reality.

There seem to be several younger Japanese directors who are making the kind of realistic films you are talking about.
Yes, directors like Hirokazu Koreeda and Ryosuke Hashiguchi, who aren't afraid to make dramas about difficult subjects, who record their own view of reality.

How was it working with Takeshi Kitano? You shot the video on the making of his latest film, Kikujiro no Natsu *(Kikujiro).*
A producer at Office Kitano asked me to take the job—I've been involved with his new film for several months now. It's helped me to pay the rent. The film itself is a departure for him—it doesn't have much violence in it. Instead it's an essay on what it means to live life to the fullest.

In his violent films Kitano explores the theme of life versus death. Violence is just a device for furthering that exploration. He does not use violence simply for the sake of using violence. His work in *Sonatine* especially is extremely realistic—the dialogue in particular is very real. It's not an ordinary gang story.

Japanese films often contain a lot of explanations—too much actually. Kitano doesn't believe in explaining—he would rather show with images.

I also found that reluctance to overexplain in Okaeri, *whose approach was diametrically opposed to that of the usual Japanese "problem drama" on mental illness.*
I didn't want to tell the audience exactly why the heroine was going insane—instead I used a more indirect approach. In Japan there's still this view that schizophrenia is something to hide. There's is still a lingering prejudice against the mentally ill. But in depicting her slide into madness, I don't give that prejudice as a reason. I don't explain—I believe if you explain everything for the audience, you don't allow them to feel anything. You've already done the feeling for them.

Instead of explaining, you use long cuts that allow the audience to directly experience the emotions of the characters.
I used long cuts because I wanted to get into the heart of the relationship of the two

main characters, the man and wife. With montage I could get some beautiful images, but I don't think I could have brought out the atmosphere of their lives as well. The drama would have gotten lost.

In making *Okaeri* My first priority was to focus on the emotions of the characters. I couldn't have maintained that focus if I had used a lot of cuts. But long cuts are not always my style—it depends on the theme and story.

To bring out the real emotions of the characters, I used a lot of improvisation with the actors playing the two lead roles. I tried to stay flexible. Of course, I rewrite my script several times before shooting. Also, I think over all the details. After that I try to forget everything I thought!

That emotion is not something you can bring out with computer graphics.
That's a problem I have with films that use a lot of computer graphics—the technology becomes more important than the people. That's what I thought was wrong with *Titanic*. You can't show the flow of emotions with computer graphics. I think computer graphics can be limiting in that way.

The most memorable scene in Okaeri *for me is the one in which the husband and wife have a highly emotional argument and reconciliation, all shot in one long take. It struck me as being so spontaneous, almost as if you were shooting a documentary. At the same time, the scene had a distinct arc.*
It's a simple scene. The wife goes into the toilet and doesn't come out. The husband sits outside the door, talking to her. Finally she comes out and he comforts her.

There was no dialogue as such for this scene. Instead, we worked it out in rehearsal. Susumu Terashima practiced until he could do it naturally. I told him to forget the script and had him create his own dialogue

Miho Uemura also did a great job on this scene. She went into the toilet and Terashima tried to persuade her to come out. Ten minutes later she came and started crying a torrent. The assistant directors were surprised—they weren't expecting something like that. Terashiima, who wasn't expecting it either, improvised—he got a towel and started wiping the tears away and comforting her. None of this was in the script. If they had done this scene exactly according to the script, it might have been boring. But they both did extremely well—the sight of Uemura crying was so beautiful. So I'm glad we tried it that way—I wouldn't have minded if we had failed. It was worth the risk to get that kind of performance.

I wanted to put as little pressure as possible on the actors, so I decided to do the whole scene in one take. If I had done it in several takes, there's no way they could have shown the same emotion. Instead, we used two cameras. The entire scene was about seventeen minutes long, and you can film for only ten minutes before you have to change the reel. So we had one camera filming for ten minutes and the other for the remaining seven or eight minutes. Then we spliced the film together in the editing room.

There's been a lot of talk recently about the revival of Japanese cinema, with Okaeri *being used as a prominent example.*
Five years ago things looked pretty dismal, but now Japanese movies are becoming interesting again. More opportunities are being created for Japanese filmmakers by hit movies like *Shall We Dance?* and *Mononoke Hime*. If the industry can produce two or

three major films like those a year, it can afford to make more minor films. Films like Kitano's are not always going to find a mass audience, but they have an originality that mass-audience films lack.

But for movies like that to get made, we need the base of support that major films provide. If everyone were to make only art films, the industry couldn't survive. Entertainment is also important. I don't mean junk like *Peking Genjin* (Peking Man), but well-made films like Masayuki Suo's *Shall We Dance?* that display a distinct directorial personality.

(September 1998)

Takeshi KITANO

Takeshi Kitano is to Japanese show business what Steven Spielberg is to the Hollywood film industry: a man who, despite his public image as an eternal Peter Pan, has been the king of his professional hill for more than two decades and extended his activities far beyond the limits of most of his colleagues. Kitano, or as he is better known to Japan's TV-watching masses, Beat Takeshi, may not run a movie studio, but he has gone from being a strip joint emcee and playing the dimwit in a comedy duo called Two Beats (thus his "Beat" stage name) to appearing on countless network TV shows, writing more than sixty books, cutting hit records, and even dabbling in the curry-restaurant business.

On the TV programs that he appears on almost nightly, he is everything to everybody, clowning on one show in sailor-dress drag, discoursing on another about the latest discoveries in astronomy. Voted Japan's most popular male celebrity in polls year after year, he is too protean to easily categorize, too talented and articulate to dismiss as just another TV buffoon. Like Woody Allen, he has moved to the grown-up table of national life and has no intention of leaving.

Abroad, Kitano is better known as the director of films that, in their understated, innovative, blackly humorous explorations of society's fringes, including Japan's ubiquitous yakuza gangs, have earned him critical praise and numerous prizes. In 1997, Kitano's *Hana-Bi* (Fireworks), a tersely told, starkly violent drama about an ex-cop's search for redemption, won the Golden Lion at the Venice Film Festival.

In person, Kitano is utterly without the usual airs and pretensions of the entertainment-world elite. Shifting mental gears with blinding speed, he leaps from subject to subject, image to image, at times with little regard for the question at hand. He is not trying to impress so much as simply give his nimble mind free rein and, not incidentally, keep everyone laughing.

John Woo said in an interview that he thought you were the next Asian director most likely to make it in Hollywood. What kind of movie would you make if you could work with a Hollywood studio and budget? Also, do you have any desire to make such a film?
I'm working on two projects now set in America. I've written simple treatments for them. One is about two members of minorities, a Japanese *yakuza* and a black American who becomes the yakuza's *kyodaibun*—his gang brother. They are fighting together

against the larger white society and realize, in the course of the struggle, that they are brothers in the real sense of the word.

Another one is inspired by Tarantino and Scorsese and other directors who are really familiar with the Italian Mafia. It's a film set in Hawaii about the Japanese *yakuza* and the American Mafia. There's this old *yakuza* who happens to get into some trouble with another old man and discovers that he's with the Mafia. They start talking in a coffee shop about why they became gangsters. The Mafia guy says that he got involved in the gangs when he was a kid. The *yakuza* says that he was poor when he was a kid and that the *yakuza* gave him a way out. Then the Mafia guy asks the *yakuza* guy what kind of ceremonies the *yakuza* have when someone joins a gang.

The story traces their lives, from the old days to the present. When they part, they agree to meet at the coffee shop at the same time next year. Then the Mafia guy takes a walk on the beach. Suddenly there's the sound of gunfire and he falls. The Japanese *yakuza* thinks the American Mafia is tougher than the *yakuza* and that's how the movie ends. These films are just in the treatment stage. If anyone is interested, I can say I have these two treatments.

So you aren't in negotiation with any Hollywood studio now.
No, not at all. I can't make movies the way John Woo does. I don't have that kind of speed. In general, I don't think that I have the kind of speed that you find in Hollywood films, so it probably wouldn't work out. I don't think it would be fair to moviegoers who come expecting to be entertained.

My movie [*Hana-Bi*] opened at a theater in Shinjuku yesterday. Usually when a screening ends people start walking out during the credits, but after *Hana-Bi* ended the audience stayed until the lights went up in the theater, so they had to delay the next screening until everyone left. The schedule got screwed up because of that.

When I saw it at the Nippon Herald screening room, the place was packed, but no one left until the end of the credits. They seemed to be lost in thought.
How can we take money for bringing people down like that? [*laughs*] The audience is going to be asking for a refund. "Hey, I thought movies were supposed to be fun." [*laughs*] "You've got some kind of strange mind, making a movie like that." [*laughs*]

Was the reaction abroad the same?
Pretty much the same I think. When they screened it at Venice, the audience was quiet until the end and I thought, "Uh oh, this isn't good." Then after the lights went up, there was some applause, so I felt relieved. "At least they're applauding it." But there was a gap between the end of the film and the applause. Finally, they gave it a big hand.

Your work is so different from what the West has been getting from Asia lately—a lot of the Hong Kong movies or Hollywood movies made by Hong Kong directors.
Hong Kong films are like a kind of dance, a show. You'll never see anything like that in real life. When they show fight scenes, they just go on and on. There's no way that people can keep punching and kicking each other like that, making it look so beautiful. In real life, there's one punch and it's over. So I don't think of my violent films as being entertainment. In Hong Kong movies, there's no realism to the fighting or shooting— it's all a show.

Whereas Hong Kong movies seem to be influenced by Chinese opera, yours seem to have a more distinctly Japanese quality. The way you use pauses reminds me somehow of Noh drama [laughs]. Your gang movies seem restrained compared to what has been coming out of Hong Kong. Did you intend to inject a traditional Japanese quality into your films?
No, not all. In the neighborhood where I grew up there were a lot of *yakuza* around. I used to see them fight each other and usually it would be over with one punch. I never saw them punching away at each other—they might trade as many three punches, then one guy would be getting the worst of it and give up. I never saw them go at each other the way you see in a cowboy movie. Usually it would be one-sided—one guy working over another. I would see one guy kicking another, that kind of thing. I never saw what you would describe as boxing match.

What about the influence of Japanese yakuza *movies from the sixties and seventies—Ken Takakura charging into a nest of rival gangsters with a sword?*
Those Ken Takakura movies were popular when the student movement was at its height. Radical students would go to the theater and applaud Ken Takakura. But I knew there was no way for that kind of thing to happen—for one *yakuza* to take on a whole rival gang with a wooden sword. It was totally unrealistic. I thought, well, it's only a movie, but when I made movies myself I could never do that. Stories like that were made into *manga*. At the end Ken Takakura says, "I'll go alone." The other guys in the gang say "Go ahead, we're not stopping you." [*laughs*].

In the seventies the Jingi Naki Tatakai *(Battles Without Honor) series by Kinji Fukasaku tried to inject more realism into the yakuza genre.*
His camerawork had a documentary feel. Now they would use a Steadicam, but back then they would shoot like a reporter chasing a TV star, with a wobbling handheld camera. Especially in the fight scenes—it would heighten the tension. Fukasaku was quite good at that.

When I saw your first film, Sono Otoko, Kyobo ni Tsuki *(Violent Cop, 1989) I thought that you were trying to get away from what had been done in the past and make a different kind of gang movie.*
The story, the camerawork—the whole process of making films has it own rules, like baseball. When I made my first film I tried to learn the rules and I followed them until *Hana-Bi*. I had pretty much figured out how to make a movie by then. In the beginning, I didn't know very much about how to move the camera and so on. So the movie turned out looking like a souvenir snapshot. After my second or third film, though, I started to figure out how to move the camera.

With Hana-Bi *I felt that you were putting in everything you had learned about film-making. It was a kind of summation.*
If I compare *Hana-Bi* to an entrance exam for a public university, where they test you on five subjects—English and Japanese and so on—I think I scored an average of sixty points on all the subjects and passed. But in some scenes I scored ninety percent and others ten percent. If I had been taking a test for a private college, where they only require three subjects, *Hana-Bi* would have scored pretty well, though. [*laughs*] But a lot of movies that apply for that national university of film score better than *Hana-Bi*.

Are you going to take a different approach for you next film? Or are you going to expand on the themes you explored in Hana-Bi?

When you think about the most popular stories with audiences, the ones that seem to work the most consistently are about parents and children. One story is a child visiting its mother during the summer vacation. They meet and various things happen, then the child goes back to its grandmother. That's a classic story. Various people have told it and each one has his own way of telling it. So now I'm thinking how I can tell it differently.

It's like a piano recital where everyone plays the same number, but one performance is somehow better than the others. I would like to try something like that once. Everyone has his own idea of how to tell a story about family relations. You have the Tora-san approach, you have the approach of Masahiro Shinoda in *Shonen Jidai* (Takeshi: Childhood Days) So I would like to try making the same kind of film and see how I could do it differently.

In the same way, I've seen a lot of younger Japanese directors try to make films like Yasujiro Ozu. They may be making a parody, but at the same time they're trying to match themselves against the master—again, like classical pianists playing the same composition.

When I see Ozu's movies, I'm impressed with the shots he gets when the characters go outside—you can't find those kinds of backdrops in Japan anymore. You couldn't make those kinds of shots today—the right scenery isn't there anymore. There's too much extraneous stuff in the background. So the only way you can still imitate Ozu now is to shoot on a set. Once you go outside it would be too difficult.

People are talking about how Japanese films are reviving, but when you compare them to what was made in the Golden Age of the 1950s by people like Ozu and Kurosawa, there's still a gap.

Japanese movies are still pretty bad. Back then there were a lot of good movies being made, so a lot of people went to see them—that's why it was called the Golden Age. The release of movies like *Mononoke Hime* (Princess Mononoke) and *Shitsurakuen* (Lost Paradise) that draw people back to the theaters is a good thing, but the films themselves are not that great [*laughs*]. To have a Golden Age you need to have both good films and a lot of people who want to see them. If we had three or four really great directors, we might have a new Golden Age, but we're not there yet.

In the past couple years a lot of young directors have been making their first features. Have you seen any that you thought were really good?

I've been collecting videos of films by young directors. I'm judging the Tokyo Sports Film Awards this year. We're totally free to pick any movies we want, whether or not they're from a major studio.

There have been a lot of "problem" films recently, especially films about *enjo kosai* ["paid dates" in which older men buy the sexual favors of teenage girls]. But I think that kind of subject would be more interesting as a documentary. When you think about the possibilities of film, that kind of subject matter seems to limit what you can do visually. I wouldn't have very much interest in watching that kind of film. I just don't like message or problem films anyway.

A lot of younger directors are coming from backgrounds other than films—music videos and TV commercials and so on. When you made your first movie nine years ago, there was a certain prejudice in the industry against outsiders directing, but that doesn't seem to be case now.

When we're looking for locations, sometimes they won't let us shoot. A temple might let Kurosawa shoot there, but not me, because I am a celebrity and they are afraid they won't be able to control the crowds. But since I've taken the prize at Venice, places like that will let me shoot there. It's become a lot easier. Before we'd get a lot of static from people saying "you can't shoot here, you can't shoot there."

But when I interviewed Kurosawa a few years ago, he complained about the same thing. Japanese bureaucrats and police make it hard for anyone to shoot movies in this country.

Japanese bureaucrats earn their bread by building roads, but the money they use comes from taxpayers like me. I can't tell them "I've paid for this road, you have to let me use it," but I would like them to give me a straight explanation for why they are saying no.

A more important problem for a lot of Japanese filmmakers, though, is to get the money to make a movie in the first place.

When you come down to it, there are only about four movie companies that finance film production. Now you also have the TV networks joining with the film companies to make big projects like *Mononoke Hime*. I think that co-financing with the TV networks is one way to go—they can do a lot to publicize a film.

That was certainly true in the case of Shall We Dance?, *which got a lot of TV publicity from one of its backers, the NTV network. The problem with the films that TV networks make is that a lot of them end up looking like TV dramas.*

There was no need to make *Shall We Dance?* as a movie—it's made the same way as a TV drama. You have a bunch of actors talking on a set—I think that film has more possibilities than that. With films you can have a bigger scale, more visual beauty—but just filming a bunch of actors talking on a set, you might as well do it with a TV camera.

Yet another problem, especially for makers of independent films in Japan, is distribution, which is tightly controlled by three companies.

Yes. Toei, Toho, and Shochiku all have theater chains, leaving only a limited number of independent theaters, such as Theater Shinjuku. But nowadays, with the growth of multiplex cinemas, you can rent more independent theaters for your films. We've been able to get *Hana-Bi* into a fairly large number of theaters—sixty or seventy—around the country. So there are ways to get around the chains.

Before you started distributing through your own company, Office Kitano, you made three films with Shochiku. With the third, Sonatine *(1993), you had some differences with the producer, Kazuyoshi Okuyama. Is that what persuaded you to start distributing your films independently?*

Yes, the wonderful Mr. Okuyama [*laughs*]. When he saw the rushes he got mad and said "This is not a movie." He said he didn't want his name on the film as a producer, so we had some trouble over that.

After *Sonatine* won a prize at the Taormina festival in Italy, he kept it a secret. Two years later, when I went to the Cannes film festival, an Italian journalist asked me how I felt about winning the prize. I said, "What prize?" Shochiku had been holding onto it all that time. I felt like saying "What do you guys think you're doing?"

Now that you've had so much success as a director, have you started to wonder what your real job should be? Do you ever think of chucking TV and concentrating on films?
Appearing on television gets me the money and fame I need to work as a director, so television has its good points. Also, if I just made movies, I couldn't eat [*laughs*]. With *Hana-Bi* I may earn enough money to make a living off my movies, for the first time ever. Before there was no way—I simply couldn't make enough money at it. So for me, being a director is a kind of hobby.

Also, because I'm a comedian, making movies and working on television gives me a lot of good material for gags. And because I have the status of being a movie director, I can get mad at people and they can't say anything [*laughs*]. So doing both jobs has a kind of synergy that's worked well for me. But it's become hard to do both in terms of time and stamina. I've got eight regular programs now and that may be too many. If I just made one film year and cut back on my TV schedule, it would be physically easier, but then I wouldn't have enough money to live on [*laughs*].

You've been working regularly on television for more than twenty years. It's amazing that you've been able to stand the pace this long.
It's because I goof off on the job—I don't work at it and I don't think about it.

But how do you make shift from the film mode to the television mode, from the serious filmmaker to the television comedian?
If you compare films and television to games, like professional football or major league baseball, you play football according to football rules, baseball according to baseball rules. In the same way being a TV talent has its own rules and so does working in films. For me comedy is the best way to go on television. But in movies, I want to do more serious things, such as play *yakuza*.

A lot of comedians have tried to make the shift from comedy to serious drama, but you're the only one I can think of who has played such tough characters in films.
Even since I appeared in [Nagisa Oshima's] *Merry Christmas, Mr. Lawrence* as a camp guard, I've been playing serious roles. Because I first came up as a standup comedian, whenever I appeared on the screen, audiences would start laughing, no matter what role I was in. It took about fifteen years until audiences started to regard me as something other than a comedian and really pay attention to what I was doing. Until then they would just laugh.

I also played a lot of bad guys on TV dramas and got a good reaction. Finally audiences started to distinguish between Beat Takeshi the comedian and Takeshi Kitano the actor and filmmaker. But it took a long time. It was as hard for me as it was for Michael Jordan to hit a home run in the major leagues.

Do you enjoy shifting from one mode to another for a change of pace?
I regard the two as being in completely different categories. It's like eating Japanese

food and Italian food. The TV and movie work influence each other, but they are completely separate.

You appeared in one Hollywood film, Johnny Mnemonic, *and it seemed that you might do more work with Hollywood directors, but since your accident, you seem to have given up those plans. What happened?*
I thought *Johnny Mnemonic* would be good chance to work in a Hollywood movie with a big actor like Keanu Reeves, but after the shooting was over I felt like a Japanese kid who had been taken to the real Disneyland in America but had to come home without riding on anything [*laughs*]. I didn't really feel like I was in a Hollywood movie. I'd be happy to do it again, but this time I want to go on some rides [*laughs*].

Why did you feel that you didn't get to go on any rides?
To be honest, I probably should have looked at the script more closely before I agreed to do the film. I should have turned it down—it was a boring movie.

Are there any Hollywood directors or actors you especially want to work with?
It's hard for me to tell about the actors—they all look good to me. I'm not a native speaker of English, so I have so read the subtitles. It hard for me to tell whether they're really reading their lines well or not. I know there are good and bad Hollywood stars, but I can't get a feel for which is which. I might read in a magazine that this or that actor is good, but that's all I know—so anyone would be all right [*laughs*].

Would you feel more comfortable about appearing in, say, a gang movie than another science fiction film?
Yes, a gang movie would be all right—either a European or Hollywood action film would be all right, but the range of what I can do is rather limited. I have to play a tough guy. Also, I make a big impact on the screen, so I have to have other actors around who can keep up with me. But if both those conditions are met, then I would be interested in seeing a script. With *Johnny Mnemonic*, I agreed to do it without first checking the script. When I got to the set I was surprised to see what was going on, but by then it was too late. So if I appear in a Hollywood movie again, I want to have a better idea of what I'm getting into.

In *Johnny Mnemonic* I was supposed to wear a *yakuza* tattoo. In Japan everyone knows what *yakuza* are and what *yakuza* tattoos are supposed to look like, so there's no problem, but over there they have unions for the technical people and the makeup people and they're very strong. They tell you what they're going to do and you have to listen to them. They wanted me to wear a tattoo like something on an aloha shirt [*laughs*]. I wondered what the Japanese audience would think when they saw that.

It would have been different if I had stated in my contract what kind of tattoo I would wear, but instead I found myself in this strange place where I didn't know the customs and they were telling me to how be a *yakuza*. I should have turned down the part. I can understand that there might be some differences, but I didn't know that it would be so different.

Speaking about different working methods, I remember being surprised when I went to the set of Hana-Bi *and heard you talking with your staff about how to end the movie. I know that you had a script but it almost seemed as though you were making up the story as you went along. Is that the way you usually work?*

Usually we have a synopsis when we start. After we begin filming, though, I don't like to force the actors to do what they're uncomfortable with, so once they get into their rhythms, the story naturally starts to change. I don't change the script on my own, but in consultation with my staff. This can create problems. One time we going to use a ferry boat and, when the story changed, we had to cancel. So one of the staff had to go to the ferry boat people and apologize. All he could say was "the director's changed his mind." That's kind of thing happens a lot. When you're faced with a choice, you have to go with the one you think is best. But when you're making a Hollywood movie, you have a script and usually you have to follow it. You can't go the people in charge and say "I don't like this." You 'll get fired [*laughs*].

Akira Kurosawa used his drawings to give his staff a feel for the kind of look and feel he wanted in the scene. They served as a kind of storyboard. You've also taken up painting—some of your paintings were used in Hana-Bi. *Did you make them for the same reason— to use as a visual guide for your staff?*

Even if I were to make a drawing of a location for the staff, it only exists in my head—I haven't been there, my staff hasn't been there. First we have to go to the actual place where we're going to film and look around. Also, I like to play it by ear so I can fool the lighting and camera directors. They want everything to be perfect, but I like the mistakes—I like changing the direction of the action so the light isn't shining where it's supposed to or the camera isn't pointing where it's supposed to. Of course, I can't ignore them completely—they're professionals who know their jobs. But they'll tell me I can't do this or that—otherwise they'll look bad. At first, I would tell them what I wanted them to do, but they wouldn't listen to me. So now I fool them. I'll shoot it the way I like, without the proper lighting, and tell them I'll throw the footage away, but later on I'll edit it in. [*laughs*].

You're involved in the whole process, from scriptwriting to editing. Do you think that editing is the most important part of the job?

Editing like making a plastic model. You have the numbered parts—the shots that you filmed—and editing is the process of putting them together. Having someone else do the editing for you is like having the people at the factory build your model for you. The job of putting the parts together is mine and for me it's the most interesting part of the whole process. Of course, sometimes you don't have the parts you need, and you have to improvise. It's like having not having a steering wheel for your model and putting a tire in its place. You just hope that people don't watch the movie two or three times—they're going to find you out ([*laughs*]).

Sometimes when my mind is really clicking, I'll be cutting in my head as I film. I think if I film in such and such a way I'll have such and such a sequence of cuts. There's one scene in *Hana-Bi* of a punk standing by a car. He throws away a box lunch and suddenly my fist flashes out and he's on the ground. I filmed it exactly that way— that's all the footage I had to work with. Ordinarily, I would have shown the punch making contact with the punk's face, but I thought it would be more interesting the other way. Usually, though, I'll film more footage for insurance and then end up throwing it away.

So sometimes you have a clear image of what you want to shoot before you begin filming?
Yes, when I'm really clicking. Before I shoot the scene, I'll be watching the movie in my head. Then I can film one scene after another; but sometimes my mind goes blank. That's when I shoot a lot of footage on the set. That's when I have the most trouble editing—it takes a lot of time to get what I want.

Do you go through the same process of visualization when, say, you're making a TV program?
Not at all. When I go to a TV station, it's just to play. I never go there to work. I never read a script. Sometimes I don't even know what program I'm supposed to be on [*laughs*].Even if you prepare, TV programs have a way of going in a different direction and you have to be ready to go with it.

With movies, you have more of a line to follow. Once I was on a two-hour program where they gave us food and booze. I starting drinking and after about thirty minutes I passed out and slept through the rest of the show. The other guests were talking about me—"Oh, Takeshi's still sleeping" [*laughs*]. I didn't mean to pass out, but it made the show more interesting. That's just the way TV is, so what's the point of preparing?

Did you ever look around at all the young faces and wonder what you're doing here and how much longer you'll be around?
Yes, the turnover is high. TV talents are always being compared with each other—"Takeshi's getting a little stale." But now Takeshi is also a movie director. That's a kind of insurance. Now that I've become famous for my films, it's easier for me to do TV. I don't have to compete with the other guys out there. I'm coming from a different place. I think it's tough for older guys who only have television to fall back on to be appearing on shows with all these young guys.

You also have books—you've written more than sixty books now. In some of them you comment on serious issues. What social issue are you most interested in now?
After the war the system changed completely and we had the high-growth era. Now that postwar system has developed a lot of problems and, fifty years after the end of the war, with all those problems coming to the surface, we can finally say that the postwar period is over.

I was born right after the end of the war and was raised on American TV sitcoms— *Life with Father* and all those other shows. Watching them I thought that the middle-class lifestyle they portrayed—the house with the yard, the big refrigerator, the nice father, the happy family with everyone talking to everyone else—was typical. In Japan we've been trying to live up to that model for so long. But we're starting to realize that not many Americans really live that way, that we been chasing after a dream.

In the same way, we been trying to imitate the good parts of the American system— democracy and human rights. But now we've having all kind of problems with that system, in education and other areas. Kids hitting teachers, kids dropping out, parents killing their kids. And when we look at America we see the same thing. The jury system that produced the O.J. Simpson trial, the criminal law system that lets criminals out on the streets. The American culture of guns and drugs. The American conflict between blacks and whites.

But for fifty years after the end of the war, we've been following in America's footsteps and heading in the same direction. When we look at the Japan today and wonder why we have all these problems between parents and children, with drug use—well, we just have to look at America and see what kind of country it's become, where their form of democracy has taken them. Parents have become scared of their own kids. It used to be that adults would scold kids who were running around and making trouble on the train, but now no one does that. When I was a kid I used get scolded by adults all the time, but that doesn't happen anymore.

We've lost the ability to distinguish between rights and duties. Now the emphasis is totally on rights—no one talks about duties any more and we're going in a very strange direction as a result.

(*Winds*, July, 1998)

Jun
ICHIKAWA

Japan's leading director of TV commercials, with a slew of industry honors to his credit, Jun Ichikawa has, since his 1987 feature debut *B*U*S*U*, embarked on a parallel career as a maker of movies that recall, in their intimate scale, understated humanism, elegant compositions, and deliberate pace, the work of Yasujiro Ozu. A longtime admirer of the director of *Tokyo Monogatari* (Tokyo Story)and other masterpieces, Ichikawa underlined this comparison with *Tokyo Kyodai* (Tokyo Siblings), a 1995 film that was a conscious Ozu homage, right down to its simple but evocative title.

But while winning recognition for his work, including screenings at major international festivals, Ichikawa found himself tagged as *jimi* (plain, unremarkable), especially by a younger generation of Japanese filmgoers. While self-deprecatingly applying this label to himself, Ichikawa has long chafed under it—one doesn't become the king of the commercial in Japan by fading away into the woodwork. Now, however, he is breaking free of it. In the following interview he describes why and how.

You're known a big fan of Ozu, but have any films by other Japanese directors impressed you recently?
I like the films of Takeshi Kitano. In the past I liked the films of Somai Shinji—he was the director of *Typhoon Club*—but recently I've been really been impressed with Kitano's work.

He's got a highly individual style—he brings something to each cut that is totally his own.
He's very concise—he doesn't do a lot of explaining, so the audience has to use its imagination.

Even so, he doesn't deliberately make his films hard to understand.
He gives the audience various things to think about—I try to do that in my films as well. So we resemble each other a little in that way. TV dramas, for example, are all explanation—I really hate that. I don't like overacting, in which everything is spelled out for you. A natural performance, in which you can't tell if the actor is an amateur or a professional, is the best. I like a professional actor who has the feeling of the amateurish in his performance.

But in Tokyo Yakyoku (Tokyo Lullaby) you used two actors—Kaori Momoi and Kyozo Nagatsuka—who have strongly individual styles. Perhaps too strong [laughs]. Did you find that a problem?
Yes, I couldn't quite kill off their individuality [laughs]. I couldn't quite control it. I had the feeling that they were beating me with their individuality, even thought I was trying to contain it. I don't like a high noise level—low is better for me. I don't want the actors to get too excited [laughs].

A lot of Japanese movies, especially by younger directors, use such loud music on the soundtrack that it's hard to tell what the actors are saying.
I don't hate music—I used quite a lot of it in *Tsugumi*, but I don't like music that explains too much. Sad music for a sad scene, happy music for a happy scene—I don't care for that kind of thing.

But you could also say that you have developed a distinctive style yourself —rather quiet, restrained, indirect.
I've made twelve films and I don't want to keep making them the same way forever. So my latest film, *Osaka Monogatari* (Osaka Story), is very energetic. Before I was too shy to work that way, but this time I'm raising the volume a bit [laughs]. Japan is in a recession now, so I want to cheer people up. During the bubble economy days, I liked to make quiet films, but now that the bubble has burst, people have lost their energy, so it won't do if my films are low key as well. I want to make films that are more positive and energetic.

Perhaps you are also showing people that, even though you are in your fifties, you still have a lot of energy left [laughs].
There are a lot of films I still want to make. Fifty is not old at all. Ozu made *Tokyo Monogatari* when he was fifty. For a director, fifty is a peak. Another example is Kenji Mizoguchi's *Ugetsu Monogatari*—he made that when he was about fifty. It depends on the director, but many of them do their best work when they are about fifty. The same is also true of foreign directors.

So for the next two or three years I want to do my best with the know-how I have. I want to make one film with Ryoko Hirosue—a popular idol. I also want to make one more film with Momoi Kaori. I have plans for a lot of films. After I finish *Osaka Monogatari* I will make a few commercials, and then make another film.

So your next film will be with Hirosue?
I shot a commercial with her for Sakura Bank, and from that connection I got an opportunity to make a film with her. A lot of the actors I use in my films are acquaintances I made doing commercials. One is Kyozo Nagatsuka, whom I first met shooting a commercial. Momoi Kaori is another one. Not only actors, but a lot of the people involved in my films I first met through my commercial work.

Are there any actors out there that you haven't worked with yet, but would like to?
One is Kimutaku—Takuya Kimura [of the pop group SMAP].

Has he appeared in films before?
Yes he has, but not a very good one.

It was that soccer movie for Shochiku—something called Shoot.

Yes, it wasn't very good—but he reminds me of Yujiro Ishihara . I haven't made a film with a male star before, so I'd like to try it. Another one is Takeshi Kaneshiro. I would like to use him in a macho-ish youth movie, with a different, more energetic approach than in my previous films.

So there are various kinds of films that I want to do—not just the same thing again and again. I would like to wait until I get a bit older before I become like Ozu and make the same kind of film every time [*laughs*]. When Ozu was young, he made films in various genres. I'm not young any more, but even so, I'd like to do something different. I can make quiet films anytime I like, but now I want to shoot a number of more powerful movies. After releasing *Tokyo Yakyoku* I made a film called *Tadon to Chikuwa* that will be released this fall. It stars Koji Yakusho and Hiroyuki Sanada. You might be surprised when you see it, but it's really violent—it's the first time I've ever made that kind of violent film.

I've been thinking about groups like the Aum Shinrikyo [a religious cult whose members gassed commuters in the Tokyo subways in 1995] and how Japanese are becoming stranger. That led me to make this movie, which is quite different from anything I've done before. It's so grotesque that it might shock you, but at the end the two main characters become energized, so it's not a depressing movie.

So you might say that it's more imaginative than some of your other films?

Not imaginative so much as philosophical. Or surrealistic—blood spurts out, but it's green and blue. It's fantastic violence.

Like I said, that's coming out this fall—a bit too late, I think. Now I'm doing another film called *Osaka Monogatari*, set in Osaka. The heroine is a girl I discovered while filming in one of my TV commercials. She's from Osaka herself and is only fifteen. The story is about entertainers in Osaka. You know Yoshimoto [the talent agency that specialies in *manzai* comedy]? It's about a pair of *manzai* comedians, but they're poor, not popular. They're the parents of the girl. So it's a story of a poor family in Osaka. I wanted to do a more violent film, but instead I ended up making another one of my favorites—a family drama [*laughs*].

Are there are plans to screen both films abroad?

Yes, the producer is working on it. My film's aren't exactly big hits in Japan [*laughs*] so it would be nice if foreign audiences liked them. I'd like to make a film that becomes a hit abroad. Maybe *Osaka Monogatari* will be the one.

Did winning the Best Director's prize at Montreal for Tokyo Yakyoku *give you the confidence that you can be accepted by foreign audiences?*

Yes, it's a festival with a long history, but still I would feel better if I could win something at Cannes, Venice, or Berlin.

Also it would be good to have more foreign distributors who supported Japanese films. It seems that all the attention is being focused on Takeshi Kitano, but it would be better if other Japanese directors could also get their film shown abroad. I'd also like to see more Japanese producers become active abroad. Now just about the only ones are Kazuyoshi Okuyama and Kaz Kuzui. It would be better if there were a lot more.

Right now the only thing I can do is make the best films I can. If I think too much about having hits or winning prizes, I can't concentrate on making the best possible films. I like films by directors like Ken Loach, Mike Leigh, and Eric Rohmer, that take place in a rich but circumscribed world. They may unfold within a small place, but they are saying some big things. The films of Ozu Yasujiro were also like that—they were small in scale, but they made audiences think of larger philosophical issues. On the other hand, you have some very large-scale movies that say very little.

On the whole, I think I like European films the best, especially those by British or French directors. My favorite, though, is probably Truffaut's *Les Quatre Cents Coups* (Four Hundred Blows). It's an old film, but no matter how many times I see it, I never get tired of it. Ozu is another favorite. Today kids may have TV games and the world around may seem to be different, but really nothing has changed. The feelings between parents and children, between brothers and sister, between husbands and wives are still the same. The essence of human beings remains the same. That's why Ozu's films never become dated.

The young people in Shibuya may look different, but young people have always disdained the ways of the generation before them and looked for something new. When you look around Japan, however, you still find a lot of Ozuesque families and people. Even walking around Tokyo, you can still find quiet traditional houses, shrines, and temples. When you look up from those quiet old places you may see high-rise buildings, but at least they still exist. One place like that is Ikebukuro, where you have a mix of modern technology and old neighborhoods.

That is the kind of place I filmed in *Tokyo Kyodai*. The father and mother of the family and the brother and sister are still living together in imitation of their parents, almost like a married couple, in an old house. I think a brother and sister like that must exist somewhere in Tokyo. *Tokyo Yakyoku* is the same way—I have the feeling that these people really exist. There may be fewer of them than there were before, but they are still around. I don't want to ignore or forget them.

It is sad that to think that Japanese have changed and that old-fashioned types of people have all disappeared. I'm always searching for old types of places and people and when I find them, it makes me happy. When you watch television or read the newspapers you know that something strange has happened to the Japanese, but I don't think people have to pay money to see that kind of thing in a theater.

In *Tadon and Chikuwa* I may be saying that Japanese people have become strange, but in *Osaka Monogatari* I'm again saying that we shouldn't give up on them—they still have good qualities.

I suppose that's same message as the Tora-san series, which also seems to be set in an older Japan, but you give it a different spin.
Just like the Tora-san series, not much seems to be going on in the foreground of my characters' lives, but in the background they are changing. For example, the younger sister in *Tokyo Kyodai* leaves home. On the surface she seems to be an old-fashioned Japanese girl, but really she very much a modern *gyaru* ["gal"—Janglish slang for liberated young women]—there is something different about her. Her neighborhood may have the same look and atmosphere as the Tora-san films, but there are different things going on in the background.

I like the Tora-san films, especially the early ones—the first ten or so. In the beginning of the series, Tora-san might really have existed. That was in the Showa thirties and forties (1955 to 1975), when types like him were still around, but now they don't exist anymore.

Also, the sentimentalism of the Tora-san series is absent in your films. In Tokiwaso no Seishun *(Tokiwa: The Manga Apartment), for example, there is a feeling of loneliness that you would never find in a Tora-san film.*
That film is about how a group of friends go their separate ways. Friends can't always stay together—a time for saying goodbye must come. You might call it a youth movie *(seishun eiga)*, but it also a film about growing up, and I feel that growing up is a lonely thing to do. Growing up is a good thing, but the more adult people become, the lonelier they get. Growing up means saying goodbye, it means losing something.

Mono no aware [*the pathos that comes from an awareness of the passage of time*] *is often decribed as distinctly Japanese, but I think that in some ways it is a universal emotion.*
That feeling is in Ozu's films—and I think that its something everyone from every country can understand. A good film can be understood everywhere. The look of his films may be very Japanese and he may be telling stories about Japanese families, but family and siblings are universal—they don't vary much from country to country. His films may be called very Japanese, but when people from other countries see them, they have no trouble understanding them. I like the films of Ozu, but I also like the relationship of the couple in Takeshi Kitano's *Hana-Bi*.

Some viewers overseas, though, found that couple a bit strange because they hardly ever spoke with each other [laughs]. *In your films, as in Ozu's, the theme of the family is very important, but whereas Ozu usually depicted ordinary middle-class families, in your films they rarely make an appearance.*
That's true now that you mention it. I guess I'll have to make that kind of film then [*laughs*]. Various kinds of families appeared in *Byoin de Shinu to Iu Koto* (Dying at a Hospital). There were even the homeless. It contained all the different family patterns you find in Japan. So perhaps the closest I've come to an Ozu movie is *Byoin de Shinu to Iu Koto*. When I was making that film, that's when I thinking the most about Ozu.

There was also *Tokyo Kyodai*, which was an Ozu homage, but in that film I was more concerned with getting Ozu into the camera angles and scenery. *Byoin* was closer in spirit to an Ozu film.

In some ways, though, that was your most experimental film, in the way you introduced montage into the narrative and the way you kept the camera at the foot of the patients' beds, never moving in for a closeup.
I didn't want to do the closeups of doctor's faces or suffering patients that you usually find in hospital films. Instead I wanted images that would be similar to a picture painted from a middle distance.

Death is an equalizer. It comes to everyone, whether they are rich or poor. All the six patients in that six-bed ward in *Byoin* were main characters. I didn't want to focus on one at the expense of the others. I wanted to view them all equally. That's why I kept the camera in one place. The camera itself has no emotion—it is simply a neutral observer. I didn't want any camera moves because I wanted to maintain that neutrality.

The camera didn't move in the hospital scenes, but in the montage scenes it was highly expressive.
The montage scenes were a kind of documentary showing the joy of life. They were like an album of photographs that tells a family history as you thumb through them. I wanted to convey both the joy of life and the reality of death in that film.

There was also a montage of black-and-white photographs in Tokiwaso no Seishun.
Taking those kind of photographs is my hobby. I feel a deep nostalgia for the Japan of my childhood, the Showa thirties (1955–65). *Tokiwaso* was set in the Tokyo of my childhood.

Also, I often use montage sequences in my commercials. I like to edit, and the editing techniques I use in commercial films end up in my films. But in my films I can do things I can't do in my commercials. For example, I could never show the hospital scenes in *Byoin* in a commercial. I used montages in commercials I did for an insurance company and for NTT. I did a lot of cutting for those.

I suppose this a question you always get , but I have to ask it. How does your film work relate to your commercial work?
Films are a poor medium, commercials, a rich one. Takeshi works as a TV talent and I make TV commercials [so that we can make films]. Even if a film doesn't make any money, I don't feel so bad about it.

Another difference is that commercials are short—only fifteen or thirty seconds long. When I do nothing but commercials for any length of time, I start to feel that I want to do something longer. When I make a film I can stretch out more, and I feel refreshed.

(Excerpts from this interview appeared in *Japan Times*, December 8, 1998.)

Takenori SENTO

Born in 1961 in Yokohama, Takenori Sento began making 8mm movies while a fresh-man in high school. After joining Wowow (Japan Satellite Broadcasting, Japan's first commercial satellite broadcaster) in 1990, he became a film programmer, and in 1992 a producer of Wowow-financed films under the J Movie Wars label. In 1993 Yoichi Sai's *Tsuki wa Dotchi ni Deteiru* (All Under the Moon), a black comedy that originat-ed as a J Movie Wars short produced by Sento, swept domestic film awards. Among other Sento-produced award-winners are Tomoyuki Furumaya's *Kono Mado wa Kimi no Mono* (This Window is Yours; Dragon & Tiger Young Cinema Award, 1994 Vancouver Film Festival), Go Riju's *Elephant Song* (NETPAC Award, 1995 Berlin Film Festival, Golden Gate Award), Nobuhiro Suwa's *2/Duo* (NETPAC Award, 1997 Rotterdam Film Festival) and Naomi Sento's *Moe no Suzaku* (Suzaku; Camera d'Or, 1997 Cannes Film Festival). In December 1998, with the backing of Wowow, Sento launched Suncent CinemaWorks to develop, produce, and manage rights for low-bud-get feature films.

This interview took place at the Suncent CinemaWorks headquarters near Toetsu Station on Tokyo's Asakusa Line. Though still not completely furnished, with its wooden flooring, open spaces, floor-to-ceiling windows, and clear partitions, it looked less like a typical Japanese office than an exceptionally sunny atelier. And with his styl-ishly casual clothes and shoulder-length hair, Sento looked less like a typical Japanese movie producer (who is hard to distinguish from a typical salaryman) than an artist, or perhaps a closer comparison, gallery owner. In conversation, however, he was the opposite of the otherworldly creator. Expressing strong opinions born of hard-won experience, possessed of boundless energy and ambition, he was the producer as get-it-done dynamo.

Why did you choose the name Suncent CinemaWorks Inc. for your new company?
There's a book by Roger Corman titled *How I Made 100 Movies and Never Lost a Cent* I liked that book—it gave me the idea of producing a lot of movies with low budgets. I also learned from Anatole Gorman, a French producer who made a lot of films with Godard. Both taught me a lot.

Corman, of course, is also known as the father of modern American cinema—many of his writers and directors later went on to illustrious careers.

Yes, people like Scorcese and Lucas learned from him.

Do you have the same kind of ambition? You've already introduced a number of directors to the world at large, including your wife [Naomi Sento, director of Moe no Suzaku].

Yes, I had that ambition from the beginning. From the moment I started J Movie Wars, that was my goal—to introduce my films to the world.

As you probably know, a lot of Japanese filmmakers say that their first target is the domestic market, that when they're making a film they're not thinking of the foreign market at all.

Yes, I know—I'm the exact opposite. I think of both as being the same. I think you're going to do better business if you think of the entire world as your market. It's better to have your movie play in a big theater in Paris than a small theater in the Japanese countryside.

There is a certain ratio between the box office in Tokyo and the box office in the provinces—usually it's two to one. In other words, the box office from the provinces will account for one-third of the total. So it's much better to have your film playing in several cities around the world the size of Tokyo, than in Tokyo and the provinces alone.

Think of it this way. It costs about the same to send a print to a one-hundred-seat theater in Fukuoka and to a three-hundred-seat theater in Paris. So it's more efficient, everything else being equal, to have the film play in Paris. There is more potential for the film if audiences from outside Japan watch it.

Of course, when you send a print abroad, you also have other costs, such as subtitling and making foreign-language promotional materials.

So you factor those costs into the production of the film from the very beginning. You don't start thinking about doing it after you've made the film.

Also, in the Japanese film industry, there's this feeling that to appeal to foreign audiences, you have to make a big-budget period film. One example is Kadokawa Haruki's Ten to Chi to.

That's an illusion. Japanese feel that to compete with Hollywood they have to make Hollywood-style movies, with big budgets. I'm completely the opposite—I feel there's no need to do that. We can incorporate traditional Japanese aesthetics into our films without spending a lot of money. Or we can do something entirely different, something that is uniquely ours. That's true of anything—if you are just trying to follow someone else, you'll never beat him, but if you go your own way and develop your own style, you'll do better.

The Japanese film industry tends to divide films into two categories: Japanese films and foreign films. I think of them as all being films. I never think that I'm making a "Japanese film." I grew up watching Hollywood and European films, so that influence is stronger. I didn't grow up watching Japanese films. But it just so happens that it's easier for me to make films in Japan. I'm not trying to imitate Hollywood or Europe. At the same time, I don't feel that I'm making "Japanese movies."

Recently there been a tendency for new directors to come from the worlds of advertising or television or music videos. The films they make are influenced by those backgrounds, such as Hiroyuki Nakano's Samurai Fiction, *which is like a two-hour music video.*

I understand what they were trying to do, but I don't think that *Samurai Fiction* is a real movie. I think that if I'm going to make a period film—and that's what I plan to do— I have to compete with traditional period films head-to-head, but at the same time I have to make it with the feeling of my generation.

I want to compete with Akira Kurosawa. If I don't think I can do that, then I'd better give up from the beginning. With *Samurai Fiction*, the filmmakers didn't think they could equal what Kurosawa had done, so they decided to try something else. I'm different— I want to go head-to-head with Kurosawa.

But Kurosawa wasn't working in a vacuum—he had the support of a studio and a staff. He needed that kind of organizational support to make his period films.

In other words, he had the right environment. In the course of making nearly thirty films that's what I've been trying to create. Of course, I've been trying to make each film as good as possible, but at the same time I've been trying to create the proper working environment. That' s my job as a producer.

Even if you produce a masterpiece, you aren't necessarily going to change the environment for the better. You can only do that by making one movie after another. That's why I think quantity is important. By making a lot of films you develop the knowhow that in turn enables you to make better films.

It sounds as though you want to return to the days of "program pictures."

That's what we have to do. Last year the Japanese film industry made 127 films. In the days when Kurosawa was at his peak, it was making 500 annually. We have to create the same conditions [that made Kurosawa's movies possible]. To produce a Kurosawa, you have be making that many films. There's a Japanese saying that "quantity gives birth to quality" (*ryo ga shitsu o umu*). I believe that, and that's why I want to make so many films.

*Of course, back then they were making a lot of genre films—*yakuza *movies and samurai movies and so on.*

Yes, it would be hard to do that now—to make a lot of movies on genre themes. Genre movies are relatively easy to turn into hits—like action movies in America. If I were to make a film to be released in 150 theaters in Japan, I would make a genre movie. A horror movie—that would probably do well here. But Japanese exhibitors are opposed to the idea—they don't think it would work.

I still think that if you're going to make a genre movie now, it shouldn't be a *yakuza* movie but a modern horror movie. They've been making (modern horror movies) in Italy and elsewhere for the past decade or so—Dario Argento's *Susperia* and so on. Japan is the only place where they haven't been making them.

There have been the horror films of Kurosawa Kiyoshi [Sweet Home, Door III, Cure].

Yes, but they haven't been well produced. There were producers for his films, of course, but they didn't fulfill what I consider to be the role of producer—developing a project and putting it on the screen.

Producer is a rather vague job description, isn't it? There are producers who are nothing more than the director's brother-in-law or the man who puts up the money. But you are obviously not one of those—you believe in doing everything.

I'm on the set, I'm in the editing room—I'm there for the whole process. I'm just not sitting around mouthing off. Now it's become a lot more difficult because I'm so busy, but I'm still there from beginning to end, from the planning stages to negotiating with the theaters. I do it all.

There are a lot of producers like me in America, but not in Japan. I don't want people to think that I'm just there to hand over the money. I'm not a sponsor or patron. In America you have the investor, who provides the money, and the producer, who makes the film. There's a clear distinction between the two. In Japan the producer is not generally considered to be one of the makers of the film. But I definitely am.

Another difference between the Japanese and American ways of making films is the amount of time and effort devoted to the script. Americans place a strong priority on this stage, while the Japanese are more inclined to scimp on it.

That's a big difference. That's where I put in a lot of time. You either make or break a film in the script stage. You have to spend whatever time it takes to do it right.

I'll spend about a year on the script for any film I make, revising it again and again with the scriptwriter and director. I don't just pay for an already completed script. That's the way it often works in Japan, though.

I'm there with my own plan. I want to make horror films because I like them. I have my own ideas about how to make them. I believe that a producer should be someone who does everything, from the script on.

In Japan there's a tendency to develop films properties from other media—from a manga or a book or a television program. There aren't many projects that are trying to break new ground.

They want to do it the easy way, they don't want to use this [points to his head]. The way I go about it is different. One example is *Moe no Suzaku*. From the very first we wanted to go abroad with it. We wanted to make a film that foreign audiences would like. We thought over various ideas, but decided that, rather than make a film specifically for foreign audiences, we would first try to thoroughly investigate what it means to be Japanese.

We also tried to think of a theme that would be universal. We considered various possibilities—urbanization, cultural change—but we finally decided on the family. One thing that people all over the world all have in common is the family. So we thought that if we made a film about the Japanese family, we could take it abroad. Audiences in both Japan and foreign countries could relate to it.

That kind of search for human communality is the true meaning of internationalization. Instead of looking for something completely new—say the problems related to computerization—I think it's better to investigate something nearer to home. The starting point is what we are as Japanese—the way we think of ourselves.

Your approach to marketing is somewhat different from the way its usually done here. First you take your films to foreign festivals and win prizes. Then you try to sell them abroad.

Most Japanese producers think of the domestic market first. They go to a foreign film festival because they hope it will help their domestic business. They think, "If (my film) wins a prize here, it will be a hit in Japan." I'm different—I feel that getting exposure at a foreign festival has value in itself. I'm thinking of both the foreign and the Japanese market.

There is also the way of New Cinema from Japan, the cooperative of independent film-makers. They have taken stands at the MIP and Berlin film markets to sell their films to foreign buyers. What do you think of their approach?
I'm not a big fan of groups and organizations. Especially anything to do with the government. I feel that it's important to succeed on your own. One reason Hollywood films have been so successful is that they have received no support from the government. If anything, the U.S. government has been the opposite of supportive. For example, after the war the government forced the studios to get rid of their exhibition chains. So the studios had to struggle hard to survive.

By contrast, French films have been getting worse and worse recently. What's the reason? Support from the government has been growing and growing. They are essentially making "national policy" (*kokusaku*) films with government support. A government bureaucrat has to first give his OK, right? So the films end up reflecting his tastes.

In Japan there are those who say that we could make more films with government support, but if that happened we would end up making films not to attract audiences, but to get a government stamp of approval.

The Ministry of Cultural Affairs is already providing some support, but the films that have received their grants are in some ways all alike.
Right, they're all the same. When you receive support from that kind of bureaucracy, there are only certain kinds of films you can make. Instead of relying on the government, I believe that the private sector has to link hands and work together. When you look at the Japanese companies that are succeeding today—the car companies and so on—they are doing it on their own, in the private sector. If Japanese filmmakers were to rely on support from the government, they would never be able to develop a film industry. I personally have no interest in that kind of thing. I can raise money on my own—I have no need of government support.

One advantage the Hollywood films have is that they're made in English—they can find a larger audience overseas simply because of that. On the other hand, Japanese films have to first be dubbed or subtitled before they can be shown abroad. Also, you often hear people talk about a culture gap that makes it difficult for Japanese films to travel abroad.
I don't believe any of that. If a film seems interesting I'll watch it, even if it's subtitled. While it's true that English-language movies have a large market, it can also work the other way around. In other words, if a foreign film is interesting, people will watch it, even if it's subtitled. Bruce Willis movies are subtitled here, but people still come to see them because they find them interesting. It not that people abroad don't want to understand [Japanese] films—the filmmakers aren't trying hard enough to make them understand.

That's certainly true—the proof that you can make them understand is Shall We Dance?, *which became a big hit in the United States. But the market share of foreign*

films in the United States is still less than two percent. There are still significant barriers to the import of foreign films.
Yes, it's less than two percent, but you have the opportunity to win over the other ninety-eight percent. In other words, you can expand your market. The business potential is larger there than in Japan. I'm not satisfied with appealing to the two percent who watch foreign films.

You also have Japanese producers, such as Amuse, who are aiming first at the Asian market, rather than the West.
That's so, but I don't make such distinctions among regions or countries. I'm not thinking in terms of Asia or North America or Europe. What they can do in Asia they can also do in Japan, but they're not doing it here, are they? If you can't make a go of it in your own country, why do you think you can do any better abroad? It doesn't make sense. That's why I produced *Ring* and *Rasen* (The Spiral)—to show what you could do right here in Japan.

What do you think of coproductions with foreign partners, such as Amuse's tie-up with Golden Harvest?
I have worked with international partners on a individual basis. For example, I've brought a Hong Kong cameraman here and I've gone to New York to work with independent filmmakers. Also, next year [in 1999] a French cameraman will work on one of my films. But I don't like partnerships between companies. I'll work together with foreign partners to make a film, but I don't need foreign investment.

It's dangerous to start with a financial partnership. It all right to think "We want to make this movie so we need this much money," but often people will do it the other way—get money together and then decide to make a movie. That's a recipe for failure. It's not enough just have the money, you also need the know-how for making films. I have both—I can't claim to have a lot of money—but I have both. There are producers who can talk about what makes a movie work artistically, but they can't raise money. There are also those who can talk about money, but have no idea how to make a film. But I can do both.

I know that you've made more than thirty films, but what I don't see in them is what might be called a "Sento style." You seem to respect the individual styles of your directors.
A producer shouldn't have his own style. He should be able to do anything—that flexibility is what makes the job interesting. I can't direct, but on the other hand, there aren't any directors who can make horror and action and entertainment films. Godard has his style and John Ford has his, but neither could direct the other's films. A producer, however, can make various kinds of films.

It's one thing to respect a director's style, but directors can also be self-indulgent, can't they?
I know—and I won't tolerate it. I've never lost money on a film. I've also never gone over budget. I think that's very important. In the Japanese film business going ten percent over budget is common practice. I won't go even one percent over budget. I understand what the director is trying to do—so I'm less likely to make mistakes about the budget.

Also, I'm from the computer generation—look at all the computers in this office. There's aren't any other film companies in Japan like this one. No one in the other companies thinks they need computers to do their jobs. But computers are required to manage budgets and do other jobs well. That's the American approach. When I went to New York to make a film [*Artful Dodgers*], everyone on my New York staff had computers as a matter of course. So I had to use one too to keep up with them.

Now that you mention it, when I go to the offices of Toei, Shochiku, Toho and other movie companies here, I never see computers.
No, you don't. I make sure that everyone on my staff has one. I also take them on location. That has become standard practice at other Japanese companies. Look at Honda or Toyota—all their employees have computers. That's what I'm doing as well.

To change the subject a bit, look at the way people in the film industry here dress—they have no fashion sense.

You're right—A lot of them of them look like salarymen [laughs].
They have no idea how to dress. They're behind the times.

They talk about remaking films that were popular thirty years ago.
Every year they're releasing films that you don't know what year they were made in.

When I went the press conference announcing the launch of Suncent CinemaWorks, I was surprised to hear you say you wanted to recruit people from outside the industry. But now I understand that you want to bring in a fresh approach.
I don't want the way of thinking that's been prevalent in this industry till now. Movies are a product—people pay money to see them. So you have to make them so that people will want to buy them. That's just common sense in the business world. You're making films for the audience, not for the director or the investors. The investors are important, but the larger the audience the better it is for them. Why should you make the film to their specifications? They aren't thinking about what will make the film interesting to the audience—which is the important thing. You need people who have a sense for what the audience wants.

I feel that I'm one of those people. I'm not originally from the film industry—I used to work for a steel manufacturer. I still have the feeling for films that I had when I was working for a steel manufacturer and watching them for my own enjoyment. You have to be able to stand in the audience's shoes.

The Japanese film industry tends to target demographic extremes—they either go for kids or old people, ignoring everyone in between.
I go for that middle, though movies aren't necessarily for any particular age. Take the movies of John Ford—you don't have to be of any particular age to enjoy them. I don't think there is such a thing as a movie for women in their twenties. That may be the audience that comes to see the film, but when you're planning it, you don't have to think of it as being for a particular age group.

But directors get labeled as making films for a particular group. Shunji Iwai, for example—he's been knocked for making films for fans of shojo manga [girls comics]. Of course, he probably doesn't think so himself.
No, he doesn't, But that happens to be his style—it's the job of a producer to know that.

I have to know that he has a *shojo manga* sensibility. I compare myself to a doctor, a director to the patient. I have to be able to diagnose the director's strengths and weaknesses. I have to have the confidence that I can do that.

Do you feel any obligation to work with younger directors? Most of the directors you want to work in Suncent seem to be of your generation.
But I also plan to work with Yoichi Sai, who's nearly fifty. I don't care about age. I'd be willing to work directors in their teens. They would be the best ones to understand how to make certain films. I want to work in various genres with various kinds of directors. Not only artistic films but entertainment films as well.

Are you only going to make low-budget films, or some with larger budgets, too?
The period drama I plan to make with Toho in 1999 will have a big budget. I can't tell you the budget. It will cost a lot of money because we have to build a town. It's based on an old neighborhood in the center of Kyoto. We can't film there, so we have to build the town.

Period dramas haven't done well at the box office recently. Sharaku, Shijushichinin no Shikaku *(Forty-Seven Ronin),* Chushingura Gaiden Yotsuya Kaidan *(Crest of Betrayal)—none of them made any money.*
They were half-assed movies.

There was also Samurai Fiction, *which did well at the box office, but it wasn't really a movie.*
It was a moving *manga*. I'm going to make a real movie. But I'm not going to make a "period drama." I'm going to make an action movie—a Japanese action movie. That means it has to be set in the past—that's the most realistic way to do it. Not pistols, but swords. Pistols don't have any reality for us. If Japanese are going to make action movies, they have to go back to past.

Recently directors like Takeshi Kitano and Tadashi Ishii have been taking the gang movie genre in new directions. Don't you have any interest in making gang movies?
No, none. I don't know anything about gangs. They don't have any reality for me. When *Reservoir Dogs* came out, everyone here was saying we have to make something like that. I didn't think so. No one in Japan is walking around with a pistol. When you see that in Japanese movies it's all a fake. That's why Ishii's films don't become hits, even though they're well made. When *yakuza* movies were at their peak, there really were *yakuza* running around, so the films had a certain realism, but now they've all disappeared.

Then you have movies like Fuyajo *(Sleepless Town) in which the gangsters are foreigners.*
Yes, Chinese gangsters. But to me the Shinjuku portrayed in that film is not the real thing. The Chinese and Koreans in that film may have been realistic enough, but not Shinjuku.

It did well at the box office, though.
But the P & A costs were higher than the production budget. I think that kind of marketing, with posters everywhere, is overdoing it. If you're going to appeal directly to

consumers, to tell them that there's this kind of film, aggressive marketing may be necessary, though. You're not going to reach them with just an ad in the newspaper.

What about the practice of printing large numbers of advance tickets to sell a film?
I don't like it. You have to get people into the theaters. There are a lot of movies out there that may sell a lot of tickets, but don't get people into the theaters. That's no good. Also, you have all the discount shops selling cheap tickets—that's no good either. Your first aim should be to make people want to pay money to see your movie.

One point I want to clarify. Wowow has fully financed your company, but you're the only one with greenlight authority, aren't you?
That's right. That was the condition I made when I started the company. Wowow is only an investor—they have a say in the management, but they have no say in how the movies are made. That's important.

That was also the case with J Movie Wars, wasn't it?
Yes, but because I was making the movies under the Wowow label, I had to listen to them. When I was making *Moe no Suzaku* people in Wowow were saying "What kind of movie is this?"

It must have been tough, especially in the beginning.
It was—I was constantly getting flack. I never heard a word of praise for what I was doing. But when we won the prize at Cannes, they had to think again.

I remember going to Wowow to do a story several years ago and mentioning J Movie Wars. The reaction was "Oh, that." I had the feeling that they ranked J Movie Wars way down here [lowers hand] *and Hollywood movies way up here* [raises hand].
That's the way it was the whole time I was there. They thought it was cheaper to buy films than to make them. But that way you end up with nothing

If you were to buy a film that took the Camera d'Or prize at Cannes, you would only have the rights for one year. Also, the price would be high. But with *Moe no Suzaku*, you have the rights forever. They have finally figured that out. They aren't very bright [*laughs*].

(December 17, 1998)

Hirokazu KOREEDA

I interviewed Hirokazu Koreeda shortly after his return from the 1999 Sundance and Rotterdam film festivals, where he had screened his latest film, *Wonderful Life* (After Life). We met at TV Man Union, where he has worked since 1987, mainly as a documentarian, and which produced his first feature film, *Maboroshi no Hikari* (Maborosi, 1995). Relaxed and confident, he was more eager to talk about the film's international prospects, which looked bright, than its themes, which he had explained again and again to the media and fans since the world premiere of *Wonderful Life* at the 1998 Toronto Film Festival. Nonetheless, he was patient with even my more obvious questions, answering with the sameattentiveness, precision, and intelligence so evident in his work.

What was the reaction to Wonderful Life *at Rotterdam and Sundance?*
Quite good—all of the screenings were sold out. Also, we've been able to arrange for general release in both Europe and America. Representatives from the distributors came to the film festivals and did PR for the film, which helped a lot. I was also glad that the audiences were laughing from beginning to end.

I'm a bit surprised to hear that the reaction was so good at Sundance—usually the only films that get any attention there are American.
Before I went I was told not to be too disappointed if no one came—screenings in the World Cinema section are usually not well attended because the focus is so much on American independent cinema. But when I went, I found that people did show up, which was a relief.

I would imagine that the reaction would have been different according to the country— that audiences in Japan would have been different from audiences in the United States.
We had the world premiere in Toronto. My biggest impression was that the Americans and Canadians in the audience really enjoyed the film. People starting laughing when they realized that [the characters in the film] had died and the laughter kept building for the first ten or fifteen minutes. Audiences in Spain were also that way, as were those in Paris and Korea. Audiences in Japan were the quietest. But when I went to a preview screening recently, people were laughing—that was a relief.

No doubt you're already thinking about your next project.
I wrote the script for *Wonderful Life* about ten years ago. There's another project that I've been thinking of doing for the past seven or eight years. It's based on a real incident that occurred in Tokyo about eight years ago. The story I've written differs somewhat from the incident, but the main outlines are the same.

There is a mother and four children living together in an apartment. All the children have different fathers and none of them have even been to school. The mother goes off with a new lover and dies, and the children are left in the apartment alone. The older brother looks after his younger sister for six months. There is no record that they are living there and none of the neighbors notice that they are there alone.

The film shows Tokyo from a child's point of view. I want to describe the Tokyo that could ignore the existence of those four children for six months. I may not use any professional actors in the children's roles. Instead, I audition amateurs—children who are not members of any theater group. I plan to spend about a year [casting the film].

Will this new film be part of the project that producer Takenori Sento is going to start this April with five younger Japanese directors—you being one of them?
Yes it will. It will be the first time for us to work together. I don't know exactly what kind of cooperative relationship we'll have, but he seems like an interesting guy, so I'm looking forward to working with him. We've been talking about doing this project for two years now.

Do you have the feeling that there's more awareness abroad of new filmmakers coming out of Japan—that there is, for lack a of better term, a Japanese New Wave?
Yes, I feel that there's a growing interest. At Toronto last year there was a section titled New Cinema from Japan. Also, we've been able to release this new film fairly widely abroad. But when it comes to moving beyond film festivals to general release, there is still a way to go. In Europe, for example, there are still barriers to a wider release [of Japanese films]. We have to try harder if we want our films to reach average filmgoers.

But the current New Wave is quite different from the one a generation ago. Directors seem to be focusing more on personal issues, less on themes like Japanese politics or history.
Yes, there does seem to be that tendency. There haven't been many since Oshima who have dealt with those themes, myself included.

Also, when you look at the career of a director like Kurosawa, there was tremendous variety in his work—he did entertainment films, serious films, and everything in between. Do you have that same desire to make a variety of films?
Very much so. I've only made two so far and I want to try making a wide variety of films. I want to make action films, period films.

Did you ever think about shooting a film in America?
Well, I have a problem with the language. But at Sundance there was a lot of talk about remaking *Wonderful Life*. I have an agent who's pursuing these discussions so we can decide how to move forward. In America there is a large pool of good actors, far larger than you would find in Japan. I would like to use them in a remake. Also, I would like to be involved in the writing of the script.

How did you get the idea for Wonderful Life?

I'd been planning to do the film for about ten years, but for various reason I couldn't. Then everything fell into place and I was able to go ahead.

Initially, I was thinking of doing it as a TV documentary. Using a video camera, my staff and I went around interviewing various people. We asked them what memory they would take with them to heaven when they died, if they could choose only one. But we got so much good material that I thought it would difficult to cut it down to a one-hour documentary. I finally decided to make it as a film, adding the stories of the three main characters. I never thought of it as a religious film. Instead, I wanted the focus to be on the importance of memory in our lives.

Wonderful Life emerged from a documentary called *Without Memory* that I made in 1994. It was about a man who had lost the ability to make new memories. It made me realize how vital memories are. Without memories, we have no identity.

I think it would be relatively easy to do a remake of Wonderful Life—*it doesn't have a viewpoint that belongs to Buddhism or any other specific religion.*

I tried to keep religion out of it as much as possible.

It has other elements, such as comedy and the love story, that could appeal to an American audience.

Yes, many of the people who want to do a remake talked about expanding the comedy and love-story elements.

I also had the impression that it could appeal to a wide age group, that older people as well as younger ones could enjoy it.

At the foreign festivals we screened it at, a lot of people in their fifties to seventies came. That's also been true of screenings in Japan—a lot of older people have come.

It also has the love story, which appeals to younger people. So there are various ways for audiences of all ages to enjoy the movie.

Another thing that struck me was the way the film stayed with me, days and weeks afterwards. I don't see many films that have that effect—often I start forgetting about them as soon as I walk out of the theater.

We had a screening of the film at TV Man Union, and the next day when I came in I found that people were still talking about it, everyone from management types in their fifties and sixties to the girls at the reception desk. They told me how much they enjoyed it and how much they had discussed it—it really made me happy.

Given all the work you put into it, including the hundreds of interviews you filmed, have you ever thought of making a sequel?

I think it would be interesting to make a Part II. When we filmed *Wonderful Life* we went out on the streets and did about five hundred video interviews with ordinary people. So we have a lot of material we could use. But maybe this time, instead of heaven, we could make a film about people who end up in hell [*laughs*].

(*Premier*, May 1999)

Takeshi Kitano (right) directed and starred in **Sonatine** (1993) as a yakuza fighting a gang war and flirting with death.

Kyozo Nagatsuka and Kaori Momoi rekindle an old flame in Jun Ichikawa's **Tokyo Yakyoku** (Tokyo Lullaby, 1997).

Dating older men for fun and profit in Masato Harada's **Bounce Ko Gals** (Bounce, 1997): Hitomi Sato, Yasue Sato, and Yukiko Okamoto.

Masahiro Motoki and Koichi Sato as losers sailing defiantly over the edge in Tadashi Ishii's **Gonin** (1995).

As the irrepressible Tora-san, Atsumi Kiyoshi saved a studio and warmed the hearts of millions. **Otoko wa Tsurai yo: Torajiro no Seishun** (Tora-san Makes Excuses, 1992) was one of the last in this long-running series directed by Yoji Yamada. (Clockwise from top) Hidetaka Yoshioka, Kimiko Goto, Jun Fubuki, Kiyoshi Atsumi.

Nobuko Miyamoto as a housewife who saves a failing supermarket—and spars with its ineffective owner (Masahiko Tsugawa) in **Super no Onna** (Supermarket Woman, 1996).

Naoto Takenaka and Koji Yakusho dance to box-office success in Masayuki Suo's **Shall We Dance?** (1996).

Cousinly love in the mountains of Nara: Naomi Sento's **Moe no Suzaku** (Suzaku, 1997).

Shigeru Muroi as enka singer Reiko Akagi, taking a last shot at the big time on an amateur song show in Kazuyuki Izutsu's **Nodo Jiman** (Proud of My Voice, 1999).

Rentaro Mikuni and Shinobu Otake as battling father and daughter in Kaneto Shindo's latest investigation into the graying of Japan: **Ikitai** (Will to Live, 1999).

Tadanobu Asano as a geek who turns the tables on his media tormentors in Satoshi Isaka's **Focus** (1996).

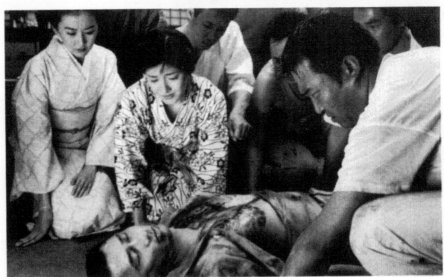

Ikuo Sekimoto's **Zankyo** (Remains of Chivalry) tries to revive traditional yakuza movie conventions—and shows why they don't work anymore.

Koji Yakusho as an ex-con trying to regain his trust in humanity, with Misa Shimizu supplying the necessary link, in Shohei Imamura's **Unagi** (The Eel, 1997).

Hiroshi Tachi as an action star campaigning, not for election, but for a driver's license, in Tomoyuki Akaishi's **Menkyo ga Nai!** (No License!, 1994).

Hiroyuki Sanada plays the eternally elusive and spectacularly talented ukiyo-e artist Sharaku in Masahiro Shinoda's **Sharaku** (1994).

Yoshinori Okada (right) as a gay youth struggling to express his true identity—and his love for his best friend (Kota Kusano, left)—in Ryosuke Hashiguchi's **Nagisa no Sindbad** (Like Grains of Sand, 1996)

The biggest Japanese box-office hit of all time: Hayao Miyazaki's **Mononoke Hime** (Princess Mononoke, 1997).

Hiroki Matsukata (right center) contemplates his next career move in Toei's "last" gang movie: **Don o Totta Otoko** (The Man Who Killed the Don, 1994).

Toshiyuki Nishida (right) helps students who have dropped through the cracks in Japan's educational system in Yoji Yamada's **Gakko** (A Class to Remember, 1993).

Susuku goes flying with a feline friend in Yoshimori Kondo's **Mimi o Sumaseba** (Whisper of the Heart, 1995).

Rentaro Mikuni and Sayuri Yoshinaga as journalists facing the personal and professional perils of modern Japanese society in Nobuhiko Obayashi's **Onna Zakari** (Turning Point, 1994).

Bette Davis in a kimono: Shima Iwashita (center) domineers and dazzles in the **Gokudo no Onnatachi** (Gang Wives) series.

Makiko Esumi (right) seeks escape from mortal loss in Hirokazu Koreeda's **Maboroshi no Hikari** (Maborosi, 1996).

The essence of underworld cool: Sho Aikawa in Takashi Miike's **Gokudo Kuro Shakai Rainy Dog** (Rainy Dog, 1996).

Film
REVIEWS

The reviews in this section span the decade of the 1990s, from July 1989 to June 1999. All of them originally appeared in *The Japan Times*, Japan's oldest English-language daily newspaper. Initially, I wrote about both Japanese and non-Japanese films for the paper, including Hollywood blockbusters. By 1992, however, I was concentrating mainly on Japanese films, with the occasional venture into European or Asian cinema. And for the past several years I have been reviewing Japanese films almost exclusively, so most of the reviews included here are from the latter half of the decade.

To fit nearly four hundred reviews into one volume, I have had to trim and revise extensively. But I have not rewritten in order to update or to change my opinions or my assessments of the films—the reviews remain faithful to the time and context in which they were written.

I would have liked to include more production credits, but space limitations made it impossible. Readers who need complete credit lists would be well advised to invest in Stephen Cremin's *The Asian Film Library Reference: Japanese Film*, a two-volume work I found invaluable in preparing this book. Also, there are films that I should have reviewed, but didn't. My only excuse is that some were in and out of the theaters before I could write about them. Others I just wasn't alert enough to spot. My apologies.

And finally, a word about the presentation of the reviews. They are listed in alphabetical order by their Japanese title, under which, in smaller type, appears an English version of the title and a release date. Many of the English titles are "official" ones given by the film's producers, and are often not direct or literal translations. When an "official" title exists, I have used it; in other cases, I have provided a literal translation of the Japanese title. Many of the films have only one title given, because the Japanese title was one using English loanwords, such as *Focus* or *Perfect Blue*.

My favorite films of the decade are marked after their Japanese titles with a star: ✷

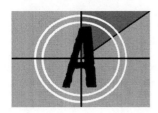

A
[1998]

Directed by Tatsuya Mori. **Produced by** the A Production Committee and Yasuoka Film. (135 mins.)

Pack journalism is hardly unique to Japan, but in Japan the pack moves with a unity and avidity seldom seen elsewhere. Once a big story breaks, the hordes descend and woe to the ink-stained wretch who arrives late or approaches the story from an unorthodox angle. He will find himself shunned or even relegated to freelancing—a dire fate in a society in which organizational affiliation is all.

Such was the fate of Tatsuya Mori, a documentarian who, in September 1995, approached the Aum Shinrikyo cult with a request to film behind the closed doors of its compounds. Six months earlier cult leaders had attempted to commit mass murder on Tokyo subways. When the police investigation began shortly afterwards, the media hordes descended, depicting cult members as deadly zombies wired to the brain waves of leader Shoko Asahara.

Not unexpectedly, Aumers had become wary of journalists, but Mori was different. Instead of faxing or phoning—the usual communications methods of the press pack—Mori wrote a letter to Aum spokesman Hiroshi Araki explaining his project and politely requesting Aum's cooperation. This was a pleasant first for Araki, who agreed to a meeting.

Mori signed a contract with a production company and began negotiating with Araki. He wanted to make a documentary that would show Aum members as they were, with no concealment of their voices or identities. He would be an objective observer, neither overtly critical or sympathetic. He would also have complete editorial control. Araki agreed to his conditions, and in March 1996, Mori began filming. Then came a devastating blow. When Mori rejected his producer's demand that he allow an anti-Aum journalist to question cult members, the production company voided his contract. Mori decided to soldier on. By this time, however, the media had beaten the Aum story into the ground. A colleague told Araki that he was wasting his time. Assuming he could finish a theatrical documentary, who would show it? Who would watch it?

Nearly two years later, Mori's *A* (a title that stands for, among other things, Aum, Asahara, and Araki) is in the theaters and, despite technical rough spots, including a soundtrack that illustrates why Japan is one of the world's noisiest countries, *A* is enjoying a *succes d'éstime*. Mori films his subjects with an unerring journalistic sense for the right question, the revealing image. His aim is not another exposé, but an investigation into why Araki and his fellow cultists joined Aum and why they persisted in their faith despite universal censure and ostracism from "normal" society.

The film's focus is Hiroshi Araki, who at the time Mori began filming was Aum's most visible member. Araki is clearly uncomfortable in his spokesman's role—he tells Mori that he would rather pursue his spiritual training—but he comes across as a tough negotiator who can quickly see through journos angling for yet another Aum scoop.

If there is a villain in Mori's film, it is the Japanese media, especially TV producers and reporters eager to goose ratings with shocking revelations, but who try to conceal that purpose from Araki with fake sincerity and squirmy evasions. Meanwhile, Araki is a surprisingly sympathetic type, whose mild manner, ready smile, and dogged persistence cannot hide his discouragement over Aum's declining fortunes and his uneasiness over the effect his cult membership has had on his family and will have on his future.

After spending time with Mori's camera inside an Aum *dojo*, it becomes evident that, instead of demons, Aumers are, in the main, ordinary enough Japanese: loyal to their group, suspicious of outsiders, tolerant of clutter, fascinated with electronic gadgetry. One begins to admire their sincerity, dedication and tenacity, however, loopy.

An Araki, one realizes, is the product of a social system that, while cultivating moral qualities in its citizens, no longer gives them a moral rationale for their endeavors. The kid who faithfully does his homework inhabits the same spiritual vacuum as the flame-haired punks dealing drugs and the shiny-domed bureaucrats betraying the public trust. Aum offered not only high-tech jobs and opportunities for rapid advancement, but also a sense of mission and fulfillment missing in Japanese life. As *A* shows us so incisively, Shoko Asahara's warped utopia is not an aberration so much as a mirror of Japan in the 1990s.

Aa, Haru
Ah, Spring [1999]

Directed by Shinji Somai. **Screenplay by** Takehiro Nakajima. **Produced by** Shochiku, Eisei Gekijo, and Tram. **With** Tsutomu Yamazaki, Koichi Sato, Sumiko Fuji, Yuki Saito, Shiho Fujimura, Keita Okada. (100 mins.)

In *Aa, Haru* Shinji Somai proposes a nonviolent cure for the recession blues, but his film is less interested in examining the ongoing collapse of the Japanese economy than in retreating to a vanished Japan so beloved by an older generation of humanist directors. Though set in the present, *Aa, Haru* seems to be taking place in a time warp, somewhat like that of the Tora-san series, with the same stress on the warm, loveable humanity of all the characters, even the most obnoxious.

The set-up, however, is that of *The Man Who Came to Dinner*. In *Aa, Haru* the unwanted guest is the long-lost father (Tsutomu Yamazaki) of Hiroshi Nirasaki (Koichi Sato), an elite salaryman at a failing securities company. Dad, who looks as though he has spent the last several months sleeping rough in Ueno Park, accosts Hiroshi one night on his way home from work and demands to be taken in. Hiroshi, however, has no memory of this drunken coot; his mother (Sumiko Fuji), who runs a short-order restaurant, told him that his father died shortly after he was born. But the old man knows enough about the past to make Hiroshi believe that he might be the real thing. Reluctantly, he invites him to spend the night. Dad, however, has every intention of staying longer.

This is an obvious premise for a comedy and Yamazaki is a gifted comic actor. But though the movie has its lighter moments, neither scriptwriter Takehiro Nakajima nor Somai have aimed primarily for laughs. Instead, they have produced a feel-good family drama that is mildly amusing, mildly heartwarming, mildly inspiring.

Dad is hardly the most welcome of visitors in Hiroshi's house, a beautifully well-preserved example of prewar domestic architecture that once belonged to his wife's father, a prosperous businessman. Now Hiroshi lives there with his neurotic, unworldly wife Mizuho (Yuki Saito), her prim and proper mother (Shiho Fujimura), and his son (Keita Okada), a small boy who loves to play in the garden with his pet chickens.

As might be expected, the sudden arrival of Hiroshi's Dad, with his uncouth ways and loud insistence on his fatherly rights, gives Mizuho a rude shock. She must already endure the loneliness of Hiroshi's workaholic lifestyle—how can she also cope with this rough stranger in their midst? Her mother is likewise alarmed—this, she seems to say with her disapproving glance, is what comes from marrying among the lower orders.

The old man is a fun-loving sort, playing a demon during the Setsubun holiday to the delight of the little boy. He is also not the best moral example, teaching the boy the art of dice and peeping at the grandmother in her bath. For the latter offense, he is thrown out of the house, but instead of disappearing, he sets up camp in a nearby park together with other elderly homeless men, who quickly become his boon companions.

As might be expected, there is soon a reconciliation, with the old man returning to Hiroshi's home. There is also a medical development that I shouldn't reveal, only to say that it draws the old man closer to his newfound family, while underscoring his essential loneliness.

The old man, like Tora-san, is a life-force figure, though Yamazaki plays him more realistically, less comically and sentimentally. While being a rogue and a lech, he represents a kind of vitality and endurance that the overeducated, overprotected Japanese of Hiroshi and Mizuho's generation have either forgotten or lost. He also serves as a reminder of the importance of family ties and human connection, in an era that devalues both.

Somai drums in his Life Goes On message by the thumpingly simple metaphor of chickens laying eggs, which in turn become chicks, which in turn... but I'm sure you get the idea. He also takes careful note of the passing of traditional holidays—Setsubun, the Doll Festival, and Children's Day—to the same obvious effect. This traditional cycle has its comforts, but it is hard to see how it can heal a society that is collapsing like a slow-motion film of a dynamited building. *Aa, Haru* may be intended as a pepper-upper for recession-weary audiences, but years from now it may well be regarded as a symptom of the strange complacency that lulled these islands before the arrival of the deluge.

Adrenaline Drive
(1999)

Written and directed by Shinobu Yaguchi. Produced by Kindai Eiga Kyokai, Gaga Communications, Nihon Shuppan Hambai, and There's Enterprise. With Masanobu Ando, Yutaka Matsushige, Hikari Ishida. (112 mins.)

Shinobu Yaguchi's *Adrenaline Drive* will look familiar to those who have seen the director's two previous features—*Hadashi no Picnic* (Down the Drain, 1993) and *Himitsu no Hanazono* (The Secret Garden, 1997). All are picaresque in form, with heroes who are lovable goofs, but *Adrenaline Drive* represents an advance.

Yaguchi has always been a crowd-pleasing idea man, whose high-concept plots could fly at a Hollywood pitch meeting, but in earlier films his storytelling reach often exceeded his technical grasp. In *Adrenaline Drive*, however, he has finally mastered the art of making every yen count on the screen. If not quite Hollywood-slick, the film is a more accomplished entertainment than anything he has attempted so far. Yet despite better film quality and smoother camerawork, *Adrenaline Drive* has story problems that in Hollywood probably would have not survived the second rewrite. Yaguchi gives his narrative game away too easily and occasionally sacrifices logic altogether. I am usually not interested in picking holes in plots—I go to movies to be seduced, not convinced—but in *Adrenaline Drive* the holes are too big to ignore. In the end, though, the ride is worth it. Yaguchi fuels his film with sharp, fundamentally sympathetic observations about his characters and the madly acquisitive society in which they live.

His hero is Satoru Suzuki (Masanobu Ando), an employee at a rent-a-car company who, distracted by the teasing of a sadistic superior, smacks a company car into the rear of a Jaguar. The driver, a menacing gangster named Kuroiwa (Yutaka Matsushige), drags poor Satoru to the gang office to extract an extortionate payment for damages.

A gas explosion at the office, however, leaves Satoru as the only ambulant survivor. He is rescued by Shizuka Sato (Hikari Ishida), a nurse who has rushed to the scene from a nearby convenience store. A mousy type in a semi-permanent daze, Shizuka is shaken out of her shock at the carnage long enough to help Satoru out of the ruined building. Satoru, however, is thinking less about saving his hide than swiping a box filled with two hundred million yen in *yakuza* loot. When the ambulance carrying Satoru, Shizuka, and Kuroiwa crashes, Satoru scoops up the spilled money, with Shizuka's reluctant assistance. Before they can make a clean getaway, they are spotted by a semi-conscious Kuroiwa.

Satoru and Shizuka soon find themselves being pursued by the gang's surviving *chimpira* (apprentice gangsters played by the Jovi Jova comedy troupe), who have little intention of turning over the loot to Kuroiwa, their erstwhile boss. They are also incompetents who let Satoru and Shizuka escape and flee to the countryside. Realizing that if he wants the job done right he has to do it himself, Kuroiwa hobbles out of the ICU in search of the fleeing couple, who by this time are enjoying their windfall at a resort hotel—and falling in love.

Satoru and Shizuka are predictably careless with the loot (Shizuka hauls her share around in a knapsack) and predictably smitten with each other. They also spend their small fortune in the usual ways—fancy designer clothes, expensive jewelry, and a room with a view—while Shizuka undergoes the usual transformation from bespectacled nerd to

babe in a red minidress. Several of the plot twists strain credibility. Why, for example, does a friendly sommelier Shizuka encounters suddenly make off with her knapsack, without knowing what is in it? But *Adrenaline Drive* does not commit the cardinal genre sin of dullness. Matsushige Yutaka is particularly good as Kuroiwa. He looks the part, with the skull-face, slicked-back hair, and doom-laden voice of a Japanese Christopher Walken. But he can also get laughs by arching his eyebrows in exasperation while trapped in a neck brace that resembles a fiendish Lego construction.

Yaguchi obviously wants to be the next Masayuki Suo—a maker of intelligently crafted, irresistibly entertaining mainstream films—but he should hire a producer with a Suo-like steel-trap mind. He is bit too much like his hero, who may win Shizuka, but can't quite keep both feet planted on planet Earth.

Afureru Atsui Namida ✳
Swimming With Tears (1992)

Written and directed by Hirotaka Tashiro. **Produced by** Cine Ballet. **With** Ruby Moreno, Masayuki Suzuki, Shiro Sano, Jun Togawa. (104 mins.)

From the title *Afureru Atsui Namida* we expect—what else?—a tearjerker. But this film by Hirotaka Tashiro seeks to evoke emotions, not manipulate them. It succeeds the way good Japanese poetry often succeeds, by packing a worldview into a single image, with sublimely artful immediacy. That view is quintessentially Japanese: human beings are fundamentally good, but live in a world of suffering.

Afureru Atsui Namida depicts that suffering with a sympathy that is all the more powerful for its restraint. The dispassionate eye of Tashiro's camera shows us the pathos of the characters' lives more clearly than if it were glazed with glycerine tears. There are tears in the film, of course, but unlike many Japanese directors, who simply use them for effect, baldly and crudely, Tashiro makes us feel that they are earned; they belong.

The story is that of Fey (Ruby Moreno), a young Filipina who runs away from her husband (Masayuki Suzuki), a close-mouthed Tohoku farmer. The coldness of the snow that she stumbles through in her escape symbolizes the state of her marriage. "My life is just hard work and sex to produce children," she wrote to her mother in Manila.

Arriving in Shin Okubo—Tokyo's mecca for Asian workers—she tries to find Maria, a Filipina friend. But Mr. Yang, the owner of the Chinese restaurant where she worked, tells Fey that Maria has already returned to Manila. Alone and lost in a strange land, Fey becomes a waitress for Yang and finds a tiny room near the restaurant, where she becomes friends with her neighbors: a university economics professor named Kokubo (Shiro Sano) and his live-in lover Asami (Jun Togawa). Both are sympathetic to Fey's plight, especially when they learn that Fey's father is Japanese. An executive at a trading company, he met Fey's mother during a posting to Manila, but broke off contact after returning to Japan more than twenty years ago. Fey wants to meet him, but he refuses to acknowledge her existence.

In addition to Fey's quest—and her father's attempts to discourage her from it—there is a subplot seemingly straight from *Sunday Mystery Theater*: the professor's ten-year old daughter, we learn, was murdered by his lover's brother, who is about to be released from jail. Rather than simply juicing up his narrative, Tashiro uses this subplot to deepen our understanding of his characters and strengthen his indictment of the society in which they live.

It is not a one-sided indictment. Fey's father stands as a symbol of the ugly Japanese who exploits other Asians and thinks that money solves all problems, but in his weary face we also see an overworked corporate warrior who longs for the Philippines' tropical pleasures. Also, though Asami and Kokubo are certainly victims of their society's intolerance, as personified by the mass-media hounds baying at their doorstep, they face a dilemma that admits no clearcut or politically correct solutions. Logically, the murder has nothing to do with them. Emotionally, it permeates their relationship to its core. Fey understands that relationship, especially Kokubo's side of it, quite well. As a fellow victim, she shares his "unreasonable" rage, that extends even to the innocent relations of the perpetrator.

The politics of *Afureru Atsui Namida* do not overshadow its individual dramas, however. Its austere beauty and its people remain, as do our tears, after the lights go up.

Ageman
A-Ge-Man: Tales of a Golden Geisha (1990)

Written and directed by Juzo Itami. Produced by Itami Films. With Nobuko Miyamoto, Ryunosuke Kaneda, Shogo Shimada, Masahiko Tsugawa, Mitsuko. (119 mins.)

The title of Juzo Itami's *Ageman* is an old Japanese word for luck. And luck is what the heroine, Nayoko (Nobuko Miyamoto), brings to the men in her life. But *Ageman* is less a success story than a love story and a penetrating look at modern Japanese mores.

Nayoko begins the film as a baby abandoned at a neighborhood shrine. At sixteen she becomes an apprentice geisha, and at eighteen, the mistress of an elderly Buddhist priest (Ryunosuke Kaneda). Three years later, when the priest dies, his mother hands Nayoko the deed to the house that the priest had used for their assignations and tells her she still has plenty of time to find a good man. Ten years later she is still looking.

Ageman is a record of that search. Nayoko does find men, including a piratical political fixer (Shogo Shimada) and a philandering bank executive (Masahiko Tsugawa), but they hardly deserve the adjective "good." This goes for nearly all her men, faces in the Itami rogues' gallery of money- and power-hungry hustlers and unreconstructed male chauvinists.

As luck would have it, Nayoko falls hardest for the worst one—the banker, who cheats on his spoiled brat of a wife (Mitsuko) with a practiced *sang froid*. When she kicks him out, Nayoko takes him in, but he cannot keep his hands off his old conquests or stop making new ones. He also cannot refuse his boss's offer of a directorship—on the condition that he make up with his ex, the daughter of an important client.

Itami handles this material with his usual wit and panache. More than most directors, he has imposed an unmistakably original vision on his films. From his is first, *Ososhiki* (The Funeral, 1984)—Itami has rarely strayed from it. But in *Ageman* he also essays straight drama (in an interview, he said he wanted the audience to "laugh ten times and cry three times"). He doesn't succeed at the latter; his attempts to jerk tears fall flat. Though Itami may dip a toe in the warm waters of Japanese movie sentimentality, he never plunges. He remains the most dry-eyed of all Japanese directors.

His bigger problem is flagging inspiration. Although Itami hasn't run out of things to say—*Ageman* is filled with fresh comic bits—he isn't saying them with the old precision or punch. His main target is the Japanese male who makes a mother of his wife or lover and then begins playing the field again once he is certain of Mommy's love—the banker being Exhibit A. Itami, however, finds this behavior is not only inevitable (boys will be boys), but charming (his banker is a *cute* rogue). In short, he likes his banker too much (or identifies with him too closely) to give him the roasting he deserves. Also, Nayoko is an all-too-willing Mommy. She picks up the clothes that the banker scatters on the floor with a motherly tut-tutting that Western viewers might find baffling, to say the least.

Judging rightly that this relationship could not carry the film, Itami takes potshots at climbing politicians, lecherous priests, and stone-hearted doctors, but he's already made better hits elsewhere. Also, this scattershot approach dissipates the film's energy: it ends not with a bang, but a dumb sight gag that could have lifted from *The Blues Brothers*. Be that as it may, Nobuko Miyamoto and Masahiko Tsugawa are two funny people in a funny cast. Also, Toshiyuki Honda contributes his usual bouncy, infectious score. But after so many times around— Honda also scored the two *Taxing Woman* films— his music has started to sound like a Greatest Hits collection. So, unfortunately, has *Ageman*.

Ai ni Tsuite, Tokyo
All About Love, Tokyo (1992)

Written and directed by Mitsuo Yanagimachi. Produced by Ai ni Tsuite Tokyo Production Committee. With Wu Xiao Tong, Asuka Okasaka, Hiroshi Fujioka. (113 mins.)

In *Ai ni Tsuite, Tokyo*, Mitsuo Yanagimachi shows us the lives of Asians in Japan from the inside, while blurring the usual PC distinction between "good Asians" and "bad Japanese." In *Ai ni Tsuite* the two sides distrust each other, exploit each other and need each other. The Japanese, being wealthier and more powerful, would seem to have the advantage in this relationship, but the film's Asians have weapons of their own: resentment, sex, and guile.

The story centers on Hojun (Wu Xiao Tong), a foppish young man who has given up a budding singing career in Beijing to work in a Tokyo slaughterhouse, killing cattle with a pistol. He lives in a rooming house with other Chinese and studies Japanese at a language school catering to Asians. Yanagimachi makes much of the slaughterhouse metaphor. He begins the film with Hojun shooting a cow between its unsuspecting eyes. And he keeps returning to this place that symbolizes the death of his characters' hopes. Though hardly beasts waiting passively to be slaughtered, the film's Chinese are gradually losing their illusions, standards, and sanity. They are in danger of becoming morally dead "economic animals" occupied only with moneymaking.

At a rooming-house going-away party, the guest of honor laments that he came to Japan to study, but learned only how to kill cattle. As he cries bitterly, Hojun begins singing a Chinese song about home. His mellow voice and stagey manner made me think, for an uncomfortable moment, that I might be watching a badly produced musical—but they also signaled the presence of a survivor.

He soon meets another, Ailin (Asuka Okasaka), an ethnic Chinese born and raised in Japan. Ailin is pretty, vivacious, and wants something more from life than waitressing at a Japanese restaurant. When Hojun heaves a chair at a cook who accuses her of dipping into the till, she is only too glad to chuck her job and go with him. Their brief idyll ends when Hojun is caught trying to cheat at a neighborhood *pachinko* parlor. Endo (Hiroshi Fujioka), the parlor's *yakuza* owner, offers Hojun a deal: he won't turn him in if Hojun introduces him to Ailin. Hojun can't refuse. Hojun appends a condition of his own, though: He wants one of Endo's *pachinko* machines to pour out its jackpot of steel balls for him every day. "I can see you've got what it takes to succeed in Japan," Endo says, smiling wryly.

Ai ni Tsuite may sound like a darkly satirical study of a young man on the make. It is not. Though Hojun may be a hustler, Yanagimachi wants us to feel the pathos of his situation, not smile at its absurdity. Even Endo is not a typical movie mobster, but a sad character who cannot perform in bed with Ailin and discovers his wife in the embrace of a young subordinate. His failure in bed is a metaphor for Japan's failure to exert any but economic domination over its former Asian colonies. Despite Endo's attempts to bully Hojun and buy Ailin, they remain disdainful and defiant. Soon they are meeting clandestinely and Ailin is dreaming of escape.

Yanagimachi integrates these metaphors into his film without distracting from its story. He is less successful, however, in sustaining mood. One problem is the musical interludes, which pull the film in the direction of bathos. Another is casting. Wu Xiao Tong can project a spoiled-boy charm as Hojun, but not much more. Asuka Okasaka's performance is more professional, but she doesn't make Ailin's motives clear. Why does she submit so readily to Endo? Why does she abandon her waitressing job to become a mistress? The traditional passivity of the Asian female is not the answer, but she doesn't supply others. Hiroshi Fujioka charges Endo with a dark masculine energy and strong core of character that are perversely attractive. Though I didn't care for Endo's opinions of the Chinese or his exploitation of Hojun and Ailin, he was more credible than either of them in his passion and rage. In this movie, the devil has the best lines.

Ai o Kou Hito *
Begging For Love (1998)

Directed by Hideyoshi Hirayama. Screenplay by Yoshinobu Tei. Produced by Toho, Kadokawa Shoten, and Sundance Company. With Mieko Harada, Kiichi Nakai, Jun Kunimura, Maho Nonami. (135 mins.)

What inspires a parent to abuse a child with beatings and belittlings that wound for a lifetime? Hideyoshi Hirayama's *Ai o Kou Hito* does not approach child abuse as a social issue or propose the usual Japanese cinematic fix-all: i.e., forgive and forget. Instead, it discovers the roots of abuse less specifically in Japanese culture than in the mysteries of human nature. Its abusive mother is not a devil in a flashy red dress, but a woman with a terrible vitality and purity. Deeply flawed, deeply wounded, she nonetheless lives fully in the moment, with an energy that overawes the ineffectual men in her life.

As played by Mieko Harada, she is a charismatic, volatile presence, who can be brutal one moment, buoyant the next. The one most caught up in this human whirlwind is her only daughter, Terue. After losing her Taiwanese father (Kiichi Nakai) to tuberculosis shortly after the end of the war, Terue is placed in an orphanage by her mother Toyoko (Harada), a cabaret hostess. Then one day, without ceremony or affection, Toyoko reclaims Terue, then five, and takes her to a shantytown—her new home. She introduces the girl to a new father and little brother—a boy named Takenori—then promptly leaves for work.

There is nothing permanent about this arrangement either. Before long, the "father" disappears and Terue and Takenori are in a rooming house more cramped than their old hovel. Toyoko's new man, Saburo (Jun Kunimura), begs in the guise of a disabled veteran. A weak-willed, kindly type, he cannot stop Toyoko from abusing Terue: she starves her, beats her, curses her, and even puts out a cigarette in the palm of her hand. Takenori also suffers, but it is Terue—so sweet, quiet and quick to smile—who receives the brunt of their mother's wrath.

While this story unfolds, we also see Terue as an adult (played by Harada as well) seeking to exorcise the ghosts of her past. A widow with a teenage daughter (Maho Nonami), she has apparently broken free of her mother's tyranny, but the scars of her childhood still remain. Her way of healing is to perform a Buddhist service for the repose of her father's soul, but first she has to find his ashes, which were lost long ago. Together with her daughter, a big, outgoing girl who speaks her mind bluntly, she begins a search that leads her to Taiwan. At her daughter's prompting, she also discovers what she is really looking for: her mother. Toyoko, she learns, is still alive and working as a beautician. Terue finds her shop and slowly, hesitantly, opens the door.

Though its theme of long-lost relatives reuniting may be a melodrama favorite, *Ai o Kou Hito* rejects easy sentimentalism. As a child Terue loves her mother, but she also hates her with a passion that becomes fiercer as the years pass. In middle age, she still smiles in the face of insult or injury, but she is reluctant to forgive the woman who so nearly ruined her life.

Returning to the screen after a decade's absence, Mieko Harada is especially good as Toyoko, whose wild, destructive vitality epitomizes the anarchic years following Japan's defeat. As Terue, Harada is more subdued, but her mouse with the prim demeanor can also silently roar her anger. The film's only jarring note is Maho Nonami as Terue's daughter. Looking as though she could crack walnuts with her teeth, she is bursting with rude health—and blithely oblivious to Terue's agony. This incomprehension, though, may be Terue's greatest accomplishment: by the end she has freed not only herself, but another generation, from the echoes of her mother's demon rage.

Ai Suru
To Love (1997)

Written and directed by Kei Kumai. Produced by Nikkatsu. With Miki Sakai, Atsushi Watanabe, Kyoko Kishida. (114 mins.)

Kei Kumai's *Ai Suru* is an unabashed tearjerker that, if audible audience reaction is any guide, must be deemed a smashing success. The festival crowd I saw it with was snuffling with abandon. At the end of the screening, one man pulled the front of his T-shirt over his face to mop away the tears.

Stylistically conservative but socially engaged, Kumai rejects cinematic fads and fashions in favor of serious themes and straight-from-the-heart storytelling. Truth be told, though, he is inclined to a plodding earnestness. Watching Rentaro Mikuni, as a boat captain, solemnly munching the flesh of one of his crew in Kumai's World War II drama *Hikarigoke*, I thought that I had never seen anyone make cannibalism look so unappetizing. Hannibal Lecter would have found him dull company, I'm afraid. In *Ai Suru*, however, Kumai has found not only a congenial subject—the decades-old prejudice and discrimination against lepers in Japanese society—but an effective method of telling his uplifting story.

Mitsu (Miki Sakai), a pure-hearted, naive sort, befriends an Okinawan box-lunch vendor named Yoshioka (Atsuro Watabe) while touring the sights of Tokyo Bay. When Yoshioka invites her to consummate their acquaintance in a love hotel, she at first reject s him, but finally takes pity on him—he limps so winningly, you see—and succumbs to his advances. This affair is short-lived: unable to trust women since being abandoned by his mother as a boy, Yoshioka disappears, while Mitsu pines. A month later, a chance meeting leads to love, this time for keeps. Then Mitsu develops a sore on her arm and is diagnosed with leprosy.

Sent to a leprosarium in the mountains, she sobs her heart out. She is lifted from this slough of despond by the kindly staff and patients, including her roommate, an elderly former pianist named Taeko (Kyoko Kishida). Mitsu is beginning to accept her fate, when she is told she has been misdiagnosed. While Taeko chokes back her tears, Mitsu leaves for the glorious world outside. Standing on the train platform, however, she has a change of heart and decides to devote her life to her now-beloved lepers. The long-suffering Taeko is overjoyed when she hears the news—and every handkerchief in the house is sopping wet. There is more, but enough to say that the climax would wring moisture from even a stony-eyed critic.

Kumai's treatment of this material is impeccably high-minded. He describes the problems of Japan's lepers, including their legal segregation from society for ninety years until 1996, without a hint of sensationalism. Also, the film earns its tears honestly, even though Miki Sakai's Mitsu seems to have been beamed down from a 1957 Keisuke Kinoshita film. Bring a towel and settle in for the best cry of the year.

Alice Sanctuary
(1995)

Written and directed by Takaaki Watanabe. Produced by Alice Production Committee. With Kazuki Sakai, Enami Sakai, Daisuke Uchida. (108 mins.)

How does one film modern-day evil? Some would argue that the documentary approach is the only moral choice; that the deeds committed in the gulags and concentration camps are beyond the reach of human imagination. Others would counter that even the most well-made documentary can tell only part of the story. To fully capture the reality of the victims' lives, inner and outer, we must imaginatively recreate them.

Japan has experienced its own horrors in recent years, caused less by an evil ideology than a spiritual vacuum. In depicting one of them—the 1989 rape and murder of a high school girl by four teenage boys, who then stuffed her body into a barrel and covered it with concrete—award-winning documentarian Takaaki Watanabe has chosen the approach of the symbolist poet rather than the investigative reporter. His first feature, *Alice Sanctuary*, does not flinch from the ugliness of rape and the brutality of the rapists, while

believing in the innocence and purity of its victims. Its pathos is wistfully austere, its message the quietly stern one that the pure of heart will be betrayed and that, pure or not, we are all finally alone.

Watanabe uses the incident on which it is based as point of departure, not a text. Instead of one girl, there are two: a pair of seventeen-year-old identical twins. Keiko (Kazuki Sakai) is deaf and Akiko (Enami Sakai) is not, but both girls share a telepathic language of the heart that can be airily poetic and brutally honest. They lead very different lives. Akiko goes to a public high school, Keiko, to a school for the deaf. Akiko has a boyfriend, a judo star named Takeshi (Daisuke Uchida), Keiko has her sister. Akiko is radiantly happy, Keiko, smolderingly jealous.

Takeshi and Akiko become acquainted with three aimless, casually criminal punks. Takeshi is drawn to these lowlifes because he's an easily-led zero, Akiko because she is in love with Takeshi and wants to like the people he likes. One day, the punks gang-rape Akiko, then laughingly present her, mute with shock, to Takeshi. There is another reason for her silence; she is really Keiko, posing as her sister to get next to Takeshi.

Instead of becoming enraged at the attackers and at Takeshi for his acquiescence, Akiko excoriates her sister for trying to live her life and spoil her relationship with her lover. She decides to continue as though nothing had happened (nothing, after all, has happened to her). Watanabe asks us to take this this decision as further proof of the purity of Akiko's love. Despite everything, she will stand by her man. I was more inclined, however, to take it as evidence of willful obtuseness. And yet the film insists, with some persuasiveness, on the pathos of Akiko's blindness to her man's essential nullity and her willingness to sacrifice herself on the altar of a one-sided love.

In telling this story, Watanabe forcefully contrasts the poetry of the sisters' secret language to the coarseness of the punk's street slang, and the safe, cozy (if parentless) haven of the sisters' home to the ugly chaos of Takeshi's room, which the punks make their own while Takeshi's parents idle about downstairs. The performances of Kazuki and Enami Sakai evoke the sisters' innocence and sensuality, while portraying twinship as a private world both comforting and claustrophobic.

But in this debut film, Watanabe also betrays his inexperience. His attempts at stylization are at times too labored, with the actors behaving like robots, while his visual metaphors are at times composed statically and sentimentally, like dried flowers behind tinted glass. Even so, Watanabe's vision of a moral wasteland persuades and disturbs. His punks are so cocksure that they can get away with murder—and I fear that, before long, they may be right. In the value-free society *Alice Sanctuary* insists is ours, who will be there to stop them, or care?

Ano Natsu, Ichiban Shizukana Umi
A Scene At the Sea (1991)

Written and directed by Takeshi Kitano. Produced by Office Kitano and Totsu. With Kurodo Maki, Hiroko Oshima. (101 mins.)

Ano Natsu, Ichiban Shizukana Umi might be called Takeshi Kitano's contribution to the beach movie genre. His's first feature, *Sono Otoko, Kyobo ni Tsuki* (Violent Cop), was both praised for its fresh take on genre conventions and criticized for its sadistic violence. Undeterred, Kitano gave his audience another rude jolt with *3-4 X 10 Gatsu* (Boiling Point), which describes the unsettling encounter of two amateur baseball players with a *yakuza* boss, played by Kitano, who is at once casually brutal and strangely charismatic.

In *Ano Natsu*, however, Kitano takes another tack entirely, into the silent world of the deaf. Both the hero, played by TV star Kurodo Maki, and his girlfriend, played by newcomer Hiroko Oshima, live in that world. For Kitano deafness is less a theme for a "problem film" than a device for getting back to the basics. Kitano uses silence to reduce life's background noise and remind us of our essential humanity. He is concerned with fundamental human emotions and simple human pleasures, including the joy of soaking in rays on a midsummer day or riding a surfboard plucked out of the trash.

Kitano is guilty of equating deafness with dumbness—his deaf characters seldom sign and never speak—and assuming that the deaf, being immune to auditory temptation, have purer hearts than the rest of us. But his film has a quirky, roughhewn charm, and after his earlier efforts comes as a welcome nonviolent relief.

The story revolves around the hero's infatuation with surfing, from his first look at a discarded surfboard to his final encounter with an unforgiving sea. Nothing much happens: the hero and his girlfriend spend much of the film traipsing silently across the screen, surfboard in hand, or staring silently out at the waves. The few incidents are of a commonplace sort: the girl becomes jealous when she sees the boy sharing a tangerine with an attractive stranger, the boy and girl become friends with a group of surfers and go with them to a surfing competition and the boy, after a misunderstanding caused by his deafness, wins a prize.

Except for brief appearances by two surfing buffoons and a stray pratfall or two, the film doesn't try for laughs. Instead, it asks us to admire the purity of the boy's struggle and the girl's devotion. (She never puts a foot in the water; instead her sole function is to fold her boyfriend's jeans and watch him as he battles the waves.)

By restricting his central characters to near muteness, Kitano risks reducing them to nonentities. If film acting, as is often said, is all in the eyes, then his boy and girl need to have talented orbs indeed; for they have little else to work with. Kurodo Maki, as the boy, has not only the right surfer's build and over-the-horizon squint, but a quiet intensity that keeps us watching, even when he is waxing his surfboard. Hiroko Oshima works well with her co-star. Together, they look like the kind of couple who really can read each other's thoughts. But her eyes tell us little; judging only from her reactions, it's hard to say whether her boyfriend is shooting a curl, flirting with a surfer girl, or riding one wave ahead of a shark.

Ano Natsu, Ichiban Shizuka Na Umi goes against the noisy grain of so many films by young directors, with their love of extravagant imagery and self-congratulatory hipness. It is almost willfully unhurried and undramatic and its surfers are mostly dull normals in embryo. Even so, it invites us to take a break from our twenty-four-hour-a-day lives, smell the surf and soak in some home truths about life's transience and tragedy. It's a hard invitation to refuse.

Aoi Sakana
Blue Fish (1999)

Written and directed by Yosuke Nakagawa. Produced by Tompu Sosakusha. With Mari Ouchi, Keigo Heshiki, Yoshino Tamaki, Miyuki Tobaru, Gu Xiaodong. (60 mins.)

Aoi Sakana, the debut film by former magazine editor, FM-radio director, and video producer Yosuke Nakagawa, gave me a new take on where media cross-fertilization might be leading. While shooting his young actors like models in a TV ad for a casual clothing line, and foregrounding Keiichiro Shibuya's evocative, if overly explanatory, piano score in the manner of a music video, Nakagawa is also hearkening back to the lyricism and romanticism of silent films. His real influences are not Gap ads so much as Chaplin and Griffith.

First, he keeps the dialogue to a minimum, particularly in depicting the romance between his two principals—a fiery-eyed beauty salon assistant (Mari Ouchi) and a laconic gangster (Keigo Heshiki). Second, he reduces his story to its basics and tells it in exactly sixty minutes, a length typical of early silent features. One could turn off the sound and still understand what is going on in nearly every scene. Third, he rejects irony in favor of poeticized intensity. As the assistant, Mari Ouchi moves with an dancerly expressiveness and burns with a pure-hearted passion reminiscent of Paulette Godard. Her scenes with the gangster are not staged so much as choreographed.

I don't want to overdraw the Griffith-Chaplin comparisons. The heroine's pursuit of her man is too bold for silent-era sensibilities—Paulette would not steal into the Tramp's room and wait all night for his return. (What she and one-time paramour Chaplin did in real life is another matter, however). Also, D.W. would not have used the long traveling shot that, in the opening scene, explores the plant life on an Okinawan back street. In the cool blue tones of Ichigo Sugawara's cinematography, this evocation of the island's beauty has an impact it would obviously lack in black and white.

Ryoko (Ouchi) works at a beauty parlor in a Naha shopping arcade. In her time off she chats with her best friend (Miyuki Tobaru), another shopgirl, and together they hang out with boys who work in the arcade. Life is easy, but to the restless Ryoko, pointless. Then one day she drops a towel to the street below, at the feet of Kazuya (Heshiki), a long-legged dreamboat. Instead of answering her call for help, however, Kazuya strides up the stairs, opens a door on the opposite side of the arcade and disappears inside. He is selfish and rude—and Ryoko can't take her eyes off him.

Kazuya is a drug dealer in cahoots with Shanghainese gangsters. They plan to muscle into the territory of the local Taiwanese mob—a dangerous game. Ryoko keeps trying to get next to Kazuya and Kazuya keeps fending her off with thousand-yard stares. Then, just as her persistence is beginning to pay off, his Taiwanese rivals burst into his room, rip off his white powder and, after issuing a few threats, vanish into the night. Kazuya takes off in pursuit while Ryoko, who is still ignorant of his true occupation, walks in the open door of his apartment and waits for his return. But will Kazuya ever come back?

From this summary, Kazuya may seem an egotistical lowlife and Ryoko, a hormone-besotted teen, but their brief encounter achieves a kind of dignity and pathos. True, Nakagawa's camera lingers too often and long on the cloud formations, narrow backstreets and other local Okinawan color, as in a tranced-out travelogue. But in the crucial scenes, it creates a mood of daybreak freshness, tropical sensuousness, and mortal sadness. And yes, Ryoko's pursuit annoys with its obtuseness—can't she see what bad news this guy is?—but Ouchi's performance is all essence, no waste. She makes *Aoi Sakana* more than a music video in a silent-movie mode.

Aozora ni Ichiban Chikai Basho
The Nearest Place to the Sky (1994)

Written and directed by Shoji Kokami. Produced by Third Stage and Right Vision. With Hidetaka Yoshioka, Tomokazu Miura, Mayumi Hasegawa, Junko Maya. (102 mins.)

What does it take to get a movie made in Japan? If you're an independent director trying to make a film about a salesman who finds peace of mind on an office-building roof, the answer is: beg, borrow, and steal, but mostly beg. For his second feature, *Aozora ni Ichiban Chikai Basho*, Shoji Kokami had to borrow his parent's retirement nest egg. He thought about asking them to take out a second mortgage on their condo, but remembered they'd already put it in hock to keep his Third Stage theater company afloat.

Was it worth it? Artistically, the answer is yes; a Frank Capra-ish fantasy with a contemporary spin, *Aozora* is an entertaining film with a lift. Yes, it's tough out there, it says, but you can get by with a little help from your friends, your guardian angels, and an occasional game of kick the can.

Kitagawa (Hidetaka Yoshioka) works as a salesman for a company that uses high-pressure tactics to push high-priced household goods on the guilible. The sales manager is a slave driver who subjects poor performers to group tongue lashings that reduces them to quivering lumps of humiliation. His star salesman, Kitagawa, is among the most merciless of the lashers.

One day, Kitagawa hears that the poorest of the poor performers, Yamaguchi (Tomokazu Miura) has jumped to his death off the office-building roof. He recalls a secret from his past he has never told anyone. While in high school, he once tried to take a similar dive off the roof of his school. Just as he was about to go over, he noticed a girl standing on the roof railing—a fellow suicide. Before he could stop her, she leapt —and he decided to live. Since then he has been haunted by the thought that she had died to save him. But why?

Kitagawa has little time to wonder or mourn, however; in addition to making his monthly quota, he is fending off bill collectors. Though he lives alone in a studio apartment, he has managed to accumulate ninety million yen in debts. Thuggish collectors are staking out his office building and, when he bumps into two of them on the way out, they give chase. Kitagawa flees upstairs to the roof, where he finds a young clerk (Mayumi Hasegawa) and a middle-aged cleaning lady (Junko Maya) happily playing a game of freeze tag. They ask him to join and he agrees. The sky is blue, the breeze is pleasant and soon he is having the time of his life. But who are these people and what are they doing here? They don't, somehow, seem to belong to this world.

Kokami's office girl and cleaning lady are as pixillated in their own way as Longfellow Deeds with his tuba was in his. But this is urban Japan in the nineties, not Capra's small town America in the thirties—the gap between the world of the roof, with its timeless play, and that of the sales section, with its brutal demands, is so great as to seem unbridgeable.

Yet, as Aozora explains persuasively, context is all. Though people create their own hells, they are not innately bad. Up on the roof, Kitagawa finds a way to live that doesn't require him to lie, cheat and humiliate. He discovers a better, gentler self. This is a Capracornish message, but Kokami delivers it with irony and artistry and without sentimentalizing about the child within or overselling the need to smell the roses (or, in this movie, sunflowers).

Many of his actors are famous faces working for scale, including several network news announcers who play journalists investigating the company's misdeeds. His lead, Hidetaka Yoshioka, displays an edge not always apparent in his other work, including his role as the mildly messed-up nephew in the Tora-san series, but he doesn't persuade as a hustler who undergoes a change of heart. The part seems to cry out for a Japanese Tom Cruise.

Kokami pushes Aozora toward Cocteauesque surrealism, without undermining its essential sweetness and sanity. I wish, though, he hadn't given his angels those big, stagy wings. We already know that they can work their miracles without them. Just give them a bit of free space—and a tin can.

Artful Dodgers
The Artful Dodgers (1998)

Written and directed by Takuo Yasuda. Produced by Wowow and Bandai Visual. With Issei Ishida, Taiji Sato, Hidetoshi Nishijima, Maiko Asano, Hitomi Hayase, Nobuko Okayasu. (96 mins.)

Takuo Yasuda's Artful Dodgers is enough to make one a believer in synchronicity. How else to account for its remarkable similarity to Yoshifumi Hosoya's Sleepy Heads? Both are first-time directorial efforts with cute-but-strange English titles about three young Japanese drop-outs comically adrift in New York. Both sets of heroes hang out at a funky eatery—a Japanese restaurant in Sleepy Heads, a Chinese noo-

dle shop in Artful Dodgers. And in both films one of the heroes meets a Japanese girl who turns his thoughts, predictably, in the direction of home.

The styles of Yasuda and Hosoya are also similar: a gloss of Big Apple funkiness and a dollop of made-in-Japan sweetness. Though their heroes may be hustling in low-rent neighborhoods, the street characters they encounter are amusingly colorful, their stories heart-warming. Trainspotting clones these movies are not. But Sleepy Heads was a TV sitcom transposed to the big screen, whereas Artful Dodgers aims to be more. Underneath its burlesque runs a current of loneliness and futility. The heroes realize that their bohemian adventures in the Land of the Free will not necessarily have a happy ending: that they are losers marking time, with the only out being a plane ticket back home.

They are Hayakawa (Issei Ishida), a sidewalk portrait artist who draws bad Picasso imitations, Kurihara (Taiji Sato), a frizzy-haired guitarist who annoys tourists with interminable solos, and Kotani (Hidetoshi Nishijima), a writer who posts kinky English porno to the Internet under a Russian pen name. The story follows the lives of the heroes for a few days at Christmas time. Hayakawa chats up a Japanese woman and discovers she is his long-lost kindergarten classmate, Saori (Maiko Asano). She is looking for her older sister, who came to New York to study, but has disappeared. Soon after, Kurihara's younger sister (Hitomi Hayase) and her friend (Nobuko Okayasu) visit from Osaka. Kurihara is not overjoyed by this intrusion, but the two girls quickly settle in and take a liking to Kotani, who looks, with his shades and black clothes, the image of the boho writer. Kotani, however, is more interested in an e-mail message from a publisher who wants to meet him.

Though his approach may be picaresque, Yasuda smoothly weaves bits of comic business and flashes of drama into his various story strands. He is better at the smaller scenes, such as the mah-jongg games with the elderly father of the noodle shop proprietor, that serve up droll comedy. In the bigger scenes, he builds tension with devices almost childishly transparent. When the suicidal sister is sitting on a beach, wondering whether to drown herself, Saori and Hayakawa hide in the weeds. When she goes to a cheap motel, presumably to end it all with pills, they take the room next door and wait until morning. What, I wondered, was preventing these would-be saviors from walking up and saying hi?

It is hard, however, to dislike the film's trio of losers. As the guitarist whose instrument seems to be permanently welded to his body, Taiji Sato gives a performance that, with his droopy eyelids, slow grin, and slurry Kansai-dialect patter, is the comic definition of beat. As the writer, Hidetoshi Nishijima alternates between deadpan cool and moments of acting out, to amusing effect. Even Issei Ishida, a spoiled mama's boy on the hustle, has his moments, as when he discovers that his supposedly secure atelier door can be opened by anything resembling a key.

It's too bad, though, that they live only to get by, get on, or as Hayakawa does in the end, get out. As bohemians they lack passion, inspiration, and conviction, however absurd. Dodgers of middle-class dullness back home, they are less artful than clueless.

Ashita
Goodbye for Tomorrow (1995)

Directed by Nobuhiko Obayashi. **Screenplay by** Chiho Katsura. **Produced by** Amuse, BSC, Imagica, and Pride One. **With** Hitoshi Ueki, Toru Minegishi, Yumi Takigawa, Rumi Shiina, Mai Hosho, Ittoku Kishibe, Tomoro Taguchi. (140 mins.)

Nobuhiko Obayashi's *Ashita* is the second installment in his second Onomichi triology. The first trilogy consisted of three *seishun eiga* (youth movies) that he shot in his native town of Onomichi in the 1980s. The second began in 1991 with *Futari*, a sweetly weepy film about a level-headed young woman who returns from the other side to guide her scatterbrained younger sister to a better life. *Ashita*, like *Futari*, is based on a novel by Jiro Akagawa and set in the Onomichi of the present. Once again, Obayashi's theme is love beyond the grave and his approach, gently humanist fantasy overlain with lots of heartwarming sentiment.

The film begins with invitations to an unexpected reunion. Several residents of Onomichi receive messages from deceased loved ones who perished in a ferry disaster three months before to meet them at midnight at the ferry dock. One is an elderly *yakuza* boss (Hitoshi Ueki) who is being hunted by former members of his gang. Another is a middle-aged salaryman (Toru Minegishi) who is carrying on a discreet affair with a young subordinate. Still another is a neurotic housewife (Yumi Takigawa) whose closest confidant was her dead husband's secretary and secret lover. Still another is a swimmer (Rumi Shiina) who set records out of love for her coach, but saw him snatched away before his death by the swim team's scheming manager. Still another is a high-school student (Mai Hosho) who pledged her eternal love to a handsome, hot-tempered classmate but lost him soon after.

These people and several others, including two young women who missed the last ferry, and two

yakuza brothers who want to whack their old boss, are at the ferry rest house at the appointed hour. The death ship arrives on time and the passengers disembark. They look and act as though they had just finished a ferry ride, not spent three months at the bottom of Onomichi harbor. They are, however, all too aware that their time is short; they must return to the ship by the crack of dawn and sink back into their watery graves, this time for good.

Obayashi adroitly juggles his various narratives, but he also annoys with his gimmicks to lighten up the film. One *yakuza* baddie (Ittoku Kishibe, who should know better) spends much of the movie sucking a bad tooth, while his younger brother (Tomoro Taguchi) plucks a jew's harp. I began to wish that they, rather than the passengers, were at the bottom of the harbor. Also, everyone arrives at top speed by a different mode of transportation—bicycle, scooter, minicar, three-wheel truck, and motorboat—creating a vehiclar stampede reminiscent of *It's a Mad, Mad, Mad, Mad World*. And the sweetly-sad pop score covers everything, like treacle.

There are moving moments—how could there not be?—but the characters' dilemmas seemed designed less to explore universal themes than to milk audience tears. Watching the salaryman's agony as he parted from his wife and young daughter—to send them to drown a second time, as it were—I could not help thinking that once had been enough. The Bible, I believe, had it right: "Let the dead bury their dead."

Asian Beat Nihon-hen: I Love Nippon
Asian Beat: I Love Nippon (1991)

Written and directed by Daisuke Tengan. **Series supervision by** Kaizo Hayashi. **Produced by** the Asian Beat Production Project. **With** Masatoshi Nagase, Ruby Moreno, Yukio Yamato, Haruko Wanibuchi. (91 mins.)

Daisuke Tengan's *Asian Beat Nihon-hen: I Love Nippon* is the first of a five-part series under the generic title *Asian Beat*. Supervised by Kaizo Hayashi, the series traces the path of a young Japanese named Tokio (Masatoshi Nagase) through several Asian countries. Each film is by a different Asian director, who continues the story, while adhering to a few ground rules (the first being that no one can kill off Tokio) and relying on his own imagination.

Tengan's first installment develops its Japan-encounters-Asia theme with offbeat humor, surrealistic imagery, and raw storytelling power. His tale of lower-depths love and intrigue in Tokyo is at times overwrought, grotesque, and silly, but it keeps us watching, right to the to-be-continued end.

Tokio is an an assistant to a sleazeball hustler who recruits Asian labor for the dirty, dangerous, and low-paid work that Japanese no longer want to do. Tokio, however, likes his clients and wants to help them. Though not a client, one foreigner that he particularly wants to help is a pretty Filipina named Banana (Ruby Moreno). Banana, he discovers, has a mysterious past and dangerous enemies. One is a flamboyant xenophobe (Yukio Yamato) whose self-imposed mission is to rid Japan of impure Asian elements. Another is a sultry businesswoman (Haruko Wanibuchi) who wants important information that Banana possesses.

What is the information and why is it important? Therein lies the tale—if not the film. While telling his cloak-and-dagger story with considerable energy, Tengan has not made a straight-ahead thriller. He lightens his narrative with buffonish humor and sharpens it with observations gained from interviewing more than one hundred Asian students and workers. I Love Nippon tells home truths about the lives of Asians in Japan, while making a plea for mutual Asian understanding. At times it does this directly; as in a series of interviews with young Asians who relate why they like or dislike Japan.

At other times, however, its way of imparting its message is subtler and more original. While Tokio and Banana make love in his rat's nest of an apartment, he tells her a story about being bitten by a dog as a boy. She replies by reciting passages from the Japanese constitution in Tagalog (subtitles provided). Though this couple would seem to have trouble communicating, the scene works. Ruby Moreno's Banana makes the ringing guarantees of human rights sound like a love poem. Masatoshi Nagase's Tokio may sound self-absorbed as he tells his childhood anecdote (which is reminiscent of Marlon Brando's in Last Tango In Paris), but he responds to his lover's caressing words. When he wakes the next morning, Banana is gone, but she has left a note: "I love Nippon."

Asian Blue:
Ukishima Maru Saikan *
Asian Blue (1995)

Directed by Hiromichi Horikawa. Screenplay by Hisashi Yamauchi. Produced by Cinema Work. With Toru Masuoka, Yuki Yamabe, Kikuko Fujimoto. (111 mins.)

Hiromichi Horikawa's Asian Blue focuses on Koreans brought to Japan to work in forced-labor

brigades during World War II. Assigned the dirtiest, most dangerous jobs in mines and on construction sites, subsisting on starvation rations and enduring beatings from sadistic guards, they were in a hell from which for most the only escape was death. Koreans have kept alive the memory of this wartime servitude—but as scene after scene so compellingly shows, many Japanese have either conveniently forgotten, or in the case of the younger generation, never learned the truth. A former assistant director to Akira Kurosawa who directed his first feature film in 1955, Horikawa has both the historical perspective and personal passion. This is a movie he wants' to be remembered for.

In structure, Asian Blue resembles such recent war films as Gekko no Natsu (Summer of the Moonlight Sonata, 1993) and Senso to Seishun (War and Youth, 1991). In all three the present frames the past, with the older characters serving as teachers to the younger ones, who serve as stand-ins for the presumably younger audience. I don't care for this approach, which smells of chalk dust. Horikawa, however, has largely avoided the sentimentalism that spoiled the other two films. He wants us to see the past whole and clear, both the worst and the best.

The film begins in a Kyoto classroom. An ethnic Korean teacher (Toru Masuoka) asks his seminar students to write a paper examining the fifty postwar years, from the perspective of the 1200th year since Kyoto's founding. The best paper is turned in by Yuko Nishihara (Yuki Yamabe), another ethnic Korean. Her topic is the fatal voyage of the Ukishima Maru, a cargo ship carrying several thousand Koreans back to their homeland shortly after the end of war. When the ship foundered on August 24, 1945 in Maizuru Bay, 549 passengers drowned. Talking with her after class, the teacher learns that he and Yuko share not only a knowledge of a tragedy of which his Japanese students are ignorant, but an interest in Korean poet Hakumo Takazawa. Her interest, however, is more personal; Hakumo was her father, who abandoned the family when Yuko was two and has not been heard from since.

The teacher and Yuko visit Yuko's older sister, Ritsuko (Kikuko Fujimoto), who shows him a wartime journal that her father kept, which describes the sinking of the Ukishima Maru and his life in a Korean labor camp in Aomori Prefecture. Though an unhappy relationship with a Korean man has left Ritsuko wary of things Korean, she agrees to join the teacher and her sister when they propose a quest to find Hakumo and learn the truth about the Ukishima Maru. Why were the Japanese authorities so anxious to get rid of the Koreans before the arrival of the Occupation forces? Why did they ignore the obvious dangers?

Though Hakumo is a fictional character, the *Ukishima Maru* tragedy is a historical fact, surrounded by ambiguity. The film does not resolve that ambiguity, but it does examine, through extended black-and-white flashbacks, what it was like to push a loaded coal cart with a guard's strap thudding against your back; to chant, while fainting with hunger, an oath of allegiance to the country that has enslaved you; to listen to a song from home that makes you fierce with longing. And yes, what it was like to search a line of corpses for a friend, knowing that you tried to save him and failed, knowing that your Japanese masters wanted him and others like him dead, so they could never tell what they had survived and witnessed. But *Asian Blue* tells this painfully well, and now, perhaps, some of us will remember.

Asu Naki Machikado

End of Our Own Real (1997)

Directed by Koji Wakamatsu. Screenplay by Toshiji Maruuchi. Produced by KSS. With Ken Kaneko, Koji Matoba. (95 mins.)

In Koji Wakamatsu's new noir thriller, the usual mix of sex and violence by this former "king of the pinks" is much in evidence, as is a rough affection for the byways of Tokyo's meaner streets. Missing, however, is an truly fresh take on his much-filmed theme of underworld betrayal and revenge. Ever the pro, Wakamatsu has produced an entertainment that should please salarymen looking to chill out with ninety-five minutes of boom-boom and bang-bang, but his approach is more reminiscent of 1977 than 1997.

Tetsuji (Ken Kaneko) operates a screw-making machine in a small machine shop by day, and works as a drug runner for a gangster named Sasaki by night. One day, however, a deal goes wrong, Tetsuji is ripped off, and Sasaki ends up dead. Realizing that he is in over his head, Tetsuji does not try to search for the killers, but the bag man for the buyers—the cold-eyed, hot-tempered Koga (Koji Matoba)—finds him and, thinking that he was in on the job, nearly fillets him with a knife. Tetsuji, however, persuades Koga that he too was a victim and together they search for the gangsters who made off with their drugs and money.

They discover that the thieves were taking orders from Koga's boss—a squat, bulldog-faced extortionist named Murakawa. Enraged, Koga and Tetsuji invade his office and Tetsuji beats Murakawa to a bloody pulp with a tire chain. He survives, however, and his crew declares war on Koga and Tetsuji. With

the heat on, the pair soon learns that each has only the other to depend on.

Wakamatsu's treatment of this tried-and-true materal is all too familiar. He films point-of-view shots with a hand-held camera reminiscent of vintage Godard, while staging quick-draw contests in drug handover scenes recycled from countless TV cop shows. More indicative, however, of his reluctance to move with times is his treatment of the film's women, who serve mainly as objects for displaying the heroes' prowess in bed. The one with the strongest character, Koga's worldly-wise lover, ends by selling him out. The sweetest trap in an unapologetically retro movie.

A Un

Buddies (1989)

Directed by Yasuo Furuhata. Screenplay by Tsutomu Nakamura. Produced by Toho Eiga and Film Face. With Ken Takakura, Eiji Bando, Sumiko Fuji, Yasuko Tomita, Mie Yamamoto, Nobuko Miyamoto. (114 mins.)

A Un refers to the beginning and end of all life—alpha and omega. The paired guardian gods of Buddhist temples and guardian dogs of Shinto shrines express this concept simply: one's mouth is open (*a*), the other's is closed (*un*). In everyday terms, the phrase implies complete understanding between friends and lovers.

Yasuo Furuhata's film of the same title tells the story of a perfect friendship nearly destroyed by a platonic love. The friends—Kadokura (Ken Takakura) and Miyata (Eiji Bando)—are old army buddies. Kadokura is the president of a small company, Miyata, a struggling company employee. The lovers are Katakura and Tami (Sumiko Fuji), Miyata's wife. Theirs, however, is a very Japanese type of love, with no caresses, kisses, or declarations. Even so, it gradually becomes obvious to those around them, including Miyata and Satoko (Yasuko Tomita), his eighteen-year-old daughter. This awareness places a subtle strain on the two men's friendship and on Miyata's marriage. When Miyata seeks consolation in the company of a young geisha (Mie Yamamoto), Kadokura becomes concerned that this affair might hurt Tami and tries to end it by winning the geisha for himself. His interference, understandably, does not please Miyata. The two men speak about the unspeakable: Kadokura's relationship to Tami.

Based on a novel by Kuniko Mukoda, the film bears a family resemblance to light-comic TV dramas in which everyone is frantically trying to prove how warmhearted they are. In fact, Mukoda, who died shortly after *A Un*'s publication in 1981, often wrote for television, and the novel was dramatized as a nine-part series on NHK.

The film is set in the Tokyo of 1937,· when Japanese armies were marching in triumph across China and militarists were tightening their hold on the government. *A Un*, however, bathes this dark time in the amber glow of nostalgia. The film is filled with references to a simpler, purer Japan. Whenever the characters walk out the door they run across a reminder of the good old days: a *kami shibai* (picture-card show) man entertaining the neighborhood children or a sweet-potato vendor hawking his wares with his very own voice instead of a taped spiel. The interior of the Miyata's house, where much of the action takes place, is like a folk museum where every detail of a bygone day has been carefully recreated, minus the dirt and stench and noise. Living in this best of all possible Japanese worlds, everyone is so filled with fellow-feeling that they bubble over, like mugging actors in a soft-drink commercial.

This Panglossian existence has to end, of course, or there wouldn't be a movie. But the serpent in the Garden—the affair between Kadokura and Tami—is a nonstarter. In fact, all the leading characters—with the lonely exception of Kadokura's whining wife (Nobuko Miyamoto)—fall in love, but no one does much of anything with anyone. One exception is Satoko, whose boyfriend (Kurando Maki) plants one shy kiss on her lips before he is hauled off for interrogation by the secret police.

This traditional Japanese reticence wouldn't matter if we could sense the fires burning beneath the smiling surfaces. But Kadokura is a decent sort, and Tami seemingly desires nothing more than a friendly flirtation. The dramatic focus of the film is not this tepid romance, but the fiery breakup of Kadokura and Miyata's friendship. From his Mr. Nice Guy routine, Takakura suddenly reverts to tough-guy type, while Bando, the heart-of-gold hubby, transforms into a feisty little fighter. In other words, they drop the buddy-buddy front and reveal their not-so-nice true feelings.

The film is billed, however, as the reunion of Takakura and Fuji, who made thirty-four *yakuza* films together for Toei before Fuji's retirement in 1972. In *A Un* Takakura projects a boyish charm oddly reminiscent of Gene Kelly: you almost expect him to cut a few *Singing In The Rain* steps as he ambles down the street. Fuji is clearly enjoying her comeback, but seems slightly above it all: she enjoys the antics of the men in her life, but refuses to take them too seriously.

That is perhaps the best way to enjoy *A Un*: not as a searing study of human emotions, but as a nice, long soak in the tub of Japanese nostalgia.

Autobike Shojo *

The Motorbike Girl (1994)

Directed by Morio Agata. **Screenplay by** Morio Agata, Jin Yamamoto, and Oji Suzuki. **Cinematography by** Tetsuya Nagata. **Produced by** Garo Cinema, Seirindo, and Tsuaito. With Natsuo Ishido, Morio Agata. (78 mins.)

Morio Agata's *Autobike Shojo* tells the simplest of stories. One day seventeen-year-old Minoru (Natsuo Ishido) decides to find her father, who left home when she was still a baby and never returned. With her mother's blessing, she travels from Tokyo to Hokkaido on an old motorbike. She finds her father, who is a *manga* artist, with a new family and a new life. There is a reunion, with the expected awkwardness and recrimination and attempt at reconciliation. There is a parting—and that's the movie.

The theme of a child's search for a missing parent is a TV-drama staple, usually climaxing in tearjerking bathos. I thus went to *Autobike Shojo* with some trepidation, but I left it with it admiration. Director Morio Agata, who is known primarily as a musician and actor, and who released his first feature film, *Boku wa Tenshi ja Nai yo* (I'm Not an Angel) in 1974, sells us no cheap tears; instead, he has made a film that is stylishly bold, lyrically moving. The film's form at times overwhelm its substance—I found myself paying more attention to the lighting than the actors' lines—but *Autobike Shojo* never loses it firm, quiet hold on the emotions. This, I felt, is the way these situations so often play out in real life: with a mixture of expectation and disappointment, anger and acceptance.

As portrayed by newcomer Natsuo Ishido, Minoru has the looks and attitude of a real adolescent in full rebellion against the adult world: short, chopped hair, leather jacket and jeans, a poker face whose expression might be variously interpreted as sullen, wary, or shy. But there is something special about Ishido as well; an intensity and sensitivity that illuminates every scene.

Agata, who co-wrote the script with Jin Yamamoto and Oji Suzuki, based on a Suzuki *manga* that first appeared in *Garo* magazine in 1973, makes extensive use of unorthodox camera angles and editing rhythms and varies the visual texture of his shots. We see characters cut off in mid-emotion or hear them speaking to each other as disembodied voices. One moment, the colors look a shade off, as though we have been suddenly transported to an alien planet at the crack of a hung-over dawn. The next, they transform into bright, primary reds and blues that make everything look fresh and new. The effect is to make us see the world through Minoru's emotions.

Though a series of brief encounters—with an old man by the sea, a young woman in a photo gallery, a boorish truck driver, a handsome young projectionist, and an eccentric middle-aged man with a literal surprise up every sleeve—Minoru gradually comes out of her girl-on-a-mission shell as she experiences the small shocks and revelations that subtlely prepare her and us for the biggest of all—her first meeting with her father.

As played by Agata, he is a shadowy figure, appearing out of the mists of the past as a stranger with an uncertain smile. He wants to be Minoru's friend, but he cannot be her father again. He can remember and try to make amends, but he can't go back. Minoru can't accept this. To her he is a betrayer, making lame excuses for his misdeeds. He has a new home and she is not a part of it.

There is an ache at the center of *Autobike Shojo* that has nothing to do with usual movie sentimentality, everything to do with growing up. There is also an awareness of the strangeness and beauty of the world that is peculiar to adolescence. Agata derives some of his cinematic sensibility from Fellini; he has the same taste for the comically bizarre, the same knack for blurring the boundaries between fantasy and reality. He has also brought something of his own to *Autobike Shojo*—a vivid sense of what is it like to be young, alone, and unbearably alive to the never-ending process of growth and loss.

Avec Mon Mari
2 X 2 [1999]

Written and directed by Kentaro Otani. **Produced by** Muro Kiichi Office. **With** Hirofumi Kobayashi, Yuka Itaya, Kaori Tsuji, Ren Osugi. (95 mins.)

Japanese cinema, it can be safely said, isn't known for talky, sophisticated romantic dramas. French cinema is, however—thus the title of Kentaro Otani's feature debut, *Avec Mon Mari*, makes eminent sense. Otani's handling of his subject—a sexual quadrangle that threatens two relationships—displays an ironic intelligence and formal structure more Left Bank than East Shinjuku. It illustrates the French proverb that, in any love affair, there is one who kisses, and one who offers the cheek.

Otani labored for nearly five years to bring *Avec Mon Mari* to the screen, rewriting the script again and again. The result is a richness of observation and shapeliness of form that rarely intrudes into the natural-seeming flow of the characters' talk. This is a film that we watch with a smile of complicity and anticipation, feeling as though we have

been taken into the director's confidence and waiting to savor the next brillantly understated comic bit. So many movies talk down—*Avec Mon Mari* includes us in the conversation as equals. It's a nice feeling.

Shot in 16mm with only the four principals in most of the scenes, *Avec Mon Mari* has the look of a bare-bones indie production. But Otani and cinematographer Kazuhiro Suzuki keep the many long scenes from degenerating into static stage drama, without resorting to the flashy busyness that many younger directors use to prove their cinematic cool. Also, the film uses only natural sound, a welcome change from the J-Pop soundtracks percolating away through so many films by younger Japanese directors. Silence, Otani proves, can be golden.

Tamotsu (Hirofumi Kobayashi), a freelance photographer, comes to the office where his wife Mitsuko (Yuka Ihaya) works as a magazine editor to beg her not to file for divorce. But Mitsuko is convinced that Tamotsu is cheating on her with Mayu (Kaori Tsuji)—a pouty minx who works as a model and is the lover of her boss, a middled-aged art director named Nakazaki (Ren Osugi). Tamotsu, who has played the home-loving wife in this relationship, insists that Mayu is merely a friend. Mitsuko has been so busy with her work that he felt, well, lonely. This classic complaint of the neglected housewife cuts no ice with Mitsuko— she gives him the heave-ho. With hardly a yen to his name, Tamotsu heads for Mayu's place.

Mayu assures him that Nakazaki seldom makes an appearance, but the older man finds out about her new roomate after overhearing a conversation between Mayu and Mitsuko. But Nakazaki is, like Tamotsu, the weaker of the partners in the relationship. Worried that Tamotsu may be getting more than a sympathetic ear, but unwilling to risk a confrontation, he decides to bring the separated couple back together. Mitsuko is unwilling to make the first move, but Nakazaki senses that she still carries a torch for her soon-to-be ex. He invites Tamotsu to his villa in Kamakura for a heart-to-heart and, when he arrives, leads him to the garden where Mitsuko is sitting. This attempt at re-matchmaking backfires, however, when Mayu makes an unexpected entrance and declares that she likes Tamotsu—not only as a friend—and Mitsuko reveals similar feelings for Nakazaki.

Otani's dialogue sounds as though he simply flipped on a tape recorder to record his actors' improvisations, but it gets the requisite laughs, while revealing character layer by layer. Also, his story, which starts as free-spiritedly as Mayu's wild-on-top hairdo, begins to fall into place with the logic and order of the garden at Versailles.

A fashion model making her screen debut, Yuka Itaya is particularly good as the acerbic Mitsuko. By the end she has convinced us that poor Tamotsu's trials and tribulations were worth it. Playing the sly, slinky, disconcertingly honest Mayu, Kaori Tsuji supplies most of the erotic steam that drives the narrative forward. As the two hapless men, Hirofumi Kobayashi and Ren Osugi provide most of the comedy. Osugi clowns a bit too strenuously playing the sexually insecure older man, but not enough to damage the film—the finest character study and the truest examination of the power balance between the sexes in today's Japan I have seen all year.

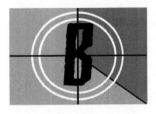

Bakayaro! 2: Shiawase ni Naritai
Bakayaro! 2 (1989)

Directed by Masahiro Honda, Gen Suzuki, Ryo Iwamatsu, and Yusuke Narita. Executive production and screenplay by Yoshimitsu Morita. Produced by Kowa International. With Nenji Kobayashi, Shin'ichi Tsutsumi, Ikuya Fujii, Keiko Oginome, Kuniko Yamada. (98 mins.)

"Don't Worry, Be Happy" says the song. But sometimes happiness is turning the air a bright shade of blue. We Westerners think we know how to do this and pity (or admire) the Japanese for their relative lack of expletives. Some Japanese words, of course, do pack a punch or invite one, including *bakayaro*, which the *Kenkyusha Japanese-English Dictionary* defines as "a fool; an idiot; a simpleton; a goose." It is also the title of Yoshimitsu Morita's latest film, *Bakayaro! 2: Shiawase ni Naritai*.

Like its 1988 predecessor, *Bakayaro! 2* is a comic anthology in which each segment ends with the main character shouting the title word. As executive producer and scriptwriter, Morita has imposed a unity of outlook and approach: the four segments make a movie, not a grab bag. *Bakayaro! 2* is the latest in a by-now long series of Japanese black comedies dealing with topical social issues. Morita, who popularized this genre with *Kazoku Game* (Family Game) in 1983, is once again humanizing the headlines by showing ordinary people acting in extraordinary

ways. *Bakayaro* is the cry of nails who refuse to be pounded down.

In the first segment, a travel agent (Nenji Kobayashi) spends his Sundays apologizing to irate clients for various foul-ups and to his family for never taking them anywhere. Downing bottles of pep tonic to maintain his workaholic pace, Kobayashi comes up with an ideal plan to get his wife and daughter off his back: a seven-day summer trip to New Caledonia. His boss, however, has other ideas. Director Masahiro Honda paces his sketch deliberately—the first laugh is a long time coming—but the final cathartic scene is explosively hilarious, with emphasis on "explosively."

The second segment by Gen Suzuki turns sharply towards the surreal. A young night clerk (Shinichi Tsutsumi) at a convenience store spends his days fending off weirdos, dining on leftover *oden* stew, and watching porno videos. Then a beautiful girl walks into the store and he sees a way out. In his overheated imagination, however, his new love joins the weirdos, and the store erupts in a wild uprising against authority. The source for this foolery is obviously the harem scene in *8 1/2*, but Suzuki welds his own quirky vision to basic Fellini. The neighborhood 7-11 will never look the same again.

The third segment also hits close to home. Two young newlyweds (Ikuya Fujii and Keiko Oginome) move into a new condo. They are giddy with happiness—they trade high fives as they do the housework—but their bubble soon bursts. Their neighbor, an audio nut, informs them that their broken-down stereo is a museum piece, their noisy washing machine a public nuisance. Embarrassed and determined to join the late twentieth century, they journey to Akihabara. They find, however, that the leading edge is a slippery place to be. After a series of disastrous encounters with high-tech gadgetry, the bridegroom shouts his *bakayaro* from the heart. His balcony monologue—a cry of protest against the electronic flood that engulfs us—is the film's most moving (and funniest) moment.

Yusuke Narita's segment deals with the film's biggest issue: sex and age discrimination. Rie Sema (Kuniko Yamada) is a twenty-six-year-old career woman who feels that life is passing her by. She quits her job, leaves her boyfriend, and returns to her home in the countryside. Her mother urges her to get married, and bored personnel managers at local companies tell her to go back to Tokyo. She takes the latter advice, but soon finds that as far as the men in her life are concerned, she is a Christmas cake on December 26—i.e., past her romantic expiration date. A popular TV comedian, Kuniko Yamada has been guilty of much idiocy, but in this segment she is a powerful presence. Her last scene—in which she verbally pounds a quintet of male chauvinists into submission—makes most Hollywood movies with feminist themes look timid by comparison. *Bakayaro*, indeed.

Beautiful Sunday
(1998)

Written and directed by Tetsuya Nakajima. Produced by Fat, Inc. With Masatoshi Nagase, Momoko Bito, Kumi Nakamura, Noriko Nagi, Kyoko Endo, Mamako Yoneyama, Teruyuki Kagawa, Matsuo Bannai, Reika Matsumoto, Kishibe Ittoku. (93 mins.)

The title of Tetsuya Nakajima's *Beautiful Sunday* is ironic. In the program notes, Nakajima says "I hate the optimistic view that 'Sunday is fun.'" In this film he sets out to show exactly how miserable that day can be.

Like *Grand Hotel*, his film weaves together the stories of strangers who happen to find themselves under the same roof, in this case a condo somewhere in Tokyo. But rather than entertain with the glamorous weariness of Greta Garbo or the sexy neediness of Joan Crawford, Nakajima has produced the blankest of black comedies, pounding across his theme—the emptiness of modern Japanese lives—like a mime spending the afternoon trying to escape a glass box.

This is not a new theme for Nakajima: his 1997 *Natsu Jikan no Otonatachi* (Happy-Go-Lucky) focused on a family whose father and mother were emotionally arrested nullities. But *Beautiful Sunday* is drier, sparer, grimmer. The outsider boy hero of *Natsu* could at least hope to grow up and escape his dismal school and family. The protagonists of *Beautiful Sunday*, however, have little to look forward to but the bluest of Mondays.

The film relates a series of incidents in which the characters impinge on each other, often with all the emotional impact of electrons in a supercollider. A dulled-out young couple (Masatoshi Nagase and Momoko Bito) try to play a game of catch, but are thwarted by a series of accidents and interruptions. Finally, a missed ball chips paint from a parked Porsche and its enraged owner (Matsuo Bannai) jumps behind the wheel and chases them with murderous intent.

Meanwhile, a half-Japanese, half-black girl (Reika Matsumoto), whose flaky mother (Kyoko Endo) is a fervent fan of actor Masaki Kyomoto, grinds away at the books and firmly ignores the ruckus being made by the adults around her. But her Sunday is ruined when a gang of neighborhood girls chase her and, later, lock her into the bathroom at the cram school she attends.

There are other odd birds in this condo from hell, including a creepy artist (Kumi Nakamura) who tries to seduce the husband in 102 by showing him a studio filled with her own self-portraits; an elderly lady (Mamako Yoneyama) who screams her head off every day at noon in order to affirm her own existence; and a narcissist (Noriko Nagi) who stares at the mirror in her darkened room, when she isn't peeking out the window at a stalker (Kishibe Ittoku).

A decade ago, when he was filming an installment in the *Bakayaro!* series for producer Yoshimitsu Morita, Nakajima might have injected this downbeat material with real laughs, as well as real insights into the moral and spiritual wasteland of present-day Japan. *Beautiful Sunday*, however, plays like bad Takeshi Kitano, including the immobile camera, the affectless acting, the flat narrative, and flashes of droll whimsy in the nihilistic gloom. I got the point ten minutes into the movie, but an hour later Nakajima was still whacking away at the same angle, with the same force.

There is much talent in the movie, most of it wasted. The one bright spot was Reika Matsumoto as the pint-sized grind. Determined to prevail in a hostile world, she glows with a fierce light. Perhaps next time out, Nakajima ought to concentrate on kids, whom he seems to genuinely like and understand, and leave the enervated, eccentric adults to Kitano and his followers. Then we might have a wonderful follow-up to a tiresome *Beautiful Sunday*.

Billiken
(1996)

Written and directed by Junji Sakamoto. Produced by Billiken Production Committee. With Tetsuta Sugimoto, Ryutaro Gan, Tomoko Yamaguchi. (100 mins).

Japan loves to imports fads and fashions from the West. What not everyone realizes, however, is how old some of those borrowed fads and fashions are, and how Japanized they have become. One example is a long-forgotten American fad of 1908, the "billiken": a seated figure that, with its pot belly, pointed head, and smug grin, is a fatter, more decadent cousin of the kewpie doll, with its slanted eyes suggesting a touch of Oriental exoticism. The billiken quickly won popularity in Japan, where he was regarded as a Western version of Ebisu, the god of wealth and good fortune.

It is in this Japanized incarnation that he appears in Junji Sakamoto's comic fantasy, *Billiken*. Once the reigning deity of Tsutenkaku Tower, an Osaka landmark, the film's billiken was long ago relegated to a packing crate in an abandoned stairwell. One night a tower employee falls down the stairs and smashes the crate to pieces.

The billiken's spirit (Tetsuta Sugimoto) is at first ecstatic at regaining his freedom. Standing at the top of the tower, he proclaims that he is "the god who brings happiness to everyone in the world." He is soon baffled, though, by the changes the decades have wrought. Hardly anyone believes in him anymore! Luckily, he still has magic powers, including the ability to become invisible. He is not an all-powerful miracle worker, however. When his first client, a *yakuza* who wants to quit the life to please his girlfriend, asks him to reattach a severed little finger, the billiken grants his request, but gets the pinky on backwards. He has better luck with an wizened collector of cardboard cartons who prays for his horse to win at the racetrack. Slapping the chosen nag to victory, the billiken earns his first convert, and when the word gets around, he soon becomes the tower's star attraction.

In struggling to grant everyone's wishes, however, he runs himself ragged, until he requires the services of a blind masseur for his aching muscles. When some of his good deeds backfire, believers quickly become apostates. Worst of all is a yuppie businessman (Ryutaro Gan), who is campaigning to bring the Olympics to Osaka. The tower, he insists, has to go—it will interfere with media helicopters. But if the tower disappears, so will the billiken's powers. How can he and his beloved Tsutenkaku survive in late twentieth-century Japan, with its anything-for-a-yen ethic?

An Osaka native whose three previous films were all set in Japan's second city, Junji Sakamoto makes Tsutenkaku Tower a central character. Old and dowdy perhaps, but possessing an air of mystery (as emphasized in vertiginous traveling shots through the tower's darker nooks) and even grandeur (as evoked in sweeping helicopter shots of its heights). Also, while Sakamoto may be grabbing for laughs, his depiction of a supernatural Good Samaritan makes a larger statement about the limited ability of even the best-intentioned of gods to satisfy the never-ending litany of human wants and needs.

Sakamoto, who also wrote the script, tells the subplot of the yuppie businessman's shenanigans with fisticuffs and other rough stuff that seem to belong in one of Sakamoto's boxing films, not the story of a supposed smooth operator. Also, the character of a spunky young daycare worker (Tomoko Yamaguchi) may be intended as a love interest for the hero, but she is more decorative than essential. The billiken, after all, is the embodiment of a spiritual yearning, not a man trying, and failing, to play God. He can help, but not humanly connect.

Even so, I couldn't help liking *Billiken*'s kinder, gentler view of the otherworldly. If all our gods, East and West, were as eager to please, perhaps we would be closer to Sakamoto's vision of a warmly human Osakan paradise in which wishes, even silly ones, can come true.

Black Jack
(1996)

Directed by Osamu Dezaki. **Screenplay by** Osamu Dezaki and Eto Mori. **Produced by** Shochiku and Tezuka Productions. (94 mins.)

Osamu Tezuka is revered by Japanese comics fans as the father of modern Japanese *manga*. One of the most enduringly popular of Osamu Tezuka's creations was *Black Jack*, whose scar-faced hero, with his two-toned shock of white and black hair, embodied the duality that Tezuka was so fond of exploring. A crack surgeon who never bothered to get a medical license, an unapologetic exploiter of his rich patients who disdained their materialism, Black Jack was an enigma wrapped in a flowing cape. An outcast hero in the romantic mold, he was the product of an unromantic age whose only faith was in science and technology, whose only gods were money and power.

After Tezuka's death in 1989, *Black Jack* survived in paperback collections, TV programs and straight-to-video *anime*. Oddly, no one ever thought to produce a full-length feature until Shochiku decided to get into the animation business with the film under review. Directed by Tezuka disciple Osamu Dezaki, *Black Jack* updates Tezuka's masterwork for the nineties. The Black Jack of character designer Akio Sugino has a bigger, rounder look than Tezuka's hero, as though he's been bulking up and buffing his bod at the gym. Though his wardrobe is the same, right down to the cape, he wears it with more macho drama, as though he's been working on his attitude as well as his pecs.

The story has a ripped-from-the-headlines flavor, while remaining true to Tezuka's central concerns, including the dangers of technology. During the 1996 Olympics, several athletes break records with stunning performances, until commentators begin calling them a "super race." Meanwhile, Black Jack gets a frantic call from the parents of a girl he'd successfully treated several years ago—she is sinking fast, for no apparent reason. Even Black Jack cannot work a miracle in this case. After the girl's death he finds that she has the body of a ninety-year old. He also learns that she became an artistic prodigy, whose paintings were fought over by gallery owners.

Soon after, he is approached by Jo Carol Braine, the beautiful, coldly brilliant administrator of the St.

Joel Research Center. She wants Black Jack to treat patients suffering from a mysterious illness called the Moira Syndrome. When he refuses, she has his pint-sized girl assistant, Pinoko, kidnaped. Momentarily under her power, Black Jack goes to the Center, where he finds members of the so-called "super race" dying the same horrible deaths as the young artist. What, he wonders, is the connection between the unusual talents these patients possess and the disease that is killing them?

Dezaki strives for a baroque efflorescence, as when the patients begin to deliquesce in agonizing slow motion and grotesque detail, but his film is the usual budget-driven compromise between *manga* and full animation. Some of the film's most striking moments, in fact, are when motion stops entirely and, in a freeze frame, we clearly see Dezaki's vision of the technological terrors waiting for us in the next millenia.

The story is dense with pseudomedical jargon and ripe with pseudointellectual significance. Nonetheless, it works well enough as medical melodrama and dark utopian fantasy, keeping us in suspense about the true nature of the Moira Syndrome, while giving us an intricately imagined look at a future that seems, in its view of human beings as another manipulatable biological material, depressingly possible. Also, Black Jack, with his loner-genius swagger and cool, is a memorable pop-culture icon.

For non-Japanese viewers, another point of interest is the depiction of the numerous foreign characters. The Westerners tend to be long in the leg and big in the nose, but the film does not regard their otherness as either outlandish or absurd. In the world of *Black Jack*, if not in real Japanese life, all men are created (and at times recreated) equal.

Boku ga Byoki ni Natta Wake
The Reason I Got Sick (1991)
Directed by Kazuki Omori, Shoji Kogami, and Takayoshi Watanabe. Screenplay by Akira Nagai and Kazuki Omori. Produced by Cinema Hauto and Suntory. With Ginnosuke Higashi, Masanobu Katsumura, Yuko Natori, Lasalle Ishii, Makoto Otake, Anna Nakagawa. (101 mins.)

Cancer, diabetes, high blood-pressure—hardly laughing matters. But taking the Big Three adult diseases as their theme, three young Japanese directors have fashioned a sardonically funny and informative comedy with dialogue that could play on an NHK medical information show

One reason for the laughs is the deft juxtaposition of the serious and the absurd. A straight talk on diabetes, complete with a chart, becomes funny when delivered in perfect, mellifluous Japanese by an elderly Caucasian gent (Ginnosuke Higashi) wearing a baseball uniform and sitting in the Tokyo Dome broadcasting booth. We laugh at not only the odd setting and the presenter's deadpan delivery, but his violation of a movie taboo: one doesn't lecture on diabetes in a movie (or a broadcasting booth, for that matter). But we find ourselves reveling in the hypochondria of it all. Diabetes, after all, is high on the list of prizes in the mortality sweepstakes. Kazuki Omori, the director of this segment, and scriptwriter Akira Nagai, a former physician, is hitting the audience, especially the older members of it, where it lives.

Another top prize is cancer, the subject of the first segment, directed by Shoji Kogami. A young man (Masanobu Katsumura) bursts into the office of a securities company flourishing a shotgun. Claiming that he has colon cancer, he demands a rare and expensive drug and says he will hold the employees hostage until he gets it. The police soon arrive at the scene, as do doctors from a nearby hospital, who try to convince him that he has a touch of constipation, not the Big C. Frantic, he refuses to listen. In addition to a gun, he has come prepared with X-rays, test results, and a family medical encyclopedia. In the ensuing confrontation, the segment poses telling questions about the vagaries of cancer diagnosis and the ignorance-is-bliss school of Japanese medicine. It goes over the top, however, until it resembles a television skit in which smirking comedians bop each other with polyurethane clubs.

In the second segment, a newscaster (Yuko Natori) is unceremoniously dumped by her fiancee, the spoiled son of a company president. She is a borderline diabetic and thus unfit to bear his heirs (Higashi, in the guise of "Dr. Langerhans," appears to assure us that diabetic mothers can give birth to healthy babies). Depressed, she binges on sweets, until she is rescued by a TV-director friend (Lasalle Ishii) who gets her a job hosting a TV food show. The resulting conflict between the ratings and the heroine's blood sugar level is painful to watch, but director Kazuki Omori adroitly lightens this material with running gags and a comic story of tabloid-crossed love.

The strongest segment is the last: director Takayoshi Watanabe's tale of a man (Makoto Otake) on his way to his daughter's wedding, and a young cellist (Anna Nakagawa) on her way to an audition who end up in the same bedroom—and at each other's throats. The situation is a direct (and acknowledged) steal of *It Happened One Night*, but Otake and Nakagawa's version of it is as funny as it is different. Otake is a hypochondriac who bears his high blood-pressure like a cross, while Nakagawa tries to take this self-imposed weight off his shoulders. ("High blood-pressure is all in your head!" she shouts.) Otake has the born-to-worry face of a natural comedian, Nakagawa, the right combination of comic energy and slinky sexuality. Together they bring *Boku ga Byoki* to a rousingly hilarious finish. The film sends you out of the theater smiling—and anxious to schedule that checkup you've been putting off.

Bokura wa Minna Ikiteiru
We Are Not Alone (1993)

Directed by Yojiro Takita. Screenplay by Nobuyuki Isshiki. Produced by Shochiku. With Hiroyuki Sanada, Tsutomu Yamazaki, Ittoku Kishibe, Kyusaku Shimada, Bengal. (115 mins.)

The salaryman comedy is an established genre, yet despite the legions of salarymen who have traveled to every corner of the earth, name cards in hand, few movies have comically chronicled their adventures abroad. The experience of scriptwriter Nobuyuki Isshiki and director Yojiro Takita in filming *Bokura wa Minna Ikiteiru* helps explain why—it took them nearly six years to make their tale of four salarymen caught up by a coup d'état in a fictional Southeast Asian country. As Isshiki admitted in an interview, it was a "dangerous, difficult, and expensive" undertaking. Was it worth spending seventy-five days and untold millions of yen on location in Thailand, battling heat, creepy-crawlies, and Bangkok traffic jams? Unfortunately, what should have been a romp in the rain forest becomes a long slog through an improbable war zone.

Bokura starts off with that old cross-cultural standby: the education of an innocent abroad. Takahashi (Hiroyuki Sanada), an engineer for a big Tokyo construction company, is dispatched for a five-day business trip to Tarckistan, a Southeast Asian governed by a corrupt military and mired in poverty. Bright, cocky, dressed for success, Takahashi is entranced and appalled by the colorful crowds, child beggars, and rumbling tanks he sees from the window of the local branch-manager's Mercedes Benz. The manager, Nakaido (Tsutomu Yamazaki), is a flamboyantly decadent character from a Hunter S. Thompson novel, living in semicolonial splendor together with three nubile native maids. But Takahashi's initial fascination with the country and the lifestyle soon gives way to annoyance and disgust. The water is undrinkable, the phones don't work, and as a final blow his Walkman is stolen, probably by one of the maids. What a hellhole! None of this would ever happen in Japan!

Takahashi's construction company is bidding for a large contract, and their main competitor is also Japanese, represented by the smarmy Tomita (Ittoku Kishibe) and the lanky, bearded Masumoto (Kyusaku Shimada). A former elite salaryman, Tomita was exiled to Tarckistan after becoming involved in a bribery scandal, while Masumoto is a gone-native individualist who has actually bothered to learn the local language. The scenes of the four rivals competing cravenly for the favor of the beribboned colonel who runs the country have a Graham Greene-ish flavor: bitter, but pungent.

Then a shell explodes at the colonel's garden party and, instead of gunning for a contract, the four salarymen are running for their lives as government and rebel forces fight it out in the streets. Takita wants to give us a real war, with blood and bodies flying through the air, but he also wants us to laugh at his heroes' frantic dash for the safety of the airport and dear old Nippon.

The result is a mishmash. The battle scenes are amateurish and phony, and the attempts at comedy are strained and unfunny. The gag of the salaryman waving their passports and business cards to escape a firefight might have worked in a *Duck Soup* kind of war, but not after we have just seen a poor salaryman, driven around the bend by his company's order to stay another two years in country, take a round in the forehead. Once the four salarymen are in the jungle the film descends to lame slapstick, tired male-bonding sequences, and clichéd action. As three of them ride to the rescue of Nakaido, who has been captured by the rebels as a government spy, we count up all the Hollywood movies *Bokura* has ripped off and reflect that Sylvester Stallone did this kind of thing better.

Then Sanada, a fine comic actor, delivers an amusing and enlightening defense of the salaryman ethic to the rebel leader and momentarily raises the film to its earlier heights. Despite his limitations and absurdities, Sanada shows us that the salaryman is also a human being who wants his sacrifice to have meaning and be recognized. On his knees before his colleague's captor, begging for his friend's release, Sanada's salaryman acquires an undeniable nobility. He saves Nakaido, of course. The film, however, is beyond help.

Bokuto Kidan *
The Strange Tale of Oyuki (1992)

Written and directed by Kaneto Shindo. Produced by ATG and Kindai Eiga Kyokai. With Masahiko Tsugawa, Yuki Sumita, Haruko Sugimura. (112 mins.)

Directors can love writers to death. The usual murder method is literalism; transferring the master's works directly from the printed page to the screen. The revered prose rolls off the silken tongue of a narrator, the beloved dialogue flows from the mouths of talented actors, but the audience is restive. The words of Joyce, Fitzgerald, or Dostoevsky don't play as well on the screen as they read on the page. They sound—how fatal the word! — *literary*. That is the greatest of cinematic sins, and the film usually pays the price: box office oblivion.

Bokuto Kidan, based on Nagai Kafu's book of the same title about his affairs with women of the demimonde and his love for a prostitute named Oyuki, is not free of that sin. Director Kaneto Shindo, who first read the book as a newspaper serial in the *Asahi Shimbun* in 1937 and spent eight years writing the script, makes abundant use of Kafu's own prose, which is unapologetically literary.

But the voice behind it—urbane, ironic, elegiac—is that of Kafu himself and the story it tells is very much his own. The film has the episodic structure of the book. Kafu was a diarist and autobiographer first, a novelist second. Instead of building fictional monuments, his talent was for recording the personal, the private, the fleetingly quotidian. *Bokuto* reflects Kafu's personality and work; instead of an intricately constructed plot, it gives us episodes from Kafu's life—primarily his erotic adventures.

As Kafu, Masahiko Tsugawa subsumes his highly distinctive and acidly funny screen persona into the character of Kafu. Instead of a standard Tsugawa turn, he delivers a finely shaded impersonation. Whether or not it is an accurate one, I have no idea, but Tsugawa's Kafu fits the story and the prose quite well. A sensual, Westernized man of the city, who haunts Ginza cafes and patronizes Yoshiwara fleshpots, he has a very Japanese awareness of the transient nature of his pleasures and a very human regret for their passing. Something of a rogue, who goes from woman to woman with an unflagging energy and unapologetic amorality, he is also something of a saint, who treats all of his lovers, even the ones he has paid for, with an unwavering gentleness and respect.

Kafu remains ever the bachelor and artist; women may enter his life, but they never penetrate the inner reaches of his stubbornly idealistic heart. He wants the right woman, or none at all. Then, one rainy night, walking through the narrow streets of a low-rent redlight district, he meets Oyuki. Played by newcomer Yuki Sumita, Oyuki is a willowy, languidly sensuous whore. But though she is good at the game—regulars flock to the house she shares with her "mother" (Haruko Sugimura)—she is not a hard case. Like the others, Kafu is attracted by her beauty, but as the years pass and their relationship deeps, he discovers the honesty and affection of the woman beneath the white-powdered mask. She is the ideal he has long been searching for.

This story may sound hackneyed—the jaded sophisticate who falls for the pure-hearted whore—but Tsugawa and Sumita keep it firmly grounded in emotional truth. We believe in their relationship, in all its slow-burning passion and lingering poignancy. Though an unabashedly erotic film, *Bokuto Kidan* does not deny the sadness of the sensual. In his fifties when he meets Oyuki, Kafu is still young enough to please her, but he knows he is taking a last fling—that with every passing year he is slipping farther down the path to a lonely old age. Yet he refuses to cling and play the fool (He is not the professor in *The Blue Angel*). At the end, we respect his decision, even as we regret its price. *Bokuto Kidan* is faithful to not only Kafu's words, but his spirit, which is of a sort quickly vanishing from our on-line, bottom-line world. I am glad to have a film that embodies it so well.

Boku wa Benkyo ga Dekinai
I Can't Study (1996)

Directed by Yasuhiko Yamamoto. **Screenplay by** Rika Nakase. **Produced by** Amuse, Fuji TV, and Tsutaya Group. With Jun Toda, Shinobu Sato. (105 mins.)

Movies can shock us into new ways of seeing. Jack Nicholson's comment that *Ferris Bueller's Day Off* made him "feel 119 years old" and "totally irrelevant to anything an audience might want" was a reaction not so much to the film itself as to its teenage hero. The incredibly glib and cocky kid played by Matthew Broderick may have been hilarious to his age mates—the film was a big hit—but to Nicholson he seemed utterly alien. (He and I) had never gone to high school with anyone like that.

My reaction to Yasuhiko Yamamoto's debut feature, *Boku wa Benkyo ga Dekinai* was similar. For an oldie, I have seen quite a few Japanese youth movies, but never one with a youth quite like Jun Toda's Hidemi Tokita. Am I simply out of touch, or is Yamamoto spinning an upscale fantasy—a Japanese version of *Beverly Hills 90210*?

A second-year student at a private high school, Hidemi rejects the pressures to study and get ahead. When the nerdy class president tells him that students who don't go on to college "will never become worthwhile people," Hidemi looks at him with eloquent scorn. "What do you mean by 'good people'—someone like you?" he asks. "But you're not popular with the girls." Though a slacker, Hidemi *is* popular with the girls. Tall, slender, flawlessly handsome, and dressed in the latest grunge styles, this kid is teenage cool personified. No working-class hero, Hidemi has own, stylishly decorated room and snazzy racing bike. He hangs with the coolest guys in class and, though he keeps his distance from their juvenile hijinks, he is their real leader. Hidemi is the rebel who seems to have it all.

His most effective weapon is his mouth, which he uses to not only put down nerds, but talk back to his teachers. He argues with one hard-shelled type who catches him with a condom, demanding to know what is wrong with protecting someone he loves: a sentiment that, however admirable, I had never before heard expressed by a kid in a Japanese movie.

Where does he get his attitude? His divorced mom is a free-spirited career women who has raised him with none of the usual hangups about getting ahead or fitting in with the group. Gramps, who takes care of the housework, is a hip old guy who borrows his grandson's fashionably baggy jacket to impress a neighborhood granny. He drops occasional pearls of wisdom, but never delivers draggy lectures. This trio behaves more like three live-in friends who happen to be of different generations than an ordinary Japanese movie family. Hidemi's nonconformity is bred in the bone.

After school, Hidemi hangs out at a plush jazz bar, where he knocks back cocktails and chats up the bartender, the smokily sexy Momoko (Shinobu Sato). She encourages his advances and, within minutes of screen time, they are in bed together in her apartment. Though Hidemi has thus realized the fantasy of millions of teenage boys, of whatever nationality or generation, he accepts it as his due. Mere sex, in his world, is no big deal. But he falls hard for Momoko, and finally proves that he is human after all. When she punctures his fantasy by returning to an old lover, he learns, for the first time, the meaning of loss and begins the long climb from dudedom to adulthood.

A TV commercial director making his first feature, Yamamoto films this climb in crisp, sensuousness colors, with spare, clever camerawork. Rika Nakase's script, which is based on a novel by Emi Yamada, portrays Hidemi's dilemma with welcome touches of offbeat humor and even a poetic flight or two (at one point, he speculates on the joys of becoming his lover's shit). But Hidemi is less a representative of contemporary Japanese youth than a deracinated Ken doll living in a dream Japan. He may be to die for, but don't bet on finding him on the streets of Shibuya tonight.

Bo no Kanashimi
Hard-Head Fool (1994)

Directed by Tatsumi Kumashiro. Screenplay by Tatsumi Kumashiro and Hidehiro Ito. Produced by Excellent Film, Unitary Kikaku, Hero, and TMC. With Eiji Okuda, Hakuryu. (120 mins.)

In *Bo no Kanashimi*, his first film in six years, Tatsumi Kumashiro shows one way to revive the flagging *yakuza* genre: fine-edged character portrayal and irony-laced nihilism that plunges us into the heart of *yakuza* darkness. Like *Reservoir Dogs*, *Bo no Kana-shimi* delivers rude shocks with calculated effectiveness, if not Tarantino's self-conscious mannerisms. "You want blood and sleaze?" it seems to say. "We'll show you blood and sleaze you'll never forget." And it does. At at the film's premiere at the 1994 Kyoto International Film Festival, members of the audience reacted to certain scenes by covering their eyes or emitting audible groans of dismay (I was one of them).

The film's focus, however, is less on sex and violence for their own sakes than the dilemma of its hero, a gangster facing a midlife crisis. After taking fall after fall for his gang and spending a total of eight years in the slammer, Tanaka (Eiji Okuda) feels that it's payback time. Instead, the boss gives him the back of his hand. The old boy's favorite is Kurauchi (Hakuryu), a smooth-talking, "business" *yakuza* who believes in making yen, not war.

Tanaka, however, is a warrior of the old school. He may look like a rumpled salaryman (a young woman he wants to turn out as a hooker tells him he looks like a "department manager at an electronics company"), but he still rumbles with the best of them. Jumped by two punks from a rival gang, he quickly reduces his attackers to heaps of writhing flesh, while barely breaking a sweat.

The boss appreciates Tanaka's talent for violence, but he also fears him. After treating him to dinner at a fancy restaurant, the boss suggests that Tanaka set up his own subgang under the umbrella of the *honke* (main gang). Tanaka rightly sees this as a ploy to ease him aside and give Kurauchi a clear path to the gang succession. He decides to fight back.

A film that turned out to be Kumashiro's last—he died soon after its release—*Bo no Kanashimi* is too episodic in structure, too distracted by its various subplots, to be a well-made gang movie, but it gives us, in Tanaka, an antihero who is as fascinating in his human complexity as he is strange in his habits and repulsive in his actions. A bit stir-crazy after his years in the slammer, Tanaka talks to himself continually, giving us a running monologue on his plans, suspicions, and fears. He also orders the murder of a skinheaded spy for a rival gang, and, together with his housewife mistress, corrupts a young woman with amphetamines and sex. In his struggle against Kurauchi, he is even capable of planning his own knifing and afterward sewing up the gaping wound.

But though scary and brutal, Tanaka is without pretensions, has no use for authority and conventions, and adheres strictly to his own code of *yakuza* conduct. He is the antihero's antihero, right down to his close-cropped (and very hard) head and his skill at tying off a suture. Eiji Okuda can be the glummest of actors—one often feels like handing him a prescription for Prozac—but in Tanaka he has found a role suited to his talent for emotional understatement and honesty.

Bo no Kanashimi offers a vivid portrayal of a gangster's inner life, but it is also, truth be told, not always pleasant to watch, unless your idea of erotic fun is a woman exciting herself to orgasm while her lover describes a stabbing in gory detail. But whether you giggle, slaver, or walk out in disgust, *Bo no Kanashimi* will leave an impression. After seeing it, I have a new appreciation for the infinite variety of human sexuality—and the possible uses of a needle and thread.

Bounce Ko Gals
Bounce (1997)

Directed by Masato Harada. **Screenplay by** Yoshitaka Sakamoto. **Produced by** Bounce Ko Gals Production Committee. **With** Hitomi Sato, Yasue Sato, Yukiko Okamoto, Shin Yazawa, Koji Yakusho. (109 mins.)

In the movie business, timing is of essence. This year's hot theme—say, space aliens—can easily become stone cold, done to death by media hype and a flood of imitative product. Then someone finds a way to do a "different" alien movie and the cycle starts again. Where to place Masato Harada's *Bounce Ko Gals* on the hot-cold continuum? Its topic—the schoolgirls (*kogyaru*) who go on "paid dates" (*enjo kosai*) with middle-aged men—has been the victim of massive media overkill. Far from being DOA at the theater, however, *Bounce* is among the most sharply observed youth films I have seen this year. Though its *kogyaru* may be hardly typical—not every sweet young thing in a plaid mini packs a stun gun, talks tough to gangsters, or earns a more in a night than her father does in a month—they impress as brilliantly realized archetypes, not ripped-from-the-headlines clichés.

One point of comparison is Danny Boyle's *Trainspotting*. Both Harada's *kogyaru* and Boyle's heroin addicts are living on the edge, in offhand defiance of society's rules. Both are resourceful and ruthless hustlers, who have a casual contempt for the square johns they fleece. Both belong to subcultures whose language and folkways are all but incomprehensible to outsiders. But whereas Boyle takes an insider's view of his outlaw characters, Harada prefers to view them from outside, as a boomer who cannot help comparing their materialistic, trendy, value-free lifestyles with his own idealistically rebellious youth. But though his editorializing is at times heavy-handed, he refuses to simplistically preach or caricaturize. He gets nearly everything right, with insight and precision.

Harada's *kogyaru* hang out in Shibuya, where anyone over twenty-five is made to feel like a dinosaur. The film chronicles what begins as a typical day in their lives. After school and a meeting with other *kogyaru* in a fast-food restaurant, chunky-faced Maru (Shin Yazawa) goes to the abortion clinic, accompanied by her friend Raku (Yasue Sato). Maru regards an abortion as a minor annoyance; she could be going to the dentist's to have her teeth cleaned. Afterwards, she meets a john—a fashionably dressed dude named Oshima (Koji Yakusho). He not only laughs at her suggested service and price (fellatio for ¥100,000) but reveals himself as a gangster who runs a stable of hookers out of a date club and regards her and her friends as unwanted competition.

One of Maru's buddies, the whip-smart Jonko (Hitomi Sato) is also into *enjo kosai* hustling, but she is not, she insists to her friends, stupid enough to actually sleep with her johns. Instead, she runs off with their money, and when they prove unusually persistent, zaps them with a stun gun. She meets her match, though, when she goes to Oshima's club to negotiate for Maru—Oshima is demanding that she pay a hundred thousand yen for trying to rip him off. A former student-activist turned mobster, Oshima has little but contempt for *kogyaru*, but wants to recruit Jonko and Maru. Jonko has no choice but to accept his offer.

Meanwhile, capering about in a school uniform for a soft-porn video, Raku encounters Risa (Yukiko Okamoto) a new girl who is trying to earn cash for a long-planned trip to New York, When a couple of punks break up the shoot and rip off Risa's savings, the two girls escape to a nearby park. Risa is in despair—how can she recoup her losses before her plane takes off tomorrow? Raku has the obvious idea—*enjo kosai*. What could be easier than to raise a few hundred thousand yen by morning?

Harada takes his *kogyaru* into the heart of the Tokyo night with a narrative and stylistic velocity that matches the pace of their own frenetic lives, while developing his story and deepening our understanding of the characters and their milieu. Although not as orderly a filmmaker as Boyle, who makes the elements of his films snap smartly into place like so many Lego blocks, Harada has given his twenty-four-hour storyline a clean, satisfying arc.

By the end, we like his *kogyaru* more than we thought we could. Children of a material world, they have an openness about their emotions and desires that many of their elders have either conveniently forgotten or carefully suppressed. Will they all end up as bored housewives and office clerks by the age of twenty-five? Perhaps, but for the moment they are changing Japanese society in ways that government white papers could never dream. *Kogyaru* rule!

Byoin de Shinu to Iu Koto *
Dying at the Hospital (1998)

Written and directed by Jun Ichikawa. Produced by Chukonen Koyo Fukushi Jigyodan, Opto Communication, Supesumu, and TV Tokyo. With Ittoku Kishibe. (100 mins.)

What is driving the spate of hospital films? More, I think, than the urge to cash in. They strike me as a reflection of Japan's aging society, or, as director Jun Ichikawa has suggested, a world afflicted by famine, AIDS, and environmental destruction. In any case, Japanese directors seem more attuned than ever to the realities of disease and death—and eager to say something fresh and true about them.

Ichikawa is one of them. Based on a book by Fumio Yamasaki, a doctor and hospice director, *Byoin de Shinu to Iu Koto* is a hospital movie that rejects the usual clichés. Like a good documentarian, Ichikawa has a keen eye for the revealing word and moment. Like a good poet, he sees the deeper truths that lie beneath the surface banalities of life and can communicate them with transparency, power, and grace.

Five cancer patients—three men and two women—receive treatment from the same doctor. We follow their progress from the time they are admitted to the hospital until their deaths. For much of the film, we are literally standing at the foot of their beds, watching their lives unfold from the middle distance. By making his camera a detached observer, Ichikawa avoids the emotionalism endemic to the genre and creates a quietly elegiac mood. Rather than wring tears with closeups of sobbing relatives, he wants us to see his patients' illness and their eventual deaths as part of a larger stream of life. Instead of exposing the defects of the Japanese medical establishment, he presents his doctors and nurses as caring, competent professionals who, like their patients, also happen to be fallible human beings. (Save for the doctor, played by Ittoku Kishibe, all the film's hospital staff are amateurs enacting their real-life roles.)

The detachment of the unmoving camera, however, can lead to tedium, and the universality of the middle distance, to indifference. Ichikawa addresses this danger by fading in and fading out each shot to add visual dynamism and emotional impact to his otherwise static *mise en scene*. Also, this technique mimics the way we remember the past; not as a continuous, clearly defined stream, but as heightened moments emerging from the background mist. As the patients' lives flicker in and out of view, we see what will remain after the dross of the everyday has faded away. In these moments, we experience the essense of their struggle against the cancer that is devouring them.

Some of the film's other moments are more typical of the genre. An old couple, both dying of cancer, meet for the last time in the wife's hospital room. A forty-year-old salaryman complains bitterly that he is not getting better and asks his doctor to tell him frankly what is wrong with him. He suspects cancer; his doctor, as is still a common practice in Japan, has been withholding the truth. In these scenes, however, there are no heroes, no villains, no jerking of tears or grinding of editorial axes. Instead we hear the salaryman expressing his regret at leaving his three young children—and his joy at seeing them during what is probably his last visit home. In another voiceover, the doctor states his wish that the hospital be a place where patients come, not to die, but live fully to the end.

The hospital scenes are interspersed with montages of ordinary people doing ordinary things: hunting for clams at the seaside, watching a baseball game, dancing at a Bon festival. The montages are visual haiku that embody, with a gesture or glance, the beauty, pathos, and preciousness of life. Ichikawa filmed them over a period of months in various locations around Japan. They are among the best moments in the film.

This is not to say that I was always in agreement with Ichikawa's methods. After an hour of watching the action from across the room, I wanted to see the actors' faces to get a better feel for their performances. Also, minus dramatic charge, the film feels overly muted. But though Ichikawa may not equal some of his contemporaries as an advocate or entertainer, he surpasses nearly all of them as an artist who can change the way we look at the world.

Byoin e Iko
Let's Go to the Hospital (1990)

Directed by Yojiro Takita. Screenplay by Nobuyuki Isshiki and Akira Nagai. Produced by Fuji Television Network. With Hiroyuki Sanada, Keiko Saito, Yasuo Daichi, Hiroko Yakushimaru. (118 mins.)

In *Byoin e Iko*, Yojiro Takita proves that a semidocumentary approach can sharpen a comedy director's satirical scalpel—having done his legwork, he can better cut to the bone. Takita, who burst onto the scene in 1985 with the comic hit *Comic Zasshi Nanka Iranai* (We Don't Need Your Stinking Comic Books!), has teamed with scriptwriters Nobuyuki Isshiki and Akira Nagai, a former internist, to make a hospital comedy that skewers everyone from goldbricking patients to stonewalling doctors. Filmed in a working hospital, it has a realistic look and sound—the doctors and nurses bandy about so much jargon that the program includes a glossary to aid the perplexed.

For all its busyness and brightness, *Byoin* is not a high-speed laugh machine, but a seriocomic drama that approaches its subject from the patients' point of view. Their common experiences humanize them and draw them together. They form a little society that has rejected the hierarchies and snobberies of the outside world; pajamas and pain are great equalizers. While stoutly resisting the sentimentalism that mars so many Japanese hospital dramas, *Byoin* concludes with a lump-in-the-throat surge of feeling. I never thought my eyes would mist over at the sight of a middle-aged man making a paper crane with one hand, but I was not expecting much of what I saw in this film.

A workaholic copywriter (Hiroyuki Sanada) comes home one night to find his lissome wife (Keiko Saito) playing a game of strip *janken* (scissors-paper-stone) with a balding stranger (Yasuo Daichi). Already down to his boxers and a pair of mouse ears, the stranger tries to escape, but the copywriter catches him and, after a brief tussle, they roll together down several flights of concrete steps. Enter the ambulance.

The private university hospital to which they are taken is not the roach-ridden chamber of horrors we might expect (or know) in Japan, but a gleaming modern edifice equipped with the latest medical gadgets. It is a training hospital, where a young intern (Hiroko Yakushimaru) confronts her first emergency room case—the copywriter. The intern greets her screaming patient with a stiff bow and a frightened "good evening" and then, in a closeup, clumsily injects a needle into his gaping wound. The effect is funny and horrifying—I wanted to laugh one moment, look away the next. Making the audience's laughter stick in its throat may violate comic convention, but Takita wants to shock us out of the easy condescension of the healthy toward the sick, to make us not only laugh at the foibles of his patients, but feel their terror and pain.

As the career-obsessed copywriter, Hiroyuki Sanada knows how to milk his comic scenes for laughs—he is a talented screamer—while playing his more serious ones with a welcome restraint. Yasuo Daichi, as the Other Man, is a comic natural—he can get laughs just by flashing a beatific grin on that big moon face. I never thought I would say the same about Hiroko Yakushimaru—a former idol star known for her kewpie-doll looks and bird-song voice. But in playing an addled innocent, she uses both attributes to advantage. She sheds her idol image and behaves like a flesh-and-blood woman. She even demonstrates that she can act.

Byoin e Iko may avoid the grimmer aspects of hospital life—we see no serious illness, no death—but it gets across its message: we are all patients under the skin.

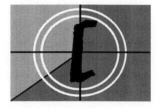

Cats Eye
(1997)

Directed by Kaizo Hayashi. **Screenplay by** Kaizo Hayashi and Tokio Tsuchiya. **Produced by** Fuji TV. **With** Kenta Uchida, Norika Fujiwara, Izumi Inamori, Yuki Uchida, Akira Terao, Kane Kosugi, Naoko Yamazaki, Jiang Wenli. (91 mins.)

Ever since Kaizo Hayashi debuted in 1985 with *Yume Miru Yo ni Nemuritai* (To Sleep, Perchance to Dream), he has been feted as a wunderkind of Japanese film. A master of the visual medium, who can assume an infinite array of onscreen attitudes, from the edgily modern to the gauzily nostalgic, with unmatched fluency and vividness, Hayashi is Japan's nearest equivalent to Hong Kong's Wong Kar-Wai. Though their films may be set in Asia, it's hard to detect anything resembling Asian values in them. They are impeccably postmodern, borderless, and above all, cool.

Hayashi, however, differs from his Hong Kong colleague in the quality of his imagination. Whereas Wong's films are grounded in the realities of Hong Kong's chaotic streets, Hayashi's seem to flow from the memory bank of a pop-culture-obsessed *otaku*. In his latest film, *Cats Eye*, Hayashi is usual weightless form, creating pure popcorn entertainment. Based on a *manga* that ran from 1981 to 1985 in the comic magazine *Shonen Jump*, the film depicts the adventures of Cats Eye, a gang of three sisters, sleek stunners all, who steal expensive paintings using ultrasophisticated, ultracool, ultrafeminine gear, including a lipstick that shoots miniature rockets and another that smears plastic explosive. Wearing skintight catwoman costumes and flying through the air with the agility of *ninja*, they are so confident of their ability to baffle the cops, including a bumbling, if cute, detective (played by pop star Kenta Uchida), that they publicize the time and place of their next job and, despite the wall of blue around the targets, invariably pull it off.

As befitting *manga* heroines, each of the sisters is an easily identifiable type. Rui (Norika Fujiwara), the oldest, is the level-headed leader who plans the group's daring thefts. Hitomi (Izumi Inamori), the second sister, is a glamorous beauty and a master of disguise. The youngest, Ai (Yuki Uchida), is a hot-blooded tomboy who is a whiz with machinery. They are not stealing paintings for fun and profit, but because they were painted by their artist father. (Akira Terao). When they were children, a mysterious gang kidnapped him and killed their mother. They are completing a collection of his work to honor his memory.

Complications ensue when the detective falls in love with Hitomi, whose day job is coffee-shop waitress, and when a handsome Taiwanese student (Kane Kosugi) develops a crush on Ai, who designs gadgets at a university lab. Also, the girls have to deal with a clever female detective (Naoko Yamazaki) who is onto their game, and a ruthless Chinese gang that, led by a mysterious old man known as the Emperor, is muscling in on their territory. But the gang's real leader, they discover, is the Emperor's concubine (Jiang Wenli), who will stop at nothing to achieve her ends.

Hayashi achieves some nifty effects, including a collective Cats Eye drop from a high ceiling reminiscent of Tom Cruise's invasion of the CIA's inner sanctum in *Mission Impossible*. Also, seen in full battle array, the Cats Eye sisters equal Michelle Pfieffer's Catwoman in slinky sexiness.

Hayashi can't do much with the cartoon storyline except camp it up, but humor has never been his strong point. His idea of funny is the concubine as Dragon Lady, complete with slit dress and evil cackle. Perhaps she will amuse the boys who deliver antiforeign tirades on the soundtrucks outside Shibuya Station. Also, a John Woo he is not. Though he tries to impress with the slickness of his heroines' moves, his fight scenes have all the punch of a Power Rangers episode. He tries to wink his way through the action stuff, but the jokiness undercuts whatever impact it might have had.

Cats Eye is typical Hayashi—i.e., a large talent expended to little effect. The difference is that, in this piece of teen-targeted foolery, he has abandoned all pretense of art. Perhaps his true ambition is not to become Japan's next internationally recognized cinematic master, but to replace Joel Schumacher as the director of the next Batman movie.

The Chugaku Kyoshi *
Games Teachers Play (1992)

Directed by Hideyuki Hirayama. Screenplay by Hiroshi Saito. Produced by Melies and Suntory. With Kyozo Nagatsuka, Tomoko Fujita. (106 mins.)

It has been more than a decade since school violence and bullying began appearing in the headlines and became topics of national debate. What is to be done? For the junior high schools that have been at the center of the storm, the answer has often been rules, rules, and more rules, enforced with an iron fist. This approach, called *kanri kyoiku* (control education), is not uniquely Japanese, but in Japan it has been carried to extremes. Some schools even regulate the amount of toilet paper students can use at one time. Who, one wonders, enforces *that* one?

The title character of *The Chugaku Kyoshi* (literally, "The Middle-School Teacher") is one of the enforcers. Shuhei Mikami (Kyozo Nagatsuka) would seem, at first glance, to be the kind of martinet kids love to hate. Unlike other teachers at Sakura Junior High, who dress casually (one of the profession's few perks), Mikami arrives bright and early every morning in a dark suit and tie. His expression is as severe as his clothes; the only time we can imagine him cracking a smile is when he is announcing a test.

Watching him work, however, we sense that beneath the stern exterior is a man determined to do the best job possible in a less-than-ideal situation. His students are at a dangerous age in an uncertain time. They have lost their childish respect for adult authority, but not their childish contempt for adult weakness.

The martinet solution would be a reign of terror. Mikami's is to have the students administer their own justice. When he catches three boys sneaking into class with a pack of cigarettes, he divides the class into five groups to discuss the offenders' punishment and then calls for a vote. The decision: the boys must come early for three days to scrub the hallway floor. Everyone is satisfied—and Mikami has not touched a hair on the offenders' heads.

The smart, dedicated teacher who wins over a class of unruly kids is a film and television staple, going back to *The Blackboard Jungle* and beyond. Too often, though, these fictional *sensei* fail to convince. We know, especially if we have spent any time classroom teaching, that they are too good to be true. Teachers may win battles, but seldom the war, especially when colleagues and parents have abandoned the fight.

The great thing about The Chugaku Kyoshi is its insistence on the realities of the classroom; Mikami is not a miracle worker, but a lonely warrior in a moral wasteland, whose only weapons are his character and the rules. Kyozo Nagatsuka, who has the dark masculine charisma of Michael Keaton in Batman, minus the pursed-lip creepiness, is ideal for the role.

The film's realism extends to its kids. Director Hideyuki Hirayama has not rehearsed his young actors so much as released them. They offer us a clear-eyed view of their teenage world, minus adult romanticizing, caricaturizing and demonizing. That world is all the more disturbing for its outward normality. The cigarette smokers and their classmates are not sneering punks, but nice kids from middle-class families. Nonetheless, they regard shoplifting as a game; extorting money from classmates, a business.

Mikami, however, is not trying the save their amoral souls, but introduce a little order and a few values. As a professional, he knows that teaching, like politics, is the art of possible. A young, free-spirited art teacher (Tomoko Fujita) considers his approach cold and unfeeling. But her own approach—playing buddy to her students—only adds to the confusion.

The confrontation between Mikami's enlightened conservatism and the art teacher's wrong-headed anarchism is the film's principal weakness. It presents us with a false choice: Mikami or the deluge. But as extreme as the art teacher may seem, she is also a character rooted in reality (I have worked with her American sister).

From this, it may sound as though the film is rather depressing. But Hirayama provides a superb catharsis in the form of a relay race that Mikami organizes. It restores the school's spirit and lifts our own. Mikami, however, knows that the battle must continue. If, as Yoji Yamada once complained to me, too many Japanese films are like strawberry shortcake—sweet but lacking in nourishment—The Chugaku Kyoshi offers substantial, well-prepared food for thought about the state of Japanese education and society.

Chugoku no Tojin
The Bird People in China (1998)

Directed by Takashi Miike. Screenplay by Masashi Nakamura. Cinematography by Hideo Yamamoto. Produced by Hone Film and Marubeni. With Masatoshi Nagase, Renji Ishibashi, Mako, Li Li Wang. (118 mins.)

Takashi Miike's Chugoku no Tojin is a journey to Shangri La from the Asian side of the Himalayan divide, with a Japanese point of view. Whereas the typical hero of a Hollywood lost paradise film is usually journeying to find adventure, escape, or New Age wisdom, Miike's two heroes—a workaholic salaryman named Wada (Masatoshi Nagase) and a short-tempered yakuza named Ujiie (Renji Ishibashi)—travel to China for reasons utterly mundane. Wada is replacing a sick colleague who has been extracting jade ore from a newly discovered deposit, while Ujiie has been dispatched by his boss, who complains that he has been cheated by Wada's colleague. He intends to collect his gang's share of the treasure, by force if necessary.

Based on a story by Makoto Shiina and filmed on location in Yunnan Province, Chugoku no Tojin traces the outer and inner journeys of Wada and Ujiie from earthbound pragmatism to the realization that life offers more than grubbing for money, status, and power; that one can soar to unknown, even impossible, heights. It is, in short, more of a Japanized Lost Horizon than a Seven Years In Tibet.

After meeting their local guide (Mako) in a frontier town, the two Japanese proceed by fits and starts into the mountain fastness of southwest China. Soon they have left behind all signs of twentieth-century civilization, including paved roads, signs, and inns. Then one night they are caught in a storm and a gust of wind carries away the contents of the briefcase Wada had lugged all the way from Tokyo. How is he going to do his job? What is he going to tell his boss?

Before he can answer these vital questions, the guide arranges for new transportation: a boat pulled by river turtles. Wada's business trip is, to his unease, becoming curiouser and curiouser. At camp that night the guide gets drunk, hits his head, and loses his memory. By now totally lost, Wada, Ujiie, and the clueless guide wander on until they encounter a hill tribe whose children wear birdlike wings. Their teacher, a blue-eyed young woman named Yan (Li Li Wang) tells the intruders that the children are learning how to fly. Impressed by her sincerity, as well as by a book on human-powered flight she claims her grandfather (a British airman downed in the war) left behind, Wada and Ujiie start wanting to believe her.

The film posits an earthly paradise in danger of extinction as the outside world edges closer. (Bearing such poisoned gifts of civilization as electronic gadgets and guns, Wada and Ujiie are unwittingly agents of that world.) Together with cinematographer Hideo Yamamoto, Miike has filmed a heavenly land of pure rushing rivers, crystal blue skies, and fancifully-shaped mountains that seem to have sprung directly from a classical Chinese landscape scroll. It is almost too perfect, this China, and Miike gives us far too much of it.

As the movie's various subplots unwind, including a tiresome search for the lyrics to "Annie Laurie," the melancholy Scottish ballad that Yan learned from her grandfather and sings in garbled English, we begin to feel that, like the heroes, we are spending years, if not decades, slogging toward spiritual revelation—or just a dramatic climax. And like Wada, we long to go home. (Ujiie, perhaps realizing that his new, peaceable persona has made him unfit for his old job, decides to stay.)

Paradise may look wonderful on travel posters, but for filmmaking refugees from modern civilization who exile themselves there, the rarefied air can disorient as well as inspire. Miike's birdmen may look lovely soaring in their mountain wilderness, but his film needs a stronger narrative tailwind.

Closing Time

(1997)

Written and directed by Masahiro Kobayashi. Produced by Monkey Town Production. With Sansho Shinsui, Mari Natsuki, Yasushi Kitamura. (81 mins.)

Some people will do anything to direct. In 1976 Masahiro Kobayashi was an aspiring twenty-two-year-old folk singer when he decided to change careers and become a film director. To support his ambition, he worked a series of day jobs while studying French, the language of his directorial heroes. In 1982 he journeyed to France to meet one of them, Francois Truffaut. Truffaut, however, was out of the country and Kobayashi, after wandering about Europe, returned to Japan and became a scriptwriter for porno films. In 1996, his longtime directorial collaborator, Toshiki Sato, released his first non-porn film, Lunatic, with a script by Kobayashi. Now, at the age of forty-two, Kobayashi has finally made his directorial debut with Closing Time, a film that he financed out of his own pocket.

Was the wait worth it? A dedicated admirer of European cinema, whose pantheon includes Renoir, Dreyer, Bresson, Godard, and Truffaut, Kobayashi has shot what is essentially a European art film, right down to its French-language credits, though the hero, played by Sansho Shinsui, is the type of romantic down-and-outer that Kobayashi favorite Tom Waits has so often hymned in his music.

Kobayashi brings off his cultural cross-dressing with a certain amount of stylistic finesse. His division of Closing Time into three clearly labeled acts, each with a title borrowed from a Waits tune, tightens the film's structure and defines its narrative arc. Also, he starts each act with a short scene of Shinsui listening, with an amused grin, as a fellow drunk

regales him with an anecdote or observation. These scenes adds a welcome touchs of offbeat humor, as well as provide a rhythmic pulse. But Closing Time is a movie-fed fantasy that stresses mood over character, while scattering its energies in too many thematic directions. Perhaps fearing that he will get only one chance, Kobayashi has crammed elements of what could have easily been several films into Closing Time. It can't bear the weight.

Shinsui plays a TV scriptwriter who has taken to drink, sponging from all and sundry. With his lined face, baggy eyes and long scraggly hair, he looks every inch the degenerate alcoholic. But rather than show us the all-too-real horrors of the drunken life, the film paints it in a glamorous light. The hero receives an endless supply of liquor from the master of an underground dive, while bedding one nubile young woman after another. Though he exudes all the sexual charisma you might expect of a tired middle-aged man with a permanent hangover, these women seem to think he is a terrific lover: Brad Pitt with a paunch.

He descends further into the depths, sleeping rough with an eccentric homeless woman (Mari Natsuki) who is, like the hero, addicted to the bottle and movies. She reels off the names of her favorite directors (who are also Kobayashi's) as they sit drinking. This is the film's best moment—Shinsui, who seems to be sleepwalking though much of Closing Time—comes alive and connects with another human being.

Then the hero encounters a young man (Yasushi Kitamura) who is homeless, gay, and dying of AIDS. The hero rejects his advances, but cares for him when he gets sick, and holds him in his arms as he breathes his last. The hero resumes his old routine of drink and sex, but the master finally brings him up short. You are, he says, living an illusion. The hero admits that the master might be right.

The hero has his reasons for his self-destructive spree—but the revelation comes too late to save the film, which has become a melange of Leaving Las Vegas, Last Tango In Paris, and Les Amants Du Pont Neuf. I hope that Kobayashi gets another chance to direct—his heart is in the right place—but that, next time, he makes only one film and that his hero stays clean and sober.

Coquille

(1999)

Directed by Shun Nakahara. Screenplay by Kota Yamada. Cinematography by Shogo Ueda. Produced by Shochiku. With Jun Fubuki, Kaoru Kobayashi, Toru Masuoka. (95 mins.)

Shun Nakahara's *Coquille* chronicles the affair of two junior high school classmates who have been reunited after a gap of three decades in the provincial town where they grew up. Though I admire Nakahara's work, particularly his ensemble pieces *Sakura no Sono* (The Cherry Orchard, 1990) and *Juninin no Yasashi Nihonjin* (The Gentle Twelve, 1991), I have a built-in resistance to movies targeted at babyboomers that are as sedate in tone and conservative in approach as their supposed audience. *Coquille*, I'm afraid, fits squarely in that category. Am I another eternal adolescent denying the passage of time? I suppose so.

Nakahara fulfills his assignment in *Coquille* with his usual attention to detail and nuance, but Kota Yamada's script, which is based on a novel by Osamu Yamamoto, develops its familiar theme in a lachrymose direction, dragging in that familiar *deux ex machina*—the traffic accident—to provide the climax. This may be comforting to over-forties who are looking for pathos in gentle doses, but this one is still immature enough to want to be surprised at the movies, not depressed at the failure of yet another pair of middle-aged lovers to find more than fleeting happiness. Just once, I'd like to see a graying couple meet the fade out with a clink of cocktail glasses on a beach in Waikiki.

Naoko (Jun Fubuki) has recently divorced her husband, moved back to her hometown, and opened a bar called Coquille (scallop shell). Appearing at her junior high-school class reunion for the first time in decades, she is all but a stranger to most of her former classmates, but she becomes reacquainted with one: the soft-spoken, straight-arrow Urayama (Kaoru Kobayashi), whom she first fell for as a schoolgirl and never forgot.

Urayama, however, has only the faintest recollection of Naoko. Supporting a wife and two children with his middle-management job at a local plant, he is too busy to dwell on a girl he once knew in junior high school. And yet there is something in the longing of her glance that awakens old memories, old feelings. While they are dancing, she reminds him that she approached him one day after his *kendo* practice at school and whispered something in his right ear—something important. He tells her that he is deaf in that ear and heard nothing. As a result, their budding romance never bloomed.

One night, he comes to Coquille with his boss (Sansho Shinsui), who promptly creates a drunken scene. Even so, Urayama becomes a Coquille regular. But Urayama and Naoko's renewed acquaintance is darkened from the beginning by their awareness of its brevity: Urayama has been transferred to Tokyo. Before he leaves, however, Naoko asks him for one last favor—a day trip to a mountain they had one

climbed as students. Urayama agrees, and they end up spending the night together at an inn. Will he choose to fulfill his duty to his wife and family—or follow the impulses of his heart?

Naoko could have easily been merely pathetic—a middle-aged woman who never had a life—but Jun Fubuki plays her with a self-awareness and self-respect that elevates and justifies her passion. Urayama, on the other hand, barely emerges from the woodwork at first, but Kaoru Kobayashi portrays, with subtle strokes, his awakening to all he has missed and all that is at stake. Toru Masuko plays Tanikawa, another former classmate who briefly becomes Naoko's lover. A brash, crass egotist, he represents all that Urayama is not. I know that *Coquille* wants me to despise Tanikawa and sympathize with Naoko and Urayama (its Good Japanese), but he brought a welcome splash of raucous color to the movie's autumnal gray—and I'm sure he would mix a wicked martini.

Cosmos
Remembering the Cosmos (1997)

Written and directed by Jun'ichi Suzuki. Produced by Film Voice. With Akane Oda, Megumi Matsushita, Jo Shishido, Tamio Kawaji, Kai Shishido, Mari Natsuki. (103 mins.)

In Japan, AIDS patients are only beginning to emerge from the shadows into which they have been cast by ignorance and prejudice. Although filmmakers here have dealt with AIDS, their work has not had the impact of Hollywood's. For one thing, such films, beginning with Jun'ya Sato's 1992 *Watashi o Daite Soshite Kiss Shite* (Hug Me, Then Kiss Me), have been few and far between. For another, they haven't been very good as popular art or effective as propaganda.

Jun'ichi Suzuki's *Çosmos* is not going to change this state of affairs. Trailing a long string of commendations from governmental organizations, *Cosmos* is the kind of high-minded, tearjerking *seishun eiga* (youth movie) that the Japanese film industry has been turning out for years. With a change of disease and decade it could have been another vehicle for Sayuri Yoshinaga who, as a teen star for Nikkatsu in the 1960s, specialized in suffering nobly and dying beautifully. But what worked at the box office for Sayuri in 1963 no longer works in 1997. Though *Cosmos* is so earnestly educational and blandly nonconfrontational that it will no doubt find a captive audience among schoolchildren—and it will no doubt do good—it could have done much better.

The story is that of Akiko Sonoda (Akane Oda), a high-school girl who returns to her native Kumamoto Prefecture after an absence of seven years. During that time she went to South America with her parents and, after being injured in a traffic accident and receiving an transfusion of HIV-infected blood, contracted AIDS.

Bright and chipper, she seems, at first, an unlikely AIDS victim, but when she runs into an old school friend, Natsumi (Megumi Matsushita) and hugs her, she learns, from the uneasy expression on her friend's face that, in this small provincial town, she is regarded as untouchable. Natsumi soon repents of her prejudice and becomes Akiko's best—and only—friend, but the rest of the community is slower to come around. Natsumi's father and boyfriend regard Akiko with ill-disguised distaste, her classmates shun her, and the leader of a parent's group (Jo Shishido) even tries to have her expelled from the school. Fortunately, she has allies, including a strong-willed vice-principal (Tamio Kawaji), a fair-minded homeroom teacher (Kai Shishido), and most of all, her fiercely supportive mother (Mari Natsuki).

The struggle, nonetheless, is not an easy one, and Akiko's health begins to fail. Then, while confronting her bitterest enemy in a driving rainstorm, she collapses. Will Akiko and Natsumi perform their long-rehearsed *manzai* comedy routine at the school festival and win the applause of their classmates? Or will death deny Akiko her long-desired triumph and final acceptance by her home town?

Suzuki maximizes hankie-wringing sentiments, minimizes unpleasant realities. Akiko and Natsumi are so relentlessly cheerful and brave in the face of adversity one longs to pinch their grinning cheeks and shake them, just to make sure their owners are for real. The pair, especially Megumi Matsushita, in an impassioned speech at the school festival for her stricken friend, certainly makes the audience snuffle into its kleenex, but will we ever see a Japanese movie about AIDS whose protagonist is gay, or that mentions the infection of thousands of hemophiliacs by corporate and bureaucratic collusion? Or will the local film industry continue to use this twentieth-century plague as fodder for perfervid melodrama?

Crepe *
(1993)

Written and directed by Jun Ichikawa. Produced by Seiyu, Toei, and Tohoku Shinsha. With Masahi Tashiro, Kaho Minami. (56 mins.)

Chibusa
Nipple (1993)

Directed by Kichitaro Negishi. Screenplay by Hiroshi

Saito. Produced by Seiyu, Toei, and Tohoku Shinsha. With Kaoru Kobayashi, Mai Oikawa, Jun Togawa. (57 mins.)

Crepe and *Chibusa* are a double bill with a difference. Both films are based on short stories by former TV-commercial director and pop songwriter Shizuka Ijunin, and both are half the standard feature length. The heroes of both are middle-aged men who have been living in the fast lane, but are brought up short by a woman in their lives. The hero of *Crepe* confronts the responsibility of fatherhood; the hero of *Chibusa*, the inevitability of separation. Both learn a lesson about the fragility and fleetingness of human relationships. Directors Jun Ichikawa (*Crepe*) and Kichitaro Negishi (*Chibusa*) film their stories with sensibilities and styles that are at once complementary and strongly individual. They have made a matched set whose components can also stand alone.

Ichikawa's approach is more lyrical, direct, and original. A hair stylist (Masahi Tashiro) receives a call from his ex-wife at the hotel where he works. His daughter, whom he has not seen in fourteen years, has passed the entrance exam to junior high school and wants to meet her father. The stylist agrees, but wonders what he has gotten himself into. He is relatively affluent, happy, and healthy. Though pushing forty, he is living with a vivacious younger woman (Kaho Minami), playing the horses, and carousing every night at a local Western-style bar. Why does he need to dig up the past? His best friend tells him that in today's high schools, girls act like adults. Is his daughter one of the crowd?

He plans this fateful encounter like a military campaign, drawing maps and scouting out the terrain. He finally decides on a French restaurant that serves crepes—a favorite, he notices, of the teenage female patrons. The meeting, as we might expect, is an awkward one. What we are not expecting is the way Ichikawa presents this key scene, with frontal head-and-shoulders shots of the characters, speaking with a painful deliberateness. Ichikawa uses these unusual line readings to strip away the surface banality of the conversation and expose the characters' innermost feelings. His meticulous stylization is effective the way Ozu's is effective: it brings the characters closer to us, until we feel it is we who are sitting across the table.

By the end of this encounter father and daughter have not erased a fourteen-year blank, but they have reached an understanding (it helps that they both like baseball). That is heartening, but somehow sad, as we see in a last shot of the father walking alone down the empty subway platform, his back to the camera. It is one of several shots from *Crepe* that linger in the mind.

Chibusa has a more worldly feel, and tries to cover more narrative and emotional ground. The hero is a hard-drinking, hard-gambling, hard-smoking pop-concert producer (Kaoru Kobayashi) who is catnip to women. A young lighting technician (Mai Oikawa) throws herself at him with a directness and persistence that he finds off-putting. At a busy street crossing, he tells her to go home and she responds by placing his hand against her breast. His resistance begins to crumble, all the way to love and marriage. He forsakes all others, including the wife of his best friend (Jun Togawa), who tries to seduce him during a two-couple campout. But then misfortune strikes; his wife informs him that she cannot have children and falls ill with leukemia. As the film begins, she is in a hospital bed, recovering from a relapse, and he is her devoted, if rather strict, nurse.

The film's flashback structure serves to reduce its moisture level, by shifting the focus from the technician's illness to her love for the producer—and the producer's change of heart. Nemoto tempers his film's sentimentality, without trashing the romanticism at its its core. Kaoru Kobayashi's performance is another plus. A versatile actor who played a farmer in the 1989 *Untama Giru* and a tombstone salesman in the 1993 *Ohaka to Rikon* (The Grave and Divorce), Kobayashi is both credibly tough as a playboy and credibly tender as his wife's nurse. Newcomer Mai Oikawa is conventionally charming and spunky—not quite a match for her partner.

Of the two films, I preferred *Crepe*. With brilliant artistry, Ichikawa depicts the unhealed ache of loneliness and loss. Negishi gives a hard, shiny gloss to an age-old romantic dream: a short, beautiful love affair and a lingering, beautiful death.

Cure *
(1997)

Written and directed by Kiyoshi Kurosawa. Produced by Daiei. With Koji Yakusho, Tsuyoshi Ujiki, Anna Nakagawa, Masato Hagiwara (111 mins.)

In *Cure* Kiyoshi Kurosawa creates a scary alternative universe where the boundaries between reality and illusion dissolve, where murder is a bad dream from which the victims never awaken. But having made this universe, he doesn't quite know what to do with it. Rather than a finale that leaves the audience in a cold sweat, he opts for an underexplained, underplayed ending that feels confusing and flat.

The film depicts a deadly contest between a police detective and a killer with a strange ability to cloud men's minds. The detective is Takabe (Koji Yakusho), who is investigating a series of mysterious murders in which the victims are slashed across the throat with an X and the perpetrators are found in a zombielike trance, with no memory of their deeds. Takabe consults a psychiatrist (Tsuyoshi Ujiki) about the links between the killings, but neither can come up with a convincing answer. Meanwhile, Takabe's wife (Anna Nakagawa) is seeing another shrink and waging a long, losing struggle against madness. Confronted with the baffling crimes and his wife's deteriorating condition, Takabe feels caught in a double bind, with no easy way out.

The scene shifts to a deserted beach on which two strangers meet—an elementary school teacher and a puffy-faced young man in a wrinkled trenchcoat (Masato Hagiwara) who has no idea who or where he is. The teacher takes the man home and tries to find the key to his mental confusion, but the man keeps asking questions with a slouching, mumbling, maddening persistence: Who are you? What do you do? What am I doing here? In the midst of this mantra, he flicks his lighter and the teacher gazes at the flame with a helpless fascination. The next thing we know, the teacher is flying, naked, from the second-story window of his house, his wife is lying dead on the floor, cut with an X, and the young man is nowhere to be found.

Investigating this case, Takabe learns the identity of this demon in human form, with his strange, hypnotic line of patter. Then he meets him and learns, to his horror, that the man knows about his wife and is trying, with all the insanely malicious art at his command, to turn Takabe into another of his remote-controlled hitmen.

Kurosawa, who also wrote the script, films this terrific thriller premise with a fine sense of timing and rhythm, starting with effects that seem, at first, to be almost as childishly simple as his killer's questions. What could be less scare-inducing in this age of flying body parts than a lighter flame wavering in a darkened room or spilled water spreading slowly on a dirty tile floor? But somehow the flame looks threatening, the water suggests blood, and the flesh starts to creep.

Koji Yakusho demonstrates again why he is Japan's most versatile male actor. His Takabe is not just a bewildered nice guy staring into the face of evil, but a man grappling with his various demons, in the depths of terror and rage. With his boneless body and slurry delivery, Masato Hagiwara initially seems to lack the menace needed for the role of the killer, but his space-punk act is, we eventually see, a cover for a subtly manipulative, utterly malevolent killer. I think David Lynch would like him. True creepiness knows no borders.

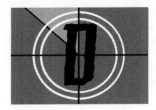

Daibyonin
The Last Dance (1993)

Written and directed by Juzo Itami. Music by Naoki Tachikawa. Produced by Itami Films. With Nobuko Miyamoto, Masahiko Tsugawa, Rentaro Mikuni, Haruna Takase. (116 mins.)

Mimbo no Onna, Juzo Itami's 1992 how-to-beat-the-*yakuza* movie, was a hit, but it nearly got him killed. Shortly after the film was released, several *yakuza* knifed him outside his house. This incident would seem to be a source of inspiration for *Daibyonin*—Itami's meditation on death. Not so, he says. In a program interview he claims that the idea came to him after witnessing the passing of a friend.

From what Itami calls the film's "catch phrase" "This is how I would like to die"—we know that we are in for another of his how-to lectures. We also recognize the infectious music by Naoki Tachikawa and the comically stylized performances of regulars Nobuko Miyamoto, as the dying hero's wife, and Masahiko Tsugawa, as his doctor. But in *Daibyonin* the didacticism and grotesquery always present in Itami's work is accompanied by a new sincerity of feeling.

His film-director hero (Rentaro Mikuni) suffers from that commonplace of Japanese hospital melodramas: stomach cancer. He is not told the truth about his condition, however—another convention of the genre—and goes on swigging whiskey and directing his latest film, a bathetic tale of a couple succumbing to cancer at the same time. The director also plays the husband in the film while carrying on an affair with the actress who is his onscreen wife (Haruna Takase).

The director begins the film convinced that his good health will last forever. When the doctor tells him that he needs an operation, he becomes angry, confused, frightened. He is in the middle of a shoot. How can he take time out for an ulcer? His wife, who is wise to his philandering and is getting ready to leave him, knows why. She feels the truth would kill him—he's such a child—and she's probably right. There is something pathetic about this man. He is aware of so little, with so little time left.

Daibyonin is about his coming to awareness. Itami handles this theme with the kind of sensitivity and sympathy we don't usually associate with his work. Perhaps it's because he has been in the director's shoes himself, and being Itami, he can put us there as well. When another cancer patient tells the director about the hospital's ruses for concealing the truth and the director, realizing that he has been a victim of those ruses himself, turns pale with shock, we hear an echo of Kurosawa's *Ikiru* (To Live, 1952) and feel a similar chill.

Itami, however, does not advocate a *Final Exit* solution. Taking a hint from his own movie, the director tries to do himself in, but it is an act of desperation and despair. His real awakening—and acceptance—begins only after he returns from the brink of death. The film relates his journey to the other side, during which he sees the faces of departed loved ones, with a straight face, and regards it as the key to the director's change of heart.

His final days illustrate Itami's precepts for a good end. After a struggle between his medical pride and his human feelings, the doctor comes to understand the director's needs. After nearly abandoning him when she discovers him enjoying one last fling with his lover, his wife decides to stay with him. Instead of pumping him full of debilitating drugs, the hospital allows him to return home, where he can die surrounded by family and friends.

Those who remember the Itami of *Ososhiki* (The Funeral)—his wickedly hilarious exposure of Japan's "death industry"— may feel that he has lost his edge. Yes, he lays on his new-found wisdom on too thick and stages his director's "good death" too slickly— the old rogue cracks jokes to the end and even expires on cue—but he makes his points with characteristic energy and humor. In his final images—the lithe, graceful movements of a young woman, the swaying, soughing expanse of a bamboo forest—he shows us what his hero has learned. Life is precious, eternity is now.

Daitoryo no Christmas Tree
The President's Christmas Tree (1996)

Directed by Kazuyoshi Okuyama. Screenplay by Masato Harada and Kazuyoshi Okuyama. Produced by Daitoryo no Christmas Tree Production Committee. With Michiko Hada, Urara Uwata, Kimiko Yo, Tetsuya Bessho. (106 mins.)

In 1994 producer Kazuyoshi Okuyama personally reshot nearly seventy percent of *Rampo*, a psychodrama based on the life and works of mystery writer Edogawa Rampo, when the director refused Okuyama's requests for extensive retakes. Okuyama did, however, have the decency to release both versions in Shochiku theaters. Not surprisingly, his own version got the better venues. But it also became the biggest domestic hit of the summer, was distributed by Samuel Goldwyn in the United States, and garnered rave reviews from American critics.

Now, Okuyama is back with his first film as a start-to-finish director: *Daitoryo no Christmas Tree*. Once again, he has shown us what he means by his frequent calls for a fresh approach to commercial filmmaking in Japan. *Daitoryo* is, first and foremost, a stylishly photographed and slickly plotted date movie for the young adults who are the core movie audience. But though the film uses a lushly melodic theme song by Boz Scaggs, a sensuously noodling jazz score, and montages of New York street scenes to create a made-in-America ambience, it does not slavishly imitate its Hollywood models. In its story of early death and unrequited love and its preference for introspective poetics over overt eroticism—no kissing scenes, please, we're Japanese—it is definitely a made-for-Japan product. The aim is less to inspire feel-good tingles over the dizzy wonderfulness of love fulfilled than sweet sighs over the aching sadness of love denied.

Kirari (Michiko Hada) comes to New York to study lighting design and visit her two expatriate sisters. The younger one, Akari (Urara Uwata) is trying to break into Broadway as a dancer while working as a waitress in a sushi shop and living a boho life in a Manhattan walkup. The older one, Kyoko (Kimiko Yo), is a writer who has recently divorced and is suffering from terminal cancer. Although Kirari tries to bring her sisters together—Akari has barely spoken to Kyoko since arriving in Manhattan six months earlier—she is far more anxious to reconcile Kyoko and her ex-husband, Haruki (Tetsuya Bessho), who lives only to play jazz piano in funky dives.

Kirari is driven by more than a conventional desire to console a dying woman. An earlier trip to Washington with Kyoko and Haruki to view the president's Christmas Tree has become her touchstone of happiness. If she could somehow bring the three of them together, she thinks, they might find that happiness again. After her sister's death, and the failure of her efforts to realize that dream, she discovers that the one she really wanted to meet at that tree was Haruki.

A co-writer of the script with Masato Harada, Okuyama tells this story with commendable restraint, given the usual wretched excesses of movies of this type. There are no tear-jerking reunions, no heart-rending deathbed scenes. But he also smoothes over the rough edges of his characters' lives with the cinematic equivalent of romantic restaurant music. Nearly everything is tinklingly pretty, nothing much lingers. There are, however, stereotyped glimpses of the urban jungle. In one scene, a streetwise New Yorker pulls out a gun and scares off a menacing derelict before escorting Kirari from his pickup to the abandoned church where Haruki is jamming.

Despite the jarring notes, Okuyama has made a film that is a hymn to New York. His Japanese expats may have to cope isolation, danger, and ruinous temptations, but they also enjoy a freedom they never had at home. That is the best present Kirari finds under the president's Christmas Tree.

Daiyonige: Yonigeya Hompo 3
Midnight Run 3 (1995)

Directed by Takahito Hara. Screenplay by Takahito Hara, Makoto Masaki, and Yukio Nagasaki. Produced by Kowa International and NTV. With Masatoshi Nakamura, Atsuo Nakamura, Toru Minegishi, Miyoko Asada, Kaori Hosomi, Kazumi Shiomi, Jun Miho, Tetsu Masuoka. (102 mins.)

The *Yonigeya Hompo* (Midnight Run) series was born of the collapse of the eighties bubble economy. In the late eighties, when everyone was going to get rich on NTT shares, comedies about an agency that helps debtors escape financial hell wouldn't have stood a chance. In the recession of the early nineties, however, they hit the topical spot. Both *Yonigeya Hompo* (1992) and *Yonigeya Hompo 2* (1993) were box-office successes.

The third entry, *Daiyonige*, wants to be a comic take on *The Great Escape*. Though as slickly produced as the first two installments, the film demonstrates why most series end. The ideas that seemed so fresh in the first installment become tired by the third, despite a grossly inflated story line, more expensive sets, and more famous faces in the cast.

The most famous is that of Masatoshi Nakamura, a singer, actor, and TV pitchman with a Mr. Nice Guy image. In the *Yonigeya* series, he plays against type as Masahiko Genji, the tough-minded manager of the Rising Sun agency, which specializes in helping debtors file for personal bankruptcy. Genji wants to do right by his clients, even though most have the self-control of five-year-olds turned loose in a candy store, but he also manages Midnight Run, which might described as a moving service for the financially distressed. Creditors try to stop Genji and his crew from going quietly into the good night, with debtors in tow, so they have to operate undercover, with the resourcefulness, precision, and intrepidity of a hostage rescue team. The idea of this valiant band aiding feckless creditors and doing battle with venal creditors is ripe with comic possibilities, many of which director Takahito Hara exploited in the first two installments, along with dispensing plenty of how-to advice on how to handle debt.

In *Daiyonige*, however, Hara has set out to a make a crowd-pleasing comedy, not a manual. Genji and his crew are back, but this time they are up against a scam artist named Isomura (Atsuo Nakamura) who is extracting profit from misery. He has Genji's clients, including the sad-sack proprietor of a sporting-goods store (Toru Minegishi), his bubbly wife (Miyoko Asada) and button-cute daughter (Kaori Hosomi), move into Niko Niko Village, a community of debtors who are working their way back to solvency with Isomura's friendly assistance. Beneath his kind-uncle exterior, however, Isomura is determined to squeeze every last yen out his charges, even if it means making them his slaves.

When an excitable cab driver (Kazumi Shiomi) and his scatterbrained wife (Jun Miho) try to escape and are nabbed by Isomura, barbed wire goes up and flashlight-wielding thugs begin patrolling the grounds. The village, which once seemed a low-rent haven, becomes a POW camp. Desperate, the sporting-goods store man sends a fax to Genji begging for help and adding that twenty other potential clients need his services. Midnight Run launches its biggest-ever rescue mission.

This mission involves much comic skullduggery, including an appearance by Genji and his right-hand man (Tetsu Masuoka) in drag, and an elaborate escape plan that borrows heavily from the John Sturges classic; all it lacks is Steven McQueen on a motorbike. But in going for big-scale action, the movie loses its satirical edge and descends to frenetic silliness. The escape scenes needed inspired lunacy to put them across. Instead, Hara relies on tired sitcom gags, including a slapstick chase through the sewer, that could have been lifted from *Hogan's Heroes*.

The film's backers probably aren't going to need assistance from Genji's real-life counterparts—*Daiyonige* is entertaining enough for the less-demanding video audience—but the series' biggest midnight run finishes out of breath.

Daiyukai: Rainbow Kids

Rainbow Kids (1991)

Written and directed by Kihachi Okamoto. Produced by Kihachi Pro, Nichimen, and Fuji Eight. With Yae Kitabayashi, Toru Kazama, Katsuyoshi Uchida, Hiroshi Nishikawa, and Ken Ogata. (120 mins.)

Daiyukai: Rainbow Kids starts cute and stays cute. It also gets laughs; I have rarely heard more titters, chuckles, and guffaws in a movie theater in Japan.

Unfortunately, few of them were coming from me.

The film's premise sounds surefire; a spunky granny (Yae Kitabayashi) kidnapped by a trio of small-time punks turns the tables on her abductors. This eighty-two-year-old widow, who lives on a forty-thousand hectare estate in Wakayama Prefecture, doesn't blanch when three young men jump out of the bushes and spirit her away in a car—she positively enjoys the experience. She soon takes command, suggesting the isolated home of her former maid as the perfect hideout and dictating the ransom demand: ten billion yen. Soon granny is running her own kidnapping, as her four children worry and fret (some more sincerely than others), the police launch a manhunt, and the media whoop up the incident into a major story.

As this description indicates, the film's focus is not the gang—the Rainbow Kids—but the granny who gives them their name from a Japanese folk tale. Yae Kitabayashi has been playing variations of this role for years and, by now, it comes as naturally as breathing. Her laconic, almost offhanded delivery lowers the film's sugar count considerably, while winning her the lion's share of the laughs. Some of the humor, however, hinges on her use of the local dialect, which is largely impenetrable to those who have seldom ventured linguistically beyond Tokyo.

Making his thirty-seventh feature, director and scriptwriter Kihachi Okamoto has also packed *Daiyukai* full of gags than don't require a knowledge of Wakayama dialect. Some are abstruse (a course in Japanese real estate law would be helpful in understanding the biggest boff of all—the reason why Granny coopts her kidnappers), while others are as obvious as a swift kick to the posterior. In addition to large helpings of humor, *Daiyukai* provides a dollop of social commentary. Targets include extortionate inheritance taxes, absurd land prices, bungling cops, and media feeding frenzies. Nothing particularly new here, but Okamoto gets off some neat shots, Granny's diabolically clever tax scam being the neatest of all. His real object, though, is to charm and even squeeze out a tear or two. The biggest charmer, naturally, is Granny, but her three kidnapers are also winsome types; dumb, perhaps, but winsome.

One look at the gang leader, played by teen heartthrob Toru Kazama, and you know that Granny is in safe hands. His tough-guy pose is nothing more than that. His two henchmen are even more harmless. Katsuyoshi Uchida gets laughs as the moonfaced goof who falls for the former maid's pretty neighbor and nearly gives the gang away by showing her his face. Hiroshi Nishikawa, who resembles his beefier and more comically talented partner, remains something of a blank. Several of the supporting actors are quite good, including Ken Ogata as the Wakayama cop who is Granny's longtime friend and would-be savior. He storms about trying to crack the case, but has an amused twinkle in his eye when he confronts the old girl and demands that she come clean. Too bad he doesn't have any gross participation points in the film—he, like Granny, would be smiling all the way to the bank.

Dangan Runner
(1996)

Written and directed by Sabu. **Produced by** Nikkatsu. **With** Tomoro Taguchi, Diamond Yukai, Shin'ichi Tsutsumi. (82 mins.)

Dangan Runner is, as the title implies, basically one long chase through the urban landscape of today's Japan. *Dangan*, which means bullet or projectile, aptly describes the frenetic, headlong quality of the action, but the aim of first-time director Sabu is not to make pulses race so much as to comment on the absurdity of violence and the oneness of humanity, especially the portion of it for whom a marathon is the ultimate high.

Yasuda (Tomoro Taguchi) is a bumbling cook who, after a series of humiliations at work and in his love life, tries to regain his self-respect by robbing a bank. But just as he is about to stride though the bank doors, Yasuda realizes that he has forgotten an important part of his disguise—a gauze face mask. Ducking into a nearby convenience store, he finds one—in a child's size. He decides to buy it anyway, but discovers that he has also forgotten his wallet. Now panicked, he stuffs the mask into his jacket pocket and is caught in the act by the store's clerk (Diamond Yukai).

After a scuffle, in which he loses his pistol, Yasuda flees the store with the clerk in hot pursuit. A speed-addicated rock singer whose career is on the skids, the clerk is also fed up with the indignities of his lot; getting ripped off by a dweebish shoplifter is the last straw. Gun in hand, he runs after Yasuda with a murderous glint in his eye. Before he can draw a bead, however, he slams into a *yakuza* (Shin'ichi Tsutsumi) to whom he owes money for drugs. The *yakuza* runs after him and the movie becomes a three-man chase from a Keystone Cops silent. Then, to top the topper, we learn that the *yakuza* himself is in hot water for allowing a hit man from a rival gang to stab his boss and ignite a gang war. Like the man he is pursuing, he has more than one reason to run.

Sabu does not, as we might expect, play this chase primarily for laughs. Keeping his camera close to the action, with shots of straining faces and pumping legs, he underlines its desperate, life-or-death quality.

By shifting the scene, in mid-stride, to his character's memories and fantasies, he shows us the reasons for their' desperation. The inner runner, in short, is as important as the outer one. The obvious point of comparison is director Shin'ya Tsukamoto, who injects his violent fantasies with fevered, twisted, yet somehow amusing life. Tomoro Taguchi, who starred in Tsukamoto's *Tetsuo* and *Tetsuo II*, brings a similar charge to *Dangan Runner*. Though his Yasuda is funny in his bumbling attempts at crime, he can chill with the darkness of his anger and the fierceness of his desire for revenge.

All of Taguchi's skill, however, cannot make the frantic rushing about amount to much finally. Sabu lacks Tsukamoto's talent for pounding his story home. There is a funny sequence when the runners pass a girl on the street—and each imagines himself in bed with her. There is a nice moment when the clerk and the *yakuza* finally catch up with Yasuda, smile at each other, and keep running. But these new-found companions have no where to go but a showdown with a silly lot of cliché gangsters. *Dangan Runner* exhausts itself before the title crawl.

Deborah ga Rival
Deborah, the Rival (1997)

Directed by Masako Matsuura. **Screenplay by** Kazuhiko Ban. **Produced by** Fuji TV and Toei. **With** Hinano Yoshikawa, Tomoe Shinohara, Shunsuke Matsuoka, Shosuke Tanihara. (94 mins.)

Deborah ga Rival stars the big-eyed, button-cute Hinano Yoshikawa, an idol in the idol mold, and Tomoe Shinohara, the rubber-faced TV comedian whose fashion sense—dozens of plastic baubles and beads decorating her person like ornaments on an undersized Christmas tree—hasn't advanced since the first grade. They play friends named Asayo (Hinano) and Shizuka (Shinohara) who enter the same college and become football cheerleaders.

Asayo soon falls for the team's star receiver, longhaired, gorgeous Igarashi (Shunsuke Matsuoka). But she discovers, to her horror, that she has a rival in the team's quarterback (Shosuke Tanihara), who is not only long-haired and gorgeous as well, but a flagrant *okama* (drag queen). Flouncing about on the field, with a pink blouse peaking out from under his jersey, he insists that everyone call him Deborah, for the divine Deborah Harry of Blondie. But he also happens to have a deadly passing arm—and his teammates love him for it.

Directed by Masako Matsuura, who also made the excellent period-drama *Hitodenashi no Koi* (1995), *Deborah* is material that John Waters might have turned into comedy totally unsuitable for viewing by impressionable teenagers. Matsuura may suggest that, far from being appalled by Deborah's acting out, the entire team is gay, but she is, after all, making a teen comedy for Toei. Shosuke Tanihara's Deborah never evolves far beyond the standard *okama* caricature for the girls in the back row to giggle at, though her ability to charm nearly everyone she meets seems convincing enough.

The film's main problem, though, is Hinano, who has a face the camera loves—she's a top teen model—but whose idea of comedy is to twist it into various goofy shapes, like a kid playing with a fun house mirror. She comes across, in fact, as too young for the role: seventeen (her real age) going on twelve. No wonder poor Igarashi can't make up his mind between her and her voguing rival. Though the female principle dominates in *Deborah*, the movie is sorely lacking in real women.

Doten
(1991)

Directed by Toshio Masuda. Screenplay by Toshio Masuda, Toshiro Ashizawa, and Yasuo Sasahara. Produced by Tomen. With Kin'ya Kitaoji, Hitomi Kuroki, Yoko Shimada. (122 mins.)

"This is *Doten*, you know," said the ticket-taker, sure that I'd walked into the wrong theater. "Yes, I know," I replied. I didn't tell her that I'd recently translated a novel set in the early days of Yokohama and wanted to see how Toshio Masuda had filmed that period. *Doten* has big-screen scale—lavish sets, a cast of thousands and a spectacular fire—but a small-screen mentality. It is, essentially, a two-hour TV special. The story and characterizations are outlined in bright, primary colors so that no one misses anything. Also, for all its ostensible earnestness and energy, *Doten* is rather bland, as though it has been processed through an NHK blender. It is mass-audience fare that goes down easily and leaves little aftertaste.

The story is based on historical fact. The hero, Nakaiya Jubei (Kin'ya Kitaoji), was a pioneering Yokohama merchant who eagerly pursued Western learning and developed many contacts among the samurai elite. He was the prototype for Konosuke Matsushita, Akio Morita, and other Japanese businessmen who built fortunes by bridging the gap between East and West, while becoming influential voices in the nation's councils. The film begins in 1858, the year that the shogun's government signed the Treaty of Kanagawa with the United States and opened Japan to commercial intercourse with the outside world. To handle its trade with foreigners

and keep their Western ways from infecting the general population, the government has built a port in a fishing village called Yokohama, a comfortable distance from the seat of power in Edo.

Among the first to see the potential of this trade is Jubei, a prosperous Nihombashi merchant. Leasing a large tract of land, he builds a big emporium of commerce in what is still a frontier town. Right from the start, he aims to stands out from the crowd, many of whom are violently opposed to the opening of the country. As long as most of the voices of reaction are *ronin* (masterless samurai), Jubei can rely on his wits and martial arts skills to survive. But when a conservative regime sweeps to power and deposes Jubei's protector, Iwase, the commissioner of foreign affairs, he faces opponents of a different order. He is brought up before a magistrate for violating the sumptuary laws and is forbidden from bringing silk—the cornerstone of his trade—to Yokohama. He decides to support a direct strike against shogunal oppression: the assassination of Ii Naosuke, the *daimyo* of Hikone and the leader of the shogun's government. The assassins succeed, but the shogunate retaliates and Jubei prepares to go down in a blaze of glory.

Veteran period-drama star Kin'ya Kitaoji plays Jubei with the requisite energy and swagger. That he has brought a similar energy and swagger to countless other films and TV programs doesn't really matter; the character—a rip-roaring Robin Hood of free trade—demands a bravado performance. Jubei is also a charmer with the ladies, including his wife Osono (Hitomi Kuroki) and his friend Oran (Yoko Shimada), the madam of a Yokohama brothel. As Osono, Hitomi Kuroki plays dewy-eyed innocence corrupted by wicked foreign influences, beginning with those twin evils, beef and wine. Her performance ranges from the mildly amusing, as when she takes her first bite of sukiyaki, to the insufferable, as when she goes on a drunken, self-pitying crying jag.

Doten is heavily populated with foreigners—all amateurs and all dreadful. But competent actors are not needed to play the cartoons who tramp across the *tatami* in this film. Despite its internationally minded hero, *Doten* panders to prejudices that go back to arrival of the first Black Ship in Edo Bay. No wonder the ticket-taker did a doubletake when she saw my face; foreigners may belong in *Doten*, but definitely not in its audience.

Don o Totta Otoko
The Man Who Killed the Don (1994)

Directed by Sadao Nakajima. Screenplay by Koji Takada. Produced by Toei, Toei Video. With Hiroki Matsukata,

Tatsuya Yamaguchi, Isao Natsuyaki, Eriko Tamura, Yumi Takigawa. (116 mins.)

For nearly three decades, *yakuza* movies have been to Toei what animation is to Disney: not only a major source of revenue but a part of the company's core identity. A Toei lineup without *yakuza* would be like Disneyland without Mickey Mouse. So when Toei announced that it was making its "last *yakuza* movie"—Sadao Nakajima's *Don o Totta Otoko*, the reverberations could be felt throughout the industry. (Toei later said that if *Don* earned more than four billion yen it would reconsider its decision. It didn't, though—the film fell far short of its target)

Instead of reinventing the genre to attract new fans, *Don* is content to repackage old clichés. It's as though John Wayne were to make his Golden Years comeback, not in *True Grit*, but the thousandth reworking of *Stagecoach*.

Horai (Hiroki Matsukata) has spent eighteen years in prison for killing a rival gang's boss. Just before his release, however, a fellow inmate attacks him with a knife. With the timely help of a young con named Kazu (Tatsuya Yamaguchi), Horai survives, but he knows that someone out there doesn't like him. Who could it be?

When he finally gets out, though, he wants, not revenge, but new life. It will not be easy. The gangster who went with him on the hit, Okido (Isao Natsuyaki), is now the boss (*oyabun*) of a nationwide syndicate. He wants to do right by Horai, who did time for them both. Through his subordinates, he offers him the position of senior advisor. Who could resist? Horai, that's who. He tells Okido's boys that they can keep their meaningless title: he still wants out. Through Kazu, he has found a job as a cook in a nightclub and, through a chance meeting, he has found a young admirer, a jazz singer named Jane (Eriko Tamura). Happiness beckons.

If this were the story of an ordinary gangster, it might end here. But Horai is not ordinary; he is a throwback to the days when *yakuza* were still romantic outlaws with a code of honor. When he gets out of prison, his first act is to visit his old *oyabun*'s grave. When he see that the kimono-clad woman offering incense at a nearby tomb is the daughter of the man he killed (he is mistaken, but no matter), he tells her that a lifetime will not be enough to work off his obligation. When he meets her later at a club—she is the above-mentioned Jane—he takes the mike and wows the young crowd with an emotion-packed *enka* number. This old guy has soul!

He really does. Matsukata, who has been playing *yakuza* roles almost as long as Toei has been making *yakuza* movies, swaggers and growls with a natural authority and style. He can play with his macho

dinosaur image, even taking a bearish pratfall or two, but when the occasion calls for it, he becomes a demon god in a baggy suit.

But even Matsukata's star presence can't overcome the film's idiot plot, juvenile action sequences, and retrograde stereotyping of its female characters. Why, for example, didn't Horai have access to information about Okido's acts and intentions while he was in the slammer? The movie paints him as a latter-day Urashima Taro (Japan's answer to Rip van Winkle), but even a slow-learning *yakuza* would eventually find out that the country's biggest boss had had a daughter with his supposedly devoted wife. When Okido's men try to whack Horai at a hot springs, why do all of them miss their point-blank target? Why does Jane, the film's representative of modern womanhood, spend so much of the movie in the weepy-clingy mode, mooning after her *otosan* (daddy)? She seems to exist solely as a wish-fulfillment object for middle-aged men.

Perhaps I'm being too harsh; traditional *yakuza* movies aren't meant to be realistic portrayals of gangs, but fairy tales for adults longing for a simpler world in which justice always triumphs. The climax of *Don*, in which Horai fights Okido's minions on his way to a showdown with the man himself, is staged exactly like the cybersocky shows for kids in which the good superheroes vaporize dozens of bad space aliens before climbing into their super-robot to battle a super-monster. Most boys, however, outgrow this kind of show by the age of seven or so. Maybe the traditional *yakuza* movie is fading away because its audience is finally maturing—or dying off. But I hope we see Matsukata again; a growl like his is a terrible thing to waste.

Door 3
[1996]

Directed by Kiyoshi Kurosawa. **Screenplay by** Chiaki Konaka. **Produced by** Aya Pro. **With** Minako Tanaka, Akiharu Nakazawa. (Running time: 85 mins.)

There's something to be said for cheesy horror movies. For one thing, they make no pretense about being anything but cheap thrills. You can put away your thinking cap and fall into a pleasant, slackjawed stupor, safe in the knowledge that almost everyone else in the theater is doing likewise. For another thing, the cheesiness can add to the creepy atmosphere. *Night of the Living Dead* was scarier for its use of grainy black-and-white instead of color, and authentic-looking amateur actors instead of pro hacks.

Kiyoshi Kurosawa's *Door 3*—the latest installment in this straight-to-video series—certainly has the requisite cheesiness, including a muddy sound track, with one long dialogue sequence nearly drowned out by heavy traffic, and a cliché-filled score by Torsten Rasch that is a throwback to the days of *The Mummy's Tomb*. At the same time, *Door 3* does not quite fall into the so-bad-it's-good category. Kiyoshi Kurosawa (no relation to Akira) knows how to build tension, create atmosphere, and vigorously milk his few effects. The result is a spine-tingling film made for late-night video viewing.

Miyako (Minako Tanaka) is an insurance saleswoman who has fallen into a slump. She tries everything, including flirting with her male customers, but though they leer and fondle, they don't buy. One day, walking down a narrow stairwell, she bumps into Mitsuru (Akiharu Nakazawa), who manages the local office of a foreign company. With long, lank hair, mascaraed eyes and the smile of a vampire that has just sniffed supper, Mitsuru is seriously weird, but he also has a gentlemanly, soft-spoken, insidiously seductive manner. When he escorts Miyako into his office to treat the ankle she bruised in their fateful encounter, the air suddenly turns hazy and the all-female staff seems to be—how shall we put it?—not altogether there. If we didn't know any better, we would swear they were zombies, who see Miyako as a new rival for the affections of their languorous boss.

Strange things begin happening to poor Miyako. Someone vomits on her front door, a mysterious woman in red flits in and out of sight and, most unsettling of all, Mitsuru tries to force himself on her over drinks one night and she finds herself falling, irresistibly, under his power. Who is this man anyway? A sicko—or a demon?

Not much of this is particularly new or Japanese. The OLs ("office ladies," in Japanese parlance) with glazed eyes are less the scary ghosts of Japanese folklore than steals from *Night of the Living Dead*, while Mitsuru is a close cousin to Tom Cruise's bloodthirsty Lestat in *Interview With the Vampire*, though he is more interested in possessing the bodies of his victims than sucking them dry. But when Tomoko Mayumi, as Miyako's insurance-selling rival, falls into Mitsuru's clutches, she becomes a zombie whose horrifying implacability is reminiscent of the *yuki onna* (snow woman) of Japanese legend. She's the best thing in the film.

The arc of the story is also familiar, leading as it does to the secrets lurking behind the big steel door in Mitsuru's mansion. For me, however, the film's biggest unsolved mystery is Mitsuru's ability to keep his company running with OLs who are—shall we say?—dead on their feet, while managing to allay the suspicions of visitors, who never seem to notice that the office is enveloped in a fog and that the employees are moving in slow motion, if they are moving at all. Does Mitsuru, like the Shadow, have the ability to cloud the minds of men? Or is Kurosawa satirizing the efficiency of typical OLs?—"flowers of the office" who, in this movie, happen to be nightshade.

Dozoku no Ranjo
The Echoes of Folkloric Traditions (1991)
Directed by Kenji Maeda. Produced by Eizo Hanul and Cine Saison. (127 mins.)

As Kenji Maeda's *Dozoku no Ranjo* reminds us, festivals in Japan are more than the colorful pageantry and rowdy highjinks the JTB (Japan Tourist Bureau) sells to tourists. Filmed in Korea, China, and Japan, this documentary examines the historical and religious roots of Japanese festivals, while challenging the myth of Japanese uniqueness and homogeneity.

This examination begins in the hill country of southern China, where the Miao ethnic minority ritually slaughter oxen as a form of ancestor worship. The film is unflinching in its depiction of this rite, showing us the agonized death throes of the helpless animal. But as the narrator reminds us in dulcet tones and scholarly language, this ancient ritual spread throughout Asia and was practiced in Japan until the beginning of this century. We may recoil from the ritual's cruelty, but we begin to understand the religious impulse behind it and that impulse's universality.

As *Dozuku no Ranjo* demonstrates so graphically, the Asia of antiquity was a borderless world, with a free flow of people, customs, and ideas. Japan was also on the receiving end of that flow. Much of what was formerly considered purely Japanese, including festivals and the beliefs that underlie them, came to Japan via the Korean peninsula. Here Maeda treads on what was once—and often still is—dangerous ground. To his credit, he addresses the issue of Korean influence on Japanese folk culture with a wealth of substantiating imagery and commentary, but without sensationalism or political grandstanding.

We learn, for example, how North Star worship, which originated in ancient hunting and fishing rituals, spread from northeastern China to Korea. Along the way it acquired an accretion of Taoist and Buddhist beliefs, then passed over to Japan, where it survives to this day in the Myoken, or North Star, festival. One such festival, celebrated in Mizusawa in northern Japan, reminds us that the gods here can be as harsh on their worshipers as the Old Testament Jehovah. In midwinter, men clad only in loincloths go down to the river, where they purify themselves with cold water. They then proceed to the courtyard of the Myoken Hall, where they wait, packed like sushi in a *bento* box, until a wooden talisman is dropped into the crowd. The one who carries it out of the courtyard is assured of good fortune in the coming year. The resulting melee resembles a huge rugby scrum, with dozens of nearly naked males writhing and twisting toward the center of a roaring, pulsating human pile. This goes beyond the usual definition of "sport." American football is a sport. The Myoken festival is a glimpse into the face of chaos—the Dionysian side of the cultural coin.

Not all of the festivals shown in the film are as life-threatening, however. In Korea, we witness what must be a Guiness World Record tug-of-war, with hundreds of participants to a side. The scene shifts to a similar contest in the Ryukyu islands, in which the tug-of-war rope sprawls out in dozens of strands, like an enormous macrame sculpture,.

A veteran documentary filmmaker, Maeda has made several feature-length documentaries about Japanese festivals. His aim is to produce a definitive statement that is exhaustive and, in places, exhausting. As thorough as a doctoral candidate taking her orals in cultural anthropology, *Dozoku* plods through example after example, in language that even the native speaker who accompanied me to the screening found hard to comprehend. At times, the film seems to bury its subject in an avalanche of fact. But then it presents an image so striking and makes its point so strongly that we have to wake up and take notice. *Dozoku no Ranjo* captures the vibrant energy of Asian folk culture, while presenting a persuasive case for its essential oneness—a case with an increasing importance in a fragmenting world.

2/Duo *
(1997)

Written and directed by Nobuhiro Suwa. Produced by Bitters End. With Eri Yu, Hidetoshi Nishijima. (95 mins.)

Breaking up, as the song says, is hard to do. It is also not easy to sit in a theater and watch two people tear at each other for two hours; a big reason why romantic comedies usually get bigger budgets and better venues than those that describe interpersonal meltdowns, such as Nobuhiro Suwa's *2/Duo*, a first feature, made for next to nothing, that is playing on a late show at one downtown theater.

In filming his story of a relationship gone wrong, Suwa rejects the devices of mainstream romances. There are no joyous scampers on beaches at sunset, no high-volume arguments in driving rainstorms, no chic young women walking alone down city streets, while tears trickle down their perfectly made up cheeks and a plaintive J-Pop theme song swells on the soundtrack. Instead, his lovers—a salesclerk (Eri Yu) in a fancy boutique and a struggling actor (Hidetoshi Nishijima) with no visible means of support—live in a nondescript apartment in an average urban neighborhood. And yet in their very everydayness, they touch us in ways that characters in the trendy dramas, with their high stylistic gloss, rarely do. We cannot help feeling that we are peering past their apartment doorway and into their innermost secrets. We become voyeurs, sympathizers, participants.

A veteran documentarian, Suwa used documentary methods in making *2/Duo*. Writing only a ten-page treatment, he relied on his actors to flesh it out with dialogue. Sitting off camera, he even interviewed his two principals at critical points on their journey to separation. While still in character, they improvised the answers. As the lovers, Hidetoshi Nishijima and Eri Yu create the illusion of naturalness and rightness. In their scenes together, they appear to have passed beyond the usual dating game maneuvers to familiarity, if not true closeness. Their characters are still children who wound out of petulance, destroy from willfulness, and cling to each other from fear of loneliness. They are able to change, but not necessarily for the better. By the end of the film, they have become more adult but, with their love shattered and dreams abandoned, somehow reduced: they are Peter Pans who have forgotten how to fly.

As the film begins, they are living in what looks to be blissful contentment. Though an irresponsible sort who can never keep a yen in his jeans, Nishijima is an affectionate, playful, hippie hunk. His little-boy-lost act has its dark side, however: he can suddenly become childishly petty and cruel, without being able to articulate why. Making sale after sale with a perky, cheerful line of patter, Yu at work presents a sharp contrast to her slacker mate. But when she returns to the apartment she shares with Nishijima, she becomes quieter, softer, and more vulnerable, as though she were shucking her on-the-job character armor the way she takes off her expensive clothes. She enjoys indulging Nishijima in his appetites and games, in the traditional Japanese maternal mold. At the same time she has begun to tire of his aimlessness, though she finds these feelings too dangerous to express.

The debacle begins when Nishijima proposes marriage and Yu refuses. He pretends not to care, but falls into a funk. One night, on returning home from work, Yu finds him sitting silently on the veranda. A moment later, he is wrecking the room and throwing her goldfish bowl to the concrete below. They fight and make up, but soon after he humiliates her in front of her friends. Enraged, Yu packs up and leaves while he is away. Nishijima looks for her and, in the course of his search, makes his long-delayed leap to adulthood. Meanwhile, Yu is living alone in a run-down apartment, working at a mindless factory job, and blanking out in despair.

While not proposing any easy answers, Suwa has created a closely observed portrait of a couple—and by inference, a generation—that seem to have it all, including an erring sense for the right style and attitude, but find adulthood a terror and intimacy hard, if not impossible, to achieve. Their emotional vocabularies aren't big enough and there isn't a cram school in the country that can teach them the words.

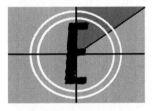

East Meets West

(1995)

Written and directed by Kihachi Okamoto. Produced by Shochiku, Feature Film Enterprise, and Kihachi Production. With Hiroyuki Sanada, Naoto Takenaka, Angelique Roehm, Scott Bachicha, Jay Kerr. (124 mins.)

The story of Kihachi Okamoto's *East Meets West*—a samurai takes on a gang of American desperadoes—may seem unusual, if not absurd, but something very similar has worked well before. The *Kung Fu* TV series, with David Carradine in the lead role, became a huge hit in the early seventies and helped launched the international martial arts boom. It's one thing, however, for Hollywood to produce an Eastern Western and another for a Japanese film company to make one. The Western is a core American film genre, with a tradition as old as the movies. The *Kung Fu* producers may have made a bad casting choice—Bruce Lee tried and failed to get the role—but when it came to genre conventions, they knew what they were violating.

Imagine those same producers putting a cowboy in a samurai film. A harder stretch, right? That, in reverse, was the same stretch facing *East Meets West* scriptwriter and director Kihachi Okamoto. This seventy-one-year-old veteran says in the program notes that, after coming to Tokyo in 1941, he developed "something of a mania for Westerns." *East Meets West* evidences a close acquaintance with

Howard Hawk's *Rio Bravo*. But for all the funny bits of slapstick and the dazzlingly choreographed action sequences, *East Meets West* is like those Western-themed restaurants in Japan that serve miniature steaks on hot plates, with prettily sliced vegetables on the side. Not exactly chuckwagon fare.

Kamijo Kenkichi (Hiroyuki Sanada) is a masterless samurai from a clan that is opposed to opening the country to foreigners. Somehow, he manages to join a government delegation bound for Washington to conclude a treaty of friendship between the United States and Japan. His object: to foil the delegation's mission by assassinating key members. When his ship lands in San Francisco he is ordered to assist in the exchange of three thousand Japanese gold pieces for American dollars. But the detail carrying the strongbox is ambushed by bandits, the gold is stolen, and Kamijo, after dicing several of the bad guys, sets off in pursuit. On discovering his disappearance and learning his true identity, the leaders of the delegation conclude that he was in on the robbery and dispatch a loyal *ninja* (Naoto Takenaka) to find him and recover the gold.

Sanada, as Kamijo, speaks his English lines with a samurai-like dignity, and slashes the baddies with the grace and style of the gymnast he once was. As the *ninja*, Naoto Takenaka entertains with broad comedy—his wiggle through the bars of a San Francisco jail to the adjoining cell of an Indian maiden (Angelique Roehm) is amusingly lubricous—but he mugs too long and too hard and finally becomes tiresome.

More problematic, however, is the plot, whose busyness works to the detriment of character development and narrative drive,. In addition to a *tour de horizon* of Japanese politics, circa 1860, with an array of famous historical faces, Okamoto gives us a cute towheaded boy (Scott Bachicha) who joins Kamijo to find his father's killers, the aforementioned Indian maiden, who becomes the *ninja*'s lover and introduces him to Indian life (while saving his ignorant scalp), and a schoolteacher (Jay Kerr), who decides to help Kamijo and drafts a gang of former students into the samurai's quest. Save for the boy, who becomes Kamijo's disciple and learns to wield a mean sword, the American characters are little more than stick-figures fitted with a comic quirk or two.

Also, couldn't the producers find enough Native American actors to play the movie's cliché Indians? It's bad enough that their lines amount to little more than "hows" and howls, but the sight of white boys clowning in warpaint strikes the wrong note of cultural insensitivity and moral obtuseness. East does meet West in this movie, hilariously at times. It's too bad they don't become better acquainted.

Edogawa Rampo Gekijo: Yaneura no Samposha

Watcher In the Ceiling (1994)

Directed by Akio Jissoji. Screenplay by Akio Satsugawa. Cinematography by Masao Nakahori. Produced by TBS and Bandai Visual. With Hiroshi Mikami, Masumi Miyazaki, No Terada, Hitomi Shimizu, Naomasa Mutaka, Kyusaku Shimada. (74 mins.)

Born in 1894, Edogawa Rampo was a pioneer of the mystery genre in Japan, just as Edgar Allan Poe was in the West. And like Poe, from whom he took his pen name, Rampo had a taste for the supernatural, a streak of perversity, and a knack for the kinds of "well-made" stories that evoke elemental fantasies and fears, and, for that reason, are still read.

The centennial of his birth has occasioned a Rampo revival. One of its products is *Yaneura no Samposha*. Based on a 1925 Rampo story, it evokes an atmosphere of stylish Taisho-era enervation and steamy contemporary eroticism, underlaid with canny insights into the baser human passions. As a mystery, it is old-fashioned—it turns, shades of Sherlock Holmes, on an amateur detective uncovering the single clue that spoils the perfect crime—but it holds our interest until the twist ending.

The film unfolds within the confines of the Toeikan, a Tokyo rooming house. As the film begins, the residents are discussing the impact sound will have on the movies. One, a languid young man named Goda (Hiroshi Mikami), is sitting apart from the others, making smoke rings and thinking how stupendously boring these people are. Better to die and be done with it!

But rather than end it all, Goda finds a new interest. One day, while playing dress-up with a woman's wig and lipstick, he accidentally loosens a ceiling board in his closet. Climbing up, he discovers a dimly lit passageway under the roof leading to the rooms of the other residents. Soon he is scampering about up there, making knotholes to better view intimacies that reveal infinitely more about his fellow residents than the intellectualities they present to the world.

There is Miss Akizuki (Masumi Miyazaki) of the sweet voice and lusciously vacuous manner, sawing away on her violin to a classical piece on her phonograph. She plays in a hotel orchestra but, from the fiercely intent look on her face, we see that she aspires to something higher—and is not quite the excruciatingly proper young lady she seems. There is the mustachioed lawyer (No Terada) who has tied his kimonoed concubine (Hitomi Shimizu) into an elaborate spider's web with hempen ropes and is now sketching her on a pad of rice paper. Wanting the final, perfect touch, he approaches her with a lit candle and slowly drips wax on her exposed breast. She quivers and screams in orgasmic delight.

There is more, much more—but, as the days pass, the delight Goda first felt from his explorations begins to fade. He needs a new stimulus. He remembers Endo the dentist (Naomasa Mutaka), a loathsome toad who once boasted of a failed *shinju* (love suicide) with the wife of a colleague and his theft of a bottle of morphine from his office. "With this," he said, "you can die easily, without pain." Goda decides to give Dr. Endo a taste of his own medicine. It would not be fair to describe how he plots the dentist's death, with an ingenuity worthy of a Conan Doyle villain, or how a lantern-jawed "researcher of human psychology" (Kyusaku Shimada) uncovers Goda's nefarious scheme. Enough to say that these two come to understand each other in way the other roomers do not.

As played by Hiroshi Mikami, Goda may be a pervert and voyeur, but he is an amusing fellow nonetheless, cleverly commenting on his victims as he peers at them through the knothole. Kyusaku Shimada is convincing as the phlegmatic researcher who believes in nothing and views his fellow beings with the same impersonal eyes as Goda's. (The difference being that his are cold, not hot, his pleasures intellectual, not sensual).

Yaneura no Samposha is not what is usually considered an art film; it belongs, after to all, to a genre that was once relegated to the drive-in. And yet there is more art—and considerably more entertainment—in this film than others from Japan that find their way onto festival programs. It is a decadently delightful walk on the wild side.

Eiko to Kyoki

Rowing Through (1996)

Directed by Masato Harada. Screenplay by Will Aitken, Masato Harada. Produced by Shochiku, Fuji TV, Pony Canyon, Dentsu, and Aska Film International. With Michiko Hada, Colin Ferguson, Pete Murnik, James Hyndman, Leslie Hope. (116 mins.)

The trip across the Pacific has not been a noticeably rewarding one for Japanese filmmakers. Films made by Japanese producers or directors in the States, such as *Iron Maze*, *Ruby Cairo*, and *Painted Desert*, have died terrible deaths at the Japanese box office. But hope springs eternal. Producer Kazuyoshi Okuyama and director Masato Harada, who gave us *Painted*

Desert, with its ludicrous Mafia trench war in the sand, are now back with *Eiko to Kyoki* (Rowing Through), the story of a rower's lonely quest to compete in the 1984 Los Angeles Olympics.

Based on *The Amateurs*, a nonfiction book by David Halberstam, the film was shot largely in Canada, with a local crew. Also, the cast, with sole exception of Michiko Hada, is North American. But what truly marks the movie as non-Japanese is its look. A former film journalist who covered Hollywood for Japanese magazines, Harada has mastered the craft of Hollywood commercial moviemaking, with its emphasis on smoothly dynamic camerawork (his swooping shots of straining rowers seem to have been filmed on a magic carpet) and a storytelling style that minimizes draggy exposition and maximizes action.

He has made a sport that this reviewer long thought of as a masochistic exercise in character building for prep-school boys look ruggedly macho, viscerally thrilling, and elegantly lovely. Selected clips would a make a terrific recruiting video for the Harvard rowing team. The film, however, has relatively little to do with the glamour of Ivy League rowing, and quite a lot to do with Japanese mass-audience expectations. It's focus is that eternal Japanese theme: the pure-hearted hero who stubbornly battles against overwhelming odds and finally goes down in sublime defeat.

He is Tiff Wood (Colin Ferguson), a Harvard rowing-team star who spends four years after graduation training for the Moscow Olympics, only to have them canceled by Jimmy Carter. A short-fused type, Tiff freaks out at the news conference protesting this decision (not one of the film's dramatic high points), but resolves to persevere another four years, until Los Angeles. When 1984 rolls around, however, Tiff is past thirty and starting to feel it. Meanwhile, younger competitors are coming up, including a natural named Bigelow (Pete Murnik) who owns the best fast-twitch muscles in the sport and a shaven-headed hulk (James Hyndman) who goes by the name Polar Bear and is into Oriental martial arts and mysticism.

On shore, Tiff is torn between Kate (Leslie Hope), a former Harvard cox who is now writing a book on the Olympic rowing team, and Slim, an older woman who runs a local bar. Kate, who keeps a picture of St. Sebastian in her room and frankly admits that she enjoys "watching men suffer," encourages him to stick it out, while Slim, frankly sensuous and worldly-wise, urges him to hang up his oars. If *Eiko* were a Hollywood zero-to-hero movie we know who Tiff would listen to and how he would respond to the threat of being cut from the team. But of course it isn't that kind of movie; it's about giving one's all

and achieving glorious oblivion: *Ashita no Joe* in a two-man scull.

A former Second City comedian playing in his first starring movie role, Colin Ferguson projects his character's stoicism and intensity by alternating between dull woodenness and freak-out hysteria. Not too many laughs, or too many insights into what makes a man sacrifice eight years for a long shot at a medal.

Though the leading man's vibes may be stupefyingly flat, the story is frantically busy, condensing enough material for a miniseries into its two-hour running length. Rather than simplify the decade of events covered in Halberstam's book, Harada and co-scriptwriter Will Aitken try to cram them all in. The result is a film full of stormy incident, oddly devoid of tension. Rather than cribbing from Halberstam, these two should have been stealing from *Rocky*.

Finally, the film is full of obscure rowing jargon and tired profanities, the latter usually shouted. Instead of Harvard men, the characters often sound like New York cabbies cussing a lane jumper. Perhaps they should have taken up a quieter, less stressful sport. Skydiving, anyone?

Eko Eko Azaraku ✳
Wizard of Darkness (1995)

Directed by Shimako Sato. Screenplay by Junki Takegami. Produced by Gaga Communications. With Kimika Yoshino, Miho Kanno, Shuma, Naoto Takahashi, Mio Takaki. (81 mins.)

School is a spooky place for a lot of Japanese kids, if the popularity of books and comics with "ghost in the classroom" themes is any indication. One reason, I suspect, is that too many schools here, with their mindless rules and mindbending tests, their beatings by the teachers and bullying by students, are horror shows to begin with. If the devil is behind the teacher's desk, who's to say what's in the restroom?

Shimako Sato's *Eko Eko Azaraku* would seem to exploit this fear. Based on a series that appears in the horror-*manga* magazine *Suspiria*, the film falls into the much-reviled, if enduringly popular, Dead Teenager genre. But though its teenage protagonists may meet terrifying ends at the hands of an evil witch, *Eko Eko* is insightful into the ways adolescents fantasize about power, sex and the unseen world. The script, by Junki Takegami, plays as though it were written by a teenager, without the usual adult filters of sentimentalizing nostalgia or condescending humor.

Also, Sato, who studied her craft at the London International Film School for two years and shot her 1992 debut film, *Virginia*, with a British staff and cast, has injected her story with a dark, edgy suspense and a hot, dangerous eroticism. Save for few spots that reveal the inexperience of her actors and the limitations of her budget, she maximizes the impact of each scene with eerie atmospherics, tight, inventive camerawork and, in the film's final showdown between good and evil, spectacular computer graphics. In short, a satisfying genre entertainment that successfully aspires to something more.

The film's heroine is Misa Kuroi (Kimika Yoshino), a transfer student with big eyes, a cool gaze, and, as it turns out, a mysterious past. She soon finds a friend in Mizuki, the cute class president (Miho Kanno), an admirer in Shindo, a handsome soccer player (Shuma) and an enemy in Mizuno (Naoto Takahashi), a loner with an unhealthy interest in the occult. When Mizuki tries to tell her about the rumored lesbian love affair between their homeroom teacher, Ms. Shirai (Mio Takaki), and a classmate—and begins writhing in pain—Misa also learns that someone in the school is practicing black magic. She should know; she's a witch herself.

The story concerns Misa's struggle to expose and defeat this opponent, while trying to clear her name of Mizuno's charge that she is the one casting the evil spells. The final showdown comes one night when she and twelve of her classmates find themselves locked in the school and begin dying off one by one. Her powers, she discovers, are useless. Meanwhile the number thirteen, which has mysteriously appeared on the blackboard, is counting down to zero.

In a typical horror flick the screen would soon be swimming in blood, as the body count builds. Sato prefers to first explore her heroine's new social environment, such as the way Misa's casting of a spell on a sexually harassing teacher make her an instant heroine—and how her success later rebounds against her when the teacher falls seriously ill. Though Sato does not try to give this material more significance that it deserves, she delivers pointed observations on the dynamics of bullying and sex in the classroom.

Does the fact that she is a woman matter? I think that fact that she displays a large, audience-pleasing talent matters very much indeed. The Japanese film industry needs more Shimako Satos if it hopes to regain its artistic credibility and box-office clout.

Eko Eko Azaraku 2: Birth of the Wizard

Wizard of Darkness 2: Birth of the Wizard (1996)

Written and directed by Shimako Sato. Produced by Gaga Communications and Tsuburaya Eizo. With Kimika Yoshino, Wataru Shihodo. (83 mins.)

In 1995 Shimako Sato made an extraordinary film in the despised Dead Teenager genre: *Eko Eko Azaraku.* Now Sato is back with *Eko Eko Azaraku II—Birth of the Wizard.* Once again the film is based on a *manga* by Shin'ichi Koga and once again the star is Kimika Yoshino, playing the teen witch Misa Kuroi. This time, however, Sato incorporates more effects, some of which are gorily spectacular. She has also abandoned the psycho-sociological explorations of the first film for full-bore thrills and chills. The sequel, in short, is a technically slicker production, but lacks the freshness of the original.

Eko II bears almost no narrative relation to its predecessor. Though still a high-school student, Misa Kuroi begins the movie unaware of her powers—quite a change from the seasoned witch of the first film. Her days as a normal teenager soon end, however, when she returns to a party after a beer-buying expedition and finds her classmates sprawled in pools of blood, their faces crushed to pulp by the hand of a white-coated assailant. His real target, though, was Misa—and he is soon on her trail, with an implacable stare not quite human. Before he can get her in his deadly grip, however, she is saved by a stranger in a black trenchcoat (Wataru Shihodo).

She doesn't trust him at first—he is too silent and secretive. But after she escapes to a nearby police box, and he rescues her again—this time from a zombielike cop who coldbloodedly murders his colleagues and trains his pistol on Misa—he finally tells her his story. His name is Saiga and he is the last survivor of a family of magicians are who were massacred in 1880. More than a century later, an archaeologist dug up the victims and unwittingly freed the evil witch responsible for the murders. Now she is after Misa. By possessing the girl's body she can unleash her terrible powers on the world. Only Misa herself, with the aid of a magic pendant, can stop her.

Sato and her staff may not have the budget of a James Cameron, but they create effects that shock us out of our just-a-horror-movie superiority. It wouldn't be fair to reveal too much; just imagine fingers that not only tear at flesh, but sink into it. Sato paces the film perfectly, never letting the action drag, while springing her big jolts at exactly the right moment. If any Japanese director is ready to make the move to Hollywood, it is Sato.

Once again Kimika Yoshino gives a performance that is as highly charged, if not quite as dark and knowing as in the first film. This actress with the big eyes and piercing gaze makes us believers in Misa's mysterious powers.

But Sato can't entirely hide *Eko II*'s thinness. For all her craft, it is just one more story about a young woman fleeing from a boogie man in an empty labyrinthine building, and a dark, handsome hero charging to the rescue. In short, the gothic in late twentieth-century Japan, with body-slashing instead of bodice-ripping. But give her credit for an ending that brings the movie's occult powers to scarifyingly operatic life. One (bloody) thumb up—and the nod to direct the next Stephen King movie.

Endless Waltz
(1995)

Directed by Koji Wakamatsu. Screenplay by Akimasa Shimma and Deru Deguchi. Produced by Shochiku. With Ko Machida, Reona Hirota. (102 mins.)

Movies that touch on personally remembered people and events are tricky to review. I overpraised Oliver Stone's The Doors because it brought back the 1960s and its Lizard King, Jim Morrison, so vividly. Stone got the clothes, the attitudes, and the music right, but failed to capture the inner demons that made Morrison's music possible. That should have mattered more than it did when I wrote the review.

Koji Wakamatsu's Endless Waltz is another screen bio centering on a talented, charismatic, but self-destructive musician, jazz saxophonist Kaoru Abe. Though Abe's decade was the 1970s, he shared Morrison's disdain for limits and his fondness for mood-altering substances. Whereas The Doors focused on its hero's public persona—with Van Kilmer's Morrison in concert bearing an uncanny resemblance to the real thing—Endless Waltz takes us deep inside Abe's marriage to writer Izumi Suzuki.

This is a commercially riskier approach, but in Kaoru Abe's case, it is the only one. Unlike Morrison, whose exploits on and off stage became the stuff of generational legend, Abe spent his nine-year career playing free jazz to a coterie audience. A music that ventured outside the conventional bounds of rhythm and melody, free jazz no doubt sounded like industrial noise to the uninitiated. To this Ornette Coleman fan, Abe's experimentations have their fascinations and familiarities, but they are not the stuff of which audience-pleasing films are made. Also, though singer Ko Machida projects a white-hot intensity as Abe on stage, a Morrison his character is not. A hardcore jazzbo, Abe plays for himself alone, disdaining rock's sexual theatrics.

In Endless Waltz, however, his offstage life is anything but asexual. He first encounters Izumi Suzuki (Reona Hirota) when she dials a wrong number, but after wangling a date with her, immediately decides she is Ms. Right and moves in. He is, he announces, a man who takes everything to the limit, including love. The attraction, Suzuki makes clear, is mutual.

Shortly after their telephone self-introductions, Abe and Suzuki are having uninhibited sex in Suzuki's apartment. But as their relationship deepens, it becomes obvious that these two have more than the hots for each other. They are soulmates, who share not only an outlook on life, but a way of being.

Though Abe plays the controlling macho male, smacking Suzuki and smashing her things when her words or attitudes enrage him, he also has a strong feminine side that expresses itself positively in the passion of his music and his sensitivity to feelings, negatively in his pettiness, moodiness, and dependency. Also, when his turbulent emotions overwhelm him, he is prone to epileptic seizures. He is, in short, often hell to live with. Suzuki initially comes across as an airheaded hippie chick who collects men the way other women buy shoes, but as her affair with Abe segues into marriage and motherhood, we see that she is the stronger of the two, with a firmer grip on life's realities and professional responsibilities. Her emotions, however, are every bit as volatile and her urge to self-destruction every bit as strong as her mate's.

In the early days of the their relationship, Abe and Suzuki are less adults in love than two wild, lost kids playing thrilling, dangerous games on the edge of the abyss. Drugs and booze are an integral part of these games, as are bitter fights, tearful separations and, in Suzuki's case, the offering of a body part to her beloved. An idealist, Abe wants Suzuki to follow him into holy poverty, for the sake of their sacred Muse. Suzuki refuses; she wants a seminormal life for herself, and later, for her daughter. This difference is never resolved. They can't live together, they can't live apart, and, finally, they decide they can't live at all.

Koji Wakamatsu, who knew both principals, recreates their lives and milieu with imaginative sympathy and period accuracy. Like Oliver Stone, he tends to overinflate and overstate (seeing the many explicit sex scenes, video shop owners may file this film in the "adult" section), but he also makes us understand the sadness and even the beauty of Abe and Suzuki's messy, disastrous, madly passionate love affair. Am I overselling this film because I knew the times and places it describes? I think not, but it makes me feel lucky that I, unlike its principals, escaped alive.

E no Naka no Boku no Mura
Village of Dreams (1996)

Directed by Yoichi Higashi. Screenplay by Takehiro Nakajima. Produced by Siglo. With Keigo Matsuyama, Shogo Matsuyama, Mikiko Harada, Kyozo Nagatsuka. (112 mins.)

Childhood is a magical time, we are often told. Yoichi Higashi's *E no Naka no Boku no Mura* reminds us that this magic is black as well as white, scary as well as delightful. It goes straight to our core and teaches lessons that last a lifetime.

Set in a remote village in Kochi Prefecture in 1948, *E no Naka* depicts the boyhood of twin brothers—Yukihiko and Seizo Tashima—who later became well-known illustrators of children's books. Simply told but richly imagined, the film offers insights into the traditional Japanese ethos and the workings of the heart, Japanese or no.

Higashi frames his film with documentary scenes of the twins, now in their fifties, discussing a book on their childhood that they are making together. Then we are in that childhood—and a Japan that no longer exists. In 1948 Japan was undergoing profound changes, but in Seizo and Yukihiko's rural backwater, life still moved to old rhythms, followed old ways. As the film begins, the boys are living in an eternal summer amidst a countryside that has not yet entered the twentieth century. Played by identical twins Keigo and Shogo Matsuyama, the boys spend their days fishing, swimming, and catching eels in the local stream—Japanese Huck Finns, right down to their wide-brimmed straw hats.

The film, however, is not a nostalgic idyll—the boys' world has its dark side as well. As twins, they are variously petted as curiosities and shunned as freaks. Their mother (Mikiko Harada), who teaches at the local elementary school, is viewed coldly as an outsider who, though dependent on local benevolence—she and the boys are living with a member of the provincial gentry while her government official husband (Kyozo Nagatsuka) is away on on business—holds herself aloof from local society. She is also criticized for selecting her sons' works for an art contest over the objections of the school principal (and is praised, reluctantly, when the boys win). Partly in reaction to this treatment and partly because they are boys, the twins are constantly getting into mischief. They cut down taro plants, break light bulbs, and, to revenge a humiliation by the school principal, toss their classmates' footwear into a nearby rice paddy.

They befriend a boy and girl in their class who are despised for their poverty and, though this is never clearly stated, for belonging to the *burakumin* caste. The boy understands the natural world in a way the twins do not. He knows how to catch fish, blow a conch shell, and swipe eels from fishermen's traps. He shares his secrets with the twins and brings them closer to that world.

As children living in a society still close to its premodern roots, the boys also encounter phenomena that can only be called magical. A white bellyband

comes to life and wraps itself, snakelike, around them; a mysterious voice invites one of the twins to wrestle while he is swimming for his life in a roiling stream; and a forest sprite pokes his head out of the bushes, frightening them both half to death. Watching over the twins' adventures, natural and supernatural, are three witches who comment like a Greek chorus on their actions and occasionally try to punish them for their misdeeds.

Though structured as loosely as the twins' summer days, these and other incidents point unwaveringly toward larger themes. How, Higashi asks, do we draw the boundaries between self and other in a society that does not tolerate difference? What do we lose by destroying the links between the human and the natural world and by cutting ourselves off from our cultural roots?

The twins' solution—to retreat into a private world shared only by the two of them—is only temporarily viable. They fight with each other, while struggling unsuccessfully against society's view of them as one personality in two bodies. Not even twinship, Higashi tells us, can completely protect us from the isolation that is our fate. But his film gives us back a bit of the magic we have lost.

F
(1998)

Directed by Shusuke Kaneko. **Screenplay by** Shusuke Kaneko and Natsu Matsuo. **Produced by** Shochiku, Shochiku Fuji and Eisei Gekijo. **With** Michiko Hada, Hironobu Nomura, Tetsuya Kumakawa, Rikaco. (102 mins.)

Seeing *F*, Shusuke Kaneko's romantic drama about a love affair conducted over the airwaves, I was reminded of Orson Welles' 1974 *F for Fake*, the master's rambling but engaging documentary on famous hoaxers. In both films the principals are smart dissemblers who learn that the games they play with the truth have consequences not always pleasant.

But the makers of *F* were thinking less of paying homage to Welles and more of reproducing the smash success of *Sleepless in Seattle*. Much like Meg

Ryan's journalist in *Sleepless*, Michiko Hada's Hikaru is a career woman more-or-less engaged to a nice, steady, dependable fellow named Shogo (Hironobu Nomura), who is about as exciting as tofu. Then while she and Mr. Not-Quite-Right are cruising around Tokyo Bay at night they run across a couple who have lost their car keys and locked themselves out of their snazzy red sedan. Shogo leaves in search of a gas station with the driver, an irritatiingly superior but insecure young woman, while Hikaru remains behind with her consort, a darkly handsome guy on crutches. A mechanical whiz, Hikaru soon manages to start the engine and heads off after Shogo, but by the time she catches up, something has clicked between her and this stranger with the searching eyes.

He is Fumiya Furuse (Tetsuya Kumakawa), a world-class ballet dancer who injured his foot while practicing in London and has returned to Japan to recuperate. To raise his profile in Japan, his manager and financee—the aforementioned young woman—arranges for him to host a radio show. Now regretting that he neglected to ask the name of his rescuer, Fumiya uses his radio show to mount a missing person search. Taking the pseudonym "Mr. F"—a reference to a word game he and Hikaru played that fateful night—he asks listeners to guess his identity. Tuning in, Hikaru decides to drop Mr. F a postcard and sign it with a pseudonym of her own—Hikari.

Soon Hikari and Mr. F are flirting on the air while listeners hang on their every word. Ratings soar, but Hikaru can't bring herself to reveal her real identity to Mr. F and break up with Shogo. He may be dull, but he represents stability, while Mr. F is a leap into the dark. Though her worldly-wise friend Yuka (Rikaco) advises her to grab what her heart desires, Hikaru hesitates. Here *F* departs radically from *Sleepless In Seattle*. In the Hollywood film, romantic love is the be all and end all, worthy of any sacrifice. Once Meg has her heart set on Tom Hanks, her lumpish fiancee hardly stands a chance. Hikaru, however, is torn between competing claims and it's not immediately clear that her love for Mr. F will tip the balance. Interestingly, the traditional balance-tippers—family considerations and future prospects—never make an appearance. Hikaru is a Meg-like romantic, but she's also more used to being carried along by the current than making waves.

The male leads in Japanese date movies are usually little more than Ken-doll figures. *F*, however, has not only reversed the usual sexual roles—Hikaru likes messing with cars and computers, Fumiya lives to dance—but created a role for ballet star Tetsuya Kumakawa that presents him as a flesh-and-blood being, albeit one larger than life as we groundlings know it. A principal dancer with the Royal Ballet

Company of London, Kumakawa performs all those dazzling leaps and spins himself. He is also a talented actor, who can not only set Hikaru's heart aquiver with his smoky aura, but look passably heartbroken when she tries to throw him over. He is, in fact, too big a talent to be contained by this *shojo manga* (girls comic) brought to the screen.

Michiko Hada is so convincing as an audience-surrogate, who is not boringly serious about her career and would drift into a safe, dull marriage save for her balletic *deus ex machina*, that it's hard to imagine what Fumiya sees in her. That, in a way, is the whole point of this glossy fantasy: that a gifted, cosmopolitan hunk would find Hikaru attractive simply because she is an ordinary woman who represents all the real Japaneseness that has been missing in his life. F, in this movie, finally stands for *furusato* (home sweet Japan).

Far East Babies

(1994)

Written and directed by Junji Yasuda. Produced by P.P.P. Project. With Jin Ueno, Shusuke Sano, Nuts Tanahashi. (107 mins.)

Punk rock, like everything else, came to Japan, but as we can see in Junji Yasuda's *Far East Babies*, it lost something in the social translation. The first thing to go, as we might expect, was the rage. The film's punk band, a trio called the Gasoline Brothers (Jin Ueno, Shusuke Sano, Nuts Tanahashi), are mugging nerds with ukuleles who strum sardonic ditties as they stroll through the architectural excess of West Shinjuku. Yes, they smash faces, but much the way the Marx Brothers used to wreck staterooms, with a demented glee more funny than scary. They are clowns without a cause.

Like the chord structure of a punk song, the story is don't-care simple. And, like a punk performance, the telling of that story is in-your-face chaotic. Who are these characters? Why are they doing these weird things to each other? Where, if anywhere, is this movie headed? Instead of answers, Uchida produces images that at first look to be eye candy of the rock-video variety—much self-consciously cool style, little discernible substance. But if one abandons the search for deeper meaning and sits in a back row seat to avoid visual overload, *Far East Babies* becomes a wacky excursion into the absurd: *Duck Soup* for Gen Xers.

The story can be summarized in a paragraph (the film's program does it in eight lines). A young man named Wakuta becomes frantic when he discovers that someone has stolen his "*obaasan*" (grandmother)

from his shambles of an apartment. This "*obaasan*," we soon discover, is a carved figure of unnamed ethnic origin. While Wakuta is digging away for it at the beach, he and his buddies the Gasoline Brothers suddenly see (have a vision of ?) another young man named Narutoshi walking off with the idol cradled in his arms. A naturalist—or obsessed beachcomber—who lives alone on an island in an A-frame hut and spends his days collecting and classifying specimens, Narutoshi would seem to be a harmless type, but Wakuta and the Gasoline Brothers set off in search of him as though he were the enemy. They pack not only their ukuleles, but a gun.

One could read this as allegory, with the Gasoline Brothers, grinning wickedly in a dimly-lit room filled with menacing machinery, representing the dark destructive forces of modern life and Narutoshi, calmly stuffing crabs into specimen bottles, standing for the spirit of light and reason. But, besides being silly, this reading simply doesn't work. The Gasoline Brothers may strap Narutoshi's fat, dull-witted brother into a chair and whirl him about like a pinwheel to extract information, but they are bad the way Harpo with a rubber bladder was bad; their leer is worse than their bite. Also, Narutoshi is less the man of science than an *otaku* loner who gets his kicks looking at bugs he has embalmed in transparent plastic. In this movie, there are no heroes, no villains—only wackos of varying descriptions.

Yes, there is violence, lot of it, it's ironic, not real. When Wakuta shoots two punks in the subway, the sound has all the impact of a convenience-store firecracker and his victims writhe about as though they were performing a horizontal slam dance. Though Uchida may do his damnedest to subvert cinematic conventions, he takes as much care with lighting and composition as any Golden Age director. Shot in black-and-white, *Far East Babies* has a visual richness that is absorbing, numbing, mind-blowing. In several scenes, the film abandons narrative altogether for a strobe-light onslaught of images. The effect is like that of a punk guitar solo; you are either swept away by the noise—or seized by an irresistible urge to leave the theater. Either way *Far East Babies* will linger somewhere in the corner of your mind—like that green and pink hairdo you saw in 1982, while waiting on a Shinjuku Station platform for a last train to nowhere.

Father Fucker *
The Girl of the Silence (1995)

Directed by Genjiro Arato. Screenplay by Goro Hayazaki. Produced by Filmmakers, HoriPro, Pony Canyon. With Mami Nakamura, Yoshio Harada, Michio Akiyama, Kaori Momoi, Ken Kaneko. (90 mins.)

When I received publicity materials for Genjiro Arato's *Father Fucker*, my first thought was that it needed a new English title (It got one—The Girl Of the Silence). My second was that it would be heavy going. I was wrong. Despite visual metaphors that are overabundant and over-obvious—too many flowers of fertility and towers of virility—the film tells its dark story with insight, imagination, and even touches of humor. Its poetic approach takes us deeper in its heroine's inner world than conventional realism, with its stress on the sordid (and its undercurrent of exploitation) would.

Fourteen-year-old Shizuko (Mami Nakamura) discovers that she is pregnant by a classmate. When her stepfather (Michio Akiyama) finds out, he rapes her as a form of "punishment," while her mother (Kaori Momoi), a slatternly cabaret hostess, silently acquiesces. As this sexual abuse becomes routine, Shizuko takes refuge in her imagination. An aspiring *manga* (comic book) artist, she sits at her desk drawing a different world and dreaming of a different life.

Father Fucker is based on an autobiographical novel by Shungiku Uchida that became a controversial bestseller. In an interview Uchida said that when she finally left home for Tokyo she and her mother severed relations. "I realized that if I were to die, by law everything I had would go to my mother... So I wrote [the book] out of spite," she said. A properly brought-up Japanese woman could not say this (even if she wanted to), but Uchida hardly had a proper upbringing. She does, however, seem to possess a dry sense of humor and an uncommonly strong will. She would rather think of herself as a survivor than a victim.

In Mami Nakamura's Shizuko we can see this survivor in embryo, especially in the glint of her large, staring eyes. But she is also a girl living in Nagasaki in the late 1960s. When her real father (Yoshio Harada) leaves and a strange man wearing a white suit suddenly appears, she quietly accepts the change, even when it becomes clear that her new *otosama* (father) is a monster. In addition to a refrigerator fetish (he loves to polish the white door and stare at the clean, cool contents), he has a thing about proper behavior, as defined by a Japanese male chauvinist, circa 1968. He is to be the master and the women his servants, jumping at his every command (and satisfying his sexual urges).

Michio Akiyama, a producer/planner who discovered Uchida and promoted her *manga* career, portrays this monster with comic attitudes and rhythms that would be perfect for the social satire of Juzo Itami. In *Father Fucker* however, they are a touch too jokey for the material. He can express the father's egotistical ugliness, but not the moral abyss into which he has fallen. Kaori Momoi gives her best performance in years as the mother. Momoi is often lazy and self-indulgent, but in this film she is superb, playing a woman whose resignation to evil becomes another form of abuse. Even the way she stolidly washes the rice, while her daughter is being raped in the next room, speak eloquently about the mother's character—or rather lack of it.

The film's best scenes, however, are those that take leave of reality altogether and explore Shizuko's inner world. Directing his first film after a long career as an independent producer, Genjiro Arato skillfully traces Shizuko's transition from wounded girlhood into defiant womanhood in symbolic images and dreams, including a series of imaginary conversations that she holds with her father (Ken Kaneko) in a younger, longhaired incarnation. This father is understanding, supportive and kind—everything the adults in her life are not. Their conversations take place in a school clinic—a "safe zone" where Shizuko can have her drawings and a big tank of tropical fish, where she can breathe freely. Her dream life, we see, enables her to fight the destructive forces in her real life and finally escape them. A movie about one of lowest acts a human being can commit ends as a testament to the strength of the human spirit.

Focus *
(1996)

Written and directed by Satoshi Isaka. **Cinematography by** Tetsuro Sano. **Produced by** Seiyu, Ace Pictures. **With** Tadanobu Asano, Akira Shirai, Keiko Unno. (73 mins.)

The image of the media in the movies has seldom been worse or more superficial than it is now. Instead of the whipsmart journos of *All the President's Men* we now have the cliché of frantic TV reporters jamming microphones in the hero's face— and the hero contemptuously brushing them off. How, one wonders, do these quoteless losers ever get their stories? The fact that the media pack does have a bite as well as a bark rarely makes it to the screen. Given that the Japanese pack is among the world's most ravening, this lacuna is particularly noticeable in Japanese films.

First-time director Satoshi Isaka has filled this gap brilliantly with *Focus*, which features an unscrupulous TV director (Akira Shirai) and his victim du jour—an introverted *otaku* played by Tadanobu Asano. Within its simple day-in-the-life structure the film comments incisively on the ills of Japanese society, from the emptiness of its youth to the manipulativeness of its media, while building steadily to its shocking denouement. Though it strips its characters to the emotional bone, it never descends to the self-

serving moralism or voyeuristic sensationalism of the media it is examining. Instead, it tells its story through the camera's relentlessly observing—and self-revealing—eye.

A TV crew is assigned to interview a young man named Kanemura (Asano) with an unusual hobby: electronic eavesdropping. Iwai, the crew's director-reporter, is a familiar type: glib, slick, and forever on the lookout for the journalistic main chance. He is accompanied by an ambitious assistant director (Keiko Unno) and an invisible cameraman (cinematographer Tetsuro Sano).

This interview, we realize as Iwai preps a nervous Kanemura on a park bench, is just another career stepping-stone. We also see that Iwai intends to make Kanemura an object of titillation. If he has to pry into the his private life, twist his words and portray him as a slavering peeping Tom, he will do it gladly, if slyly. Though at first ignorant of Iwai's agenda, Kanemura is no fool. He resists Iwai's phony camaraderie, resents his leading questions and refuses to allow him inside his apartment. He cannot, however, do the smart thing—walk away from the interview. Iwai is too persistent, the lure of the camera's eye too strong. Even an *otaku* whose only connection with the world is his electronic eavesdropping gear longs for his fifteen minutes of fame.

While listening to the babble of voices in Kanemura's car, Iwai overhears a conversation about a smuggled gun. Suddenly, this routine assignment becomes a hot story. After finding the gun in a coin locker, Iwai stages a fake "discovery" scene, with Kanemura as a reluctant supporting player. Before Iwai can savor this triumph, however, a trio of skateboarders pop into the frame, demanding to know what the crew is up to. When Iwai tries to shoo them away and the skateboarders retaliate by jumping on the car, Kanemura cracks. The next moment a skateboarder is breathing his last on the pavement and the camera is recording a horror-show of violence and rape, with Iwai and his assistant as the unwilling stars.

As Iwai, Akira Shirai gives a pitch-perfect performance that will make a more than a few media types squirm in self recognition (though most will grin, shrug, and keep on doing what they do). As Kanemura, Tadanobu Asano displays a range not always apparent in his recent Gen X films. His transition from put-upon wimp to murderous rageball feels inevitable. When the nerd turns, we realize that Kanemura's anger had always been roiling beneath the surface, that his eavesdropping was not as innocent as he tried to make it appear. Though Iwai's victim, he was also, in ways he did not understand, his colleague.

By using one cut per scene and viewing the film's events through the crew's camera, *Focus* creates the illusion of being behind-the-lens participants. More than just a strategy for drawing us into the action, the film's point of view provides a powerful commentary on our own complicity with the media. Iwai and Kanemura, says Satoshi, are our creations, whose only roles are user and used, in a film whose final climax is spiritual degradation and death. But we can't stop watching—or can we?

Fukai Kawa
Deep River (1995)

Written and directed by Kei Kumai. Cinematography by Masao Tochizawa. Produced by Shigoto and Fukai Kawa Production Committee. With Hisashi Igawa, Kumiko Akiyoshi, Yoichi Numata, Eiji Okuda. (108 mins.)

Based on a novel by Shusaku Endo, Kei Kumai's *Fukai Kawa* (Deep River) tells the stories of three Japanese tourists in India who are on spiritual quests: a salaryman (Hisashi Igawa) who recently lost his wife to cancer, a divorcée (Kumiko Akiyoshi) bothered by a guilty conscience, and a former Imperial Army soldier (Yoichi Numata) haunted by the memory of dead comrades. No longer comforted by traditional beliefs in a Japan whose god has been the GNP, they are searching for something that will give their lives meaning.

Fukai Kawa makes this search compelling. In powerful images it expresses the elusiveness of the quarry and the rewards of discovery. The most powerful image is that of India itself. The scenes Kumai and his staff shot in Benares, where the Hindu faithful come to perform ablutions in and commit their dead to the Ganges, are disturbing and stunning. The first Japanese filmmakers to attempt extended location shooting there, they capture India in its squalor and vibrancy, chaos and beauty .

Isolated and cosseted in their tourist-bus bubble, the film's Japanese at first seem too self-absorbed to respond vitally to Indian life. But as flashbacks reveal, three of them have good reasons for being here. The salaryman is looking for the reincarnation of his wife (before she died she told him that she would be reborn and made him promise to search for her); the divorcée wants to reunite with a priest (Eiji Okuda) she had tempted and abandoned years ago; the former soldier wants to know why he lived, while his comrades died in the the Burmese jungles. These quests may seem irrational and quixotic to their fellow Japanese (including a honeymoon couple who personify the ugly Japanese abroad), but in the context of Benares they make sense. These tourists are really pilgrims, even if they don't quite know which god they are worshiping.

Scenes shot in Japan, France, and Israel are not as successful. The story of the divorcée and the priest, especially, suffers from a certain bookishness. Despite deeply felt performances by Okuda and Akiyoshi, the authorial and directorial puppetry is too obvious. The characters become strained literary symbols, with the priest standing for conflicted spirituality and the divorcee, guilty sensuality and empty materialism.

Also, the flashbacks of the thirty-eight-year-old Akiyoshi as a vampish college girl and the forty-five-year-old Okuda as a nerdish college boy verge on the bizarre, as when they engage in an impromptu drinking contest at a fancy club, with a flutist in a tux and a harpist in an evening gown noodling classical melodies in the background. Where, I wondered, did Kumai hang out in college?

Though this lapse indicates a fatal lack of humor, Kumai's passion for the material carried me along. The climatic scene of Akiyoshi's immersion in the Ganges overwhelmed me. She embodied a woman in the throes of spiritual transformation with whole-spirited conviction (she also reportedly rose from a sickbed to film this scene). It's a performance that justifies a career—and demonstrates the power of love.

Fuyajo
Sleepless Town (1998)

Directed by Lee Chi Ngai. Screenplay by Lee Chi Ngai and Hisashi Nozawa. Produced by Kadokawa Shoten and Ace Pictures. With Takeshi Kaneshiro, Mirai Yamamoto, Sihung Lung, Kippei Shiina, Eric Tsang, Shu Ken. (122 mins.)

Fuyajo is essentially a vehicle for Takeshi Kaneshiro, the half-Japanese, half-Taiwanese actor who first came to attention in the films of Wong Kar-Wai and has since become one of the hottest actors in Asia. In the film he plays a hustler of his own ethnic background who becomes mixed up in a Chinese gang war in the Kabukicho entertainment district of Tokyo, while pursuing a passionate, volatile affair with the former lover of a man he is trying to kill.

Based on a best-selling novel by Seishu Hase, who worked as a bartender in Golden Gai, the seedy heart of Kabukicho, and met many of the underworld types he later wrote about, *Fuyajo* accurately depicts the ethnic stew that Kabukicho has become, as well as the growing influence of its Chinese gangs.

Filming on an open set that recreates Kabukicho right down to the barfing salarymen, Lee has created a vision of Japan's most notorious play spot that is at once familiar and strange. This disjunction is not due so much to atmospherics—though Lee sees

Kabukicho through a filter of gaudy exoticism absent in most local films about the place—as approach. His film is a glimpse of a new borderless world in which Japan is merely a backdrop to the war of its Chinese gangsters.

But that war has little in common with the usual ultraviolent dustups in Hong Kong films. Instead, *Fuyajo* focuses on the labyrinthine intrigues of its three contending gangs and the love affair of its two principals, saving most of its bang-bang for the last fifteen minutes. It is finally more romance than thriller, though its two narrative strands tend to cancel each other out, leaving a not-so-romantic romance and a thriller not so thrilling. The main problem is the lack of chemistry between the principals. Kaneshiro gets it on with co-star Mirai Yamamoto in scenes of frenetic lovemaking, but he doesn't connect with her. For most of the film he regards her more as an annoyance or threat than a lover. It's as though Leo were to spend most of *Titanic* treating Kate as excess baggage.

As the film begin, Liu Chien-yi (Kaneshiro) is scraping out a living fencing stolen goods in Kabukicho. A former protege of Yang Wei-min (Sihung Lung), the don of the local Taiwanese Mafia, he went independent when he realized that his mixed blood barred him from full acceptance by clannish gang society. He becomes embroiled in its quarrels, however, when Wu Feng-ch'un (Kippei Shiina), a former fellow gangster, returns to Tokyo after killing the top lieutenant of Yuan Ch'eng-kuei (Eric Tsang), the dome-pated boss of the Shanghai Mafia. Yuan assigns Liu to hit him in turn, with the proviso that, if he can't whack Wu in three days, Yuan will whack him instead. When Liu goes to his old godfather for help, Yang refers him to Tsui Hu (Shu Ken), the hot-headed leader of the Beijing Mafia. Liu quickly realizes, however, that only his own survival skills, including his talent for deceit, can save him in the gangs' Machiavellian battle for supremacy.

At this worst possible moment, Wu 's Nagoya girlfriend, Natsumi (Yamamoto), slinks into his life. Claiming that Wu abused her, she tells Liu that she has come to sell him out—and Feng-ch'un has followed her to Tokyo to stop her. It soon becomes apparent, though, that Natsumi sees Liu as not only an instrument of revenge, but a replacement lover. Liu, however, can't help wondering if she is playing the same head games with him that she plays with everybody else.

A mid-shoot replacement for Reona Hazuki, who left the set citing artistic differences with Lee, Yamamoto is so blatantly flirty and clingy that she comes across more as a Kaneshiro groupie than a woman of the world plotting his seduction. Also, she lacks the dangerous aura that made Hazuki so ideal

for this *femme fatale* role. Kaneshiro gives no indication that Yamamoto's lack of star wattage bothers him, but he ends up supplying enough for both. What should have been a poignant story of love and betrayal becomes a slickly produced, oddly bloodless one-man show.

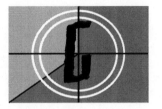

Gakko *
A Class to Remember (1993)

Directed by Yoji Yamada. **Screenplay by** Yoji Yamada and Yoshitaka Asama. **Produced by** Shochiku. **With** Toshiyuki Nishida, Eiko Shin'ya, Nae Yuki, Weng Huarong, Kunie Tanaka, Keiko Takeshita. (129 mins.)

There must be times when Yoji Yamada wonders about the irony of his career. This maker of movies about the outsiders of Japanese society has become the most successful director in the history of Japanese cinema. Though called Japan's Frank Capra, Yamada has enjoyed a far longer run at the top than the director of that flop *It's A Wonderful Life*. In addition to reeling off forty-eight Tora-san episodes, nearly all of which became hits, he struck box-office gold with several non-Tora-san films. Also, unlike Capra, who was a rock-ribbed conservative off the set, Yamada has remained a defender of progressive ideals.

Now, after fifteen years of planning, he has finally brought *Gakko*, his latest non-Tora-san project, to the screen. A drama about teachers and students at a night school in the Tokyo *shitamachi* (the old working-class district on the banks of the Sumida River), *Gakko* has the atmosphere we have come to expect from the Tora-san films: unabashedly sentimental, doggedly optimistic, warmly humane.

The film features yet another common-man hero who, like Tora-san, represents the best of the *shitamachi* ethic. Kuroi Sensei (Toshiyuki Nishida) may dress unfashionably, be grossly overweight, and have a distressing habit of plucking his nose hairs, but he is conscientious and dedicated to a fault. When the principal insists that he accept a transfer to a top-rated junior high school—a posting that most teachers would kill for—Kuroi refuses. He wants to stay on so that, years from now, former students will be able to see a familiar face when they return.

Toward his current students, he feels a strong sense of *giri* (responsibility); he visits their homes, listens to their personal troubles and is always ready to talk about more pressing concerns than the lesson: the death of a student or the meaning of happiness. A bachelor, he seems to have no life outside the classroom. But though he may be a paragon, he is not a know-it-all. Bursting with *ninjo* (warm human feelings) he doesn't mind playing the fool, and his students love him for it.

They are in night school because they fell through the cracks of the Japanese educational system and failed to get a junior high school diploma. In Japan's credential-obsessed society, they are outcasts, doomed to a life on the fringe. They include Omoni (Eiko Shinya), a Korean woman who runs a *yakiniku* barbeque restaurant, Midori (Nae Yuki), a former paint-thinner addict who wants to become a beautician, Kazu, a janitor for a building maintenance company, Eriko, a nice middle-class girl who refused to attend her junior high school classes, Chan (Weng Huarong), a Chinese man who came to Japan five years ago with his Japanese war- orphan mother, and Ino-san (Kunie Tanaka) a laborer who has a phenomenal memory for racetrack trivia, but never learned to read and write.

As the students labor over their graduation essays, Kuroi recalls incidents in their year together. There was Omoni, beaming with pride at the safe arrival of her first postcard written in Japanese. There was Midori, huddled by the school gate, wondering whether to walk in. There was Eriko, sitting meekly as her mother answered Kuroi's questions, but hitting a volleyball to her new classmates with a fierce delight. There was Kazu, taunting Kuroi for his easy life behind a desk, but changing his mind after his teacher followed him one day on his exhausting rounds. And finally, there was Ino-san, trying hard to master *kanji* (Chinese characters) and win the heart of Kuroi's attractive colleague, Tajima Sensei (Keiko Takeshita).

Yamada combines these individual sketches into a cohesive group portrait. Along the way, he squeezes out the expected tears, while providing instructive glimpses into the problems the students face as outsiders in Japanese society. Also, though sympathetic to the students' plight, he is clear-eyed about their weaknesses. Chan rightly complains about the Japanese preference for white-skinned foreigners, but he exposes his own ignorance of Japanese mores when he taunts a prospective boss for his low wage offer and, in doing so, embarrasses Tajima, who had arranged the interview.

It would be easy to dismiss *Gakko* as *shitamachi* corn, but Yamada's look at Japan's underclass evidences deep preparation and personal passion. Too many movies are all calculated surface. This is one from the heart.

Gakko 2
The Learning Circle (1996)

Directed by Yoji Yamada. **Screenplay by** Yoji Yamada and Yoshitaka Asama. **Produced by** Shochiku, NTV, and Sumitomo Corp. **With** Toshiyuki Nishida, Masatoshi Nagase, Hidetaka Yoshioka, Hiroshi Kambe. (122 mins.)

Gakko 2 is the sequel to *Gakko*, Yoji Yamada's idealistic 1993 film about a bumbling but lovable nightschool teacher and his troubled but lovable students. Infused with Yamada's trademark sentimentality and informed by his understanding of his characters' lives, *Gakko* swept domestic film awards, including a Japan Academy Award for Best Picture, and became yet another of Yamada's box-office hits.

Gakko 2 again stars Toshiyuki Nishida as a teacher, but the setting has changed from Tokyo's *shitamachi* (old downtown) to a small town in Hokkaido, and the character Nishida plays has changed as well. Ryu Sensei (*sensei* is an honorific meaning "teacher") spends his days, and often his nights, working at a school for the disabled.

Also, Nishida is less of a scenery-chewing clown than he was in *Gakko*. He still plays a self-sacrificing type as before, who will spend a day of his vacation surf-fishing with a close-mouthed student, but he no longer grabs cheap laughs by scratching his enormous belly, plucking stray hairs from his nose, or otherwise acting the slob.

Compared with *Gakko*, the narrative focus has widened and become more complex. Ryu Sensei does not carry the film's teaching load alone, but is aided by Koba Sensei (Masatoshi Nagase), who is, like Richard Dreyfuss's music teacher in *Mr. Holland's Opus*, a reluctant recruit to the profession.

Gakko II begins with an argument between Ryu Sensei and his teenage daughter over her future. He wants her to study for her college entrance exams at home and can't understand why she would rather go the to the big city and become a musician. His attention, however, soon shifts to two students who have left their dorm without permission and must be found. One, Takeshi (Hidetaka Yoshioka), came to the school an emotional wreck. Bullied at his previous school, he retreated into himself until he would not even answer to his own name. The other boy, the mentally disabled Yuya (Hiroshi Kambe), was

Takeshi's opposite. Unable to control his tantrums and rages, he drove his teachers, particularly Koba Sensei, to distraction.

But now Takeshi and Yuya are on their way to a pop concert in a nearby town, and, as the film shows us in extended flashbacks, they have been dramatically transformed. Takeshi has emerged from his shell to become one of the school's prize pupils, even winning an award at a student speech contest. Yuya, meanwhile, has become totally devoted to Takeshi, whom he regards as an older brother, and the tantrums and rages have disappeared. This transformation was not the work of a miracle-working teacher, but the result of a serendipitous bonding that Koba and Ryu did little more than midwife. Also, when Takeshi and Yuya first ventured out into the world, with the school's support and encouragement, this transformation was less than complete. Takeshi could not adjust to his job in a dry-cleaning plant, where his bosses and fellow workers saw him as stupid, sullen, and slow. Yuya, we feel, will not easily recover when he and Takeshi come to their inevitable parting of the ways.

While refusing to go for the usual feel-good payoffs, Yamada does not hesitate to wring the expected tears. During Koba's passionate farewell speech at a classroom graduation party, the sound of snuffling could be heard throughout the theater (and this reviewer was contributing to it). This is what the audience came for, but they also got Yamada pushing the boundaries of Japanese commercial cinema, while again demonstrating his considerable storytelling powers.

Gakko no Kaidan
School Ghost Stories (1995)

Directed by Hideyuki Hirayama. Screenplay by Sadoko Okudera. Produced by Toho and Sundance Company. With Shiori Yonezawa, Hironobu Nomura, Ayako Sugiyama. (100 mins.)

The recent spate of films about ghosts in the schoolhouse may, as the program notes of Gakko no Kaidan suggest, be a reflection of fin de siècle unrest. The ends of the Heian, Muromachi, and Edo periods, when spiritual and social turmoil rose to new heights, also produced a surge of supernatural tales. But a more immediate inspiration are the best-selling books for children that retell the schoolhouse equivalent of urban legends. One six-volume series of such compilations by Tetsu Tsunemitsu on which Gakko no Kaidan is based, has sold a million copies.

What Hideyuki Hirayama's Gakko no Kaidan sug-gests, though, is that the scary stories Japanese kids are telling each other in 1995 closely resemble the ones their great-grandfathers were telling in 1895. Despite all the Nintendo games and Disney videos, kids still imagine schoolhouse ghouls in forms handed down from age-old folk tales: a female teacher whose terrifying smile splits her face or a janitor who has the disconcerting habit of transforming into a giant crab. Though the Japanese crested ibis may face extinction, the Japanese collective unconscious, with its rich store of spooky archetypes, is alive and well.

The story concerns a group of children who, one sunny day at the beginning of summer vacation, find themselves trapped in the dark, dusty, abandoned wooden schoolhouse next to their new concrete elementary school. According to school legend, this shuttered old rattletrap is haunted by the ghost of a girl named Hanako. What the children do not know is that Hanako is not the school's only supernatural inhabitant.

Once past the preliminaries, including a mysterious bouncing ball that lures an unsuspecting second-grade girl (Shiori Yonezawa) into the clutches of Hanako herself, we discover that we are in a cinematic version of an *obake yashiki* (haunted house). The story is little more than the children's frantic search for a way out, while a male teacher (Hironobu Nomura), the twin brother of one trapped boy, and the motorbike-riding mother (Ayako Sugiyama) of another look frantically for a way in.

Hirayama, whose credits include the 1992 *The Chugaku Kyoshi* (The Games Teachers Play), handles this material with a light comic touch, while tingling spines with well-timed shocks. He also draws performances from his young actors that are credibly kid-like. Adult moviegoers who shudder at the thought of Macaulay Culkin may rest assured. The real stars of this film, however, are the ghouls and goblins. Some are straight steals from *Ghostbusters* (a pinkish, glowing gorilla-like creature) or Disneyland (a hologram Beethoven), but most have a distinctly Japanese flavor. One of the most impressive is a giant who tromps down the hall with huge, thundering steps, but is in the frame only from the knees down. Somehow this is scarier than seeing the whole giant—an expression, perhaps, of the traditional Japanese aesthetic that less is more?

But compared with Shimako Sato's *Eko Eko Azaraku* (Wizard of Darkness, 1995), which takes the inner terrors and obsessions of its teenage characters seriously, *Gakko no Kaidan* is mild stuff indeed. The ghosts in its corridors are so many computer-generated jack-in-the-boxes—external to its characters' lives and, once the initial shock of seeing them is past, more charming than frightening. As a special effects *obake yashiki,* the movie entertains, but unless you are impressionable indeed, it won't haunt your dreams.

Gambatte Ikimasshoi ∗
Live It All (1998)

Written and directed by Itsumichi Isomura. Produced by Fuji TV, Pony Canyon, and Altamira Pictures. With Rena Tanaka, Mami Shimizu, Wakana Aoi, Kirina Mano, Emu Hisazumi, Tomoko Nakajima, Masatoshi Matsuo. (120 mins.)

I was not expecting much from Itsumichi Isomura's *Gambatte Ikimasshoi*. Though produced by Masayuki Suo, who had been hugely successful with the zero-to-hero sports-themed film (*Shiko Funjatta*; *Shall We Dance?*), I wondered how much freshness anyone could bring to the story of a struggling girls' rowing crew in mid-seventies Shikoku. It recalled a hundred sweetly sad, soddenly nostalgic *seishun eiga* (youth movies).

But Isomura, a co-founder of Suo's Altamira production company in 1993, has made a film that reflects the real pains and joys of adolescence, while rejecting the genre's endemic sappiness. He has a keen eye for the small crises that loom so large in teenage life, and the large disappointments that so often turn out to be more important than the occasional successes. He also creates the precisely right tone of remembrance; a look back from a middle distance that is neither frigidly objective nor cloyingly emotional, and that leads at the end to exactly the needed moment of catharsis.

Mono no aware, that distinctly Japanese pathos in contemplating the irretrievability of time and the inevitability of loss, is an overworked term in the criticism of Japanese arts. *Gambatte*, however, exemplifies it. Or perhaps I am just a big sucker for a well-done zero-to-hero movie. I cried at the end of *Rocky*, and I had wipe away the moisture as the credits rolled for *Gambatte* as well.

Etsuko Shinomura (Rena Tanaka) is a first year student at a high school near the Shikoku side of the Inland Sea. Not a grind like her big sister, who has since gone off to a university in Tokyo, not interested in the usual club activities, she feels a void widening before her as she begins the new school year. Then one day, on the beach, she sees the boys' rowing crew cutting through the waves in their five-man shell and finds poetry in motion. She wants to be out there too. There is one problem: the school does not have a girls' rowing crew. Etsuko decides to start one, even though she has never wet an oar. Displaying a commendable stubbornness, she gets permission from the boys' coach and recruits members for the

crew, while learning the basics of the sport from a male *sempai* (upperclassman).

At the same time, she discovers new feelings for Sekino (Masatoshi Matsuo), a childhood friend who has joined the rowing crew—and has transformed himself into a rugged specimen of young manhood. But though the attraction is mutual, old antagonisms and a new awkwardness get in the way of its expression.

At first the crew's five girls can barely move the shell from its boathouse supports, but soon they are flailing through the water and becoming closer in ways that only fellow sufferers can understand. They are still a long way from competence, however, when they get their first real coach (Tomoko Nakajima), a former ace rower who looks elaborately bored, even as she works the girls to exhaustion. Etsuko thinks the coach has what used to be called a "past" and she is right.

· If this were a standard *seishun eiga*, the battling-through-adversity scenes would lead to a heart-warming, if hardly credible, triumph. *Gambatte* is more realistic; the crew members overcome major obstacles, including in Etsuko's case, anemic fainting spells and a bad back, but they remain ordinary girls and mediocre athletes. The best they can hope for is to rise, however briefly, from the bottom. Nonetheless, instead of bailing out after their first, humiliating season, they stick it out for another grueling year. They also share experiences, such as a midnight romp with fireworks, that may be nothing extraordinary, but somehow epitomize their friendship, their youth.

In the course of then film they emerge as strongly realized individuals, including the tall, sarcastic Dakko (Kirina Mano), the chubby, childish Imochi (Emu Hisazumi), the sweet, motherly Lee (Rie Yano) and the cute, tenacious Hime (Mami Shimizu). The most affecting, however, remains Etsuko, played by newcomer Rena Tanaka. A generation and a sensibility removed from the cool *kogyaru* (high-school girls) of contemporary Tokyo, she has a naive determination that may be born of desperation, but brings her a moment of heroism, a bitter taste of defeat, a beginning of love.

Gamera 3: Jashin Irisu Kakusei
Gamera 3: Awakening of the Demon-God Iris (1999)

Directed by Shusuke Kaneko. Screenplay by Kazunori Ito. Special effects supervision by Shinji Higuchi. Produced by Daiei, Tokuma Shoten, Nippon Television Network, Hakuhodo, and Nihon Shuppan Hambai. With Ai Maeda, Shinobu Nakayama, Ayako Fujitani, Nozomi Ando, Senri Yamazaki, Toru Tezuka. (108 mins.)

Remember when Japanese monster movies used to be cheesy camp, good for a few giggles among serious cinephiles? Now the trash of an earlier generation has become the obsession of overseas fans and thesis fodder for graduate students. Is this madness or what? Daiei's contribution to the genre is its Gamera series, whose star, a giant flying turtle, was first wakened from his eons-long sleep by atomic testing in the 1966 *Daikaiju Gamera*. Gamera appeared in seven films before going into hibernation in 1971.

In 1995, he returned in Shusuke Kaneko's *Gamera Daikaiju Kuchu Kessen* (Gamera, the Guardian of the Universe)—a film that featured Gyaos, the batlike nemesis from the earlier series, but offered fans snazzier effects and a new heroine in Ayako Fujitani, the daughter of Steven Seagal.

Now the big guy is back for a third installment. The budget is small compared with Hollywood effect shows, but the results are by no means shabby. Though working again with clunky models instead of computer graphics for much of the film, special effects supervisor Shinji Higuchi has created eye-popping illusions, such as the fiery battle royal between Gamera and his latest multi-story-tall opponent. Also, instead of space-opera for kiddies, the story offers a blend of ancient folklore and modern pseudoscience that should delight the hearts of pop-culture buffs and academics everywhere. "Cheesy," as an adjective, no longer cuts it.

The film begins with the arrival of orthinologist Mayumi Nagamine (Shinobu Nakayama) in a remote Philippine village to investigate a dead Gyaos. The revolting buggers have been multiplying like, well, bats. How to stop them? Meanwhile, a teenaged girl named Ayana (Ai Maeda) is recalling Gamera's tromping of Tokyo four years earlier—a rampage that killed both her parents, while sparing her and her younger brother. Understandably she has developed an invincible loathing of the monster.

Living in countryside with relatives, she is seemingly safe from further monster attacks, but one day, a gang of bullying classmates force her to enter a cave where a fierce dragon god is said to be sleeping. There Ayana discovers a large rock that looks like a scaly egg. To her astonishment and delight, it cracks open to reveal a cute baby monster with long, wiggly tentacles. Is this the ally against Gamera she has been praying for?

Flashback to Tokyo. Mayumi attends a meeting of a government anti-monster task force, where she meets Mito Asakura (Senri Yamazaki), a deeply strange government researcher who is working with a deeply strange, but brilliant game designer (Toru Tezuka) on a computer simulation of monster behavior. While the meeting is still in session, Gamera and

a Gyaos suddenly appear in the heart of Shibuya, locked in mortal combat. Crowds run screaming in terror as monsters thrash and buildings burn. At this dark moment, Mayumi encounters an intense young woman who has been up-close-and-personal with Gamera before: Asagi Kusanagi (Ayako Fujitani). The mass spawning of Gyaos, she says, has been caused by an earlier battle between Gamera and another monster, Legion, that upset the balance of the natural world. "Worse is yet to come," she warns.

To fans of Hollywood SF films that link their fantasies, however tenuously, to scientific fact, this may all seem campy nonsense. Those, however, who have lived through a few Japanese natural disasters, including the inevitable earthquakes and volcanic eruptions, can better understand why monster movies have had such a deep and enduring impact here. The bombings of World War II added to the general insecurity—the feeling that one is living under threat from large, inhuman, and horrifically destructive forces—but they certainly didn't create it.

Gamera 3 expresses the psychology of that insecurity, including its mythological underpinnings, with more clarity than the usual genre outing. It also has some awesome battle scenes, edited for maximum impact: director Kaneko has evidently been woodshedding with Steven Spielberg tapes. Snicker if you will at the overacting, groan if you will at the clichés, but Gamera, that green giant with the atomic breath, still has it all over that overgrown iguana from Manhattan.

Gekashitsu
The Operating Room (1992)

Written and directed by Tamasaburo Bando. Produced by TV Asahi, Shochiku, and Arato Genjiro Jimusho. With Sayuri Yoshinaga, Masaya Kato. (50 mins.)

Gekashitsu tells of a platonic love affair between a middle-aged countess (Sayuri Yoshinaga) and a young doctor (Masaya Kato) that begins with a glance exchanged in a park and ends nine years later with the countess on the doctor's operating table about to undergo life-threatening surgery.

Based on a short story by Meiji-era writer Izumi Kyoka, the film is an experiment. Though playing in downtown theaters, it is only fifty minutes long and costs only one thousand yen to see. It thus violates two ironclad rules of the Japanese movie business: (1) ticket prices must be the same for all films, even if one is a Hollywood blockbuster and another a zero-budget Japanese comedy, and (2) a film must have a running time of at least ninety minutes to be considered a stand-alone feature. Shochiku was right to violate these arbitrary rules. It has also been justified commercially: *Gekashitsu* has become a hit.

The story is no more than a sketch, its essence, that one life-changing glance. Two eyes meet across a pond on a perfect spring day and two hearts join across the chasm of age, status, marital ties. Their union grows in strength through the years, though the two lovers never speak or meet again, until that fatal day at the hospital. The countess refuses anesthetic because she is afraid that, under its influence, she will blurt out the secret of her love. Grimly, the doctor accedes to her wish, despite the protests of her family. Silently, he approaches the table, knife in hand.

First-time director Tamasaburo Bando, a famed Kabuki *onnagata* (player of women's roles) has has the sensibility, background, and talent needed for this material. He understands that *Gekashitsu* is the countess's story and he knows how to present it from her point of view. More importantly, he is not embarrassed by the story's high romanticism. Kabuki, of course, is drenched in it, and it is but a step from the love suicides of Chikamatsu to the operating-room tragedy of *Gekashitsu.*

Though he has brought the deliberate pace and electric intensity of Kabuki to the screen, Bando has left its unabashed artifice on the stage. Instead, he has recreated the atmosphere of the period, the mood of that fateful day in the park. The countess's carriage, her kimono, the lacy umbrella that she uses to shade her fashionably pale face, are straight from a Meiji-era print. The lush red camellias, shimmering spring grass, and warm sunlight falling across a path evoke an earthly paradise. In this world, all things, even love at first sight, seem possible.

Sayuri Yoshinaga totally inhabits her role as a woman of Meiji, with her iron reserve and passionate heart. As the doctor, former fashion model Masaya Kato is not required to do much more than look broodingly handsome. He does that quite well, though we don't believe for an instant that he is a real surgeon. But at the pond, we see why Yoshinaga's countess might be willing, nine years later, to die for him. The teenagers who loved *Pretty Woman* would probably find *Gekashitsu* slow and staid. In its own way, however, it is as fantastic as Richard Gere's encounter with the ideal prostitute. But romantics of whatever age will enjoy this pervervid reverie, with a message that could have come straight from D.W. Griffith's lace valentine heart.

Gekko no Natsu

Summer of the Moonlight Sonata (1993)

Directed by Seijiro Koyama. **Screenplay by** Tsuneyuki Mori. **Produced by** Shigoto. **With** Mayumi Wakamura, Norikatsu Nagano, Minoru Tanaka, Misako Watanabe, Kiyoshi Yamamoto, Tatsuya Nakadai. (112 mins.)

Some movies are almost impossible to review honestly without feeling like a heel. Panning Tadashi Imai's *Senso to Seishun* (War and Youth, 1991), a woodenly acted, tearjerking melodrama about a mother and child separated by the firebombing of Tokyo, I knew I would sound callous and unfeeling to readers who lived through that time and loved the film for the righteousness of its sentiments. It was like panning a memorial service. Seijiro Koyama's *Gekko no Natsu*, which focuses on the fates of two *tokkotai* (special attack unit) pilots who visit a Kyushu elementary school just before the end of the war, presents a similar dilemma.

The pilots have heard about the school's rare German-made grand piano and ask a young teacher named Kimiko Yoshioka (Mayumi Wakamura) if they might play it. She can hardly refuse; they are "living gods" who will soon make the ultimate sacrifice for their country. As the children and teachers watch, one of the pilots (Norikatsu Nagano), a former student at a Tokyo music school, plays Beethoven's "Moonlight Sonata." His friend (Minoru Tanaka), who once studied at a teacher's college, plays a Japanese children's song as everyone sings along. The pilots then bid the teachers and students an emotional farewell; they will soon be flying on their first and last mission against the U.S. Navy.

Based on an actual incident, this section of *Gekko no Natsu* is surefire. If a director can't coax tears from a Japanese audience with a story like this, he ought to turn in his megaphone. Seijiro Koyama succeeds: his young heros glow with a youthful purity and passion that has the audience reaching for its collective handkerchief.

The Japanese have long revered young heroes who struggle sincerely in a losing cause. As symbols of core values, the *tokkotai* pilots (never called "kamikaze" by contemporary Japanese) were direct descendants of the legendary heros of antiquity. In the closing days of the war, the country's military leaders hoped that, inspired by the example of those pilots, the nation would rally to victory—or extinguish itself in a blaze of glory. The leaders were wrong, but in *Gekko no Natsu*, those values are still very much alive. The film, however, is resolutely antiwar. It shows us the ugly face of the Japanese military, which regarded all Tokkotai returnees as cowards, as well as the pain of the survivors, who feel guilty for not going to their deaths with their comrades.

Flash to the present. Yoshioka Sensei (Misako Watanabe), who is now retired, learns that the school is about to scrap the pilots' piano. She offers to take it and, when the principal asks why, tells their story.

When she repeats it before a school assembly, it becomes news. Led by a freelance writer (Kiyoshi Yamamoto), the media begins searching for the two pilots.

The player of the "Moonlight Sonata" never returned. The other pilot (Tatsuya Nakadai) is found living in Kagoshima Prefecture. but he refuses to answer the writer's questions. "I've forgotten about all that," he says. The movie is about his coming to terms with the past. Tatsuya Nakadai movingly portrays the old pilot's wariness and pain, but the film shows him as a conventional TV documentary might: the subject of a media quest.

Even so, a flashback to his final hours with his comrades conveys important truths about the pilots: they were very young and, in their heart of hearts, wanted very much to live. The scene in which these boys, some of them barely old enough to shave, sing a song about saying farewell to home, knowing the next day would be their last, is surprisingly strong. More than all the film's sentimentalizing about the departed heros, the sight of those faces—so alive and so soon to be dead—brings home the war's cruelty and waste.

Goaisatsu *
Greetings (1991)

Directed by Toshio Terada, Jun Ichikawa, Kaori Momoi. Screenplay by Toshio Terada and Jun Ichikawa. Produced by Sony Music Entertainment and Center Promotion. With Keizo Kanie, Mamako Yoneyama, Kaori Momoi. (98 mins.)

Most of us who have been in Japan long enough to attend a wedding ceremony, farewell party, or kindergarten reunion know the meaning of goaisatsu. The dictionary definition—"greeting or salutation"—doesn't begin to express the central role goaisatsu play in Japanese social life. As speeches, they are often hodgepodges of overripe compliments, tired homilies, and rambling reminiscences that are as excruciating to the native speaker as the struggling language student. But as devices for deploying the formidable arsenal of keigo (polite language) they are unsurpassed. Occasionally, they can enlighten, entertain, or even move. The directors of the anthology film Goaisatsu try to do all three, but in radically different ways, with radically different results.

The first of the three segments, "Iroiro Arimashite" (Various Things Have Happened) is a social satire of the type often found in comic anthology films, beginning with the 1988 Bakayaro! This time the target is office and sexual politics. When a young clerk leaves the company to marry, she makes a goaisatsu to her coworkers, in which she remarks that "various things have happened" (iroiro arimashite) during her period of employment. This apparently innocent observation stirs up a storm of speculation. What was she referring to? An affair? Sexual harassment? A dirty corporate secret? Worried that all this smoke might mean fire, her former bosses dispatch a middle-aged salaryman (Keizo Kanie) to get to the bottom of the mystery.

As the salaryman searches for a clue he uncovers the underside of office life—the petty jealousies, the furtive lusts. He also finds himself sinking into a personal and professional morass. His wife feels abandoned, his bosses are growing impatient. What else can he do but go to the source? Scriptwriter and director Toshio Terada tells this story the way a good stand-up comedian structures a routine; not only zinging us with funny bits, but telling home truths.

The second segment, Jun Ichikawa's "Kayo," is a cinematic essay on aging, loneliness, loss, and friendship. It is also very nearly a silent film; the only extended dialogue comes at the end, when the heroine (Mamako Yoneyama) makes her goaisatsu.

Kayo is a kiosk obasan, one of the legions of blue-uniformed, largely middle-aged women who tend the newstands in train stations. She leaves her tiny apartment every day at the crack of dawn, rides the train to her tiny stand, works long hours and then rides the train back again. We see her industriously performing her duties, while realizing what tiring duties they are—making change all day is no fun. We also catch her stealing a sip from her coffee mug, casting a disapproving glance at a trio of teenage punks, and taking a welcome load off her aching feet. In the course of her day, we come to understand her loneliness, sadness, and quiet strength.

There is no plot. Kayo studies calligraphy, watches sumo on TV, and meets her newsstand colleague for a walk along the riverbank. Finally, she attends her colleague's wedding, at which she makes a goaisatsu. Ichikawa's direction is so gently lyrical and pantomimist Yoneyama Mamako's performance so silently eloquent that we never miss the usual narrative machinations. The final scene is a revelation that, after all the talk of their decline, Japanese films can still be this good.

The last segment is one reason for that talk. Actress Momoi Kaori directs and stars in the story of a thirtysomething woman who attends a chaotic high-school class reunion. The segment is much like Kaori's performance; charming in a Annie Hall-ish way, but sloppy, self-indulgent, unfocused—a waste of an undeniable talent. When Kaori finishes making a heartfelt but nearly incoherent speech—and finds herself alone in a empty room, we understand her classmates' feelings perfectly.

Godzilla vs. Destroyah

(1995)

Directed by Takao Ogasawara. **Screenplay by** Kazuki Omori. **Produced by** Toho Eiga. **With** Takuro Tatsumi, Megumi Odaka. (103 mins.)

Over the years, Godzilla has become an instantly recognizable symbol of Japan to the world at large. Folks in the American heartland who wouldn't know Akira Kurosawa from an Achilles tendon know Godzilla as the giant mutant lizard that stomps Tokyo.

In 1992 Tristar Pictures bought the international rights to the character from Toho with the idea of filming an American Godzilla movie. Rather than compete with this high-powered Hollywood newcomer and cannibalize the revenues from distributing it in Japan, Toho decided to bow out of the Godzilla business. In July 1995 Toho announced that the entry for this year's New Year's season—*Godzilla vs. Destroyah*—would be the last, for the time being at least.

The Big G is going out with a bang. He not only has a glowing reactor in his stomach, but a sidekick, Godzilla Junior, who resembles Big G as he looked in 1954. Even the film's humans, including an adolescent genius whose father survived Godzilla's first rampage and later studied under famed Godzilla expert Dr. Yamane (played by Takashi Shimura), have connections to the original cast. The story also reprises the first film in that the two Godzillas fight their climatic battle in Tokyo. Instead of the Ginza, however, they demolish the bubble-era buildings of Tokyo Bay.

Despite these harkings back, *Godzilla vs. Destroyah* is very much a Godzilla movie of the 1990s, trying to overawe with big effects, heavy-duty technobabble and a wackily overblown story line. Godzilla is getting ready to melt down and take the world with him. Meanwhile an organism called the Oxygen Destroyer has sprung to life after a 2.5-billion-year sleep and is rapidly mutating into scary, Tokyo-Dome-sized maturity. What can mere humans do to stop these engines of destruction? Well, what the Self Defense Force has done, while we thought it was protecting Hokkaido from the Russians, is build the Super X-III, an airborne fortress that can withstand a nuclear attack and deliver super-low-temperature rays able to freeze even a Godzilla in his tracks.

This is all rather silly and, despite some impressive images, including Godzilla's demise in a chaos of fire and smoke, the effects are not up to Hollywood standards. Instead of superreal computer-generated creatures, we get a man splashing about Tokyo Bay in

a Godzilla suit. Still, fans are buying tickets and Toho has yet another hit on its hands. Can this really be the end—or is Godzilla just going into hibernation until his American cousin dies at the box office? Somehow, I think we have yet to hear the big guy's last roar.

Gogo no Yuigonjo *

A Last Note (1995)

Written and directed by Kaneto Shindo. **Produced by** Kindai Eiga Kyokai. **With** Haruko Sugimura, Nobuko Otowa, Kyoko Asagiri, Hideo Kanze. (112 mins.)

What does it mean to be old in today's youth-mad society? That's the question eighty-three-year-old director Kaneto Shindo poses in *Gogo no Yuigonjo*, a film about an aged actress's unusual summer vacation at a mountain villa. His message, Kaneto says in the program notes, is "to live life to the fullest as long as one is alive." His elderly characters exemplify that message by being completely human, with all the accompanying caprices, frailties, and cruelties. They never become clichés or, worse, ancient icons basking in the glow of their own self regard.

Though *Gogo no Yuigonjo* clearly has something serious to say, it is anything but preachy. Kaneto mixes in jokes and even touches of slapstick to create a light mood. In some scenes, the film threatens to cast off its moorings to the real world altogether and become a whimsically uplifting entertainment of the TV sitcom sort. Such lapses are minor, however; Kaneto makes us care about his people and understand their actions, without passing judgments on their rightness. There are no pat conclusions; only the injunction to live fully in the moment, even in the face of debility and death.

Gogo no Yuigonjo was conceived as a vehicle for Haruko Sugimura, a favorite supporting actress of Ozu, Kurosawa, and Naruse. Playing an actress who is still working in her eighties, Sugimura is elegantly dressed, perfectly coiffed, and entertainingly tart-tongued. But beneath her Great Lady of the Theater manner is a woman curious about and connected to the life around her. Arriving at her mountain villa for a ten-day stay, she is shocked when her caretaker of many years (Nobuko Otowa) tells her that her old gardener committed suicide in a coffin of his own making, leaving only a cryptic note and a round rock for pounding in the final nail. The actress has the caretaker take her to the river to find a similar one, and has the caretaker's grown daughter carry it home. She thinks that it would make an excellent prop for her own final public performance.

Soon after, she receives another reminder of mortality: a rare visit from a former fellow actress (Kyoko Asagiri) and her Noh-actor husband (Hideo Kanze). After giving up her career decades ago to take care of her husband, her old colleague is now in need of care herself; a victim of Alzheimer's disease, she is nearly mute and helpless. Her husband hopes that a visit to her acting *sempai* (senior) will return her, however temporarily, to a semblance of normality.

What happen next is not normal, however; the villa is invaded by an escapee from a psychiatric ward. Improbably, the former actress wrests a knife from him and the cops move in for the arrest. Now a heroine, she receives a commendation from the police (and plants a kiss on the cheek of the presenter). But though her visit to the villa does not restore her to her senses, it inspires the caretaker to tell the actress a long-kept secret that shocks her far more than any knife-wielding madman.

Those expecting a quiet, sensitive film about the problems of aging may find these injections of absurdist comedy and melodrama distracting. But in exposing his elderly characters to the wild winds of reality, Kaneto invigorates them, while demonstrating that they are still capable of riding those winds.

Among the most impressive riders is Nobuko Otowa. Kaneto's wife and a frequent actress in his films, Otowa was suffering from liver cancer when shooting began. Soon after the film wrapped, on December 12, 1994, she died. On screen, however, she is ever the professional, bearing up brilliantly to the end. A courageous performance in an extraordinary film.

Gohime
Princess Go (1992)

Directed by Hiroshi Teshigahara. Screenplay by Hiroshi Teshigahara and Gempei Akasegawa. Produced by Shochiku and Teshigahara Production, TV Asahi, Hakuhodo; With Rie Miyazawa, Tetsuya Nakadai, Toshiya Nagasawa. (142 mins.)

If *Gohime* had been released a year ago, we would have thought of it first as the latest film by Hiroshi Teshigahara, the director, artist, landscape designer, and head of the Sogetsu school of flower arranging. This modern-day Renaissance man has the whole of Japanese culture and history in his breath and bones, and in *Gohime* he creates a living dialog between the sixteenth century and the twentieth. While bringing traditional Japanese arts gorgeously to the screen, he relates a medieval moral drama whose principals are both very much of their period and very much like ourselves.

But in the spring of 1992, after the publication of a nude photo book featuring Rie Miyazawa and the subsequent media feeding frenzy, I watched *Gohime* wondering how Miyazawa would handle the biggest role of her career. Was she just another teen idol whose real talent was self-publicity? Or could she act? The answer to the latter question is yes; Miyazawa brings a youthful verve and sensual fire to the role of Princess Go reminiscent of Misa Uehara's full-bore performance in *Kakushi Toride no San Akunin* (The Hidden Fortress), the 1958 Akira Kurosawa film that was an inspiration for *Star Wars*. Not bad for a cutesy *tarento* who was once on her way to becoming her generation's Brooke Shields.

It was not an easy leap to make; in the course of the film, Miyazawa ages twenty years, from the arrow-shooting, horse-riding tomboy striding about the estate of adoptive father Toyotomi Hideyoshi, to the mature woman who lives in lonely, defiant isolation with her memories. She shares this journey with Hideyoshi's master of tea, Furuta Oribe (Tatsuya Nakadai). A disciple of Sen no Rikyu, the tea master who had also served the temperamental warlord—and been forced to commit suicide by him— Oribe is a man divided between his desire to practice his art freely and his need to adapt to the dangerous political climate around him. He is stubborn by temperament, subtle by necessity.

The princess is more daring by choice. When she hears that officials trying to curry favor with Hideyoshi have displayed Rikyu's head in public in a gesture of contempt, she rides to retrieve it with Usu (Toshiya Nagasawa), Oribe's stud-muffin gardener. They succeed, but Usu decides to leave his master's service for fear of implicating him in their deed. Before he goes he makes love to the Princess—and is saved by her and his master from vengeful samurai.

The bonds uniting this trio are strong ones, but all must endure long years of exile. When they finally meet again, after two decades, Oribe is in the service of Hideyoshi's rival, Tokugawa Ieyasu, Usu is a mountain hermit, and the Princess is living at the home of her natural father's family, the Maeda clan. The Maedas, however, are the defeated and still feared enemies of Ieyasu. By asking Oribe to preside at a spring tea ceremony at the Maeda's, she is again tweaking authority's nose. But this time, it is Oribe's head and possibly her own that are at stake.

How, Teshigahara asks, can the living ideals of art coexist with the deadly practicalities of politics? How can individual conscience challenge absolute power? He finds answers in the character of the Princess. She may bow to the realities of her time—to the exile of her husband or the suppression of her family and friends—but she refuses to be broken. Her tea party is a necessary gesture, a defiant affirmation of the spirit.

Despite excellent performances by the principals (Nakadai delights with his mordant wit and aristocratic disdain), *Gohime* is, at nearly two-and-a-half hours, too long. We start to feel that we are in exile with poor Usu. Also, is it necessary to pretend that, in her later scenes, the Princess is in her forties? We look at Miyazawa's white-powdered face and see the same vibrantly zaftig young woman who posed, notoriously, in a best-selling nude photo book. It's as though the young Marilyn Monroe were to play the Bette Davis role in *All About Eve*. A charismatic actress, a terrific part, and yet they are, in a fundamental way, wrong for each other. It is to Miyazawa's credit that we still see the character, not the absurdity.

Gokudo Kuro Shakai Rainy Dog *

Rainy Dog (1998)

Directed by Takashi Miike. Screenplay by Seigo Inoue. Produced by Daiei. With Sho Aikawa, He Jianxian, Chen Xianmei. (94 mins.)

More Japanese films has have been taking on an Asian complexion, as Japanese contacts with the region grow and Asians flood into Japan in increasing numbers. Takashi Miike's *Gokudo Kuro Shakai Rainy Dog* seems to be following this trend in its Taipei setting and its contingent of Taiwanese actors, but instead of simply adding Asian spice to his product, Miike explores's Taiwan's underworld from the viewpoint of an insider, albeit one alienated from the human race. He makes no attempt to exoticize or caricaturize his Taiwanese for Japanese consumption. Instead, he allows them be themselves, assuming rightly that his gangsters and whores need no cross-cultural filters to be understood.

Though lacking the hard-boiled flair of a John Woo, he tells a noirish tale of a Japanese hitman's life on the edge that exudes attitude, with spare but stylish atmospherics. Like its hitman hero, *Gokudo* makes no excuses and takes no prisoners. Though suffused with macho romanticism, it goes easy on the macho self-regard and self-pity. The ending hits exactly the right note: stark, downbeat, zero cool.

Yuji (Sho Aikawa) scrapes out a living as a hitman for a Taipei gang. Living in a shabby apartment and surfing the Internet on his computer, he is a loner who seems to have little need of or use for human contact. When his boss—a crude, dangerously explosive man—calls him his son, his face remains an unreadable mask; all he cares about is the cash. One day, a former girlfriend appears at his door and,

with a desperate abruptness, leaves him with a boy (He Jianxian) she claims is his son.

While the boy tags after him, Yuji goes calmly about his business: blowing away a rival gangster who is eating lunch with his family, and after collecting his payment, taking home a pretty young hooker named Lily (Chen Xianmei). Meanwhile, the boy is sleeping on flattened cardboard in the rain, snuggling a puppy he found in the street.

Child abuse? Certainly, but Yuji smiles with amusement at the boy's persistence and throws him a towel for his drenched body. After Yuji finds a briefcase full of cash following a hit on a rival boss, he even becomes generous, offering to fulfill Lily's dream of fleeing to a place drier than her monsoon-soaked homeland. Together with the boy, they escape to a lonely beach with the gang's remaining members in hot pursuit. Taking shelter in a wartime pillbox, they wait for the neverending rain to stop. During this enforced closeness they begin to show traces, however faint, of family feeling. Then the skies clear and the deadly chase resumes.

Rain is a constant presence in the film; it both circumscribes Yuji's life and symbolizes his essential dilemma. Continuing for days and weeks, it seeps, inexorably, into everything. In Taiwan's climate—and underworld society—the stranger can never quite come out of the rain. It finds him, and if he is in the wrong place at the wrong time, can kill him.

As Yuji, Sho Aikawa combines mute stoicism with glimpses of minimalist charm and flourishes of cool-dude theatrics, including the neat way he whips his piece out from behind his white trenchcoat. He may well be bound for better things. I just hope he takes his shades along—with them, he looks debonairly menacing, without them, he has the face of a dissipated choirboy. Anybody know where I can get a pair?

Gokudo no Onnatachi: Kejime

Gang Wives: Decision (1998)

Directed by Sadao Nakajima. Screenplay by Hiroji Takada. Produced by Toei. With Shima Iwashita, Rina Katase, Riki Takeuchi, Fumie Hosokawa. (116 mins.)

One day in 1986 Toei producer Goro Kusakabe was on the train thumbing through weekly magazines when he came across an article by a journalist named Shoko Ieda about the lives of gangster girlfriends and wives. Ieda had spent a year living among her subjects, becoming their friend and confidant while having several close encounters with an ongoing gang war.

Kusakabe saw that many of the women in Ieda's stories were neither exploited products of the sex industry nor squelched victims of feudalistic relationships, but strong personalities who had learned to assert themselves in a macho world. Here, he decided, was a movie.

That movie, *Gokudo no Onnatachi* (Gang Wives), became a hit following its release in November 1986. One reason for its success was its unusual subject matter: Another was its realism; *Gokudo* followed the outlines of Ieda's reportage fairly closely. Still another was star Shima Iwashita. Elegant and stately, possessed of a steely will and cool intelligence, Iwashita's gang-boss wife was a match for any *yakuza* tough guy. Though more imperious queen than woman warrior, she could hold her own in a knock-down-drag-out fight with her younger sister (Rina Katase) that was reminiscent of the classic brawl between Marlene Dietrich and Una Merkel in *Destry Rides Again*. After starring in seven of nine series installments, and thoroughly implanting her gang-wife image in the public mind, Iwashita decided that her tenth *Gokudo* film, with the subtitle *Kejime* (Decision), would be her last.

Directed by Toei veteran Sadao Nakajima, Iwashita's farewell performance is of a piece with her others, even though she is not playing a continuing character (given the high mortality rate of the male characters in the series, this is understandable). Once again, she impersonates the wife of an Osaka *oyabun* with a swagger and haughtiness that defines the essence of camp. Picture Bette Davis in a kimono. But unlike Davis, who often swept everything before her like a natural force, Iwashita is an ensemble player who shares the spotlight with several other actresses, notably the voluptuous and equally formidable Rina Katase.

In the latest installment, Iwashita's husband heads the Idei-gumi, a large gang with a base in South Osaka and three subgangs that have formed a close alliance. One day a perfectly permed stud named Ginji (Riki Takeuchi), the boss of a subgang, is murdered while working out in a gym. Following this hit, the gang's cohesion begins to erode. As it turns out, Ginji borrowed money from a local trust bank for a resort hotel he was building. Then the economy turned sour. Drowning in bad debt, the bank went belly-up and stopped payment on his loan. Desperate for funds, he decided to use his last trump card: information he had secretly obtained about a five-billion-yen stash a gang director had accumulated on the sly.

Now the question is, who ordered the hit? The cops arrest the hitman, a "guest" member of the Idei-gumi, who promptly snitches on Idei for putting out the contract. Idei's wife (Shima Iwashita) believes that her husband has been set up: Ginji had been like a son to him. But if he didn't order the hit, who did? She decides to find the real culprit and prove her husband's innocence. Naturally, she enlists the support of the other gang wives.

The story serves as yet another star vehicle for Iwashita, while supplying enough action thrills and sexual oomph for the genre's core male fans. The film's women are thus a varied lot: the wives played by Iwashita and Katase project an admirable firmness, while a *zaftig* bank teller (Fumie Hosokawa) who becomes the plotter's accomplice is made of baser, more pliable clay. Those hoping to see their first feminist *yakuza* film will have to wait. Also, those hoping to revel in ultraviolence will be disappointed. Nakajima may film bang-bang scenes in operatic slo-mo, but a John Woo he is not.

Nonetheless, the film has Iwashita. Watching her calmly squeeze off a round at an assault-weapon-wielding gangster, without mussing a hair of her impeccable coiffure or crinkling a line on her still exquisite face, one has to admire a presence that goes beyond mere acting. Now in the fourth decade of her career, she is still the reigning diva of Japanese film.

Gonin ✳
(1995)

Written and directed by Tadashi Ishii. Produced by Bunkasha and Image Factory IM. With Koichi Sato, Naoto Takenaka, Jimpachi Nezu, Kippei Shiina, Masahiro Motoki, Takeshi Kitano. (109 mins.)

Tadashi Ishii's *Gonin*, tries to shock the unshockable much the way *Pulp Fiction* did, with violence that is not just in your face, but at your throat. He differs from Tarantino, however, in his approach to his material and his attitude toward his audience. Whereas Tarantino is the hip trickster, subverting genre conventions and playing with his audience's head, Ishii is an *otaku* of sex and violence who puts his obsessions on the screen and takes his audience to the end of the night. To put it another way, Tarantino directs from the neck up, Ishii from the neck down, with a particular emphasis on the region of the solar plexus.

In making an action film about a gang of losers and outcasts who take on the *yakuza*, Ishii is a riding on the wave of "new *yakuza*" films flooding the video shops. But *Gonin* is also definitely an Ishii film. While assaulting the senses with violent, erotic, and hallucinatory imagery, it explores the borderlands of revenge, lust, and sanity. Few directors venture so far, or know the terrain so well. Those expecting to unwind with two hours of mindless bang-bang are in for some rude jolts.

The story is as timely as the latest financial page headline. Bandai (Koichi Sato), a disco owner who was once a bubble-era comer, is now up to his handsome jowls in debt to the *yakuza*. They harass him, humiliate him, and threaten his life. Desperate for a way out, Bandai encounters others at the ends of their ropes: a strung-out salaryman (Naoto Takenaka) who has been restructured out of a job, a former police detective (Jimpachi Nezu) who has just been released from the slammer, a hotheaded ex-boxer pimp (Kippei Shiina) who is on the outs with the mob, and a gay blackmailer (Masahiro Motoki) who is still in love with Bandai, though he suspects that the disco manager sold him to the cops. Bandai recruits this motley crew to rob the *yakuza* office at gunpoint. Amazingly, they make off with nearly a hundred million yen, and the enraged *yakuza* hire a hitman (Takeshi Kitano) to hunt them down, one by one.

The standard recipe for movies of this kind calls for a dollop of macho humor, a pinch of redeeming qualities for the good guys, and a fiery climax, in which the star and a buddy or two emerge victorious. In making *Gonin*, however, Ishii threw the recipe away. The good guys are not charming scapegraces (though Saito, Nezu, and Motoki are convincing hard guys) and the big confrontation with the *yakuza* degenerates into a bloody mess. The ending? Don't ask, but I doubt that Hollywood will buy the remake rights.

What the film lacks in clichés, it more than makes up in high-charged drama. Ishii's directorial trademark is intensity, and in *Gonin* he screws it up to the max. He pushs his actors to their limits, until they reek of sweaty fear and vibrate with hot rage, and edits for speed, tension, and immediacy, until we feel that we are running across the tabletop, heart in mouth and gun in hand, toward an ashen-faced gang boss.

In other scenes, however, Ishii abandons grass-is-green realism for flights of sophisticated dream (or nightmare) imagery. We may have seen his techniques, including cuts of subliminal brevity, on MTV, but Ishii usually uses them for a good narrative reason, not flashy effect, and he usually gets what he is looking for.

Does he go over the top with ultra-violence? Does he indulge in displays of macho melodrama? Does he oversell his movie's dark, bleak, nihilistic message? Yes, yes, and yes. But, to paraphrase Blake, the road of excess leads to an extraordinary film. Go figure, or go see *Gonin*.

Gonin 2
(1996)

Written and directed by Tadashi Ishii. Produced by Eisei Gekijo. With Ken Ogata, Yumi Takigawa, Kimiko Yo, Shinobu Otake, Yumi Nishiyama, Yui Natsukawa, Mai Kitajima. (105 mins.)

In 1995 Tadashi Ishii made a film called *Gonin* about five ill-assorted losers who ripped off a hundred million yen from the local *yakuza* and paid for their rashness with their blood and lives. In *Gonin 2* the five misfits are all women. The film is not so much a feminist statement, however, as an attempt to add the spice of sex to the story's already strong action brew.

The debt-ridden owner of a small metal-working company (Ken Ogata) borrows from *yakuza* loan sharks. One night, after buying a birthday present for his wife (Yumi Takigawa), he returns home to find gangsters waiting to collect. They rape his wife as a warning and beat him when he tries to interfere. Her reason unhinged, she searches frantically for his birthday present—a set of earrings—in the grass and, later that night, while her husband sleeps, she hangs herself.

We then meet other women in desperate straits: a bankrupt fitness-club owner (Kimiko Yo) who has been discarded by her patron, a sailor-suited hooker (Shinobu Otake) who is hitting bottom at age thirty-seven, a housewife (Yumi Nishiyama) who has just discovered her husband in bed with another woman, and an OL ("office lady," or female office worker) played by Yui Natsukawa, who still dreams of a rape by a ski-masked attacker when she was only fifteen.

These four angry women happen to be in a swank jewelry store when a gang of ski-masked robbers invade it. In their rush to hoover up jewelry, the robbers fail to notice that the jilted housewife and the man-hating OL are not cowering in a corner with the others. When a robber finally spots them, the OL zaps him with a stun gun and the housewife wallops his confederate with a nightstick. A mélee ensues. When the dust finally clears, our four heroines are beating an escape with the loot, together with a store employee (Mai Kitajima) who, unbeknownst to them, is in cahoots with the robbers. On the way out, they pass Ogata, who has just sliced and diced a nest of *yakuza* and is on his way to buy the present his dead wife really wanted: a five-million-yen ring. He follows after them, bloody sword in hand.

What we have here is the basic jewelry-heist-gone-wrong scenario that has has become familiar since *Reservoir Dogs*. Unlike Quentin Tarantino, however, Ishii is not into stylized irony. Instead he takes a more straight-ahead approach, making heavy use of atmospherics (most of the movie takes place in either dark buildings or driving rain) and old-fashioned ultra-vee, including the cliché of the good guy who, though ventilated by the bad guys' guns, stays upright though sheer samurai willpower. The film also takes the conventional view that in dealing with macho gangsters its heroines require the assistance of a macho hero. It is as if Thelma and Louise were to fight their battles with a sword-wielding father figure by their side.

Gorotsuki *
Tough Guys (1992)
Written and directed by Yasuhiro Horiuchi. Produced by Hero Communications. With Masanori Ikeda, Yoshiyuki Omori, Naoko Amihama, Aiko Asano. (97 mins.)

Gorotsuki is a yakuza buddy movie with a difference. Akira (Masanori Ikeda), a smart-mouthed college student and Ryo (Yoshiyuki Omori), a lunk-headed reform-school graduate, meet cute in a Roppongi disco. Just released from juvenile detention, Ryo bulls his way in and begins dancing wildly to celebrate his new freedom. Akira scolds him for breaking the house rules. Soon they are outside, trading insults and punches.

As they are tumbling about beside a Mercedes Benz, a rolled up magazine makes contact with Akira's skull. The two boys look up into the angry face of fat, long-haired, loudly dressed yakuza. From this beginning, with its humor, violence and clever camerawork (shots of Ryo's beat-up sneakers tramping through puddles alternate with shots of stylish footwear vamping on the dance floor), we expect a tongue-in-cheek, action-filled look at gang life.

Not quite: Gorotsuki has too many rough edges and too much gritty honesty to be just another funny-gangster movie. Its yakuza are not scar-faced clowns or noble outlaws, but lowlifes. Director Yasuhiro Horiuchi may have shot Gorotsuki on the cheap, but its technical flaws, if anything, enhance its semidocumentary feel.

Unknown to each other, the boys end up in the same gang, Akira because he wants money and women, Ryo because his father forces him to join, in the hope that gang discipline will straighten him out. The boys are set to answering the phones, cleaning the office and performing a myriad of other chores. Inevitably, they screw up and incur the wrath of their seniors. With their slaps upside the head and comic books thrown across the room, these scenes are funny in a Three Stooges sort of way.

But while getting laughs at the boys' expense, the film shows us how their relationship changes and how they make the choices that will determine their lives. In most movies about bad boys the characters' criminality is a given; they start bad and become worse. In Gorotsuki the bad boys are not sure that they want to become bad men. The rewards, including overseas trips and yakuza groupies, are often outweighed by the unpleasantness. Confessing their doubts to each other, they become friends.

As they graduate from gofer status, they are introduced into the gang's real work, and punished with kicks and blows if they fail to do it well. Akira is sent to collect money from an old woman living alone; Ryo is told to rape a young girl for the filming of a porno video. Horiuchi presents these scenes minus any moralizing. This, he seems to be saying, is what the yakuza do; this is the kind of men they are. Instead of angels with dirty faces, we see thugs with dirty souls.

The boys find themselves caught up in a gang war and drafted as hitmen. Akira is ordered to shoot a helpless gangster who has been tied, tortured, and stabbed. He is not a Michael Corleone making his first hit—there is no danger, no glory in the deed. Instead, he takes a gut-wrenching leap into a moral abyss. Afterwards, he sits in a phone booth chanting "if they made me do it, it's not a sin" as though he were praying for—and failing to find—absolution.

The two leads work well together. As Akira, TV-drama star Masanori Ikeda projects the pretty-boy charm of a classic nimaime (romantic lead), but he is also tough enough to be a credible yakuza recruit. Katsuyuki Omori plays Ryo as a bullheaded wildman. This, we think, is the type who was born to be a yakuza. But Ryo also wants to live. Is being a gangster, he asks, worth getting killed for?

It from such basic questions and unvarnished answers that Gorotsuki is made. Shoko Ieda, the journalist who wrote the book on which it is based, spent two years living among the gangs. Yasuhiro Horiuchi got his start as a porno director, a profession not free of underworld connections. His first straight feature may be too down-and-dirty for fans who prefer the genre's romantic illusions and ironclad conventions. For the rest of us, though, Gorotsuki will be a sobering initiation into the mean, messy reality of the gangsters' world.

Gunhed
(1989)
Written and directed by Masato Harada. Produced by Toho, Sunrise, Bandai, Kadokawa Shoten, and Imagica. With Masahiro Takashima, Brenda Bakke. (100 mins.)

Walking out of Masato Harada's Gunhed I felt as though I were coming off the shift at the foundry where I used to work. There was the same feeling of numbness and relief. This is not to say that *Gunhed* relies only on brute sensory overload for its effects—it has an incredibly busy story line—but that the end result of all the banging and clanging was exhaustion.

Harada has exploited a Hollywood trend without understanding its roots. The trend in question began with *Star Wars*, George Lucas's paean to the sci-fi serials of his youth. The film spawned a host of successors who may have abandoned Lucas's calculated cuteness for jack-in-the-box horror (*Alien*) or murky twenty-first-century angst (*Blade Runner*), but retained his look of grubby realism and his expectation—expressed most vividly in the character of Hans Solo—that our descendants will still be recognizably, even degenerately, human. Shiny cities on the hill are conspicuously absent in these films. In some, such as *Robocop*, the outlook is frankly pessimistic. Hobbes' war of all against all has become a grim reality.

Gunhed is set inside an artificial island—a dimly lit jungle of pipes, beams, and industrial junk—where a mad supercomputer reigns. The island's evil genius is the Biodroid: a powerful "living robot" programmed to do the computer's dirty work, including the killing of unwanted intruders. The intruders come anyway and meet sudden, horrible ends. Two, however, survive—an ex-pilot named Brooklyn (Masahiro Takashima) who has landed on the island with a gang of cutthroat treasure hunters (the treasure in this case being computer chips), and a female security officer named Nim (Brenda Bakke), who has arrived with her elite unit—the Texas Air Rangers— in pursuit of the renegade Biodroid.

The parallels with *Alien* are obvious. Harada tries to create the same feeling of edgy camaraderie and the same atmosphere of gut-wrenching suspense, but falls far short of his model. His failure is both technical and cultural, and given the poorly structured storyline, probably inevitable. Brooklyn needs only about fifteen minutes of screen time to discover the true nature of the treasure hunters and kill most of them off. These action scenes, presented in a choppily-edited blur, make it hard to tell who is doing what to whom. This confusion is compounded by the dialogue. The American actors speak in hardboiled English clichés, and the Japanese actors in standard Japanese. As a consequence, the characters often appear to be talking at, but not with, each other, an impression strengthened when they mispronounce phrases in each other's languages.

In not only its English but its look, such as the treasure hunters' B-17 and their leader's World War II–vintage flight cap, *Gunhed* tries to evoke a *Star Wars*–like nostalgia for the movie past, but it is an alien past, imperfectly understood. Lucas made his

takeoff of old serials work because he had grown up with the material, had real affection for it, and knew its limitations. Harada either uses his American influences trivially—as a design motif—or in odd-ball earnest. Before the penultimate battle the hero's robot delivers a rousing speech on the glories of the old Brooklyn Dodgers (!). The effect is jarring and sad, like spotting an old Armed Forces–edition paperback, alone and out of place, in a Jimbocho used book bin. Even sadder, however, is the acting of Brenda Bakke, yet another minimally talented *gaijin* carrying too large a dramatic load in a Japanese film. Cast as a macho wonderwoman, she impresses as a supremely bored waitress. Her partner in adventure, Masahiro Takashima, is an easygoing hunk who has neither the intensity nor charisma the part requires.

The real star of the movie is Gunhed—the fighter robot that Takashima's Brooklyn uses to defeat the forces of evil. When he appears in all his clanking splendor the movie's real inspiration becomes apparent—the good-robot-versus-bad-robot TV shows that Japanese boys teethe on. The conclusion of these shows is always the same—a robot battle-royal that ends with the good robot vaporizing his opponent. A similar battle is also the heart of *Gunhed*, despite a plot the program devotes eight pages to summarizing. If I were ten years old I might daydream through the dull parts, sit enthralled through the climatic scenes and then rush out to buy my very own Gunhed (sold, thoughtfully, by Bandai). Not being ten, I simply suffer—until the noise stops.

Hachigatsu no Rhapsody
Rhapsody in August (1991)

Directed by Akira Kurosawa. **Screenplay by** Akira Kurosawa and Ishiro Honda. **Produced by** Shochiku and Kurosawa Films. **With** Sachiko Murase, Mitsunori Isaki, Tomoko Otakara, Richard Gere, and Hisashi Igawa. (98 mins.)

"It was a very strange summer." So begins Akira Kurosawa's thirtieth feature film, *Hachigatsu no Rhapsody*. The foreign reaction to this tale of an old woman's search for her past during a summer holiday with her four grandchildren has also been passing strange or, perhaps I should say, sharply divided. The audience at the Cannes Film Festival applauded *Rhapsody* and its director loud and long, but foreign reporters at a pre-Cannes press conference in Tokyo bombarded him with questions about the film's historical one-sidedness. Why did the *Rhapsody* make so much of the Nagasaki bombing, so little of Japan's deeds during World War II?

"It isn't that kind of film," Kurosawa replied. He was right: *Rhapsody* is about family relationships and remembrance, not the war as such. But after four decades, the bombing still shapes those relationships. *Rhapsody* is a didactically political film, with a message familiar to anyone who has sampled the many Japanese TV programs and movies about the events of August 1945: remember the victims and end the wars that produce them. Kurosawa states this message simply and poignantly, with signature touches.

The film may offend certain American sensibilities. When the children are looking at the memorials to the bombing victims erected by foreign countries in the Peace Park, the younger boy (Mitsunori Isaki), asks why there is no American memorial. "Of course there's no American memorial," his older sister (Tomoko Otakara) replies, as though stating the obvious. "They're the ones who dropped the bomb."

Is Kurosawa trying to cast America as the villain and Japan as the victim? The answer, I think, is no. Experiencing the reality of the bombing for the first time, the children are understandably shocked and angry at what they consider to be the perpetrator: America. But the grandmother (Sachiko Murase), who lost her husband in the bombing, tells them that war itself, not America, is to blame. She has gone beyond anger at the bombers, if not sorrow at the tragedy they brought.

The children have a chance to meet a real American when Clark (Richard Gere), the son of the grandmother's long-lost older brother, pays a visit. The brother, who went to Hawaii as a young man and made a fortune in pineapples, is now dying and wishes to see his sister one last time. Clark has come to escort her to Hawaii. Gere may not look right for the part, but he represents a casting coup for Kurosawa. Fresh from the success of *Pretty Woman*, he can help the film at the international box office. Whether he helps the film artistically is more debatable. He tries hard to blend in with the Japanese cast, but he comes across as a Hollywood star visiting the set. With his big smile and easygoing ways, he is an American all right, but not a credible Nisei relation.

His All-Americaness, however, is perfect for his key scene; a heart-to-heart talk with the grand-mother. Clark, who has just heard that her husband was killed in the Nagasaki bombing, expresses his apologies ("America was wrong"). The grandmother tells him that he has nothing to apologize for. This U.S.-Japan reconciliation scene rubbed some members of the American press the wrong way. Why should only the American have to apologize? they asked. But it was Clark's uncle, not an anonymous victim, who died; his words of sympathy and regret sound natural and right.

Kurosawa doubtless knew that his latest cinematic statement about the atomic bombings would be a gamble. His earlier film on the same theme, *Ikimono no Kiroku* (Record of a Living Being, 1955), was a critical and box office failure. That he went ahead and made another anyway is admirable. *Rhapsody* is minor-key Kurosawa; it lectures too much, engages too little. But it is still Kurosawa. Who else could have filmed the children's sobering encounter with a jungle gym twisted by the nuclear blast? Or the final, tragic run in a driving rainstorm? In these, and other scenes, Kurosawa shows that he can still make moments of what he calls "real cinema." I hope he can give us many more.

Hadashi no Picnic
Down the Drain (1993)

Directed by Shinobu Yaguchi. Screenplay by Shinobu Yaguchi, Takuji Suzuki, Yasunobu Nakagawa. Produced by Pia and Pony Canyon. With Saori Serikawa, Akane Asano, Miwako Kaji. (92 mins.)

Shinobu Yaguchi's *Hadashi no Picnic* begins as a comedy of errors; Junko Suzuki (Saori Serikawa) is a high school girl who is secretly dating a college boy, taking driving lessons, and riding the train for free. One day a conductor catches her, but she manages to escape, leaving her bag behind. The station notifies her mother, who comes to retrieve it and apologize abjectly to the station men.

Meanwhile, Junko is aboard another train, on her way to see her grandmother. But when she arrives, she finds only an empty house where, exhausted, she promptly falls asleep. That night she is awakened by her parents; granny has died and they have come for the funeral.

On the way home, disaster strikes again as their car collides with a motorcycle. Her parents are hospitalized and Junko finds herself alone with granny's urn. Walking to the station, she drops it and it promptly disappears under the brushes of a street sweeper. What is a girl to do?

The logical thing to do from this point, one would think, is escalate: i.e., subject poor Junko to a succession of ever greater, ever more hilarious, catastrophes. Yaguchi, however, wants to make a statement about the absurdity of it all, including the absurdity of action. Junko becomes a rag doll in the hands of fate and the film becomes one damn thing after another. After her unfortunate encounter with the street-sweeper, she is nearly poisoned by a kindly noodle-shop proprietress, taken on a tour of unoccupied houses by a eccentric woman (who leaves her in the lurch when the owners return), and beaten by classmates who don't like her attitude. It is hard to say, however, what her attitude is: she has long since lapsed into a depressed, near-catatonic state.

Yaguchi has injected youthful energy into this farce, but, except for a few comic gems (the look on Junko's face as the sweeper sucks up granny's ashes), it is energy without clear direction. Saori Serikawa, the newcomer who plays Junko, is little more than a pretty blank who spends most of the movie schlepping about in a dowdy dress and peering owlishly through oversized spectacles. One wants to tell her—and Yaguchi—to get a grip.

Hana-Bi *
Fireworks (1998)
Written and directed by Takeshi Kitano. Produced by Bandai Visual, TV Tokyo, Tokyo FM, and Office Kitano. With Takeshi Kitano, Kayoko Kishimoto, Ren Osugi. (103 mins.)

In his latest film, *Hana-Bi*, Takeshi Kitano proves again that he has an original directorial mind able to brilliantly reimagine hackneyed genre material and make it unquestionably his own. Also, from the violent extravagances of *Sono Otoko Kyobo ni Tsuki* (Violent Cop) whose cop hero, played by Kitano, spent much of the film kicking, punching, and otherwise abusing hapless victims, he has evolved into a cinematic stylist who gets his effects with the utmost economy of means and the least possible melodramatic fuss.

The macho romanticism of the first film still suffuses the seventh, but is refined almost to the point of abstraction. Instead of ramming a pistol barrel up a punk's bloodied mouth and giving him a cold-steel flossing in medium closeup, his cop hero in *Hana-Bi*, beats up a punk offscreen. while the camera watches his friend's reaction of slow-witted shock and surprise. Yes, Kitano's cop once again proves that he is a mean dude, but with a welcome touch of understated humor.

Nishi (Kitano) is a veteran cop who is wrestling with a personal crisis—his wife (Kayoko Kishimoto) is dying of cancer—and a guilty conscience. After he left his partner, Horibe (Ren Osugi), at a stakeout to visit his wife in the hospital, Horibe was shot and paralyzed from the waist down. Now he lives alone with no job, no family—his wife left him, taking their daughter—and seemingly no hope. Nishi feels that if he had stayed on the job his partner might have avoided this disaster.

Stunned by these double blows, Nishi moves through life like a mute sleepwalker whose body is wired to explode. When the punks he encounters in his daily round annoy him, he crushes them with the impassive ferocity of a man swatting a buzzing fly. Meanwhile, after years of chasing bad guys, Horibe is becoming reacquainted with the beauties of nature, the existence of an inner life. Hesitantly, he begins to paint. Soon, pictures of animals and people, most with blooming flowers in place of faces, are appearing in rapid succession, painted with a primitive authority, in bold colors. (All are actually the works of Kitano himself). From death, Horibe starts to move toward life.

Nishi, however, is heading in the other direction. To take responsibility for what he sees as his derelictions of duty and compensate those who have been affected, including the young widow of a murdered junior dectective, he quits the police force and robs a bank. But in abandoning his old life, he rediscovers his love for his dying wife. Together, they set out on a final journey, as his former colleagues close in.

In delineating the arcs of Horibe and Nishi's lives, Kitano rejects the usual underlinings and exclamation points of cop-thriller melodrama. Instead, he reduces his two cops to their human essence and then, with a directorial gaze coldly observant, if wryly sympathetic, watches as that essence expresses itself, for better or worse. Nishi is the more fully realized and interesting of the two: he is both a prototypical Japanese stoic, who lets his Quixotic actions speak louder than his cryptic words, and a naughty kid in a man's body, who expresses his defiance of fate by goofing around at the edge of the abyss. He is, in other words, a typical Kitano hero; a man who fights, loves, laughs, and dies without regrets, excuses, explanation, or apologies. No longer the sadistic bully of *Sono Otoko*, he attains, in the end, to something approaching grace. Kitano may not yet be the Ozu of the nineties—the director of *Tokyo Monogatari* would have never used that girl romping with the kite in the last scene (an in-your-face symbol if there ever was one)—but he has become, after winning the Golden Lion in Venice for *Hana-Bi*, the leading Japanese filmmaker of his generation. Will Kitano justify the confidence of John Woo, who has said that he will be the next Asian filmmaker to make it big in Hollywood? Perhaps, but after the operatic excesses of Woo and his fellow Hong Kong action directors, Kitano's off-beat reductionism—the cinematic equivalent of Theolonious Monk's jazz—will strike American audiences as different indeed. And somehow, it's hard to imagine him working with John Travolta.

Happyaku Two Lap Runners
Boo Two Lap Runners (1994)

Directed by Ryuichi Hiroki. Screenplay by Masato Kato. Produced by Suntory, Pony Canyon, and New Century Producers. With Shunsuke Matsuoka, Miwako Kawai, Eugene Nomura. (110 mins.)

Former soft-porn director Ryuichi Hiroki makes a successful transition to straight filmmaking with *Happyaku Two Lap Runners*, a selection for the 1994 Berlin Film Festival. But for all its gently ironic lyricism and knowing insights into the tangled emotional and erotic lives of its adolescent characters, the film is an illustration of what might be called the Laws of Cinematic Reaction for graduates of Nikkatsu and other porn factories.

The first law is that, having spent your formative years filming sweaty couplings, you all but abandon eroticism in your straight feature debut. *Happyaku* tells the story of two teenage boys—a rich kid from Shonan Beach and a poor kid from Kawasaki—who become rivals on the track, unlikely friends off it and participants in a sexual roundelay. The film, however, is unlibidinous. Its teenagers may take sex for granted—the girls call up the boys for trysts as casually as though they were ordering out for pizza—but their couplings are usually either failures or devoid of heat.

The rich kid, Kenji (Shunsuke Matsuoka), is torn between his obsession with a dead track-club *sempai* (senior), with whom he once had a sexually charged moment, and his romance with the equally obsessed Kyoko (Miwako Kawai), who was the *sempai*'s lover. She wants him, he wants his memories. Also, he is an intellectual type, who would rather discuss the mechanics and metaphysics of running than chase girls. When Kyoko finally drags him to bed, his performance is unspectacular, his reaction surprisingly cool. The movie, we see, is less about Kenji's sexual awakening, than his coming to terms with his past. He reaches out to Kyoko as a way of remembering his *sempai*. There is longing, but no passion, in his touch.

When Kenji does get it on, Hiroki films the lovemaking ironically, as though Kenji and his partner were bouncing marionettes, with biology pulling the strings. Even Kenji's poor-boy rival, Ryuji (Eugene Nomura), who has an ample supply of male libido, spends most of the movie pursuing a pretty long-legged hurdler who only has eyes for Kenji. Then, when Ryuji finds himself in a love hotel with Kenji's kid sister, he can't make her; she looks too much like her older brother. So they spend the afternoon singing *karaoke* and finding solace from their loneliness. Hiroki has excised teenage lust from his characters not out of prudery, but because it would disturb his film's coolly elegiac mood, its austerely poignant celebration of the neo-romantic purity of contemporary youth.

The second cinematic law is that, after filming closeups of your actors' various parts in your porn factory days, you keep your camera as far away from them as possible now that you are an auteur. While his shots of runners in action have a youthful energy that bursts from the screen, Hiroki films most of his emotional highlights from atop a moving crane or aboard a whirling helicopter. He uses long shots to effectively reveal his characters as universal figures in an ongoing cosmic drama. But he overdoes them, until we feel not only distanced but excluded. We hear expressive voices, but see only inexpressive backs or human dots in vast landscapes.

This strategy may make it easier for Hiroki to establish his creds as a serious stylist— no hack, after all, would wait an hour to give the audience its first close look at his leading lady—but it also slows the action to a crawl and drains the big scenes of emotional power, until we become too aware of the director's technique, too unconcerned about his characters' dilemmas.

Good performances emerge from the distance nonetheless. I particularly liked Eugene Nomura as Ryuji. The kid may have an inflated opinion of his prowess in bed and on the track, but he is also unpretentious and full of beans. Listening to the infectious doo-wop theme and watching Ryuji's amusingly disjointed run around the track in the opening scene, I thought that *Happyaku* would belong to him. I was wrong—it belongs too much to Hiroki—and his crane operator.

Haru
(1996)

Written and directed by Yoshimitsu Morita. Produced by Kowa International. With Masaaki Uchino, Eri Fukatsu. (118 mins.)

Japan started in the slow lane on the information highway, but is fast getting up to speed. How fast is evident in Yoshimitsu Morita's *Haru*, in which a man in Tokyo and a woman in Morioka meet, become confidants, and fall in love, almost entirely on line. If nothing else, the film provides an interesting jumping-off point for cross-cultural comparison. Confronted with a new techno-fad, Hollywood immediately thinks "thriller." This hacker/VR/ Internet stuff can be dangerous! The resulting movies are essentially paranoid fantasies: the big, scary "what if."

Morita, who once produced the brilliant social satire of *Kazoku Game* (Family Game), has since become a purveyor of date movies. *Haru* is a typical Morita product of the 1990s: feel-good entertainment that is at once strenuously with-it and timelessly romantic. In short, save for a scheduling slip, the perfect cinematic present for Valentine's Day. Instead of inspiring visions of personal crisis or global doomsday, the film's high tech serves only as a shiny ribbon, as it were, to tie everything together while concealing the final, too-perfect twist.

Despite the sticky softness of its center, *Haru* resurrects the ghost of Morita the cinematic innovator, compelling storyteller, and insightful delineator of character. His young lovers are likable people with more than two dimensions, and it's hard to resist the tug at the heartstrings when they finally meet. Also, by telling a large chunk of the story by e-mail—made easy to read by a blue background—Morita has created a new hybrid: the film/novel of linked letters. *Haru* is a movie you read, a novel you see. But the story itself is a facile sell—an alert ad director could quickly boil it down to a thirty-second spot for a computer maanufacturer—and this consumer couldn't quite buy it.

Haru is the handle for a young salesman (Masaaki Uchino) who joins an online movie chat group to forget his disappointment at the sudden end to his athletic career when he injured his knee playing American football. He addresses most of his private e-mail to Hoshi, a male member of the group who is unusually sympathetic to Haru's personal problems, including his troubled relationship with his long-time girlfriend.

Then Hoshi makes a startling confession; he is really a she—a Morioka department store clerk (Eri Fukatsu) haunted by the memory of a dead lover and burdened with the unwanted attentions of the lover's friend. Hoshi hid her sexual identity to avoid harassment, but she trusts Haru enough to come out of the closet. A friendship blossoms. Hoshi keeps changing jobs to avoid her persistent suitor, until as a "companion"—a woman who decorates corporate functions with her youth, beauty, and charm—she meets a young executive (Kazushi Yamashita) who makes her an unusual offer: a platonic relationship leading to a marriage without illusions or love. She agrees to give it a try. Meanwhile, Haru begins a relationship with Rose, a hot-blooded, free-spirited dental assistant. He tells Hoshi the details of this affair, including the physical. Hoshi replies with confessions of her own about her dates with the exec.

These relationships are but distractions—Haru and Hoshi are about as likely to go permanently off line as Tom Hanks and Meg Ryan are about to be eternally disconnected in *Sleepless in Seattle*. On the way to the denouement, however, Morita distracts us with e-mail messages that read as naturally as an overheard coffee-shop conversation, but have an adroitly constructed romance-novel arc. He is too clever by half, though, throwing in plot twists that ring more of box-office calculation than artistic fascination with this strange new method of communication—so intimate, so anonymous, encouraging the boldest of truths, the baldest of lies.

Hashi no Nai Kawa
The River with no Bridge (1992)

Directed by Yoichi Higashi. **Screenplay by** Yoichi Higashi and Soo-Kil Kim. **Cinematography by** Koichi Kawakami, Naoko Otani. **Produced by** Galleria and Seiyu. **With** Naoko Otani, Tamao Nakamura, Tetsuta Sugimoto. (139 mins.)

Burakumin (literally, "village people") are racially, culturally, and linguistically identical to the Japanese around them, but since the beginning of the seventeenth century, when the Tokugawa government divided the population into a rigid hierarchy of social classes, they have occupied the bottom rung. Burakumin did work that other Japanese considered ritually unclean, such as disposing of dead animals, tanning hides. and making footwear. So they were called *eta*, which means "filth," and forced to live in segregated villages, called *buraku*, where many of the three million *burakumin* still live today.

Seventy years ago, a group of young *burakumin* organized the National Levelers Association (Zenkoku Suiheisha) to fight for equal rights. Today, the Buraku Liberation League, successor to the NLA, continues that struggle. Together with Seiyu, the BLL has produced a film to celebrate its seventieth anniversary and dramatize its origins: *Hashi no Nai Kawa*.

Based on a book by Sue Sumii and directed by Yoichi Higashi, *Hashi* tells the story of two brothers who grow up in Komori, a *burakumin* village, in the early years of this century. It traces their development from boys who innocently believe that *"eta"* is a term of abuse for *burakumin* children, to men who see it as a badge of pride.

Hashi, however, is not a "problem film" in the usual sense. Shot in warm earth colors by cinematographer Koichi Kawakami, *Hashi* has the incongruous look of a rural idyll. The people in

Komori may be desperately poor, but they live in a setting that, with its glittering green paddies, sparkling river, and picturesquely thatched cottages, could illustrate a Japan Travel Bureau calendar.

Higashi takes a naturalistic approach to his story. Instead of building to a big, dramatic confrontation, the film is a series of small epiphanies. For two hours we become part of their community and learn something of what it was like to be a *burakumin* in Meiji and Taisho Japan. It was, we imagine, akin to being black in the Jim Crow–era South. The Komori *burakumin* live in intimate contact with their "betters" —their children go to the same rural school— and experience discrimination on a daily basis. In one scene, the boys' mother (Naoko Otani) helps a farmer with his rice harvest. When the harvesters take a tea break, she is given a "special" cup. And when they queue for their pay, she is told to leave the line. Instead of handing her her coins, the farmer smilingly places them on the doorsill and slams the door in her face.

It is the *burakumin* children who are the most vulnerable to this discrimination. They see their tormentors every day at school but lack adult defenses for dealing with them. One teacher explains to his class that *burakumin* are officially equal because the Meiji Constitution has declared them *shinheimin* ("new commoners") but explodes at *burakumin* boys who reply to the taunts of their classmates with their fists. How dare they strike their superiors?

As these scenes indicate, *Hashi no Nai Kawa* is explicit in its indictment of anti-*burakumin* prejudice. Despite its postcard prettiness, it expresses a reality that many Japanese, even today, would prefer to keep hidden.The lack of narrative focus weakens the impact of that reality, however. There are three sets of brothers—as children, adolescents, and young men—and enough subplots to supply a miniseries. As the years passed on the screen—the film begins in 1908 and ends in 1922, with the foundation of the National Levelers Association—I began to feel the minutes crawl in the theater. Higashi made me better understand the *burakumin*'s plight, but after witnessing the endless string of indignities they suffered (and continue to suffer), I wished he could have hit harder at their oppressors—and made more of his mainstream audience spill their "clean" cups of tea.

Hatachi no Binetsu *
A Touch of Fever (1994)

Written and directed by Ryosuke Hashiguchi. Produced by Pia and Pony Canyon. With Yoshihiko Hakamata, Masashi Endo, Reiko Kataoka, Sumiyo Yamada, Ryosuke Hashiguchi. (114 mins.)

What, as Tina Turner once asked, has love got to do with it? To prostitutes the answer is usually "not much." Why sell your heart along with your body? At the end of Tamasaburo Bando's *Yearning*, a Meiji-era *oiran* (courtesan) played by Sayuri Yoshinaga confesses to her young successor that she has never really liked any of her customers. This said after one has killed himself for her and another has saved her from a life of dissipation and penury.

In *Hatachi no Binetsu*, first-time director Ryosuke Hashiguchi depicts hustlers of another sex, generation and attitude. Constants remain, however. His hero, a blandly handsome college boy named Tatsuru (Yoshihiko Hakamata) cares nothing for his customers at the gay bar where he is on call part-time. He cares nothing, really, for anyone. He is reminiscent of the existential murderer in Camus's *The Stranger*, but rather than another human being, he has killed the potential for feeling in himself.

Outwardly Tatsuru looks much like the hundreds of other nice young men living uneventful lives in characterless single rooms. He has his admirers, including Shin (Masashi Endo), a teenage runaway who works at the same bar, and Yoshiko (Reiko Kataoka), who belongs to the same marketing club at school. But Tatsuru keeps his distance and can be quite hard when someone ventures too near. (To a customer who asks him if he "can get it on with a man," Tatsuru replies "I don't care if it's a woman or a man; I can have sex without liking someone.") A similar character in an American or European film might give off a smell of danger or corruption. Tatsuru, however, is odor-free. (In the program notes, director Jun Ichikawa comments that Tatsuru and his fellow hookers are "boys who look as though they could be rubbed out with an eraser.") We want to see him dirtied up and that affectless mask torn away.

A winner of a Pia Film Festival Scholarship in 1989 for *Yube no Himitsu* (Secrets of the Evening), Hashiguchi shapes each scene for maximum impact. Even the scene-ending blackouts zap us ironic flashes of beauty and insight, like punchlines of visual haiku. In the setup to the first, a customer asks Tatsuru his name. As he opens his mouth to utter what will no doubt be a lie, the screen blackens and we hear Yoshiko calling him. Next we see Tatsuru and Yoshiko in bathing suits, dangling their feet into a crowded swimming pool. Even with a conventional transition, we would understand that Tatsuru is leading a double life, but the blackout underlines that fact with a darkly humorous twist.

Why is he hustling? Shin, alone with no friends in the big city, needs the money, but Tatsuru is in no such financial straits. Even so, he tells everyone that he is only doing it for the yen. Sensing, in his cool passivity, the disgust he feels for his customers, we suspect there may be other, darker reasons as well.

Though *Hatachi* focuses on gay life, it is unself-conscious about gayness. Instead of loudly trying to change our presumed attitudes, the film quietly assumes that its characters are the same tangle of desires and dreams as the rest of us. More than the consequences of sexual orientation, the film is concerned with the neverending grope in the dark towards love and happiness, in whatever form. Shin likes Tatsuru, but when the older boy makes a pass at him, Shin recoils. He doesn't want sex until he is surer of Tatsuru's friendship. Yoshiko can't make up her mind whether she wants Tatsuru for a friend or a lover, even after he kisses her in a car at a gas station. Somehow, though, she senses that something is amiss. Only Tatsuru seems to glide through this tangle of emotions relatively unscathed. He does suffer a shock when Yoshiko invites him home for dinner—and he discovers that her father is one of his customers—but the scene seems to belong in a different film.

The glide ends when a customer (Hashiguchi) hires Tatsuru and Shin for a threesome. Young, good-looking, and hip, the customer doesn't need to buy sex, but he wants to play games that ends in the boys' humiliation and tears. In one long take, shot with a handheld camera, Hashiguchi achieves a documentary rawness and impact as the customer strips away the boys' lies and evasions. *Hatachi no Binetsu* was Hashiguchi's Pia Film Festival Scholarship film. He has graduated from his apprenticeship with flying colors.

Heisei Musekinin Ikka Tokyo Deluxe
Tokyo Deluxe (1995)

Directed by Yoichi Sai. **Screenplay by** Yoichi Sai and Chong Ui Shin. **Produced by** Amuse, Cine Qua Non. **With** Moeko Ezawa, Ittoku Kishibe, Goro Kishitani, Kazuya Takahashi, Dave Kureiken, Shigeru Nakano, Hitomi Ishii. (108 mins.)

In 1993 Yoichi Sai made *Tsuki wa Dotchi ni Deteiru* (All Under the Moon), a black comedy about an ethnic Korean cab driver trying to find romance and a Filipino bartender trying to find a life in today's Tokyo. An ethnic Korean himself, Sai skewered his Japanese and Korean characters with equal relish. His talent for caricature, nose for controversy, and freshness of approach made him Japan's answer to Spike Lee. *Tsuki* swept major awards and became the year's biggest independent hit.

Now Sai is back with *Heisei Musekinin Ikka Tokyo Deluxe*, a comedy about a family of flimflam artists. But though intended as mass audience entertainment—imagine Spike Lee remaking *The Sting*—it retains Sai's stylistic stamp and personal outlook. The world of *Tokyo Deluxe* is divided between hustlers and marks—and the borders are constantly shifting. Who can you trust? The answer, in this movie, is "no one." It's message—the family that scams together, stays together—may sound upbeat enough, in its own sardonic hipster way, but we can't quite buy it. It is Sai genuflecting in the direction of the box office.

The clan matriarch is Matsu (Moeko Ezawa), a feisty bulldozer whose motto is "It's better to con than be conned." Of the men in her family, including husband Kimio (Ittoku Kishibe) and four sons by various fathers, the only one she can rely on is second-son Minoru (Goro Kishitani), who dreams up most of the scams and holds this fractious clan together by the force of his personality. Minoru, though, is tired of the life, which has more downs than ups. Also, he is occasionally afflicted with twinges of what may be a conscience.

As the movie begins, the family is sixty million yen in the hole after backing the wrong candidate in an election-betting scheme. Instead of paying up, they run off to Tokyo. Though third-son Susumu (Kazuya Takahashi), whose specialty is marriage fraud, assures everyone that the metropolis is his backyard, it is Minoru who finds the family a rent-free refuge; a barbershop run by the naive parents of a former one-night-stand. Swayed by Minoru's emotional spiel—within minutes of walking in the door he is calling them "mother" and "father"—they allow him and fourth-son Jun (Dave Kureiken), a half-Japanese, half-American teenager, to stay the night. Soon after, the entire family moves in and takes over. But how can they grab the brass ring that always seems just beyond their grasp?

The story is a picaresque chronicle of their attempts to hit it big. Oldest son Takashi (Shigeru Nakano) and wife Nobuko (Hitomi Ishii) solicit clients for a phony celebrity sperm bank, Minoru persuades a gay-bar manager to advance cash for a nonexistent condo contract, and Jun promises (but doesn't deliver) underage delights to a middle-aged man with a Lolita complex. Although Sai has done his homework on these and other scams—many of them are based on actual incidents—he presents them mostly in short scenes that distance us from the action and sometimes leave us guessing. Instead of pulling away the Wizard's curtain, he gives us suggestive peeks.

This fragmentary, episodic approach mimics the life-rhythms and thought-patterns of the flimflammers, who live from one score to next and never bridge the yawning disconnect between their big talk and squalid lives. As he did in *Tsuki*, Sai refuses to draw the usual distinctions between good and bad; he paints everyone various shades of gray. If the family is voracious, unscrupulous, and clannish, their victims are equally grasping—and many end up clutching worthless contracts or phony gold bars. Justice, in a way, is served. But in trying to please a mass audience while remaining true to the viewpoint expressed in *Tsuki*, Sai ends up with a film that is at odds with itself. It's like a con that starts brilliantly, but is too cute for its own good. This mark couldn't fall for it. Perhaps after his attempt to pull off *The Sting*, Sai will *Do The Right Thing* in his next film. We need him more as Japan's Spike Lee than its George Roy Hill.

Heisei Tanuki Gassen Pompoko

Pompoko (1994)

Written and directed by Isao Takahata. Produced by Tokuma Shoten, NTV, Hakuhodo, and Studio Ghibli. (119 mins.)

The Japanese love the cute, especially in exotic, furry form. This category includes pandas and koalas and that big-eared inhabitant of the Urayasu landfill, Mickey Mouse. Creatures closer to home, however, tend to have a more ambiguous rep. The *tanuki* (badger-dog) may appear in folklore as a fat, jolly fellow slapping a round belly and holding a jug of *sake*, but he is also known as a metamorphosing trickster who loves to fool and frighten unsuspecting human beings. There is, in Japanese eyes, something mysterious and eerie about this otherwise loveable creature.

The *tanuki* would thus seem to be out of place in modern Japan, which is rapidly transforming countryside into condos, leaving little room for four-legged creatures of any kind, real, or legendary. Isao Takahata's *Heisei Tanuki Gassen Pompoko* protests this trend, from the *tanuki* point of view. The film also offers a pointed, rather despairing commentary on how Japanese society has divorced itself not only from nature, but its folklore and traditions. The film's *tanuki*, it would seem, are the only real Japanese—and they are in danger of ending as roadkill on the Superhighway to Progress.

As the film begins they are battling each other for dwindling food supplies, but they soon realize who the real enemy is: the developers who are transforming their idyllic forests in Tokyo's Tama Hills into soulless suburban sprawl. Oroku Baba, a stout, gruff-voiced matron, proposes a plan: use the traditional *tanuki* arts of metamophosis against the enemy. They will literally never know what hit them.

Soon young *tanuki* braves are changing into tarpaulins that fall mysteriously over windshields or into concrete blocks that suddenly appear on roads. Trucks crash, bulldozers tumble over cliffs. The *tanuki* celebrate wildly, joyously. Victory is theirs! But it isn't. New trucks and bulldozers appear, progress marches on. What to do? That is the question the *tanuki* keep asking themselves, but they struggle throughout the film to come up with satisfactory answers.

This is not typical mass-audience storytelling; in any contest of good and evil, especially in the world of *anime*, we would expect good to win, triumphantly and overwhelming. But Isao Takahata, who wrote the script and directed, sets his *tanuki*-vs.-human saga in a real place and time. How can a small band of animals hold back the bulldozers indefinitely? Even with the help of the supernatural, it's not easy. Despite the film's eco-moralizing— its glorifying of the good old days when man and *tanuki* lived in harmony with each other and with nature—it does not treat its heroes solely as an endangered species. They are a lively, close-knit bunch, who may behave foolishly from time to time, but are tenacious in their defense of home and hearth. They are the filmmakers's idealized image of the old-time peasant village.

The *tanuki* also represent all that is magical and sacred in traditional culture. (When an elder perishes from his transformational exertions, buddhas sweep down on a cloud to carry him up to heaven.) But when the *tanuki*, with the aid of three ancient masters, flood the neighboring suburb with goblins, the human residents want to treat it all as a weird but spectacular show. The next day, when an amusement park developer lyingly takes the blame—he wants the publicity—everyone, even those who were scared out of their wits, accept his story. The poor *tanuki* are wonderful at what they do, but hardly any one is willing to believe that they can do it. Even so, the many and varied metamorphoses are the highlight of the film. The *tanuki* are like furry magicians who pull themselves out of the hat, in a show that builds from the comically clumsy to the delightfully spectacular.

All the *tanuki*'s tricks, however, cannot disguise the rambling narrative. We see many inconclusive skirmishes between the *tanuki* and humans and many meetings of the *tanuki* elders, but we do not get a climax. The story resembles the environmental damage suits that drag on for decades. Even so, children, older ones especially, will enjoy the film's goofy comedy, slambang action, and spectacular effects. They will also like the *tanuki*: through thick and thin, the little guys stick together—and keep dancing.

Helpless

(1996)

Written and directed by Shinji Aoyama. **Produced by** Wowow, Bandai Visual. **With** Ken Mitsuishi, Tadanobu Asano, Kaori Tsuji, Yoichiro Saito. (80 mins.)

Shinji Aoyama's debut feature *Helpless* tells the by now familiar story of young protagonists who float without direction, resort to violence on impulse, and view their deeds with a casual indifference. Also, it is fundamentally sympathetic toward its protagonists, viewing them not so much as the degenerate products of a sick society as outsider antiheroes.

Director Aoyama says that, in writing the script, he was inspired by the work of Arthur Rimbaud—the original rebel without a cause. And yet, in the extremity of its violence, *Helpless* represents a departure for the youth-film genre—not altogether a welcome one. It is the fantasy of a movie-saturated imagination that sees murder less as a deed with consequences than a kind of stylistic statement.

The story begins like a thousand *yakuza* movies: a gangster named Yasuo (Ken Mitsuishi) is released from the slammer, only to find his boss dead, the gang in disarray, and his own future in doubt. After hearing the bad news, he spots Kenji (Tadanobu Asano), a high-school classmate, speeding by on a motorbike. Together with his welcoming committee—a young punk and a stylishly dressed gangster with a huge port-wine birthmark—Yasuo catches up with his friend at a family restaurant and they reminisce about old times. But when the gangster makes a wisecrack about the boss that rubs him the wrong way, Yasuo shoots him. End of scene.

After paying a visit to his sick, severely depressed father in the hospital, Kenji goes to the cabin in the mountains where Yasuo is burying the body. (How he did get it out of the restaurant without cops crawling all over him?) There he finds Yasuo's spacey younger sister Yuki (Kaori Tsuji), whose reaction to the corpse is to slap her brother petulantly on the shoulder. Yasuo drives off in search of more information about his boss, while Kenji puts Yuki on his motorbike and speeds away in the other direction.

When Kenji, wanting to call his father, stops at a roadside cafe, he runs into another former classmate, Akihito (Yoichiro Saito), a jokester who likes taking candid shots with his Polaroid. Kenji, however, is in no mood for laughs, especially when he hears that his father has hanged himself. When he returns to the cafe and discovers that the cook has been accusing the clueless Akihito of sleeping with a *yakuza*'s sister, his ugly mood turns violent. What

had begun that morning as a reunion between friends becomes a journey into hell.

As Kenji, Tadanobu Asano is appropriately blank, but his heavy-lidded good looks, dark charisma, and coiled energy make him compellingly watchable. Those expecting action with a stylish edge will be disappointed, however. Kenji and Yasuo attack their victims as though a switch had been flipped, hurtling them into frenzies that feel arbitrary and unreal. Also, the camera tends to look away at crucial moments, undercutting the violence. The intent may be to suggest rather than brutally present, but the effect is to drain these moments of impact.

Despite amateurish lapses and auteurist pretensions, Aoyama is onto something real about the character of his generation and the shape Japan's future is taking. One can only hope that he is wrong.

Hero Interview

(1994)

Directed by Michio Mitsuno. **Screenplay by** Shinji Nojima. **Music by** Chage & Aska. **Produced by** Fuji TV and Hori Pro. **With** Honami Suzuki, Hiroyuki Sanada, Yumi Adachi. (106 mins.)

The "trendy drama" genre, which depicts the love troubles of fashionable upwardly mobile young urbanites, was born in the late eighties, when Japan was ascending, like Dorothy, into an Oz filled with gourmet meals, fancy foreign cars, and to-die-for fashions. Then came the Wicked Witch in the form of a recession and we all fell back to earth (if not precisely Kansas).

The trendy dramas, however, kept coming—and attracting young female viewers. Among the most successful was *101 Kaime no Propose* (The 101st Proposal), the funny-tender tale of a homely middle-aged man's pursuit of a modish young woman that garnered monster ratings for Fuji TV in 1991. Scriptwriter Shinji Nojima, director Michio Mitsuno, producer Toru Ota, and singer-songwriters Chage & Aska shot to fame, while solidifying their hitmaker reputation. They have assembled those talents again for *Hero Interview*, a film that depicts, not the impossible dream of the bubble years, but the gritty realities of the less-than-effervescent present.

The heroine, Kasumi Sawaki (Honami Suzuki), hardly strikes us as a recession victim, however. In addition to her flawless features and exquisitely tailored designer clothes, she has a working-woman's dream job: reporter for a leading business newspaper.

She even has a dream boyfriend, a tall, handsome coworker on the career fast track, and a dream dwelling, a spacious, beautifully furnished apartment with no snoopy relations hanging about (though Mr. Right is there to comfort her when she comes back from a hard day at the office).

Then disaster strikes. Kasumi is transferred to the sports section. This, on a paper that worships the Nikkei average, is equivalent to exile in Siberia. What has the poor girl done to deserve it? Become engaged to Mr. Right, that's what. The transfer is a hint to quit her job and become Mrs. Right. Instead of taking it, Kasumi soldiers on, despite her boorish colleagues, whose uncouth behavior shocks her to the depths of her primly proper soul, and a clownish ballplayer named Jinta Todoroki (Hiroyuki Sanada), who jokingly feeds her a phony story that she swallows whole. When she shows it to her colleagues, their scornful laughter makes her wish she had never seen the inside of a ball park or the grinning face of a certain ballplayer.

This being a trendy drama, in which reality takes a holiday, we know that Kasumi will see that Todoroki has a good heart behind that muddy shirt. She will fall for this washed-up former homerun hitter, who has become ball-shy after a pitcher beaned and nearly brained him three years ago. Together with his button-cute daughter (Yumi Adachi), she will try to give him back his homerun-hitting dream. And Mr. Right? Well, we know what happens to Mr. Right in movies like this one, don't we?

Hero Interview runs through the complete catalog of trendy drama clichés, including 360-degree shots that whirl about Kasumi at key moments, a helicopter shot of Kasumi and Todoroki together in Tokyo Tower, a long shot of Kasumi and Todoroki having their first spat in a downpour, and a closeup of a distraught Kasumi walking alone, framed by headlamps shimmering like soft-focus fireflies. And all the while the pop melodies of Chage & Aska shimmer with their romantic glow, like Muzak at a department store fountain.

For much of the movie Honami Suzuki plays the spoiled daughter of the elite, who can't work up a passion for either her job or her ballplayer. When she finally does embrace him, she places one hand firmly on his chest, as though to keep the lout from mussing her clothes. Forced to put on a one-man show, Hiroyuki Sanada's Todoroki becomes an acrobat, magician, and clown, who treats the game as show time. It's a comic ham turn with the spice of desperation.

Though their characters may be clichés, the popularity of this movie suggests that Sanada and Suzuki have struck a chord. Perhaps in their hitless hitter and careerless career woman audiences see a

mirror image of their own—and their society's—situation. No longer booming, no longer confident (or some would say, arrogant), Japan faces the future with diminished expectations. Like Todoroki, it sits fondling its trophies—and wondering whether it can ever hit the long ball again.

Hikarigoke
Luminous Moss (1992)

Written and directed by Kei Kumai. **Produced by** Herald Ace and Nippon Herald. **With** Tetsuta Sugimoto, Rentaro Mikuni, Taketoshi Naito. (118 mins.)

Extreme acts provoke extreme reactions. We laugh when, in *The Gold Rush*, Mack Swain takes Charlie Chaplin for a chicken; we shudder when, in *The Silence of the Lambs*, Anthony Hopkins tells Jodie Foster that he devours his victims with the appropriate wine. We find it hard to view the act of eating human flesh as just another human failing; the cannibal must be a grotesque figure of either fun or horror. There can be no middle ground.

That middle ground, however, is what director Kei Kumai has staked out in *Hikarigoke*. While transporting supplies to an army base, the captain and crew of a cargo boat are shipwrecked on the Hokkaido coast. It is midwinter in the middle of the World War II and the nearest village is several days' walk away. They take refuge in a cave, but have no food. They face slow death by starvation. Gosuke (Tetsuta Sugimoto) has already been weakened by near-drowning. To his horror, he realizes that his crewmates, led by the captain (Rentaro Mikuni), are waiting impatiently for his death so they can consume his flesh.

The film is framed as true story: In the opening scenes, a writer (Taketoshi Naito) goes with the principal of a Hokkaido high school (Rentaro Mikuni, again) to investigate the luminous moss in a local cave. The principal tells the writer about the crew's ordeal— and the captain's arrest for cannibalism. The story is not true; it is based on a novel by Taijun Takeda. But it is one that Kumai has waited nearly three decades to film. That wait suggests a personal obsession; for Kumai the crew's cannibalism is a path into the depths of the human heart, not an excuse for comic hijinks or camp horror.

But how heavily he treads that path! After two hours in his dank, dark cave, I was longing for a ray of light and a breath of fresh air. Kumai is dealing with Big Questions here. Is survival alone enough or does life have higher ends? Is the captain evil or merely human? If we were in his shoes, would we also succumb? He drives home his answers with lugubrious earnestness and heavy-handed symbolism. A halo of luminous moss glows around the heads of the cannibals just as a scarlet letter blazed on the adulterous person of Hester Prynne. I got the point all right—that we are, in a fundamental sense, all guilty of the captain's crimes—but I also started to feel that the real problem in the cave was a lack of, not food, but fog-clearing oxygen.

Everyone overacts furiously, as though they were playing to the last row in the Imperial Theater balcony. The worst scenery chewer is Kunie Tanaka, the Japanese Ernest Borgnine. As the captain's opponent, he played salt-of-the-earth goodness with such overwrought awfulness that when the captain carved him up, I had an unkind thought: the ham was getting sliced.

Hikarigoke also has Chishu Ryu. The eighty-seven-year-old star of Ozu's masterpieces plays the judge at the captain's trial for cannibalism, which seems to take place in a dream or the afterlife. When the judge asks him to speak in his own defense, the captain says that he is "bearing the unbearable," meaning the trial. That is also a famous line from Emperor Showa's surrender speech and the Captain's use of it scandalizes the court. Then the air raid sirens sound and everyone but the judge and the captain run to the shelters.

The two men look silently into each other's eyes. Mikuni is wearing the same hangdog expression he has worn throughout the film, but Ryu gives him a look at once impishly stern and sagely tolerant. A current flows between the two men and they have a moment of simple human understanding—the first such moment in this high-minded, leadenly pretentious film.

Himeyuri no To
Eternal Monument (1995)

Directed by Seijiro Koyama. **Screenplay by** Seijiro Koyama, Nobuyo Kato. **Produced by** Toho. **With** Kumiko Goto, Yasuko Sawaguchi. (121 mins.)

For generations of Japanese, the Battle of Okinawa, in which one-third of the native population—120,000 people—lost their lives, has been symbolized by the sufferings of the students of the Okinawa Kenritsu Daiichi Koto Jogakko, a teachers college for women popularly known as Himeyuri Gakuen (Lily School).

On March 23, 1945, as the students were preparing for graduation, American warships began shelling the island. With invasion imminent, the students were enlisted into the Himeyuri Student Corps and sent to work on the front lines as nurses. After the American invasion on April 1, some were felled by shells, others by exhaustion and illness. When the Japanese defenders were fighting with their backs to the southern coast of the island, with U.S. troops closing in, the Himeyuri Student Corps was disbanded. Many of the students were subsequently either killed or committed suicide to avoid capture. Only a handful survived.

The sacrifice of the Himeyuri students has inspired four feature films, the first by Tadashi Imai in 1953, the second by Toshio Masuda in 1968 and the third by Imai again, in 1982. The fourth is Seijiro Koyama's *Himeyuri no To*. Made nearly fifty years after the events it describes, it is as full of stock pieties as a politician's speech at a government-sponsored war memorial service.

For many of the film's young actresses, the numerous scenes of tending the wounded in dim, overcrowded caves or tramping about the countryside in the dark, with loud explosions going off everywhere, seem to have been the equivalent of an unpleasant part-time job, like working the Saturday night shift at the Kabukicho MacDonald's. War is hell, but so is watching Kumiko Goto mime noble suffering, while obviously dying for a hot bath and a cold Perrier.

Director Koyama tells his sad story with a plodding earnestness and a numbing lack of imagination. Those looking for Japanese war-movie clichés will find the entire lot here, from the beautiful young teacher (Yasuko Sawaguchi) who selflessly sacrifices herself for her students (and dies touching the fingers of one in a pose reminiscent of Michelangelo's God and Adam) to the student who runs out of a cave to retrieve a fatal water bucket. (The less reverent will be tempted to shout, "Don't do it! No, do it!") His twenty-one heroines are not required to act so much as portray Innocence Sacrificed in various forms and attitudes: some perish with high-minded platitudes on their lips, while other revert to infancy to escape the horrors they see around them.

There is a possible feminist subtext to the students' story: that in this trial by fire, they often behaved heroically and proved, tragically, that they could give their lives as readily as any man. But the film portrays them as *kawaiso* (deserving of pity), not *kakkoii* (deserving of admiration). *Himeyuri no To* is discouraging proof that, half a century after the tragedy of Okinawa, Japanese filmmakers still view it through a haze of patronizing, mythologizing tears.

Himitsu no Hanazono
The Secret Garden (1997)

Written and directed by Shinobu Yaguchi. **Produced by**

Toho and Pia. **With** Naomi Nishida, Go Riju, Takako Kato. (83 mins.)

Getting rich quick is among the commonest of fantasies. Seeking to capitalize on this universal dream (and get rich quick themselves) filmmakers have made the hunt for fortune a favorite theme. Examples range from the sublime (*The Treasure of the Sierra Madre*) to the ridiculous (*Dumb and Dumber*).

Shinobu Yaguchi has added to this list with *Himitsu no Hanazono* (The Secret Garden), a film about a bent young woman's fanatical pursuit of a sunken treasure. I found it loopily engaging, if rather poky and thin. It resembles its heroine, a bank teller named Sakiko Suzuki (Naomi Nishida).

First, Sakiko takes us on a quick tour of her past, narrating deadpan comic sketches illustrating the highlights of her early life. Although in many ways ordinary, Sakiko has a personality quirk that sets her apart: she is obsessed with money and will do anything, short of committing murder, to get next to it.

Her idea of entrepreneurship, however, is to apply for a teller's job at a bank. Though a slack-jawed, rail-thin, lank-haired mouse, who seems to be missing a few dots on her dice, Sakiko gets hired because, when the bank managers inquire about her hobby, she gives them the perfect answer: "Counting money." Soon after getting her dream job, though, Sakiko becomes bored with it. Counting money is no fun if you can't keep it. She longs to become a hostage in a bank robbery. Anything to break the routine.

One day, she gets her wish when bank robbers whisk her out the door and lock her in the trunk of the getaway car, but in their haste to escape, the robbers drive off a mountain road. On hitting bottom, the car bursts into flames and Sachiko is thrown free. Landing in a mountain stream, she grabs a bright yellow suitcase and clings to it as the current sweeps her away. After plunging over a waterfall, she is sucked through an underground passageway to a large grotto, with a hole opening to a blue sky. The suitcase—filled with five hundred million yen in cash—sinks and Sakiko passes out. When she comes to she is floating near a riverbank, looking into the surprised eyes of a family of picnickers.

The rest of the movie records Sakiko's struggle to recover the loot and live out her dreams of wealth. If she succeeds, it will be the perfect crime. The police and media assume that the cash was burned to ashes, together with the robbers and their car. The grotto, however, turns about to be frustratingly inaccessible. What is a girl to do?

The film draws the comic contrast between the pre-robbery Sakiko—a friendless, money-grubbing nerd—and the post-robbery Sakiko, still friendless,

still money-grubbing, but steadily transforming herself into a superwoman as she single-mindedly pursues her goal. She enters a university to study geology, joins a rock-climbing club, signs up for a driving school, and takes scuba-diving lessons. She also attracts the attention of a time-serving assistant professor (Go Riju) and the jealousy of the prof's slithery student girlfriend (Takako Kato).

Yaguchi, who directed the 1993 *Hadashi no Picnic* (Barefoot Picnic), another comedy of errors about a fabulously unlucky young woman, slows the pace after a fast start and turns to self-referentially pawky humor. Imagine Jim Jarmusch directing a Laurel and Hardy comedy.

Naomi Nishida creates the right boneless, nerveless persona for Sakiko, but her performance stays as flat as her character's vibes. The gawky grimaces that were funny in the first reel become tiresome by the last. Also, though the film's air of amateurishness—the mannequin going over the waterfall that looks like a mannequin, the clay model of the underground passageway that looks like a clay model—may be a knowing dig at Hollywood slickness, the goofs start to look less clever than clumsy.

Watching *Himitsu no Hanazono*, I couldn't help thinking that it had possibilities. What about a remake with Jim Carrey in the lead role and a budget of fifty million dollars instead of five million yen? It was time to get out of the theater, call my agent, and start writing that script.

Hisai
Secret Ceremony (1998)

Directed by Taku Shinjo. **Screenplay by** Shintaro Ishihara. **Produced by** Shinjo Taku Jimusho. **With** Gitan Otsuru, Mitsuko Baisho. (103 mins.)

Who are the Japanese, really? Shohei Imamura has spent a career looking for the answers to that question, mainly on society's fringes. The resulting body of work constitutes a group portrait radically different from Western stereotypes of stoic samurai and twittering geisha. In Imamura's Japan, Westernization is but the thinnest of overlays, while the values of village society still rule. Instead of sacrificing self for the country or company, his Japanese are more likely to indulge their desires to the limit, avidly grasping for money, sex, and power. Instead of catering to the male ego with displays of coy submissiveness, his women tend to be lusty, vital types, who overwhelm feeble male attempts at domination.

Despite Imamura's affection for his characters, he is also aware of the darkness at the heart of his villagers' world view, born of poverty, insularity, and age-old fears of the unknown. One cinematic portrayal of that darkness was the 1968 *Kamigami no Fukai Yokubo* (The Profound Desire of the Gods) which tells the story of an engineer sent to a small island in the Okinawan chain to build a modern water system. Instead of the tropical paradise of his imagination, he finds a society riven by all the passions of the one he has left behind, while still adhering to the most ancient of human beliefs, including the magic efficacy of ritual murder.

Taku Shinjo, who worked as an assistant director under Imamura and now teaches at his film school, has made *Hisai*, a film about a salaryman sent to a small island in the Okinawa chain who also encounters a culture both enchantingly and eerily unchanged by the twentieth century. Given the long, close association between master and disciple, it's not surprising that *Hisai* displays the Imamura influence, down to a storyline that reads like a rewrite of *Kamigami no Fukai Yokubo*. The film, however, is not simply an Imamura homage.

Shinjo is an Okinawa native—his first film was the 1983 *Okinawan Boys*—who views the local culture from the inside, while Imamura prefers to film his subjects from a distance, like an entomologist squinting at specimens through a microscope. Also, Shinjo is conventionally lyrical in a way that the determinedly iconoclastic Imamura is not. The two lovers in *Hisai* enjoy a rapturous *pas de deux* on a secluded beach in the moonlight, while in an Imamura film they would mostly likely spend at least one scene rolling in the mud.

There is another element in the mix that is definitely non-Imamura; *Hisai* is based on a novel by Shintaro Ishihara, the novelist-turned-politician who is known for his right-wing views. But in a program essay Ishihara frankly acknowledges the origins of Okinawan culture in Polynesia and Melanesia. He also contrasts it favorably with what he describes as the "vulgarity and absence of values" so prevalent in mainstream Japanese culture. There is, he implies, a true Japaneseness about the Okinawan islanders that the Westernized, modernized majority is in danger of forgetting.

Takamine (Gitan Otsuru) arrives on a tiny island to sell its seventeen inhabitants on the advantages of mass tourism. His predecessor was about to sign a contract with them for the building of a resort hotel, but died in mysterious circumstances. Now Takamine has come to finish the job. The mostly elderly islanders seem friendly enough, but Takamine finds it impossible to talk business. "Become an islander," one advises him and that is what Takamine, over the coming months, sets out to do, helping the women with their planting, the men with their fishing. The suit and necktie disappear, together with the

workaholic ethic. Takamine begins to understand the hold the place has its people, even though he knows that they will always regard him as a stranger.

He becomes a frequent visitor to the house of the village headman, whose spinsterish daughter, Takako (Mitsuko Baisho), seethes with frustration and whose mentally disturbed son Minoru is kept chained in a pen, howling his loneliness and rage. One night Takako leads Takamine to a secluded beach, where they romp naked in the surf and make passionate love. Their affair, however, does not go unnoticed by the islanders, who are alarmed at the possible defection of their chief *miko* (shrine maiden).

During the annual festival, whose penultimate rites are conducted in secret, the island is invaded by a boatload of outsiders, including a TV camera crew. The crew and village youths clash, and a young woman is raped and her boyfriend beaten for wandering too near the incessantly beating drums. When the outsiders leave, Takamine stays, not only to finish his job, but to pull away the veil from longfestering evils. In drawing that veil, however, he is breaking the most fundamental of taboos.

Laboring under incredible difficulties—both his production company and distributor went bankrupt during the six years it took to bring *Hisai* to the screen—Shinjo has produced a film that, for all its celebrations of natural beauty and tradition, has a chill at its core reminiscent of Shirley Jackson's *The Lottery*. While rediscovering the essence of Japanese culture in his remote island community, Shinjo has expressed an archaic truth: we mortals invade the precincts of the gods at our peril. They guard their secrets jealously and, when angered, teach us the meaning of terror.

Hitodenashi no Koi *
Secret Liaisons (1995)

Written and directed by Masako Matsuura. Cinematography by Yasushi Sakakibara. Produced by Shochiku and Bandai Visual. With Michiko Hada, Hiroshi Abe, Nana Horie. (86 mins.)

In 1994, Kazuyoshi Okuyama's period mystery *Rampo* became Shochiku's biggest summer hit. Wanting to make another film based on the work of Edogawa Rampo, but not wanting to direct again, Okuyama recruited Masako Matsuura, a graduate of Shochiku's screenwriting program and a well-regarded TV commercial director. But instead of taking up where *Rampo*'s heavy-breathing eroticism and splashy computer-graphics effects left off, Matsuura's *Hitodenashi no Koi* (An Inhuman Love) tries to recapture the spirit of Rampo's early Showa era (the late 1920s and 1930s), when the ghosts of the premodern past were still alive in the Westernized present.

Many directors have recently made films set in the same between-the-wars period, but few have captured its domestic beauties with Matsuura's feeling for detail and atmosphere. The house and grounds of which her young heroine (Michiko Hada) is mistress embody traditional Japanese aesthetics as practiced by the educated upper middle-class; the place exudes tranquillity and refinement. The heroine, attired in a lovely kimono, charmingly modest in word and gesture, fits in well with her surroundings. This is the Japan that we still glimpse in glossy women's magazines, but, unless we are fortunate indeed, rarely see in our urban daily lives.

The story, one of Rampo's best known, is the familiar one of the entry into paradise and the discovery of the serpent. Kyoko (Michiko Hada), a young art student, develops a crush on her handsome, long-limbed teacher (Hiroshi Abe), but before she can muster the courage to say hello, he quits teaching to concentrate on his art. Then, by an incredible stroke of luck, former student and teacher are joined in an arranged marriage. Kyoko is overjoyed. Her new husband is not only a girls-comic hero in the flesh, but gentle, sensitive, and considerate. Their new house, a gift of his wealthy father, is a dream. Yes, *danna-sama* (hubby) doesn't talk much and often seems lost in a world of his own, but he is an artist, after all. If she wants companionship she can turn to the cheerful, lively teenage maid (Nana Horie), who is deeply fond of her mistress, but not obviously envious of her good fortune. Life is wonderful.

Danna-sama, however, leaves the bedroom in the middle of the night and returns hours later, smelling of a strange perfume. One night Kyoko follows him to his atelier and, huddling beneath the attic trap door, hears the husky voice of an older woman telling her husband she will never leave him. Paradise has just become hell. The movie, however, is not another tale of an amorous hunk cheating on his innocent bride. Though we know that something is dreadfully wrong with this marriage—and *danna-sama*—Matsuura keeps us guessing until the shocking denouement.

In her first starring role Michiko Hada is almost too perfect as the naive, trusting bride. Abandoning her own art career, her Kyoko trills her devotion to her lord and master, until we begin to feel, unkindly, that she deserves the disaster we know is coming. But after *danna-sama* begins his midnight strolls, she metamorphoses into a suspicious, jealous, and finally vengeful woman in a delicately layered, impressively strong performance. Meanwhile, Hiroshi Abe's

danna-sama remains a passive, distant blank to which Kyoko attaches her fantasies. His absence leaves a hole that all of Matsuura's beautifully composed shots cannot hide. Before showing up on the set he should have rented a copy of *Psycho* and stolen freely from Anthony Perkins. He would have learned that there are more interesting varieties of madness than catatonia.

Hong Kong Daiyasokai: Touch & Maggie
Hong Kong Nightclub (1997)

Directed by Takayoshi Watanabe. Screenplay by Nobuyuki Isshiki. Produced by NTV, Amuse, Bapp, and Nihon TV Ongaku. With Anita Yuen, Shingo Katori, Goro Kishitani, Stephen Au. (110 mins.)

The latest in a recent spate of pan-Asian co-productions is *Hong Kong Daiyasokai: Touch & Maggie*, which takes its narrative inspiration from *Some Like it Hot*, the 1959 Billy Wilder comedy about two Prohibition-era musicians who witness a mob rubout and, in their ensuing escape from the enraged hitmen, dress as women and join an all-girl band. In *Hong Kong Daiyasokai* the musicians have become a gay reporter (Goro Kishitani) and a young photographer (Katori) who have come to Hong Kong to do a piece about the local underworld. The reporter is attracted to the photographer, but before he can make his intentions known, they are caught in the act of recording a gangland murder and are chased by the killers, who go by the name of the Black Society. To shake their pursuers, the reporter hits on the brilliantly devious idea of dressing his colleague in women's clothes and posing as a honeymoon couple.

The honeymooners flee into a nightclub and somehow find themselves on stage as the principals in an magic act. The management is impressed with their impromptu performance—especially the "husband"'s frantic concern for his "wife" while she is drowning in a water tank during a botched disappearing act—and offers them a spot in the show. The "husband" becomes Touch and the "wife," Maggie. Further troubles ensue, however, when the Maggie falls for the club's singer (Anita Yuen), the singer's childhood friend (Stephen Au) falls for Maggie, and the singer falls for Touch who, of course, only has eyes for his hunky "wife." Meanwhile the club's new act attracts the attention of the Black Society boss. How can Maggie and Touch escape the mob's clutches—and Maggie save her virtue—before the final credits roll?

Scriptwriter Nobuyuki Isshiki, who was responsible for two other comedies with Southeast Asian settings—the 1992 *Sotsugyo Ryoko* (Graduation Trip) and the 1994 *Nettai Rakuen Club* (The Tropical People)—and director Takayoshi Watanabe, who helmed the 1995 hit romantic comedy *Izakaya Yurei* (Ghost at a Drinking Joint) and its 1996 sequel, combine the film's various romantic entanglements with knockabout farce and slambang action in a way more reminiscent of contemporary Hong Kong comedy than classic Hollywood farce.

Also, the homosexual element of the story, which Wilder could only hint at in 1959, becomes blazingly apparent in Watanabe's remake. We are even treated to a scene of Touch trying to rape the helplessly prostrate Maggie, filmed with an explicitness that make Joe E. Brown's pursuit of Jack Lemmon look positively courtly. Where Wilder was stingingly clever, Watanabe is obvious and crude, as though he were slamming out a lowest-common-denominator TV variety show. Even so, Goro Kishitani projects a cool self-possession and comic manic energy as Touch, while Shingo Katori is both amusingly clumsy and stunningly gorgeous in drag—think of a more muscular Goldie Hawn. Anita Yuen is no Marilyn Monroe; her sprightly normality pales against the outrageousness of her Japanese costars.

Hong Kong Daiyasokai scatters a few funny moments amidst campy excess and formulaic dross. I'll take the one of Katori trapped in the water tank on stage. As a drowning woman he gives an excellent imitation of a bewildered goldfish. Are we watching Japan's Jim Carrey in the making?

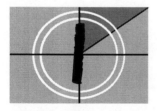

Ichi-ichi-kyu *
119 (1994)

Directed by Naoto Takenaka. **Screenplay by** Naoto Takenaka and Tomomi Tsutsui. **Produced by** Shochiku, TV Tokyo, and Image Factory IM. **With** Kyoka Suzuki, Naoto Takenaka, Hidekazu Akai. (115 mins.)

Naoto Takenaka's *119* (the emergency number for the fire department in Japan) is a film about fire-

fighters in a seaside town that has not had even a one-alarm blaze in eighteen years. This is a world familiar to us from Takenaka's *Muno no Hito* (1991); poky, eccentric, and lost in a fifties time warp. The good folks of Harari seem to be drowsing in an eternal present, in which a stuck desk drawer rates as the day's big event. The boys of the town's No. 2 Engine Company are so desperate for action that when a neighboring station gets a call they chase after its fire trucks in their civvies and nearly get run down for their trouble. When they arrive at the scene they find the members of a senior citizen's club sedately folk-dancing around a campfire.

They dutifully polish the fire truck and perform their drills, but they have plenty of time to kill. They play *shoji* and fall asleep, mouths gaping, between moves. They dance with each other to old Japanese pop music at a waterfront bar. They are not gay, just lonesome; all the eligible young women have left town.

Then something happens that wakes them out of their torpor; two university biologists come to study crabs at the local seashore. One is a goateed chap who looks like a professor from a Meiji-era faculty photo. His assistant, however, is a vision of purity and loveliness named Momoko Hibino (Kyoka Suzuki). Two of the firemen fall hard for her: the big, brawny, Ishii (Hidekazu Akai) and the small, shaven-headed, Tsuda (Naoto Takenaka), the fire chief.

In their rivalry are echoes of the 1986 Steve Martin comedy *Roxanne*, which was in turn based on *Cyrano de Bergerac*. Once again we have the picture-postcard setting, the wacky but lovable firemen, the chief with his endearing peculiarities (Tsuda's his antique toy fire engine collection), and the big lunk too shy to pitch woo to his socially superior lady love. Takenaka has also appropriated Martin's whimsy, grotesquery, and romanticism.

But though he may borrow, Takenaka makes *119* his own. Tsuda urges Ishii to write daily love letters to a nurse who his infatuation of the moment, but he does not serve as the big guy's epistolary stand-in. Later, when Ishii transfers his affections to Momoko, he courts her without Tsuda's assistance (though Tsuda gives him a toy fire truck that Ishii later presents as a love offering to Momoko). Also, Tsuda lacks Cyrano's blistering eloquence, haughty pride, and dazzling martial skills. A widower who lives in with his chubby son and his cagey coot of a father, he is comfortable with his nothing job and his humdrum milieu. Like Cyrano, however, Tsuda is a dreamer and romantic who will risk his life for strangers, but lacks the courage to pursue the love of his life.

The story unfolds at the pace of small-town life. The jokes revolve around minor upsets and misunderstandings and the rivalry between the principals is so low-key at be almost undetectable. Takenaka's attitude is closer to the deadpan hipsterism and oddball nostalgia of Aki Kaurismaki and Jim Jarmusch than the frenetic buffoonery of Steve Martin. He is not merely goofing on his firefighters' oddities, however, but doing the more difficult job of revealing their humanity.

Momoko is a latter-day Setsuko Hara heroine; intelligent, refined, and modern, but also cheerful, hardworking, considerate, and polite to a fault. Kyoka Suzuki brings a natural radiance to this traditionalist's ideal. By the time she walks off into the shadows for the last time, I shared the firefighters' infatuation. I also understood their affection for their job, comrades, and town. In *119* Takenaka has given stressed-out urbanites a glimpse of paradise. Lift your foot off the pedal, kick off your shoes, and enjoy the scenery.

Ie Nakiko
Sans Famille (1995)

Directed by Hidenobu Hosono. Screenplay by Toshiya Ito. Produced by NTV. With: Yumi Adachi, Yosuke Saito, Rumiko Koyanagi, Koichi Domoto, Takako Sakurai, Masato Hiruoya, Ayaka Nishida, Masaki Kyomoto. (92 mins).

Movie reviewers ought to occasionally mingle with the people who pay for tickets; sometimes audiences surprise you. That was my thought as I watched *Ie Nakiko* (Sans Famille), the film based on the hit NTV drama series about a much-put-upon waif played by Yumi Adachi. From the show's high ratings—a 37.2 percent for its last episode—I had imagined a tearjerker with a cross-generational appeal, but the crowd at the screening I attended was overwhelmingly the same age and sex as Adachi. Many of these girls seemed to have come more for the star than the film; they laughed in the wrong places and, at the end, there wasn't a wet eye in the house. There is hope for the younger generation yet. In lining up to see this film, they were doing what came naturally. Not long ago they had been standing in similar queues to see feature-length versions of their favorite TV *anime*. Also, *Ie Nakiko*—with its cartoonish characterizations and lurid story line, resembled the girls' comics they devoured. Their whole pop culture past had prepared them for this movie.

There was also Yumi Adachi, who is to the Japanese entertainment industry what Macauley Culkin was until recently to Hollywood: a pint-sized superstar whose magic touch turns even dreck into ratings and box-office gold. Adachi first proved she had the touch in *Rex*, a syrupy tale of a girl and her pet Tyrannosaurus Rex, but it was as Suzu, the spunky twelve-year old heroine of *Ie Nakiko*, that Adachi shot to superstardom.

In the TV series, Suzu was beaten by her stepfather, bullied by her classmates, and orphaned by the death of her mother. But with her indomitable spirit, she managed to prevail, even if she had to break society's rules. She stole from her classmates to pay for her mother's heart surgery and schemed to get her mean stepfather sent to prison for arson. Shirley Temple was never like this. In the film Suzu is still at it, swiping a Christmas cake so that she and her faithful dog Ryu can share some holiday cheer in public park. Now, she is not only parentless, but homeless. Not for long, though; she falls into the hands of Isogai (Yosuke Saito), the Shylock-ish owner a small circus, most of whose performers are runaways like herself. He also happens to be the new husband of her aunt Kyoko (Rumiko Koyanagi), a dreadful woman who, together with her ex, had once plotted to kill Suzu's mother.

Forced to join the circus against her will by this nefarious couple, Suzu finds friends in Minoru (Koichi Domoto) and Megumi (Takako Sakurai)—brother-and-sister trapeze performers with their own problems. Megumi has a weak heart, but the Isogais, fearing the loss of a top money earner, are denying her proper medical treatment and making her take to the air.

With Suzu's help, Minoru asks his natural father, a corrupt politician (Masato Hiruoya), to pay for Megumi's surgery, but he refuses to acknowledge the boy as his son. Then Suzu has a idea; send Ryu to fetch the doctor who operated on her mother! While Ryu is crossing the countryside on his mission of mercy, Suzu and Minoru are falling in love—and tempting the jealous wrath of Mayumi (Ayaka Nishida), the Isogais' terror of a daughter.

For *Ie Nakiko* fans, this story will be *déja vu* all over again; many of its characters and situations appeared on the television series. For this non-fan, watching the film was like sitting in on another family's long-running quarrel; no one stopped to explain why these people were being so nasty to one another. Also, scriptwriter Toshiya Ito and first-time director Hidenobu Hosono seem to have overdosed on *Oliver Twist*. The plot relies upon coincidence to an absurd degree ("of all the circuses in the world," Suzu might well say to herself, "I had to pick this one"), the baddies are straight out of Victorian melodrama (Rumiko Koyanagi's Isogai alternates between oozing insincerity and slithering malevolence) and a pure young woman dies a lingering, pathetic death (with her hand on her heart and noble sentiments on her lips).

The movie departs from Dickens, however, in the character of Suzu. Disdaining Oliver's passive, innocent victimhood, Suzu is the spunky, rule-breaking fighter. But she is also a one-note character who neither changes nor grows in the course of the film. Another departure from Dickens is the dog—the most intelligent character in the movie. He traverses hundred of miles of strange country without once asking for directions and persuades a young doctor (Masaki Kyomoto) to return to the circus with him, without even showing him a National Health Care card. That, I thought, showed uncommon wit, resourcefulness, and cunning. Perhaps they ought to sign him to produce the sequel.

Ikinai *
(1998)

Directed by Hiroshi Shimizu. **Screenplay by** Duncan. **Produced by** Office Kitano, Bandai Visual, TBS, Tokyo FM, and Nippon Herald. **With** Duncan, Nanako Okochi. (100 mins.)

The title of *Ikinai* (literally, "Not to Live") the debut feature by Hiroshi Shimizu, may be a play on the title of the Akira Kurosawa masterpiece *Ikiru* (To Live), but *Ikinai* is a Takeshi Kitano film by proxy. This is not surprising: Shimizu worked as Kitano's first assistant director on his last three films and *Ikinai* is the first non-Kitano film to be made by the director's Office Kitano production company.

This is also nothing to be ashamed of. While recalling the Kitano style in its puckish deadpan humor, spare narrative structure, and shotmaking economy, *Ikinai* is not baldly imitative. I was reminded of Masayuki Suo, another director who learned his trade at the feet of a master—in his case Juzo Itami—but whose own films softened the harsher aspects of his *sensei's* style, including his strident grotesquerie. *Ikinai* is likewise Kitano without the rough edges, including the sadistic violence and bad-boy jokes about sex and bodily functions. Shimizu also lacks Kitano's talent for shocking us into new ways of seeing and feeling, but has his own knack for making his narrative points with the least possible fuss, much like the simple but evocative Peruvian flute music of *Ikinai* soundtrack composer Maya. His is a minimalism that, with its absence of directorial ego, is in some ways more palatable than his master's.

In *Ikinai* ordinary Japanese faced with a crushing burden of debt decide to commit group suicide for insurance money. If life is a journey that ends in death, the film asks, how would you react if the journey were compressed to the length of a three-day bus tour of Okinawa? Would you stoically wait for the bus to sail off a cliff or frantically try to cram in as much living as you can?

The leader of this unusual group tour is Niigaki (Duncan), who is suitably somber in demeanor, inflexible in purpose. Having signed his charges to their fatal contracts, he is determined that they carry them out. Then he is confronted with a disruption to his plans in Mitsuki (Nanako Okochi), a young woman who has come in place of her uncle. Eager to enjoy her tour, Mitsuki has no idea of the bus's final destination. Leading her nine reluctant fellow tourists in a word association game, she breaks the ice. As the tour takes in the standard sights, the members tell each other their stories and speak frankly about their desires and fears. A solidarity develops that releases them, temporarily, from their dread of the trip's end. They are not Tokkotai suicide pilots going willingly to their doom for a cause, but men who have lost hope and resigned themselves to the inevitable. With Mitsuki serving as a catalyst, however, they begin to appreciate what they are about to lose. But the bus rolls on. Who, if anyone, can stop it?

Ikinai develops its Eros vs. Thanatos premise with finesse and ingenuity, as well as plenty of stops along the way to reveal the personal quirks of its thirteen characters. I expected to be annoyed by Nanako Okochi as the film's effervescent life-force, but I was not. She's a comic natural whose concern for her suicidal companions is unexpectedly touching. No wonder the male passengers, especially the younger ones, start to want to get off that bus alive.

As the film's *eminence gris*, Duncan gives a pared-down performance reminiscent of Kitano's in his various tough-guy incarnations, but he is no match for his boss as a commanding presence. In a way this is fortunate. Kitano in the tour conductor role would have killed the suspense. With him in charge, the question would be not if the bus would fly over the edge, but when.

Ikitai
Will to Live (1999)

Written and directed by Kaneto Shindo. **Produced by** Kindai Eiga Kyokai. **With** Rentaro Mikuni, Shinobu Otake, Hideko Yoshida, Akira Emoto, Masayuki Shionoya, Naoko Otani, Masahiko Tsugawa. (119 mins.)

First came *Ikiru* (To Live), Akira Kurosawa's 1952 classic about a dying bureaucrat's search for meaning and redemption. Then came *Ikinai*, Hiroshi Shimizu's 1998 black comedy about a bus tour en route to group suicide in Okinawa. Now we have *Ikitai*, Kaneto Shindo's seriocomic essay on aging in modern Japan. At the very least, they might teach foreign film fans how to decline the Japanese verb *ikiru*. As their titles imply, the heroes of these films are all questioning the course their lives have taken. Was it worth it? A huge mistake? How should they spend their remaining time?

For Shindo, who at eighty-six is one of the last surviving members of his directorial generation, these questions seem to have special urgency. *Ikitai* is spiritual autobiography, as well as an editorial on the graying of Japan. Now that he is reaching the end of his journey, Shindo has discarded the usual inhibitions about speaking one's mind directly, while viewing his characters and their predicaments with a wry but sympathetic eye. *Ikitai* combines high earnestness with black comedy to entertaining, if at times overly didactic and sentimental, effect.

Yasukichi (Rentaro Mikuni) is a retired chemist who lives with his forty-year-old daughter Tokuko (Shinobu Otake) in a ramshackle old house. A nasty drunk, Yasukichi loudly laments the younger generation's shabby treatment of the aged while making a nuisance of himself at his favorite bar. The *mama-san* (Naoko Otani) scolds him, but Yasukichi keeps pouring out the venom and pouring down the booze until he loses control of his bladder and slides to the floor. Enraged, the *mama-san* throws him out.

Waking up in a hospital under the care of a doctor (Akira Emoto) who ran across his prostrate form on his bicycle, Yasukichi transforms into a sweetly pathetic old chap who bewails his fate in the accents of injured virtue. Tokuko will have none of it—she knows his tricks too well. The old monster has alienated her younger brother and sister, while turning her into a manic depressive. She would love to leave him in the hospital—and says so to his face. But the doctor tartly informs her he is not running an old folks home. Yasukichi will have to go.

This miserable situation reminds Yasukichi of a recent visit to the village of Obasuteyama in Nagano Prefecture where, legend has it, inhabitants used to carry their old folks to a nearby mountain and leave them to die. Terrified and fascinated by this legend, Yasukichi is convinced that nothing has really changed in the intervening centuries—for Obasuteyama, substitute nursing home. That, he knows, is where he is headed.

While pulling out the dramatic stops in telling this gloomy story, Rentaro Mikuni and Shinobu Otake are also aiming for smiles with their histrionics. This kind of irony can backfire—if the actors are laughing at their characters, why should the audience care about them?—but they use it to make what would otherwise be unbearable, bearable. Mikuni may go overboard with the buffoonery, but he brings to life that familiar figure: the tyrannizing father slowly reverting to tyrannizing infant. Otake, who

can irritate with her purer-than-thou act, turns in a pitch-perfect performance as Tokuko. Like her father, Tokuko expresses herself with a nakedness both comic and revealing. She explodes with a frustration and rage that strips away Yasukichi's pretenses and exposes the dysfunctional reality.

The parallel story of Okoma (Hideko Yoshida), an old woman who goes to Obasuteyama, is likewise told with dryly ironic stylization, but in mythologizing black-and-white. Okoma is overjoyed to be chosen in a lottery overseen by the village headman (Masahiko Tsugawa); by village custom, her eldest son (Masayuki Shionoya) will be allowed to take a bride in compensation for carrying her to the mountain. She supervises the preparations with an energy that is verges on the burlesque—she seems less on her last legs than likely to outlive her two strapping sons. There is also something to admire in her stoicism, based on an unshakable faith, but as Mikuni reminds us so well, we moderns can no longer easily imitate it.

Inu, Hashiru
Dog Race (1998)

Directed by Yoichi Sai. **Screenplay by** Yoichi Sai and Chong Ui Shin. **Produced by** Central Arts and Toei Video. **With** Goro Kishitani, Makoto Togashi. (110 mins.)

A second-generation ethnic Korean, Yoichi Sai had his biggest critical and commercial hit with the 1993 *Tsuki wa Dotchi ni Deteiru* (All Under the Moon) a black comedy about the picaresque adventures of a jaded Korean cabby. But Sai had no desire to be tagged as a "Korean" filmmaker. His next two films were commercially unsuccessful attempts to please the mainstream. Now he has returned to the Asians-in-Japan theme in *Inu, Hashiru*.

Nakayama (Goro Kishitani) is a tough, cynical police detective, and Hideyoshi (Ren Osugi) is a timid, weak-willed Korean gangster who share a disregard for the rules and an affection for Momo-chan (Makoto Togashi), a lithesome Shanghainese hooker. The story is a blend of frenetic comedy and action, with the aim being less edification than fast-paced, taboo-free entertainment. *Inu*'s take on its underworld milieu is refreshingly smart and un-PC, but it promises more than its delivers. What is left at the end is the pathos of two unlikely friends who find that, though they may cross boundaries, they cannot rise above their roles. This most iconoclastic of movies is about the way society—in both its legitimate and criminal incarnations—crushes its outcastes with an inexorable logic that has little to do with right and wrong.

Nakayama and Hideyoshi begin the film as cop and snitch who may exploit each other for money, but have built a bridge of trust across enemy lines. They also both have a thing for the spunky, slinky Momo-chan, though it is cool-dude Nakayama who actually beds her, while shy, fumbling Hideyoshi makes his move a beat too late. Momo-chan, however, likes them both and, together, they form an uneasy triumvirate. Unbeknownst to Nakayama, however, Momo-chan and Hideyoshi are united by more than palship—together with her younger brother Kenyu, they are involved in scams that include smuggling illegal immigrants into Japan, and money into China. Their boss is Gonda, the *oyabun* (godfather) of a Korean gang who has a direct pipeline to the police via Hideyoshi and Nakayama.

Though Nakayama may not go by the book, he gets results, busting a drug-dealing Westerner (and sampling his white powder) and a school girl prostitution ring (after enjoying the favors of a teenage hooker). His young partner (Teruyuki Kagawa), who is at first a disapproving straight-arrow, begins to follow his senior's infectious example. Nakayama can seemingly do no wrong.

Then Hideyoshi finds Momo-chan in his house, lying on his bed—a corpse. The movie doesn't lose its comic momentum after this startling development—if anything it accelerates as Hideyoshi and Nakayama lug Momo-chan's body around Kabukicho in search of the killer. But in crossing the line to farce, the film begins to lose its bearings. The sharp observations about the survival tactics of Asians in Japan give way to a long, tiresomely goofy chase sequence

Sai wants *Inu, Hashiru* to be fun—and there's nothing wrong with that—but he would have better succeeded if he had been more satiric, less frantically silly. The rabbit this dog is chasing isn't quite worth the race.

Ippai no Kakesoba
One Bowl of Kakesoba (1992)

Directed by Katsumi Nishikawa. Screenplay by Ai Nagai. Produced by Toei, FM Tokyo, Sony, Dentsu, Tohoku Shinsha, Hokkaido Hoso, and Kinema Tokyo. With Tsunehiko Watase, Yoshie Ishige, Pinko Izumi, Masaya Obi, Hidetsugu Takiguchi. (99 mins.)

The Japanese have always loved a good cry. Before the war, there was even a three-handkerchief system for rating a film's effectiveness at making its audience blub. By that measure, Katsumi Nishikawa's *Ippai no Kakesoba* is at least a two-and-a-half. It isn't a good

movie by any means, but it gets the job done; the eyes of audience I saw it with were misting over quite satisfactorily—and mine were as well.

Ippai began life as a children's story by Ryohei Izumi. In 1988 it became a best-selling book, and on New Year's Eve of that same year, was broadcast as a radio play. A longer version of the play was broadcast in January 1989 and attracted a large, appreciative audience. Izumi had created an instant classic. Like Dickens in *A Christmas Carol*, Izumi uses a seasonal motif and a poor-but-winsome little boy to tug at the heartstrings. But because this is a Japanese story, the season is New Year's, and fate, not a crabby old miser, is the main cause of the boy's poverty.

The story begins in the days of the first Oil Shock of the late 1970s, when the Japanese were wondering whether their economic miracle might indeed be over. At the Hokkaitei *soba* noodle restaurant in Sapporo, business is still booming, however. The stonefaced master (Tsunehiko Watase) and his ever-smiling wife (Yoshie Ishige) are at work from morning till night, making and serving *soba* to their loyal customers.

That New Year's Eve, just as they are about to close, a mother (Pinko Izumi) and her two young sons (Masaya Obi and Hidetsugu Takiguchi) poke their heads in the door. "Can we order one bowl of *kakesoba*?" the mother asks hesitantly. The master, out of sympathy for this forlorn-looking trio, throws an extra handful of noodles into the pot. The smaller of the two boys brightens up when the *soba* arrives. It is, he proclaims, delicious. He shares it with his mother, his brother, and the shop's cute little dog.

One year passes and the family returns. Once again the mother orders one bowl of *kakesoba*, but this time the master puts in enough noodles for two helpings. He remembers them, of course—even the dog does—but he wonders who they could be. So does his wife; the boy so resembles their son, who was killed by a truck three years ago.

They finally find out the third year. The mother and her sons have been coming to their shop to honor the memory of the boys' father, who died in a traffic accident shortly after promising to take them to Hokkaitei for *toshikoshi soba*—a traditional New Year's dish. Since then they have been working hard to pay compensation to the accident's victims. The one thing that had kept them going was the memory of Hokkaitei's *kakesoba* and the wife's cheery "Happy New Year!"

The plot, in Japanese tearjerker terms, is foolproof. Everyone suffers nobly and no one is really to blame. And it is the younger boy, played by child star Hidetsugu Takiguchi, who is the noblest and most blameless of all. When he reads an essay in class about how his yearly bowl of *kakesoba* has helped him and his family bear up under their burdens, every mother in the classroom—and the audience—reaches for her hanky.

Despite its 1970s setting, *Ippai no Kakesoba* has the mental atmosphere of the early postwar period. Nishikawa's direction reinforces the film's anachronistic feel. A veteran who began his career with Shochiku in 1939, Nishikawa gives every scene the look of a perfectly exposed, numbingly bland Kodachrome snapshot, circa 1959. Every cut, every gesture is impeccably conventional, completely predictable. This is one film that will make the transition to the small screen quite easily.

But we don't go to *Ippai no Kakesoba* for innovative filmmaking. It we go at all, it is to be moved without being made to think; to have our values confirmed without having to confront their disappearance. If we are non-natives, we might go to better understand the mainstream culture's schlock sentimentality and, if we are so inclined, to have a good cry.

Iron Maze
(1992)

Written and directed by Hiroaki Yoshida. Produced by Mazev Pressman/Stone Productions. With Jeff Fahey, Bridget Fonda, Hiroaki Murakami, J.T. Walsh. (102 mins.)

A small but growing number of young Japanese directors believe that to make successful international films they must first internationalize themselves. They are enrolling in Western film schools and studying under Western directors. One is Hiroaki Yoshida, who enrolled in Robert Redford's Sundance Institute in 1988. His second feature film, *Iron Maze* not only has a international cast, but the look of mainstream Hollywood product. American mall moviegoers unaware of the film's origins would probably never guess that it was made by a Japanese director with Japanese money.

Yoshida takes his plot from Ryunosuke Akutagawa's "In A Grove," the same story that inspired Akira Kurosawa's *Rashomon*. Both films are about the mutability of truth in the cauldron of human lust, pride, and fear. But while Kurosawa's film broke new cinematic ground, Yoshida's is aimed squarely at the American box office. *Rashomon* inspired critical rhapsodies about Toshiro Mifune's raw, sweaty performance and Kurosawa's groundbreaking camera work. *Iron Maze* is more likely to pique teenage interest in Jeff Fahey's moody macho persona and puzzlement at the film's convoluted plot.

A wealthy Japanese businessman (Hiroaki Murakami), accompanied by his American wife (Bridget Fonda), comes to a depressed Pennsylvania mill town to negotiate the construction of an amusement park. There the couple encounters a studly bellhop (Jeff Fahey) who wins the wife's affections. The husband discovers the couple *in flagrante delicto*—and winds up in the hospital in a coma. Who tried to do him in—and how? The local cops question the the wife and bellhop and hear two radically different versions of the truth. Instead of Akutagawa's wood, the main events of the story take place in an abandoned steel mill. Rising in rusty grandeur, like the cathedral of a dead religion, the mill stands as a symbol of all that has gone wrong with America.

Yoshida does not exploit the metaphorical possibilities of his setting, however. Instead, he uses the mill as a neat backdrop for chases and stunts and the display of Jeff Fahey's pecs and lats. The film's plot reduces Akutagawa's ironic juxtapositions to the formulas of the thriller genre. The question is not so much "What is truth?" as "Who done it?" By crosscutting between the characters' conflicting stories Yoshida makes the latter question briefly intriguing. By the time the plodding chief of police finally unearthed the truth, however, I had long since ceased to care.

If the bellhop and the wife had been more honest in their lust, I might have understood them better and liked them more. Instead Yoshida contrasts the "natural" behavior of the American lovers with the "unnatural" foreign ways of the Japanese husband. The guy deserves what he gets, he seems to say: Besides being filthy rich, he talks funny, acts funny, and insults the pride of the town's real Americans by threatening to tear down their beloved mill and replace it with an amusement park that will pump millions of dollars into the local economy. No wonder the bellhop rises up in defiant rebellion against this intruder: he is a latter-day John Wayne defending a bankrupt Alamo. Murakami's wooden performance is partly responsible for the film's anti-Japanese undercurrent. The one most to blame, though, is Yoshida, who in trying to attract an American audience, panders to Yellow Peril racism and xenophobia. *Iron Maze* gets lost in a moral maze and never finds it way out.

Izakaya Yurei
Ghost at a Drinking Joint (1994)

Directed by Takayoshi Watanabe. Screenplay by Yozo Tanaka. Produced by Suntory, TV Asahi, Tohoku Shinsha. With Ken'ichi Hagiwara, Shigeru Muroi, Tomoko Yamaguchi. (110 mins.)

Unlike most movies about the supernatural, Takayoshi Watanabe's *Izakaya Yurei* targets adult, not adolescents, with humor that is medium-dry. Also, instead of trying to cash in on a trend with scary effects, the film is more interested in the conflict between the hero's loyalty to his dead wife and his need to get on with the business of living. In its last thirty minutes, it becomes a feel-good TV drama, but it also has flashes of *Topper*-ish wit. For that, I suppose, we should be grateful.

Shotaro (Ken'ichi Hagiwara) is the proprietor of a funky Yokohama *izakaya* (pub) that is a neighborhood gathering place. There is little cheer in Shotaro's life, however. His wife Shizuko (Shigeru Muroi) is dying of a mysterious disease. Before she expires, she make him promise to never take another wife. "Otherwise, I'll come back and haunt you," she jokingly warns.

After her death, however, Shotaro finds himself short-handed and lonely. His older brother proposes a solution—a childless young widow named Satoko (Tomoko Yamaguchi). Shotaro, remembering his promise, doesn't go for the idea at first, but his resistance melts when Satoko tells him that she liked him from the moment she first saw him. (He was, we see, also checking her out and liking what he found.) Satoko is soon happily serving customers at the *izakaya* as Shotaro's new missus. This, it would seem, is a marriage made in heaven. Shizuko doesn't see it that way, however. One night she appears to the startled couple and announces that she has come back to stay. "This is my house, after all," she says, giving Satoko a meaningful look.

In Hollywood comedies with ghostly protagonists much of the humor derives from the semblance of normality; Cary Grant in a tux instead of a sheet, wisecracking instead of rattling chains. Shizuko, on the other hand, first appears as a traditional Japanese ghost in kimono and long flowing hair, with a weird gleam in her eye and an unearthly glow. But unlike the female ghosts in traditional ghost stories, she is not vengeful. Instead she is miffed that Shotaro did not keep his promise. Her repeated appearances are less attempts to horrify than the ghostly equivalent of nuisance calls. Shotaro and Satoko have to get rid of her, but how?

Having set up this comically promising situation, the film is not quite sure what to do with it. There are some mildly amusing gags, as when the couple trap's Shizuko's spirit in a hanging scroll and ships it off to the local temple. But when Shotaro persuades Shizuko to play Good Samaritan and patch up the messy lives of his regulars, the movie goes gooey. We meet an estranged couple and their cute eight-year-old boy. We become acquainted with a pure-hearted young woman who is searching for her long-lost father. We know how they will solve their various problems, with help from above.

A former rock star, Ken'ichi Hagiwara gives an effortlessly accomplished performance as Shotaro. He is one of the few Japanese leading men who looks truly comfortable with his leading ladies; no macho grimaces, no wimpish grins, just Hagiwara turning on the charm. Is it too much of a stretch to imagine Cary Grant pouring *sake* instead of cocktails? Perhaps, but Shoken (Hagiwara's nickname) comes closer than most.

Like the bar in "Cheers," Shotaro's *izakaya* is intended as an ideal of its type: secluded, intimate, and old-fashioned, with a scrumptious-looking pot of *nikomi* stew always bubbling on the stove. The beer of choice? Suntory Malts. Guess whose TV beer commercial the star appears in, and who helped finance the movie? *Kampai!*

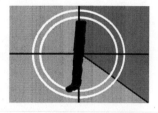

James Yama no Riran
Riran of Mount James (1992)

Directed by Nobuaki Inozaki. Screenplay by Hisashi Nozawa. Produced by '92 M.M.I., Capitol Network, Kyasutosu, and Apollon. With: Yuko Natori, Mikihisa Azuma, Jimpachi Nezu. (114 mins.)

In his essay "The Real Disneyland," Donald Richie noted the Japanese "passion, amounting to near genius, for kitsch." Why, he asked, did Japan need Disneyland—America's greatest contribution to kitsch culture—when it had so many Disneylands of its own? Examples abound: a cluster of "Early American" boutiques in Jiyugaoka, a love hotel in Kichijoji that sports a replica of the Statue of Liberty on its roof. Presiding over it all is Tokyo Tower, an "improved" version of its Parisian model.

James Yama no Riran is photographed almost entirely in such settings. Even the title, with its foreign-monikered mountain, signals that we are about to spend two hours in a Japan as Japanese as a Shakey's "old-fashioned" pizza parlor. Based on a novel by Shunkichi Higuchi, *James Yama* tells a tale about a storm-tossed love of a younger man for an older woman. It might have been a vehicle for Bette Davis in her Margot Channing period. It takes itself very seriously indeed.

Riran (Yuko Natori) is a ripe Chinese beauty with one arm who lives in a old Western-style house atop a hill in Kobe called Mount James. Yosuke (Mikihisa Azuma) is a young bartender at a Western-style club that caters to off-duty GIs. His boss and mentor is Paul (Jimpachi Nezu), an American Nisei who embezzled money from the U.S. Army to start his nightspot—and is always on the lookout for inquisitive MPs .

The time is 1952, when the GHQ still ruled Japan and many Japanese, including the employees of Paul's club, found themselves in close contact with foreigners for the first times in their lives. Japanese popular culture often portrays those early postwar encounters in Us versus Them terms, with stalwart Japanese defending their homeland against *tatami*-tromping barbarians. In *James Yama* the barbarian is General Leon, a jug-eared lout to whom Riran owes a large sum of money. Yosuke would like to be her defender—he falls in love with her at first sight, when she beats him in a poker game—but first he has to win her. He discovers that Riran shares his love of Hollywood movies. Soon they are exchanging dialogue from *High Noon*.

First-time director Nobuaki Inozaki lets us know, early on, that Riran has a past, and not a pleasant one. (How could it be, minus that arm?) She endures her mutilation stoically, but she has become suspicious of men, especially young studs like Yosuke. Like Bette Davis in *All About Eve*, she is also obsessed with the thought that time sweeps all, even her still-considerable beauty, away. Though Yuko Natori is the right age for the part, she is no Bette Davis; she sighes with heavy resignation where Davis would have steamed with fiery indignation.

Not only her character, but the film dies a lingering death. It really ends with the climatic poker game between Yosuke and the General. Yosuke wins enough to free Riran from her debt, but instead of ending the film on this upbeat note, Inozaki shows us the now-united couple slipping into old age in scene after lugubrious scene.

He is trying, evidently, to make a statement about the fleeting nature of beauty, life, and love. But Inozaki substitutes emoting for emotion, trendiness for style. *James Yama* is an elegantly empty melodrama played out in surroundings that underline the phoniness of the proceedings. This may be the only Japanese film I have even seen in which the characters never take off their shoes in a *genkan*, slide open a *fusuma*, or do other recognizably Japanese things.

Walt Disney may have much to answer for, but he never would have staged *Mary Poppins* in Main Street. Even kitsch has its rules.

Juninin no Yasashii Nihonjin
The Gentle Twelve (1991)

Directed by Shun Nakahara. **Screenplay by** Koki Mitani and the Tokyo Sunshine Boys. **Produced by** New Century Producers, Suntory, and Nippon Television Network. **With** Kazuyuki Aijima, Etsushi Toyokawa. (116 mins.)

When I interviewed Shun Nakahara in 1990, he told me that he wanted his next film to be a comedy. "That's the test of a real director—to make a Japanese audience laugh," he said. Now he has made a comedy called *Juninin no Yasashii Nihonjin* and the Japanese audience I saw it with laughed; faces were glowing when the lights went up. Inspired by Sidney Lumet's 1957 *Twelve Angry Men*, and based on a play by Koki Mitani, *Juninin* is less a remake of a Hollywood classic than a seriocomic study of Japanese group dynamics that is entertaining and enlightening.

Those dynamics differ radically from those of the twelve angry men in Lumet's juryroom melodrama. Instead of Henry Fonda's lonely struggle to persuade his eleven fellow jurors of the defendant's innocence, Kazuyuki Aijima plays an earnest, bespectacled fellow who attempts the opposite. The defendant—a twenty-one-year old bar hostess—is accused of murdering her ex-husband by pushing him into the path of an oncoming truck. Did she mean to do him in or was she acting in self defense? The jury quickly decides she is innocent and Aijima's nameless character just as quickly has second thoughts. "Let's talk about it," he says. Up goes a groan—everyone has places to go, things to do. How could the defendant be guilty? She has such an innocent-looking face! But Aijima insists—and the movie begins.

As in *Twelve Angry Men*, the action remains confined to the jury room and its environs and takes place in real time. But while the earlier film was explosively emotional, the new one aims to amuse, while teasing the intellect. We never learn the names or occupations of the jurors—self-introductions not being part of the deliberation process—but we come to see each of them as distinct individuals. There is the shy, motherly woman who believes the defendant is innocent because "she could never do a thing like that"; the sharp-tongued intellectual who scorns emotional arguments but likes to play mind-games; and the tall, forbidding young man (Etsushi Toyokawa) who stares out the window while others debate, but plunges in at a crucial moment to turn the tide.

In *Twelve Angry Men*, the battlelines were sharply drawn between the forces of good, led by the upright Henry Fonda, and the forces of evil, led by the bigoted Lee J. Cobb. In *Juninin*, however, the lines are blurred. Aihara, the lonely fighter for justice, would seem to be on the side of the angels, but as he begins to win adherents we see that the struggle is not so simple. Even the most bullheaded of the jurors are not villains, but decent folks who can't bring themselves to condemn a long-suffering single mother. "Why, we're all nice people here," a bubbly young woman proclaims at one point, apropos of nothing. We smile, but she is speaking the truth.

The jurors *are* "gentle Japanese" for whom the pursuit of an abstract truth is less important than the promptings of their (basically good) hearts. Even if those promptings led to heated arguments and angry accusations, the ultimate aim is harmony and consensus—not victory. This may sound stereotypical, but Nakahara, working with a wonderful cast recruited from Mitani's Tokyo Sunshine Boys theater troupe, breathes a winningly diverse life into the proceedings. We may nod with recognition as we watch the "typically Japanese" reactions of some of the characters, but the film also shows us the range of that "typically Japanese" humanity. It is both wider—and more familiar—than we might have imagined.

Junk Food *
(1998)

Written and directed by Masashi Yamamoto. Produced by Junk Food Connection, Stance Company, and Transformer. With Miyuki Iijima, Yoshiyuki, Mia, Ali Amed, Onimaru, Kanji Tsuda. (84 mins.)

In *Junk Food*, Masahi Yamamoto examines society's lawless fringes with the stark depictions of sex and violence that may revolt and disturb, but are undeniably true—voyeuristic, perhaps, but true. Also, though they may be little more than scum on the Japanese social pond, his characters have a raw vitality that the gray-suited masses around them have either lost or never had.

Junk Food resembles its characters in its disdain for conventional narrative forms. It begins quietly enough, with the morning rituals of an elderly blind woman (the director's mother) who lives alone in a tiny apartment, including her offering to the departed spirits in the family Buddhist altar. Then, with no explanation, we are in a ratty apartment where a sullen beauty named Miyuki (Miyuki Iijima) is smoking what looks to be crack cocaine. She then strangles her sleeping lover, for reasons known only to the mind of a degenerate addict, and troops off to her office job. She writhes in the agonies of withdrawal during a boring meeting, frantically cruises the streets for a fix during her lunch hour, and finds more than she bargained for in the arms of a psychotic dealer.

Once again the scene changes, this time to a Yokohama red-light district where Hide (Yoshiyuki), a frizzy-haired rocker, hires the services of a Chinese-American hooker named Myan (Mia). Though Hide speaks little English and Myan no Japanese, they hit it off and go out together into the night. Next to appear is Cawl (Ali Amed) a Pakistani whose dissatisfaction with his marginal existence turns to murderous rage when his Japanese lover rejects his offer of marriage. When he seeks help from the Pakistani broker who brought him to Japan, the broker demands another payment on his loan. Cawl explodes again—and finds himself with more blood on his hands.

Then we meet Ryo (Onimaru), a longhaired *chiima* ("teamer" or gangbanger) who is hanging out with his gang of lowriders when he is approached by a *sempai* (senior gang member) named Sato (Kanji Tsuda). Blonde-haired and hot-tempered, Sato wants Ryo's help in finding his girlfriend, whom he claims has been kidnapped by a car thief. Sato's two punk associates, however, dis Ryo's gang and soon a battle is raging. Sato ends up with butterfly knife in his thigh, but Ryo, who has remained above the fray, agrees to help him. Then Ryo discovers that Sato's quest is not what it seems and, once again, all hell breaks loose. Yamamoto has made an impressive find in Onimaru, a real-life *chiima* who makes most tough-guy actors look like poseurs.

There is more, including vignettes of a Mexican female pro wrestler's farewell to Japan and a Japanese druggie's long nod-out on the Yamanote Line. The characters are mainly the same international types that Yamamoto introduced in his 1996 black comedy *Atlanta Boogie*. His take on their stories, however, is darker and, in several scenes, as blatantly exploitative as a mail-order SM flick.

Nonetheless, unlike other young directors whose view of the social margins is largely derived from other movies, Yamamoto has a personal acquaintance with his onscreen milieu. Rather than play the role of gimlet-eyed social anthropologist, as Shohei Imamura did in so many of his films, Yamamoto is more than a little in love with the heroin chic and macho cool of his characters. In places, he seems to be making an in-groupy home movie for the apocalypse.

Despite its lapses into self-congratulation and self-indulgence, *Junk Food* is a powerful examination of a generation that has abandoned old moralities, while replacing them with little more than new trends in consumption, including drugs and crime. It goes beyond the fevered headlines and hand-wringing editorials to present an intimate portrait that supplies in insight what it lacks in focus. More than most recent Japanese youth movies, *Junk Food* delivers the beef.

Jutai *
Traffic Jam (1991)

Directed by Mitsuo Kurotsuchi. Screenplay by Mitsuo Kurotsuchi and Mineyo Sato. Produced by Mitsubishi Corp., Suntory, and New Century Producers. With Ken'ichi Hagiwara, Hitomi Kuroki, Eiji Okada, Emiko Azuma, Ayaka Takarada, Shingo Yazawa. (109 mins.)

Jutai (Traffic Jam) sounds like a premise for a TV comedy sketch: a typical Japanese family (Mom, Dad, older sister, and younger brother) leave Tokyo before New Year's for Dad's home island off Shikoku. On the way, they encounter a typical Japanese disaster—a traffic jam that starts in Tokyo and ends in Kyushu. This is only the beginning: if bad things happen to good people, the Fuji family must be the best people on the Kanto Plain. Younger brother's bladder becomes inconveniently full. Mom misses a turn on the map. Dad nearly has a headon with a truck full of pigs. But this family farce alone does not a movie make. Do we really want to spend two hours with these people, watching their nightmarish holiday unfold? Won't the jokes, like the traffic jam, quickly get old?

Director and scriptwriter Mitsuo Kurotsuchi understands the problem and provides original, if occasionally sentimental, solutions. He takes us on a trip not only to sitcom land, but inside his typical couple's marriage and their feelings about the Japanese Way of Life. He makes us enjoy and appreciate the ride.

Former rock idol Ken'ichi Hagiwara plays Dad as a bullheaded blusterer who is a nice, sexy guy underneath. These are hardly rare attributes for a fictional Japanese father (save for the "sexy" part), but Hagiwara gives his portrayal an ironic edge and throwaway charm. The guy even has a comically stylish way of jumping puddles. He works well with his co-star, Hitomi Kuroki. Her Mom may not be as funny as his Dad—Japanese movie moms seldom are—but the way she laughs at his jokes and steams at his insults make us believe that they are a real couple. The current flowing between them propels the film, despite the banality of argument and reconciliation scenes straight from a thousand TV soaps.

I also liked the way the movie stripped away its characters' *tatemae* (outer face). On the job in an Akihabara electric store, Dad is all smiles and bows

and customer service, but after a horrendous day on the road, during which his car runs out of gas and his son runs a fever, Dad angrily mutters "I work hard—Why do I have to have put up with this crap just to go home?" This *cri de coeur* would seem to indicate a new level of frustration with the inconveniences and indignities of modern Japanese life.

One thing that never changes is the Japanese fascination with *furusato*, the native place that all city dwellers supposedly long for. Dad has what must be the ultimate *furusato*, an island in the Inland Sea so out of the way that he has not been back for five years. Waiting patiently for his return are Grandpa (Eiji Okada), who is going senile, and Grandma (Emiko Higashi), who is so bright-eyed and bushy-tailed that we want to throttle her. Kurotsuchi would have us believe that Grandpa and Grandma and all the other good folks on the island live in an earthly paradise, in stark contrast to the Fuji' all-hassle holiday. He has a point; almost anything would be better than the mass exoduses that regularly afflict these islands. But he also lays it on thick. The entire island turns out to cheer when the ferry bearing the Fujis finally pulls into port. It's as though the Fujis had survived a war, not just an accident-prone car trip.

Even so, anyone who has served a holiday weekend on Japanese roads will find the Fuji family and their misadventures easy to identify with. *Jutai* is the real Japan, red lights and all.

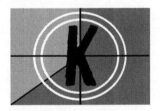

Kamikaze Taxi
(1995)

Written and directed by Masato Harada. Produced by Pony Canyon. With Kazuya Takahashi, Mickey Curtis, Koji Yakusho, Reiko Takahashi. (150 mins.)

Masato Harada's *Kamikaze Taxi* depicts the plight of ethnic Japanese from South America who have come to Japan to find a prosperity denied to them in their land of their birth. As we learn from the interviews with returnees that open the film, they often encounter prejudice in finding housing and work, even though they are Japanese by blood and statute. The reasons? They talk funny and act funny, they listen to different music and eat different food. They aren't "real" Japanese.

Kamikaze Taxi touches other thematic bases at well, including the meltdown of Japanese politics, the Neanderthalism of certain Japanese politicians, the spread of drugs in Japanese society, and the rise of of self-help movements, including the inevitable spiritual snake-oil peddlers. But though he may probe, at times quite sharply, at society's ills, Harada's central concerns are the universal ones of friendship and loss, love, and revenge. His characters are searching for meaning and connection on society's fringes, but finding both in short supply. The price of the search, they discover, can be isolation and even death.

Tatsuo (Kazuya Takahashi) is a cocky *chimpira* (apprentice gangster) whom his *yakuza* bosses are grooming as a pimp. But the first hooker he supplies to an elderly conservative politician returns from her date beaten nearly half to death. When Tatsuo's girlfriend protests, a pony-tailed boss named Animaru (Mickey Curtis) kills her as Tatsuo looks on. Enraged, Tatsuo seeks revenge by breaking into the politician's house with his *chimpira* cronies and stealing a large pot full of money.

Their gang *sempai* (seniors) soon trace them to the countryside villa where they are hiding out and begin executing them one by one. Firing at his pursuers, Tatsuo makes his escape, together with several of his buddies. He is the only one to emerge from the woods alive, however. Vowing to stage a kamikaze raid on the gang headquarters, he finds a taxi and orders the driver to take him to a town on the Izu Peninsula. But the Japanese-Peruvian driver (Koji Yakusho) can't read the map. "A foreigner!" Tatsuo groans.

Calm where Tatsuo is excitable, quiet where Tatsuo is loud, the driver seems at first a Third World innocent, lost and out of place in midst of First World sophistication and corruption. But as they travel the countryside, stopping for occasional gun battles, the driver emerges as a tower of inner strength. Tatsuo and the hooker (Reiko Takahashi), who later joins their odyssey, come to respect that strength. The driver, in turn, takes Tatsuo's side. By the time Tatsuo makes his kamikaze raid, they are no longer passenger and driver, but allies.

The driver is a familiar type in Hollywood films; the minority father or older brother figure (African-American, Native American, you name it) who sets the young majority hero straight. But the *Kamikaze Taxi* takes us beyond surface ethnicisms to the heart of contemporary Japan. The ride is long, winding, and occasionally bumpy, but the sights along the way are extraordinary. I'm glad I went along.

Kantsubaki
Winter Camelia (1992)

Directed by Yasuo Furuhata. Screenplay by Michiko Nasu. Produced by Toei. With Yoko Minamino, Masahiro Takashima, Toshiyuki Nishida. (115 mins.)

Kantsubaki is a typical mass-audience entertainment, costume-drama division. It features familiar TV faces (Yoko Minamino, Masahiro Takashima, Toshiyuki Nishida), a big budget, much of which was spent on the gorgeous costumes and lavish period sets, and a reliable hack director (Yasuo Furuhata). It is also an installment, the sixth, in a series based on the works of popular historical-romance writer Tomiko Miyao. Launched in 1984 with *Kiryuin Hanako no Shogai* (The Life of Hanako Kiryuin), the series spurred a *yakuza* genre revival. But instead of the gangsters themselves, its focus is the women who lived with and loved them in the early decades of the century.

The heroine of *Kantsubaki* is Botan (Yoko Minamino), a geisha in a Kochi brothel. Like many geisha in 1932—the year the film begins—Botan entered the profession against her will. Her gambler father sold her to a pimp named Tomita (Toshiyuki Nishida), who in turn passed her on to the master of the brothel. Botan is beautiful, pure, and passive. *Katsubaki* invites us to sympathize with her sufferings, despise the beastliness of the gangsters who abuse her, and admire the manliness of the gangsters who rescue her. It is a woman's picture of the unapologetically retrograde type.

The main cause of Botan's many sufferings is the rivalry for her favors of two powerful Kochi politicians. Both are trying to win election to the Diet with the help of *yakuza* gangs. Botan becomes a pawn in their nefarious games. In the classic *yakuza* movie, the story usually revolves around a clash between bad *yakuza*, who are strictly in it for the money, and good *yakuza*, who uphold *ninkyo*, the traditional code of chivalry. In *Kantsubaki* the good guys are Tomita and Nioyama (Masahiro Takashima), an ex-sumo wrestler. Tomita may be deep into the life—so deep, in fact, that his wife leaves him, taking their ten-year old son—but he has a soft spot for Botan. When he first meets her, she is a bus conductor in a smart blue uniform—a *moga* (modern girl) if there ever was one. Her father, though, is a crawling reptile who would as soon sell his daughter as pawn his watch. Her innocent beauty touches Tomita's jaded heart; her father's attitude stirs his chivalrous rage. As played by Toshiyuki Nishida, an overacter who specializes in warm-fuzzy roles, Tomita is a gruff but kindly bear who always looks out for Botan's best interests.

Botan's paramour, however, is Nioyama (Masahiro Takashima), who belongs to one of the gangs involved in the political tug of war. A handsome lout, Nioyama's passion for Botan is almost comically out of control. He spends half the movie busting heads and bursting though doors to be with her. But are we supposed to laugh when he rapes her, tearing off her kimono bit by ravishingly photographed bit? Are we supposed to be relieved that she likes it? Though foreign feminists might howl at this soft-focus celebration of rape, distributor Toei no doubt hopes that the Japanese women who are the film's target audience will smile indulgently on Nioyama's pure-hearted impulsiveness.

But are they smiling? *Kantsubaki* has disappointed at the box office. Perhaps even the mass audience is tiring of the prettied-up emptiness of films like this, and their tiredly nostalgic view of what must have been a sordid reality. Japanese studios, however, are not likely to traverse the distance between *Kantsubaki* and *Thelma and Louise* anytime soon.

Kanzen Naru Shiiku
Perfect Nurture (1999)

Directed by Ben Wada. Screenplay by Kaneto Shindo. Cinematography by Hoshi Sakakibara. Produced by Tokyo Theater, Marubeni, and Times, Inc. With Naoto Takenaka, Hijiri Kojima, Kazuki Kitamura, Shin'ya Tsukamoto, Shigeru Izumiya, Asami Sawaki, Eriko Watanabe. (96 mins.)

The story of Ben Wada's *Kanzen Naru Shiiku* (Perfect Nurture) plays like Bill's fantasy of what he would have done with Monica if he hadn't been encumbered by that inconvenient wife and job. Instead of trying to consummate their passion in fugitive moments between meetings with foreign dignitaries, the film's forty-three-year-old salesman and eighteen-year-old schoolgirl enjoy days and nights of uninhibited lovemaking in the blissful obscurity of a rundown rooming house.

Like the saga of Monica and Bill, Ben Wada's second feature is sure to divide audiences between loathers and, if not quite lovers, defenders. The salesman, Iwazono (Naoto Takenaka), kidnaps and drugs the schoolgirl, Kuniko (Hijiri Kojima), while she is out on an evening jog and brings her back to his room. There he ties her to a bed and tells her that he wants her to join him in a perfect union of body and soul. From brutality, in other words, he expects love to bloom.

Why and how did he pick Kuniko? Did he hang around her school in a soiled trenchcoat? Take candid snaps and bring them back to his room for solitary revels? Kaneto Shindo's script ignores these questions. Instead it portrays Iwazono as a true, if

twisted, romantic, who failed to find his ideal union in a marriage with a former coworker (easy to believe given that he raped her before the wedding), but now hopes to achieve it with Kuniko.

This time, however, he is going to do it right. Yes to ropes and tape, but no to rape. He may threaten her with a knife when she starts to scream, but he also caters to her every whim, including bagfuls of goodies from MacDonald's. To further mask the reality of this sordid situation, the filmmakers spice it with comic relief. When he is not trying to have his way with Kuniko, Iwazono is having amusingly squirmy conversations with his widowed landlady (Eriko Watanabe), who is trying to find out what is going on in his room—and lure him into her futon.

Not only the horny landlady, but all her boarders are wacky eccentrics, including a gay salesman (Shin'ya Tsukamoto) who mascaras his eyes while hawking bottles of spring water on his cell phone, a racetrack cleaning man (Shigeru Izumiya) who scours the stands for winning tickets, and an S&M bar hostess (Asami Sawaki) who brings her work home—and throws it down the stairs. But as funny as these folks may be, kidnapping a teenager with the aim of indulging one's sexual fantasies is, *ipso facto*, the act of a brute.

Be that as it may, *Kanzen* convinces us that Iwazono and Kuniko find the erotic paradise Iwazono has so long desired. First, there is genuine chemistry between the two principals. Kuniko may be something of a lumpish ditz, but to Iwazono's hungry eyes she is a fleshy garden of earthly delights. Meanwhile, Kuniko is a tolerant sort, who starts to fall for her captor as she discovers that he is generous, accommodating, and, with his lithe, tanned body, kind of sexy (if decidedly short).

Second, Iwazono leaves the erotic initiative entirely up to her, to the point of self-destructive masochism. As he reminds her several times while fending off her insincere advances, he is not after forced submission, but love, freely offered. When Kuniko realizes that he is serious—and that the feelings he has tried so hard to nurture really exist—the fireworks explode.

This is not the PC choice, but her decision feels right, given all that has gone before. It was also the decision made by the girl in Michiko Matsuda's docu-novel, which was the basis for Kaneto's script. None of this should be surprising—the phenomenon of kidnapees and hostages falling under the spell of their abductors has been well documented. Also well known is the reluctance of Eros to follow the PC line.

More importantly, however, the love scenes between Takenaka and Kojima, a former child actress who is Japan's taller Christina Ricci, are among the most the joyously carnal I have seen in

Japanese films, porno or otherwise. Not a comment I'd make about a movie I walked into the theater expecting to hate—but it happens to be true.

Kanzo Sensei *
Dr. Akagi (1998)

Directed by Shohei Imamura. Screenplay by Shohei Imamura and Daisuke Tengen. Cinematography by Shigeru Matsubara. Produced by Imamura Production, Toei, Tohoku Shinsha, and Kadokawa Shoten. With Akira Emoto, Kumiko Aso, Jacques Gamblin, Kotsuke Sera, Juro Kara. (129 mins.)

Hollywood has rediscovered an interest in World War II, thanks to Steven Spielberg's *Saving Private Ryan*. In Japan, however, directors have been making films about the war and its aftermath throughout the decade—Shohei Imamura's *Kanzo Sensei* being the latest example. Most of these directors, the seventy-two-year-old Imamura included, are old enough to remember the war. But rather than Spielberg's brand of hyperrealism, they prefer indirection and symbolism. Instead of the killing zones at the height of the conflict, they often prefer to report on the home front, in the last days of the war. At their worst these films are cinematic war memorials, characterized by inflated sentiment, received opinions, gauzy nostalgia, and selective forgetting.

Kanzo Sensei is not a memorial service, but is also no exception to the general rule. Imamura takes an approach to his story about an eccentric doctor in wartime Okayama Prefecture that is ironic, distanced, avuncular. He has not made another *Madadayo*—Akira Kurosawa's celebration of a beloved teacher that plays like a testimonial dinner—but he is also no longer the fearlessly iconoclastic maker of *Buta to Gunkan* (Pigs and Battleships) and *Fukushu Suru wa Ware ni Ari* (Vengeance Is Mine). Instead he is fondly recalling an innocence and purity whose passing he regrets.

Seeing his film immediately after *Saving Private Ryan* is like walking directly from the combat zone to a sunlit veranda where an elderly uncle is holding forth with anecdotes about a neighborhood character. He is an accomplished raconteur, this uncle, and his stories are instructive on the workings of the heart and the nature of war, but he is brightening them with soft pastels from his fictionalizing brush.

"Kanzo Sensei" (Doctor Liver) is the nickname bestowed on Dr. Akagi (Akira Emoto), a gent in a white suit and straw hat who runs from patient to patient at a full trot, shouting out greetings to passersby. But though a paragon of dedication,

Akagi Sensei has one peculiarity: no matter what the patient's complaint, his diagnosis is always the same: hepatitis (*kanzoen*). Even so, his patients love and trust him. Through one of them, he acquires a nurse—an orphaned hoyden named Sonoko (Kumiko Aso) whose mother was a whore. From her, Sonoko received an unusual piece of advice—to give her favors to only one lover and demand hard cash from the rest. She soon decides that the lucky one will be Akagi, but when she makes her declaration he is shocked. He has no inclination for anything but his *idée fixe*: discovering a cure for hepatitis.

Sonoko brings a Dutch soldier (Jaques Gamblin) into the clinic. An escapee from a local prison camp, he is a mass of bruises and wounds. Knowing that return to the camp will mean certain death, Akagi decides to hide him. A camera-lens technician in peacetime, the soldier repays this kindness by helping prepare the lens of a recently acquired microscope to examine the hepatitis virus. If he can only see the enemy at first hand, Akagi knows he can beat him! With the help of a morphine-addicted colleague (Kotsuke Sera) and an alcoholic Buddhist priest (Juro Kara), he begins the biggest battle of his career.

Though told with a light touch, made lighter by Yosuke Yamashita's punchy jazz score, *Kanzo Sensei* is more than just a whimsical home-front comedy. In the end, all Akagi's dedication can not save him and those around him from the war's devastation. Like the hepatitis virus, we see, the seeds of war are sown deep in our cells and are hard, if not impossible, to eradicate. The cloud that rises over Hiroshima at the film's conclusion is not, in the doctor's eyes, a mushroom, but a huge diseased liver. More than half a century on, we are, like the doctor, still treating the symptoms, still looking for a cure. No wonder that, after living with these symptoms so long, Imamura has resigned himself to the possibility that this particular ailment will survive him, will survive us all—if it doesn't kill us first.

Kappa
(1994)

Directed by Tatsuya Ishii. Screenplay by Masumi Suetani. Cinematography by Genkichi Hasegawa. Produced by Cappadocia. With Keisuke Funakoshi, Tatsuya Fuji, Takanori Jinnai. (118 mins.)

Several years ago, Japanese movie studios decided that since professional directors were having trouble making hits they would turn over the job to amateurs who were celebrities in other fields. The rationale: the celeb director's fans would show up for the movie, however awful. Also, the more optimistic reasoned that the celeb might bring a natural talent and fresh approach to an all-too hidebound business.

The latest result of this strategy is *Kappa*, a big-budget, effects-heavy eco-fable conceived and directed by Tatsuya Ishii, lead singer of the Kome Kome Club pop group. Technically, the backers got their money's worth. All those yen are on the screen, in the form of gorgeous visuals (credit to cinematographer Genkichi Hasegawa) and superrealistic effects (credit to special-effects producer Katsuyuki Sugimura). The film, however, is a self-indulgent music video stretched, intolerably, to feature length. Though it strives for poignancy and significance, it only reminds us why it still pays to hire a professional.

The story centers on a family of what the locals call *kappa* (water sprites), trying to survive in the Japanese countryside of 1953. They are not the mischievous water imps of legend, however, but shy, kindly space aliens. In appearance, they are E.T.s with goiters, right down to the birdlike motions of their big green heads and the flutters of their long, scaly fingers. The aliens—Mom, Dad, and Junior—live, *kappa*-like, in a gloomy, watery underground cave. Dad labors away at a contraption that looks like a self-exploding junk pile, while Mom wastes away inside what looks like a discarded space capsule. Junior follows Dad around and makes cute noises.

They are harmless creatures, but to a boy named Yuta (Keisuke Funakoshi), who surprises Junior and Dad one evening near a lake, they are wondrous beings indeed. Inspired by the stories his grandfather has told him about the *kappa* that are said to protect their village (and will destroy it if they are harmed), he tracks them to their lair. Unfortunately, the villagers are also on their trail—and are bent on destroying what they cannot control or understand.

There is also a framing story about Yuta forty years on. Now a famous photographer, Yuta (Tatsuya Fuji) returns to the village with his grown son (Takanori Jinnai) to meet Junior once more, knowing that this will be his last chance. This pair puts in occasional appearances throughout the film, but we never really get to know them. Obsessed and weird, Yuta seems to be reprising the Dennis Hopper role in *Apocalypse Now*. His son seems to be wondering what he is doing here (and so do we).

As it turns out, Yuta and the other characters are actors in a morality play. The message: selfish, thoughtless, unloving people are bad for the environment and the creatures that inhabit it. Ishii drives it home by filming his baddies—the villagers who torment Yuta's spineless father, the bullies who torment Yuta and his scaredy-cat best friend—as strident grotesques, who grimace buffonishly and growl boorishly.

More than its message, however, *Kappa* is really about attitude and style. Because this is fantasy, it seems to say, we needn't worry about things like character development and narrative coherence. Sincerity will carry the day. Who cares that the aliens speak in incomprehensible twitters and shrieks and that, as a result, we have absolutely no idea what they are really doing in the cave. (Reporting on earth-creature activities for a possible alien invasion?)

The camera swirls, zooms, and otherwise tries desperately to impress us with its cleverness. To Ishii, filmmaking would seem to be a kind of stage performance. Keeping shaking it, and perhaps they won't notice you have nothing to say.

Karada mo Kokoro mo
Body and Soul (1997)

Written and directed by Haruhiko Arai. Produced by Tohoku Shinsha and Toei Video. With Eiji Okuda, Rina Katase, Akira Enomoto. (126 mins.)

Haruhiko Arai's debut feature, *Karada mo Kokoro mo* describes a sexual roundelay involving four middle-agers who were once student radicals in the sixties—an era that now seems as distant as The War of Jenkin's Ear.

As befits a first film by a veteran scriptwriter, *Karada* is almost defiantly talky. But though Arai knows how to construct dialogue that is emotionally rich and narratively revealing, he succeeds only sporadically in making his movie come visually alive. Even the numerous sex scenes, which provide virtually the only action, have a sameness that is finally tedious, until I began to think less about the characters' dilemmas and more about the lack of imagination in their bedroom antics. (Arai should have hired Dr. Ruth as a technical advisor.)

Also, the men come across as so tired of it all that I felt like slipping them a few bottles of Yomeishu—the Geritol of Japan. Granted, they don't have much to celebrate. Sekiya (Akira Emoto), a scriptwriter, has separated from his wife and and fallen from favor with TV-drama producers. They want stories that appeal to twentysomething females and fortysomething Sekiya can no longer write them. Reduced to editing a dictionary for schoolchildren and house-sitting for an old college buddy Okamoto (Eiji Okada), he is at the end of his personal and professional tether. Okamoto is having more professional success—he has been invited to teach Japanese literature at a university in New York—but his marriage to the beautiful-but-sharp-tongued Aya (Rina Katase) is under strain. She considers him a mama's boy and has no desire to spend a year in a foreign country catering to his needs. He persuades her to accompany him but she lets him know that she is going against her will.

Soon after Sekiya begin his house-sitting chores, he receives an unexpected visitor: Reiko (Eiko Nagashima), a designer friend of the Okamoto's who has agreed to help at Aya's coffee shop while she is away. The same age as Aya, Reiko has never married. She finds Sekiya attractive and soon they are making passionate love in their employers' bedroom.

All seems to be going swimmingly when Aya suddenly returns from the States, fed with up with being her husband's nursemaid. She also wants to see Sekiya. Lovers in their student days, they were forced to part when Sekiya was arrested in a demonstration and sentenced to three years in prison. During his time in the slammer, Aya took up with Okamoto, who left his then lover, Reiko, for her. To assuage their guilt over these ancient betrayals, the Okamotos had schemed to throw Sekiya and Reiko together.

But now Aya is back to reclaim Sekiya and escape from her failing marriage. Sekiya, who has been carrying a torch all these years, responds to her advances. While these two are beginning a torrid affair, Okamoto suddenly returns—and promptly makes a pass at Reiko. But this quartet discovers that the past is not easy to recover—or forget.

With his trademark hangdog face and weary voice, Akira Emoto is glaringly miscast as a leading man in a drama of turbulent passion. Also, while sensitively probing the desires, regrets, and illusions of his characters, Arai stages his bedroom scenes as though he were filming a porno video. The contrast is not only sharp, but unintentionally absurd. One moment Emoto is engaged in a soul-baring conversation and looking as though the seduction were the furthest thing from his mind, the next he stolidly humping away in medium closeup, looking as though he could use a membership in a good gym. These scenes are a reminder that, after a certain age, some things are better suggested than nakedly expressed. Thankfully, a few more films like *Karada mo Kokoro mo* may kill the craze for movies about middle-aged lovers. What next? Jane Austen anyone?

Kaze no Katami
After Wind Has Gone (1996)

Written and directed by Yukiko Takayama. **Produced by** Kihachi Production, Studio TYT, and Fourtacks. **With** Kaori Takahashi, Hiroshi Abe, Shinobu Sakagami, Ittoku Kishibe, Toshiya Nagasawa, Shima Iwashita. (98 mins.)

Few filmmakers have dwelt longer in development hell than Mineko Okamoto. Though successful in

her career as a screenwriter and producer, whose highlights include a Fujimoto Award for producing husband Kihachi Okamoto's hit 1991 film *Daiyukai* (Rainbow Kids), she struggled long and hard to make a movie from *Konjaku Monogatari*, a 1968 historical novel by Takehiko Fukunaga. Now, twenty-eight years after first reading the novel, she has realized her dream in *Kaze no Katami*. The film's first-time director is also a woman, Yukiko Takayama, who worked as a scriptwriter for director Tetsutaro Murano. This combination of a woman producer and director is as rare in Japanese films as lifetime employment is for Hollywood studio execs.

But while representing a welcome advance, *Kaze no Katami* is a Japanese woman's picture in the traditional mold. Its heroine—an aristocratic beauty of Heian Kyoto named Princess Hagi (Kaori Takahashi)—is a living *emaki* (picture scroll) painting in her gorgeous multilayered silk robes. She lives behind reed screens with her attendants and pines for the love of Yasumaro (Hiroshi Abe), a high court official who is as cold and dissolute as he is handsome. Unfortunately, she has been promised as the concubine of the Emperor—a great honor she dreads, but cannot reject.

Meanwhile, Jiro (Shinobu Sakagami), the son of a provincial lord, has come to capital to seek his fortune. Young, pure-hearted, and by Kyoto standards, uncultivated, he takes up residence in the palace of Hagi's father (Ittoku Kishibe) and falls in love with the princess. But Hagi sees him only as an amusingly tongue-tied bumpkin who plays the flute beautifully. There is a third contender for Hagi's hand—a mysterious thief named Fudomaru (Toshiya Nagasawa), who is determined to take the princess by any means necessary, including rape. There is also a strange presence overseeing and influencing these proceedings: a shaman (Shima Iwashita) whom Jiro first encounters one night on his way to the capital. Separated from his companions, he discovers her, together with a burly shaven-headed assistant, burning a statue of the Buddha. "Aren't you afraid?" Jiro asks. "It is also the way of the Buddha to give warmth to those who are cold," she answers with a seductive smile.

Rather than supply that warmth, Takayama's approach is that of a conventionally-minded museum curator mounting an exhibition on the Heian era: beautiful objects frontally presented and impeccably lit to show every detail. Even though much of the action takes place at night, with only small oil lamps for illumination, we see Princess Hagi with the clarity of a mannequin in a diorama. In its storytelling and acting as well, the film has a preserved-under-glass feel. *Kaze no Katami* is an artifact of a fimmaking tradition that has long since substituted the assurances of ritual for the unruly impulses of creation.

Because Takayama is such a conscientious preservationist, however, *Kaze no Katami* has value as a document of not only Heian culture but of period-drama narrative styles. Though Princess Hagi may be, to modern sensibilities, annoyingly passive, she is true to type, as are the other characters, from the stouthearted Jiro to the blackhearted Fudomaro. Also, there is Shima Iwashita, perfectly cast as the weaver of spells and the teller of the future. She injects a creepy, campy charge into the otherwise predictable proceedings. But even Iwashita cannot blow all the dust off this particular display case.

Kaze no Uta ga Kikitai
I Want to Hear the Wind's Song (1999)

Directed by Nobuhiko Obayashi. Screenplay by Nobuhiko Obayashi, Kyohei Nakaoka, and Chuji Naito. Produced by PSC, Toshin Enterprise, and Pride One. With Ryo Amamiya, Yuri Nakae, Jimpachi Nezu, Ittoku Kishibe. (161 mins.)

Kaze no Uta ga Kikitai is based on a true story about deaf youngsters triumphing over adversity to find fulfillment and true love. The deaf have been the subjects of Japanese films before, including Takeshi Kitano's 1991 *Ano Natsu, Ichiban Shikuza na Umi*, but Obayashi goes farther than Kitano in showing us what it means to be disabled in a society that too often punishes difference with exclusion and isolation.

Over its 161-minute running time, the film details, with a fidelity that is admirable but trying, the lives of a deaf couple who met as penpals and now compete together in triathlons. With the onscreen years slipping by in what seemed to be real time, I began to long for a pair of editing shears.

Also, *Kaze* is not only a plea for tolerance, but a call to return to bedrock values. Accordingly, it won the recommendation of the Ministry of Culture and other government agencies. One imagines bureaucratic types nodding approval as the hero hymns the joys of working on the Nissan assembly line and the heroine glows with the pleasure and pride of young motherhood. But while unabashedly plumping for the *gambaru seishin* (stick-to-it spirit), *Kaze* does not portray its couple as unblemished saints. In junior high school, Masahiro (Ryo Amamiya) was a self-described delinquent who once drew a suspension for carousing with his dorm buddies after hours, while Namiko (Yuri Nakae) was a tenderly raised *ojosan* (young miss) who, soon after enrolling in a design school in which she was the only non-hearing student, came running home in tears.

The film shuttles back and forth between the present, in which Namiko is giving birth to her first child while Masahiro competes in a triathlon, and the past, starting from their childhoods in widely separated corners of Japan.

While attending a junior high school for the deaf, Masahiro writes letters to potential pen pals, asking them to enclose photos in their replies. Choosing the cutest girl among his respondents, he writes her a letter. A beautiful friendship has begun.

Romance, however, is longer in blooming. Though they continue to correspond throughout their high school years, Namiko as "Mickey" (for Mickey Mouse) and Masahiro as "Rock'n'roller Jimmy" (for James Dean), they meet only once, when Masahiro pays a brief visit to Namiko in Hokkaido. After graduation, Masahiro takes a job in a Nissan plant near Tokyo, while Namiko enters a design school in Sapporo. They continue to go their separate ways, with Masahiro joining a deaf triathlon club and making the rounds of the discos (he may not hear the music, but he loves to boogie) and Namiko becoming close friends with a hearing classmate. Then, when Namiko comes to Tokyo to find a job—and finds the walls of prejudice frustratingly hard to breach— she and Masahiro move past the "just friends" stage to love, cohabitation, and finally (with a prod from Namiko's worried parents) marriage.

Screen newcomer Ryo Amamiya's performance as Masahiro is refreshingly unaffected. When stars play disabled heroes they usually crank up the histrionic machinery to the highest possible pitch. With Amamiya, however, we can't hear a single gear click—an accomplishment that occaisionally lifts *Kaze* above mere earnestness to art.

Kegareta Maria
Defiled Maria (1998)

Screenplay and direction by Takahisa Zeze. Produced by Kokuei and Shin Toho. With Akira Yoshino, Yota Kawase, Shoko Kudo, Taro Suwa. (79 mins.)

In Japan, former porno directors often shy away from overt sexuality in their straight films. Whatever their motives—an eagerness to prove their credentials as serious auteurs or a reluctance to run through familiar paces—many have made movies as chaste as a Booth Tarkington novel. There are, however, prominent exceptions to this *noli me tangere* rule, including Takahisa Zeze. In his latest film, *Kegareta Maria* (Defiled Maria), this former "king of the pinks" shows why he deserves the title, in scenes of fervid lovemaking that make the bed-scene choreography in most Hollywood movies look restrained.

There is, however, more to the film than the sum of its sexual sprints to the finish line. *Kerageta* takes the murderous passion of its heroine—a ruby-lipped, ferret-eyed bookkeeper for a beauty salon—to extremes both disturbing and absurd. Though based on a true story, the film soars beyond sordid realism into a stylized realm that may bear little relation to waking life, but has a persuasive dream logic. It is Janus-faced Eros at its outer limits, where murder follows lust in a downward spiral leading to moral exhaustion and a longing for easeful death.

Zeze subverts—or rather completely ignores—filmmaking conventions, while pursuing a personal agenda more concerned with reaction than action, poeticized emotion than plot points. He takes what would be a key scene in a Hollywood thriller—the bookkeeper's murder of her rival for her lover's affections—and guts it of suspense or terror. One moment the victim is walking out of her apartment, the next the bookkeeper is dragging her bloody body to the bath. Imagine watching *Psycho* minus the shower scene: an enormous hole opens in the film. Zeze, however, uses that hole to make an important point; for the clerk, the act of murder is nothing, the fact of passion everything.

Though his trashing of standard cinematic grammar has its payoffs, Zeze not only betrays expectations, but tests patience. In whipping through the drama of jealousy and retribution that begins the film, he may be expressing his disdain of thriller genre scene-setting, he also makes it hard to tell who to doing what to whom and why.

The bookkeeper, Fumiko (Akira Yoshino), is conducting an affair with Sakai (Yota Kawase), a stylist in the salon. Meanwhile, another stylist, the voluptuous Mayumi (Shoko Kudo), is sleeping with the shop's owner. When she announces that she is quitting to set up on her own shop, the owner persuades her to celebrate her leavetaking with a night of hot love. The next day, however, Fumiko takes one look at Mayumi's secretly smiling face and decides that she is also having sex with Sakai. Enraged, she lures Mayumi to her apartment and, while her salaryman husband is at work and her son is at daycare, murders her, dismembers her, and deposits her remains in neighborhood dumpsters.

Then comes a devastating blow: Sakai tells Fumiko that he wants to break it off and claims he had nothing to do with Mayumi. Soon after, Mayumi's husband, a bearded taxi driver named Yukio (Taro Suwa), shows up at the salon to beat her lover into a pride-salvaging pulp. Instead, Yukio loses the fight and Fumiko treats his wounds. When she hears that the police have found one of her trash bags, she decides to take Yukio to a snow country hot springs to "search" for the missing Mayumi—and murder him as well.

This search becomes the heart of the film, in which Yukio discovers not only the truth about

Mayumi and her killer, but a disturbing passion for the woman who murdered his wife and would now have him dead. As lust-besotted as Fumiko, he is torn between a desire to ravish and kill.

Zeze stages this psychodrama in a snow-covered wilderness across which his two principals wander like lost souls locked in their strange dance of fate and fatality. Yes, Fumiko's attempts to murder Yukio verge on the absurd, as do his attempts to punish her (in one scene he whacks her with a ball bat and, in the next, she is sitting across the table from him, a bandage on her head, calmly sucking down a bowl of noodles), but their dance speaks the lawless, contrary language of desire. Once again, Japan's dirty movie business has produced an extraordinary filmmaker.

Keiho Daisanjukyujo
Naked Law (1999)

Directed by Yoshimitsu Morita. **Screenplay by** Sumio Omori. **Produced by** Kowa International and Shochiku. **With** Shin'ichi Tsutsumi, Kirin Kiki, Naoki Sugiura, Kyoka Suzuki. (133 mins.)

In *Keiho Daisanjukyujo*, Yoshimitsu Morita has made a 180-degree turn from the crowd-pleasing melodrama of *Shitsurakuen* to a deep-think psychodrama about a murderer with a split personality, aimed at the festival and art-house circuit. But screening in competition at the 1999 Berlin Film Festival, *Keiho* divided the critics and left empty-handed.

I found the film heavy going, not only because dialogue was dense with legal and psychiatric jargon and the plot was as tangled as the hero's psyche, but because the lead characters were all either bizarre, eccentric, or clinically depressed. By the end, I felt fogbound myself, with no catharsis in sight.

The story is that of the 1995 Richard Gere thriller *Primal Fear*—an open-and-shut murder case that, as investigators delve into the killer's motives, becomes more complex than it first appears. The victims are a pregnant woman and her husband, the killer a stage actor named Masaki Shibata (Shin'ichi Tsutsumi) who stabs them in their apartment soon after they return from his one-man show. When cops find his prints on a ticket stub and a bloody knife, Shibata quickly confesses, but claims he has no memory of being in the couple's apartment.

When his court-appointed lawyer (Kirin Kiki) visits him in prison, she finds not one client but two—a sensitive, mild-mannered artist, and after a shocking transformation, a frothing, fiery-eyed madman. Which one is she representing? When the judge asks Shibata to state his guilt or innocence at the hearing, he erupts into incoherent rage. Is the man mad? The court asks a psychiatrist (Naoki Sugiura) and his assistant (Kyoka Suzuki) to examine him in prison. All goes well with the interview until the assistant begins to question Shibata and read a passage from his one-man play. His hands tremble and his expression changes. Suddenly he pushes his interrogator to the wall and threatens her in the coarse language of a hardened criminal. This new Shibata also expresses his disdain for the wimpy actor with whom he shares a body—and whom he vows to eliminate.

The shrink says the poor fellow is a case of split personality. Under Article 39 of the Japanese legal code, which mandates special consideration for the mentally incompetent, he cannot be executed for his crimes, however much he may desire the ultimate punishment. But the assistant, the aptly-named Kafuka Ogawa, doubts whether Shibata is what he seems. She has an intimate acquaintance with mental illness: her father committed suicide before her eyes and her mother has become an obsessive-compulsive who hides her fears behind enormous meals. Meanwhile, Kafuka has retreated behind a mousy exterior and an air of permanent mourning, but she also knows acting when she sees it. She claims in court that Shibata is a fake. How can she make anyone believe her?

In telling this story, Morita prefers the small shocks that reveal character to the racheting of tension that is standard for the genre. Also, instead of Hollywood extroversion, he opts for—can we say it?—Kafkaesque mystification. Nothing is quite what it seems—including Kafuka herself. But where Kafka's nightmarish interior world evokes our worst fears with uncanny accuracy—one doesn't read Kafka so much as dream him—Morita succeeds only in casting a pall over what could have been a gut-grinding psycho-thriller. The usually excellent Kyoka Suzuki spends most of the film in a low-energy funk, wearing the same spinsterish glasses and hang-dog expression. I usually groan at the cliché of the brown mouse morphing into a raving beauty, but in Suzuki's case I longed for it.

Shin'ichi Tsutsumi executes Shibata's Jekyll-Hyde transformations with force and precision, but he needs to open up his character more. Robert De Niro's more memorable wackos—Travis Bickle in *Taxi Driver* and Max Cady in *Cape Fear*—are scary because they are alive in all dimensions. They are not assemblages of actor's tricks, but monsters who live down the street—or inside our heads. Shibata never leaves the stage. At the end of his performance, I applauded his virtuosity, but I left the screening room with a sigh of relief. *Keiho* handed down a longer sentence than I cared to serve.

Keiko Desukedo
My Name Is Keiko (1997)

Written and directed by Shion Sono. Produced by Anchors Production. With Keiko Suzuki. (61 mins.)

Shion Sono is a filmmaker in the tradition of Andy Warhol, that master of cinematic banality and boredom. In his 1993 *Room*, an old gangster with a robotic young female real estate agent in tow spent an interminable amount of screen time searching for the perfect place to commit suicide. But whereas Warhol filmed his banalities with tongue in cheek, Sono presented his with a straight face, as though letting us in on Important Truths. In *Keiko Desukedo*, Sono still evidences the Warholian influence, but from the period when Warhol disciple Paul Morrisey took over the direction of Warhol's films and injected semblances of conventional cinematic structure into them.

Keiko Suzuki (Keiko Suzuki) is living alone in Tokyo and working as a waitress. Her father, she tells us, died of cancer several years ago and in three weeks she will be twenty-two. She is obsessed with time and its passage, reeling off not only the number of days (8,036) and hours (192,864) she has been alive, but the running time of the film we are watching (one hour, one minute, and one second). "I want to make an accurate record of these three weeks," she says. "As much as possible, I want to to record this time with the accuracy of 'one hour equals sixty minutes.'"

Instead of accuracy, however, the film presents an impressionist account of Keiko's loneliness, ennui, and fantasies as the minutes tick, tick, tick away. Though counting out time the way a miser counts out coins, she spends much of the last three weeks of her twenty-first year doing little or nothing. We see Keiko staring at the camera, staring out the window, wiggling her fingers, wiggling her toes, writing the words "I am" and then crossing them out.

While presenting Keiko in her various moods as she struggles for meaning and identity, Sono is investigating the nature of time and reality. In the course of that investigation, his heroine becomes a symbolic figure in a cinematic landscape stripped to the narrative and visual bone. No longer a woman but Woman, no longer a character, but a counter in Sono's artistic and philosphical games.

As he did in *The Room*, Sono uses tedium to underscore the emptiness of his central character's world. But in *Keiko* he is less self-importantly programmic, more creatively playful and—dare I say it?—entertaining. In one sequence of "news programs" Keiko dresses up in goofy costumes, including a blonde wig and frilly ball dress, to read bulletins about her mundane daily adventures. These "programs" may illustrate the plasticity of this concept called "Keiko," but as blackout sketches they are also loopily amusing. Likewise, in painting Keiko's room and its furnishings in bright primary colors, Sono may be demonstating the banality of her existence, but they also give the film a comic undertone. Presented in a cheery red box, even her father's bones begin to look absurd.

Keiko Desukedo is a film for those still young enough to find the fleetingness of time more an abstract idea than a present reality. That said, I have to admit that Sono timed his film exactly right—it ended not a minute too soon.

Keisho Sakazuki
Succession Ceremony (1992)

Directed by Kazuki Omori. Screenplay by Hiroo Matsuda. Produced by Toei. With Hiroyuki Sanada, Ken Ogata, Yuko Kotegawa. (119 mins.)

Because they tend to take themselves with such awful seriousness, gangsters are natural subjects for comedy. (Mack Sennet once made the same observation about cops.) Making funny gangster movies is tricky, however. Turn *yakuza* into clowns and nobody will take them seriously as gangsters. Make them behave like real gangsters (pummeling underlings, knifing rivals) and they suddenly aren't funny any more.

Kazuki Omori's *Keisho Sakazuki* tries to resolve this dilemma in several ways. The story, which concerns the arrangements for a gang succession ceremony, lends itself to comedy; a screwed-up gangland social event, especially one staged by fanatically perfectionist thugs, is potentially funnier than, say, a screwed-up gangland execution.

Second, the hero is a funny fellow. A college grad and former stockbroker, Shoichi Yoshinari (Hiroyuki Sanada) is an unlikely *yakuza* to begin with. Sanada plays him with a frenetic eagerness that is amusingly right, not irritatingly wrong. Perhaps it's his gift for physical comedy—a former gymnast, he's got an amusingly desperate way of running. Perhaps it's his blend of boyish charm and roguish calculation. He is like Michael J. Fox in his better roles. But taller.

When an elderly boss of bosses decides to step aside in favor of a younger underling, Yoshinari is assigned to persuade the *oyabun* (godfather)of an affiliate gang to serve as the *baishakunin*—a kind of emcee—at the succession ceremony. His job is a tough one, because he is asking the *oyabun* to fill in,

the first choice for *baishakunin* having fallen ill. Being considered second-best is an unbearable blow to *yakuza* pride.

When, after several mishaps, Yoshinari arrives at the country home of the *oyabun* (Ken Ogata), he finds him to be a pleasant, amiable type. He also discovers that the stunner he tried to pick up on the way over is the *oyabun's* wife (Yuko Kotegawa). His troubles don't really begin until this pair arrives in Tokyo. The geezer who was the first choice makes a miraculous recovery, and Yoshinari has to tell the *oyabun* that his services are no longer needed. Now the *oyabun* is really insulted. He gets roaring drunk, crashes a funeral and, confusing the funeral altar with the one used in the succession ceremony, starts a one-man riot. Soon after, the geezer collapses again and the *oyabun* gets another chance. By now Yoshinari knows that he will need a miracle of his own if he is to shepherd his *sake*-loving charge successfully through the ceremony.

Hiroo Matsuda's script has promise, but the film doesn't realize it. The beginning, with its wild race through the countryside—Yoshinari and his frantic superior are late for an appointment with the *oyabun*—points *Keisho* in the direction of farce, but it soon turns back toward soapish melodrama.

The *oyabun*, it so happens, is a not a W.C. Fields comic drunk, but a Ray (*Lost Weekend*) Milland tragic drunk who becomes painful to watch. His wife, understandably, becomes fed up. A former office clerk, she once embezzled seventy million yen for him and spent three years in prison as a result. Now look how he is paying her back! This veering between the silly and the serious keeps *Keisho* from taking off. We cringe at the confessions and keep waiting for laughs that never quite arrive.

The key scene, however, is the ceremony itself, and Ken Ogata brings it off splendidly. We may have sat, paralyzed with boredom, through too many Japanese weddings to work up much enthusiasm for yet another overpriced, overprepared ceremony, but Ogata illuminates the spirit behind the mummery. Though his hands may tremble with the DTs, he guts through, calling on his reserves of *yakuza* pride. Throughout the film we have seen the gangsters' buffoonish side. Now we get a different, more intimate view of their world. I was reminded of sportswriter Bill Murray's observation about a Hell's Angel: "Planted on the back of his hog, this oaf acquired instant grace." Ogata's *oyabun* undergoes a similar transformation, one that expresses not only an individual will, but group continuity and solidarity. For one moment in a less-than-revealing movie, we see the glue that holds the gangs together.

Kichiku Daienkai

Satanic Banquet (1998)

Screenplay and direction by Kazuyoshi Kumakiri. Produced by Oni Pro. With Yuji Hashimoto, Sumiko Mikami, Tomohiro Zaizen, Kentaro Ogiso, Toshiyuki Sugihara, Shigeru Bokuda, Shunsuke Sawada. (108 mins.)

It's tough to make it in the movie business nowadays, with all those Quentin Tarantino and Oliver Stone wannabees out there. One way of breaking through the static is that of Quentin and Oliver—pushing the envelope of sex and violence. Such was the strategy of twenty-three-year-old Kazuyoshi Kumakiri in making *Kichiku Daienkai*, his debut feature about the bloody dissolution of a radical student group in the 1970s. It has worked well, both critically and commercially. After winning second prize at the twentieth Pia Film Festival and being screened at the 1997 Berlin Film Festival, *Kichiku* became an art-house hit..

Made as Kumakiri's graduation project for an Osaka Art University film course, *Kichiku* has the look of a student production, complete with blotchy closeups, ragged sound, choppy editing, and effects that verge on the unintentionally comic. It is also the work of a genuine—and genuinely perverse—talent. *Kichiku* is not just a testing of limits, but a frontal assault on them, whose killers celebrate their murders in obscene orgies of blood and gore that revolt and defile. One walks out of the theater with an intense desire to take a mental shower.

But while descending toward the level of the snuff film, *Kichiku* tells unpleasant truths about the nature of madness and evil and provides an unmediated view of the flip side of the Japanese group harmony ethic. I was reminded of George Orwell's comment about the work of another *enfant terrible*, Salvador Dali: "It should be possible to say, 'This is a good book or a good picture, and it ought to be burned by the public hangman.'" I would not like to see *Kichiku* burned, but if Kumakiri commits a sequel, he ought to be slowly boiled in his own prop blood.

The film begins as an examination of a seventies radical sect in crisis. The sect's charismatic leader, Aizawa (Yuji Hashimoto), is in prison, and his lover Masami (Sumiko Mikami) has taken command. Though not a conventional beauty, she rules her mostly male followers with an unabashed sexuality and a fiery will. When her lover of the moment, the pudgy, bearded Yamane (Tomohiro Zaizen), flails out at two members who robbed a post office on her orders, she snaps back. The two lovers launch into a shouting match while other members look mutely on.

But when Yamane makes a slighting comment about Aizawa—an unforgivable breach of sect etiquette—Masami slaps him, the other members jump him, and soon Yamane is stumbling out the door, disgraced and expelled. Yamane is soon replaced by the silent, shaven-headed Fujihara (Kentaro Ogiso), who is Aizawa's friend from prison, and the nerdy Sugihara (Toshiyuki Sugihara), who is the college buddy of Kumatani (Shigeru Bokuda), a long-haired, guitar-strumming member who is the quintessential seventies radical.

Life goes on in the grubby apartment that is sect's hideout. Members collect weapons, including a shotgun that Masami fondles intently, and have an impromptu party, during which Masami dons a Chinese lion mask and performs an orgiastic dance. That night she also takes a new lover: Kumatani.

Then the sect hears news of Aizawa's death—he cut his stomach in his cell—and its group solidarity, always fragile, implodes. They need a scapegoat to restore it, however temporarily, and they find it in Yamane, whom they discover brawling with Kumatani in Kumatani's room. After beating their former comrade senseless, they throw him into a car and drive off to a forest where, on a beautiful spring day, they engage in an orgy of violence that ends with two dead bodies and a writhing, blood-spattered victim, his penis severed and his mind gone. The instigator of this orgy, Masami, finds a ready accomplice and new paramour in the handsome, pitiless Okazaki (Shunsuke Sawada), but their idyll does not last long. Having unleashed blood lust, they cannot easily contain it.

Kumakiri captures the look and feel of the period quite well. He is aware, as many are not, that hardcore student radicals were a remarkably unattractive crew, by intent as much as by nature. He also evokes the hysteria of the true-believer, which is universal, but particularly virulent in Japanese sects, where *wa* (harmony) depends on everyone holding rigidly to the same beliefs, however absurd, and where deviation is punished with ferocity.

But while the descent from the teasing frolic of Masami's *matsuri* dance to the black chaos of her final madness has few false notes—Sumiko Mikami portrays the unstable fascist personality to cold perfection—*Kichiku* wallows in the bloody muck with an autointoxicated joy that crosses the line from art to voyeurism. In short, a film that degrades the victim, besmirches the spirit. Dali himself could not have done it better.

Kids Return *

(1996)

Written and directed by Takeshi Kitano. Produced by Office Kitano, Bandai Visual. With Ken Kaneko, Masanobu Ando. (108 mins.)

Takeshi Kitano's *Kids Return* is ostensibly about the attempts of two present-day high school dropouts to make their fortunes on society's fringes, but its point of view is that of a middle-aged man looking back at his own younger days with hard-won wisdom and telling the kids in the audience that life is tough and unforgiving. Its mood, however, is anything but harsh. Though Kitano is famously fed up with the younger generation, he has an evident affection for his two no-account heroes. They are, as he mentions in the program notes, modeled on boys he grew up with—1960s throwbacks in 1990s dress.

Despite its air of being suspended between eras, *Kids Return* is the most observant, poignant, and nuanced of Kitano's six films, though it shares their wry understatement and quirky, even pranksterish, inventiveness. Like most of us, his heroes find it easier to change their circumstances than their characters. Whether wearing a boxer's trunks or a *yakuza*'s luminescent silk shirt, they are forever the teenage punks whose idea of a good time is to defiantly weave around the schoolyard on a bike while their classmates endure a trigonometry lesson.

Though Kitano has been guilty of gratuitous violence (as in the 1989 *Sono Otoko Kyobo ni Tsuki*), patronizing sentimentalism (as in the 1991 *Ano Natsu, Ichiban Shizukana Umi*) and auteurist self-indulgence (as in the 1993 *Sonatine*), there has always been a welcome strain of emotional and intellectual honesty in his work. Unlike directors whose only aim is to make us feel good, Kitano's is to express how he feels, without worrying too much about whether the mass audience will accept the often nihilistic messages of his films.

Kids Return, however, tries harder to meet mainstream expectations halfway, while refusing to soften its downbeat story line. Its two buddy-heroes—the loudmouth Masaru (Ken Kaneko) and his quiet follower Shinji (Masanobu Ando)—exhibit the same raunchy, cruel sense of humor familiar to viewers of Kitano's innumerable TV comedy shows. They dangle a handmade doll, complete with bobbing penis, from the school roof to their classroom window, or shake down classmates for spare change by forcing them to jump up and down like so many jammed piggy banks. Their aim in life is to spend as little time as possible in class and as much time as possible eating noodles, drinking beer, and sneaking into dirty movies.

One day, a favorite victim brings a protector—a professional boxer—who promptly wipes the sneer off Masaru's face and dumps him on his arrogant rear. Soon after, Masaru drops out of school to train at a local boxing gym. Shinji tags along and discovers, to his surprise, not to mention Masaru's, that he is a natural boxer. After Shinji cleans his clock in a sparring bout, Masaru quits the gym in disgust and becomes an apprentice *yakuza*.

The two friends drift apart. Shinji continues to move up the boxing ranks, while Masaru learns the gangster's violent trade. The film also follows the post-high-school careers of the boys' "victim" classmates, including a meek loner who longs futilely for a pretty coffeeshop waitress and ends up driving a cab, and two fledgling *manzai* comedians who crack lame jokes about their high school teachers to audiences of uncomprehending pensioners.

It's not hard to guess the Shinji and Masaru's respective fates: the movie is framed as flashback from their unpromising present. Ironically, the only ones who succeed are the *manzai* duo—Masaru and Shinji's former marks. As a full house roars at their jokes, we can see Kitano looking back at his own past as a *manzai* comedian—and hear him having a film's last laugh.

Kike, Wadatsumi no Koe
Last Friends (1995)

Directed by Masanobu Deme. Screenplay by Akira Hayasaka. Produced by Toei, Bandai Visual. With Naoto Ogata, Yuji Oda, Toru Kazama, Toru Nakamura, Ken'ichi Endo. (129 mins.)

When I heard that three major Japanese studios—Shochiku, Toho and Toei—were planning films to commemorate the fiftieth anniversary of the end of the war, I wondered what they could say about World War II today that hadn't been said a thousand times before. Now that the films are in the theaters, the answer is—not much.

Kike, Wadatsumi no Koe (Last Friends), Toei's remake of a 1950 Hideo Sekikawa film of the same title, tries to make the war understandable to the younger generation and tell truths about it that certain members of the older generation may not want to hear. Nonetheless, the overall tone is that of a cinematic war-memorial service that views its fallen heroes through a mist of platitudes. They are less fallible human beings than pure vessels for the expression of uplifting sentiments, usually in the film's many death scenes that relentlessly milk the pathos of it all. Instead of the raw horrors of a *Platoon* or the bitter ironies of a *Paths of Glory*, we get attitudes received from five decades of World War II melodramas. The stylization is as rigid as that of a Kabuki drama.

Akira Hayasaka's screenplay introduces a new twist in the character of Tsuruya (Naoto Ogata), a university rugby player who is tackled hard in practice one summer day in 1995 and wakes to find himself in uniform and marching in the rain with thousands of other students in a war rally at Jingu Gaien Stadium. "What is this all about?" he asks one of the other students. "War," is the reply. Having lost their deferments, these college boys are about to be shipped off to the killing fields. The date is October 21, 1943.

The story quickly shifts from its time-travel framing device—the dazed Tsuruya retains no memory of his 1995 existence—to a drama of men at war. The men are three of Tsuruya's fellow marchers who, though hailing from different elite universities, share a passion for rugby. There is Katsumura (Yuji Oda) from Meiji University, who marries his hometown sweetheart before shipping out as a second lieutenant to the Philippines. There is Aihara (Toru Kazama) of the University of Tokyo, who rejects his industrialist father's offer of a cushy rear-echelon post and joins the army as a lowly private (Guess whose unit he ends up in?). Finally, there is Akutagawa (Toru Nakamura) from Waseda University, who ships out as a pilot, leaving behind his mother, his younger sister and his tuberculosis-stricken girlfriend. Though he considers the war a mistake, he decides to join the *tokkotai* (special attack units), whose targets in the closing days of the war are U.S. Navy ships lying off the coast of Okinawa. "If 'my country' means my family, my friends, and the beautiful mountains and rivers [of Nagano], then I'm willing to throw away my life to save it," he says.

Director Masanobu Deme gives us a big emotion-drenched scene every ten minutes, while ploddingly developing his three main story lines: the struggle of Katsumura and Aihara's unit to survive in the hell of the Philippines, the preparation of Akutagawa and his fellow pilots for their first and final *tokkotai* flight, and the wanderings of Tsuruya following his decision to desert rather than fight a war he opposes. None of these men are gung-ho types brimming with *Yamato-damashii* (Japanese spirit). Their "war aims," as Akutagawa's comment indicates, are strictly personal and local; their basic attitude, pacifistic. They, together with the nurses who tend the wounded in the Philippines and the wives, sisters, and mothers who wait anxiously at home, are the film's "good Japanese." The bad ones include the brutal first lieutenant (Ken'ichi Endo), who orders Katsumura to abandon the unit's field hospital patients to the mercies of the enemy and laughingly approves his men's attempt to rape the nurses. The baddies, however, are clearly exceptions, and by the end most of them are dead.

Despite the film's PC gestures—particularly its depiction of the sufferings of "comfort women" in an army brothel—it is conventional in its approach and message: though there were bad, cruel men on Japan's side, most Japanese soldiers and civilians were decent people defending their homes and loved ones in a valiant, if hopeless, struggle. Far from being meaningless, their sacrifices were noble, inspiring, and worthy of imitation. Such sentiments may suitable for a memorial service, but I wonder how much they will help young Japanese understand why, fifty years after the war's end, so many of their fellow Asians still suspect Japanese motives and doubt the sincerity of Japanese repentance.

Kikujiro no Natsu
Kikujiro (1999)

Written and directed by Takeshi Kitano. Cinematography by Katsumi Yanagishima. Produced by Office Kitano, Bandai Visual, Tokyo FM, and Nippon Herald. With Takeshi Kitano, Yusuke Sekiguchi, Kayoko Kishimoto, Kazuko Yoshiyuki. (121 mins.)

In making his eighth film, *Kikujiro no Natsu*, Takeshi Kitano could have continued in the same hard-edged, off-beat, minimalist vein that have made him the most internationally acclaimed Japanese director of his generation. Instead, he has taken a different tack entirely, in the direction of sentiment, slapstick comedy, and dream sequences made with computer effects. In short, he has risked falling flat on his face. I admire his courage, but foreign supporters who have hailed him as Japan's Tarantino may find *Kikujiro* a puzzling letdown. It's as though Quentin had followed *Pulp Fiction* with *A Perfect World*.

Kikujiro's problems begin with Kitano's direction of young co-star Yusuke Sekiguchi. The boy spends much of the movie shuffling about with his eyes pointed glumly downward, giving the impression that he can't act. Also, several of the slapstick routines fall embarrassingly flat, like lame TV skits that even the studio audience strains to find funny. And the dream sequences feel glaringly out of place, as though beamed from the mind of Suzuki Seijun at his most theatrically surreal. That said, Kitano creates an on-the-road ambiance flavored with puckish humor and tinged with a loneliness and longing that feels like the essence of summer. Like many of Kitano's films, it is something of a wish-fulfillment for its director, but more than his hyper-violent fantasies, it is one that more of us can share, even those who have never run away from home with only a few riceballs.

Masao (Sekiguchi) lives alone with his grandmother in the Asakusa district of Tokyo. Summer vacation is starting and he has no one to play with, nothing to do. Then he has an idea—visit his mother, whom has not seen her since he was a baby, in

Toyohashi. Just as he is about to set off he encounters a neighbor couple on the street. When the wife (Kayoko Kishimoto) hears where he is going, she urges her husband (Takeshi Kitano), who has no known occupation, to accompany him. The grandmother gives her permission and the boy and his new *ojichan* (uncle) set off on their big adventure.

But instead of Toyohashi, the *ojichan* heads for the bike track, where he wins big on numbers the boy gives him. The next day, after blowing a wad on hostesses and a hotel, he tries his luck again and proceeds to lose everything. The *ojichan* then proceeds to lead Masao on a trek filled with absurd perils, strange encounters, and plain idiocy. That night he beats up a bald pedophile who was making a pass at the boy in a park restroom, steals a taxicab, and ruins the engine with his incompetent driving. The following morning, now wheelless and broke, he bullies his way into a resort hotel.

After a short-but-eventful stay, the desk clerk gets wise to him and deposits his unwanted guests at a bus stop. The *ojichan* promptly gets into a fight with a surly truck driver, but manages to hitch a lift with a young surfer couple. They deposit their passengers in the middle of the countryside, with Toyohashi still a glimmer in the distance.

There is more in the same shambling comic vein. The *ojichan* always has a scam percolating through his brain, but he is constantly coming up one card short of a full deck. Also, we discover that he is making this journey for reasons similar to Masao's. For all his tough-guy bluff, he is still a lonely kid himself. Finally, together with a wandering poet and a pair of local bikers, the *ojichan* and Masao enjoy an summertime idyll. This chance assembly of strangers in the wilds of Shizuoka becomes more of a family that either of them have ever known—or maybe ever will know.

If *Hana-Bi* was Kitano's vision of himself as Don Quixote, the romantic loner proceeding stoically to his chosen doom, *Kikujiro* is his vision of himself as Sancho Panza, the loser clown who uses any means necessary, however low, to get his way. And yet there is something to admire in this character as well—more than most of the other adults in Masao's life, he understands and, by the end, cares. Will he change and become Masao's guardian angel for keeps? Kitano isn't saying, but he has given us a summer worth remembering. Naked freeze tag, anyone?

Ki no Ue no Sogyo
Fishing from the Treetops (1997)

Directed by Junji Ishikawa. **Screenplay by** Chiho Katsura. **Produced by** Whiz Shuppan/M.M. **With** Tadashi Nishikawa, Takami Yoshimoto, Mitsuo Hamada. (86 mins.)

Gender-crossing is becoming more common in pre-millenial Japan. In addition to such traditional pop-culture phenomena as the all-female Takarazuka troupe, whose "male" stars thrill female fans with their princely charms, we now have the gorgeously androgynous Takuya Kimura of SMAP getting his face smeared with lipstick for a cosmetics ad campaign, and teenage boys parading about the streets of Shibuya in long skirts. But what of hermaphroditism? Not boys dressing in girls' clothes, but boys who are also girls—and vice versa. How does one make a movie about a hermaphrodite hero/heroine? Shock with grotesqueries, as Tod Browning did in his classic *Freaks*? Or amuse with bizarre black comedy, as John Waters did in *Pink Flamingos*?

In *Ki no Ue no Sogyo* Junji Ishikawa opts for neither approach, taking instead an earnest, idealized view of his unusual subject. He knows his target audience: the same young women who buy Kimura's cosmetics, attend Takarazuka's stage shows, and devour *manga* about cute guys who turn out to be gay. For this reviewer, however, the experience was somewhat similar to watching a *Peter Pan* for the nineties and knowing that, by the end of the show, the actress playing Peter would whiz through Never-Never Land in a skirt.

Based on a novel by Yuji Usui, *Ki no Ue* concerns the unusual friendship that develops between the rugged Wataru (Tadashi Nishikawa), a high-school judo athlete, and the delicate Hiroshi (Takami Yoshimoto). They are sons of rival politicians—Hiroshi father's is successful, Wataru's is not—and should be enemies, but when Wataru encounters Hiroshi one morning, fishing from high in the branches of a tree near the riverbank, he feels an attraction he can't explain. He returns with a fishing pole to deepen his acquaintance, but when he snags a large fish, Hiroshi accuses him of stealing it, jumps down from the tree and lunges at him with a knife. Wataru sidesteps his charge and Hiroshi falls on the blade, plunging it into his chest. Rushed to the hospital, he barely survives.

Eight years pass. After a chance meeting, Wataru helps Hiroshi find a job at the video shop where he is working. Despite everything, he still wants to be friends. Suspicious at first, Hiroshi begins to reciprocate. But he also attracts the attention of Natsue, who was a nurse at the hospital where he recovered from his stabbing. Natsue's interest in her old patient is not romantic, however; she asks Wataru to persuade Hiroshi to undergo what she describes as a life-or-death operation. Born a hermaphrodite, he must soon become a woman or risk dying as a man.

When Hiroshi learns that Natsue has discovered his secret he is at first furious, but nature begins to take its course and Hiroshi, with Natsue's aid, resigns himself to the inevitable. The one who cannot accept this change is Wataru. Has his friendship, he wonders to his horror, been tainted all along with forbidden feelings?

With a few exceptions, such as a flamboyant video shop owner (Mitsuo Hamada), everyone is almost excruciatingly straight-faced. But it is also obvious that Takami Yoshimoto is a girl playing a boy. The lack of all but the most rudimentary dramatic subterfuge—Yoshimoto wears her hair short and tries to look stern, but is otherwise unmistakably feminine—is at first disconcerting, especially when Takami Yoshimoto's Wataru treats her as just another guy. Is he blind or, as the shop owner suspects, not as hopelessly hetero as he pretends?

This gap between appearance and reality creates some strange vibes, but Ishikawa, an assistant director for Teruo Ishii, Tadashi Ishii, and Seijun Suzuki (who appears in a cameo as a goaty old sex-change doctor), knows what he is doing. As are Takarazuka's princes, Hiroshi (who becomes Hiromi) is living out the audience's romantic and erotic fantasies. *Ki no Ue no Sogyo* may dip its line in the turbulent waters of contemporary trends, but its head is in the clouds, dreaming of a love beyond time—and gender.

Kira Kira Hikaru *
Twinkle (1992)

Written and directed by Joji Matsuoka. Produced by Fuji Television Network. With Hiroko Yakushimaru, Etsushi Toyokawa, Michitaka Tsutsui. (103 mins.)

Joji Matsuoka's *Kira Kira Hikaru* is a ground-breaking film about a gay couple and an alcoholic woman who comes into their lives. She is played by Hiroko Yakushimaru, a former idol star who was enormously popular in the eighties. Her films were mostly forgettable, but she was not. With her heart-shaped face, waiflike eyes and bird-song voice, Yakushimaru was a child-woman who personified idolhood as then defined. She may have been cast to help *Kira Kira* at the box office, but she has matured into an actress who can convincingly play a troubled character, without sacrificing her trademark charm. Etsushi Toyokawa and Michitaka Tsutsui are also excellent as the gay couple.

But what truly sets *Kira Kira* apart is it's approach to its subject matter—no camp, no cashing in on controversy, just an honest, sympathetic portrayal of three people who don't fit Japanese society's rigid definitions of normality. In its opening scenes, the film plays like Japanized Neil Simon: slickly clever, comfortably daring. Shoko (Yakushimaru) is a twenty-seven-year-old translator and alcoholic.

Mutsuki (Toyokawa) is a thirty-year-old doctor and homosexual. They meet cute, through an *omiai* (meeting for the purpose of marriage) arranged by their desperate parents. Convinced that no normal man would want her, Shoko picks a fight with her would-be fiancee. They part, meet again by chance and discover that they have their "abnormality" in common. They decide that they would make a perfect couple, if not for reasons their parents would approve.

The marriage of convenience is the stuff of classic farce, in *Kira Kira* the partners in deception really like each other and truly want their unconventional relationship to work. Mutsuki comes home every night from the hospital with a big grin on his otherwise poker face. Shoko sings sweetly as she irons his sheets every night, just before he goes to bed. They are the picture of a happily married couple.

But they are also playing house; their marriage does nothing to alter their deeper natures. Shoko still turns to the bottle, Mutsuki to his lover, a college student named Kon (Michitaka Tsutsui). Though the film gives us more comic scenes, including Kon's first visit to the love nest, easy ironies gradually give way to the darker realities of the characters' lives. Not a few Japanese directors have trouble making this kind of transition, plunging directly from slapstick into bathos. Matsuoka does it with ease. Shoko and Mutuski are complex beings who behave in ways they themselves don't fully understand, but can't help. (They behave, in other words, much like us.)

Shoko knows, as a woman, that her marriage with Mutsuki is incomplete, but she can't bear the thought of leaving him. Mutsuki knows that he is hurting Kon, but he can't give up Shoko. And Kon, though he likes Shoko, worries that she might replace him in Mutsuki's affections. The characters' contradictory impulses suddenly surface when Shoko's parents learn about Kon and accuse of Mutsuki and his parents of trying to deceive them. Should Mutsuki and Shoko do the "right" thing and divorce? Here the movie veers briefly toward perfervid home drama, but Matsuoka steers it away in time. He also drives home his message: we can get by with a little help from our friends—as long as we know who they are.

Kiri no Shigosen
The Meridian In the Mist (1996)

Directed by Masanobu Deme. Screenplay by Machiko Nasu. Produced by Toei Tokyo. With Sayuri Yoshinaga, Shima Iwashita, Koji Yamamoto, Koji Tamaoki. (106 mins.)

In 1962, when Hollywood paired Bette Davis and Joan Crawford for the first time, it cast them as scarifying harridans, though both were still in their mid-fifties. The movie, *What Ever Happened to Baby Jane?*, revived their careers, but it also reinforced the Hollywood stereotype that, for a woman, the onset of middle age meant the beginning of a rapid transition to hagdom.

In Japan, however, two over-fifty female stars—Sayuri Yoshinaga and Shima Iwashita—still command big followings, especially among older moviegoers. What could be more natural than casting them together in a film? What indeed? Courtesy of Toei, we now have Yoshinaga and Iwashita in Masanobu Deme's *Kiri no Shigosen*. This is the first-ever on-screen pairing of these actresses, even though they have each made more than a hundred films. But unlike Crawford and Davis, they get to play women of their own age who find a second chance at love, while pursuing fulfilling careers and living amidst surroundings taken from the pages of a glossy interior decorating magazine. You've come a long way, baby.

Kiri, however, is in many ways the kind of traditional women's picture Crawford and Davis made in their heyday. Its elegantly dressed and coiffed stars suffer stylishly for love in gorgeous settings, with the object of winning audience admiration for their wounded nobility and wringing audience tears over the beautiful sadness of it all. It also shows us why Yoshinaga and Iwashita long went their separate ways: their on-screen images are like oil and water. Yoshinaga has portrayed the male ideal of Japanese femininity—an eternally virginal vision in a kimono—in film after film, while Iwashita has had some of her greatest successes in bitch-goddess roles.

In *Kiri* Yoshinaga and Iwashita, improbably, play best friends who have kept up with each other since their days as student activists. Kiyoko (Iwashita) is a reporter on a Hakodate newspaper, who lives alone with her teenage son Mitsuo (Koji Yamamoto) and is conducting a discreet affair with a colleague, the bumbling-but-sexy Takao (Koji Tamaoki). Yae (Yoshinaga) is a former TV newscaster who has become a teacher of *chigiri-e* (pictures made by pasting bits of colored paper in a design) but is suffering from a mysterious wasting illness.

When Yae comes to Hakodate to teach *chigiri-e* classes, she meets Kiyoko to talk about old times, including a secret they have kept for the past twenty years: they once shared the same lover, a radical student leader named Awaji. To escape arrest, Awaji left the country, never to be heard from again. He also left behind a child—Mitsuo. Now Mitsuo is demanding that Kiyoko tell him his father's identity and she doesn't know how to answer him. The truth might be unbearable; a lie, untenable. Soon, she faces another potential disaster: Takao takes an interest in Yae, and her lonely, fatally ill friend falls in love, for what may be the last time.

Machiko Nasu's script, based on a novel by Nobuko Takaki, tailors Yoshinaga and Iwashita's roles to their star images. Yoshinaga is quietly touching as the dying artist with a hunger for life, Iwashita, briskly convincing as the career woman trying to juggle the demands of her job and personal life. But the film's oil does not mix well with its water. Instead of the gloriously bitchy fireworks of Davis and Crawford, we get soggy protestations of undying friendship, with Iwashita overdoing the hysterics, until I was reminded of Mommie Dearest on a bad wire-hanger day.

Also, the film's concept of its student radicals struck me as bizarre. Did the women really make little self-renunciatory speeches while picking up bricks to throw at cops? Did the men really look soulfully skyward while embracing a pair of lovers, as though posing for park statuary? The "mist" in this movie evidently clouded not only the filmmakers' judgment, but their memory.

Kiriko no Fukei
de Chirico's Landscape (1998)

Directed by Tomoyuki Akaishi. Screenplay by Yoshimitsu Morita. Produced by Nikkatsu. With Tetsuta Sugimoto, Masanobu Katsumura, Go Riju, Satomi Kobayashi. (105 mins.)

Call Yoshimitsu Morita what you will (and I have called him unkind things over the years), he has long been a nurturer of talent. In 1994, he turned over one of his scripts, for the driving school comedy *Menkyo ga Nai!*, to long-time assistant director Tomoyuki Akaishi. In his second feature, *Kiriko no Fukei*, Akaishi uses another Morita script, but this time the take on the material is quite different. The film, which depicts the fumbling attempts of a former con artist with psychic powers to reunite with his ex-wife, is rich in comic potential, but Akaishi sacrifices most of it to make weighty points about the inscrutable mysteries of the human heart.

The film's use of grotesquery is reminiscent of *Kazoku Game* (Family Game), the 1983 Morita breakthrough film that skewered middle-class family values. But in *Kiriko* the characters' antics are more subdued. The aim is not to evoke belly laughs but to lighten mood and elicit sympathy. Usually, I would applaud such an aim—in trying to be audience-friendly, too many otherwise serious Japanese films indulge in ungainly displays of mugging. Akaishi, however, has sat on his actors too hard. Bits of comic business that should have provoked at least a smile fall flat, not from a want of competence so much as from an excess of restraint. Perhaps Akaishi was respecting his boss's script too much, trusting his own instincts too little.

The story derives from an epiphany by Morita that he could sense "the DNA in everything," from his pen and PC to the Inokashira-line trains. He was, in other words, experiencing the age-old insight that all is connected, all is alive. This kind of insight can lead to either transcendence or madness. In Morita's case, it led him to Hakodate in Hokkaido, where a "sadness and crispness in the atmosphere" reminded him of the landscapes of Giorgio de Chirico. Thus the setting and the unusual title for his script.

Kiriko, however, is not only the Japanese pronunciation of the Italian surrealist's name, but Kiriko (Satomi Kobayashi), the ex-wife of Muraishi (Tetsuta Sugimoto), a former fire-extinguisher salesman who was sent to prison for fraud. Having served his time, he has returned to Hakodate to find Kiriko and pick up the pieces of their lives. He has help in this search: the ability to read the minds and hearts of strangers, and to intuit whether the condo where they live is "sick" or "healthy."

Naturally, this ability makes him an eccentric in the eyes of his fellow citizens, a fate he quietly accepts. He enlists two of them—a taxi driver (Masanobu Katsumura) and real-estate agent (Go Riju) in what he tells them is a hunt for an apartment. When, detecting bad vibes, he strides grimly into a condo unit and tells the flutteringly nervous woman who lives there to return her stolen goods, they think him a nut. When the woman confesses, they begin to change their minds. After a few more proofs of his powers, they are ready to become his fast friends.

Muraishi, however, is no superman: Kiriko eludes him. Now working as a *mama-san* in a posh club and living with a new lover, she has little time for memories or regrets. The sympathetic vibrations Muraishi is seeking simply aren't there. Muraishi eventually unearths Kiriko, but discovers that her new lover is closer to him than he could have ever imagined. He also begins to confront his past, when his only talent was conning naive housewives. In dealing with these dilemmas he finds that his powers are of little use. Instead he has to call on qualities that are the true measures of his change of heart: understanding, forbearance, courage. What he is really looking for, we see, is a way to say good-bye.

As Muraishi, the long-faced, heavy-browed Tetsuta Sugimoto has the right presence and intensity, but his performance also has a heaviness that wears. More appealing is Satomi Kobayashi as Kiriko. A former child actress, Kobayashi has since matured into a delightfully insouciant comedian. Down to earth, level-headed, wise to the ways of the heart and the world, she provides a needed ballast to Sugimoto's extrasensory flights. The film could have

used less de Chirico, more Kiriko, but what we have is reason enough to climb on board.

Kishiwada Shonen Gurentai *
Boys, Be Ambitious (1996)

Directed by Kazuyuki Izutsu. **Screenplay by** Chong Ui Shin and Masayoshi Azuma. **Produced by** Shochiku and Yoshimoto Kogyo. **With:** Takashi Okamura, Hiroyuki Yabe, Nanako Okochi, Nenji Kobayashi, Ryu Haku. (106 mins.)

Japanese filmmakers would seemingly find it hard to make a local version of *Boyz N The Hood*. Aren't Japanese kids docile, nonviolent types, whose rebellious poses are little more than fashion statements? But take a glance at *Be Bop High School* or other *manga* featuring sneering schoolboy punks. The stories depict high school as a war zone, with turf battles as fierce, if not as deadly, as any in South Central L.A.

Fantasy? Perhaps not, if Kazuyuki Izutsu's *Kishiwada Shonen Gurentai* is any indication. Based on an autobiographical novel by Riichi Nakaba, a long-distance trucker turned author, the movie is a nearly plotless account of youths growing up in Kishiwada, a working-class district of Osaka. The time is the mid-seventies, the violence, nearly nonstop. The two heroes—Kotetsu (Takashi Okamura) and Chuba (Hiroyuki Yabe)—are forever either beating the bejesus out of some hapless punk or getting the bejesus beaten out of themselves. There is no rhyme or reason to this tit for tat, other than the age-old commandment of gang warfare: do unto to others before others do unto you.

Usually, films about boys gone bad have an arc—the heroes either go down in a blaze of antisocial glory or arrive at the edge of the abyss and pull back. *Kishiwada*, however, has almost no arc at all. Kotetsu and Chuba like fighting the way Ichiro likes swinging a bat and Nomo likes throwing a ball. It's their release, their form of self-expression, their *raison d'etre*. Like baseball players, they follow certain rules in their war games. Kotetsu may smash a gang boss in the face with a brick and Chubu gong a punk on the head with a steel plate cleverly concealed in his school bag, but neither would do anything truly nasty, such as bully a wimp or whack a rival. They are restrained less by a moral strictures than the gut feeling that going over the line would spoil their fun. (The price of sticking a shiv into someone, Chubu reminds Kotetsu, is a long, dull stretch in reform school.)

This utter lack of melodrama or moralizing, combined with realistic action (the actors evidently accumulated plenty of genuine bumps and bruises in the course of filming) and naturalistic dialogue (the characters' Kishiwada dialect is occasionally impenetrable) gives the film an air of authenticity. Also, the performances by the Kansai *manzai* (standup comedy) duo Ninety-Nine as Chuba and Kotetsu adroitly combine straight dramatic acting and comic caricature. Even when a rival gang ties them to a fence and pelts them with stones, Chubu, Kotetsu, and their buddies keep making wisecracks and hurling insults at their tormentors. This is not made-for-TV slapstick; the stones hurt, the anger and defiance are real. Our heroes are funny guys, to be sure, but they are also tough guys, who live by their own don't-care code.

Director Izutsu, whose previous credits include *Gaki Teikoku* (Punk Empire, 1981), a film that resembles *Kishiwada*, is after more than nostalgia. His film is essentially a cry of defiance against the stifling middle-class ethic of work hard, get ahead, follow the rules (the English title *Boys, Be Ambitious*, is ironic). His heroes are layabouts who ride the academic escalator from public junior high school to bottom-of-the-barrel commercial high school. From there they drift into the fringes of the underworld and through a series of menial part-time jobs. Chubu, who wears a semi-permanent look of ironic boredom, conducts a desultory relationship with Ryoko (Nanako Okochi), a transfer student from Tokyo, but his real interests lie elsewhere, in headbanging and daydreaming about exotic, faraway places, like the Kurobe Dam. He is, however, going exactly nowhere—and Izutsu clearly approves of him not setting foot on the fast track. The film, in fact, overglamorizes the heroes' feckless lifestyles, making the beatings with various blunt objects look as dangerous as a Three Stooges routine.

Kishiwada also shows us the origins of the rough-and-tumble Kansai style of comedy that dominates the TV airwaves. The next time I see one TV comedian slap another upside the head and let fly with a few choice insults in Kansai dialect, I'll reflect that they probably didn't pass the exams to the right schools, but are now making more money that ten of their Tokyo University–graduated contemporaries combined. There is a kind of justice in this world.

Kizuna
Tirs (1998)

Directed by Kichitaro Negishi. **Screenplay by** Teruhiko Arai. **Produced by** Toho. **With** Koji Yakusho, Yosuke Saito, Yoshihiro Kato, Ken Watanabe, Yumi Aso, Katsuo Nakamura, Hoka Kinoshita, Mansaku Ikeuchi, Kumiko Tsuchiya, Ikuko Kawai. (123 mins.)

Though advertised as a *yakuza* thriller, Kichitaro Negishi's *Kizuna* is really more a social melodrama of a familiar type, in which the gunplay is less important than the tangle of relationships that bind the hero, a *yakuza*-turned-businessman who returns to the life for a personal mission of vengeance.

The film does not untangle those relationships until the end: the mass audience loves a puzzle, the more convoluted the better, and *Kizuna* gives it to them. While the police are busy chasing clues, the hero moves inexorably toward his destiny, driven by love, friendship, and a sense of duty that is all the more noble for its selflessness. He is, like so many Japanese heroes, ultimately alone, ultimately doomed.

Though a conventional entertainment, *Kizuna* features an unconventional performance by Koji Yakusho in the central role. In forgoing the macho stereotype to create a living individual, Yakusho evokes not only admiration for the hero's stoicism, but empathy for his self-chosen predicament. While the plot is busy explaining, Yakusho does something more difficult and important: he tell us, without a word, why his character is willing risk everything for a woman who does not even know he is alive.

He plays Takaaki Ise, a former *yakuza* who is president of Ise Shoji, a company that manages clubs and restaurants in Ginza and Roppongi. He still has close ties, though, to his old gang, the Sasaki-gumi. When a longtime Sasaki confederate, Fuda (Yosuke Saito) shows up at his door, stabbed in a gang dust-up, Ise comes to his aid. The gang is fighting a turf war with the rival Kuhara-gumi and Fuda is one of the casualties. After taking his friend to a gang-affiliated clinic for treatment, Ise meets Fuda's wife, Kyoko, (Yumi Aso), a old flame whom he has been trying, without much success, to forget. With her marriage unraveling, she is eager to renew her acquaintance with Ise.

A few days later, Ise reads in the paper about the murder of a scandal-sheet writer (Yoshihiro Kato). The headline says the gun in the slaying is the same as the one that had been used to murder the president of a loan company ten years earlier. The gun had been his. He had given it to a younger friend (Hoka Kinoshita) from the orphanage where he had been raised, with orders to throw it into the ocean. Why is it turning up now? He goes to the friend, who is now a restaurant manager and cook, to find out.

Meanwhile the cops, led by the glinty-eyed Detective Sako (Ken Watanabe) and his eager subordinate, Okubo (Mansaku Ikeuchi), are hot on the trail of the killer. They discover that not only the victim's notebook is missing, but learn that he had thirteen million yen in the bank. They question his club-hostess girlfriend (Kumiko Tsuchiya), who tells them that the writer had suddenly come into money. They begin to suspect that he was killed because he had put the arm on the wrong person.

It doesn't take Sako long to dig up a suspect—Ise. But he also discovers that there seem to be two Ises, one of whom may be dead, the other a fake.

Why did the writer end up with a bullet in his heart ? Why does Ise want to return to a business he had no taste for? The answers lie deep in the past, in a house on the Inland Sea, where the hero lived with a seaman stepfather, who taught him the flute, and a younger half-sister, who later became a famous violist. Now his only living relative is this half-sister, Kaoru (Ikuko Kawai), with whom he has lost all contact and who has no idea that he is willing to sacrifice everything to save her reputation.

Director Negishi does a workmanlike job of transferring Toru Shirakawa's bestselling novel, *Umi wa Kawaiteita* (The Sea Dried Up), to the screen. Given all the twists and turns of the plot, it's not surprising that the film plays slower than the usual Hollywood cop thriller, but Negishi keeps the focus squarely on the film's central relationships. In one key scene, he stops the action entirely as Koji Yakusho's ex-gangster watches his sister perform on stage. In its mixture of loving pride and aching regret, remembrance and determination, his face tells us all we need to know about his motivation—and ultimate fate.

Koi no Tasogare *
(Breakable) (1994)

Written and directed by Takayoshi Yamaguchi. Produced by Far East Films. With Hironori Hirabayashi, Satoko Abe, Keiko Sugano, Tsubame Mita, Yumi Waei. (70 mins.)

To baby-boomers who tasted the privations of postwar Japan, participated in the upheavals of the sixties, and are now dedicated corporate warriors, the materialism, self-absorption, and slacker ethic of young Japanese makes them somehow not Japanese at all: they are a *shinjinrui* (new breed). Like any generational label, *shinjinrui* contains a grain of truth, a lump of distortion. What is this "new breed"? In *Koi no Tasogare* first-time director Takayoshi Yamaguchi supplies an answer, with a cool intelligence and critical eye. He films the lives and loves of his postadolescent characters as an insider who can not only hear the music, but dance to the beat. It's a low-key but impressive performance. I walked out of the theater feeling that there was a direct connection between what I had seen on the screen and what I was seeing on the streets. The under-twenty-five "aliens" didn't look so alien any more.

Yamaguchi achieves this *satori* through specificity. Instead of fantasy figures, he gives us a real twenty-five-year-old *manga* editor falling out of love with his real twenty-four-year-old girlfriend. As the film begins, they both sense that they approaching a cusp in their two-and-a-half-year relationship. Will they marry or go their separate ways? Minoru (Hironori Hirabayashi) is unhappy as an editor for a girls' comic and Kyoko (Satoko Abe) is restless as an unemployed office clerk. They are looking for something else, but don't quite know what.

Minoru begins to find an answer when he is assigned to a difficult-but-talented *manga* artist named Emi, whose previous editor broke down from "work-related stress," and meets her twenty-year-old sister, Yumi (Keiko Sugano). Yumi is younger, prettier, and spunkier than the mild-mannered Kyoko. Though she may serve as her older sister's assistant (all the others have quit), she refuses to take her guff. "You've got to talk tougher to her," she says to Minoru when he makes his first, ineffectual attempt to extract a manuscript from Emi. He is surprised and charmed. After driving back with Yumi from another failed attempt to meet her sister, he kisses her before they get out of the car.

Meanwhile, Kyoko is creating complications of her own. Fumiko (Tsubame Mita), an artist at the studio where Kyoko is modeling, asks if she can borrow Minoru's car for a trip to Hokkaido. Though Kyoko barely knows Fumiko, she agrees. She starts to have her doubts, however, when she notices that Fumiko has trouble operating the car's stick shift. She is distracted from her worries when a visiting cousin from Osaka invites her to travel together to Brazil. It sounds like a grand adventure and Kyoko wants Minoru to go along, but he is cool to the idea. The next day, she receives another, harder blow when she walks into her friend Nanae's studio and finds her sitting alone, nervously smoking a cigarette. "Please don't get mad," says Nanae. "Fumiko came back from Hokkaido without your car." How can she explain this disaster to Minoru? How can Minoru tell her that it's all over?

Hironori Hirabayashi, a stage actor appearing in his first film role, says in a program interview that he modeled Minoru on macho superstar Yujiro Ishihara. Minoru tries to play the man of the world, always in charge and in control. But after seeing him cringing before Emi, larking with Yumi, and lying to Kyoko, we realize that he is something of a poseur, who is wearing adult clothes that don't fit. When, at the end of the film, Emi casually remarks to Nanae that he is unreliable, we know exactly what she means.

But Emi, who never meets a deadline, is no one to talk about "reliability." Worse, though, is Fumiko, who after casually telling Kyoko and Nanae that she abandoned the car in a Hokkaido snowdrift, refuses to apologize. When she flounces away, annoyed that her friends have pestered her about a matter so beyond her control, we start to understand why older Japanese worry about the future of the country. Yamaguchi does not make a blanket indictment of a generation, but incisive observations about a few individuals. He suggests rather than explains, enlightens rather than bludgeons. Though filmed in black-and-white with unknown actors on a zero budget, *Koi no Tasogare* has the look and sound of a generation.

Kokaku Kidotai *
Ghost In the Shell (1996)

Directed by Mamoru Oshii. Screenplay by Kazunori Ito. Music by Kenji Kawaii. Produced by Kodansha, Manga Entertainment. Voices by Atsuko Tanaka, Akio Otsuka, Tetsusho Genda. (85 mins.)

"Japanimation" is not a new word—Western fans of Japanese animation began using it nearly two decades ago—but it has recently become a buzz word. One reason is Mamoru Oshii's *Kokaku Kidotai*. Released in 1996 in Japan and lasting all of four weeks in its Tokyo first run, this dark fantasy about deadly intrigue and existential angst on the Net in the year 2029 later played on eighty screens in the United States and, in August, climbed to number one on the Billboard sell video chart—a first for a Japanese film.

Though *Kokaku Kidotai* may resemble *Terminator 2* and other Hollywood dark-future films in its emphasis on high-powered weaponry and its pessimism about what the next millennium holds, it is ambitious to not only entertain, but to engage in deep thinking about the increasingly equal—and uneasy—relationship between humankind and its digital servants. Based on a Shirow Masamune *manga* known among cognoscenti for the complexity of its storyline and the density of its information-per-frame, *Kokaku Kidotai* makes few concessions to the casual viewer. The international version, which has been dubbed into at-times-jarring American English, manages to spin enough plot and subplot into its eighty-five minutes to fill a nineteenth-century Russian novel, though Tolstoy never wrote about a secret-service unit of partly human cyborgs trying to thwart a murky governmental conspiracy and nab a superhacker who possesses no physical body and claims that he (she? it?) was born in "a sea of information."

The leader of the aforementioned unit, called the Shell Squad, is Major Motoko Kusanagi, whose perfectly formed titanium body is a product of the lat-est cyborgian engineering, but whose brain is partly human, with its own "ghost," or human identity. At the beginning of the film, Kusanagi and her cohorts, including a Schwarzenegger-ish right-hand man named Batou and a mostly human newbie named Togusa, become caught up in the machinations of the Ministry of Foreign Affairs to protect a super-secret hacking program from leaks or break-ins. Called Project 2501, the program aids the Ministry in its digital snooping and political maneuverings.

While trying to get to the bottom of the Ministry's dirty dealings, which include bribes in the form of ODA to the leaders of a new third-world dictatorship, Kusanagi and the Shell Squad encounter the Puppet Master, a cybernetic supercriminal spawned by Project 2501. Capable of hacking into even the "ghosts" of his prey and substituting digitally generated memories for their human originals, the Puppet Master would seem to rule the Net. But the Puppet Master is not satisfied; it wants to live in a corporeal body and replicate its kind. For its mate, it chooses that ultimate fusion of the human and the machine—Major Kusanagi. What it proposes, however, is not just a marriage, but a melding.

Though its story may be labyrinthine, *Kokaku Kidotai* is ultimately less concerned with plot points than philosophical questions of identity in a society whose definitions of human and nonhuman have become blurred. At times the speculations of Kusanagi and other characters on these questions stop the film dead in its narrative tracks, but they also intrigue and disturb. Unlike the space fantasies that have come to characterize Japanimation in the West, *Kokaku Kidotai* has the feeling of an all-too-plausible future reality.

But director Oshii also supplies enough of the high-powered action, high-tech machinery and highly detailed backgrounds—this time of a Hong-Kong-like urban hell—to satisfy the most demanding *anime otaku* (animation geek). Despite its various complications and pretensions, it's entirely possible to enjoy *Kokaku Kidotai* with the sound turned off, as an example of state-of-the-art Japanimation in all its Baroque technoglory. Among the film's high points, however, are the dialogueless musical interludes by Kenji Kawaii that use thuddingly insistent synthesized rhythms and ethereal female voices to create, together with Oshii's images, a vision of a future both alluring and haunting, vibrantly alive and spookily empty. In that future, we won't just surf the Net, but subside into it, abandoning our archaic carbon-based humanity for a silicon-based immortality or, depending on how we view it, extinction. Whatever, a septuagenarian Bill Gates will no doubt be selling us our operating systems.

Kokkai e Iko *
Let's Go to the Diet! (1993)

Directed by Haruo Ichikura. **Screenplay by** Hiroshi Saito, Kazuaki Takano. **Produced by** Bandai Visual and Right Vision. **With** Eisaku Yoshida, Ken Ogata, Tatsuo Matsumura, Masumi Miyazaki. (110 mins.)

Political satire is not common in Japanese popular culture, but recently bribe-taking, influence-peddling Japanese politicians have become the targets of acerbically funny *homegoroshi* (killing-with-compliments) campaigns. Now director Haruo Ichikura, together with scriptwriters Hiroshi Saito and Kazuaki Takano, have also taken aim at them in *Kokkai e Iko*, which views the current scene much the way H.L. Mencken viewed the indictable buffoons of the Ohio Gang; with a mixture of amusement, contempt, and a shrewd reportorial eye. It is not just a send-up, but an expertly guided tour through the inner workings of the Nagatacho underworld (Nagatacho being Tokyo's equivalent of Capitol Hill).

The story resembles that of Frank Capra's *Mr. Smith Goes to Washington*. But instead of a small-town crusader shaking up the Senate, Naochika Kawai (Eisaku Yoshida) is a part-time deliveryman who happens upon an auto accident. Pulling a barely conscious man out of the wreckage, he rushes him to the hospital. Kawai thinks nothing of it—he has only done the right thing. But one night, he finds the man he rescued waiting for him at his apartment, together with half the reporters and camera crews in Tokyo. Shigenori Matsudaira (Ken Ogata), a Lower House Dietman and a leading member of a ruling-party's Diet faction, has come to thank his benefactor. He has also come to offer Kawai a job: personal secretary.

Like Capra's 1939 classic, *Kokkai* is about a young man's political education. But in this film the young man starts at the bottom and undergoes an immersion course in the underside of political life. He rushes from funerals to weddings to present envelopes stuffed with cash, and later watches, horrified, as a senior secretary accepts similar envelopes from constituents begging favors. The politicians and their staffs, we learn, are not the stony-faced mannequins we glimpse on TV but smart, tough, down-to-earth people who can be hard to dislike, even when they are counting their ill-gotten gains.

Matsudaira seems, at first, to be a typical member of the breed, who can play the money-for-favors game without batting an eye. Kawai is appalled by his behavior and soon decides that this is not the life for him. Here is where Ichikura takes leaves of Capra and his simplistic good-versus-evil formula.

Matsudaira, we discover, is a reformer manqué, who proposed an anti-corruption bill twenty years ago, only to have it shot down by a former prime minister (Tatsuo Matsumura) who heads his party's largest faction. Since that defeat, Matsudaira has played the Nagatacho game and bided his time. When Kawai learns about his boss's noble intentions, he is once again ready to fight the good fight.

Then Matsudaira and the former prime minister are named in a scandal involving crooked land and stock deals. Meanwhile, Kawai falls for the ex-prime-minister's secretary (Masumi Miyazaki), who is as lovely as a fashion model and worldly wise as an old pol. Guess who her uncle is? Throughout the plot's twists and turns, Ichikura keeps the the pace quick, the comic timing sharp. When Matsudaira finally decides to risk his political life for reform, *Kokkai* develops a emotional charge. The debate on Matsudaira's bill in a Diet committee, the arrest of the construction company's president, and the pitched committee-room battle between the reform and anti-reform forces may have a comic spin, but the film also makes us feel the electricity generated when stakes are high and the game up for grabs. By the end we see why politicians become so addicted to the life, despite the humiliations, defeats, and the always-present possibility of professional oblivion.

Ichikura, however, was less successful in convincing me that a twice-born reformer could split the ruling party and lead a nationwide campaign for political change. This is feel-good filmmaking in the Capra mold—and the history of Japanese politics doesn't hold out much hope for a Capraesque ending. Perhaps the popularity of *Kokkai* is an indication that the Japanese people really are getting fed up. It is more likely, however, that the recent victories over the old order are, like Matsudaira's, only temporary ones and that a long, twilight struggle lies ahead. As the movie warns us, individuals can do nothing alone. We all have to go to the Diet.

Koko Kyoshi
High School Teacher (1993)

Directed by Ken Yoshida. **Screenplay by** Shinji Nojima. **Produced by** Tokyo Broadcasting System. **With** Toshiaki Karasawa, Kyoko Toyama, Anju Suzuki, Keiko Oginome. (105 mins.)

The TBS television drama *Koko Kyoshi* produced an impact beyond that of the usual hit show, with subject matter that included rape, incest, and homosexuality. But most thrilling of all to its young viewers was its frank treatment of a love affair between a troubled high-school student, played by Yukiko

Sakurai, and her troubled PE teacher, played by Hiroyuki Sanada.

The film version of *Koko Kyoshi* has the same director (Ken Yoshida) and scriptwriter (Shinji Nojima). But instead of answering the question posed in the show's final episode—did Mayu and Kazuki commit *shinju* (love suicide)?—it covers some of the same ground as the TV drama, with new twists. It also gives us new faces: Kyoko Toyama is now Mayu and Toshiaki Karasawa, Kazuki. This change seems not to have bothered *Koko Kyoshi* fans; the movie has also become a hit. It goes farther than the series—there are still things that can't be shown even on Japanese TV—in updating a traditional theme: forbidden love and its consequences.

The film treads a dangerous line. One step in the wrong direction and it becomes a pedophilic exploitation flick. It doesn't take that step; there is not one leer in the entire movie. If anything, *Koko* goes too far in the opposite direction. The love between the two principals is impossibly pure, their story, clichéd melodrama. What begins as a psychologically insightful, visually imaginative trip down the back ways of love becomes a trudge down a familiar path. Chikamatsu did this kind of thing better.

Kazuki, a former rugby star who quit the sport after tackling his best friend in a game and turning him into a vegetable, discovers a student at his girls high school shoplifting a toothbrush at a convenience store. He sidles up to her, swipes a toothbrush himself and whispers "Let's get out of here!" The girl runs from the store in confusion, with the teacher close behind. Outside, he tells her "We're in it together now" and tosses her his prize. Relieved, she tells him her class and name: Mayu. Kazuki is in no mood for dallying, however; he still in mourning for his friend and angry at himself. Mayu also has a past. Her mother died giving birth to her and her businessman father never forgave her. Now he lives in London and, though he pays for Mayu's education, never calls or sees her. She keeps a picture of him—with the face torn out—above her bunk at the school dorm.

Yoshida reveals all this in a series of flashbacks. At this stage, however, all we know is that this gangly, beautiful teenager has a crush on her dashingly handsome teacher. One day, she follows him home. Kazuki spots her, invites her in, and tries to rape her. She resists until, ashamed, he finally relents. When Kazuki storms out of the apartment, Mayu puts on his clothes to replace her torn dress and smiles in a strangely satisfied way. Now that she has found her way into his life, she wants to stay.

The story is really Mayu's: she is the first to see her teacher's loneliness and pain (it resembles her own). She is the one who directs the course of their relationship (Kazuki is too lost to care). Finally, the bar-

riers between them fall, until they are no longer teacher and student, or even man and woman, but two lost souls who have found each, reeling in a precious space beyond society's mores.

Their paradise is soon lost. Mayu's dorm mother (Keiko Oginome) makes life hell for the girl. A spying, sadistic horror, she stands for the forces of convention that crush the spirit. Meanwhile, Kazuki must fend off the advances of his friend's sister, a clinging, scheming woman who wants him to resume his rugby career and take her into his life. Here the film takes a melodramatic turn and dissipates its emotional energy. As I watched it run through the standard changes, with the standard paraphernalia of guns, knives, car crashes, and body bags, I regretted opportunities lost.

Kyoko Toyama perfectly embodies her character's precocious wisdom and fugitive charm. Though her Mayu is no Lolita, I have the feeling that Humbert Humbert would have enjoyed her performance. I know that, as the patron saint of Japan's *roricon* (Lolita complex) brigade, he would have found her country a heaven on earth.

Kowagaru Hitobito
Uneasy Encounters (1994)

Written and directed by Makoto Wada. Produced by Suntory and Shochiku. With Hiroyuki Sanada, Mieko Harada, Mami Kumagai, Frankie Sakai, Haruhiko Saito, Ryuko Hagiwara, Kaoru Kobayashi, Hitomi Kuroki, Ken Ishiguro, Kyusaku Shimada, Eriko Watanabe. (117 mins.)

Kowagaru Hitobito is a Japanese *Twilight Zone: The Movie*—an omnibus film built around the premise that weird, wonderful and even funny things can happen at the ever-shifting border between reality and the imagination. One difference is that, instead of four directors competing to take us on the best trip to the Twilight Zone, Makoto Wada has scripted and directed segments from five stories by four different writers. Another is that, whereas the *Twilight Zone* movie and TV series tried to give a moral and intellectual gloss to their scarifying tales, *Kowagaru* is content to entertain with black humor and *kaidan* (Japanese ghost-story) atmospherics.

The first segment, about a man and a woman trapped in an elevator at night, is a modern urban folktale. The man (Hiroyuki Sanada) is a bit drunk. The woman (Mieko Harada) is tight-lipped and tense. As the camera examines her lingeringly from toe to head, we can also see that she is attractive. When the elevator stops and the lights go out, we would seem to have the beginning of a romantic comedy. But during the long wait for help to arrive, the woman starts accusing the man of plotting to stop the elevator. When the man protests his innocence, she attacks him with a switchblade knife. Finally, we find out what is bothering her; enough to say that it is in the bag that she lugged into the elevator. Wada does a good job of making the elevator a small, sweaty corner of hell. But the ending, which features Shiro Sano in yet another creep role, is a cop-out; instead of a release, we feel had.

The second segment is a story within a story within a story. A young woman (Mami Kumagai) desperately seeking work meets another young woman who offers to help her. The letter of introduction this stranger writes to a male friend seems to be the door that our heroine has been looking for, and yet, as she rides a boat downriver to meet her prospective savior, she remembers a storyteller (Frankie Sakai) from her girlhood who used to enthrall the neighborhood children with tales of the supernatural. One was about a boatman who, on his way to see a Buddhist priest, is asked by a mysterious stranger to deliver a letter. When he arrives at the temple, the priest asks to see it. Puzzled, he hands it over. As the priest reads it, an expression of horror spread across his face; the letter asks the recipient to... but perhaps you've guessed already. With her mobile features and big, staring eyes, Kumagai is ideal for the role of a woman on the edge of a terrifying revelation. Her segment, however, takes leave of her so long for its subplots that we almost forget about her.

The third segment tells the story of a novelist (Haruhiko Saito) who is returning to his native village for a visit. After stopping off to visit an old friend, he hopped back on the train without a ticket. He had intended to buy one from the conductor, but forgot, and now here he is, trying to explain all this to the station man (Ryuko Hagiwara) and failing. The station man not only mistrusts him, but resents his nice clothes, his profession, his apologies, and even his clumsy attempt at bribery.

The comedy and horror in this segment cut closer to the bone than in the others; we can imagine being in the novelist's shoes. Also, Saito and Hagiwara, both actors with distinctive presences, make a good comic pair. In the end, unfortunately, the segment's psychological realism gives way to Grand Guignol theatrics.

The fourth segment is in the classic *kaidan* mold. Based on a story by Yoshie Hirayama, it is about a drygoods dealer (Kaoru Kobayashi) and a former concubine (Hitomi Kuroki) who meet in a driving rainstorm and end up sharing a room in a countryside inn. In the course of the night, they become lovers—and the dealer learns that the concubine suffers from terrifying visions. By dawn, he is sharing them. The sensuousness and period beauty of this

segment serve to deepen its horror. An evil fate seems to be pursuing the heroine; we can feel it breathing down her lovely kimonoed neck.

The last segment is another comedy, but this time the action is slapstick, the ending a dumb joke. A writer (Ken Ishiguro) and photographer (Kyusaku Shimada) are on assignment for a terror of an editor. Stranded on an island in a typhoon, they are desperate to make their deadline. Their only hope, they learn from two local farmers, is a rickety plane piloted by a daredevil named by Gorohachi. But when the plane finally arrives, the pilot is Gorohachi's wife (Eriko Watanabe), with a baby strapped on her back. Though a good-natured sort, she flies the plane as though it were a grocery cart. Her nonchalance, even as the plane plunges over a cliff, distresses the writer, terrifies the photographer. Enough to say that the men meet quite different fates. One could have come from the brain of Gary (*The Far Side*) Larson—on a bad day.

Kurenai no Buta
Porco Rosso (1992)

Written and directed by Hayao Miyazaki. **Produced by** Tokuma Shoten, Japan Airlines, Nippon Television Network, and Studio Ghibli. **Voices by** Shuichiro Moriyama, Tokiko Kato. (93 mins.)

Japanimation has legions of devoted fans, of all ages. Not only the kids, but Dad, stretched out on the *tatami* with his Kirin beer, watch cartoon shows on the tube. So it should come as no surprise that animation director Hayao Miyazaki should make a film aimed at, as he wrote in a joking memo to his animators, "tired middle-aged men." *Kurenai no Buta* (Porco Rosso) tells the story of Porco Rosso, an Italian World War I flying ace of the porcine persuasion. Though approaching middle age, Porco is hardly tired; instead, he flies his snazzy red hydroplane, scouring the skies for air pirates. The year is 1920 and the airspace over the Adriatic Sea is infested with gangs of cashiered fliers who prey on cruise-ship passengers. Porco make his living by saving the pirates' victims and collecting rewards.

Miyazaki's is a Mickey Mouse world, in which reality takes a vacation, but though the hero may be a pig, he is no cousin to Porky. He blows cigarette smoke with a Continental insouciance, carries a torch for a thrice-widowed *chanteuse*, and lives alone on a desert island in disillusioned retreat from the world. Starting life as a dashing young man in love with a pretty girl (the *chanteuse*), he later decides to grow a snout and triangular ears in contrition for the deaths of his wartime comerades. This, clearly, is no ordinary animation hero, and Miyazaki is no ordinary animation director. Like another master, Walt Disney, Miyazaki is something of a genius and something of a flake—and it is sometimes hard to tell which is which. Who decided to attempt the kind of adult, personal theme until now reserved for live-action films?

Commercially, this decision was a stroke of genius: *Kurenai* has become Miyazaki's biggest-ever hit. Artistically, however, I have to wonder. Stripped of its wonderfully realized animation, *Kurenai* is both mock-Hemingway, with Porco as a macho Papa figure, and thirties B-picture, with a story that could have been lifted from an *Action Stories* comic.

It revolves around a rivalry between Porco and an Errol Flynn-ish American pilot who flies with the pirates. Defeated by his rival in a dogfight, Porco takes his battered plane to Milan. When he arrives at the repair hangar, he is greeted by the wizened proprietor and his saucy young granddaughter, Fio, who is an aircraft designer. We are not surprised when Porco, a male chauvinist pig, at first refuses her services, or when he later succumbs to her charms. We are surprised, however, when Grandpa hires local women to rebuild the plane (all the men are away, working in distant cities) and Porco sits contentedly watching them and absentmindedly rocking a cradle. Here we see Miyazaki's talent for humanizing his cartoon heroes.

Then the plane takes off, with Fio aboard, and we head back to comic-book country. After the pirates jump them at the island hideaway, Fio spunkily dresses down their leader (How dare he destroy the plane they worked so hard to build!) and challenges the American to fight Porco in an aerial duel. The showdown itself, with its carnival atmosphere and its two "prizes"—Fio for the American, a bag full of loot for Porco—is low comedy straight from TV-cartoon land.

But the film also tells the story of Porco's mysterious past (Why did he become a pig?), his ambiguous relationship with the *chanteuse* (Can she love him as a pig as much as she did as a man?), and his ongoing argument with the human race (Will he reject it or rejoin it?). This story is more atmospherics than substance; we begin to long for Porco to get a grip and take to the air again.

The flight sequences are the film's glory. An aviation buff, Miyazaki has a true love and understanding of old airplanes and has brought them to exhilarating life on the screen. Just as his hero risks everything in the air, he and his Studio Ghibli animators have taken the art of animation to new heights. They achieve a beauty beyond mere realism; this is the way flying ought to look and feel. Miyazaki's amazing flying machines are an excellent reason to see this animated fantasy, with all its wildly swinging moods. In *Kurenai no Buta* there is no angst above the clouds.

Kuro no Tenshi, Vol. 1
Black Angel, Vol. 1 (1998)

Written and directed by Takashi Ishii. Produced by Shochiku. With Reona Hazuki, Reiko Takashima, Jimpachi Nezu, Yoshiyuki Yamaguchi, Miyuki Ono. (106 mins.)

Takashi Ishii's *Kuro no Tenshi, Vol. 1* is frank escapism for unreconstructed action fans, with one of the genre's hoariest themes: revenge for the murder of a father. Taking a hint from *Nikita, Natural Born Killers*, and other films whose murderous protagonists are women, Ishii makes his vengeful child a daughter, not a son—the "Black Angel" of the title—and turns her into a relentless killing machine.

The first of a series bound for the video shelves, *Kuro no Tenshi* bears Ishii's visually extravagant, emotion-charged stamp in every scene. He also has Reona Hazuki to project the right combination of steamy sexuality and cold menace. *Kuro no Tenshi* is trash with attitude that thankfully aspires to be nothing more. Slap it into the machine, pour a finger of Jack Daniels, and turn the left brain on low.

The story begins, appropriately, with the assassination of the heroine's father—a gruff, gray-haired *oyabun* (gang boss)—in his own home by a pair of hitwomen. Six-year-old Ikko is asleep when the shooting starts, but witnesses enough of the bloodshed, including the horrifying killing of her mother, to be permanently traumatized. Saved by Mayo (Reiko Takashima), a fearless hitwoman belonging to her father's gang, she is spirited to the United States, where she spends the next fourteen years.

Cut to the present. The gang boss is now Nogi (Jimpachi Nezu), a former subordinate of Ikko's father. Smart, dapper, and utterly ruthless, Nogi ordered the hit that brought him to power—and Ikko knows it. Getting off the plane at Narita with a gay Japanese-American companion named Jil (Yoshiyuki Yamaguchi) she has only one thought—kill Nogi and anyone who gets in her way. Nogi, however, is a hard target. In addition to the phalanx of underlings who shadow his every move, he has an ally in Ikko's sister-in-law (Miyuki Ono), who has, to Ikko's disgust, become his lover. Ikko soon discovers another disturbing change: Mayo, the woman she once admired so fervently, has become Nogi's drug-addled sex slave.

Enraged, Ikko blasts her way into Nogi's headquarters—a spare, spacious warren that looks like a modern art museum with most of its collection on loan. Naturally, she fails in her mission and is captured, but rather than do the intelligent thing—kill her as he would a rabid beast—Nogi decides to toy with her. Bad mistake, of course. Soon, Ikko is on the loose and plotting her next move, Meanwhile, Mayo, her nearly moribund will stirred by Ikko's return, begins to free herself from her addiction and realize where her true loyalty lies.

When these two women warriors finally join forces, even a *yakuza* army could not stop them. Nogi is a few divisions short. But though the ending is never in doubt, Ishii provides plenty of flagrant sex and flamboyant violence to distract us on the way. In his equal-opportunity world, big, strapping *yakuza* are easy marks for not only the bullets, but the flying kicks and slamming punches of Ikko and Jil. Though the lithesome Hazuki is no Demi Moore, Ishii stages her fight scenes with Chinese operatic energy and flair. Also, as the gay street kid Jil, Yoshiyuki Yamaguchi displays an explosive fighting style inspired more by breakdance moves than karate *kata*, but looks devastating nonetheless.

Ishii supplies the right noirish atmospherics for the film's action, much of which takes place at night in smoky dives or driving rain. He is also adept at using the off-kilter camera angle or traveling crane shot to heighten tension and deepen suspense, though he cannot completely disguise the familiarity of the proceedings. Given his affinity with the material, Ishii will no doubt make other volumes in the *Kuro no Tenshi* series. I hope, though, that next time he sends his Black Angel on a less clichéd assignment.

Kusa no Ue no Shigoto
Work on the Grass (1993)

Written and directed by Tetsuo Shinohara. Produced by Pia Corporation and Pictures Up. With Naoki Goto, Hikari Ota. (42 mins.)

Oinaru Gakusei
I Find Myself Getting Smaller and Smaller (1993)

Written and directed by Takashi Koike. Produced by Pia Corporation and Pony Canyon. With Ryo Iwamatsu, Eriko Aso, Takashi Koike, Yasunobu Nakagawa. (50 mins.)

The films sharing this review originally shared the same double-bill as films made with Pia Scholarship grants, but differ radically from one another in tone, approach, and quality.

The jobs that most people really do seldom appear on the screen. Blasting bad guys, yes, bagging groceries, no. But, as Tetsuo Shinohara's *Kusa no Ue no Shigoto* demonstrates, hard, dirty work can also make

for compelling, even poetic, cinema. A self-described "lawnmower man" and a fledgling writer spend a day cutting tall grass in a rolling field in the middle of nowhere. We never find out why they are there—brush-fire prevention perhaps?—but the Sisyphean nature of their task both appalls and fascinates. How can they cut all that greenery with what look to be whirring metal detectors? But cut it they do.

The lawnmower man (Naoki Goto), a rugged, athletic type, sweeps his blade through the grass with a casual assurance, while the writer (Hikari Ota) looks dubious—he has never done this kind of work before. This incompetence irritates the lawnmower man; why did the agency inflict this loser on him?

The film, however, is about, not just another dull day in the life, but the two men's relationships with their work, each other, and themselves. Shinohara tells their story with the precision of one who has been there himself and wants to get it right. He puts us behind the handles of the mower and shows us the swishing of the grass, lets us hear the roar of the motor. All that's missing in his point-of-view close-ups is the sweat. He also cuts quickly to the central issues of his characters' lives. By the end we know where they've been, who they are, and where they are going. Nearly every scene, every line of dialogue tells.

Taking cigarette breaks, the men begin to talk and break down the barriers that divide them. The lawnmower man is a physical, sensual, affective being for whom the good life is being out in the fresh air and using his muscles, but he suffers from loneliness. The writer may be a terrible mower, but he is more emotionally self-contained and intellectually self-assured. Though the lawnmower man does most of the talking, he ends by deferring to the writer, who is older, better educated, and more at home in the big world beyond their grassy field.

Being so far from civilization, they are freer to shake off its restraints: the emptiness, the exertion, the soughing of the grass are an unspoken invitation to bare all. One scene, in which they lie together on the freshly cut grass, has an unmistakable erotic charge. But rather than fall into each other's arms, they describe early childhood encounters with sex. Rather than become cinematic voyeurs, we experience their heady intermingling of nature, memory, and eros as though it were our own. A job well done.

Oinaru Gakusei, the second film on the bill with *Kusa*, is set in a future world in which human beings are dominated by unseen aliens and a mysterious "Earth Patrol." It wants to be an *Alphaville* for the nineties, but instead of Godard's dark vision, it presents a dippy fantasy that could have been filmed by mildly demented undergraduates.

While on his way to a funeral, a vague young man named Komori (Takashi Koike) encounters the exuberant, rotund Ueda (Ryo Iwamatsu). Komori, it turns out, is a hopelessly fuddled illiterate, while Ueda in not only Komori's long-lost kindergarten classmate, but a teacher of sorts who is engaged in a one-man protest against the building of a new spaceport. There is something strange about Ueda and his world, however. His classroom is a tumble-down shack and the spaceport's building site is a weed-grown field surrounded by a few strands of barbed wire.

Koike gets a few laughs from his low-rent, high-tech future world. While driving Komori in his junker, Ueda takes his hands off the wheel and announces that he has turned on the "automatic drive"—a gag so dumb that it's funny. But the whimsy wears thin when we realize that there isn't going to be a story, just a lot of fey mucking about with heavyweight themes. Koike is trying to say something about the limits of intellect, the need for connection, and the absurdity of the modern world's faith in technology. He has also made a movie that is unapologetically silly, if hard to dislike. In how many other SF thrillers do the characters take a break from a rock-throwing protest against invisible aliens to fight a few bouts of *sumo*?

Kyohansha
Partners In Crime (1999)

Written and directed by Kazuhiro Kiuchi. Cinematography by Seizo Sengen. Produced by Toei, Toei Video, and Tohoku Shinsha. With Naoto Takenaka, Kyoko Koizumi, Yuya Uchida, Masataka Naruse. (102 mins.)

Kazuhiro Kiuchi's *Kyohansha* has "international" written all over it. The look and mood are reminiscent of nineties Hollywood thrillers at their most baroque, from David Fincher to John Woo. The hero, a Japanese-Brazilian gangster, sprinkles his fluent, if hardly polite, Japanese with Portuguese. The villain, a blond-haired hitman of indefinite origin, prefaces his equally flawless Japanese with phrases in tough-guy English. Also, both characters sport sexy customized weaponry that looks lifted from Arnold Schwarzenegger's personal collection.

I doubt, though, that *Kyohansha's* producers have international ambitions. The film is pitched squarely at a domestic audience, who will presumably not care (or notice) that its "foreign" characters are about as authentic as Japan's version of beef curry. The story, as one might expect from Kiuchi—the creator of the popular *Be Bop High School* comic—is pure *manga*, in which the realities of international crime in Japan count for far less than macho romanticism, cool stylistics, and violent action.

The film plays briskly and presents striking images, including shots of Kyoko Koizumi's bare feet as she silently stalks the hitman that carry a surprising erotic charge. (Are Kiuchi and cameraman Seizo Sengen foot fetishists, or is it just me?) But a John Woo Kiuchi isn't—the flamboyant inventiveness that the material demands isn't quite there. Instead, he opts for standard thriller situations, concluding with a midnight showdown in a warehouse, that make the cartoonish characters look overblown, if not absurd. Picture Wesley Snipes' futuristic superpsycho from *Demolition Man* showing up in *L.A. Confidential* and you begin to get the idea.

Kyohansha is a sequel to Kiuchi's 1991 *Carlos*, a Toei film, unseen by me, about the title character's one-man battle with a *yakuza* gang, in which he wreaks bloody havoc and winds up with an eight-year prison term. As *Kyohansha* begins, Carlos (Naoto Takenaka) is back on the streets, a man without a country. Brazil has rejected him for deportation. Adrift, Carlos decides to finish his beef with the Yamashiro-kai, which has not only recovered, but become obscenely wealthy and powerful.

Before plunging a knife into the first available Yamashiro-kai belly, he stops at a *soba* restaurant for his first post-prison noodles. Just as he is about to dig in, however, a wooden sandal plops into his bowl. Its wearer—a waitress named Satomi (Koizumi)—is being beaten by her husband. Carlos takes the sandal, slams it down on the husband's forearm and, with screams of pain echoing in his ears, casually makes his exit. Satomi is close behind, determined to escape her marriage and learn more about her savior.

Now a fellow outcast, she joins Carlos in his quest. Driving in her car to a gang office, they encounter Kaji (Masataka Naruse), a sub-boss who became a drug addict after Carlos drilled a slug into his forehead. Carrying a cash-filled suitcase and dripping with blood from the bullets of his former comrades, Kaji offers his prize to Carlos and asks him to take care of his two underlings. Carlos reluctantly agrees and Kaji is snuffed by his pursuers. After a gun battle, they retrieve the money, but Carlos isn't going to give it up so easily. He declares war on the entire gang, unless they give it back. Rather than risk another fight, the Yamashiro-kai boss hires a pair of hitmen: the fearsome brothers Elder (Yuya Uchida) and Younger Gilyak (Mikio Osawa). They plan to spring a trap on Carlos and his allies—with the suitcase as bait. Naturally, a dustup ensues. It is bloody but inconclusive and the survivors regroup for a final clash. By this time, the rivalry between Carlos and Elder Gilyak has become personal, with more than money or professional pride at stake.

Naoto Takenaka has become known for playing comic grotesques, from the Latin-music-mad dancer of *Shall We Dance?* to the self-intoxicated song show contestant in *Nodo Jiman.* He has also been effective in a wider range of roles, from the wistfully lovelorn fireman in *119*, to the sex-besotted kidnapper in *Kanzen Naru Shiiku.* He may be an acquired taste—his theatrical self-regard can grate—but he is also a gifted chameleon who brings a dark rage and explosive force to his portrait of Carlos. I would have believed in him more, though, if he had dropped the bad Portuguese and called himself Suzuki.

Kyoko

(1996)

Written and directed by Ryu Murakami. Produced by Della Corporation and Concord/New Horizon Corporation. With Saki Takaoka, Carlos Osorio, Scott Whitehurst. (100 mins.)

Foreign directors have long been fascinated with America for its extremes of personal freedom and random violence, cultural diversity and racial enmity. Some, such as Aki Kaurismaki in *Leningrad Cowboys Go America* and Percy Adlon in *Bagdad Café*, have filmed those extremes in strikingly original ways. How many American directors could have created Marianne Sagebrecht's *hausfrau* in *Bagdad Café*, with her amusing blend of lumpishness and grit, bourgeois bustle and freespirited adventurousness? How many would have even suspected her existence?

Japanese directors have also tried to put their own Americas on the screen, but the results, from Hiroaki Yoshida's *Iron Maze* to Masato Harada's *Painted Desert*, have been mostly lamentable. Instead of entering into the heart of their American settings and characters and interpreting them through their own sensibilities, they have borrowed heavily from Hollywood and the media to produce mishmashes that resemble American reality about as much as a Kichijoji coffeeshop with beef curry on the menu and a Wurlitzer jukebox in the corner.

Produced in association with Roger Corman, Ryu Murakami's *Kyoko* follows in this less-than-distinguished tradition. The film, which tells of a Japanese woman's sentimental journey to America to search for the Cuban-American soldier who taught her to dance the cha-cha-cha as a child, tries opportunistically hard to be hip and PC, but succeeds only in demonstrating that director and scriptwriter Murakami just doesn't get it. What he doesn't get, first of all, is the language. Although Murakami has the sole screenwriting credit, I could detect a ghostly hand transforming his script into

the kind of English conversation-class dialogue penned by foreigners who have been in country too long. The effect is to give the film's urban, ethnic characters linguistic lobotomies. As Kyoko, Saki Takaoka drops a few articles to add authenticity, but her line readings suggest less a non-native speaker struggling with an unfamiliar tongue than dialogue coaching aimed at conveying the impression of fluency to a Japanese audience.

The road-movie story also has it peculiarities. The trusting Kyoko parts with a large chunk of her precious savings for a limo ride from Manhattan to the AIDs hospice in Queens where her old dance teacher, Jose (Carlos Osorio), lies dying. The African-American limo driver (Scott Whitehurst) is a rip-off artist, but Kyoko doesn't think the worse of him when she discovers his cupidity, as she might of a Tokyo cabbie. Ralph, after all, is just being an American. (Luckily, he is also a prince, who goes out his way to help this Japanese damsel in distress.)

We encounter this attitude again when Kyoko finds her teacher—who does not remember her—bundles him into a rental van and drives him to Miami for one last visit home. (One wonders whether a plane flight might not be easier on the mortally ill man, but a road movie must have a road.) At a rest stop, an African-American boy tries to steal the teacher's AIDs drugs for their narcotics. When Kyoko catches him, she scolds him as though he were a kid caught with his hand in the cookie jar and, when he complains of being stranded, invites him, with a sigh of elder sisterly irritation, to ride in the van. The implicit assumption—that we Japanese shouldn't expect these people to have our morality—is ostensibly large-hearted, actually patronizing. Also, her behavior is, given the reality of crime in America, dangerously naive.

But worse than the lame dialogue, the stereotyped, condescending view of the American characters, and the tired tearjerking storyline, is the big, yawning hole at the film's heart. When Kyoko struts her stuff—either alone in a Cuban-American bar or with a group of rich, elderly white folks she encounters on the road—she has the moves, but not the fire. Her cha-cha-cha is a Cuban version of a Japanese festival dance. Jose should have told her (and someone should have told Murakami) to shake it, not fake it.

Kyoso no Tanjo

Many Happy Returns (1998)

Directed by Toshihiro Temma. Screenplay by Yuji Kato and Hideko Tanaka. Produced by Right Vision and Pony Canyon. With Kiyoto Hagiwara, Koji Tamaoki, Takeshi Kitano, Ittoku Kishibe. (94 mins.)

For many Japanese, religion seems to be little more than a Shinto wedding ceremony, an annual New Year's temple visit, and, eventually, a Buddhist funeral. And yet Japan is also the land of the New Religions, where dozens of faiths have sprouted and flourished in the postwar years.

Kyoso no Tanjo explores the phenomenon of the Newly Religious with the expected black humor and an unexpected sympathy. First-time director Toshihiro Temma and mentor Takeshi Kitano, who stars in the film and wrote the book on which it is based, have a special fellow-feeling for the con artists of God. For them religion is an inescapably human enterprise; faith may move mountains, but its keepers walk the same earth as the rest of us—and some have very clayey feet indeed. But even their spiritual snake-oil peddlers want to believe, in at least one corner of their minds, that they are doing God's work.

The hero is a young drifter named Kazuo (Kiyoto Hagiwara), whom we first meet on a ferry, casting a critical eye at a group of New Religionists. "There's something phony about them," he remarks to a pony-tailed fellow passenger (Koji Tamaoki). The ponytail, however, happens to be one of "them." He says, matter-of-factly, that they have joined because God has shown them the Way. "He's nearer than you might think," he adds. After disembarking, Kazuo encounters the group again, proselytizing in a city park. A gangsterish man (Takeshi Kitano) introduces an elderly party as their *kyoso* (sect founder) and announces that, among other talents, he can cure chronic illness. As if on cue, an old woman in a wheel chair is pushed to the front of the crowd. "Can you cure me?" she asks. The *kyoso* makes a few passes and bolts of blue light leap from his palms. The old woman stands and walks. A miracle! Or is it?

Later, Kazuo happens to board a train with the New Religionists and sees the old woman running to catch it before the doors close. Something is fishy, but Kazuo is curious. He asks the gangsterish man, whose name is Shiba, if he can join them. Despite the objections of a slithery-looking fellow named Kure (Ittoku Kishibe), Shiba agrees—and the group gains a new member.

The story centers on Kazuo's transformation from a kid who joins the sect as though it were a traveling carnival to a youth with a fervent belief in his religious vocation. Throughout his spiritual journey, two forces are contending for his soul. The ponytail, whose name is Komamura, knows that Shiba picked the *kyoso* out of a gutter and keeps him supplied with *sake*, but he still believes in its creed. God is within us. We shouldn't abandon our search for Him, even though some of His earthly messengers may not be angels. Kure, other hand, sees this

New Religion strictly as a vehicle for gaining power, wealth, and fame. "Just listen to us," he tells Kazuo, "We'll take care of you." Right, kid. Shiba stands somewhere in between. Though the group's chief con artist and enforcer, he tells Kazuo with a straight face that the old man has worked real cures and their faith is not a total crock.

Kazuo skillfully segues from tag-along to committed member to *kyoso*. He is an obedient type, who keeps doing the scutwork even after he is installed as the group's new figurehead. But he also believes in religion's higher ideals. After undergoing austerities in the mountains, he returns a transformed man, who really can heal the sick and become the sect's spiritual leader in deed as well as name. But will he clean out the crooks—or accommodate them?

Director Temma, who served as Kitano's assistant director in his first four films, tells this story with a smart comic spin, but never quite explains why Kazuo is a charismatic figure able to attract worshipers by the hundreds and thousands. Adept at presenting New Religion's underside, he fails to grasp its power. Perhaps he is too much his former boss's man: *Kyoso no Tanjo* is very much a Kitano movie, in which the devil gets all the best lines.

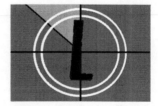

Level

(1994)

Directed by Tetsuya Matsushima. Screenplay by Tetsuya Matsushima and Takuro Fukuda. Produced by Image Factory IM. With Toru Nakamura, Bengal, Shiori Sakura, Ryo Ishibashi. (84 mins.)

Japanese hardboiled thrillers flourish mainly on video, as a look at all the *yakuza* snarling down from the racks attests. But some glint with an insider's insight into the underworld life and glow with filmmaking energy. One of these is Tetsuya Matsushima's *Level*. A vehicle for action-star Toru Nakamura, *Level* explores its world of Tokyo *pachisuro* parlors with the macho romanticism and spare, gritty realism found in the novels of Elmore Leonard.

Level's theme is classic Leonard—a man living on the fringes of the underworld who becomes caught in its grip. Tomita (Nakamura) is a salaried drone working for a company that designs computer games. When his estranged father dies, he inherits his *pachisuro* parlor and the problem of what to do with it. Though Tomita has never even tried the game (a made-in-Japan marriage of the pinball-like game of *pachinko* with a slot machine)—he finds himself attracted to the business, especially when the parlor manager (Bengal) shows him how to rig machines so the tokens pour out. Also, he is a softhearted type who cannot leave the parlor's loyal employees in the lurch. He decides to change careers.

It doesn't take Tomita long to realize that more customers will come if he gives them slightly better odds, and that his employees will work harder if he treats them as partners, not factotums. (He even gives them inspirational morning pep talks.) Soon, the money is rolling in and everyone is happy. Everyone, that is, except Tomita's sloe-eyed girlfriend (Shiori Sakura), who is worried about his change from easygoing Mr. Average to money-obsessed boss; the local *pachisuro*-parlor owners, to whom Tomita's success is a threat; and the local *yakuza*, who want their share of the take. Tomita, however, is a loner who insists on doing things his own way. One day he finds himself in a parking lot, with a garbage bag over his head and pointed shoes thudding into his kidneys. Where does he go from here?

Matsushima, a first-time director with a background in theater, TV, and music videos, films the ensuing struggle between Tomita and the local gangsters with a cool understatement, while keeping genre clichés to minimum. Like Leonard, he is an accomplished storyteller who knows how to plot, pace, and ratchet up the tension, but his real interest is character. *Level* is not just a male fantasy of a lone hero taking on the *yakuza* bad guys, but the story of a man wrestling with his dark side and not always winning. "Desire is a dangerous thing," Tomita says at one point. By the end of the film, we know what he means.

As Tomita, Nakamura is the latest pretender to the crown of the late Yujiro Ishihara—the legendary Tough Guy of film and TV. He has Ishihara's long legs, good looks, and aura of explosiveness lurking beneath the boyish surface. But whereas Ishihara tended toward traditional macho emotionalism, Nakamura is a chilled-out product of the nineties. A tough guy, yes; a warm, wet, sentimental guy, no. He charges up the film with his scorn and rage.

In the hardboiled genre the female roles are usually filler—and *Level* is no exception. As the girlfriend, Shiori Sakuri is given little to do but pull long faces and fret. The best of several strong supporting performances is that of Ryo Ishibashi, an actor/musician whose credits include Sean Penn's *Crossing Guard*. In a cameo as a *yakuza* boss, he is a scary presence who transforms a cane into a weapon of terrifying power. In many Japanese movies, the mob is little more than a pose or a joke. In *Level* it is a malevolent reality—and another reason for firing up the VCR to watch this most promising debut.

Lie, Lie, Lie
[1997]

Directed by Shun Nakahara. **Screenplay by** Aki Itami and Satoru Sawatari. **Produced by** Toei, Pony Canyon, and Hakuhodo. **With** Etsushi Toyokawa, Koichi Sato, Honami Suzuki, Miwako Kawai. (123 mins.)

Lie, Lie, Lie, a caper comedy based on a novel by Ramo Nakajima, seemingly has a lot going for it. The director is Shun Nakahara, whose credits include the acclaimed *Sakura no Sono* (The Cherry Orchard, 1991) and *Juninin no Yasashi Nihonjin* (The Gentle Twelve, 1991), while the cast is headed by Etsushi Toyokawa, Koichi Sato and Honami Suzuki, big stars all. The object was to update *The Sting*—i.e., produce a cleverly written, slickly produced entertainment about a team of cute scam artists.

But while being clever and slick enough, *Lie, Lie, Lie* is less entertaining than exhausting, like listening as a motormouth spritz a shaggy-dog story into one's ear on a flight from Tokyo to Detroit. One longs to wield a sharp pair of editing shears—on the would-be comedian's script, if not his tongue. The actors deliver their reams of dialogue well enough—Nakahara rehearsed them intensively prior to filming. Also, talkiness itself is hardly a sin, as Preston Sturges so abundantly proved, but in *Lie, Lie, Lie* the verbiage proliferates until it brings the film to a dead halt, like the weeds that block Humphrey Bogart's riverboat in *The African Queen*.

The problem lies in not only the film's verbiage, but its construction. *Lie, Lie, Lie* gets off to a slow start, loses momentum during a long, silly flashback sequence, and does not introduce the third member of its scam artist trio—a jaded, sodden, but sexy editor played by Honami Suzuki—until nearly an hour into the film. As Sturges demonstrated so eloquently in *The Lady Eve*, a caper comedy requires, first and foremost, speed and pace; in *Lie, Lie, Lie* the quips fly, but the story drags.

It begins with a reclusive phototypesetter named Hatano (Koichi Sato) who is scratching out a living in a funky bayside studio. One day his routine is rudely interrupted by a visit from Aikawa (Etsushi Toyokawa), a high school classmate he has not seen in more than a decade. In the meantime, Aikawa has become the managing director of a trading company that specializes in fresh foodstuffs (his present for his old buddy is a baggy full of shellfish). But when this seemingly successful young businessman takes up what looks to be permanent residence on the studio couch, Hatano begins to have his doubts.

Aikawa is quick to seize the main chance, however. Over a cup of coffee with a printer acquaintance of Hatano's, he presents himself as a seasoned hand in the book business and sells himself and Hatano as a production and editorial team who can help the printer win a competitive bid for a book project. The printer bites and the two friends are on their way. They are, of course, running a scam, hardly the first for Aikawa. Prior his reunion with Hatano, he had made a big score in Hokkaido by bamboozling a wild rich girl (Miwako Kawai) who got her kicks shooting guns in her postmodern mansion.

One morning Aikawa discovers a long printout on the studio floor—a novel that Hatano spun off under the influence of sleeping pills. He has a brainstorm: sell Hatano's semi-conscious ramblings as writings from the spirit world. An editor (Honami Suzuki) at a large publishing house likes their idea, but quickly sees through their ruse. She calls them on it—and asks to join the gang. The boys agree and the scammers, now a threesome, prepare to launch the biggest bestseller of the year on an unsuspecting world.

As Aikawa, Etsushi Toyokawa is properly slippery, but a bit too slimy to be likeable—a Paul Newman he isn't. As Hatano, Koichi Sato is appropriately woolly and winsome, but reeks too strongly of sincerity to be a real grifter. As the editor, Honami Suzuki does little but be Honami Suzuki—the obscure object of desire in all those trendy dramas of the departed bubble days. Unimpressive as a comic drunk, she is at her best as the goddess in designer clothes who promises, but never delivers. One could build, as Luis Buñuel did, a comic masterpiece around that maddening elusiveness (which her frustrated male admirers might call the ultimate scam). Unfortunately, *Lie, Lie, Lie* isn't it.

Love & Pop *
(1998)

Directed by Hideaki Anno. Screenplay by Akio Satsukawa. Produced by Love & Pop Production Committee. With Asumi Miwa, Yukie Nakama, Kirari. (110 mins.)

Hideaki Anno, who scored in 1997 with the *Evangelion* animated TV series and films, has made his first live-action film, *Love & Pop*. Once again Anno makes a lonely, conflicted adolescent his cen-

tral character, and fills the screen with a blizzard of images, text, and dialogue. The influence of the *anime* on the film is hardly an accident: Anno began work on his feature about high school girls tempted into the risky business of *enjo kosai* ("paid dates") while he was still drawing his visions of a future apocalypse, and admits in a program interview that *Love & Pop* is an *Evangelion* carryover.

But Anno also has that rare commody—a visual and storytelling imagination totally indifferent to received ideas about what can and can't be done with film. Working from a novel by Ryu Murakami, he first thought of filming *Love & Pop* as a pseudodocumentary, but changed his mind after seeing *Focus*, Satoshi Isaka's superb essay on media excess filmed entirely from the point of view of a documentary crew's cameraman. Instead, he recast *Love & Pop* in the form of a day-in-the-life narrative about a gang of four sweet sixteens in minis who roam Shibuya extracting ¥10,000 notes from the wallets of strange men for services that run the erotic gamut, but rarely enter the zone of conventional sex.

One of the men invites the girls for a session of *karaoke*, but after the obligatory crooning, he produces a large case, from which he carefully extracts ripe grapes, one for each of the girls. He has them bite the grapes, just enough to break the skin, then stores and labels them as though they were biological specimens. The other men who pony up for the pleasure of their company, including a slimily obsequious gourmet and a loudly censorious salaryman, are just as warped and pathetic, if not as original.

One girl, Hiromi (Asumi Miwa), has a special reason for being on the game: she wants to buy a beautiful topaz ring to hide what she is convinced are ill-shaped hands. She promises the clerk she will bring the money for the ring before the store closes for the day and, with the help of three friends, goes out to earn it the quickest, easiest possible way: *enjo kosai*. A girl from a typical (if comically clueless) middle-class family who goes to a typical (if comically chaotic) girls high school, Hiromi hardly fits the usual sex-worker profile—and would be horrified if anyone thought she did. But she plays along with her more experienced friends' hustles, then ventures out alone to earn her ring with a nonchalance that borders on arrogance. As might be expected, she meets customers who teach her harsh lessons about the degradations and dangers inherent in her new profession.

Though *enjo kosai* has become the victim of media overkill, Hiromi is not a media-generated composite. Newcomer Asumi Miwa brings a winning naturalness to the role—she seems almost blithely unaware of the camera—while adeptly negotiating the widening gap between Hiromi's on-top-of-it attitude and her out-of-control emotions, including her distress at losing not only her self-respect but her very sense of self.

Anno's treatment of his story may provoke, but it is his technique that dazzles. Using a small digital camcorder, he explores every corner of Hiromi's world, from every conceivable angle, in a giddy procession of quick cuts. We spend much of the movie looking under tables at wiggling feet, from inside microwave ovens at peering faces and from the floor at the insides of passing miniskirts. Anno's stylistic intent is less titillation—voyeurs will find the movie a crashing bore—than ironic comment on his characters and their fragmented, materialistic, chimerical transactions. In using techniques that may derive from *cinema verité*, but subvert its documentary pretensions by their blatant eccentricity, he risks producing the cinematic equivalent of a joke greeting card. Rather than trivialize his subject and trash his story, however, Anno's methods serve as an witty running commentary on a world in which nothing lasts, nothing is what it seems, and the only value is the gratification of appetites that have grown monstrous and absurd. For all its funhouse distortions, it is world that we recognize, and more than we may want to admit, symbolizes what we are in danger of becoming.

Love Letter *
(1995)

Written and directed by Shunji Iwai. Cinematography by Noboru Shinoda. Produced by Fuji TV. With Miho Nakayama, Etsushi Toyokawa. (117 mins.)

Human memory, as Shunji Iwai's *Love Letter* reminds us, is not a computer chip processing data on command, but a cluttered attic, where treasures from the past are often buried under the trivia of the present. The ardous task of uncovering and understanding those treasures is the movie's central concern.

A thirty-two-year-old with a background in music video and TV drama, Iwai brings a supremely nineties sensibility to this, his first full-length feature film. He uses fast, quirky cutting rhythms the way music-video directors do—to seduce us out of our objectivity and into his characters' emotional world, to get us moving to their beat. He also injects the perfervid romanticism of trendy TV dramas, while rejecting most of their stylistic clichés. Like most successful mainstream directors, Iwai is both deeply in touch with his audience and slightly ahead of it, showing them the familiar in ways that feel new and right for the moment. His tale of two women who come to know each other and them-

selves through their memories of a dead boy they both once loved has become a hit with the kind of audience Japanese films too seldom attract: young, hip, and female.

The story skirts the border of *Ghost* country, where so many Japanese pop films have explored the agonies and ectasies of love beyond the grave. Returning from a memorial service for her dead fiancee, who was killed two years before in a mountain-climbing accident in Hokkaido, Hiroko (Miho Nakayama) visits her fiancee's mother and, thumbing through his junior high school yearbook, reminisces about old times. Carried away by longing and loneliness, she writes him a letter from her hometown of Kobe and sends it to an Otaru address she found in the yearbook. Then, she gets a reply.

There is no postman bearing messages from loved ones in the Great Beyond. Instead there is a young woman with the same name as the fiancee—Itsuki Fujii (Miho Nakayama, again)—living in the same Hokkaido town, who gets the letter by mistake. Down with a bad cold and possessing an impish sense of humor, Itsuki types a heavenly missive to her Kobe correspondent on her word-processor. "I am fine," she writes. "How are you?"

Iwai's script carries cinematic contrivance to new heights; it asks us to believe not only that there were two Itsuki Fujiis—one male and one female—going to the same junior high school, but that the male Fujii later fell in love with his female counterpart's double and left neither of them the wiser. It also resorts to familiar formulas, including the woman who, obsessed with her dead lover, spurns the love of a new suitor, in this case Etsushi Toyokawa as a Kobe glassmaker who was the financee's climbing buddy.

But as overblown and even absurd as this story may sound on the page, Iwai manages to bring it off. Working with cinematographer Noboru Shinoda, Iwai uses his camera conventionally enough to advance his narrative, but he also employs it expressively to plumb his characters' moods. Nakayama's Hiroko initially comes across too dully ladylike to let her real emotions show, but Iwai's quick crosscutting illuminates her inner struggle between old memories and present desire.

In playing Hiroko and her Otaru double, super-idol Miho Nakayama draws the standard contrast between the prim, modest Good Girl (Hiroko) and the bold, sassy Bad Girl (Itsuki), but as the film's focus shifts to Itsuki, Nakayama's portrayal of a woman in the throes of self-discovery becomes sexy, penetrating, and amusing. Hiroko may be the image that Nakayama's legions of male admirers want, but Itsuki, I think, is the woman who signs the checks. Wisely, Iwai allows Itsuki's story to dominate this most romantic of fantasies.

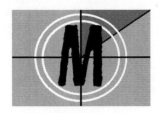

Maboroshi no Hikari ✱

Maborosi (1996)

Directed by Hirokazu Koreeda. Screenplay by Yoshihisa Hagita. Cinematography by Masao Nakabori. Produced by TV Man Union. With Makiko Esumi, Tadanobu Asano, Takashi Naito. (110 mins.)

The Japanese film industry is forever bemoaning the indifference of foreign audiences and critics to its products, especially now that other Asian cinemas are enjoying worldwide popularity and acclaim. The old excuse—that Japanese movies are too Japanese—won't wash anymore, so the current lament is that Japanese filmmakers lack their former vitality and themes.

But if one agrees with this critique, and I don't disagree with it entirely, how to explain the success abroad of a first feature film by a young director from a TV production company? The film, *Maboroshi no Hikari*, was selected for the competition section of the 1995 Venice Film Festival. Foreign critics hailed the director, Hirokazu Koreeda, as a cinematic heir of Yasujiro Ozu, Hou Hsiao-Hsien, and Theo Angelopoulos. After its triumph in Venice, *Maboroshi* went on to win the Grand Prize at the Chicago Film Festival, and Koreeda the Dragon & Tiger Young Cinema Prize for best new director at the Vancouver Film Festival.

Though the influence of the aforementioned directors may be evident—Koreeda even used Hou's favorite composer, Chen Ming-chang, to supply his film's delicately insinuating score—another valid point of comparison is Kohei Oguri's *Doro no Kawa* (Muddy River), which enjoyed similar critical accolades on its release in 1981. Both films are based on the work of Akutagawa-Prize-winning novelist Teru Miyamoto and both are deliberately paced, exquisitely photographed evocations of a materially simpler, spiritually purer life. But whereas Oguri's film is frankly retro—it is shot in black-and-white and set in the 1950s—Koreeda's takes place in a timeless present that looks and feels more like a waking dream than the Japan most of us know. The *pachinko* parlor, video-game, white-tile condo side of modern Japanese life is almost totally excluded. The colors are tastefully muted, the light is a late-afternoon haze, the settings are traditionally Japonesque. The few discordant sounds—distant traffic noise, the raucous laughter of a comic variety show from an elderly neighbor's apartment—only underscore the film's fundamental emotional tones of loneliness and longing.

In creating this world in the midst of 1990s Japan, Koreeda risks of succumbing to Parco shop-window preciousness. He does not entirely avoid it. With her long legs, boyish figure, big eyes, and direct gaze, leading lady Makiko Esumi looks disconcertingly like a model in a Comme des Garçons ad as she walks soulfully down empty streets in her dark stylish dresses. But there is also a sincerity of purpose and intelligence of execution that carries the film through. Koreeda's theme is mortal loss, in all its arbitrariness and finality, and in exploring it, he strikes chords that are less fashionable than universal. His world may not be the one we see when we reel through Shinjuku at one in the morning, but it lives, somewhere, inside us.

His story is of Yumiko (Makiko Esumi), who lives a poor but happy existence in Osaka with her factory-worker husband Ikuo (Tadanobu Asano) and their infant son. She also constantly dreams of her dead grandmother, who walked out her life when Yumiko was twelve. Then one day, for no good reason, her husband also walks out of her life and into the lights of an oncoming commuter train. His only legacy is the key from a bicycle he stole just before his suicide.

Five years later Yumiko marries Tamio (Takashi Naito), a widower who lives in a fishing village on the Noto Peninsula with his eight-year-old daughter. Though her life in the village is idyllic and her new husband kindly and well-meaning, Yumiko cannot escape the feeling that she is somehow destined to lose those she loves. That premonition is reinforced when she returns to Osaka for her brother's wedding and revisits the scenes of her unfortunate past. What can relieve her dread, her never-ending sense of loss?

This summary may make the film sound unduly depressing. It is not. Newcomer Esumi is a vital presence, whose Julia Roberts smile is as winning as her air of pathos is affecting. Also, Koreeda, working with cinematographer Masao Nakabori, gives us urban and rural landscapes that feel both warmly inviting and hauntingly remote, as though we had inhabited in them in childhood or a previous existence. We are, the film seems to say, living in a dream, and though death may tempt us with its unearthly light, we must hold onto it—it's all we have.

Not a feel-good message, exactly, but it sounds right and not just for the 1990s, either. If a few more Koreedas come along, the doomsayers of the Japanese film industry may have to look for new reasons—or a new line of work.

Madadayo

Madadayo: Not Yet (1993)

Written and directed by Akira Kurosawa. Produced by Daiei, Dentsu, and Kurosawa Production. With Tasuo Matsumura. (134 mins.)

Madadayo has a celebratory mood, as it should: the release of Akira Kurosawa's thirtieth feature film marks his fiftieth year as a director, and his is a career worth celebrating. Beginning with *Rashomon* in 1950, Kurosawa's films have earned more international honors and influenced more foreign filmmakers than those of any other Japanese director. Even the title of his latest film sounds a cry of defiance against advancing age. Kurosawa has often said that he is determined to work until the last clapper comes down, simply because there is still so much that he wants to say.

In *Madadayo*, however, the social concerns, storytelling energy and shotmaking brilliance of his best films are nowhere in evidence. Instead he has made a feature-length testimonial dinner for his hero, writer and educator Hyakken Uchida. Kurosawa's intent was to make a film about a type of man and a type of student-teacher relationship that no longer exists.

Born in 1889 in Okayama, Uchida studied German literature at the University of Tokyo and became a member of novelist Soseki Natsume's circle. After graduation, he joined the faculty of Hosei University, where he taught for eighteen years. Among his books are the best-selling *Hyakken Zuihitsu* (Hyakken's Essays) and *Nora ya* (Nora, My Lost Cat). He died in 1971, at the age of eighty-two, after rejecting induction into the Japan Academy of Arts, saying "I don't want to because I don't want to."

The film introduces us to Uchida (Tatsuo Matsumura) at his last lecture before retiring. After he announces his departure to his all-male class, a student at the back rises. "A teacher is a teacher, even if he is no longer a teacher at school," he says. "*Sensei* (our teacher) is pure gold—gold without any impurities." We are not five minutes into the movie and already the tone is worshipful, uncritical, nostalgic. That is the way it stays.

We outsiders, who have wandered into this love feast uninvited, can sense that the *sensei* is a real Mr. Chips—charmingly childish and funny in a donnish way—but instead of showing us his heart of gold, the film keeps telling us about it. Who is this man, we wonder, and why are all these people making such an unholy fuss about him?

A nadir is reached during the *sensei*'s sixtieth birthday party at an Occupation-era beer hall; the first of what were to become annual *madadayo-kai* ("not-yet" parties). Everyone is having an uproari-

ous good time, singing and shouting and rushing about as though synaptically connected. The *sensei* is proclaiming that he is "not yet" ready to shuffle off this mortal coil (who would want to with such students?) and we are wondering what this endless scene, which points to nothing and goes nowhere, is doing at the beginning of the movie.

This is not to suggest that Kurosawa retrace his artistic steps; that would be impossible in any case. But in trying to reproduce the tone of Uchida's essays on the screen, he has substituted droll anecdotes for dramatic conflict, quaint attitudes for layered characters. In his search for the simplicity and goodness of the past, he has become lost in a nostalgic haze. Kurosawa's heroes once battled the evil in the world and in their own souls; Uchida weeps for his lost cat. Incredible as it may seem, his search for poor Nora is the dramatic heart of the film. Watching the tears trickle down his withered cheeks as four of his most loyal students ponder glumly, I felt as though I had wandered into yet another movie about cute animals aimed at preadolescents.

The kitty stays lost, but another appears and life goes on. The students build *sensei* a new house to replace the tiny hut he has lived in, with his ever-patient wife (Kyoko Kagawa), since the fire-bombing of Tokyo. In the garden is a donut-shaped pond, so the carp can never reach the end of their wanderings. A gangster who wants to build a three-story building that puts the *sensei* and his carp in the shade is foiled by the students and the kindly landowner.

The years roll on. Finally is time for the seventeenth *madadayo-kai*. The students are now middle-aged and prosperous, but as devoted as ever. Though white-haired and bent, the *sensei* is still able to put away a huge glass of beer at one gulp—an annual rite. Something is different about this celebration, however. Instead of his students, Uchida addresses a few remarks to their children: "Find out what you really want to do and then do it with your whole heart," he says. Soon after, he collapses, but recovers to give his shocked students a parting word: "*madadayo*."

Like his hero, Kurosawa will also soldier on. He is already planning his next film, but if it is another *Madadayo* it might be time for his fans—and that includes anyone who cares about the art of film—to say "*mo ii yo*." Isn't enough, enough?

Mainichi ga Natsuyasumi *

Summer Holiday Every Day (1994)

Written and directed by Shusuke Kaneko. Produced by Pioneer LDC and Sundance Company. With Jun Fubuki, Shiro Sano, Hisako Saeki, Hitomi Takabayashi. (94 mins.)

Based on a *shojo manga* (girls comic) by Yumiko Oshima, Shusuke Kaneko's newest film, *Mainichi ga Natsuyasumi* mixes lighter-than-air comedy with weighty drama and pointed observations on the current state of Japanese society. Though its family may be odd and its story, a stretch, *Mainichi* amuses, engages, and even inspires. Its message: do your thing, not the right thing, and never mind the neighbors.

The Rinkaijis—Mom (Jun Fubuki), Dad (Shiro Sano) and teenage daughter Sugina (Hisako Saeki)—live in a pleasant commuter town. Dad works at an elite company, where he is on the fast track. Sugina goes to an elite girls school, where she gets excellent grades. Mom is a busy, contented housewife, whose neighborhood friends compliment her on her good fortune. Both Mom and Dad have been married before, and Sugina is Dad's stepdaughter, but they look the picture of upwardly mobile normality.

One day Dad and Sugina discover each other eating box lunches in a park when Dad is supposed to be at work and Sugina, at school. Dad, it turns out, has quit his job because he can't stand his coworkers and Sugina has stopped going to school because the other girls bully her. Her glowing report card was a fake. Dad experiences a revelation: after ten years of living together, he and Suguna hardly know each other. What can he do to set things right?

His first solution is to ask friends and colleagues for a job—and demand that Sugina accompany him to work. When this results in nothing but envelopes stuffed with sympathy money, he starts a family business, with Dad as president, Sugina as vice president, and Mom as auditor. They will be *nandemoya* (jacks-of-all-trade). This, in Mom's view, is ridiculous. What will happen to their upwardly mobile lives? What will the neighbors say?

Kaneko provides plenty of gags to move the action along. Some are sitcom standards. But others are more revealing of character, as when Dad discovers that Sugina knows a lot more than he does about beating a *futon*, preparing seaweed, and microwaving dinner. Instead of blustering with embarrassment, he humbly acknowledges her superiority.

All the principals are quite good, particularly Shiro Sano. His seeming deadpan can convey a range of emotional shadings, from blank abstraction to bug-eyed wonder. In *Mainichi* his Dad is at once a straight-arrow suit—all business even when nursing a squawling baby—and a wacky rebel saint, who stubbornly rejects everything his elite colleagues stand for and manfully bears their ridicule at a mock "farewell party." Despite his android surface, Dad is the most engagingly human character in the movie.

Jun Fubuki is a talented comedian who happens to have the looks of a Japanese Sally Fields and has

accordingly been typecast in sexless mother roles. In *Mainichi* she has undertaken a thankless task—that of playing airheaded, clueless Mom—and turned in a charmingly off-center, surprisingly affecting performance. When an upwardly mobile couple politely snigger at her family's dilemma as they drive her to the "farewell party," her look of friendship betrayed is so pathetic that we want to forgive her for all her past obtuseness and see her tormentors tormented. (But because the film is, in its own way, true to life, we never do).

Newcomer Hisako Saeki is in some ways a standard-issue ingenue—perky, spunky and sassy in a "nice" way —but she also has big, unblinking eyes that can pierce and defy. Sugina is the film's voice of truth, who lets us know that Dad's ex (Hitomi Takabayashi) has more in mind than chores when she calls on his services. Her narration is full of similar blunt, on-target remarks about people and events.

A subplot about Dad's ex threatens to pull the movie in the direction of sodden TV drama, but Kaneko soon returns to his core theme: the love and understanding that grow between father and daughter as they pursue their idiosyncratic destinies in a world that would deny their individuality. *Mainichi* proves, persuasively and entertainingly, that there really is life beyond the textbook, the manual, and the fast track.

Majo no Takkyubin *
Kiki's Delivery Service (1989)

Written and directed by Hayao Miyazaki. **Produced by** Tokuma Shoten, Yamato Transport, and Nippon Television Network. (103 mins.)

Hayao Miyazaki started his career with Toei Animation, the largest animation studio in Asia, more than two decades ago. In the course of that career, he has developed a distinctive style that blends freeform fantasy with a meticulously observed reality. His animals talk and his children fly, but they live in a world in which windows stick and the heroine catches cold in the rain.

In *Majo no Takkyubin*, which he wrote, produced, and directed, Miyazaki strives not only a physical but psychological verisimilitude of a type usually considered the province of live-action movies. His heroine, Kiki, is more than a witch with a shaky command of her broom—she has a distressing habit of bouncing off buildings—she is also a very real thirteen-year-old girl. In addition to displaying courage and spunk— standard stuff for a cartoon heroine—Kiki is by turns bored, depressed, and embarrassed.

Miyazaki's way of evoking the last state is particularly interesting. After spending her first night at the home of a baker and his wife, Kiki wakes up and, still in her nightgown, steps outside. From her second-story room, she can see an outhouse in the courtyard below. She trots down the steps, dashes into the outhouse and, a few moments later, peeps out. To her surprise, she sees the baker—a stolid young giant—stretching his muscles and walking slowly across the courtyard to a storeroom. The moment he is out of sight, she scampers back up the steps, dives into her room and shuts the door, breathing hard.

This scene does nothing to advance the plot and the humor in it is low. Disney would reject it out of hand, but in Miyazaki's hands it becomes a small triumph of understated observation that eloquently expresses Kiki's youth, vulnerability, and isolation. For one clear moment, we see into the heart of an adolescent girl.

Though sprinkled with similar moments, *Majo no Takkyubin* is also very much an entertainment— and entertain it does. The story centers around a quest. Kiki's mother, who happens to be a witch, sends her witch-in-training daughter on a year-long journey alone to complete her apprenticeship. After spending a rough night riding her broom through the rain and sleeping in a boxcar, Kiki arrives at a city on the seacoast. The local police, however, do not appreciate her aerial acrobatics and hotels do not accept under-age witches. But instead of spending the night on a park bench, Kiki uses her broom to help a baker's wife return a pacifier to a forgetful customer. The wife makes her an offer: she will give Kiki room and board in return for delivering baked goods to customers—by broom of course. Kiki agrees.

Thus the title and the premise for much of the story. While on her rounds Kiki meets an eighteen-year-old artist who becomes her best friend, an elderly woman who takes an interest in her welfare, and a thirteen-year-old boy who makes a pest of himself. These new acquaintances become a surrogate family; one that she needs when, midway through her stay, she loses her powers. Her black cat no longer talks to her, her broom no longer rises into the air. In depicting Kiki's struggle to regain those powers the film portrays her desperation, despair, and eventual triumph with striking vividness. But the most telling scenes are the smaller ones that, like Kiki's race from the outhouse, contain nuggets of emotional truth.

The setting of her story has the cultural coherence of Japanese shopping-bag prose. The port city that she calls her temporary home is a jumble of European styles, with a dash of San Francisco

thrown in. Also, anachronism reigns; the streets are filled with old-time cars, the houses, with modern gas ovens. These "mistakes," however, give the city a pleasantly bizarre blend of old-fashioned charm and up-to-date convenience. A young witch with a Walkman hanging from her broom can fit right in.

More than just a place to park the kids for two hours, *Majo no Takkyubin* is a gently moving triumph of the animator's art.

Marks no Yama
Marks (1995)

Directed by Yoichi Sai. Screenplay by Yoichi Sai and Shoichi Maruyama. Produced by Shochiku and Amuse. With Kiichi Nakai, Yuko Nattori, Masato Hagiwara, Nenji Kobayashi. (138 mins.)

When a black comedy about a don't-care Korean cabby called *Tsuki wa Dotchi ni Deteiru* swept domestic film awards in 1993, I compared director Yoichi Sai to Spike Lee. Both were members of minorities—Sai is of Korean descent—and both had a talent for caricature, a nose for controversy, and a fresh, individual approach.

Sai's next film, *Heisei Musekinin Ikka Tokyo Deluxe*, was a feather-light outing about about a family of scam artists that lacked the impact of *Tsuki*; it was Sai's genuflection to the gods of mainstream success. In *Marks no Yama*, Sai not only bends the knee but builds an altar. If *Tokyo Deluxe* was Sai trying to remake *The Sting* on the cheap, *Marks no Yama* is his attempt to rework *The Fugitive*. But in bringing Kaoru Takamura's best-selling novel to the screen, Sai wanders deep into thickets of plot, tangles of abnormal psychology and rank pools of blood and gore. *Marks no Yama* has distinctive Sai touches, including satiric takes on the inner workings of the Japanese police, but the overall effect is oppressive and off-putting, like spending a rainy afternoon in the police morgue watching an autopsy on an unfresh corpse.

The story revolves about a series of brutal murders, committed by driving a pointed object through the victim's skull. The first is of a small-time gangster, which the cops investigate with bored professionalism, but when an elite police bureaucrat in the Ministry of Justice turns up with a hole in his head, battalions of detectives scour the city for clues and end up fighting a turf war over the investigation. A hard-nosed, lone-wolf detective named Goda (Kiichi Nakai) figures out the connection between the two cases, but is stumped by the motive. Why would someone kill two men of such totally different backgrounds?

Also unfolding is the parallel story of a lonely thirtysomething nurse (Yuko Nattori) and her young mentally unbalanced lover (Masato Hagiwara). One stormy night years ago, his family committed suicide in the mountains of the Southern Alps, leaving him as the only survivor. Since then, he has been obsessed with "the dark mountain" and spent much of his time in mental institutions.

Meanwhile, a lawyer (Nenji Kobayashi) with links to both dead men—he represented the gangster in court and belonged to the same university mountain climbing club as the elite cop—makes his entrance. He also has a violent past as a student radical that he wants to hide. An amateur climber himself, Goda knows that the answers to these murders are in the mountains. First, though, he has to find the right mountain and learn the identity of a mysterious caller who identifies himself only as "Marks."

In filming a novel a director faces a fundamental choice: be faithful to the original material or follow his or her own vision of what is cinematic (or box office). Sai, who co-wrote the script with Shoichi Maruyama, has opted for the former alternative, filling the screen with dozens of characters and plot complications galore. He glories in the grubby, complex, often comic realities of urban life. His cops may be tough, competent pros, as are hundreds of their fictional counterparts, but they are also expert bureaucratic infighters, who are not above using strong-arm tactics to cow opponents and score points. Seeing them undercut and upstage each other at investigation sites and the endless meetings that seem to occupy most of their professional lives, I felt that I was getting a rare inside look at Japanese police work.

But listening to the professional chitchat about entry wounds, I began to wonder what the movie was really about. Was Goda simply trying to solve a puzzle and prove a point, or was there something more? The best cop movies are often really about relationships. What begins as just another case becomes a personal crusade, in which cop and criminal push each other to the limit and come to know each other in ways that are oddly intimate.

In Marks no Yama, however, Sai opts for hardboiled nihilism, in which the bickering continues, the body count builds and the conflict between the pursuer and the pursued is never clearly personalized. Instead, we are treated to lingering shots of mutilated bodies and subjected to tired tricks of the genre, including the most objectionable of all: the corpse that refuses to die. But where, in all the splatter, is the movie? Sai finally finds it, in the mountains, but by that time we are longing for breath of fresh, unbloodied air. The Sound of Music, anyone?

Marutai no Onna
Woman of the Police Protection Program (1997)

Written and directed by Juzo Itami. Produced by Itami Productions. With Nobuko Miyamoto, Masahiko Nishimura, Akira Nagoya. (132 mins.)

Through the long dry years of the past decade, Juzo Itami regularly topped the box office with social comedies for adults. He has had his stumbles, including a flopped adaptation of brother-in-law Kenzaburo Oe's novel Shizukana Seikatsu (A Quiet Life), but he recovered nicely with Super no Onna (Supermarket Woman), a 1996 hit comedy about a housewife, played, as always, by his wife Nobuko Miyamoto, who turns around a failing supermarket with grit, determination, and sharp eye for stale produce.

Now Itami is back with Marutai no Onna, whose Japanese title recalls those of Marusa no Onna (A Taxing Woman, 1987) and Mimbo no Onna (The Gentle Art of Japanese Extortion, 1992). The latter film, a comedy about a female lawyer's battle with the yakuza, nearly got Itami killed when a gang of punks knifed him outside his home. He recovered, but his brush with death—and his outrage at what he considered an assault on the right of free expression—inspired him to make Marutai, whose heroine witnesses a brutal murder and becomes the next target of the fanatic cult that ordered it.

As close as the film's subject may be to his heart, Itami is first and foremost a showman intent on appealing to a mass audience and Marutai is in many ways a standard Itami product: the film's take on its subject is light, its pace sprightly, its narrative trajectory as clean as that of a space shuttle heading into orbit.

But where, in fact, is the film going? Itami wants Marutai to be not only a comic romp, but a serious commentary on the dangers of standing up for one's beliefs in Japanese society. In Marusa no Onna he combined the dual role of entertainer and social gadfly to good effect, but the balancing act was never an easy one. In Marutai he veers from goofy slapstick to cold-blooded violence, while failing to deliver either laughs or chills. What could have been a bitingly amusing film, made with conviction by one who has been there, is lacking in content and jarring in tone.

The title heroine, Hiwako (Nobuko Miyamoto), is a middle-aged actress with an outsized ego who happens upon a murder while doing her breathing exercises on a lonely hilltop road. The victim is a lawyer who has been investigating the activities of an Aum-Shinrikyo-like cult, the killer is a cult member. While getting the scare of her life, Hiwako takes a good look at his face, and, when the police ask her testify for the prosecution, she quickly agrees. She also makes her intention known to the mass media and, though them, the cult leaders. They promptly dispatch a hit squad to dispose of her, while the police send two young officers to protect her: a gushing fan named Chikamatsu (Takehiro Murata), who loves his new assignment, and a tight-lipped macho type named Tachibana (Masahiko Nishimura), who hates it.

From a pampered star who lives her life, including her secret life with a married lover (Masahiko Tsugawa), exactly as she pleases, Hiwako becomes a pursued quarry, whose only protection from a hitman's bullet is her odd cop couple. Initially viewing her bodyguards as unwanted accessories, she comes to regard them as allies and respect them as professionals, while they come to admire her steadfast dedication to her craft—and the truth—even when the cult threatens to wreck her career by splashing her scandalous affair all over the front pages.

Nobuko Miyamoto gives an amusingly knowing performance as Hiwako, an aging prima donna who projects a spoiled arrogance and steely will in equal measures. She is a caricature, but one based on an close acquaintance with the real thing. Nearly everyone else mugs away frantically. There are some amusing bits, however, such as Tachibana's stint as an Egyptian spear-carrier in a lavish production of *Anthony and Cleopatra*. At first a reluctant onlooker in a big battle scene, he suddenly transforms into a Bruce-Lee-like ball of martial-arts fury. But then the film gives us an assassination scare weakly ripped off from *The Man Who Knew Too Much,* and the comic momentum gets lost.

The Marx Brothers, I couldn't help thinking, did this kind of thing so much better. *Tampopo*—still Itami's best film—will make you feel like digging into a bowl of noodles. *Marutai no Onna* will make you want to rent *A Night at the Opera.*

Memories *
(1995)

Directed by Koji Morimoto, Tensai Okamura, Katsuhiro Otomo. Screenplay by Katsuhiro Otomo. Produced by Bandai Visual, Shochiku, and Kodansha. (113 mins.)

Katsuhiro Otomo first came to international attention with *Akira*, a 1988 animated film based on his best-selling SF *manga* that became a cult hit. A dazzling exercise in future-world imagineering, it rivaled *Blade Runner* in its boldness of vision, artistic unity, and fanatic attention to detail. Though the plot was overly busy and occasionally incoherent, the dynamism of the animation and impact of the hyperviolent action made mainstream American animated features look timid and bland. *The Little Mermaid* just didn't cut it any more.

Now Otomo has taken that art to another level with *Memories*. A three-part omnibus, the film presents stories of outer space in the distant future, Japan in the present, and an Orwellian fantasy land where time has come to a stop. The animation is stunning; Otomo has lost none of his talent for bringing his fantastic dreamscapes to highly realized life. Also, advances in animation technology have enabled him and his co-directors to expand their imaginative reach. In the third episode, "Cannon Fodder," which Otomo both scripted and directed, he uses a single traveling shot throughout the film's twenty-two-minute length, soaring and swooping in a technical tour de force. What impresses most about *Memories*, however, is the way Otomo uses his formidable technique to not only overawe, but intelligently entertain. Too many SF *anime* seem to be made by *otaku* for *otaku*. Loaded with pseudo technojargon, futuristic hardware, and ponderously intricate storylines, they leave the uninitiated feeling baffled and overwhel-med.

In the first two segments of *Memories*, however, Otomo takes an approach that is reminiscent of *The Twilight Zone* at its mind-bending best. The first, "Magnetic Rose," begins as a whimsically humorous tale about four space bums in the year 2092 who travel about in a cosmic garbage scow disposing of old satellites. One huge piece of rose-shaped space junk they encounter, though, is different from the rest. Entering one of the petals, two of the crew members discover a nineteenth-century opera house that opens into a sun-drenched garden. They hear a soprano voice bursting gloriously into an aria. It belongs, they learn, to an early twenty-first century diva who leads a ghostly existence amid the ruins of her former triumphs and exerts a fatal attraction on all who come near her. Though this summary may sound simply bizarre—the gothic goes to deep space—Otomo and director Koji Morimoto create a phantasmagoric realm where the boundary between reality and illusion, human and inhuman, death and life dissolves to chilling and memorable effect.

The second segment, "Stink Bomb," starts as the lightest of the three, but the joke, by the end, is on a society that can mount massive displays of police power, but fail to stop a lone bearer of mass chaos and destruction: a young reseacher who accidentally swallows a capsule that turns him into a human stink bomb. Wherever he goes, people and animals keel over from the fumes, but unable to smell them himself, he remains clueless—and highly (though not fatally) dangerous. As he advances on Tokyo to deliver top secret materials to his boss, the Self Defense Force descends on him as though he were Godzilla. The gas, however, proves the stronger and the researcher, mounted unsteadily on his scooter, putters on as official panic reigns. Director Tensai Okamura presents this comedy of errors with spectacular visuals, including explosions worthy of *Die Hard 3*, but the subtext of official bungling and paranoia seems more inspired by *Dr. Strangelove* and headlines about the subway gassings by the Aum Shinrikyo cult.

The last segment, "Cannon Fodder," which Otomo both scripted and directed, is the strangest and most unsettling. The setting is a vaguely European city whose sole occupation is shelling distant targets with hundreds of cannons. The story is of a man who serves on the crew of a monster cannon called Number 17 and his son, who dreams of growing up to be the cannon's firer—the most prestigious job of all. There is a family resemblance to *1984*: endless war, universal obsession with an unseen enemy, and a wan-looking populace systematically programmed to perform a single task. The city of cannons, however, is less a possible future than a metaphor for the banal, tenacious horrors of modern war. The mindless power of the cannons is finally as empty as the men who tend them, but the children—already fanatic little warriors—will carry on their fathers' work.

Menda Sakae: Gokuchu no Sei

Sakae Menda: A Life in Prison (1998)

Directed by Masato Koike. Produced by Siglo. (88 mins.)

James Cagney used to do a great death scene. Who can forget his last walk to the electric chair in *Angels with Dirty Faces*, in which his tough-guy character undergoes a sudden transformation to sniveling coward? He did it to scare the Dead End Kids onto the straight-and-narrow, but he also gave us a taste of the fear that death-row prisoners live with day after day, year after year.

In Japan, the one who lived the longest with that fear was Sakae Menda. Charged with the murder of a family of four in Kumamoto Prefecture, he was convicted and sentenced to death in 1950. Though Menda protested that the police had forced him to make a false confession, the courts continued to uphold the sentence. Finally, in 1983 a judge of the Kumamoto Eighth District Court found him innocent of all charges. After thirty-four years and six months behind bars, Menda was a free man. During that time he had seen seventy of his fellow inmates die—he was first from death row to walk out the

prison gate alive. Now, after three years of planning and filming, documentarian Masato Koike has completed an account of those years.

Using interviews, official documents, photographs, and the letters Menda sent to family and supporters, Koike tried to recreate Menda's long years on death row, to give a sense of what it was like to live a few steps from the noose. To those used to watching crimes-in-progress on CNN, this approach may sound staid, but Menda, who is on camera for nearly the entire film, is a riveting presence.

A stocky, balding man in his late sixties, Menda has the dark intensity of great obsessives. Given a chance at an ordinary life, he might well have been ordinary, but in nearly three decades on death row he became an extraordinary man, with a single, unshakable purpose—to win his freedom and clear his name. In Koike's film, he pours out the story of those years, reliving every emotion, remembering every setback and triumph. He doesn't, however, weep; he would rather be understood, justified.

The film begins with Menda reading from a letter sent by the prison to his family in 1952, asking whether they would like to collect his ashes after his execution. "I didn't think I could escape this," he told Koike. With the help of his lawyers and friends who believed his innocence (his own father thought him guilty), Menda appealed the sentence. Finally, in 1956, a judge granted his request for a retrial. He was, he says, delirious with joy. But the Kumamoto prosecutor's office filed a protest, and a higher court overruled the judge. The death sentence stood.

A crushing blow, but Menda kept submitting appeals. During this period, he and his death row companions lived surprisingly normal lives. They cared for animals, raised vegetables, played baseball. Menda was an enthusiastic player on a death-row team for nearly a decade, until it disbanded. He remembers Aoyama, a close friend and excellent pitcher who ended his life on the gallows. Group activities for death row inmates are no longer permitted, but they kept Menda alive and sane.

Work was another outlet: he made braille books for a school for the blind. "Doing this helped me forget my fear," he says. But remembering was also important; Menda kept a detailed journal, including a chart of executions. He listed name, date, and noted whether he considered the sentence "doubtful." Quite a few of the listings are followed by the word "doubtful."

In 1979, the Fukuoka High Court finally granted his request for a retrial. Menda's lawyers presented evidence supporting his alibi and testimony of police torture during his interrogation. On July 15, 1983, the judge declared him innocent. Surrounded by jubilant supporters, Menda left the courtroom to face the media—his case had become a national *cause célebre*—and start a new life.

Today, nearly a decade later, he lives quietly in a small Kyushu town. At the end of the film, we see him fishing with a net in a nearby river. Again and again he casts his net and pulls it in, empty, but shows no disappointment. He looks, instead, happy and content. Perhaps he, more than anyone, can sympathize with the ones that got away.

Menkyo ga Nai!
No License! (1994)

Directed by Tomoyuki Akaishi. Screenplay by Yoshimitsu Morita. Produced by Towa International and NTV. With Hiroshi Tachi, Junko Igarashi, Toru Emori, Tsurutaro Kataoka, Yuki Sumida. (102 mins.)

As anyone who has driven on the four-lane parking lots called expressways knows, Japan is a highly motorized country. Nearly half of all Japanese—sixty-four million to be exact—have driver's licenses. But what of the other half? If Tomoyuki's Akaishi's *Menkyo ga Nai!* is any indication, not a few have developed an inferiority complex the size of the trade surplus. Here, as in many other motor-mad societies, a license is seen as a ticket to adulthood, and, for many males, a proof of manhood.

Hiroshi Nanjo (Hiroshi Tachi) is no exception; a popular action star, he owes much of his macho image to scenes in which he blasts around in a sexy sports car. But the truth, as his slinky costar (Junko Igarashi) discovers one day, is that this bronzed, jut-jawed hunk is, at the age of forty, license-less. Nanjo is humiliated— and decides to become a real driver, no matter what. Even though he is still shooting his newest film, he tells his manager (Toru Emori) that he wants to get his license—now.

A gangster type—he even has an intimidating way of hitching up his pants—the manager storms into the studio chief's office the next day and browbeats him into giving his client a three-week leave so that he can obtain his precious piece of plastic. Nanjo's star ego and the real world, in the form of a provincial driving academy, are about to collide

Menkyo is more a comedy of character than an exercise in four-wheeled slapstick. Scriptwriter Yoshimitsu Morita filters an obscure corner of everyday Japan through a sensibility that is comic but essentially sympathetic. An assistant director to Morita in six films, Akaishi has faithfully transferred this sensibility to the screen, so much so that *Menkyo gai Nai!* feels like a Morita film in all but name. In doing so he has stretched what might have been a punchy segment in a Morita *Bakayaro!* anthology

into a thin feature-length comedy. We get the joke long before the inevitable rousing ending.

Nanjo is the last to realize that learning to a drive a car is not a matter of life and death. While the twenty year-olds in the driving school dorm are laughing it up as though they were on a school excursion, he edges into the dining room in nerd mufti with a meek, nervous expression on his suddenly middle-aged face. He is about to undergo an ordeal and he isn't sure he will survive.

The ordeal arrives in the form of a diminutive instructor (Tsurutaro Kataoka) with a bad attitude. When Nanjo slides behind the wheel, the instructor tells him his breath stinks of garlic. When he goes sailing over the top of a practice hill he calls him an idiot. Definitely not star treatment. Further character tests arrive in the form of a miniskirted instructor (Yuki Sumida) and a granite-faced instructor (Tokuma Nishioka); Nanjo can't keep his eyes off the former, or please the latter. He makes every mistake in the manual—and seems headed toward disaster.

Finally, Nanjo decides to reveal his real identity and call on the reserves: the film crew that has been anxiously waiting his return. Suddenly his classmates, who have ignored his existence, are fawning on him, and even his instructors are looking at him with new eyes (Miss Miniskirt's are distractingly seductive). But he still has to pass his driving test and his tester, as luck would have it, is Granite Face. Nanjo flunks, miserably. Will he quit—and confine his road warrioring to the back lot—or find the will to press on?

In a way very Japanese, Nanjo realizes that he cannot let down his supporters, or make it without them. He also discovers that, once inside a driving school car, a klutz is a klutz, even if his face is on billboards. Though his star ego is shattered, a humbler but stronger human being emerges from the wreckage. In this slick, surfacy comedy, Nanjo's victory over himself is an unexpectedly moving moment. For those in the audience who have survived driving school hell, it may be a familiar one as well. Not everyone can be a star, but there's a little Nanjo in all of us.

Mimi o Sumaseba
Whisper of the Heart (1995)

Directed by Yoshifumi Kondo. Screenplay by Hayao Miyazaki. Produced by Tokuma Shoten, NTV, Hakuhodo, and Studio Ghibli. Voices by Yuko Honda, Kazuo Takahashi. (110 mins.)

Like Disney, Hayao Miyazaki's Studio Ghibli has become a brand name whose animated films appeal across age boundaries. Like Disney's "prince and princess" romances, Ghibli films have formulaic elements that identify them as surely as a brand logo. There is usually a spunky young heroine on the brink of adolescence, a feline familiar (in *Tonari no Totoro* the cat took the form of a four-legged bus), vaguely European settings created by a free-associating sensibility, and most distinctively of all, flying scenes animated with a breathtaking dynamism and infectious joy.

Scripted by Miyazaki and directed by Yoshifumi Kondo, *Mimi o Sumaseba* (Whisper Of the Heart), is a characteristic Ghibli product. The heroine, Suzuku Tsukishima is approaching the last summer of junior high school. A voracious reader, she harbors ambitions to write. But though she shares her efforts with her best friend—including new lyrics to that karaoke standard, "Country Roads"—at home she shuts out her parents and nagging older sister and slips into a shell. It's not that Mom and Dad don't care, but Mom is busy taking university classes, and Dad, when not working at a local library, is busy writing books about local history. They can't spare the time to find out what the girl in the shell is thinking (though Dad, an insightful sort, can usually guess).

Suzuku is thus something of a Belle in embryo, but instead of a Beast, she meets Seiji (Kazuo Takahashi), a boy whose blunt talk upsets and annoys her ("You'd better not use that line about a 'concrete road,'" he advises her). She also encounters a kindly old man who runs an antique shop stocked with wonderful treasures, including a cat statuette with strange, glittering eyes. The old man, she learns, is Seiji's grandfather. Seiji, she discovers, harbors a secret ambition of his own: to make violins in Cremona, Italy,

The story is staple boy-meets-girl: Suzuku and Seiji quarrel until they fall in love. There are no disapproving parents, jealous rivals, or evil spells to overcome, however. There is only a trial of sorts. Determined to emulate Seiji, who is working hard to realize his dream, Suzuku decides to write a story in which the old man's prize—the cat statuette—comes to life. Will she win his praise, or learn that she is just another talentless wannabe?

This is not much on which to hang a film, but plot has never been the real point of Ghibli movies anyway. Instead, Miyazaki and first-time director Kondo conjure the usual Ghibli magic, in a familiar Japanese setting (though the old man's atelier could .have come from the neo-Mediterranean port of another Miyazaki feature, *Majo no Takkyubin* [Kiki's Delivery Service]). The film develops Suzuku's character though an accretion of details, including the way she fumbles for the alarm clock and keeps forgetting her things. There are also moments, such as her pensive walk down a shaded street, with the light

and shadow playing on her slender form, that celebrate her youth, with all its promise, hope, and uncertainty. A Disney film, forever hurrying on to the next plot point, would spare little time for such moments, but they are the very heart of *Mimi o Tsumaseba.*

Mimbo no Onna
The Gentle Art of Japanese Extortion (1992)

Written and directed by Juzo Itami. Produced by Toho and Itami Film. With Nobuko Miyamoto, Akira Takarada, Yasuo Daichi, Masahiro Murata. (123 mins.)

Juzo Itami is nothing if not clever. He does more than make films about topics in the news; he has a way of making the films themselves news. One reason is skillful PR. Take the title of his latest film, *Mimbo no Onna*: it's a classic teaser. Not long ago, if you had asked the average Japanese what *mimbo* meant he or she would have probably answered with a blank stare. A contraction of *minji kainyu boryoku*, the term *mimbo* is cop talk for gangsters ripping off nongangsters through various scams. Punchy and racy, it sticks in the mind while evoking the movie's world.

Another reason is the public persona of Itami himself. Looking stylish in a kimono, with a charming twinkle in his eye, he gives interview and after interview about *mimbo* and his latest film. Though hardly the first director to go on the promo circuit, Itami is among the best at it. Unlike auteurs who drone on about their art, Itami actually has something to say, and says it entertainingly and persuasively: he's a born crusader, showman, and raconteur.

But what about *Mimbo* the movie, as opposed to *Mimbo,* the product? As do all his other films, it stars his wife, Nobuko Miyamoto. She is the *mimbo no onna,* a lawyer who specializes in helping businesses deal with the *yakuza. Mimbo* begins as a wittily crafted, nimbly acted comedy. A high-class Tokyo hotel loses a bid to a rival to host a summit meeting. The reason? The *yakuza* are conducting their busines, including shakedowns of clients who have fallen behind in their loanshark payments, in the lobby. The hotel manager (Akira Takarada) assigns two employees—an athletic bellboy named Wakasugi (Masahiro Murata) and a wiseacre pencil-pusher named Suzuki (Yasuo Daichi)—to a *yakuza* task force. Wakasugi and Suzuki haven't got a clue how to handle the boys in the razzle-dazzle suits. The *yakuza,* who sense weakness the way sharks smell blood, soon realize that the hotel is easy meat.

Although the initial confrontations between the bumbling good guys and sneering bad guys are funny enough, Itami also wants to educate us.

Mimbo is a manual of a movie: the first part is the "how not to" chapter, the second, when the lawyer finally appears on the scene, is the "how to" chapter. Dressed impeccably in Armani, the lawyer soon sets the two-man task force on the right track. Their attempts to pay off the *yakuza*, she tells them, are as futile as throwing bits of meat to a hungry shark. Firmness—and electronic gear for catching the gangsters in the act—are essential.

But won't the *yakuza* retaliate, they ask? Feed them to the fishes? She laughs in their faces. Gangsters almost never use violence against non-gangsters, she explains. Roughing up civilians is not only against the gangster code, but bad for business. For all their bluff and bluster, gangsters are businessmen first, who have no desire to spend unnecessary time in the slammer. This is good to know, but a movie it does not make. Unfortunately, Itami's didactic impulses overwhelm his movie-making instincts. We get the point long before his film winds its way to its foregone conclusion.

Like all self-help books, *Mimbo* wants to give us confidence that we can solve a problem we once considered overwhelming, but like so many of those books it makes the solution seem unrealistically easy. Itami's gangsters are posturing caricatures. They are clever enough, in a low sort of way, but they aren't very bright. They make indictable threats for the hotel's video camera, even though they know it is recording their every snarl. The movie's plunges into deep dramatic waters also fail to convince. We can laugh at Itami's cartoony characters, but when he asks us to shed a tear for them, we balk. We see the manipulative hand of the cartoonist too clearly.

Itami did his homework for *Mimbo*; he interviewed dozens of *yazuka*-afflicted businessmen and *mimbo* experts. He has also made *Mimbo* an event: theaters were packed. But he couldn't surpass *Ososhiki* (The Funeral) or *Tampopo*. Those early films were fresh, funny, delightfully shrewd. *Mimbo* seems to come from the tape recorder—and an exhausted imagination.

Minna Yatteru ka?
Getting Any? (1995)
Written and directed by Takeshi Kitano. Produced by Office Kitano and Bandai Visual. With Duncan, Takeshi Kitano. (110 mins.)

Takeshi Kitano has directed six feature films since his debut in 1989 with *Sono Otoko Kyobo Ni Tsuki* (Violent Cop). All, however, have have been art, not the kind of often raucous and occasionally inspired

comedy that he provides almost nightly on television. In his sixth film, *Minna Yatteru ka?*, Kitano has finally brought his comic mind out of the hiding and—surprise! surprise!—it is the same mind that we know and love (or loathe) from TV. Much of the movie's humor is of the numbskull school, with gags so lame-brained that I had to laugh at the sheer brass of Kitano's putting them on the screen and charging admission. Structurally, it is a grab-bag, with nothing holding it together but attitude. You've heard of *Dumb and Dumber*? This movie ought to be titled *Dumbest*. But, as in the films of Aki Kaurismaki and Jim Jarmusch, there is also a method—and message—behind the madness. Kitano, whose act is the opposite of PC, has made a movie with a strong, if absurd, feminist subtext.

Asao (Duncan) is an amiable half-wit whose only ambition in life is to get laid. One morning, after dreaming of a cool dude making it with a babe in a Porsche, he has a revelation: to get a girl, he needs a car. In the next scene, we see him in the showroom, asking the blandly smiling salesman if he has anything that would be suitable for *kaasekkusu* ("car sex"). The salesman is eager to oblige and Asao is soon driving out of the lot in something that looks like a bumper car designed by Sanrio. He tries to pick up the first girl he sees. "Wanna ride?" he asks. She replies with a few choice insults. This, he realizes, is going to be harder than he thought.

Asao's quest continues—and leads him down one wacky blind alley after another. When his car-sex fantasy doesn't pan out—his vehicles end up flattened by a truck or flying through a billboard—he decides to steal money so that he can fly first-class and receive what he imagines to be first-class service from a female flight attendant. When his career as a bank robber fails to take off—a teller responds to his gun by asking him to take a number—he tries acting. After all, women will do anything to get next to an actor, won't they? But not one who, playing a blind swordsman, misplaces his weapon and accidentally douses the baddies with manure. By the end, poor Asao has run through the entire catalog of male illusions about what women really want—and has gotten no nearer his goal. Finally, he tries to become an invisible man; in short, a voyeur. Because this is a Kitano movie, he gets his wish—and more than he bargained for.

In telling this black comic tale, Kitano throws in a raft of movie references, including the *Waka Daisho* series, the *Zatoichi* series, *yakuza* flicks, monster movies, and porno, while filling the soundtrack with old *enka* numbers, *min'yo*, and even *taiko* drumming. He is seemingly emptying his mental attic of all the pop culture junk he has stored there over the years, while working out various obsessions, sexual and otherwise, on the screen. This may be Kitano's most personal film, in which he takes off the masks of intellectuality and says what he feels about the world with a simplicity and directness that is disarming. It's easy to groan at *Minna Yatteru ka!*, hard to dislike it.

But what are the foreign critics going to say? Just when they thought they had discovered the next Tarantino, Kitano makes a movie whose idea of fun is an invisible man leering at naked women in a public bath. He shouldn't worry, however. After *Minna Yatteru ka!* he ought to be on the Hollywood A-list to direct *The Naked Gun Goes to Japan*.

Mirai No Omoide: Last Christmas

Last Christmas (1992)

Written and directed by Yoshimitsu Morita. Original story by Funio F. Fujiko. Produced by Kowa International and Fujiko F. Funio Pro. (110 mins.)

What happened to Yoshimitsu Morita? *Kazoku Game* (The Family Game) was a wonderfully acted, neatly pointed satire on the Japanese obsession with getting junior into a good school. His latest film, *Mirai No Omoide: Last Christmas*, however, is a fantasy with the sensibility of a girls' comic book, aimed squarely at a young female audience. (Not surprising considering its origins: the treatment on which Morita based his script was written by Funio F. Fujiko, half of the two-man team that created *Doraemon* and dozens of other well-known *manga* characters.) Morita gives us food for thought about the meaning of life and death, with a sugar coating of sentimentality and an intellectually hollow center. It is *Ghost* made nice, with all the zany humor, tingly suspense, and sensuous romanticism carefully excised.

Its two young heroines get what we all dream about: a second time around. Yuko (Misa Shimizu) is a struggling cartoonist. The one time she gets a marketable brainstorm for a series, a rival beats her to the editor's desk with an idea that is suspiciously similar. Ginko (Shizuka Kudo) is an empty-upstairs OL who has a crush on a hunk of a fashion designer (David Ito), but ends up marrying a fast-talking securities salesman whose real love is his job.

These two meet in the Ginza on Christmas eve and quickly become friends. Soon after, they both die suddenly and improbably; Yuko of a heart attack on a golf course while hitting a hole-in-one, Ginko of a blow on the head from what looks to be a falling cube of light.

Yuko wakes up at her desk, not in paradise, but in 1981. Morita, sensibly, does not try to explain; he is making a fantasy, not a documentary about journeys to the Other Side. The comic potential of this mate-

rial is obvious—one can imagine a film in which the heroines wickedly and amuzingly scheme to become rich and famous. Morita, however, has made *Mirai* to teach us Lessons about Life. The film's didactic intent might have been bearable if he had taught his lessons with orginality and wit. Instead, he recycles MTV clichés (including the one of the fun-loving couple in evening clothes falling backwards, in slow motion, into a swimming pool) and parades his reborn women in an array of designer clothes.

Once Yuko gets over her shock at being back among the living, she begins to plagiarize the hit *manga* of the future. Ginko, who had spent her previous existence pouring tea, becomes a successful financial guru. We know that Lesson One is coming: money and fame are not enough, especially for a woman. One must also have love. Yuko meets a young *kyogen* performer (Motoya Izumi), while Ginko reintroduces herself to her designer friend.

But the dread year 1991 approaches. Our heroines both look as dewy fresh as they did ten years ago, and as innocent of any deepening experience. Both walk straight into the waiting arms of the Grim Reaper. This, we think, is dumb. Couldn't Yuko have gotten a pacemaker before venturing out onto the golf course? Couldn't Ginko have taken a cab?

Their second returns, however, are essential for the imparting of Lessons Two and Three: Be True To Yourself and Stand By Your Man. Yuko stops plagiarizing and becomes a famous cartoonist in her own right, with a character who looks suspiciously like Doraemon. Ginko stops giving stock-market tips, but uses her insight into the future of fashion (the "body conscious" look will be in) to propel her designer boyfriend to a brilliant career. She has learned the secret of true happiness—unselfish devotion to the man of her dreams—but can she reap the rewards of her hard-won knowledge? Or will she take another hit on the head? If she does, she deserves to be reborn into the period in which she might feel most at home: the 1950s.

Misty

(1997)

Directed by Kenki Saegusa. Screenplay by Yumiko Inoue. Produced by Gaga Communications. With Takeshi Kaneshiro, Etsushi Toyokawa, Yuki Amami. (98 mins.)

In the movie business, nothing is sacred. Colorize *Casablanca*? Why not! Everyone knows black-and-white is boring. Shoot a sequel to *Gone With the Wind*? OK! We all want to know what happened to Scarlet after Rhett walked out the door, don't we? While loathing the very thought of colorizing

Casablanca, I realize that the tradition of the movie remake is, for better or worse, a long one. Also, many films, including more than a few great ones, are adaptations from other media.

In Japan, one of the most enthusiastic borrowers from other media has been Akira Kurosawa. Among his sources are Shakespeare (*Kumonosujo* from *Macbeth*, *Ran* from *King Lear*), Dostoevsky (*Hakuchi* from *The Idiot*) and Gorky (*Donzoko* from *The Lower Depths*). The film that launched him to international fame, *Rashomon*, was based on "In a Grove," a short story by Ryunosuke Akutagawa about the trial of a robber accused of murdering an aristrocrat and raping his wife. But in filming this story about the elusiveness of truth in Heian Japan, Kurosawa made it, unmistakably, his own. He was, Japanese critics complained at the time, flagrantly unfaithful to the mood and substance of the Akutagawa original. The result was a masterpiece of world cinema.

If Kurosawa could interpret Akutagawa in own his light, why not another director? Also, forty-seven years have passed since *Rashomon*'s release. To today's young audiences, Kurosawa is a dim figure, his films, even his greatest, are little known. Isn't it time for a new film version of "In a Grove" or, if you prefer, a remake of *Rashomon*? Thus the thinking of the producers of *Misty*. A coproduction of the Nikkatsu film studio and the Amuse talent agency, *Misty* was conceived, as *Rashomon* was not, as an Asian movie that could attract audiences in Hong Kong and Taipei as well as in Tokyo.

Much of this international appeal is provided by the duskily handsome Takeshi Kaneshiro, who has become a hot talent throughout Asia for his work in the films of Wong Kar-Wai, the definitively hip director of the day. To draw local crowds, the producers cast Etsushi Toyokawa, the lean, craggy-faced actor who, as magazine polls have revealed, ranks high as a man Japanese women most want to sleep with. Still another casting coup is Yuki Amami, a former Takarazuka theater star making her screen debut.

But though this package may set turnstiles spinning, *Misty* is the cinematic equivalent of touching up the Mona Lisa with Day-Glo crayolas: a feeble joke or, if one is in a unforgiving mood, a banal desecration. Kenki Saegusa, a television director for NHK making his feature debut, does not reinvent so much as reduce. All of what was intriguingly paradoxical, stunningly vibrant, and intoxicatingly mysterious about *Rashomon* is gone, replaced by steamy looks, macho posturing, vulgar clowning, and overripe atmospherics. It's as though the filmmakers took a popularizing steamroller to the Kurosawa film, flattening it to a two-dimensional form easily consumable by a generation raised on the insipid grotesqueries of *manga* and TV.

Does this sound too harsh? After all, most movies could no more stand comparison with *Rashomon* than a gnat could sit on one end of a balance, with an elephant on the other, and expect to register. But *Misty* invites the comparison by blatantly ripping off the original, from its light-through-the-trees shots to Toyokawa's parodistic interpretation of Mifune's robber—one of his greatest roles. Fans may sigh at Toyokawa's bronzed, rugged form, but where Mifune was incandescently vivid, Toyokawa is embarrassingly vapid. *Misty* tries to distinguish itself from *Rashomon*, but such efforts, including an obligatory sex scene between Toyokawa and Amami in an atmospherically lit forest bower, only remind us, again, that Kurosawa did it all so much better.

Even so, *Misty* will serve a purpose if it makes its target audience, whose personal experience of Kurosawa is of an old man in decline, curious to see the original. But the majority, I'm afraid, will prefer the cheap brilliance of Miki's Day-Glo to the rich sonorities of Kurosawa's black-and-white. What else will be coming soon to a theater near you? A remake of *Citizen Kane*, with Brad Pitt in the title role? In color, with a computer-generated Xanadu, of course.

Mitabi no Kaikyo
Three Trips Across the Strait (1995)

Directed by Seijiro Koyama. **Screenplay by** Seijiro Koyama and Masato Kato. **Produced by** Mitabi no Kaikyo Production Commitee. **With** Mikuni Rentaro, Lee Jong Ho, Toshiyuki Nagashima, Daisuke Ryu, Yoko Minamino. (123 mins.)

Why the flurry of movies with Asian locales and heroes? This year we have seen the release of Kei Kumai's *Fukai Kawa* (Deep River), with its Japanese tourists discovering eternal verities in India, Kazuki Omori's *Kinkyu Yobidashi: Emergency Call*, with its Japanese doctor serving the poor of Manila's Smoky Mountain slum, and Hiromichi Horikawa's *Asian Blue*, with its Korean slave-workers struggling to survive in wartime Japan.

Seijiro Koyama's *Mitabi no Kaikyo* is the latest example of this trend. Based a novel of the same title by Hosei Hahakigi, the film resembles *Asian Blue* in theme and approach. Once again a Japanese filmmaker explicitly takes the side of his Korean characters and forthrightly dramatizes Japanese wartime atrocities. Even the structure of the film, with its framing device of an old Korean man searching for his past in present-day Japan, is similar.

But midway through, *Mitabi* becomes a melodrama of star-crossed love and, in the modern story, of justice triumphant. Though this shift may be faithful to the novel's rambling narrative, it dissipates much of the impact the film has so carefully built in its first hour. In the first half of *Mitabi*, Koyama strives hard to accurately present not only the crimes but contradictions of the era, during which Koreans also oppressed Koreans, and the closest country to Japan became the most distant, culturally and politically. As evidence that he and co-scriptwriter Masato Kato achieved the historical perspective that seems so elusive to Japanese politicians, the *Mitabi* crew was allowed to shoot on location in Korea—a rare concession from a government that still bans the theatrical screening of Japanese films. [Note: The Korean government partially lifted this ban in October 1998.]

Mitabi begins with the modern story. Han Shigun (Mikuni Rentaro), a Pusan businessman, accepts an invitation from an old wartime comrade to return to Japan after a fifty-year absence. After crossing the strait to Kyushu, he goes to the town where he worked in the mines, one of the thousands of forced laborers brought to Japan during the war. A visit to an abandoned Korean cemetery near the mines revives memories—and a long-buried desire to reconnect with his past.

Those memories, as we see in extended flashbacks, were hardly pleasant. To fuel the Japanese war machine, the young Han (Lee Jong Ho) and his Korean comrades are forced to work impossible hours in dangerous conditions, and, when they falter, are beaten mercilessly by their supervisors, some of whom are Japanized Koreans. Finally, the miners, led by the fearless Kim Dong In (Toshiyuki Nagashima), rebel and present a list of demands to the mine boss, the cool-headed, coldblooded Yamamoto (Daisuke Ryu), who accepts them without a struggle. Soon after, however, Kim is found hanged in the barracks—with his private parts missing.

Convinced that Yamamoto was responsible for the murder and mutilation, Han decides to run away. While escaping, he kills a supervisor, but finds help and a new life in a nearby village. There he meets Chizu (Yoko Minamino), a beautiful Japanese widow—and *Mitabi* becomes a different movie: relentlessly heart-rending, tiresomely predictable. Do Han and Chizu fall in love and marry? Do they encounter opposition from Han family when he takes her back home after the war? Does she finally leave, with her infant son, never to return? I didn't have to puzzle over the answers, but I did find myself liking Minamino. Though this former idol has appeared in dreadful schlock (examples include *Kantsubaki* and *Watashi o Daite Soshite Kiss Shite*), her performance as the widow is uncluttered and dignified.

Back in the present, Han meets his long-lost son and prepares for a final showdown with Yamamoto, who has just been elected mayor on a promise to obliterates all traces of the now-abandoned mines and—his own, unspoken agenda—the graves of the Koreans, whose spirits still haunt him. We can also guess how the final, titanic battle between the two old enemies will end—and why Han will never make his fourth trip across that fateful strait.

Mizu no Tabibito: Samurai Kids
Samurai Kids (1996)

Directed by Nobuhiko Obayashi. Screenplay by Masumi Suetani. Produced by Fuji TV, Office Two One, and Toho. With Tsutomu Yamazaki, Ryo Yoshida, Ayumi Ito, Jun Fubuki, Itokku Kishibe, Tomoyo Harada. (106 mins.)

The Japanese have one of the richest fantasy literatures in the world: tales like "Momotaro," "Urashima Taro" and "Issunboshi" are equal to anything in the Brothers Grimm. So why not use the best of Japanese folk tales to compete against the best of Hollywood? That, it seems, was the thinking behind *Mizu no Tabibito: Samurai Kids*, Nobuhiko Obayashi's film version of the "Issunboshi" story, based on a novel and script by Masumi Suetani.

Hollywood can rest easy. *Mizu no Tabibito* is an odd marriage of didactic melodrama, hyperbusy camera work, and special effects that range from the excellent to the laughably amateurish. If *Jurassic Park* is a theme-park ride, *Mizu no Tabibito* is a J League soccer game: noisy, colorful, and second-rate.

The hero is not the pint-sized young adventurer of "Issunboshi," but an old warrior who seems to be in the throes of a terminal illness. Instead of story's lacquered soup bowl, his craft is a dirty hunk of hollowed out driftwood. Also, unlike Issunboshi he is not journeying to find fame and fortune, but to float out to sea and die.

Mizu no Tabibito is a modern environmental cautionary tale. The old man, Suminoe Sukunahiko (Tsutomu Yamazaki), is a water spirit. His ill health is caused by polluted water. Without help of some kind, he will never reach the sea to be reborn. Help arrives in the form of Satoru (Ryo Yoshida), a boy who, in trying to retrieve a baseball from the river, and pulls in poor Sukunahiko instead. Satoru takes this new treasure home and puts him in his desk drawer for safe-keeping.

The samurai soon begins exploring his new world. He takes a wild ride on an electric knife, carves up a cockroach with his sword and is nearly carried off by a crow. Some of the effects are amusingly well done, as when Sukunahiko jogs in place on an old phonograph. But the crow is a transparent fake who looks as though he wandered in from an old William Castle movie. Also, odd camera angles and jerky editing rhythms undermine effects that might have otherwise worked.

I should qualify—Obayashi's methods work well in expressing the emotionally claustrophobic atmosphere of Satoru's household. Watching the rapid cutting between closeups of Satoru's nagging mother (Jun Fubuki), sententious father (Itokku Kishibe), and irritable sister Chizuko (Ayumi Ito) I understand why the poor kid was constantly escaping to his room. After the ordinary madness of family life, the extraordinary, in the form of a miniature samurai, must be a relief.

The wimpy Satoru learns the code of the samurai from Sukunahiko, and a few environmental lessons. He stops kicking cans into the river and is emboldened to fend off a dalmatian who growls menacingly at his sister. The climax is water-logged melodrama. While on a school campout, Satoru goes off to discover the source of a stream; he hopes its pure waters will revive Sukunahiko. Miyuki, his sister's tomboyish archrival, tags along but becomes buried in a rockslide. When Satoru's smarmy teacher (Tomoyo Harada), his sister, and other campers notice that the two children are missing, they sound the alarm. Soon, Satoru's mother, father, and an army of rescuers are on the way as the rain pours down. Sukunahiko, mounted on Satoru's cat, is not far behind.

Once again, Obayashi goes overboard with cross-cutting, like a VCR clicked on fast-forward. Perhaps he is competing for a new, mad Guiness record: for the most camera set-ups in a single movie. I felt a quiet relief when the pyrotechnics finally ended (though the last scene, to give it credit, is a dazzler) and the credits started crawling slowly, ever so slowly, down the screen.

Mizu no Naka no Hachigatsu
August in the Water (1995)

Written and directed by Sogo Ishii. Produced by Mizu no Naka no Hachigatsu Production Committee. With Rena Komine, Shinsuke Aoki, Masaaki Muroi, Reiko Matsuo, Naho Toda. (117 mins.)

Back when I was a longhaired commie-pinko-hippie-freak, movie fans of my persuasion would rave about what they called "head movies." Be it *Fantasia* or *2001: A Space Odyssey*, a good head movie was more than the sum of its groovy images; it had to tune into the music of spheres, give off good vibes. Whether it made any logical sense to a non-expanded consciousness was beside the point.

In *Mizu no Naka no Hachigatsu*, Sogo Ishii has made a head movie for the nineties. But whereas Stanley Kubrick and Walt Disney thought that they were making serious films for adults, not mind candy for longhairs with glazed eyes, Ishii has frankly made a film about adolescents, for adolescents, especially those in the palm-reading, crystal-gazing, mysterioso-sensitivo stage.

Those who have graduated from that stage, or never entered it, may become impatient with the film's pseudo-profundities about the mysteries of death and regeneration, humankind's violations of the natural order, and the sacrifice of innocents to appease unknown gods. Or they may become irritated with the film's sudden shift from a realistic-enough story of teenage love to a wooly sci-fi fantasy of supernatural powers and extraterrestrial intervention in human affairs.

Those able to turn off their minds, relax, and float downstream will better enjoy the ride. Ishii has filmed some beautfully evocative images of earth, air, fire, and water, of athletic grace and skill, of youthful love and loss. But this reviewer found found himself not floating or streaming so much as wishing that Ishii had made his film shorter (I got the point of this cinematic mood piece long before I got to the end) and turned down the electronic hum and growl on the soundtrack that renders so much of dialogue barely intelligible.

Ishii's heroine is Hazuka Izumi (Rena Komine), a teenage high diver who is training for the Universiade, and eventually, the Olympics. When she transfers to a Fukuoka high school she meets two boys, the dishy-looking, soft-spoken Mao (Shinsuke Aoki) and the goofy-grinning, fast-talking Ukiya (Masaaki Muroi). Best buddies, they become rivals for her affections. Unluckily for Ukiya, a soothsayer friend (Reiko Matsuo) tells him that, according to the stars, he and Izumi are not meant to be, but that Mao and Izumi are. Ukiya reluctantly gives way and love, shyly, begins to bloom.

Fukuoka, however, is suffering from a severe water shortage and a strange plague that causes people to drop in their tracks. As if that weren't bad enough, Miki warns Ukiya that the signs are not good for Izumi's upcoming diving meet, while Izumi's older sister (Naho Toda) is worried that Izumi might cracking under the pressure. But she decides to compete anyway, and cracks in a way that no one expects. While soaring in the air, she sees the water below her turn into a solid sheet of rock. She bellyflops onto it.

Recovering from her nearly fatal injuries, she notices that the world around her looks glowing and fresh. She also senses new powers and a new mission. She must go to the mountains to find the source of the water that once flowed into the city, and by placating the forces that control it, save her world from destruction.

There is not much science in this fiction, or much of what Hollywood would consider production values. People afflicted with the plague collapse in the middle distance, through a filter of heat-distorted air, but we never see them up close. We hear much about Izumi's supernatural powers, but never see her demonstrate them. (The logical types around her think that she has lost her mind.)

Ishii, long a leader of Japan's independent film scene, is an accomplished visual artist. There are shots—of Izumi twisting and somersaulting through the air, communing with tankful of dolphins through a pane of glass, or walking into a lake in the moonlight—that shimmer with a strange loveliness. You needn't to be a head to enjoy them, but to help you over the inanities, a bong wouldn't be a bad idea.

Moe no Suzaku *
Suzaku (1997)

Written and directed by Naomi Sento. Produced by Bitters End. With Jun Kunimura, Machiko Ono, Sachiko Izumi. (95 mins.)

Many films, and not always the ones with the biggest effects budgets, lose something important in the transition to the small screen. Just how important I discovered when I saw Moe no Suzaku for the second time at a wonderfully restored movie palace in Honolulu called the Hawaii Theater. My first viewing of Naomi Sento's debut feature hadn't impressed me strongly. A beautifully photographed, carefully crafted, deliberately paced film set in the mountains of Nara, with insects buzzing and branches soughing on the soundtrack, Suzaku played, on the Kawakita Foundation's TV screen, as a mood piece in a minor key. On the big screen, however, those mountains loomed large in a drama of a family whose connection to the land—and the spirits that inhabit it—is generations deep. They spoke to me in ways that, on the small screen, they could not.

That family, the Taharas, still make their living from the forests of Yoshino cedars that surround them, as their ancestors did for centuries Their three-generation household includes the father's elderly mother and two children, three-year-old Michiru and eleven-year-old Eisuke—the son of the father's sister—who never seem to watch television or read manga. Instead they grow up playing in the midst of a sylvan paradise.

Then the father, Kyozo (Kunimura Jun), suffers a blow when construction on a railroad tunnel, which he had hoped would revive the village's declining economy, is suddenly abandoned. He falls into a depression and the family's paradise starts to crumble. When the film flashes forward fifteen years, he is still living in a state of limbo. To support the family, the mother takes a job at the local inn where Eisuke works. Meanwhile, Eisuke and Michiru, who is now a high school student, begin to feel more than a cousinly affection toward one another. One day, Kyozo disappears, taking his beloved 8mm camera. Later the family gets a call from the police: they have found a vagrant with the camera. Kyozo is presumed dead, and his survivors go their separate ways.

A documentarian who won acclaim for her autobiographical 8mm films, Sento shot Moe no Suzaku (whose title refers to the Chinese god of the south) in a village in rural Nara Prefecture that was experiencing the economic crisis described in the film. A Nara native herself, she researched conditions in the village for years, and had her staff live there for six months prior to shooting, repairing an old farmhouse that was to be the Tahara family's home. Finally, all of her cast, save for Jun Kunimura, whose credits include Ridley Scott's Black Rain and John Woo's Hard Boiled, were non-professionals.

Sento uses documentary methods with a subtle boldness to impart a sense of lived reality. Her non-actors do not attempt to emote. They are, in fact, taciturn almost to point of incomprehensibility. At times one can follow the story only by reading their faces and gestures—the dialogue gives only the barest of hints. But their their actions have an expressiveness that comes from character, not dramatic coaching.

There is also a sense, rare in recent films by young Japanese directors, that these characters are part of the larger world around them, a world that urbanized, Westernized Japan has largely forgotten. That world, with its ancient forests and folkways, is shown as isolated and dying. Moe no Suzaku offers no easy hope, only an elegy for what once was and might have been. But in its honesty and artistry it gives us confidence that, in Sento's hands, the best traditions of Japanese filmmaking still survive.

Mononoke Hime *
Princess Mononoke (1997)

Written and directed by Hayao Miyazaki. Produced by Tokuma Shoten and NTV. With Yoji Matsuda, Yuriko Ishida, Akihiro Miwa. (133 mins.)

Hayao Miyazaki has been called the "Walt Disney of Japan" for the excellence and popularity of his animated films, but a closer comparison might be Steven Spielberg. Both are master entertainers who have produced megahit after megahit, and in the process have acquired unprecedented power in the industry and control over their artistic destinies. Through astute choices of material they have been able to widen their popular appeal while enhancing their critical reputations. The main difference between the two is that Spielberg has conquered the world, while Miyazaki remains largely a local hero. That may change, however, with Miyazaki's latest feature, *Mononoke Hime*, which Disney will distribute worldwide.

Mononoke Hime represents a departure for Miyazaki; none of his earlier Studio Ghibli films were set in the Japan of the premodern era. Also, none of his films have cost as much to make. *Mononoke Hime*'s budget of two billion yen sets a new record for a domestic animated feature. Much of this money went for computer graphics sequences—another Ghibli first.

The result is animation with far more fluidity and realism of movement than the standard products of the Japanimation industry. Critics will still be able to say that Disney does it better—nothing in *Mononoke Hime* equals the spectacle of the stampede in *The Lion King* or the swirling beauty of the ballroom dance in *Beauty and the Beast*— but it offers its own brand of animation dazzlement, including fight scenes of an inventiveness and verve to equal the best of Jackie Chan (though even Jackie could not pull off the disappearing tricks of the title heroine).

Sheer movement, however, has never been what Miyazaki is about; strongly realized characters and brilliantly imagined fantasy worlds were, and in *Mononoke Hime*, still are. Once again we have a spunky young heroine—the princess of the title, though she is usually referred to as San. This time she is fighting to save the forest she loves, as well as the animal gods who have nurtured her and watch over her, from the depredations of the Tatara, a clan of ironworkers and weaponsmakers led by the imperious and beautiful Lady Eboshi. The save-nature-or-die theme is a Studio Ghibli favorite, but Miyazaki's treatment of it in *Mononoke Hime* is more ambiguous than colleague Isao Takahata's in his 1994 eco-fable *Heisei Tanuki Gassen Pompoko*. The humans that Princess Mononoke battles are not bad people—even Lady Eboshi, who would be cast as the villain in the Disney remake, has her good qualities. Yes, their destruction of the environment is wrong-headed, but they are also working hard to make better lives for themselves and their families— much like the Japanese of Miyazaki's generation who created Japan's economic miracle while fouling the air and poisoning the water.

What the film proposes is not a choice between black and white, but a search for the middle way. The personification of this search is Ashitaka, a youth from the northern Emishi tribe. He is on a journey south to free himself from a curse placed on him by a dying boar-god who had been wounded by one of Lady Eboshi's bullets. On his way, he encounters San and her three-hundred-year-old wolf familiar, who are engaged in a valiant but losing struggle against human encroachment, and the Tatara Clan, whose female leader saves women from the bonds of prostitution and gives them work usually reserved for men, including soldiering and ironworking. He finds himself liking members of both sides—and seeking ways to bring them together.

From this summary, it may seem as though Miyazaki is trying to impose today's PC values on Japan's middle ages, but with his lushly drawn landscapes and strange and fearsome forest gods, he recreates the natural and mythopoetic world of premodern Japan with a characteristic sympathy and passion. Miyazaki has again made, not merely a product for mass consumption, but a work of highly individualized animation art.

Mothra
(1997)

Directed by Okihiro Yoneda. Screenplay by Masumi Suetani. Produced by Toho. With Megumi Kobayashi, Sayaka Yamaguchi, Nagare Hagiwara, Aki Hano, Maya Fujisawa, Hitomi Takabayashi, Kenjiro Nashimoto. (95 mins.)

Series are hardly rare in the Japanese movie business, but a thirty-five-year hiatus between episodes is not exactly common. Toho, however, had sound business reasons for making its first Mothra film since 1961 (though the title character later appeared in other films in supporting roles). Having temporarily retired its Godzilla franchise to avoid cannibalizing returns from Tristar's Godzilla film, which it will distribute in Japan in the summer of 1998, the studio was faced with a large hole in its New Year's schedule. What better way to fill it, Toho execs reasoned, than with another classic movie monster from the company stable?

So now we have a new *Mothra*—but with a different story and, as one might expect, improved special effects. Even so, Mothra herself has remained largely the same—a winsomely strange creature that could only find a home only in Japan. Instead of the pointy teeth, bulging muscles, and metallic roar of the usual towering terror, Mothra is a giant female moth with brightly colored wings and a fuzzy, round, six-thousand-ton body, who makes hardly a sound other the flapping of her fifty-meter wings. Created by H-bomb tests on the remote Pacific island where she was born, she is basically a nonviolent type, who wrecks havoc, via laserlike beams shot from her wings, only to protect her loved ones, including a pair of fairies, the Aliases.

As the film begins, Mothra and the Aliases are living peacefully on Infant Island in a huge domed grotto. Elder sister Moll (Megumi Kobayashi) and younger sister Lora (Sayaka Yamaguchi) trill a song of praise to Mothra, who has just given birth to a giant egg. The race will continue! Meanwhile, men working for a logging company in Hokkaido discover a strange outcropping of rock and, on it, a mysterious pendant. When a helmeted section manager (Kenjiro Nashimoto) pries out the pendant with a screwdriver, he uncovers a brightly lit hole—and unwittingly unleashes a powerful force for evil.

Back on Infant Island, the Aliases intuit that something terrible has happened. They must return the pendant to its rightful place or the world, including their quiet corner of it, will be destroyed. Flying to the home of the manager and his family in Tokyo's Tama New Town, they find the pendant, now the plaything of the manager's daughter (Maya Fujisawa). They also meet an old nemesis—a black-clad fairy named Belvera (Aki Hano)—riding a winged lizard and trying to snatch the pendant for herself. The ensuing battle wrecks the house, but far worse devastation is soon being wrought in Hokkaido, in the form of a three-headed fire-breathing monster named Death Ghidora. This, the sisters decide, is a job for Mothra!

This story is the stuff of childish fantasy and, to their credit, director Okihiro Yoneda, scriptwriter Masumi Suetani and special effects director Koichi Kawakita treat it as such. Unlike the Godzilla films, *Mothra* goes light on the pseudo-scientific jargon and pseudo-thriller scenery-chewing. But to fans of Hollywood effects shows, much of the techno geewhizzery of *Mothra* will look like second-hand gimcrackery. When the toys came to life in Drew Barrymore's room in *E.T.* we were impressed, but when the same effect is repeated in *Mothra* we squirm. This is less the quoting of a classic than the mouthing of a tired cliché. The entire film has a recycled feel, from the storyline, in which Mothra rides to the resue yet again, to the musical interludes, in which Moll and Lora croon like pintsized idol singers, right down to the coyly stylized hand gestures. There is a CD for sale in the lobby.

The acting is numbingly pedestrian, with the manager's kids looking as though they had wandered in from the school play, while Kenjiro Nashimoto as the manager and Hitomi Takahashi as

his wife emote like the principals in a bad TV soap.

Of course, the non-human stars of *Mothra* received most of the filmmakers' attention. But though she may have her camp charms and even serve as a role model—at last, a movie monster a girl can look up to!—Mothra is lacking in personality, being little more than an animated stuffed animal. Death Ghidora would seem to be a suitably scary villain, with his three snakelike heads, but he is a too-familiar face, having appeared, under different names, in two other Toho films of the nineties: *Godzilla tai King Ghidora* and *Yamato Takeru*. This casting choice may represent canny studio management—three monsters for the price of one—but it also symbolizes the by-the-numbers thinking that characterizes the whole project. If *Mothra* is the best Toho can put up against the behemoths of Hollywood, the Japanese monster-movie genre may be flapping towards the box-office flame.

Muno no Hito
Nowhere Man (1991)

Directed by Naoto Takenaka. Screenplay by Toshiharu Maruichi. Produced by KSS, Shochiku, and Daiichi Kogyo. With Naoto Takenaka, Jun Fubuki, Kotaro Santo. (107 mins.)

Naota Takenaka's *Muno no Hito* has one of those titles that ask for it and sometimes get it. If Dorothy Parker could famously quip that "'The House Beautiful' is the play lousy," we might write "*Muno no Hito wa mugei no eiga*"? ("Nowhere Man is a nowhere movie"). But it wouldn't be right. Naoto Takenaka, an actor making his directorial debut, is a better maker of films than his hapless hero—played by Takenaka himself—is a maker of money. In fact, *Muno no Hito* won the FIPRESCI prize at the 1991 Venice Film Festival.

Photographed in warm sepia tones, *Muno* has an air of nostalgia for a vanished world. Takenaka's world, however, is not the past—the film is set in today's Japan—but a *manga* fantasyland. The *manga* on which the film is based, by Yoshiharu Tsuge, tells of a cartoonist named Sukezo Sukegawa (Naoto Takenaka) who falls out of favor with the public, then fails at twice at business (first at selling old cameras, then antiques) before finally hitting on what he hopes will be the key to success: rocks.

Japanese, after all, have a passion for rocks, both cut and polished and in a natural state. Rocks in the latter category are often said to resemble something else: Mt. Fuji, or a couple locked in a passionate embrace. Surely a cartoonist, who makes his living conjuring up fantasy worlds, would have leg up in this business? Sukegawa finds his rocks on the banks of the Tama River and builds a rickety little stand from which to sell them. He is not mad, but lacking in common sense. Who is going to buy river rocks when they are everywhere, free for the lifting? The answer, of course, is no one, even when the Sukegawa's apple-cheeked son is helping to hawk them.

The film itself is something of a sell; Takenaka wants us to take his hero as seriously as we took Anthony Quinn's strongman and Guilietta Masina's waif in *La Strada*. Like the characters in Fellini's masterpiece, the rock-seller represents all the "nowhere" people whose dreams are crushed by an indifferent world. But Takenaka's Nowhere Man conceit is almost as hard to swallow as Sukegawa's wares. The story of a failed artist selling worthless rocks by a riverside might have worked in a setting of poverty—Japan in the early postwar period. But at a time when jobs are going begging—or being filled by Iranians with tourist visas—the hero's choice of occupation seems not only absurd, but terminally precious.

Takenaka keeps his story simple, his emotions basic. Sukegawa meets an eccentric rock dealer (Taro Maruse) and attracts the amorous attention of his creepy wife (Miyako Yamaguchi). The former tells him of an auction where he can sell his rocks, the latter visits him at his shop, where she tries to seduce him. Neither the auction sale nor the seduction work out as expected, but during the course of his misadventures Sukegawa meets a mysterious bird-seller (director Tatsumi Kumashiro in a cameo) who sets him on a different, if not more lucrative, path. He also has the support of his long-suffering wife (Jun Fubuki), who comes to hate rocks, but can't bring herself to leave her rock-headed husband. With the exception of his wife—who serves as the film's beacon of sanity—the people the hero encounters are as eccentric as he is, if not more so. Most seem to caught in a time warp; though the calendar says 1991, they dress, live, and act as though it were 1951.

Takenaka makes us care about his characters and laugh at their foibles. The auction, where the hero hopes to makes a killing with a rock his son has found holding down a sewer lid, has an unforced pathos and wry humor. But he irritates with his heavy-handed whimsy and exasperates with his slow-footed pacing (even the Bird Man walks as though his feet were bound). He also seems to think that grinding poverty is quaintly poetic. Perhaps, like his hero, he should have spent a night sleeping rough in Shinjuku—without his crew to film his snores or the security crew to keep the real poor folk away.

Musuko *
My Sons (1992)

Directed by Yoji Yamada. **Screenplay by** Yoshitaka Asama and Yoji Yamada. **Produced by** Shochiku. **With** Rentaro Mikuni, Masatoshi Nagase, Emi Wakui. (121 mins.)

Yoji Yamada is best known for his longest-running Tora-san series, which has set a Guiness-book record and occupied most of his energies since the first installment in 1969, but the workaholic director has embarked on several non-Tora-san projects as well. One, *Kofuku no Kiroii Hankachi* (The Yellow Handkerchief) won an Japan Academy Award for Best Picture in 1977. His latest, *Musuko*, is in the down-home vein of the Torasan films, but its story is more firmly anchored in the bittersweet realities of the present than the idealized glories of the past.

As in the Tora-san series, Yamada's focus is a working-class family, but instead of being nestled in the *shitamachi* (Tokyo's old downtown), it is scattered to the four winds. As the film begins, the family's three children return to their home in Iwate Prefecture for a Buddhist service commemorating the first anniversary of their mother's death. The last to arrive, in a Hawaiian shirt, is Tetsuya, a waiter at Shinjuku pub. Tetsuya is the youngest child and the biggest thorn in his father's side. The boy, he feels, is wasting himself, while Tetsuya has only scorn for the old man's values and way of life. Why slave on a farm when you can earn a cool eight hundred yen an hour drawing mugs of draft beer? The two quarrel and separate.

Generational conflict is a common theme in postwar Japanese cinema. Rentaro Mikuni, *Musuko*'s Father, was already playing the hardheaded patriarch in Miyoji Ieki's 1957 *Ibo Kyodai* (Stepbrothers). But Yamada, whose script is based on a book by Makoto Shiina, takes an unconventional approach to this theme, dividing the film into three parts. Father and Tetsuya quarrel after the memorial service in Part I, Tetsuya learns the meaning of work and love in Part II, and Father stays, lost and lonely, in the Tokyo condo of his elder son in Part III. Towards the end, Tetsuya and Father meet again. They are both changed people, who are more willing to accept differences in others. Yet the ending is not all sweetness and light; in a very Japanese way, Father realizes that everything passes, even hearth and home.

In telling his three stories Yamada keeps the seams from showing and our attention from wandering. His style may be unpretentious—the cinematic equivalent of *takuan* pickles and rice—but he has a sure grasp of his story and solid understanding of his characters. *Musuko* is Japan with its real feelings on display. For two hours, it brings us into the family circle. It also comes closer to the Japanese audience's image of itself than films by many ostensibly more serious directors. Yamada may be guilty of sentimentalism, but he heads straight for the heart of the Japanese mythos.

With his shaggy gray hair and big, round shoulders, Rentaro Mikuni plays Father as a bearish old man, growling his displeasure at his younger son's insolence and his older son's insistence that he leave his Iwate home. Mikuni, however, is a subtle bear, who can make the father's simpleheartedness seem funny without turning him into a clown, and express his pathos without reducing him to an object of pity. Playing Tetsuya, Masatoshi Nagase starts as a don't-care punk, but after finding a job in a metalworking shop and falling in love with a pretty deaf office girl (Emi Wakui), he grows as a human being. We start by looking down on this arrogant kid, and end by admiring his inner strength. Nagase even makes credible Tetsuya's sudden conversion to the gospel of hard, sweaty work.

Yamada has described *Musuko* as a film that he "wanted to make and had to make." He added that, "it's usually hard for me to combine both motives." That is unfortunate; if he could devote more of his talents to non-series projects, we would be better off for it. Tora-san could take a much needed rest—and so could the record-keepers at Guiness.

Muteki no Handicap
Invincible Handicapped (1994)

Directed by Daisuke Tengan. Produced by Head Office, Garo Cinema, and Muteki no Handicap Production Committee. (80 mins.)

If we are right-thinking people, we applaud the lowering of physical and social barriers for the physically disabled. But in Japan, where conformity to group norms is not only expected, but rigorously and sometimes brutally enforced, there is still a large gap between the right-thinking gestures—the ramps in the train stations and the sympathetic TV documentaries—and the social and psychological realities. Daisuke Tengan's documentary *Muteki no Handicap* examines that gap with an honesty that is raw, disturbing, liberating. If nothing else, the film brings us face-to-face with our real feelings. They may not be as righteous as we may have hoped.

For what Tengan shows us are not heart-warming role models, but a group of disabled and volunteers in Setagaya Ward who have started their own professional wrestling association. The members of

the Doglegs—a non-PC name if there ever was one—approach the sport with deadly seriousness. They lift weights, practice throws, wear costumes, and adopt outlandish stage names (Sambo Shintaro, "Beast God" Magnum Namikai, Antithesis Kitajima, Big Van Volunteer), just like the real thing. Their first matches, held in April 1991, drew all of five spectators, but they quickly attracted a following. A year later, when Tengan began filming them, a crowd of 130 came to what had become a wrestling extravaganza, complete with a string-bikini-clad emcee., a bow-tied referee, and trophies for the winners.

The first wrestlers into the film's ring are both cerebral palsy victims—and they both fight for real, not show. They punch, kick, strangle, draw blood. Tengan films their struggle in grainy, blurry closeups that intensified my feelings of strangeness and discomfort. Wasn't this a variation of the carnival geek show? Wasn't the crowd paying money to gawk at human misery? And wasn't Tengan, like Tod Browning in *Freaks*, presenting decadent shock horror in the guise of a sympathetic study?

The answers, I realized, were "no." The wrestlers are there, as they later emphasize in on-camera interviews, because they enjoy it—and to make a statement. Through wrestling they are graphically challenging the stereotypes of the disabled as weak and helpless. And instead of hiding in the "safety zone" that Japanese society has made for the disabled, they flaunt their physicality and test the limits of their strength.

The disabled M.C., who also appears in the ring as "Beast God" Magnum Namikai, performs a Schwarzeneggerian muscleman routine before the matches begin. He also flings out a challenge to the crowd: "We Doglegs are here to fight for all we're worth, so you'd better watch for all you're worth!" Through Tengan's camera, that's exactly what we do. We find ourselves not only in the ring, but in the wrestlers' lives. Watching the interviews with parents, volunteers, soapland sex workers, and the wrestlers themselves, we begin to understand what it means to be disabled in today's Japan. "They are strong-willed people," says one soapland masseuse of her disabled clients. I had to agree.

But I still had to wonder about another aspect of the Doglegs' show; bouts between healthy volunteers and the disabled. One volunteer, whose ring name is Big Van Volunteer, plays a smirking, gap-toothed punk who vows to "put the cripples in their place." During one practice session, he slaps and kicks his disabled partner, Sambo Shintaro, with the glee of the schoolyard bully. The volunteer founder of the Doglegs, Gyotoku Kitajima, tries nervously to explain that, even though Big Van may be acting, he has to make it look as real as possible if his performance is to be effective.

But why do healthy volunteers have to step into the ring in the first place? The answer, says Kitajima, is that, despite a decade of volunteer work, he always felt that the disabled regarded him as "the other." Through wrestling, he has been able to narrow that gap. We see what he means when he meets Sambo Shintaro in a "challenge bout" (with Shintaro issuing the challenge). This contest, the climax to the film, leaves both contestants bloodied, exhausted, and undeniably closer than before. We may debate the means and recoil from the images; but we cannot deny their effectiveness and power. The film's message is best expressed by "Beast God" Magnum Namikai: "We are all disabled." *Muteki no Handicap* may present the ultimate comprehension challenge for non-native-speakers—it does not supply subtitles for its interviews with speech-impaired wrestlers—but it makes that message loud and clear.

Nagare Ita Shichinin
Seven Wandering Cooks (1997)

Directed by Seiji Izumi. Screenplay by Hiroji Takada. Produced by Toei. With Hiroki Matsukata, Kiyoshi Nakajo, Ayumi Ishida, Miki Sakai. (114 mins.)

The gourmet boom has been us with so long that to the younger generation food fanaticism must seem a permanent part of the Japanese cultural landscape (cherry blossoms, Mt. Fuji, the Iron Chef). In Seiji Izumi's *Nagare Ita Shichinin*, the men (seldom women) who prepare the costliest cuisine of all— Japanese gourmet food—belong to a subculture that is deeply, almost stubbornly traditional. No New Age food trendies these. Their hierarchies as strictly graded as those of a *sumo* stable and they adhere strictly to the values of *giri-ninjo*, which means doing right by those to whom you are obliged and following the warm impulses of the heart rather the cold dictates of reason. Apprentices serve under all-powerful *oyakata* (bosses) with feudal devotion and

loyalty. Their *heya*, or cooking crew, provides everything from material sustenance to moral compass. Women have a place in this subculture as maids or geisha or *josho* (mistresses) of the *ryotei* (teahouses) where the men cook. They are the face of the establishment, while the men are the heart. Neither can live without the other, but their roles are strictly defined. The atmosphere is purely Japanese, with the Westernized modern world carefully excluded. This, the movie implies, is the way it ought to be, but too seldom is.

The plot of *Nagare* could have come from another tradition—the Toei *yakuza* movie. The *oyakata* of a long-established *ryotei* is losing his grip due to poor health; the quality of the food is declining and customers are turning away. Knowing that his time is short and his *heya* in danger, he writes to a former apprentice named Ryuji Rindo (Hiroki Matsukata), asking for help. The owner and chef of a small restaurant in Okayama Prefecture, Ryuji answers his old master's call, but when he arrives in Tokyo he finds the *oyakata* dead and the members of his *heya* scattered. The proprietress has replaced them with a new crew headed by the master chef of a famous Kyoto *ryotei*, the imperious Akihiko Hokota (Kiyoshi Nakajo).

Ryuji is about to return home when Kinu Inamura (Ayumi Ishida), an agent who represents the *oyakata* and his *heya*, and her headstrong daughter Hanae (Miki Sakai) persuade him to fill in for an absent chef at another restaurant. Knowing his reputation, Kinu and Hanae want to see him in action. Ryuji obliges and wows the restaurant's patrons with his cooking, which uses only the best and freshest ingredients, incorporates natural flavors and seasonal variations, and, most important of all, comes from the heart.

As one might expect, the film's climax takes the form of a cooking contest between Ryuji and Hokota, judged by an old patron of the *ryotei* (Tatsuo Matsumura) and his gourmet friends. There is more than pride at stake; if Ryuji wins, the crew will regain their old jobs at the *ryotei*, under Kinu's representation. If Hokota wins, Kinu will give up her agency and become the *ryotei*'s mistress and Hokota's employee. Why would she take such a gamble? She is deeply, if quietly, in love with Ryuji.

Nagare's culinary showdown has a recent precedent—the 1996 *Oishimbo* (Taste Quest) featured a contest to prepare the Ultimate Menu. As in the previous film, director Izumi serves up gorgeously photographed feasts, but its inspiration are all those Toei *yakuza* movies about a loner gangster, usually played by Ken Takakura, who comes to the aid of an old *oyabun* (boss) in his struggle with a rival gang. I was half expecting Hiroki Matsukata—a veteran *yakuza*-movie star—to slice and dice a few of the bad guys with his carving knife.

That might have been preferable to the movie's actual denouement, which is clichéd and tame. Izumi provides plenty of well-researched insights into the *itamae* (cook) subculture and Japanese *haute cuisine*, but he tells his story without the passion or flair that informed that classic of epicurean cinema, *Babette's Feast*. What we get in *Nagare* are not fresh ideas, imaginatively presented, but old genres and stars, conventionally repackaged and stale on delivery. Unfortunately for film fans, movies don't come with dates of expiration. Then again, it might be strange if a movie released in 1997 came with a label saying "Do not consume after 1968."

Nagisa no Sindbad *
Like Grains of Sand (1996)

Written and directed by Ryosuke Hashiguchi. Produced by YES. With Yoshinori Okada, Kota Kusano, Ayumi Hamazaki, Kumi Takada. (129 mins.)

Once in a while a film tells us how teenagers really think, feel, and act, and for adults, the truth can hurt. We grownups tend to demonize, patronize, or idealize teenagers, and it can be a jolt to find out how little we know about them and how completely they are living in their own world, hostile or indifferent to our values and mores.

In 1992 a thirty-year-old director named Ryosuke Hashiguchi revealed a seldom-explored part of that world in *Hachigatsu no Binetsu*, a film about gay hustlers. The film had technical rough spots, but Hashiguchi knew his characters' story from the inside and told it well. He has set his second film, *Nagisa no Sinbad*, in an ordinary high school, not a gay bar. Instead of hustlers, his teenagers are seemingly ordinary kids, going through the ordinary agonies of growing up. As in *Hachigatsu*, however, Hashiguchi goes behind his characters' normal fronts to the present the truth about their not-so-normal feelings. He approaches his material much as a documentarian might, rejecting the cliches of the *seishun eiga* (youth film) genre, including the sticky coating of sentimentalism that many use, like cotton candy, to brighten and soften their cardboard centers.

Shuji Ito (Yoshinori Okada) is a gay high-school senior who has fallen in love with his best friend, Hiroyuki Yoshida (Kota Kusano). Ito can't tell Yoshida, or anyone else, about his feelings—he's afraid of ruining everything, including his carefully maintained facade. Yoshida, a straight-arrow innocent, doesn't have a clue. Meanwhile, Yoshida is attracted to Kasane Aihara (Ayumi Hamazaki), a new student who has a secret of her own: a rape that traumatized her and made her incapable of responding to Yoshida's advances. Her experience has also made her impatient with her classmates' catty social games. A truth seeker and truth teller, she finds herself without friends and with more than a few enemies. To further complicate this romantic tangle, Ayako Shimizu (Kumi Takada), another straight-arrow type, is fond of Yoshida, while Aihara is drawn to Ito. Somehow, she senses a fellow loner with a big secret. To Ito's annoyance and discomfort, she is determined to pry it out.

Hashiguchi writes dialogue that sounds like uncensored teen talk, while revealing character and advancing the story. Also, he takes big risks with his material and makes them pay off. His biggest is the scene in which Ito reveals his feelings to Yoshida. Their classmates have just teased them for being lovers and now they are alone in the classroom. This humiliation has given Ito courage; he asks Yoshida to kiss him. Embarassed and shocked, Yoshida does not know how to respond. Most directors would force a conclusion quickly and move on. Hashiguchi, however, draws this scene out, almost unbearably, to make us experience the awkwardness of the moment and the weight it carries in its characters' lives.

It is such scenes, in which destinies seem to hang on a gesture or word, that make *Nagisa* memorable. While rejecting illusions about about the innocence of youth and asking uncomfortable questions about the nature of sexual identity, Hashiguchi also leaves us adults with a feeling of affection and admiration for his wounded-outcast heroes. They still have the inconvenient virtues of sincerity and honesty and the reckless desire to live according to their instincts instead of their interests. Seeing this movie, we feel better about the future of the strange new world they are creating.

Nanmin Road
Refugees Shoot Japan (1992)

Written and directed by Takumi Igarashi. Produced by Premiere International and Suntory. With Truong Thi Thuy Trang, Le Manh Hung, Emi Sato, Vu Hoang Phuong. (101 mins.)

Young Japanese directors are become more aware of the presence of other Asians in their midst and what that presence says about Japanese society. Like many of these films, Takumi Igarashi's *Nanmin Road* shows us the exploitative, exclusionist face Japan so often turns toward non-white strangers. It is, however, the first Japanese film to tell its story almost entirely through those stranger's eyes. Its four main characters are all Vietnamese boat people, three of whom are played by Vietnamese refugees living in

Japan. But what, we might ask, does Igarashi, a twenty-three-year-old TV and music video director making his first feature, know about his characters and their culture? How can he make his Japanese audience emphasize with the foreigners up on the screen?

His answers to these questions are less than satisfactory. First, the Vietnamese characters speak Japanese, even among themselves. In a program interview Igarashi explains that he wanted to show that the characters are trying hard to adapt to Japanese society. Even so, we can't help feeling that commercial considerations are influencing their choice of language. This impression is strengthened by the film's storyline and the director's style. *Nanmin Road* sets up its melodramatic situations with strident obviousess. Igarashi's sensibility is still that of the TV director who underlines everything twice for the mass audience.

The characters are representative types. Lam (Truong Thi Thuy Trang) is an office clerk who is studying hard for a college entrance exam. Her older brother Tok (Le Manh Hung) is a steel-mill worker who is drifting through life. His live-in lover Kim (Emi Sato) is a half-Vietnamese, half-American woman who works in a bar catering to foreigners and dreams of going to the land of her father. His best friend Yon (Vu Hoang Phuong) has become an apprentice gangster and drug-money bagman.

Tok, the most "typical" character, is the film's center. Like many Asian workers in this country, he is an illegal, but he became so in an unusual way. When he and Yon were boys, they ran away from their refugee camp. A policeman chased them, but the boys wrestled his gun away and Tok shot him. This incident makes it easier to understand why Tok rejects his lover's pleas to go with her to America and why he withdraws a million yen from his sister's bank account so that Yon can replace a lost drug payment. But this nine-year-old shooting, which affects all of Tok's subsequent actions, also makes him a highly untypical refugee—and threatens to transform the film into an another tearjerking melodrama.

Fortunately, Igarashi's determination to see Japan from his refugees' point of view saves his film from this fate. However imperfectly, he and his refugee actors offer allow us to enter into the lives of Vietnamese in Japan. Toward the end, Yon dies in Tok's arms—the result of a shootout with his *yakuza* brethren. The two Vietnamese actors play this scene in their own language, with a rawness that seems born of personal experience. Had they witnessed similar scenes in their childhood, I wondered? How much better might the film have been if they had been in the director's chair, telling us their own story?

Natsu no Niwa
The Friends (1994)

Directed by Shinji Somai. Screenplay by Yozo Tanaka. Produced by Yomiuri TV. With Yasutaka Oh, Ken'ichi Makino, Naoki Sakata. (113 mins.)

In *Natsu no Niwa*, Shinji Somai injects the story of three boys' creepy, thrilling, enlightening encounter with mortality with his usual knowing insights into the workings of the preadolescent mind, leavened by touches of humor, but he also turns the film down the same introverted, gloomy, and sentimental path taken by so many before him. He has made essentially two films: one centered on his young heroes, another on the lonely old man who is the object of their fears, and eventually, friendship. The first film, after a promising start, is left underdeveloped and unresolved. The second, which reprises the themes of countless war-survivor melodramas, is geriatric cinema, tired, creaking, unconvincing.

The "friends" of the English title are three boys living in Kobe. Kawabe (Yasutaka Oh) is small and bespectacled, with a high-pitched voice and a high-strung disposition. Yamashita (Ken'ichi Makino) is a *sumo* wrestler in embryo and fishmonger in training. Kiyama (Naoki Sakata) is tall, good-looking, and chronically short of sleep. Having heard that human beings breathe from six hundred million to eight hundred million times in a lifetime, he spends his nights counting his breaths.

But it is Kawabe, whose father died shortly after he was born, who is most obsessed with death. When Yamashita returns to school from his grandmother's funeral, Kawabe grills him. Was it interesting? Was the crematory fire hot? Then he has a great idea for an adventure. He has overheard his mother saying that the old man who lives alone in a tumbledown house near their apartment building is on the verge of death. Wouldn't it be neat to catch him when he is actually croaking? He persuades his reluctant companions to stake out the house, which is buried in a stinking, creepy-crawly filled jungle of weeds.

Somai, who is known for his work with children (his 1993 *Ohikkoshi* [Moving] is an excellent example), is adept at capturing the atmosphere of boyhood, including the mixture of terror, fascination, and disgust with which his heroes stalk their quarry. Using a Steadicam, he makes us a member of the gang and takes us over the old man's wall, into a haunted corner of a forgotten world. What the boys find there is a white-haired bear of a man (Rentaro Mikuni), who is lost in a dream of the past. This bear, however, stirs to life when he discovers the boys invading his lair. They flee, screaming, but soon return, to the old man's annoyance and amusement, and a cross-generational friendship begins. Almost without knowing why, the boys begin hanging the old man's clothes on the line, pulling his weeds, and planting his garden. Their reward is a watermelon and a glimpse down a well, to which the old man consigns the corpses of dead butterflies.

The boys do not have the combination of individuality and authenticity of their counterparts in Rob Reiner's *Stand by Me*. Their performances range from the gimmicky and one-note (Yasutaka Oh's Kawabe wears Harold Lloyd glasses and talks at the top of his voice throughout the entire movie) to the dull normal (Naoki Sakata's Kiyama, who narrates the film and is its emotional center, is little more than a nice, average kid spending his vacation in a strange way).

Would that Somai had developed *Natsu* the way he did *Ohikkoshi*, with that film's profound awareness of the mysteries of growing up. Instead, he changes the focus to the old man and his wartime past. After committing atrocities in the Philippine jungle ("We had to do it to survive," he tells the boys), he did not return to his wife and child in Japan. For nearly fifty years he has lived alone, lamenting and regretting. But unbeknownst to him, the boys' pretty teacher has a grandmother who… but enough said. The coincidences involved in bringing these two together strain credulity, and the climatic reunion scene goes shamelessly for the tear ducts. Somewhere along the line the boys become supporting players in their own film, who learn that death is a pretty butterfly winging its way up from a dark well. In the final shot, their faces are wreathed in smiles—and we wonder about opportunities missed.

Natsu Jikan no Otonatachi
Happy-Go-Lucky (1997)

Written and directed by Tetsuya Nakashima. Produced by Fat, Inc. With Keiichi Hidaka, Hiroko Taguchi, Ittoku Kishibe, Noriko Saiki. (73 mins.)

The Japanese title *Natsu Jikan no Otonatachi*, which literally translates as "Summer-Time Adults," is misleading. Although the film is set in the summer and adults, especially the parents of a precocious school boy named Takashi, play a central role, it is more concerned with how childhood traumas form character and how the inner child influences the life of the outer adult. "Adults don't grow up," director Nakashima said in an interview, "They simply grow older." The reverse, he believes, is also true; "There isn't much that is really 'childish' about children." In short, his grownups may be Peter Pans, but his kids have little use for Never-Never Land. They are more concerned with surviving in a world that is forever

manipulating them, misunderstanding them, or frightening them with its obscure and mysterious terrors. In *Natsu*, Nakashima creates a vision of childhood that may have its humorous oddities, but also feels much like the real thing.

Takashi (Keiichi Hidaka) is a born outsider who is constantly critiquing the other inhabitants of his world (including, in the case of the female inhabitants, the size of their bosoms), but refuses to obey their rules, written or unwritten. One of those rules, he discovers to his chagrin, is Thou Shalt Perform a Back Flip on the Playground Horizontal Bar. His teacher, the stern Mr. Kimura, assures his charges that if they fail this important test of character, they will become failures in life. Unfortunately, Takashi and four of his classmates flail their legs skyward to no avail. Mr. Kimura orders them to keep trying until they succeed. Four of the five, including the leggy, strong-willed Tomoko (Hiroko Taguchi), practice hard to erase their shame and rejoin their classmates on the upward path. The fifth, Takashi, grips the bar moodily and wonders why a backflip is the key to his future happiness and prosperity. Obviously, this kid has problems.

Takashi and his problems are not enough to carry the film, so Nakashima also focuses on Takashi's parents, including their messed-up childhoods. Dad (Itokku Kishibe) runs a small electric-appliance store, Mom (Noriko Saiki) is a housewife. Both, as we see in extended flashbacks, endured childhood traumas and are still living with the consequences. Despite their outward normality, something is out of joint. Recovering from a whiplash suffered in a traffic accident, Dad stares out the second-story window, not even stirring when he sees a teenage girl being brutally hazed by classmates. Meanwhile, Mom is downstairs, glued to a TV soap about a love triangle. The only thing special about her, Takashi observes, is her youth.

As children, however, their lives were not so empty and vicarious. They faced crises that may now seem trivial but then loomed large. Though less actors than acted upon in these crises, they had choices, and made what in retrospect were the wrong ones. They were, in other words, very much like their son.

Nakashima films this generational drama with a leisurely pace well-suited to its small-town, summertime setting. Despite his film's comic undercurrent, he does not treat his characters as stick figures for playing his directorial games. He stays in the background, giving them room to breathe and lopsidedly grow. Takashi may be a weird kid, but his dilemma feels familiar, even if we were whizzes on the horizontal bar.

Natsu ends with a very Japanese moral. Takashi will still be Takashi, horizontal bars or no. Life will go on, with the bent twigs of childhood growing into the bent branches of adulthood. Even so, as Takashi notes at the end, there is still reason to hope: he will get taller and the girls' bosoms will get bigger. What more can a boy ask for?

Nazo no Tenkosei *
The Dimension Travelers (1999)

Directed by Kazuya Konaka. Screenplay by Sadayuki Murai. Produced by Bandai Visual and Tsuburaya Eizo. With Chiharu Niiyama, Yasue Sato, Satoshi Tsumabuki, Ken Nishida, Masaaki Takarai. (95 mins.)

Kazuya Konaka's *Nazo no Tenkosei* is the latest and most mind-bending example of a genre long popular in Japan: sci-fi fantasies with teenagers in the starring roles. Based on a novel by Takashi Mayumura and a nine-part drama series broadcast on NHK in 1975, *Nazo* takes us on a trip through parallel worlds that, to the more rationally minded, might well produce vertigo. Bring Dramamine and grab those armrests. To those tolerant of its narrative leaps and logical stretches, *Nazo* will be an absorbing, if giddy, ride into the unknown. Ultimately, the film is less about the possibility of slipping through wormholes in the time-space continuum than with the search of its adolescent heroines for friendship and love. Their dimensional travels become metaphors for that search. Though targeted squarely at teenagers, *Nazo* is exceptionally well scripted, well acted, and well made. It deserves more attention than it is likely to get.

Midori (Chiharu Niiyama) is a lonely romantic who tries to fit with her high school classmates, but secretly can't stand their insincerities and pretensions She is also head over heels for Yamazawa (Masaaki Takarai), a brooding dreamboat who barely acknowledges her existence. Meanwhile, she is being hotly pursued by Koichi (Satoshi Tsumabuki), an outspoken, undreamy classmate whom she has seemingly known forever and regards dismissively as "just a friend."

One day, while riding on the elevator to her apartment in a "New Town" high-rise, she encounters a new resident—an exotically beautiful girl with piercing eyes. She is Mayumi (Yasue Sato), who introduces herself in Midori's class the next day as a transfer student. When the teacher asks her about her hopes for the future, she replies evenly that "it would be nice if this world isn't destroyed." Later, when Mayumi calmly reels off an explanation of Heisenberg's uncertainty principle to her flummoxed physics teacher, Midori gazes at her with undisguised fascination. This is the soulmate she has

been searching for! Mayumi has been thinking the same thing. "You and I are a lot alike" she tells Midori, after discovering her secret hobby of pressing flowers in school library books. She then tells her own secret; she has come from another dimension. She and her mother made the jump just as their own world was being destroyed in a nuclear holocaust. When Midori expresses her envy of her new friend's unusual powers, Mayumi tells her that she has them too—and offers to demonstrate.

What Midori discovers when she makes the dimensional leap, however, is not just new worlds, but new lives. Who is she really, she wonders in astonishment and terror, the girl enduring the usual tribulations of adolescence, the new recruit in a resistance movement to save a dying world, or the soul-shattered inmate of a nightmarish madhouse, whose resident shrink tells her that her "real life" is nothing but a delusion? In the course of her journeys, she uncovers the answers to these questions, as well the truth about Mayumi and the enigmatic Yamazawa. Slowly, she begins to find her feet and make her way in this strangest of all possible universes.

Director Konaka, whose credits include the *Ultraman* series, deftly probes the eternal themes of adolescence: the feeling that one is living in an alien world, the need to affirm one's identity through friendship, and the belief that the truth, in the immortal words of *The X-Files*, is "out there."

Chiharu Niiyama's Midori and Yasue Sato's Mayumi are opposites—the former hot, dreamy innocence and the latter cool, worldly experience—that naturally attract. I was particularly taken with Sato, who also starred in the excellent *Bounce Ko Gals*. She brings a teenage witchery to her onscreen persona that makes her a mesmerizing otherworldly guide. Get your ticket—the last tour leaves shortly.

Nejishiki *
Wind-up Type (1998)

Written and directed by Teruo Ishii. Produced by Ishii Production. With Tadanobu Asano, Miki Fujitani, Tsugumi, Mika Aoba, Kaoru Mizuki. (87 mins.)

Watching *Nejishiki*, Teruo Ishii's eighty-first film and his second based on the work of *manga* artist Yoshiharu Tsuge, I found it passing strange that these two veteran representatives of the *eroguro* (i.e., "erotic and grotesque") side of Japanese popular art should have been so long getting together.

One reason was box-office realities. Though Ishii first read and admired *Nejishiki* when it appeared in *Garo* magazine in 1967, its offbeat tale of a struggling cartoonists's journey between dream and reality, Eros and Thanatos, would have been a hard sell to Ishii's studio bosses. In the late seventies, Ishii's career stalled, and he retreated to directing TV dramas. Ironically, the project that returned him to the big screen, after a gap of fourteen years, was *Gensenkan Shujin*, a four-segment omnibus based on Tsuge's *manga*. Now he is back again with *Nejishiki*.

Ishii begins with an opening sequence of writhing semi-naked flesh inspired by Hieronymus Bosch. Yet the film is less a tour though a garden of earthly delights than a trip through a borderland where the spiritual wounds of waking life fester in the night mind. It is a world of loners and losers, where sex becomes a frantically absurd assault across the gulf that separates the sexes, where a failed suicide attempt is regarded less than a melodramatic cry for help than a blackly comic foul-up. The underlying tone of the film, however, is gently tolerant, not mocking; sympathetic, not supercilious. Rather than simply impress with the twisted brilliance of his images, Ishii tries to locate the wellsprings of our common humanity in places we visit in the darkest hours of dreams.

The hero is a cartoonist named Tsube (Tadanobu Asano) who finds himself evicted and broke. His live-in lover, Kuniko (Miki Fujitani), becomes a housekeeper at a company dormitory for single men, while Tsube crashes with a sign-painter friend. This solution to the housing problem, however, is far from satisfactory; Tsube's friend cuddles him in his sleep, while Kuniko drifts into a friendship with a smirking creep at the dorm that drives Tsube wild with jealousy. They finally break up, not over the creep, but Kuniko's one-night stand with a customer at a bookshop where she used to work. In despair, Tsuge tries to kill himself with pills, but wakes up in a hospital bed, with a nurse putting a diaper on him, while his roommate and landlord look on with amusement.

Tsube recovers in the countryside, while having a series of erotic encounters that include a wide-eyed hostess (Tsugumi) at a country tavern who thrusts Tsube's hand down the front of her *yukata*, a sultry model (Mika Aoba) in a "nude studio" who mocks Tsube for his indifference, and the spinsterish proprietress of a seaside eatery who enjoys a night of torrid love-making with Tsube, then promptly forgets his existence.

He falls into a dream in which he is bitten on the arm by a jellyfish and searches desperately for a doctor to bind his severed veins together and save his life. After bizarre encounters with a fox-faced train engineer and an old woman who has made the world's longest *kintaro ame* confection, a sexy obstetrician (Kaoru Mizuki) eases his pain in ways the Japan Medical Association would not approve.

The most riveting of Tsube's erotic partners is Mika Aoba, who plays her scene nude, with a *sang froid* that Sharon Stone might admire. Taking Tsube on a teasing guided tour of her nether regions ("Here is Shiba Park and here's Tokyo Tower"), she generates more heat than all the film's futon gymnastics combined. In the work of the seventy-three-year-old Ishii, the erotic principle is still alive and well, with no help needed from little blue pills.

Nemureru Bijo
House of the Sleeping Beauties (1995)

Directed by Hiroto Yokoyama. Screenplay by Toshio Ishido. Produced by Hiroto Yokoyama Production. With Yoshio Harada, Haruko Wanibuchi, Yuka Onishi, Masayuki Shida. (110 mins.)

Freely adapted from a novel by Yasunari Kawabata, Hiroto Yokoyama's *Nemureru Bijo* is not the most pleasant of films. It dwells gloomily on the inevitability of decline and death, takes a disturbingly necrophiliac view of sex, and makes even the act of giving birth seem perverse. The film strives for the catharsis of Greek tragedy, but instead gives us the chill of lifting up a rock and seeing forbidden desires skitter away from the light.

After spending nearly a decade in development hell—he bought the rights to Kawabata's novel in 1986—Yokoyama knew what he wanted on the screen and how to put it there. Despite the film's dark, grainy look—it was shot in 16mm and blown up to 35mm—it has moments of striking erotic beauty and emotional impact. Yokohama, however, has lived with his story too long. His movie too closely resembles its played-out hero.

That hero, Eguchi (Yoshio Harada), is a classical music critic and DJ who, at the age of seventy, is at the peak of his career, with editors badgering him for copy and women throwing him admiring glances. But the sudden death of a long-time crony—a former Supreme Court judge—sends him into a funk. What, he wonders over drinks with two other old friends, has age done to them? Casual sex strikes him as simply embarrassing. How can he expose his wreck of a body to the scrutiny of a woman?

His deceased friend, he learns, found a solution to that dilemma: a discreet establishment that offers its elderly patrons a night in bed with a young woman who has been drugged into uncritical oblivion. There is one condition, as the establishment's beautifully kimonoed mistress (Haruko Wanibuchi) makes clear: patrons cannot have sex with their living-dead dolls. On a whim, Eguchi gives her a call and that night finds himself in a perfectly appointed

Japanese-style room, examining a sleeping woman with a magnifying glass.

If this were all, the movie would be little more than a darkly comic study of advancing age and retreating potency, the persistence of desire and the impossibility of fulfillment. But Yokoyama and scriptwriter Toshiro Ishido give us more, too much more. Eguchi's daughter-in-law (Yuka Onishi), who is on the point of leaving her cheating twit of a husband (Masayuki Shida), falls in love with her father-in-law. She sees him as not only a kind, caring man, but a solution to a problem: after five years of marriage she and her husband have yet to produce a child. When she learns about the house of the sleeping beauties, she decides to apply there for a very special part-time job. She gets it, and the fruit of her labor would make great tabloid headlines. But the ensuing melodrama revolving around betrayal, extortion, and incest are not, I think, what Kawabata had in mind.

That said, Yuka Onishi's unembarassed gaze and frank sensuality are perfect for the role and generate the movie's few moments of true erotic heat. Yoshio Harada tries hard to convince as a seventy-year-old, but his frail geezer makeup can't hide his stud's body. Together Onishi and Harada would have made a terrific pair of screen lovers—if only Harada had first ditched that gray wig.

Nemuru Otoko
Sleeping Man (1996)

Directed by Kohei Oguri. Screenplay by Kiyoshi Kemmotsu. Cinematography by Osamu Maruike. Produced by Nemuru Otoko Production Committee. With Ang Song Hi, Christine Hakkim, Koji Yakusho. (103 mins.)

Whatever happened to the real Japan? Foreign visitors have been asking that question for generations, but now more Japanese directors are posing it as well. Their definition of what constitutes the "real," however, tends to be broader, their stake in the answer more personal.

Kohei Oguri's *Nemuru Otoko* excludes everything objectionable in today's Japan—no computer games, rap music, or white tile condos. Instead, we get Japan as an exquisitely photographed poetic dreamscape, whose verdant rice fields, dramatic seascapes, and homely farmhouse interiors belong to a land that exists only in the imagination.

Nemuru Otoko is also explicitly the product of a single personality, who is all too seriously engaged in creating Art with a capital A. This is not to imply that Oguri is a bombastic poseur. Shot for shot, *Nemuru Otoko* is among the most strikingly beautiful of recent Japanese films. Working with cinematograph-

er Osamu Maruike, Oguri achieves lighting effects that illuminate the soul of their objects. Falling snowflakes glow with an unearthly radiance and even streetlamps shine like beacons to another world.

Among his themes are the relationship between man and nature, the past and present, the living and the dead. Oguri approaches them in ways Buddhist, animist, traditionally Japanese. In image after transcendent image he expresses the livingness of all things, the unity of all life, the sadness at the heart of this everchanging, eternally mysterious world. His characters are anonymous figures in a landscape scroll, whose dialogue is less explanatory than evocative. We are being invited not to watch a narrative unfold, but to participate in a ritual in which the lines between the present and the eternal, the personal and impersonal, the human and the divine, are blurred and, finally, fused.

Takuji (Ang Song Hi) returns to his native village after a long sojourn in foreign climes, but after an accident in the mountains, falls into a deep sleep from which he cannot be awakened. His aged parents care for him, while in life in the village goes on. A young boy listens to tales of long ago at the feet of an old man, as a giant waterwheel turns. A mysterious beauty from Southeast Asia (Christine Hakkim), who works at a local bar, communes with nature and has soulful talks with village residents. A local electrician (Koji Yakusho) who was a school classmate of the stricken man, muses about his past, telling of boyhood journeys with Takuji to the home of an old man and woman in the mountains. Those mountains are still calling to him, just as they called so fatally to Takuji. The stories of these characters intertwine, but there is no big tying up; the mystery of the sleeping man—and his dreams—remains.

I'd like to say that this mystery enchants to the end, but Oguri's village is like a stylized stage set screaming with meaning (all those Waterwheels of Life, Rainbows of the Soul). He has assembled an excellent cast that includes Ang Song Hi from South Korea and Christine Hakkim from Indonesia, but supplies only rare glimpses of their faces, preferring the perfectly composed long shot to the messily dramatic close-up. Also, he has a weakness for the conventionally picturesque: the old man telling tales in the old mill, the nursing mother in the hot springs bath, and the inevitable Noh performance. In this film, the real Japan begins to look a lot like a JTB travel poster.

Nettai Rakuen Club
The Tropical People (1994)

Directed by Yojiro Takita. Screenplay by Nobuyoshi Isshiki. Produced by Shochiku and Pony Canyon. With

Misa Shimizu, Kiyoto Hagiwara, Morio Kazama, Hakuryu, Naomi Takagi. (104 mins.)

After years of heading West, Japanese are taking a greater interest in exploring their own backyard: Asia. Many have but one objective: indulging themselves to the Gold Card limit. Some Asians see these innocents, who may be loaded, but lack street smarts, as easy marks. "International exchange" takes on a new meaning when the bills you get from the street-corner moneychanger turn out to be worthless paper.

Thus the premise of *Nettai Rakuen Club*, a comedy from the hit-making team of director Yojiro Takita and scriptwriter Nobuyoshi Isshiki. Like their previous film, *Bokura wa Minna Ikiteiru* (We Are Not Alone, 1993), the setting is Southeast Asia, the tone light and bright, with occasional veerings into social commentary. But unlike *Bokura*, which told the story of three salarymen who become embroiled in a shooting war in a fictional country, *Nettai* is set in a clearly identified Thailand and puts more stress on entertainment than social commentary.

A professional tour guide, Misuzu Kono (Misa Shimizu) is rapidly approaching burnout from pampering boorish, demanding Japanese tourists. Her latest lot includes an elderly couple who makes her push their overloaded shopping carts and a pudgy middle-aged lecher who sends her out at midnight to shop for condoms so that he won't contract AIDS from his Thai hooker. Then disaster strikes: the hotel loses her charges' passports. After slaving for two days so that they can return to Japan, Misuzu gets her reward: dismissal from her job. What to do?

Having retrieved the passports (the hotel cashier had mislaid them) Misuzu ventures into the soda shop of two petty-scam artists who recently gouged her for a bottle of Coke: a Japanese college student named Tondabayashi (Kiyoto Hagiwara) and the shop's half-Thai, half-Japanese owner, Joy (Morio Kazama). She wants them to help her sell the passports on the black .market. The two crooks are thrilled by the idea of breaking into the big time. The gang gets its third member.

Taking hints from the nothing-sacred school of screwball comedy writing, scriptwriter Isshiki peppers his film with clever high-energy gags and takes equal-opportunity aim at the foibles of his Japanese and Thai characters. Meanwhile director Takita gives the jokes the right amount of snap and the love triangle that develops between the three principals the right blend of comedy and poignancy (more of the former than the latter). The resulting concoction is frothy commercial filmmaking, with a contemporary bite.

Misuzu delights in her misdeeds; she never got this kind of kick from shepherding tourists through customs. As played by Misa Shimizu, Misuzu is a combination of sophistication and innocence, fragility and toughness, who charms without being cloying. As the student, pop idol Kiyoto Hagiwara projects a boyish freshness, but little perceptible acting talent. Perhaps he is present to improve the film's female demographic. As the Japanese-Thai con man, Morio Kazama is short of the necessary grit and drive. A real gangster would have him for lunch. It is hard, though, to dislike this amusing smoothy, who leaves his victims smiling. The two *yakuza* this trio scams with a phony gun-running scheme are Blues Brothers clones who left their brains on the baggage carousel. Like their American models, this pair, played by Hakuryu and Naomi Takagi, goes straight over the top.

The film's real interest, however, lies less in its slapstick car chases and travel-ad beach idylls than in its skewed view of two cultures in collision. It also offers some savvy tips for surviving your next trip to Southeast Asia with wallet and good memories intact. Hint number one: think twice before accepting that Coke from a smiling stranger.

Night Head *
(1994)

Directed by Joji Iida. Screenplay by Joji Iida, Takeo Kasai. Produced by Fuji TV and Pony Canyon. With Etsushi Toyokawa, Shinji Takeda, Hijiri Kojima, Eisuke Sasai, Yoshie Minami. (107 mins.)

"Standing Room Only" signs seldom appear at theater ticket windows for Japanese films, but Joji Iida's *Night Head* is an exception. At the afternoon screening I attended, standees occupied almost every square centimeter of free floor space. What, I wondered, was going on here?

What was going on is a local version of the *Twin Peaks* boom. *Night Head* is based on a Lynchian late-night show that became a cult hit on Fuji TV in 1992, which described the mind-tripping adventures of two brothers with psychic powers. The younger, Naoya, could read minds and foretell the future, while the older, Naoto, could move—or destroy— objects and people with the force of his anger or tears. These powers were so extraordinary that the boys found it impossible to live normal lives. Constantly swept by the waves of other people's thoughts and feelings, Naoya withdrew into himself. Unable to express his emotions for fear of harming others, Naoto became cold and distant on the surface, tormented within.

The boys found a savior in Dr. Mikuriya, a psychic investigator who gave them a refuge at his research center in the mountains of Gifu Prefecture and taught them, however imperfectly, to control their powers. As the film begins, Naoto (Etsushi Toyokawa), twenty-eight, and Naoya (Shinji Takeda), twenty-one, have escaped from the center and are living together in a city that looks very much like Tokyo.

A viewing of the series is not essential for understanding the film. All that is needed is a willingness to enter into the brothers' inner world. Despite the Gothic tangles of the storyline, mood and atmosphere are all. Iida, who conceived and directed the *Night Head* TV show and its various antecedents, is playing a "what if" game in this film, but he is also, as the program notes make clear, a believer in psychic powers. This sincerity gives his film a dark, persuasive force. *Night Head*, Iida seems to say with every shot, is just not cinematic flim-flammery, but the straight dope about the powers inside our skulls.

The film's theatrics, however, owe more to the imaginings of *manga*-land than the findings of clinical tests. The brothers become involved in the dilemma of Sakie (Hijiri Kojima), a high-school girl they discover floating in the school swimming pool, together with the bodies of five classmates. She confesses that she inadvertently killed them with her psychic powers after they had bullied her beyond endurance. The brothers' efforts to help her recover her mental balance are thwarted by Mikumo Gengo (Eisuke Sasai), a psychic sleazeball who wants to use her powers for his own nefarious ends. But the one who comes closest to taking over the girl's innocent mind is a grandmotherly psychic (Yoshie Minami) with a kindly smile and an unholy ambition.

Using MTV editing tricks to voyage through his characters' inner worlds, Iida brings back messages from the dark side of the psyche that can disturb sleep, if not upset reason. He makes no attempt to create the usual psycho-thriller settings. Most of the heroes' psychic wanderings and confrontations take place in ordinary urban places, in the clear light of day. When Naoto and Mikumo Gengo do psychic battle on a busy shopping street on a summer afternoon, the scene has more immediacy and impact than if they were to meet on a deserted moor (especially when the street is suddenly awash in blood). The extraordinary, *Night Head* suggests, is as near as the neighborhood Kentucky Fried Chicken, as everyday as a Big Mac. A thilling thought for the bored suburban kids who are the movie's target audience.

Etsushi Toyokawa is a suitably dark and brooding Naoto. As Naoya, Shinji Takeda has the requisite sexual intensity and androgynous looks, yet another reason for *Night Head*'s large female following. As Mikumo Gengo, Sasai Eisuke is the creepiest Japanese screen villain since Shiro Sano. Evil in this film is a pasty face, a thin-lipped smirk, and a smooth, seductive rap that seems to reek of bad fast food, even as it invades your mind.

Nihonsei Shonen
The Boy Made in Japan (1995)

Written and Directed by Ataru Oikawa. **Produced by** M&M Films and Nihonsei Shonen Production Committee. **With** Mikio Osawa, Kaori Shimada, Ikko Suzuki. (105 mins.)

It's time to call a moratorium on Hollywood road movies about lawbreaking young lovers. What can filmmakers do to raise the sex and violence ante? Have their young, feral pair launch mortar attacks at commuters on the Santa Monica Freeway, while making passionate love on the back of a flatbed truck?

If Ataru Oikawa's *Nihonsei Shonen* is any indication, however, the Japanese version of this subgenre has not yet graduated from adolescent angst to mass murder. *Nihonsei Shonen* is less a road movie, with the requisite wind-in-the-hair feeling of freedom, than a long, tiresome journey to the end of a self-pitying teenage night.

The journey starts out promisingly enough. Yamato Tanaka (Mikio Osawa) is a young dropout from Hokkaido who halfheartedly hunts for work in Tokyo, but is in deep rebellion against social pressures to conform. One day, he encounters Kaoru (Kaori Shimda), a sexy pixy in a stocking cap who is handing out tissue packs on a busy street. After taking one, he tries every pick-up trick he can think of, including punching himself on the nose to draw blood and evoke sympathy. Won over by his antics, Kaoru takes him back to her office and introduces him to her boss. At long last, Yamato may get the job he has been looking for.

The boss, however, is a small-time hood named Matsuura (Ikko Suzuki) for whom tissue paper is but one of several hustles. Kaoru and her colleagues are also dial-a-hookers and Matsuura is selling paint thinner to teenagers as a cheap, brain-destroying high. Yamato agrees to become his dealer. At first, underworld life is rosy for Yamato and Kaoru. They are in love, Matsuura's Chinese girlfriend cooks terrific meals, and everyone in the "advertising office" is one big, happy family. Then one day it all blows up. Yamato and Kaoru find themselves on the run, with Yamato packing a Beretta 935. It's only a matter of time until he uses it.

In a Hollywood road movie, the body count would soon begin to mount, but director and scriptwriter Oikawa would rather examine his couple's tortured psyches in the moral wasteland of modern Japan. His takes on that wasteland are, in the opening scenes, knowing and incisive. Yamato and Kaoru's millieu, with its fragile generational camaraderie, its blank look of emotional numbness, and its vast ennui in the face of a no-hope future, will be familiar to anyone who has walked the streets of Shibuya at one o'clock in the morning.

Instead of settling for low-key realism, however, Oikawa overloads his film with heavy-handed symbolism. Kaoru is not merely another teen in trouble, but a self-described "bionic girl" with a rare heart disorder who is kept alive by a pacemaker. Though her battery is about to run out, she is in no hurry to replace it. While not exploiting this gimmick to wrench tears, Oikawa uses it to underline, with numbing obviousness, Kaoru's death-in-life predicament. He also inflates Yamato's attempted parricide by comparing it with celebrated crimes of the recent past that symbolize the hollowing out of Japanese values. Yamato (whose name shouts "Everyman" to the rafters) is thus presented as a brother to the *ronin* student who, in 1980, killed his father with a metal baseball bat and the teenage boys who, in 1989, tortured a teenage girl to death and stuffed her body in a barrel. But, as played by Mikio Osawa, Yamato is less a moral monster than a buff-looking rebel with attitude.

In short, no sale. Worse than the film's solemn self-importance, though, is its attempt to emphasize the emptiness of its characters' inner world by draining their outer one of incident and interest. In scene after draggy scene we watch Yamato and Kaoru wander aimlessly through desolate landscapes and listen to them lament the meaninglessness and boredom of it all. One would like to point them in the direction of the nearest game center—or slip them two plane tickets to the United States. There, in the land of Oliver Stone's *Natural Born Killers*, they might find the vital charge they so obviously need.

Niji no Hashi
Rainbow Bridge (1993)

Written and directed by Zenzo Matsuyama Produced by Ogawa Kikaku. With Masanobu Takashima, Kunio Murai, Emi Wakui, Kotono Shibuya, Akiko Kana, Maki Mizuno, Kunie Tanaka, Kin'ya Kitaoji. (115 mins.)

At its peak, the American musical was an exuberant celebration of the national ethos. The audiences for "Oklahoma" and "Seven Brides for Seven Brothers" may have known that their rosy depiction of life on the frontier was hardly realistic, but the songs, dances, and energy carried the day. Even wishy-washy liberals walked out humming "Oklahoma," glad, for once, to be a citizen of the good old U.S.A.

Zenzo Matsuyama's *Niji no Hashi* would seem to be a very different sort of movie. Set in the Kyoto of the Edo period, it tells the story of a group of children who grow up in the same *nagaya* row house to families of humble tradespeople. Not much frontier spirit there, we would imagine. In its own way, however, *Niji no Hashi* is every bit as celebratory and idealizing as a Rogers and Hammerstein musical. Everyone is bursting with sincerity, warmth, and physical beans. Though impulsive, quarrelsome, and occasionally violent, these simple folk are the salt of the earth.

They are also, the film tells us, real Japanese, living real Japanese lives, uncorrupted by Western influences. Those lives are hardly easy: the *nagaya* houses are tiny and flimsy, with privacy an unknown word, and though the kids may play and sing with strenuous abandon, they start working at the age of five and leave home at the age of ten to start long unpaid apprenticeships. Nonetheless, the *nagaya* folk could not imagine living any other way. They are one big, happy family: drinking, laughing, celebrating, and mourning, in a community founded on traditional beliefs and mores. The men are fiercely dedicated to their work and good at it; the umbrellas and fans that flow out of the *nagaya* are works of superb craftsmanship. The sons burn to follow in their fathers' footsteps and become *ichininmae* (full-fledged craftsmen) themselves. When apple-cheeked Shukichi, the son of Tadashi the umbrella-maker, becomes the apprentice of a temple carpenter, he is beside himself with joy. "You can hit, beat me—I don't care," he tells master carpenter Nagaemon. "I will work unceasingly, with all my heart." The Japanese work ethic, we realize, is not a recent development.

But *Niji no Hashi* cannot only celebrate Japaneseness; it must have a story. Though based on a novel by Fujiko Sawada, it seems to have been cribbed from Chikamatsu. It really gets underway seven years after the opening scenes. Fujita (Masanobu Takashima), the big, strapping son of lantern-maker Kyubei (Kunio Murai), is apprenticed to a maker of *geta* (wooden clogs), while his two sisters, Chiyo (Emi Wakui) and Kiku (Kotono Shibuya), remain at home, learning the *shamisen* and *nagauta* from their stepmother (Akiko Kana), a scheming former bar girl whom the girls cordially despise. Their pretty friend Kiwa (Maki Mizuno), whose father is a drunken but talented painter of fans, has been apprenticed to a pickle maker. The other children have also grown to young adulthood and gone their separate ways.

One day, the *nagaya* residents hear shocking news. Discovering that his parents were planning to sell his sisters to a brothel, Fujita ran home, confronted them, and, after his father showed him the money he had received from the brothel keepers, stabbed them to death. The kindly magistrate tries to have Fujita's sentence lightened, but the higher authorities order his execution—a pardon, they say, would disturb the public order. He is, however, able to have the girls apprenticed to the motherly proprietress of a prosperous fish shop.

Flash forward three years. The girls hear that the sentence of execution has been carried out. Then, at a *nagaya* memorial service for Fujita, they learn that Kiwa has been sold to the same brothel they had so narrowly escaped. The tears streaming down her cheeks, Chiyo decides to help her friend. During her quest she must confront a *yakuza* who is trying to extort money from the fish shop, and choose between the dissolute son of the proprietress, who vows to turn over a new leaf, and Shukichi the apprentice temple carpenter, who is poor but has loved her since childhood. Since this choice is not obvious to a woman of Edo—Chiyo is obligated to the proprietress—I will not reveal it. Enough said that the ending is tinged with a typical Japanese sadness at the workings of fate.

Niji no Hashi beats us over the head with its life force, but it also shows us how the Japanese glorify themselves when they think outsiders aren't looking. I think Rogers and Hammerstein would approve. But they would be right in wanting to set it to music.

Niji o Tsukamu Otoko
The Man Who Caught the Rainbow (1997)

Written and directed by Yoji Yamada. **Produced by** Shochiku. **With** Toshiyuki Nishida, Yuko Tanaka, Hidetaka Yoshioka, Kunio Tanaka. (120 mins.)

When Kiyoshi Atsumi died in August 1996 at the age of sixty-eight, he left a yawning gap in the line-up of Shochiku, which produced all forty-eight episodes of the Tora-san series in which he starred. Playing a wandering peddler from Tokyo's Katsushika Ward, Atsumi became Japan's own Chaplin—a comic actor inextricably linked to his most famous character, a cinematic institution who transcended mannerism to embody an ethos.

Once Atsumi was gone, the series had to end; he was as essential to Tora as Chaplin was to the Tramp. But his passing left a hole in the schedule that had to be filled. Series director Yoji Yamada has filled it, more adequately than might have been expected, with *Niji o Tsukamu Otoko*. Although the Japanese title is the same as that of the 1947 Danny Kaye film *The Secret Life of Walter Mitty*, the true inspiration for *Niji* is the 1989 *Cinema Paradiso*, Guiseppe Tornatore's sentimental journey to the heyday of the movies as a community rite and an

individual passion, and his melancholy story of that rite's decline.

Katsuo Shirogane (Toshiyuki Nishida) is the owner and manager of the Odeonza, a movie theater in rural Tokushima Prefecture. The Odeonza has seen better days, but for Katsuo, a man who lives for movies, it is his lifeblood. Every Saturday night he screens classic films and presides over a circle of local film fans, who are enthralled by Katsuo's vivid retellings of his favorite plots. Intimately familiar with the work of Rene Clement, Henri Colpi, Yasujiro Ozu, and Keisuke Kinoshita, he is not a film scholar but a fan, whose approach is anything but stuffy. He is also, to tell the truth, a frustrated ham. The rainbow he is running after is made of tinsel.

Katsuo is in love with Yaeko (Yuko Tanaka), a widow who runs a coffee shop called Casablanca and always attends the Saturday night screenings, sitting by Katsuo's side. But she regards Katsuo as an older brother, not a potential lover. Poor Katsuo, who is desperately shy, cannot tell her his real feelings. To anyone who has ever seen a Tora-san film, this should sound familiar. Katsuo is Tora with a good film education, but without the wanderlust. Series fans will also note that many cast members, including Hidetaka Yoshioka as Katsuo's young factotum and Kunio Tanaka as a gruff-but-lovable projectionist, are members of Yamada and Tora's extended film family. Even Tora himself, played by a double, gets a cameo.

Yamada has frankly acknowledged that *Niji* is intended as a homage to Atsumi and the Tora-san series and a homage is what we get. As worthy as Yamada's intentions may be—anyone who tries to reacquaint the Japanese mass audience with the pleasure of seeing good movies in a real theater is deserving of praise—they aren't a prescription for vital filmmaking. Yamada, however, is not just strolling down a cinematic memory lane. He remains an adept pusher of mass-audience buttons, and in *Niji* he gets his usual results—a smile here, a tear there—with his usual efficiency.

Yes, he goes overboard with the bumpkin humor and the bittersweet sentiment, but he also creates a world that is an inviting place to be. Even Toshiyuki Nishida, usually a gross, mugging clown, displays under Yamada's direction a talent for spellbinding that Atsumi himself might have admired. Pull up a seat and listen.

Nijuseiki Nostalgia
Twentieth-Century Nostalgia (1997)

Directed by Masato Hara. **Screenplay by** Masato Hara and Goro Nakajima. **With** Ryoko Hirosue, Tsutomu Marushima. (93 min.)

Japan has the highest per-square-meter ratio of pop singers on earth and a film's J-Pop theme song often has a significant impact on its box office, but it's rare indeed to see anyone in a Japanese movie bursting into song anywhere but on a stage, in a *karaoke* club, or in other "proper" settings. Thus my surprise at seeing the teenage heroine of Masato Hara's *Nijuseiki Nostalgia*, played by superidol Ryoko Hirosue, dance artlessly and trill ingenuously against trendy postmodern backdrops in Tokyo Bay. But the effect was closer to India's tuneful Bollywood flicks than the Hollywood that produced *Singin' in the Rain*.

The film, however, is more than the sum of its frothy musical interludes. A prominent figure in Japan's independent film scene for nearly three decades, Hara has created, in his long-delayed feature debut, a paean to young love that is at once irredeemably twee and intriguingly acute. More than most Japanese films about modern adolescence, it is aware that while the transition from childhood innocence to adult sexuality is as bumpy as ever, teens raised in this media-saturated society can experience it at one remove, as though it were a video whose images they can endlessly manipulate.

Hirosue plays Anzu, a high school girl who, as the movie begins, is in the dumps because her boyfriend, Tetsu (Tsutomu Marushima), has left with his family for Australia. They had spent their summer vacation together making a video movie, but now that he is gone, she can't bring herself to edit it. Then, with the encouragement of her best friend and a sympathetic woman teacher, she begins to slap tapes into the editing machine, watch, and remember.

Anzu and Tetsu— a fey-looking kid in a white floppy hat—meet cute, of course, on a bridge in Tokyo Bay. Holding a camcorder, Tetsu proclaims that he has been "bodyjacked" by an alien named Chunse who has come from space to study the earth's destruction. Though taken aback at first, Anzu soon joins Tetsu in his game. Touching fingers with her new friend, she allows herself to be invaded by another alien, Pouse, who has split off from Chunse. Together these two aliens, whose names are taken from Kenji Miyazawa story *Futago no Hoshi* (The Twins' Star), begin to explore their new world, camcorders in hand. They also start to film and discover each other. Hara no doubt intends this exploration to evoke sighs of nostalgia for the innocence and purity of youth. This nostalgia is common enough among older Japanese directors, but Hara also shows how the guises and gadgets that allow these two adolescents to be together without embarrassing each other end by keeping them apart. His cloying little romance contains a shrewd commentary on the current state of human relationships among Japanese youth.

Though an agile fantasist, Chunse/Tetsu is a strange, lonely kid whose only means of connecting with the world is his camcorder. When Pouse/Anzu begins to hint that aliens can also fall in love, he rejects her offer of human contact. He wants her to stay safe inside his viewfinder, an image he can play with rather than a young woman who is becoming aware of her own sexuality. He is also an alien in another sense; knowing that his family is about to depart for Australia, he is floating between worlds, unwilling to commit to either. It's too bad Hara felt compelled to cover this coming-of-age story in the pink candy glaze of middle-aged wish fulfillment. This summer's action movies, with their thunderous Dolby soundtracks, may well give you a headache. *Nijuseiki Nostalgia*, with Hirosue mugging against the futuristic relics of bubble-era Tokyo, is more likely to give you a toothache.

Nijuseiki Shonen Dokuhon
Circus Boys (1989)

Written and directed by Kaizo Hayashi. **Cinematography by** Yuichi Osada. **Produced by** CBS Sony Group. **With** Shu Ken, Hiroshi Mikami, Moe Kamura. (106 mins.)

Circus films have gone the way of the big top, but the circus is redolent of a spirit of freedom, adventure, and romance that has yet to fade from the collective memory. Kaizo Hayashi plugs into that memory in his second feature, *Nijuseiki Shonen Dokuhon*. Set in the early postwar period, the film traces the fortunes of two brothers who perform in a small circus traveling the Japanese countryside. The nostalgia, however, comes more from old TV shows and movies, including Fellini's *La Strada*, than Hayashi's memories of sawdust between the toes. This detachment— this view of the circus through a black and white haze of remembered images—gives *Nijuseiki* a wistful, dreamy, *déja vu* mood. I did't watch it so much as float through it. It's a film student's reverie.

Based on a novel by Takeshi Kawanishi, *Nijuseiki* begins with the two brothers, Wataru and Jinta, as boys, dreaming of the day when they can take their place on the flying trapeze. The dream ends when Masaru falls off the high wire onto Jinta, crippling him.

Years pass, and Masaru (Shu Ken) becomes a trapeze artist; Jinta (Hiroshi Mikami), a clown. Overshadowed by his younger brother, Jinta limps away from the circus to seek his fortune in the outside world. A fast talker, he sets up as a traveling pitchman, selling bogus goods to credulous country folk. He also runs afoul of the *yakuza*, who don't want him poaching on their territory. They beat him, nearly behead him—and offer him a place in the gang. Jinta's talents, they feel, shouldn't go to waste. He has little choice but accept. Meanwhile, back at the big top, hard times hit. The ringmaster dies, audiences fade away and, one by one, the performers leave, until only five, together with one old elephant, remain. Nonetheless, Wataru is determined to keep the circus going until his brother returns.

In directing his circus scenes Hayashi manages to evoke pathos without plunging into sentimentality. Dipping occasionally, but not plunging. He also has a knack for picking the right image that is the cinematic equivalent of perfect pitch. Together with cinematographer Yuichi Osada and lighting director Tatsuya Osaka, he creates a gauzy black-and-white look that perfectly expresses his story's yesterday-once-more mood.

If anything, Hayashi is concerned more with the film's tone and look than its heart. Too sophisticated to simply remake La Strada, he is also too much the pop-cultural archaeologist to generate the immediacy and vibrancy of Fellini's classic. Instead, thinking perhaps that age has improved them, he resorts to clichés that were mildewed when Fellini was still learning to look through the right end of a camera. In one chase scene, Jinta and the boss's moll (Moe Kamura) run through a forest to escape the boss's henchmen. The moll, as ethereal as an Utamaro beauty, becomes too exhausted to go on. So, of course, she and Jinta sit and rest, and of course the gang catches up with them, just as they used to do in all those irritating Hollywood B-movie scenes of a girl and guy on the run.

There are other lapses, including the kindly old elephant that looks too much like a kindly old prop, but one gift: Hiroshi Mikami as Jinta. Mikami cuts through the gossamer with a performance that is intelligent, nervy, darkly sensual. Though hampered with a limp—a sympathy-getting schtick that should have gone out with Gunsmoke—he shakes the film out of its self-absorbed torpor.

Like the circus itself, Nijuseiki offers something for everyone: a smile, a sigh, and a post-modern stroll down a universal memory lane.

Nobody

(1994)

Written and directed by Toshimichi Okawa. Produced by New Wave. With Riki Takeuchi, Hideo Nakano, Masaya Kato, Hiromi Nakajima, Jimpachi Nezu. (100 mins.)

The steady decline of the domestic film industry and the continued strength of the video market has generated an interesting class of hybrids: gang films that are targeted primarily at the video fans, but which have the stars and production values of theatrical features.

Screenwriter and director Toshimichi Okawa indicates that he is aware of this fact in by shooting much of his first feature, Nobody, in TV-friendly closeup. But he has also made a stylishly menacing thriller that gets beneath its characters' skins and in its audience's face in some original ways. As its approaches its violent climax, it becomes manipulative and slightly absurd, but Nobody never loses its grip.

Three friends are having a drink in a trendy bar. Former chimpira (apprentice gangsters), they are now junior execs at a big advertising company, designing ad campaigns for a home-security company. Reminiscing about the bad old days, Nambu (Riki Takeuchi) makes a snide remark about three yakuza sitting at the next table. The yakuza, however, have rabbit ears. The ensuing confrontation ends peacefully enough, and the three men leave the bar unscathed, but when Onishi (Hideo Nakano) returns to retrieve his umbrella, he gets stomped by the wise guys. Their gangsters instincts aroused, the ad execs vow revenge.

Okawa peels this scene down to the emotional core. As the camera closes in, we see every flicker of fear, anger, and male pride on his heroes' faces. The pacing is deliberate, the air of danger, palpable. Though Okawa's story of little actions that have large consequences may be ordinary enough, he charges it up to a high, visceral pitch.

Revenge, however, does not come easy. Onishi and Taki (Masaya Katoh) start to have their doubts; chasing around after gangsters is not something adults do. But when they encounter one of the yakuza in a dark underground passageway, they beat him, Nambu kills him, and the victim's pals find out. The hunters become the hunted.

The pace picks up, the plot twists multiply and the tension escalates. Finally, Taki is left alone to confront his barroom acquaintances. Along the way to this life-or-death showdown, he meets a model (Hiromi Nakajima) who won't take no for an answer and a cop (Jimpachi Nezu) who seems to know more than he is telling.

Okawa leans too heavily on thriller clichés, including the unforgivable one of the never-say-die villain, but he builds an atmosphere of omnipresent terror. I've seldom seen a Mercedes Benz look so scary, like a low-slung, wide-jawed, grey metal beast of destruction.

Nodo Jiman *

Proud of My Voice (1999)

Directed by Kazuyuki Izutsu. Screenplay by Teruo Abe and Kazuyuki Izutsu. Produced by Cine Quanon, Toho,

Nikkatsu, and Pony Canyon. With Kyoko Asakiri, Daikichi Sugawara, Naoto Takenaka, Kohei Otomo, Ayumi Ito, Kazuo Kitamura, Shigeru Muroi, Isao Bito. (112 mins.)

When I started watching the *Nodo Jiman* amateur singing program, two decades ago, I naively thought that, since tone-deafness was as common among the contestants as gray hair at a thirtieth class reunion, NHK must have had a hard time finding the requisite twenty-five (now twenty-two) acts. Weren't the Japanese, as products of a shame culture, fearful of the fatal gong?

The short answer provided by Kazuyuki Izutsu's *Nodo Jiman*, which depicts the human comedies and tragedies behind the show, is a big, resounding "no." Out of nearly two thousand applicants, NHK chooses 250 to appear for an audition. Of this number fewer than one in ten survive to face the mike on the Sunday show. No wonder the film's contestants treasure an audition invitation. It's their admission into a select group, their validation that they are what they have long secretly considered themselves to be: starbound.

Izutsu unabashedly exploits the comic and musical potential of this material, giving us a cute granny (Kyoko Asakiri) warbling "Ginza Can Can Musume" with the air of dance-hall chorine, a hyper-sincere salaryman (Daikichi Sugawara) emoting "Ans Toi Mamie" in fractured French, and a self-intoxicated cabby (Naoto Takenaka) belting out "Sayonara o mo Ichido" with the pinky of his mike hand pointing skyward.

Some of the clowning is very funny indeed, while some of it is mechanically cartoony. One example of the latter is the mad rush of a middle-aged *yakitori*-stand trainee (Kohei Otomo) to reach the stage before the auditions end. He takes a header to the floor, slams his knee against the stage, and rises, phoenix-like, to his feet as he begins his number, but his agonies are more reminiscent of a TV *gaman taikai* (endurance contest) than a well-executed slapstick routine.

To their credit, Izutsu and scriptwriter Teruo Abe are more interested in getting at the core of the show's human appeal than running easy comic riffs on its corniness. Their heroes sing for reasons more important than a winner's trophy and rise above their limitations as a result. They may lack the pipes of their professional betters, but they are up there singing not only lyrics, but their entire lives.

Though crowded with contestants, *Nodo Jiman* focuses on four: Araki, the aforementioned *yakitori* (chicken kebab) man, who croons as he empties slop buckets; Satoka (Ayumi Ito), a high-school girl who is the star of her local *karaoke* club; Kotaro (Kazuo Kitamura), an old *shiitake* mushroom grower who wants to cheer up his autistic grandson with a song;

and Reiko (Shigeru Muroi), a struggling *enka* singer who wants, at least once in her life, to perform in a real concert hall.

Reiko's story is the most fully developed. As the film begins, she is returning to her hometown in Gumma Prefecture with her long-suffering manager (Isao Bito) to plug her latest record. But her audience at a local record store consists of staring schoolkids, blank-faced oldsters and two uncomprehending South Asians. When she visits her stern-faced father (Nenji Kobayashi) at his barber shop, she begs for a loan and tells him that she is thinking of quitting. Then she finds a *Nodo Jiman* audition invitation on the floor and decides to grab a last chance at redemption.

Meanwhile, Araki has failed at everything he has tried; Satoka comes from a dysfunctional family; and Kotaro is about to be abandoned by his businessman son, who has been transferred to Sao Paulo. But though the story set-ups may be those of conventional tearjerkers, Izutsu's development of them is true to life. He understands working-class Japanese from the inside—not just the markers of language and style, but the way they act with each other when they shut the *fusuma* and put away their public faces for the day.

Shigeru Moroi is especially good as Reiko. A skilled comedian who scuffled through nearly a hundred low-budget indie films before rising to stardom with the hit TV drama *Yappari Neko ga Suki* (Yes, I Like Cats) in 1988, she expresses Reiko's deep weariness and fierce pride with a precision honed by her own experience. Also her climactic rendition of Mayo Okamoto's "Tomorrow," which she filmed after leaving a sickbed with a high fever, is a do-or-die stunner. See *Nodo Jiman* and gain a new appreciation for Japanese soul.

Nude no Yoru
A Night In the Nude (1994)

Written and directed by Takashi Ishii. Produced by New Century Producers and Herald Ace. With Akiko Yo, Naoto Takenaka, Jimpachi Nezu. (110 mins.)

In his eighteenth feature, *Nude no Yoru* Takashi Ishii's theme is once again male-female relationships and once again his two principals are named Nami and Muraki. Normally such constancy would be a sign of (1) creative paralysis, (2) commercial success, or (3) some combination thereof. Ishii, however, is different. A *manga*-artist-turned director who got his start making soft porn for Nikkatsu, Ishii had a critical and popular triumph in 1992 with *Shindemo Ii* (Original Sin), a take-off on *The Postman Always*

Rings Twice that had a powerful visual excitement and an erotic charge. At the age of forty-five, Ishii had taken a major career step forward.

Nude, which stars Akiko Yo as Nami and Naoto Takenaka as Muraki, recalls Ishii's heavy-breathing cinematic past. (It also reflects his present; he based the script on a "rape *manga*" that he still draws.) Nami is that standard genre figure; the sexy but intellectually challenged woman of indeterminate age who falls for the wrong man and pays heavily for her mistake. We get the first indication that Nami isn't playing with a full deck when she walks into an agency that claims to "do anything" and asks the bedraggled manager, Muraki, to take her on a tour of Tokyo. Dressed in a black gang-moll outfit, she pretends to be a out-of-towner who wants to hit the high spots, including Roppongi Crossing.

While we are still asking ourselves why, instead of taking the Hato Bus tour, she has hired the bemused Muraki to be her driver/guide, she checks into a fancy hotel, changes into a red micro-mini, slips a knife under the pillow and waits for the arrival of her gangster lover (Jimpachi Nezu). In the first scene, in a deserted night club, he had ordered her to strip and then raped her, as a young underling (Kippei Shiina) looked on. We understand the knife; she wants to pay him back for this and other humiliations. We don't understand why she has gone to all the trouble. Why the rube ruse? Why the oddball agent? Why the room with double beds? If she lands on the wrong one, her knife will be out of reach. (Sharon Stone would never have made the same mistake).

The gangster arrives and—wouldn't you know it?—discovers the knife. He beats her, rapes her, and takes a nice, long shower to cool off, leaving the knife stuck in the carpet. Having seen *Psycho,* we know what is coming next and Ishii delivers the expected bloodbath with a grisly effectiveness. Now there is a body and a problem. What is a girl to do? Desperate, she calls the agency: she has a large piece of luggage she wants delivered. This is material for a black comedy but Ishii tries to return to the mood of *Shindemo Ii,* with its hypercharged eroticism and violence. Given the script—and his pretensions—he succeeds only sporadically.

As Muraki, Takenaka initially seems to be reprising his whimsical loser role in his own *Muno no Hito,* but by the end he has transformed into a noir antihero. As Nami, Yo aspires to comic flakiness, but spends most of her screen time in the state of delicious helplessness and undress that kept Nikkatsu fans slavering for decades.

The rest of the film is Theater of the Absurd, Grand Guignol division. Muraki packs the body in a suitcase and lugs it to his office. The poor goof has no choice about this particular assignment; he registered the room in his own name. Unfortunately, one of the gangster's underlings tracks him down and beats him to a pulp. He thinks, rightly, that Muraki has had a hand in his boss's disappearance. Muraki in turn tracks down Jun, who thoughtfully wrote her real name and address on the rent-a-car application, and forces her to take back the body. The scene in which he wheels the suitcase, with mist from the dry ice seeping from the seams, through a Tokyo subway in pursuit of Nami, is one of the film's bizarre highlights.

We soon see that the fates of Nami and Muraki are intertwined. When the underling finds her and threatens revenge for his boss's murder, Muraki becomes her protector, savior and, finally, lover. The film is really a story of star-crossed love. But given all the foolery that has gone on before, it is not easy to take this story seriously. Also, Takenaka's Muraki and Yo's Nami may have much in common, including a lack of common sense, but they generate few sparks together. Even so, *Nude no Yoru* has become a hit. Perhaps fans think they have discovered Japan's own David Lynch. But rather than recycle Lynch's brand of cold-blooded weirdness, Ishii would do well to rediscover the heat of *Shindemo Ii.*

Nurse Call

[1993]

Directed by Shin'ichi Nagasaki. **Screenplay by** Keiko Nobumoto. **Produced by** Apollon and Right Vision. **With** Hiroko Yakushimaru, Yuki Matsushita, Hiroko Nakajima, Toshie Negishi, Gitan Otsuru, Atsuro Watabe. (105 mins.)

Shin'ichi Nagasaki's *Nurse Call* wants to be a "problem film" that tackles pressing issues, while appealing to its female audience with a weepy tale of turbulent romance. Like so many films that try to have it both ways, it is a hodgepodge—on-target observations about the lives of its nurses juxtaposed with hackneyed melodrama. It is also the first mass audience film by Nagasaki, a leading independent director. This is a disappointment, but given the big (for Japan) budget and big-name talent in the cast, he was no doubt obliged to deliver a product that TV drama fans could watch without spilling their popcorn.

Kozue (Hiroko Yakushimaru) is a nurse at a large university hospital who is burning out and feels guilty about it. At twenty-seven, she is searching for a new direction. The obvious one—marriage—does not appeal to her. There is something about the job that holds her. ("We've been saying we're going to quit since nursing school, but we can't do it," she says, sighing, to a colleague.) Her polar opposite is Natsumi (Yuki Matsushita), a dedicated type who is constantly dispensing cheer-up advice. Among her other colleagues are a tender-hearted neophyte (Hiroko Nakajima), a tough-as-nails superior (Toshie Negishi) and a handsome young doctor (Gitan Otsuru).

We've seen their type in other hospital movies, but scriptwriter Keiko Nobumoto—a former nurse—makes them talk with a gritty realism. As the film's promo tag line ("We're no angels!") points out, Nobumoto's nurses are not selfless paragons, but professionals who are overworked, underpaid, and underappreciated. They have all the interests of ordinary young women, including young men, but because they work in intimate contact with human pain, they have a different take on life than many of their contemporaries. In one of the film's more amusing scenes, Kozue gazes at a gory horror flick with dispassionate interest, while her date cringes.

When a dishy soccer player (Atsuro Watabe) arrives in the emergency ward with a broken leg, *Nurse Call* degenerates into drecky TV drama. The soccer player has a malignant tumor in his fractured limb and must undergo painful chemotherapy. He starts to feel sorry for himself and push the nurse call button every other minute. Watching the inner struggles of a self-pitying hunk is not my idea of a good time, but I might have better endured his scenes if one of the nurses had put him firmly in his place. Instead, they indulge his every whim and worry endlessly about his progress.

Some of this interest is only natural—he is a good-looking guy—but they feel guilty instead of angry when he fails to come around. When he calls Natsumi a "robot" and she resigns from her job in a fit of self-doubt, I began to feel angry for them. Then the soccer star accidentally starts a fire in his room. When Kozue tries to rescue him, he fights her and whines that no one cares about him. Soon after, Kozue tells the head nurse that she is leaving. Like Natsumi, she feels she is a failure. I was thinking the same thing—but about the film, not her.

The soccer star comes around finally. A rousing match between former cancer patients and gruff words of wisdom from a male doctor straighten him out. Also, Natsumi and Kozue have second thoughts about their decision to quit and Kozue begins an awkward courtship with the handsome doctor. All of this, however, comes too late to save the movie. The final scene, with the nurses walking through the wards holding candles and singing *Silent Night* on Christmas Eve, is lovely and touching. In an program interview, Nagasaki said that seeing a similar procession at a Tokyo hospital inspired him to make *Nurse Call*. It's unfortunate that his inspiration carried him only through the last five minutes of the film—and not the first hundred.

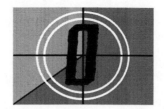

Odoru Daisosasen *

Bayside Shakedown (1998)

Directed by Katsuyuki Motohiro. **Screenplay by** Ryoichi Kimizuka. **Produced by** Fuji TV. **With** Yuji Oda, Toshiro Yanagiba, Eri Fukatsu, Chosuke Ikariya, Miki Mizuno, Kyoko Koizumi. (119 mins.)

Can Japanese movies compete with Hollywood? As the smash-hit detective drama *Odoru Daisosasen* (Bayside Shakedown) has proven so convincingly, there are other ways to fight the Hollywood juggernaut than crank out yet another *Doraemon* episode. One is to give local audiences more of what they already liked on television. *Odoru* began life in January 1997 as a hit Fuji TV series that climbed as high as 32.2 percent in the ratings.

Another is to make a real stand-alone movie, not a TV special for fans. Prior acquaintance with the show—which relates the seriocomic adventures of a salaryman-turned-detective played by pop star Yuji Oda—is helpful but not necessary to understanding the movie. Also, director Katsuyuki Motohiro and scriptwriter Ryoichi Kimizuka—both TV veterans with many hit shows on their resumés—may have lightened *Odoru* with TV-friendly slapstick, but they have also incorporated production values richer than any TV cop show could afford. Finally, despite its familiar elements, from the inevitable J-Pop theme song to the hero's Columbo-like trench-coat, *Odoru* succeeds in bringing a fresh approach to a genre in desperate need of it.

Its approach resembles that of Yoichi Sai's 1995 *Marks no Yama*. Both films explore the inner workings of the Japanese police, including nitty-gritty about bureaucratic infighting and career building, but whereas *Marks* is filled with jargony chitchat about entry wounds and other arcana, *Odoru* uses its realism about police hierarchies and procedures to bring its central relationships and situations into sharper, closer focus.

Also, *Odoru* avoids the usual genre ploys for keeping audience fingernails digging into armrests: there are no explosions, no car chases, no villainous corpses that suddenly return from the dead. Instead, the sight of a real loony holding a real gun is enough to send an entire stationhouse into a panic. Shooting the loony is, of course, a last resort. The hero of this incident, as it turns out, is not a cop but a public-spirited wacko in cop drag.

The hero of the film, however, is a thirty-year-old *junsa bucho* (inspector) at a Tokyo bayside station. A mid-career hire who once worked for a computer software company, but chafed at the rank-pulling and games-playing of the salaryman life, Shunsuke Aoshima (Oda) now finds much the same shenanigans at his new job. Instead of chasing crooks, his colleagues spend much of their time searching for lost receipts or jockeying for a better box lunch. Casually contemptuous of this routine, Aoshima is nonetheless romantic enough to want to be a crime-busting cop, not a ladder-climbing careerist.

This daily round is rudely interrupted by the discovery of a corpse floating in a nearby river, with a white teddy bear inserted in its stomach. Soon after a high-ranking police official is kidnapped in front of his bayside house in broad daylight. What criminal mastermind would be daring—or stupid—enough to pull off such a stunt? This is a obviously a case for the elite bureaucrats of the National Police Agency, who invade the station house like a dark-suited army. The bureaucrat in charge of the investigation is Shinji Muroi (Toshiro Yanagiba), a grim-visaged former colleague of Aoshima's who may be far higher in status, but remains faithful to a promise they once made as brother cops: Aoshima would battle it out on the street and Muroi would support him from the bureaucratic trenches.

Aoshima needs that support when he and others not content to be water boys (and girls) for the NPA, including the feisty Onda (Eri Fukatsu), the weary-but-wise Waku (Chosuke Ikariya) and the soft-spoken Kashiwagi (Miki Mizuno), begin to investigate on their own and discover, via the Internet, that their two big cases are connected. This is heresy to the NPA higher-ups, whose own theories about the case are strictly by the book. The battle, we see, is not between bad guys and good guys so much as between different concepts of what it means to be a cop.

Odoru does not paint this conflict in overly simplistic shades. On the other hand, it does not go to other, quintessentially Japanese, extreme of endowing everyone, even the ostensible bad guys, with hearts of gold. Also, while being precise and detailed (if occasionally absurd), it is never preachy or dull. The most popular Japanese live-action film of the year is, both as an entertainment and an essay on the Japanese organizational mind, among the most satisfying.

Ohaka ga Nai
I Don't Have a Grave (1998)

Directed by Takahito Hara. Screenplay by Sumio Omori. Produced by Kowa International and Fuji TV. With Shima Iwashita, Yumi Adachi, Hitomi Takahashi, Isao Hashizume, Yoshihiko Hakamada, Renji Ishihashi. (109 mins.)

Shima Iwashita would seem to have no more worlds to conquer. After nearly four decades, this veteran star is still at the top of her profession, one of the last of the movie queens. But she had never starred in a comedy until she saw the script for *Ohaka ga Nai*, which describes an eccentric actress's search for the perfect grave, and decided to make it her 128th film.

Though *Ohaka* lacks the headlong energy and comic edge of director Takahito Hara's better work, it is an enlightening, if only mildly amusing, essay on a very real problem for many Japanese: the ultimate destination of their last remains. Iwashita is Setsu Sakurazaki, an actress playing the mother of a teenage girl (Yumi Adachi) dying of cancer in a weepy melodrama. During the shoot, she learns that she has cancer herself—and only three months to live. Though she soldiers on, breathing not a word about her condition to her manager (Hitomi Takahashi) or studio boss (Isao Hashizume), she has a worry that preys on her mind. What will happen to her bones after she is gone? She has no family grave.

The obvious solution is to simply buy one. Surely graves are just another commodity on the open market, like condos with a slightly smaller floor space? But Setsuko wants only the best, and after years of being waited on hand and foot, is not wise to the ways of the world. Disguising herself as a kimonoed granny, she joins a bus tour of a large suburban cemetery and promptly shocks the salesman/guide with her upfront questions and outrageous behavior. (To get a better look at the goods, she tries to push away the stone over the funerary urns—a gross violation of etiquette.) An earnest young salesman (Yoshihiko Hakamada) agrees to take her on as a client, the most demanding of his short career. Meanwhile, the director (Renji Ishihashi) is steaming —where is his star? The manager, who is one of the few able to stand up to her boss, goes out to look for Setsuko and bring her back to her senses.

Iwashita is playing a caricature of her public image—a diva who is worshipped by her fans and employers, respected and feared by her underlings (save for her spoiled young co-star, who regards her as just another clueless adult). In her granny guise, she is given a chance to stretch beyond this persona, but even with a gray wig, Iwashita is still, inevitably, Iwashita. She doesn't play so much as play at comedy, while letting us know that she regards this little charade as a pleasantly amusing game.

Perhaps overawed by Iwashita, the rest of the cast, including Yoshihiko Hakamada as the young salesman, tend to defer to her. The film becomes, not a comedy of manners, but a comedy with manners. Laughs, not unexpectedly, are few and far between. Based on a book by scriptwriter Omori, *Ohaka* does get off good hits at the snobbery of temples, who admit only the well-connected to their cemeteries, and the greed of priests, who sell posthumous Buddhist names at outrageous prices. It also strips away the smarmy exterior of cemetery hucksters to reveal their calculating commercial hearts.

There are several funny turns by the supporting cast, including Tomoro Taguchi as a slick cemetery salesman and Hitomi Takahashi as Setsuko's hyper manager. Iwashita, however, should regard *Ohaka* as an interlude and get on with what she does best; dominating everyone around her with merest flicker of those still mesmerizing eyes. When you can command obedience, why sweat for laughs?

Ohaka to Rikon
The Grave and Divorce (1993)

Directed by Ryo Iwamatsu. **Screenplay by** Masahito Kagawa. **Produced by** JVC and Nippon Herald. **With** Kaoru Kobayashi, Yoshiko Tanaka, Sachiko Hidari. (107 mins.)

Ohaka to Rikon sounds as though it might be a title for a Woody Allen comedy. The first feature by director Ryo Iwamatsu, however, examines the relationship between two major life events with a style and humanism reminiscent of Yasujiro Ozu and an overlay of gently spacey humor reminiscent of Robin Williams. Scene after scene glows with small gems of emotional truth, but after an hour or so, I started to wonder what it all meant and where it was all heading. Then, at long last, the climax arrived with a bang inspired more by Albee than Ozu. Somehow, I wish that it had come sooner.

The film begins with Yoshinori (Kaoru Kobayashi), a middle-aged cemetery plot salesman, listening as his wife Atsuko (Yoshiko Tanaka) tells him she has met a man she "likes." "Don't threaten me!" he shouts. Why should he feel threatened? Aren't married women allowed to have platonic friendships with members of the opposite sex? When Yoshinori learns that the friend is a classmate in a culture center leather-working class, he is relieved—perhaps his suspicions are groundless. But something has changed.

That change has been a long time coming. Yoshinori and Atsuko married ten years ago over the objections of her parents, who felt that she could have done better. The couple left their native Kofu for Tokyo to make a new start, but Yoshinori is still working at a low-status job and they still have no children. Sitting alone at her worktable in her tiny apartment, Atsuko has a drawn, distant look. She's not ready to take a lover—quite—but she is suffering from a bad case of midlife blues.

Yoshinori, meanwhile, buries his marital dissatisfactions in a frenzy of work; he is a star salesman who really believes in his product. "Erecting a monument while the couple is still living does not just ensure a resting place after death," he tells a tiny birdlike woman (Sachiko Hidari) who is shopping for a plot with her husband. "It affirms that they will remain together in the future." Following his wife's announcement, however, Yoshinori begins to question the rut he fallen into. How to escape? A fellow salesman announces his engagement to a college classmate and asks Yoshinori to serve as his go-between. Later, at a pub, he speculates about what married life might be like. "Married people don't have sex, do they?" asks his co-worker, teasingly. Yoshinori confesses that he and his wife only do it once a week. "It's not me," he blurts. "It's both of us." That night, even though it isn't Tuesday, he goes to his wife's bed.

The unexpected keeps happening, however. A man in an orange suit who call himself Shuzenji (Kiyoshiro Imawano) tells Yoshinori he wants to buy a plot in a Tokyo ward with a view of Mt. Fuji—an all-but-impossible request. Though Shuzenji is obviously a loon, Yoshinori finds himself being drawn into his unpredictable orbit. Then his mother-in-law, whom he loathes, arrives for a visit; a rare trip to the movies with Atsuko ends in disaster; and the little woman with the raspy voice keeps changing her mind about the plot. Finally, after a night of drinking with two co-workers—the engaged salesman and the office clerk he jilted—Yoshinori ends up sleeping with the clerk.

Feeling harassed, guilty and suspicious, Yoshinori finally meets his wife's friend—a longhaired pixy who looks as though he wouldn't hurt a fly. But when Atsuko tells him deepest secret (that they can't have children because of her husband's sterility) Yoshinori picks a quarrel with him and storms out. Things have come to a breaking point and break they soon do—spectacularly.

This summary may sound cohesive enough, but the film is a jumble of discordant elements that never quite coalesce. Shuzenji, especially, has been dropped down from outer space. What, I wondered, is this guy doing here, other than to serve up a bit of comic relief and gnomic wisdom? Also, though Atsuko's malaise is genuine enough, she is an irritatingly passive schlump who doesn't seem to deserve Yoshinori's emotional investment. Why not admit her wants and try to satisfy them? Leathercraft doesn't seem to do it.

Iwamatsu, with extensive experience as a TV and stage director, knows how to get the most out of his actors, but I wanted him to get more out of his script. Big themes demand a stronger treatment. Ozu and Robin Williams with water isn't enough.

Ohigaramo Yoku Goshusho-sama
Congratulations! Condolences (1996)

Directed by Seiji Izumi. Screenplay by Hirokazu Fuse and Seiji Izumi. Produced by G Company, Hori Pro, Toa Kogyo, and Erusenu. With Isao Hashizume, Tatsuo Matsumura, Chiharu Niiyama. (105 mins.)

We've all had days when everything seems to go wrong, but few of us are as unfortunate as Mr. Tanaka in Seiji Izumi's *Ohigaramo Yoku Goshusho-sama*, who must serve as a *nakodo* (go-between) at a wedding and prepare for his father's funeral, all on the same day. Meanwhile, his elder daughter is hugely pregnant and her husband conspicuously absent, while his younger daughter makes, on this day of all days, an appointment to meet a mysterious male friend. What more could could happen to this hapless man? Plenty, as it turns out.

One way to approach this material would be as a black comedy about two Japanese rites of passage that bear an uncanny resemblance to each other. (Many of the grim-visaged photographs on funeral altars, for example, have been cropped from formal wedding portraits.) Another way is to make a heartfelt "human drama" with both smiles and tears. This is the safe, conservative approach and *Ohigaramo* adopts it unhesitatingly. But despite its conventionality and predictability—as soon as we see the pregnant daughter we know how the film is going to find the required upbeat ending—*Ohigaramo* is not the feel-good product one would expect. Its underlying theme is the howling isolation of modern Japanese, in the midst of their ordinary middle-class lives.

Mr. Tanaka (Isao Hashizume) is a middle-aged obsessive-compulsive who wants to do the right thing, but hasn't a clue as to what is really going on, either in his own life or the lives of those around him. While he is grimly practicing his *nakodo*'s speech for the upcoming wedding of a subordinate, his elderly father (Tatsuo Matsumura) is secretly preparing to travel to Hokkaido alone, and his younger daughter (Chiharu Niiyama) is secretly planning to fly off on a tropical holiday with her secret boyfriend. No one tells Dad anything!

Then the day of the wedding arrives and Tanaka finds his father dead in his futon, the apparent victim of a heart attack. Rather than do the natural thing—arrange for the funeral—Tanaka decides to do his corporate duty by attending the wedding, but he cannot suppress his unruly emotions. When his big moment arrives and he reaches for his speech, he draws a blank. In the confusion of the morning he forgot to take it. As he stumbles on, *extempore*, we see from the puzzled and angry looks on the faces of the guests that poor Tanaka knows virtually nothing about the young man he is extolling. His function as *nakodo* is simply a formality, whose emptiness is now blazingly apparent.

Returning home from this disaster, he finds a posthumous letter from his father explaining the reason for his trip. He wanted to find the mountain hut where he first met Tanaka's mother nearly sixty years ago. Tanaka never heard this story from his father's lips. He never had much time for the old man when he was alive. Where has he been all these years?

At this point, with the soundtrack violins swelling, the audience hauled out its collective hankie. But as *Ohigarmo* continued to juxtapose the mildly comic with the snuffly sentimental, I started to wonder about missed chances. Juzo Itami could have had great fun with this gimmicky material, so reminiscent of the 1984 *Ososhiki* (The Funeral), his comic look at the Japanese way of death. Yasujiro Ozu might have made a seriously moving study of failed communications within the family circle. Instead, we get a ready-for-prime-time script by popular TV scenarist Hirokazu Fuse and workmanlike direction from Seiji Izumi, who has made several video action pics for Toei. We also have Tsutomu Hashizume as Tanaka, in his first starring role. A versatile character actor who has played everything from tough cops to fumbling businessmen, Hashizume is more credible and entertaining in his flustered, corporate drone stage than when he finally sees the light through tear-clouded eyes.

Am I saying give *Ohigara* a miss? Not necessarily; the film offers good pointers on how to behave at Japanese weddings and funerals. The most important: make sure your speech is in your pocket—or your head—before you take that fatal step out the front door.

Ohikkoshi *
Moving (1993)

Directed by Shinji Somai. Screenplay by Sadoko Okudera. Cinematography by Toyomichi Kurita. Produced by Yomiuri TV. With Chieko Tabata, Junko Sakurada, Kiichi Nakai. (124 mins.)

Shinji Somai's *Ohikkoshi* depicts the breakup of a marriage and a family, but instead of the warring couple, Somai focuses on their only daughter, twelve-year old Renko (Chieko Tabata). Though she begins the film as that standard figure of family melodrama, the child who tries to bring her parents back together, Renko learns that her real task is to let go of the past and find a new, more independent self. *Ohikkoshi* is really about her journey of discovery and her arrival at the gates of adulthood. It's a grown-up film that, with clarity and compassion, touches the child in each of us.

Ohikkoshi begins with Renko's parents, Nazuna (Junko Sakurada) and Ken'ichi (Kiichi Nakai) sitting around the dinner table discussing their upcoming separation. The table—a postmodernist triangle pointed like a dagger and painted a liverish green—symbolizes their mood.

The next day Ken'ichi—a goateed nonconformist who drinks from a hip flask and likes to spar playfully with his daughter—drives off with his belongings to his new apartment. Renko tags along, but however much she might wish that her wardrobe and her father's were magically connected (a reference to C.S. Lewis?), she must return to reality and a new life with her mother. Though Nazuna tries to make that life as friction-free as possible—she draws up a house "constitution" and even tries to take over as Renko's boxing partner—her daughter still longs for the old days and tries to bring them back.

Her first effort, however, is less than successful. At the suggestion of a classmate, she decides to lay siege to her father's apartment, but her mother comes home from work early and discovers her stuffing supplies into a knapsack. Renko escapes her questions by locking herself in the bathroom. She stays there for hours, until her father comes to persuade her to come out—and ends by quarreling with her mother. The ensuing scene—with both partners boiling over into violent recrimination—is a plunge past the veil of civility into a seething hellbroth of a raw emotional ganglia. Finally, when she can stand it no more, Renko cries out "Why was I born?" Neither of her parents have a good answer. (Nazuna's is to drive her hand through the bathroom's glass door.)

Despite the horror of her parent's quarrel, Renko can't give up her dream of a happy family; for all their faults, her parents genuinely like her and want to make her happy. They are, we feel, bright, sophisticated people with humane values, who happen to hate each other's company. Renko tries once more to unite her family, by arranging a "surprise" meeting at a fancy resort hotel on Lake Biwa, but Ken'ichi's awkward attempt at reconciliation provokes tears from Nazuna. Renko runs away (everyone does a lot of running in this movie) and when Ken'ichi finds her outside the hotel, he confesses that he really wants to be alone. Renko's dream is shattered and she runs again.

Up to this point, *Ohikkoshi* has been a conventional enough family drama, with exceptional moments. But its final scenes, in which Renko wanders alone through the town and countryside at festival time, are truly extraordinary. Following a dreamlike idyll with an old couple, who advise her to forget the sad things of life, and a brief encounter with her frantic mother, whom Renko tries to reassure ("Don't worry—I'll grow up quickly"), she plunges into a dark bamboo forest to come to terms with change and the inevitable loneliness of growing up. This part of her story is told almost entirely with images: Renko watching a country fire festival with rapt eyes, seeing a vision of her family and their past happiness by the shores of Lake Biwa, and, finally, letting go of that past with a gesture of poignant simplicity.

Toyomichi Kurita's photography beautifully evokes the mystery and wonder of Renko's transformation, while Chieko Tabata's performance as Renko is appealingly feisty and fresh. But Renko's nighttime journey is, like all of what Kurosawa once called "real cinema," more than the sum of its excellences. We find a magical catharsis of our own: for a moment, everything, even forgiveness, seems possible.

Okaeri *
(1996)

Directed by Makoto Shinozaki. Screenplay by Akira Yamamura. Produced by Comstock. With Miho Uemura, Susumu Terajima. (99 mins.)

What happens when the honeymoon is over? That question has a special poignancy for young wives from the provinces living alone with their husbands in Tokyo. Without that essential badge of adult womanhood in Japan—a child—they find it hard to mix with the mothers in their building or neighborhood. Without a job that gets them out of the house, they are trapped in the cages of their white-tile condos. With hubby working or playing until all hours, they usually have no one to talk to but the walls. It's a wonder more wives don't start climbing them.

That, basically, is the dilemma of Yuriko (Miho Uemura), the heroine of Makoto Shinozaki's debut feature *Okaeri* (whose literal translation is "Welcome Home"). A former classical pianist, she spends her days transcribing tapes for an agency and waiting for her husband to come home from the cram school where he teaches. The film does not tell us why she gave up the piano; it begins in the second year of her marriage and does not, save for a few glimpses at a photo album and a box of her concert tapes, look back. What it does show us is her descent from deep loneliness to acute psychosis and the beginning of her long journey back.

This is a serious subject and Shinozaki, whose day jobs are projectionist and film journalist, treats it seriously. His methods of telling his story are subtle, indirect, and go against the entire grain of Japanese commercial moviemaking. They also happen to make for a most accomplished and moving film.

First, and to frequent viewers of recent Japanese films, most noticeably, there is no music constantly thrumming and swelling in the background, rising to crescendos in key scenes and all but drowning out the dialogue. Instead, from Yuriko's window we hear the hammering of carpenters and the voices of children. In the living room we hear her tapping on her computer keyboard and, in the kitchen, chopping, stirring, and frying food for dinner. These everyday sounds underscore the loneliness and emptiness of her existence; she has no part in the vibrant, distant life outside and her food, so lovingly prepared, remains uneaten when her husband, Takashi (Susumu Terajima), goes out drinking with a colleague instead of coming home.

Second, there is no attempt to hype the film with perfervid melodrama or speechifying. In its opening scenes, *Okaeri* gives us only the smallest hints that anything is wrong—a certain unease and inwardness in Yuriko's glance, a certain odd stiff-backed purposefulness in her long walks about the neighborhood. Takashi, an easygoing male egotist, ignores these signs until Yuriko flares out at him for his absence and indifference, and as the grip of her madness tightens, begins to speak the need to "patrol" to thwart the evil designs of the "organization." Takashi finally realizes the seriousness of Yuriko's illness when she runs away from him in the street (she is terrified that he will stop her "patrolling"), steals a car, and drives aimlessly about, with Takashi in pursuit.

We do not get the impression, however, that Shinozaki is simply trying to enliven his otherwise static film with a chase scene. Rather, we have become so well acquainted with the characters that we feel as we might were we to find friends in this situation: empathy, sadness, and an inescapable chill.

Third, Shinozaki's camera is not frantically trying to impress with technique. Instead, the austere beauty of his compositions—long shots of Yuriko walking alone on a windswept grassy hill, or down a narrow road toward a single smokestack soaring in the blue winter sky—unobtrusively but effectively symbolize her inner world. Also, Shinozaki makes abundant use of long cuts that take us deep into his characters emotions, without forcing them down our throats.

In one key scene Yuriko, afraid that Takashi will commit her to a mental institution, locks herself, crying, in the bathroom. Takashi pleads with her to come out and, sitting on the kitchen floor, slumps with exhaustion. Then Yuriko appears silently by his side and he comforts her. Shinozaki uses only one medium close-up, while allowing his actors to act as they might in real life, with no attempt to hurry or shape this intimate scene.

Both Susumu Terajima, an actor who has played supporting roles in Takeshi Kitano's films, and Miho Uemura, a screen newcomer with a large talent and a strikingly pure beauty, give inspired performances. Yes, this scene makes a conventional plot point—that Takashi is a nice guy who cares for his wife—but it also goes beyond it to demonstrate, with an unembarrassed directness, the healing power of love.

Okoge *
Fag Hag (1992)

Written and directed by Takehiro Nakajima. Produced by Tokyo Theater. With Misa Shimizu, Takehiro Murata, Takeo Nakahara. (120 mins.)

The near simultaneous release of *Kira Kira Hikaru* and *Okoge* is enough to make one believe in synchronicity. Both films are about a triangular relationship involving a gay couple and a young woman. Both depict gay life with frankness and sympathy and reach out to a wider audience than the gay community.

In *Okoge*, director and screenwriter Takehiro Nakajima does not explain or exploit his gay characters. What we see on the screen are not stereotypes, but men whose emotions run the gamut from passion and love to jealousy, loneliness, and despair. Though some of his images have a raw impact, Nakajima's intent is not to sensationalize but to provoke thought, invite understanding, and not incidentally, entertain. I think he largely succeeds.

The film begins with a striking image: a long row of near-naked gay men sunning themselves on a concrete embankment at a beach. As it roves slowly, sensually among the bare flesh, the camera's eye shows us everything from powdered queens to preening musclemen. This, Nakajima seems to say, is how gay men are when they are with their own, away from society's disapproving stare. How do you like them?

Sayoko (Misa Shimizu), an actress who does voiceovers for TV cartoons, likes them just fine. When she sees a husky young man and his mustachioed middle-aged companion exchange a tender kiss, she is transfixed. She begins to haunt gay bars, until she meets the couple again. The younger man, Go (Takehiro Murata), is a bag designer; the older man, Terasaki (Takeo Nakahara), is a married businessman. When she hears that Go's mother has recently moved into his place, their usual rendezvous, she offers them the use of her own apartment. They accept and a triangle is formed.

This relationship, with Sayoko happily thumbing through a book of Frida Kahlo reproductions while her two friends make passionate, graphically depicted love upstairs, is as idyllic as it is unusual. Go and Terasaki don't know what to make of this young woman, but they like her energy and are amused by her enthusiasm. They also know her type. She is an *okoge*, a woman who likes to associate with gay men. Sayoko accepts this tag gladly; she finds them a refreshing and unthreatening change from the men in her childhood who abandoned and abused her.

Takahiro Murata as Go and Takeo Nakahara as Terasaki project the strength and inevitability of their characters' affection for each other. Murata's intelligent, sensitively crafted performance recalls that of William Hurt in *The Kiss of the Spider Woman*, minus the layers of self-dramatizing artifice. Nakahara, a newcomer to films, may not have his partner's dramatic talent, but makes us sympathize with Terasaki's plight. Initially, I didn't know what to make of Misa Shimizu as Sayoko. Was she just another idol airhead? But she has a needy intensity that helps explain Sayoko's unusual behavior and convinces us that she belongs with her unlikely friends.

The idyll doesn't last; Terasaki's wife learns that he has a male lover and comes, in a rage, to destroy his love nest. Go subjects himself to an embarrassing *omiai* (meeting for the purpose of arranging a marriage), then tells his family that he is gay. His mother goes into shock. Go and Terasaki separate and Go becomes depressed. Sayoko tries to cheer him up by arranging a match with a moody, handsome ex-soldier who ends up raping her. She bears his child, while Go cares for his now bedridden mother. Several years later, they meet again.

Nakajima's plot machinations are not entirely convincing. Why would Sayoko willingly live with a man who is a brutal reminder of her nightmare past? Why does she indebt herself to loan sharks? These developments provide the excuse for the climatic scene—a battle between a pair of gangsters and Sayoko's gay friends—but they don't jibe with what we know of her character. And some of the minor characters, including Go's mother (Noriko Sengoku), with her idiotic laments and operatic tirades, are straight-from-TV burlesques. The film doesn't need this kind of clowning.

Okoge's excellences outweigh its lapses, however. Nakajima has made a film that goes beyond the usual cinematic boundaries into a world that many Japanese are only barely aware of and woefully misinformed about. In a time of AIDS hysteria, it is a much-needed corrective.

Omocha

The Geisha House (1999)

Directed by Kinji Fukasaku. **Screenplay by** Kaneto Shindo. Cinematography by Daisaku Kimura. **Produced by** Toei and Rising Production. **With** Maki Miyamoto, Kaho Minami, Mai Kitajima, Ryoko Gi, Yumiko Nagawa, Mariko Okada, Masahiko Tsugawa, Sumiko Fuji. (113 mins.)

Pity the poor geisha. In addition to being a hoary cliché of tourist poster Japan, she is saddled with a job description decidedly un-PC. Accomplished though she may be at *shamisen* and *buyo* (traditional dance), her clients often hire her to play a role in certain erotic or romantic or power scenarios and she must satisfy them, though her performances do not necessarily climax in the futon. That she can command large fees for her services—one must usually occupy the upper echelons of business or government to afford the pleasures of a Gion teahouse—does not alter the fact that she is a relic of a feudal system that placed her and her *mizushobai* ("water trade") sisters far below their male lords in the social pecking order.

But as Kinji Fukasaku's *Omocha* (The Geisha House) reminds us, even in early postwar Japan, geisha were hardly the childishly twittering love dolls of male fantasy and feminist scorn. Instead, they were hard-headed businesswomen who ruthlessly, if charmingly, extracted outrageous sums from their besotted paramours, while laughing up their silken sleeves at the idiocy of the male species.

What a racket—and what a strange movie to be appearing at the end of the millennium. Scriptwriter Kaneto Shindo and director Fukasaku, who is best known for the explosively violent *yakuza* actioners of the *Jingi Naki Tatakai* (Battles Without Honor) series, have produced a highly colored, archly stylized celebration of a vanished postwar world that plays like a film shot in 1969, not 1999. It's as though Steven Spielberg were to make a World War II epic with a nineties technical gloss, but with the atmosphere and viewpoint of *The Longest Day*.

The *Omocha* (literally, "Toy") of the title begins the film as Tokiko (Maki Miyamoto), a servant girl in the Fujinoya, a Kyoto geisha house. While running errands for the mistress, the elegant, unflappable Satoe (Sumiko Fuji), she is learning the secrets of her future trade from her three *onesan* ("older sisters"). Visions out of a woodblock print when they leave the house for nightly parties or assignations, the Fujinoya's geisha become, in the daytime, young women who may belong to a feudal world, but are under no illusions as to the fuel that makes that world run: cold, hard cash—and plenty of it.

The daughter of a poverty-stricken weaver, Tokiko is also only too happy to sell her body if she can provide more money for her family. Cheerful, hardworking, filial and unselfish, she is, as Fukasaku makes clear in nearly every scene, a paragon of young Japanese womanhood. Her brother, a union man and a socialist who is alienated from his traditionalist father, rates her harshly for catering to the erotic whims of the capitalist bosses, but his brief appearances in her life pass like summer thunderstorms, leaving her unshaken in her resolve to follow her chosen path.

And why should she abandon that path? Fukasaku paints the geisha life in the glowing colors of generic nostalgia. Its every aspect, from private girltalk to performances in the futon, unfolds amidst resplendent Japanesque settings, while nearly everyone archly, frantically overacts in their stereotyped roles.

As Tokiko, Maki Miyamoto presents a refreshingly naturalistic, low-key contrast to the agitated goings-on around her. A former Takarazuka star appearing in her first film, the twenty-one-year-old Miyamoto plays her younger character with a fresh-scrubbed charm, while displaying the needed evidence of inner steel.

As the plot unfolds and Omocha moves unblinkingly toward her deflowering at the wrinkled hands of a seventy-eight-year-old sybarite, we realize that, despite its knowing sympathy with the geisha's lot, Omocha is finally an exploitation film that celebrates, with the rosy tints of its vaselined lens, the buying and selling of young virgin flesh. More than the hopes and dreams of the geisha themselves, it unwittingly offers insights into the psychology of the Japanese men who seek their dream Lolita in Third World slums. Instead of inspiring sighs of regret for lost sensual splendors, it left me with a lingering case of the creeps.

Omoide Poro Poro
Only Yesterday (1991)

Written and directed by Isao Takahata. Produced by Tokuma Shoten and Nippon Television Network. Voice characterizations by Miki Imai, Toshiro Yanagiba, Yoko Honda. (119 mins.)

To foreigners, the popularity of animated TV sitcoms like *Sazae-san* and *Chibi Maruko-chan* may seem puzzling. Where, they might ask, are the action, the antics, the goofy surrealism? Where are the kicks for kids? One answer is that these shows aren't only for children. Set in the early 1970s, *Chibi Maruko-*

chan was originally targeted at adult women who grew up at the same time as its third-grade heroine. Based on a *manga* that Machiko Hasegawa drew from 1946 to 1974, *Sazae-san* is a nostalgic feel-good show intended for the whole family, from the grandmothers who are Sazae-san's real contemporaries to the tots who will watch anything that moves.

Producer Hayao Miyazaki and director Isao Takahata were perhaps encouraged by the popularity of these shows when they decided to make *Omoide Poro Poro* based on a *manga* by Yuko Tone and Kei Okamoto. The story of an office clerk's solitary journey to the countryside—and her past—it also reaches out to a wider audience than do most animated features. Like *Chibi Maruko-chan*, it focuses on the misadventures of a young girl and caters to nostalgia for simpler times. *Omoide Poro Poro*, however, looks back farther, to 1966, when hemlines rose to fantastic heights, the Beatles played the Budokan, and its heroine entered the fifth grade.

It also strives harder for psychological and visual realism, while avoiding self-conscious cuteness. Taeko, the heroine, is a bored with her job and uncertain about her future. Now twenty-seven, she senses that she is at a turning point, but doesn't know which way to go. Marriage? Perhaps, but she has no particular candidate in mind. Without knowing why, she begins to remember her tenth year and rediscover a self she had long forgotten. She seems a complex, three-dimensional woman, not a *manga* character.

Though the countryside she visits is that of a city-bred imagination—all lush green loveliness and friendly salt-of-the-earth farmers—its trees, flowers and people are drawn with painstaking realism. This meticulousness extends to the narrative. When Taeko arrives in Yamagata Prefecture after an all-night train journey and begins to help her in-laws with their work of making lipstick coloring from safflowers, the film describes the process with the exhaustiveness of an NHK documentary.

Given the filmmakers' obsession with the actual, why use animation at all? Why not film real rocks, trees, and people and save the labor of drawing them? The answer, I think, is that Miyazaki and Takahata see animation as a valid medium for depicting subjects formerly reserved for film. They want their art to take its rightful place at the grownup's table. They state their case vividly, charmingly, poignantly. The flashbacks, especially, work well; they not only have the right period look, down to Taeko's ballerina in her round plastic case, but the right period mood as well. Taeko's first encounters with romance, stage fright, and the mysteries of menstruation are told with humorous touches and a sharply observant eye. Her adventures as an adult, however, are less amusing, more predictable. From the moment she meets a bright-eyed young farmer, the cousin of her brother-in-law, we know how her anomie is going to end. The farmer delivers speeches on the decline of the countryside and the potential of mechanized farming. He's good and earnest and sincere—and he made me long for 1966.

Omoide Poro Poro pushes the envelope of animated art, but in a very Japanese way. It's true inspirations are not Mickey Mouse and Bugs Bunny, but the introspective, reflective prose of the "I" novel. Not Walt Disney, in other words, but Naoya Shiga.

Onibi *
The Fire Within (1997)

Directed by Rokuro Mochizuki. **Screenplay by** Toshiyuki Morioka. **Produced by** Gaga Productions. **With** Yoshio Harada, Sho Aikawa, Eiji Okuda, Reiko Kataoka. (101 mins.)

Rokuro Mochizuki's *Onibi* (literally, "will-o'-the-wisp"), a film about an aging hitman who wants to go straight, may cover familiar ground, but it quietly becomes a complex, incisive character study of a man on the cusp of a new beginning—and the edge of an abyss.

Yoshio Harada's performance as the hitman is his best in years. Harada has long played macho life-force types, at times with a swagger that verges on self-parody. In *Onibi*, however, his hitman is human in a weary, end-of-the-tether way. Competent at his grisly trade, he wants to start a new life, but still exemplifies old-fashioned gangster virtues. Though a sad figure, the underworld equivalent of the restructured lifetime employee, he is at the same time noble, going to his self-appointed doom with his eyes open, defiant to the end. There is no strut in his walk, but there is a slouching dignity in his bearing.

Onibi begins with that prototypical *yakuza* movie scene: the ex-con, fresh out of prison, offering incense at the grave of his old boss. The ex-con, Noriyasu Kunihiro (Harada), wants no part of his old gang, however. After serving a stretch for murder, he wants to go straight. He knows that two-time losers in his line of work get the noose. He needs a job, though, and when a junior member of his old gang (Sho Aikawa) offers him one as a gang chauffeur, he takes it. The boss (Eiji Okuda), a coolly urbane type, apologizes to Kunihiro for this demotion in status. "It's only until you get your touch back," he says.

Kunihiro proves that he never lost it when, at the boss's request, he walks into the office of a rival gang that has welshed on a loan. Grabbing a gun jammed against his forehead, he turns it on the welshers and forces them to pay. This display of bravado wins him the gratitude of the boss and the reward of a night

with the pretty young pianist at a hostess club. Unexpectedly, he and the pianist (Reiko Kataoka) hit it off. Also unexpectedly, the gang cuts him loose; the boss wants to avoid a war with the customers Kunihiro so rudely interrupted—bad for business, don't you know. So Kunihiro has to go.

This termination is a blessing in disguise. Together with the pianist, he moves into a new apartment and, before long, finds a new job as a journeyman printer. But his old calling has a hold on him he can't resist. His first client is his new lover.

Onibi has a narrative arc of a thousand other *yakuza* flicks, as well as such Hollywood movies as *Straight Time*, but it is less a throwback to genre conventions than a brilliant reworking of them. Director Rokuro Mochizuki and scriptwriter Toshiyuki Morioka provide tension and thrills for their often-told story—the staging of the gunplay scenes is as crisp and realistic as any I've seen in recent Japanese films—but given the theme, the amount of bloodshed is surprisingly small. Instead of racheting up the body count, Mochizuki and Morioka create a character who is far more than another cool-dude icon. By the end of the film, we feel a kinship with this middle-aged man who does not want to give up hope, but cannot shake off his past. Though his line of work may be unusual, his dilemma is familiar, his end, tragic. His will-'o-the-wisp is one we are also chasing.

Onna Keiji Riko:
Seibo no Fukaki Fuchi
Riko (1998)

Directed by Satoshi Isaka. **Sceenplay by** Rika Tanaka. **Produced by** Ace Pictures. **With** Ryoko Takizawa, Toru Kazama, Toshiya Nagasawa, Takeo Nakahara, Kazuma Suzuki. (99 mins.)

Satoshi Isaka builds time bombs of onscreen tension that suddenly explode in showers of revelation. Midway through his first film, the 1996 *Focus*, an introverted electronic eavesdropper played by Tadanobu Asano turns the tables on a TV reporter trying to present him as the geek of the week. What began as an incisive essay on media manipulation suddenly becomes a horror show of freak-out retaliation. Isaka has so carefully prepared the way, viewing the film's events through the TV crew's camera and using only one shot per scene, that we feel we are not only witnessing this show unfold, but taking part in it—voyeurs who can't help watching.

Isaka's second film, *Onna Keiji Riko: Seibo no Fukaki Fuchi* covers a similar arc in telling a story about detective on a baffling murder case who finds herself becoming a victim. Also, the table-turner is another deceptively mild-mannered young man with a mean streak, this time played by Kazuma Suzuku. But whereas *Focus* was an edgy, innovative attempt to examine the consequences of media excess, *Riko* is content to be a straight-ahead cop-on-a-mission movie, with a few New Age twists. It's the difference between a personal film on a passionately felt theme and a competently completed assignment.

The title character is Riko Murakami (Ryoko Takizawa), a smart, seasoned detective who also happens be the single mother of a two-year-old boy. While investigating the case of a woman brutally murdered in a hotel room, she endures what strikes her as a sterner test of her fortitude: her "park debut" with her son. A relative newcomer to the neighborhood, she finds the stares of the other moms disconcerting. Fortunately, she sees a welcoming smile from Sachiko (Keiko Unno), another young mother whose son, she says, is in the hospital. Soon they are trading child-care war stories and becoming friends.

Then Riko learns that the principal suspect in her latest case is Sachiko's businessman husband and that, instead of recuperating in the children's ward, Sachiko's son was the victim of a kidnapping several years ago and has since been given up for dead. The sweetly smiling Sachiko, in other words, is missing a bead or two off her abacus.

The case, she discovers as she questions everyone connected with it, including the husband himself and a kindly cop-turned-P.I. (Takeo Nakahara) who was in charge of the kidnapping investigation, has wheels within dangerously spinning wheels that soon produce another beautiful corpse for the coroner's squad. Riko is drawn into those wheels, until she is no longer an in-control cop, but an abused and threatened woman, a mother desperate to protect the life of her child. She refuses to play the victim, however. Stubbornly, relentlessly, she digs in deeper, fights harder.

The idea of making the detective hero a woman who trundles her child off to daycare is a clever one, but it only works if she is credible in both her roles—a hard stretch given the male-dominated realities of Japanese police work. As Riko, Ryoko Takizawa makes that stretch with ease. With her steady, unflinching gaze and tough, no-nonsense manner, she is a believable cop, but she can also play the less-than-flawless woman behind the badge, who can't easily give up her married lover (Toru Kazama)—the father of her child—or control her terror when her child is threatened.

Her male co-stars also stretch their characters beyond genre clichés. Takeo Nakahara is particularly good as the P.I., whose nice guyness cannot hide his

troubled past and disturbing secrets. He inhabits the role as comfortably as he wears casual clothes around his ramshackle office, but he also strongly conveys the guilt that still haunts and the professionalism that still drives his P.I., even at the risk of his life. Also, impressive is Kazauma Suzuki as the pretty-boy gangster who can shift from choirboy to killer in a rudely jolting instant. Nonetheless it is Takizawa, a relative newcomer whose previous credits include Sogo Ishii's *Angel Dust* and Sabu's *Dangan Runner* and *Postman Blues*, who transforms what would have otherwise been a cut-above-average thriller into a fascinating portrait of a modern Japanese woman. A generation ago a Riko would have been hard to find in Japanese films, let alone the Japanese police. Takizawa makes us hope that, in the not too distant future, she might have more company.

Onnagoroshi Abura no Jigoku
Oil-Hell Murder (1989)

Directed by Hideo Gosha. **Screenplay by** Masando Ide. **Produced by** Shochiku, Fuji TV, and Kyoto Eiga. **With** Kanako Higuchi, Shin'ichi Tsutsumi, Miwako Fujitani. (113 mins.)

Chikamatsu, the great dramatist of the Genroku era (1688–1703), has been called the Shakespeare of Japan. But rather than royals like Hamlet and Lear, he often wrote about commoners, particularly members of the merchant class who thronged to see his plays. He often based them on true stories of passionate, fatal love and deadly crime—the kind of thing that we find today on the morning "wide shows." But however sordid their subject matter, Chikamatsu's dramas have endured in the mediums of Bunraku, Kabuki and, now, film. They have remained popular because they touch deep, quintessentially Japanese chords. Chikamatsu's dramas of love suicide are perhaps the ultimate expressions of the eternal Japanese struggle between *giri* and *ninjo*—the demands of duty and the promptings of the heart.

Hideo Gosha has based his latest film, *Onnagoroshi Abura no Jigoku* on a play that Chikamatsu first staged in 1721. But though this version differs significantly from its illustrious model, it retains the Genroku-era love of the flamboyant, sensuous, and violent. As in the original, the central scene is a murder; Okichi (Kanako Higuchi), the middle-aged wife of a prosperous Osaka oil dealer, is found dead in her shop, in the midst of a pool of blood and oil. Who killed her and, more importantly, why?

We soon guess the answer to the first question. The answer to the second, however, is longer in coming. The film, we realize, is not a murder mystery, so much as the story of how an older woman's attraction to a younger man becomes obsessive and finally fatal.

The younger man is Yohei (Shin'ichi Tsutsumi), the orphaned son of an Osaka oil dealer who gave Okichi's husband his start in the business. When Yohei was a child, Okichi served in his family's shop and even nursed him. But Yohei's father died when he was four and he went to live with the shop's head clerk. Now he is a stud with a wild streak. As played by Tsutsumi, a popular TV actor, Yohei has a smoldering, punkish charm. We immediately understand why Okichi—a sensuous woman with an indifferent husband—would find him irresistible. This is where Gosha departs from the play: Chikamatsu's Okichi is a virtuous woman whose murder is as inexplicable as it is unjustified. Gosha's Okichi, however, is a schemer. While scolding Yohei for his wicked ways like an indulgent aunt, she is plotting to free him from the grip of his latest infatuation, the young daughter of a rich oil dealer (Miwako Fujitani). Far from ruining Chikamatsu's story, this departure makes it more comprehensible to us corrupt moderns. Watching the steam rise as the three principals interact, we can tell exactly what is on everyone's mind without looking up *giri* and *ninjo* in the dictionary.

Gosha films his actors in sensuous soft-focus closeups, especially when they are writhing about in their gorgeously Genroku hideaways, but he takes us beyond surface eroticism. His real theme is less the struggle between duty and desire—Okichi loses little sleep over her unfaithfulness—than the age-old battles between youth and age, men and women, the intellect and the emotions.

A film director since 1964, Gosha has a reputation for flamboyance and in *Onnagorishi* we see why he deserves it. The lavishly detailed period sets, the beautifully photographed kimonos and the sexually charged acting of the principals make the film undeniably watchable. Yes, his repeated use of full-frame closeups, slow motion, and other clichéd devices bring the film dangerously close to self-parody, but Gosha manages to put his stamp on his classic story while remaining faithful to its tabloid heart. Despite the ghostly presence of Chikamatsu, *Onnagoroshi Abura no Jigoku* is not great art. Instead, it is a popular entertainment of the seductively dissolute kind. If you liked *The Postman Always Rings Twice*, in either of its cinematic incarnations, this might be just the movie for you.

Onna Zakari *

Turning Point (1994)

Written and directed by Nobuhiko Obayashi. **Produced by** Shochiku. **With** Sayuri Yoshinaga, Rentaro Mikami, Masahiko Tsugawa, Miki Fujitani, Yumeiji Tsukioka, Tadao Takashima. (118 mins.)

Where to place Nobuhiko Obayashi on the stylistic spectrum? His talent is so large and wayward, his work so various, in both genre and quality, that he is hard to label. Even so, the sensibility running through his work is unmistakably Obayashi. It is playful yet sophisticated, in love with the anarchy of life, the richness of language, the potential of film to shape the way we see and feel. It's tempting to compare him to Robert Altman, another aging *enfant terrible* whose work has been uneven but impossible to ignore. Obayashi, however, lacks Altman's talent for satire. He is more of a sentimentalist, who sets film after nostalgia-tinged film in his native Onomichi.

In *Onna Zakari* (Turning Point) he takes what could have been a change-of-life melodrama about a middle-aged woman journalist and produces instead a film almost comically dense in language, character, and incident. He turns the conventions of commercial filmmaking on their head, with great brio and a conspiratorial wink or two at the audience. "I'm assuming you're as smart and articulate and complex as the people in this movie," he seems to be saying, "and I'm going to treat you that way." He can't quite bring off the film, however. About halfway through I realized that it was not going to tie its many narrative strands into a big, bang-up climax that it was going to be all too lifelike in its shapelessness and inconclusiveness. Nonetheless, I was carried away by its audacity.

Yumiko (Sayuri Yoshinaga) is a journalist who, after twenty years working on the women's page, is finally getting her big break: a transfer to the editorial department. Despite being on the far side of forty she still resembles a bright-eyed, eager-to-please grad student. At her first editorial meeting she raises her hand to ask the editor's permission to speak, as though he were her seminar prof. But she also comes prepared, reeling off facts and figures for a proposed editorial. The editor, impressed, gives her the assignment. Only her first day on the job and she is on her way. But the editorial, which criticizes a former prime minister's anti-abortion stance, causes unforeseen repercussions. A religious group exerts pressure on one of her bosses to have her removed from her editorial duties (Not, however, for the reason you might think; as I said, this movie is complicated).

Also, another newcomer to the editorial department, a former society page reporter (Rentaro Mikami) who has a nose for news but never learned to write, develops a crush on her. She likes this careless, eager bear of a man—he is still something of a boy, despite his gray hair—but she already has a lover, a married naturalist (Masahiko Tsugawa) with a sophisticated manner and corrosive wit.

Yumiko, we come to see, is a seasoned reporter with a mind of her own. Instead of meekly surrendering, she digs in her heels and tries to save her job. She also make friends with her fellow editorial newbie, without giving him hope for anything more. But this balancing act is not an easy one—or one that she can perform alone. In Japanese society, connections are all and Yumiko has them in spades; her lover, her grad-student daughter (Miki Fujitani), a retired movie queen aunt (Yumeiji Tsukioka) and a *yakuza* boss (Tadao Takashima) give her advice and pull strings on her behalf. But she is the one who ultimately must decide whether the battle is worth it.

Based on a novel by Saiichi Marutani, *Onna Zakari* may have a women's movie structure, but Obaybashi films it like an investigative documentary, pursuing his characters relentlessly with his handheld camera and editing to catch every reaction, gesture, and reference. Also he gives his characters reams of repartee to spin off with hardly a pause for breath. These directorial strategies give the film an extraordinary, if exhausting, immediacy and vitality. Obayashi takes faces that, over the years, have become familiar to every Japanese and, by filming them as though they were real people, not TV icons, makes them fresh. There is no such thing as a star turn in this movie (given the hyper editing, there is hardly time for a turn, period). There are, however, fine performances from unexpected sources, including Sayuri Yoshinaga, who has long been embalmed by her image as Japan's Sweetheart. In *Onna Zakari* we see not only her patented schoolgirlish charm, but the smarts, energy, and passion that have carried her through a thirty-year career.

Obayashi reveals his characters' lives in all their aspects, innner as well as outer, with far less of the *tatemae* (front) of polite banalities that clutter so many Japanese films. *Onna Zakari* gets right down to *honne* (true feelings) in take after take. Its theme may be aging—the way the passage of the years change perceptions and priorities, for the better and worse—but it is primarily valuable as an insider's tour through the tangled thickets of modern urban lives.

Oroshiyakoku Suimutan
Dreams of Russia (1992)

Directed by Jun'ya Sato. Screenplay by Jun'ya Sato, Tatsuo Nogami and Fumio Jimba. Produced by Daiei, Dentsu, and Toho. With Ken Ogata, Toshiyuki Nishida, Oleg Yankovskii. (123 mins.)

The spectacle often gets a bad critical rap. The usual complaint is impersonality: we may see a cast of thousands rampaging across the Cinemascope rec-

tangle, but no memorable faces. David Lean, the best of the big picture directors, gave us the enigmatic face of Peter O'Toole in *Lawrence of Arabia*—and we have never forgotten it.

But how many spectacle directors have Lean's talent or daring? When big money is at stake, especially in the risk-allergic Japanese movie industry, producers usually choose a safe story and hire a reliable hack to film it. That is the path the producers of *Oroshiya Suimutan* followed. Yet this Jun'ya Sato film about an Edo-era castaway stranded in Russia, which cost nearly forty million dollars to make, turned out better than we might have expected.

First, there is a recognizably human face. It is that of Daikokuya Kodayu (Ken Ogata), the captain of a ship that was carrying a cargo of rice from Ise to Edo (premodern Tokyo) when it was blown off course by a storm and landed, nine months later, on the Kamchatka Peninsula. The year was 1782. Instead of boarding the next Aeroflot flight home, Kodayu and his crew had to endure the horrors of eighteenth-century transportation, the Siberian winter, and the Russian bureaucracy. Accompanied by one member of his original seventeen-man crew, Kodayu returned to Japan in 1792, after an exodus of ten years.

During that time he learned Russian, made a hazardous sea voyage in a boat he had designed and built himself, traveled across the tundra to Irkutsk in the dead of winter, and, after a grueling 6,200 kilometer journey, met Catherine the Great at her palace in St. Petersburg. Ironically, when he finally set foot again on Japanese soil, he was arrested by shogunal authorities. By leaving Japan, however involuntarily, he had violated the law and the punishment was death. Kodayu, however, survived this ordeal, just as he had survived all the others. He was, in short, an extraordinary man who had an extraordinary adventure in an extraordinary land. His was a story that had to be a spectacle. But his goal throughout his decade-long odyssey was a simple and human one—to go home.

The producers made a wise decision when they cast Ken Ogata as Kodayu. Best known abroad for his work in Shohei Imamura's *Narayama Bushiko* (The Song of Narayama), Ogata doesn't give a marvelously strange Peter O'Toole-like performance, but he does make Kodayu humanly likeable, while revealing his strength of will and his growth as a man. He transforms what could have been a walking monument into flesh and blood. Unwisely, the producers also cast Toshiyuki Nishida. Playing a member of Kodayu's crew, Nishida serves up the biggest slice of ham acting I have seen in many a movie. When he began loudly lamenting the loss of a gangrenous leg, I longed for a volume control and regretted the skill of his Russian doctor.

As in any spectacle, the actors share top billing with the production values. In *Oroshiyakoku*, which was filmed entirely on location in Russia, those values are first-class. We get to see a real blizzard filmed during a real Siberian winter, a meticulous reconstruction of eighteenth century Irkutsk, and the extravagant rococo architecture of Czarist Petersburg, including the interior of Catherine the Great's palace (which is appearing on film for the first time). We also get close-up views of individual Russians, including a scholar, played by Oleg Yankovskii, who befriends Kodayu and goes with him to St. Petersburg. Making a Russian a main character and a friendship between a Russian and Japanese the film's central relationship gives the film's claims to being an "international" production credibility. The direction by spectacle-specialist Jun'ya Sato is competent enough, though there are no inspired moments like the snuffed out match that becomes the Arabian desert in *Lawrence In Arabia*. In the end, *Oroshiyakoku* fills the screen satisfactorily, if not spectacularly.

Osaka Story ✳
(1996)

Directed by Toichi Nakata. **Produced by** the National Film and Televison School. (75 mins.)

Autobiography is common almost to the point of absurdity—all those home pages on the Web, Advertisements for Myself jostling for attention and not finding it. Few filmmakers, however, use their own lives as material and their own bedrooms as sets. A camera, after all, is more intrusive than the usual tools of autobiography. Also, a cinematic autobiographer must work, not with malleable memory, but the often intractable raw material of life. How do you make art of the home movie?

Osaka filmmaker Toichi Nakata has attempted to answer these questions in his 1994 documentary *Osaka Story*, which focuses on his own bicultural and highly dysfunctional family. Although Nakata deftly captures moments of high emotion while crisply editing his story to the narrative bone, it is also obvious that he wants to expose his wealthy, tyrannical, philandering Korean-born father. Nakata does not one-sidedly savage the old man—he readily acknowledges his human side—but he paints an unsparing portrait of the damage he has wrought and issues a quiet-but-ringing declaration of independence.

The film begins as a homecoming. After entering the National Film and Television School in London in 1989, Nakata made *Minoru and Me*, a video documentary about his relationship with a physically dis-

abled man that was screened at festivals in Switzerland, Vancouver, and London. As the subject of his graduation film, he decided on his own family, particularly his father's troubled relationship with his mother.

So when he greets his father at the airport on his return from a monthly trip to Korea, he comes complete with sound equipment and British cameraman Simon Atkins to record his questions and his father's embarrassed answers. His father, he tells us in a voice-over English narration, had gone to his home country not only on business, but to visit his Korean wife and children. This double life is no secret to Nakata's Japanese mother or his six siblings. It is also something that they don't talk about, at least with the father. But Nakata is determined to bring this and other family secrets out into the open, not only for the sake of his film, but to clarify his own feelings and make his own decisions.

Though his approach is often indirect and impressionistic, he captures the essence of his subjects. Watching his father give a speech and sing an *enka* number at a rare family gathering Nakata has arranged, we learn more about his stubborn pride, sentimental self-pity, and pessimistic view of life ("Just about the only time human beings are really happy," he says memorably, "is when they are asleep") than we ever could from a one-on-one grilling by an "objective" stranger.

We learn that his father broke off relations with Nakata's younger brother for joining the Moonies and marrying a Korean woman in a Moonie mass wedding. (He has since been restored to his father's good graces because the old man wants him to take over his money-lending business and three *pachinko* parlors.) We also learn that his mother is upset with his father's apparent intention to be buried in Korea, apart from her. "If you are unhappy with him why don't you leave him?" Nakata asks. "I only have three or four years left to live anyway," she says, with a sigh of resignation. But he also shows us a woman who loves to shop, lords it over her Korean daughter-in-law, and plays a central role in her husband's business. She would not, we feel, readily give all this up.

Though *Osaka Story* may have its therapeutic and even ameliorative aspect—Nakata seems to hope that, by make this film, he can shame his father into being more considerate of his mother—it does not attempt to force solutions or tie the lives it depicts into a neat narrative package, complete with a happy ending. It concludes, in fact, with a violent off-screen argument between Nakata and his father and a confession to his mother that she cannot expect heirs from her first-born son: Nakata is gay. At the same time, there is a sense of closure. Nakata will break free from his father, build his own life abroad, and no doubt make more films. But he will not easily find a theme so compelling, characters as engaging. For this filmmaker, at least, there's no place like home.

Otokotachi no Kaita E
The Man With Two Hearts (1996)

Directed by Hidehiro Ito. Screenplay by Tatsumi Kumashiro and Hidehiro Ito. Cinematography by Noboru Shinoda. Produced by Excellent Film. With Etsushi Toyokawa, Yuna Natsuo, Keiko Takahashi. (120 mins.)

Etsushi Toyokawa is Japan's hottest male movie star. One indication is that his fans now call him simply "Toyoetsu," thereby elevating him to the ranks of the superstars who, like royalty, need only a single name for instant identification (Elvis, Marilyn, Kimutaku). Given his following, it was inevitable that someone would produce a Toyokawa vehicle. That someone, as it turned out, was Hidehiro Ito, a former director of soft porn for Nikkatsu and a long-time associate of Tatsumi Kumashiro, a Nikkatsu colleague.

Kumashiro was originally going to film his script of *Otokotachi no Kaita E* a study of a *yakuza* with a split personality, but died of pneumonia in February 1995, before he could begin shooting. Ito took over the project for his production company, Excellent Film. *Otokotachi* is thus a Kumashiro film *in absentia* with the same mentally unstable *yakuza* hero, shock violence, SM sex, and nihilism tinged with black humor present in Kumashiro's last film, *Bo no Kanashimi* (Hard-Head Fool, 1994). But whereas *Bo* was a gritty, downbeat character study, *Otokotachi* relies heavily on visual atmospherics and plot gimmickry for impact.

Toyokawa's hero is Dr. Jekyll and Mr. Hyde in modern *yakuza* dress. In his primary incarnation, he is Sugio, a wimpish former piano tuner who has somehow become an underling in a *yakuza* gang. With his conservative suits, boyishly tousled hair, and meek demeanor, Sugio is as out of place as a nun in a Las Vegas casino. We know, however, that the film is not going to be a *yakuza* version of *Sister Act* when Sugio's cheek starts twitching in a coffee shop and he transforms into a sneering tough-guy who abuses the waitress for bringing him the wrong (i.e., Sugio's) order. This is Matsuo, Sugio's other half, who is a sub-boss in the same gang and who, with his flashy clothes and take-charge attitude, does belong in the *yakuza* milieu.

Toyokawa manages his Jekyll-Hyde metamorphoses well, and inhabits both characters thoroughly. He is equally convincing as the Sugio who mildly accepts a contemptuous brushoff from his girlfriend (Yuna Natso) and as the Matsuo who later brutally

beats and rapes her, while coverting her to the delights of sadomasochistic sex. (The conversion, a loathsome convention in movies of this type, does not convince.)

But instead of exploring the very real difficulties of living with what has come to be called Multiple Personality Disorder, *Otokotachi* plunges us into the macho melodramatics of a gang war and Sugio/Matsuo's tangled romance with a vampish nightclub singer (Keiko Takahashi). Working with cinematographer Noboru Shinoda, Ito uses muted color tones and feathery tracking shots that underline Sugio/Matsuo's confusion and anxiety. He also enlivens the film with tightly choreographed fight scenes (though Sugio/Matsuo gets jumped in dark alleyways far too often) and steamily photographed bed scenes.

Otokotachi, however, cannot overcome the strangeness of its premise: two gangsters in one body and, incredibly, one gang. Ito tries to get around this absurdity by making the other characters, including Sugio/Matsuo's confederates, regard his transformations with barely a blink of the eye, as though the poor fellow were suffering from an annoying tick. It's as though Clark Kent were to change into his Superman outfit at a *Daily Planet* editorial meeting while Perry White cracks wise about Kent not needing carfare. Ito may have filmed his former mentor's script as a tribute, but he should have first thought seriously about a rewrite, beginning from page one.

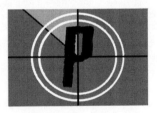

Painted Desert
(1994)

Directed by Masato Harada. Screenplay by Masato Harada and Rebecca Ross. Produced by KSS, Shochiku, Daiichi Kogyo, and Wowow. With Nobu McCarthy, Kazuya Kimura, James Gammon, Priscilla Pointer, Andreas Katsulas. (95 mins.)

Foreign directors have a terrible time getting Japan right. Often they parachute in, preconceptions already in place, shoot the exotica that will amuse or shock the average mall moviegoer, and after a few weeks, board the plane back to L.A. The view of Japan that results is absurd, grotesque, or just plain offensive.

But are Japanese directors any better at capturing America? From the evidence of Masato Harada's *Painted Desert*, the answer is no. This is unfortunate; Harada studied directing and scriptwriting in the United States and, as a film journalist, reported on the American movie scene for Japanese magazines. He is hardly a parachutist. But his view of America is one that you might find in a Kichijoji coffee shop. Bits and pieces of Americana (a weatherbeaten roadside cafe, a weatherbeaten Indian chief), borrowings from films set in the Southwest (*The Petrified Forest, Bagdad Café*) and old cowboy music (Gene Autry, Roy Rogers) mingle uneasily with a story and characters that might have come directly from one of the wilder Japanese comic books. Atmosphere is all, credibility and coherence next to nothing.

European directors such as Percy Adlon, Wim Wenders, and Aki Kaurismaki also invented their own America, quite successfully, but they were cultural guerrillas, who plunged beneath the surface and brought back something of essence. Harada's vision of America is less found than borrowed, primarily from *Bagdad Café*. Once again, we find ourselves in a funky cafe in the middle of the desert. But instead of a tough African-American woman, the proprietor is a tough Japanese-American woman named Sari (Nobu McCarthy), who also serves as the place's irritable waitress and indifferent cook. And instead of a German *hausfrau* wandering in from the desert, Sari finds a young *yakuza* named Jiro (Kazuya Kimura) crawling out from under the sagebrush. How he gets there, with a shoulder wound, is not really explained—the first of several such lacunae—but soon he is at the Desert Rose Café, whipping up fabulous meals. A trained chef, he replaces pork chops with *nouvelle Japonaise* concoctions that look like Mondrian reproductions on a plate.

The customers for this cuisine are odd birds blown in by the desert wind. Here the film departs from *Bagdad Café* and begins to echo *The Petrified Forest*, Archie Mayo's 1936 melodrama about a gang holed up in an Arizona cafe. Instead of Humphrey Bogart as the cynical Duke Mantee, we have James Gammon as Al, a mobster with a bearish manner and a heart of gold. Together with his lowlife associates, he is guarding the desert estate of his boss. Tired of eating Italian food day after day, he tries the cafe for a change of pace. Despite an unpromising beginning—Sari chases him out with a shotgun when he wanders into her personal quarters and discovers Barbara (Priscilla Pointer), her mentally disturbed live-in companion—he ends up falling in love with the food and the proprietor.

This could have been the beginning of an offbeat comedy; Al and his companions are clearly members of the Gang That Couldn't Shoot Straight. Harada, however, films the mobsters as American archtypes, the café as an American icon, and Sari as victim of American prejudice. He ladles on color and and significance with a trowel. But the mobsters talk a dated lingo and tell dumb jokes, the café looks like a Dentsu art director's idea of American funk, and Sari's tale of wartime woe—she was arrested for making Japanese propaganda broadcasts—drops out of the blue and lands with a thud.

More damaging than the wrongness of tone, however, is the lack of focus. Though the ostensible hero, Jiro quickly fades into the background; and spends most of the film silently whipping up masterpieces in the kitchen. The love story between Sari and Al takes forever to get off the ground and the showdown between the two gangs is long in coming. While the tension ebbs away, we get scenes of the boys pigging out on the food and playing a clownish game of baseball. What, I wondered again and again during the first hour, is this movie about? Finally the rival gang attacks the hideout like an invading army. (Ever hear of Mafiosi going over the top? They do in this movie.) Al and his boys fight back with a strange assortment of weaponry, including a 1930s-vintage Tommy gun, while the boss (Andreas Katsulas) enjoys Jiro's cuisine in his basement bunker. He is, as Katsulas' campy performance makes clear, a Sicilian Nero. The scene is a hoot, but Harada presents it as big-scale action.

By this time, I had realized that *Painted Desert* wasn't going to about anything but stylistic sampling and auteurist posturing. There was more, including another buffoonish gun battle, but my mind was already wandering out of the theater; I was thinking how bad movies can sometimes teach more about the art of filmmaking than good ones. From *Painted Desert*, for example, a beginning director might learn about the importance of a good script and what might be called a feeling tone. Without the former, there's no film, period. Without the latter, you're just making pretty pictures that no one is going to care about or believe. And, to paraphrase Louis Armstrong on jazz, if you don't know what it is, you'd better not mess with it.

Parasite Eve

(1997)

Directed by Masayuki Ochiai. **Screenplay by** Ryoichi Kimizuka. **Produced by** Fuji TV and Kadokawa Shoten. **With** Hiroshi Mikami, Riona Hazuki, Tetsuya Bessho. (120 mins.)

Haruki Kadokawa was Japan's own Sam Goldwyn— a nationally-known master showman. But whereas Goldwyn's public image was that of a lovable, if irascible, mangler of the English language, Kadokawa got his name in the papers for torching his career. Following his arrest for cocaine smuggling in August 1993, he quickly became an industry nonperson, though he had been responsible for some of the most successful Japanese films ever released. But while Kadokawa remains among the industry undead, the publishing company that he ran for nearly two decades—Kadokawa Shoten—has started producing movies reminiscent of the hits its former president once turned out. The most recent is Masayuki Ochiai's *Parasite Eve*, whose theme is reminiscent of Kadokawa's 1980 *Fukkatsu no Hi* (Virus), a disaster movie about a world ravaged by nuclear war and plague.

The force that threatens humanity in this film comes, not from without, in the form of living-dead zombies or an all-devouring blob, but from within, in the form of mutant mitochondria—the rodlike structures that live in the cytoplasm of cells, and as the film's scientist-hero explains to everyone who slept through high-school biology class, manufacture the energy that living organisms needs to function. In *Parasite Eve*, the mutants decide to no longer serve the humans in which they live, but to dominate them.

Before humanity joins battle with its subcellular foe, however, we have to endure various preliminaries, beginning with the traffic accident that destroys the brain of the scientist's wife (Riona Hazuki) on the day of their first wedding anniversary. The grief-stricken scientist (Hiroshi Mikami) cannot bear to part with his wife, even after he is told that she registered as an organ donor—and the transplant of one of her kidneys could save the life of a terminally ill twelve-year-old girl.

Driven to desperation by his loss, the scientist conceives of an unusual trade—he give his wife's kidney and gets her liver. The girl's doctor (Tetsuya Bessho), who is equally desperate, agrees. Clutching the metal box containing the organ and scuttling past his wondering colleagues like Igor in a Frankenstein movie, the scientist enters his lab and begins preparing petri dishes for the cultivation of his wife's liver cells—the beginning of a twisted attempt to keep her alive not only in memory but in actuality. He labels the dishes "Eve." But he soon discovers, to his wonderment and horror, that though his wife's mind may have died, her mitochondria are still very much alive—and determined to assert their will, by any means necessary.

Playing the wife, in both her pre- and post-accident incarnations, Riona Hazuki burns with a dangerous erotic brilliance reminiscent of Jessica Lange's Goddess of Death in *All That Jazz*. As the scientist, Hiroshi Mikami creates another sincere but strange genius on the order of his Kenji Miyazawa in the 1996 biopic *Miyazawa Kenji: Sono Ai*. Using computer graphics to animate the rogue mitochondria and edgy, surrealistic camerawork to mimic the hero's troubled state of mind, Ochiai has produced a stylish entertainment aimed at dating couples out for a bit of a turn-on and a bit of a thrill. But in shooting for its target audience, *Parasite Eve* goes soaring over the top with a story of cosmically doomed love, with all the operatic trimmings. Credibility, never great to begin with given the movie's strained They-Come-From-Within premise, gets left far behind.

The turnstiles, however, seem to be clicking and, looking on from show-biz limbo, Kadokawa must be amused by the irony. As mitochondria are to the body, he is to *Parasite Eve*: an energy source whose name is nowhere on final product.

Pekinteki Suika *
Beijing Watermelon (1989)

Directed by Nobuhiko Obayashi. Screenplay by Yoshihiro Ishimatsu. Produced by Maxdai and BSC. With Bengal, Masako Motai, Toru Minegishi, Takashi Sasano, Akira Emoto, Wu Yue. (135 mins.)

Topicality is tricky. Sylvester Stallone's one-man war in Afghanistan in *Rambo III* might have suited the Evil Empire mentality of the early 1980's, but in 1988, with Russian troops rapidly withdrawing from the country, it was ludicrous. Rambo was battling a Cold War ghost.

Pekinteki Suika, which tells the story of a Chiba vegetable seller's encounter with Chinese students, was also overtaken by events. Filming scheduled for Beijing had to be canceled because of the tragedy at Tienanmen Square. But instead of plugging away as though nothing had happened, director Nobuhiko Obayashi seized the opportunity to comment on that tragedy and make one of the most original, moving films in recent memory.

Based on a true story, *Pekinteki Suika* has a documentary feel, with none of the chaos of real life excluded. In the many group scenes all the characters are talking at once, off the top of their heads. This *cinema verité* style of scripting is not new—it is a trademark of Robert Altman—but results have been mixed. In Altman's films, improvisation at times becomes an end in itself—an in-groupy exercise in self-indulgence.

Obayashi, however, uses the seemingly aimless chit-chat to reveal character and advance the story, while creating an intimate, unbuttoned mood that brings out the best in his cast of amateurs and professionals. Freed from running through scripted paces, they project a naturalness that gives the film immediacy and vitality. It is not acted so much as lived.

The story is that of the Good Samaritan. Haruzo Horikoshi (Bengal) and his wife Michiko (Masako Motai) run a small vegetable shop in Chiba Prefecture. One day a tall, gangling Chinese student (Wu Yue) comes to the shop and complains, in halting Japanese, that the prices are too high. He has only ten yen to spend—too little to buy anything but a three-minute phone call. Haruzo refuses to give him a discount but the student stubbornly stands his ground. Michiko—an understanding sort—suggests that they play *jankenpon* (scissors-paper-stone) to settle the argument. Haruzo loses, but his life begins to change.

A few days later—after refusing to play another round of *jankenpon*—Haruzo finds the student in a state of collapse from malnutrition. He rushes him to a hospital and learns, from one of the boy's friends, about the harsh economic realities Chinese students face in Tokyo. Haruzo—a typical horse-playing, *sake*-drinking, middle-aged man—begins selling discount vegetables to all the Chinese students at a nearby dorm and taking them on tours of Tokyo and Kamakura while his wife minds the store.

The students call him their "Japanese father," the neighbors say he has caught the "Chinese disease." His wife and children feel that he is neglecting them and ruining the business. But despite his own doubts, Haruzo keeps helping his new Chinese friends. He doesn't stop even when the tax men come to confiscate the furniture and his wife, in tears, begs him to think of his family. Finally, he collapses from exhaustion, but he now has a dorm full of Chinese friends ready to save their Japanese father from his own excesses.

This may sounds like typical heart-warming TV-drama fare, but Obayashi's treatment is anything but conventional. While giving his actors free rein, he shapes the ensuing conversational melée to create a tone both dryly humorous (the audience was laughing more than they usually do at straight-ahead comedies) and determinedly unsentimental. Also, though he hews fairly close to the facts in bringing his true-life story to the screen, when the occasion demands it Obayashi abandons the illusion of realism altogether.

Towards the end, when Bengal and Masako Motai step out of character to explain why they weren't able to go to Beijing to shoot the final scenes, the film takes on a new dimension. It comments on the events at Tiananmen Square in an understated, but effective manner without losing track of the original story. The scene is a virtuoso turn that few other directors could even imagine, let alone bring off.

Pekinteki Suika is another indication that Japanese directors are still making some of the most innovative films on either side of Pacific.

Perfect Blue *
(1998)

Directed by Satoshi Kon. **Screenplay by** Sadayuki Murai. **Produced by** Rex Entertainment. (81 mins.)

What is your worst nightmare? To be trapped in a dream and know that you can never wake up? To realize, to your horror, that you may not be you, that there is another self—at once alien and familiar—struggling to replace the automaton in the mirror? Or perhaps to discover that you have committed the act you most dread, without even knowing it, until you glance down at your bloody hands?

It is from such sweat-drenched dreams that the makers of *Perfect Blue* have made what they are calling the first psycho-horror animation. Members of the team that created Katsuhiro Otomo's grounding-breaking omnibus *Memories* (1995), they are well qualified to attempt such a genre-stretching exercise. The film's first-time director, Satoshi Kon, wrote the screenplay for "Magnetic Rose," a *Memories* segment about an opera diva in outer space that blurred the borders between reality and illusion, human and inhuman, death and life. *Perfect Blue* is an ambitious extension of the themes that Kon explored in the earlier film.

The script by Sadayuki Murai, which is based on a novel by Yoshikazu Takeuchi, tells yet another tale of a nubile young woman in jeopardy, in this case an idol-singer-turned-actress named Mima Kirigoe. The villain is that old acquaintance, the obsessed fan who will do anything to get near the object of his twisted affection. Kon and his colleagues have gone beyond the usual shocks and scares, however, to examine the inner workings of Japanese show business and the outer reaches of the psyche in a wired age, whose virtual idols infiltrate the very souls of their models.

They have done the seemingly impossible—make a gripping psychodrama from the same basic animated materials that Disney used to create Ariel, Belle, and Esmeralda. Thus the obvious question—why use animation? Why not film a real nubile young actress whose simulated terror will presumably grab the audience in ways that her animated counterpart can't? There is no answer that is going to satisfy the animation skeptic, to whom the medium is "just for kids" anyway. Actually, the script could probably make the transition to live action, though the special-effects budget might give even Disney pause.

That said, the makers of Perfect Blue have developed a visual style for their unusual subject matter that not only vividly expresses it, but ironically comments on it. In the world of the cartoon, as we have known since the days of Ub Iwerks, everything and anything can happen. Kon has simply taken that insight one big step farther. By turning the smiley-cutesy conventions of the shojo manga (girls' comic) genre on their head, he has created a phantasmagoric world in which a sweetly grinning doppelganger in a frilly pink minidress can become the embodiment of implacable evil.

Mima Kirigoe begins the film as the lead singer for a struggling idol trio whose core male fans are loyal but whose records are going nowhere. At the urging of her talent agency, she decides to break into acting— a career move that disappoints her admirers, particularly one sallow-faced computer geek. Soon after Mima starts her first acting job—a bit role in a TV drama about a serial killer—she discovers a fan's Web page called Mima's Room that details her every move, including what she bought for dinner the night before. Standard idol-fan stuff, one would think, but then she notices that the online diary is also describing what is happening inside her one-room flat and, even more scarifying, her mind. Then she starts to catch glimpses of herself in her idol incarnation. Is she overstressed and simply imaging things? But her double begins to speak—and announce that she is the real Mima.

Meanwhile, the fictional crimes of the TV drama start to find their counterparts in real life, with the victims being people associated with the program. Inspired by the hall-of-mirrors horror show her life is becoming. Mima's acting improves and her part grows, but as the boundary between reality and fantasy dissolves, she finds herself lost, alone, losing her mind and, eventually she fears, her life. This boundary dissolves so completely, with mind-twisting shifts from scene to scene, that it becomes hard to distinguish between what Mima is dreaming or hallucinating and what is actually happening. Kon can be accused, with some justification, of playing manipulative games while losing track of his film's narrative thread, but these transitions also whirl us into the heroine's existential vertigo.

It helps, of course, to be an alien to one's own environment and one's own life, to fantasize living a parallel existence in another time and place—and

feel that existence impinging on one's unreal daily reality. If there was ever a Japanese film made for the local expat community, it is Perfect Blue.

Picnic (1996)

Written and directed by Shunji Iwai. **Cinematography by** Noboru Shinoda. **Produced by** Fuji TV and Pony Canyon. **With** Chara, Tadanobu Asano, Koichi Hashizume. (72 mins.)

In 1995 Shunji Iwai's debut feature, Love Letter, drew packed houses and made Iwai a media star. Love Letter, however, was not the first film Iwai made for theatrical release. In the summer of 1994, together with cinematographer Noboru Shinoda, he shot Picnic, a seventy-two-minute film about three young patients of a mental institution who escape one day by, not going over the wall, but walking on top of it. The world, they are convinced, is going to end, and they want to have one last fling before the apocalypse.

Iwai is in tune with the zeitgeist in a way that many of his older colleagues are not. Instead of an auteur director creating his own vision and disdaining what he sees as lesser forms of visual expression, Iwai is a self-described "visual artist" (eizo sakka) who makes little distinction between film, television, and music video. Criticizing an Iwai film for looking like an MTV video clip or a TV drama is rather beside the point. He is simply expressing what a lot of his young audience instinctively feels: the image is the thing, never mind the source. In Picnic his images are surrealistically whimsical, darkly romantic and bizarrely bleak. The film, which treats mental illness as a rebellion of pure but troubled youth against a mad, cruel adult world, has its predecessors, including King of Hearts, the 1966 Philippe De Broca movie about a World War I soldier who wanders into a French town where the escaped inmates of an insane asylum have created an oasis of freeform fantasy and undefiled spirituality.

To Iwai's credit, the madness of Picnic's trio is not as whimsically self-congratulatory as that of De Broca's inmates. Koko (rock singer Chara) is a wild, impulsive crow-woman, complete with a sexy black minidress and crow-feather stole. She believes the world began when her parents made her and will end when she dies. Tsumuji (Tadanobu Asano) murdered his bullying teacher and is plagued by horrific visions of his ghost. After receiving a Bible from a Japanese priest, he becomes convinced that the world is going to end. Satoru (Koichi Hashizume) is Tsumuji's constant companion and the most timid of the three. Though willing to walk on the hospital's wall, he is afraid to break the rules by going beyond it in the unknown.

Vehicles for Iwai's thoughts on the spiritual emptiness of present-day Japan, this trio and their journey have an appeal that transcends the film's thuddingly obvious allegory. Who hasn't, as a kid, walked on a wall and wished it would go on forever? Iwai captures that delightful feeling of freedom. His trio is not so much escaping as taking a picnic excursion to the end of the world. But the trio's picaresque journey can't continue forever; the wall borders on the abyss. The conclusion Iwai arrives at—that even love may not keep us from slipping into will not please the more tenderhearted among his fans, but fits in well with his film's mood of stylish nihilism.

Pineapple Tours *
(1992)

Written and directed by Tsutomu Makiya, Yuji Nakae, Hayashi Toma. **Music by** Rinken Teruya. **Produced by** Sukoburu Kubo, Ryuei, and Pineapple Pictures. **With** Hayato Fujiki, Reiko Kaneshima, Megumi Tomita, Saburo Kitamura, Go Riju, Yuko Miyagi, Shin'ichi Tsunami, Aino Nakasone. (118 mins.)

"This is not a Japanese film!" proclaims the ad for *Pineapple Tours*. Right in more ways than one. This movie by three young Okinawan directors not only presents an Okinawan culture distinctly different from that of mainstream Japan, but does so with an energy and warmth seldom found in films by young Japanese directors. I walked out of *Pineapple Tours* glowing, as though I'd just spent two hours plugged into a natural energy source. Much of that energy comes from the music supplied by Okinawan musicians under the direction of Rinken Band leader Rinken Teruya. Okinawan music, for those who have never heard it, is Asian bluegrass played on *shamisen* and *taiko*: lively, infectious, and rootsy.

The film is a three-part omnibus whose connecting thread is the search for a dud bomb dropped on the island during World War II. The bomb is a reminder of the island's tragic history and a hidden force with the power to both destroy—and protect. The three segments are linked by not only theme, but sensibility. The directors are all still islanders at heart; they create their characters from living models (all are played by Okinawans) and laugh at their foibles as members of the community, not patronizing outsiders. The movie's island, it should be noted, is not Okinawa, but a smaller, fictional neighbor that is ripe for spoilation by the agents of progress.

In the first segment, directed by Tsutomu Makiya,

one of those agents arrives aboard a ferryboat, together with a large, grinning, papier-maché pineapple. A bundle of nerves with a stutter, Hika (Hayato Fujiki) represents a big development company that wants to build a hotel on the island. The pineapple, with "Welcome" blazed across its base in English, is a beacon for the tourists the company hopes to attract. On the same boat is Reiko (Reiko Kaneshima), an opera singer who has unaccountably lost her voice. A native of the island, she has returned, together with her daughter Yumiko (Megumi Tomita), to recover it.

These two characters represent two opposing forces: the destructive one of Mammon (Hika) and the creative one of Art (Reiko). Yet both are cut off in a fundamental way: Hika, from the land and the people; Reiko, from her music. The lives of Hika, Reiko, and the islanders soon become linked by a dud bomb buried somewhere on the island. Hika has to find it because it interferes with his plans; Reiko because an island *yuta* (fortuneteller) has told her that her father, an American pilot, dropped it during the war. By locating the bomb, she can repay a karmic debt and regain her voice. The boundaries between myth and reality, animate and inanimate are indeterminate, ever shifting. "Together with the gods, the bomb is protecting this island," says the *yuta*. "When it's no longer needed, it will appear." The bomb also has the potential to destroy, however. When Sanra the island drunk (Saburo Kitamura) is in his cups, he bitterly recalls how he cowered from the bombing in the stone-lined crypt that has since become his home. "Don't get angry," warns the ferryboat captain. "The dud in your heart is ready to explode." Makiya's segment is not as heavy going as it sounds; he wants us to first enjoy it sensually, comically, humanly. Analysis can wait.

Yuji Nakae's middle segment is a farcical interlude that tells the story of a *Yamatonchu* (Japanese) boy (Go Riju) who becomes unwillingly—and comically—entangled with an island girl (Yuko Miyagi). But for all its buffoonery, including a wild post-wedding chase of the reluctant groom through narrow streets, Nakae's segment also touchs on the film's main themes. Once again, the outsider from the dominant culture is a clueless fool, but this time the islanders trick him into joining the community. This behavior this may seem contradictory, especially after they subvert Hika's plans, but perhaps the islanders would rather have a larger gene pool than more tourist yen.

Hayashi Toma's final segment brings the search for the dud to a riotous, bangup finish. The principal searchers are a punk-rock duo composed of a dreadlocked boy (Shin'ichi Tsunami) and redheaded girl

(Aino Nakasone). Although their motive is logical enough—they want to collect the development company's one hundred million yen reward and fly off to London—their methods are less so. What, after all, do they hope to accomplish by burying poor Hika up to his neck in the sand? *Pineapple Tours* ends with an joyous lift, as justice, in the form of an airplane-flying granny, triumphs. And Reiko, as we always knew she would, lifts up her voice in glorious, triumphant song.

Poppoya
(1999)

Directed by Yasuo Furuhata. **Screenplay by** Yoshiki Iwama and Yasuo Furuhata. **Produced by** Toei, TV Asahi, Sumitomo Corporation, Shueisha, Asahi Shimbunsha, Tokyo FM, and Tohoku Shinsha. **With** Ken Takakura, Ryoko Hirosue, Nenji Kobayashi, Teruko Naruoka. (112 mins.)

Poppoya is one of those high-concept projects that, to Toei executives, must have looked as surefire as a *Star Wars* prequel. The first selling point is Ken Takakura, the sixty-eight-year-old star of dozens of hit *yakuza* films for Toei. Takakura may have been less than boffo in his last few outings, but he is an icon who still has legions of devoted, if graying, fans. Think Clint Eastwood with a Japanese sword.

Second, *Poppoya* is set in Hokkaido in the dead of winter—the setting and season of some of Takakura's greatest triumphs, beginning with *Abashiri Bangai-chi*, the 1965 Teruo Ishii film about an escaped convict on the lam that launched a successful eighteen-part series. Third, *Poppoya* co-stars Ryoko Hirosue, the reigning idol of the moment, whose sweetly smiling face has graced countless magazine covers, TV commercials, and newspaper ads. As is usual with idols, the attention is all out of proportion to the talent, but Hirosue is huge, meaning tickets sales to legions of under-twenty-fives. Fourth, the film is based on a novel of the same title by Jiro Asada that won the prestigious Naoki Prize and became a bestseller. Thus the long list of corporate backers and the massive hype, with *Poppoya* posters plastered in seemingly every JR station in the country.

The film itself, however, is a glossy melodrama designed to draw tears from stones. Also, instead of the younger core audience, director and co-scriptwriter Yasuo Furuhata has targeted primarily men of his elder star's generation. Moviegoers under fifty may feel as though they've stumbled into an old-timers reunion to which they have not been invited.

Otomatsu Sato (Takakura) is the master of a train station in a dying Hokkaido mining town. The line is scheduled to close and Sato, to retire that year. He is a *poppoya*, a nickname for the railroad men who came in with the steam engines and are now relics in this high-tech world. Every day, even when the thermometer hits thirty below, Sato stands tall on the platform, awaiting the arrival of the next train. He is also a man haunted by memories. Seventeen years ago, his two-month-old daughter died after a brief illness and then his wife (Shinobu Otake), whose health was never strong, followed her to an early grave.

Now he is sustained by the friendship of Senji Sugiura (Nenji Kobayashi), a *poppoya* who served as Sato's fireman when he was a train engineer, and Mune Kato (Teruko Naraoka), the salty proprietress of a local restaurant. Sugiura offers Sato a job at a resort hotel he is planning to manage, but Sato doesn't want to leave his station—and his beloved dead. Then one day, he receives a visit from a little girl who reminds him uncannily of his daughter. She leaves behind a Japanese doll that her twelve year-old sister comes to claim—but forgets again. Finally, the two girls' seventeen-year-old sibling (Ryoko Hirosue) pays a call—and Sato realizes that she is not who she appears to be. This charming stranger seems to have been living inside his heart all these years. Soon, she is calling him "father"—and Sato is about to embark on the most unusual night of his life.

The movie is Japanized Frank Capra—a warmingly sentimental fantasy about a small town hero who, as one can see from the first frame, will always be what he's always been. But whereas Capra's heroes were usually eccentric All-American idealists, Takakura's Sato is the straightest of straight-arrows, devoted not to the Common Man, but to his job. Takakura embodies this character with the kind of star charisma that cannot be taught, and the kind of dignity that cannot be faked. Though the ultimate company man, he is not just punching a timecard but living a life he genuinely loves. He makes his paralyzing routine look as romantic as marching off to conquer Asia for the Asians. This is a performance that's going to lengthen the lines at the Japan Railways employment office.

As the spirit of Sato's departed daughter, Ryoko Hirosue gives the camera five coy expressions where one will do. I felt battered by this charm offensive, as though I had spent two hours watching Glico candy commercials. Even so Hirosue has a born affinity for the camera, as well as a knack approaching genius for exploiting her fresh-faced charm. One imagines middle-aged salarymen stirring out of their mid-afternoon slumbers when she trips with such calculatingly uncalculated gaiety across the screen. Is *Poppoya* worth seeing for anyone else? Railroad buffs, certainly. Takakura fans, obviously. Workaholics, however, had better stay away. Killing yourself for the company never looked cooler.

Porno Star *

(1999)

Written and directed by Toshiaki Toyoda. **Produced by** Little More, Tokyo Theater, and Filmmakers. **With** Hiroshi Chiharu, Onimaru, Akaji Maro, Rin Ozawa, Tetta Sugimoto. (98 mins.)

The title of *Porno Star* is misleading. Instead of a made-in-Japan *Boogie Nights*, Toshiaki Toyoda's debut feature is a violent fantasy about the life and death in the lower depths of Shibuya. Also, while populated by recognizable Shibuya types, from the speed-rapping hustlers to the kids on skateboards, the film is yet another romantic essay on the macho rites of blood and brotherhood that has as little to do with the realities of the Shibuya scene circa 1999 as *The Good, the Bad, and the Ugly* did with realities of life in the Old West.

Porno Star's hero is Arano (Hiroshi Chiharu), whom we first meet striding through the Shibuya streets carrying a mysterious gym bag and knocking aside passersby with brute indifference. A tall, rangy kid in a hooded khaki jacket, with a hawklike face and an impassive gaze, Arano looks so out of it as to be scary—and darkly funny. Arano is a Clint Eastwood-like stone killer, who knifes a bad-mouthing *yakuza* and, after his victim stumbles into the office of a gang boss (Akaji Maro) and collapses, casually steps over his writhing body, while the boss and his underlings look on with wide eyes and gaping mouths.

Arano, however, meets his match in not only the boss, a bald growler who runs a discount ticket shop as a front, but in Kamijo (Onimaru), a long-haired *chimpira* (apprentice gangster) who operates a date club with his gang of Shibuya bad boys. Business has been falling off, however, and the boss has been turning up the heat; Kamijo is open to anything that brings in the yen. Though better-socialized and better-focused than Arano, he is equally cold-blooded. Kamijo knows Arano may be a nut, but feels that he also has his uses. Soon Arano is running with the gang, while continuing to seethe with blank, dangerous rage.

There is a story of sorts, which revolves around a stash of LSD that Kamijo and his boys snatch from a pair of foreign dealers, and a rivalry with a gang of grown-up *yakuza* in colorful suits headed by a lantern-jawed boss (Tetta Sugimoto). The real focus, however, is on the uneasy relationship between Arano and Kamijo and Arano's quixotic pursuit of his own justice, whose code is "if it bothers me, kill it." He is searching for a kind of purity—his battle cry is *"yakuza wa iranai"* (I don't need *yakuza*)—but finds his sword of righteousness turned against him.

First-time director Toyoda tries to inject pathos into this story, but he also wants to be a Tarantino-esque purveyor of hardcore violence, who maintains the black comic tone while piling up the bodies. His execution is anything but even, however; where *Reservoir Dogs* delivered massive but cleverly aimed, jolts *Porno Star* settles for lame gags and crude shocks. The film, however, contains more than its share of peak moments. One occurs while the gang is celebrating its snatch of the stash with an orgy that features a dip in a hot tub with a floating hookah. What is striking about this scene are not the writhing bodies, but the hundreds of tomatoes floating in the tub and scattered all about the floor, like so many symbolic victims waiting to be squashed. Another happens after Arano and a date club employee named Alice (Rin Ozawa) make off with the stash and she leaves him alone in an alley while she goes to sell it. Hours pass but she does not return. Arano looks up at the night sky and a shower of knives rains down on him. The knives turn into raindrops and Arano gets thoroughly drenched—and feels spiritually cleansed.

There are other such moments, but do they add up to a movie? Not quite, but both Hiroshi Chiharu, a member of a popular *manzai* comedy act, and Onimaru, a former real-life gangbanger who made his acting debut in *Junk Food*, are strong, distinctive presences. Also, Toyoda, despite his indulgences, knows how to connect with an audience. I only wish that he would put away the *manga* and the Tarantino tapes for a while and get better acquainted with his true cinematic soul brother: Jean Cocteau.

Postman Blues

(1997)

Written and directed by Sabu. **Produced by** Nikkatsu. **With** Shin'ichi Tsutsumi, Ren Osugi, Kyoko Toyama, Keisuke Horibe. (110 mins.)

Why do dull jobs attract indie directors? In his second film, *Postman Blues*, Sabu gives us a letter-carrier whose stultifying routine is interrupted by life's chaos. His hero, however, is less a victim than a rebel who breaks free of his daily round to find friendship, love, and death. In telling his story, *Postman* slowly loses touch with reality and ascends into the ether of the absurd. As in Sabu's 1996 debut, *Dangan Runner*, the characters are caught in a life-and-death chase, in which the pursuer and the pursued become odd-lot companions who gradually let go of their obsessions and fears and give themselves up to the joy of movement. After developing terrific narrative momentum, however, *Dangan Runner* exhausted itself in silly genre clichés. *Postman* follows a similar arc.

Sawaki (Shin'ichi Tsutsumi) is young, lonely, and stupendously bored with delivering the mail. One day on his rounds, he runs across Noguchi (Ren Osugi), an old high-school friend who has become a *yakuza* drug runner. Despite the hazards of his occupation, which include the occasional severed finger, Noguchi waxes eloquent on its joys. "It's hard to feel excited about anything after the age of thirty," he says, "but being a *yakuza* is one thrill after another." Deciding to share those joys with his school chum, he slips a packet of drugs into Sawaki's mailbag. Unbeknownst to them both, Noguchi's little finger rolls off the table and falls into the bag as well.

This accidental meeting produces a profound change in Sawaki's life. Returning to his bachelor's flat, he rips opens his letters and reads one by a girl named Sayoko (Kyoko Toyama), who is dying of cancer in a nearby hospital. The next morning, on the pretext of delivering her letter, he meets her and is immediately smitten. He also encounters another cancer patient, a professional hitman named Joe (Keisuke Horibe) who is that rare creature: a totally honest man. Elated by his brushes with love and friendship, Sawaki vows to return the next day.

The police, however, suspect that he is a drug runner for the mob and, after discovering Noguchi's severed finger in his flat, a serial killer. The cops become determined to stop this fiend in postman's form by any means necessary. The next day dawns and Sawaki pedals off to a new life and an unsuspected doom.

Sabu, whose pre-directorial incarnation was as actor Hiroyuki Tanaka, films the opening scenes of *Postman* as deadpan comedy. Shin'ichi Tsutsumi plays the postman hero as a somewhat likable, somewhat bland, somewhat discontented everyman. Ren Osugi's gangster and Keisuke Horibe's hitman, by contrast, are comic grotesques who serve to prod the postman out of his rut by quirky word and example.

The pace is deliberate, the colors somber, the ironies obvious. But as the cops begin the close in, Sabu rams a directorial pedal to the metal. With the velocity high, he is in his element, giving the extended chase that fills the film's second half a giddy visceral rush and a batty comic energy. Finally he has the postman, hitman, and gangster where he wants them: hurtling down a road together on bicycles toward a police roadblock. It's the neatest image of the movie (as was the shot of the three runners abreast in *Dangan*) but then he goes cute with histrionics, like an overworked *manga* artist milking an ending to make his monthly quota. For his next

film, perhaps he ought to take a hint from Jan (*Speed*) De Bont: place a big inflammable object in a wide open space, light the fuse, and stand back. Better to go out with a bang than a tired wink.

Pride: Ummei no Toki
Pride (1998)

Directed by Shun'ya Ito. **Screenplay by** Tomoo Matsuda and Shun'ya Ito. **Produced by** Higashi Nihon House. **With** Eiji Okada, Ayumi Ishida, Masahiko Tsugawa, Scott Wilson. (161 mins.)

Most Japanese movies barely register a blip on the mental radar screen of the local foreign community. One Japanese film, however, is getting the plenty of attention from outlanders—nearly all of it negative. That film is *Pride: Ummei no Toki*, a biopic that focuses on the wartime career and subsequent warcrimes trial of former prime minister Hideki Tojo. When I first heard about the production of the film, underwritten by a home-building company whose chairman is a notorious rightist, I thought it was a sick joke, comparable to an aging German industrialist with neo-Nazi sympathies financing a Broadway revival of "Springtime for Hitler."

But no, the makers of *Pride* are in deadly earnest, and far from being a cheap whitewash, their film is a lavish production with elaborate period sets, location scenes shot in India with thousands of extras, and an all-star cast headed by Masahiko Tsugawa, who pulls out all stops as Tojo. This formidably gifted veteran, a regular in the comedies of Juzo Itami, has gone on the promo campaign trail to plump for the film's historical accuracy, while excoriating his countrymen for losing their *Yamato-damashii* (Japanese spirit) and forgetting *bushido* (the way of the samurai). Clearly for Tsugawa, as well as for director Shun'ya Ito and others involved in the production, *Pride* is not a straight soul-for-cash deal with the devil, but a labor of conviction, even love.

What is that conviction? To put it simply, far from being the arch-demon of Allied wartime propaganda, Tojo was a staunch patriot, able leader, and warm-hearted family man who personified the samurai spirit of loyalty and self-sacrifice. Meanwhile, the film presents the Tokyo Trial, at which an international panel of judges heard the cases of twenty-eight defendants charged with war crimes, as a vehicle for victor's revenge. It also makes the claim that Japan was fighting, not for its own aggrandizement, but to free the subject peoples of Asia, particularly Indians, from the yoke of their colonial masters.

Though I sat through *Tokyo Saiban* (Tokyo Trial), Masaki Kobayashi's excellent, if trying, four-and-a-hour 1983 documentary, I cannot claim to be an expert on either Tojo or his trial. What I can say, from my own limited research, is that the film is not totally off the mark. Tojo did have admirable qualities, including a rock-solid integrity of a kind in short supply among today's bureaucrats and politicians, and a razor-sharp mind that tore many of his prosecutors' ill-informed arguments to shreds. Also, the film's portrayal of his trial is, as far it goes, fairly faithful to the outline of the historical record, including the refusal of GHQ authorities to permit publication of the minority opinion of Indian jurist Radhabinod Pal, the only judge to find the defendants innocent of all charges (and who is, not incidentally, the film's sole non-Japanese hero).

Pride is not content, however, to correct errors and distortions that have crystallized over the decades into received opinion. Instead, it presents a one-sided view of its hero and his deeds that may have many precedents—the Japanese film industry has been releasing nationalistic war films for decades—but goes beyond most in its unapologetic revisionism.

One could take issue with the way the film massages its depictions of events to fit its particular mold. More important, however, are its omissions. The film presents Tojo as the embodiment of traditional Japanese virtue, who stoically undermines his own defense to save his Emperor. We never see the blinkered, rigid ultranationalist who failed to fully calculate the costs of the war or the chances of success, to the grief of millions. It portrays chief prosecutor Joseph Keenan as an arrogant, ignorant, politically motivated score settler whose case against Tojo depended on fragmentary anecdotes and baseless insinuations. It conveniently omits testimony by prosecution witnesses, including eyewitnesses to the Rape of Nanjing, that offered ample evidence of Japanese aggression and brutality.

Instead it presents scenes of pure-hearted Japanese soldiers and their Indian allies, led by Subhas Chandras Bose, advancing gloriously against the British imperialists on the India-Burma border in 1944. It does not show us the outcome: confused retreat, despite direct orders from Tokyo to hold ground, followed by disease, suicide, and a complete breakdown in discipline. It also does not present the fruits of Japanese "liberation" in Asia—a hatred and distrust of Japan that endures among survivors and their descendants to this day.

What is really needed to counter *Pride*, however, is not outraged reviews in English-language newspapers, but a Japanese film that presents the whole

truth about Tojo and his co-defendants, that effectively revises the revisionists. But who would finance it and film it, especially to the tune of *Pride*'s ¥1.5 billion? Hard to imagine anyone being so foolish, isn't it? There's a market for *Pride*, but not a nation's shame.

Pupu no Monogatari
The Story of Pupu (1998)

Written and directed by Kensaku Watanabe. Produced by Little More, Tokyo Theater, and Filmmakers. With Sakura Uehara, Reiko Matsuo, Hayato Kunimura, Yoshio Harada, Seijun Suzuki. (73 mins.)

Trailers usually promise more than the movie can deliver. Sometimes, though, they promise less. The trailer for *Pupu no Monogatari* falls into the latter category. With its mugging young woman pushing a baby carriage, its grinning kid in a spangled costume flourishing a chrome-plated six shooter, and its cutesy-cute narration, it gives the impression that Kensaku Watanabe's debut feature is an exercise in fey whimsy.

But Watanabe, a former assistant director to Seijun Suzuki, has instead created a fable of modern alienation that simultaneously celebrates and subverts road-movie conventions, while supplying a lesbian subtext to its characters' search for love. Yes, *Pupu* has its share of whimsy, but its refusal to take itself seriously is refreshing. Also, its faux naive goofiness is, finally, more revealing than annoying, exposing, as it does, the supreme self-absorption at the heart of the Peter Pan (or Hello Kitty) ethic. Like his mentor Suzuki, who appears in a cameo, Watanabe playfully celebrates the absurd, while firmly rejecting grass-is-green realism. Though a good apprentice, he is also a talented original, who can pull off the difficult trick of making contemporary Japan look like a field of dreams.

Suzu (Sakura Uehara) and Fu (Reiko Matsuo), together with a baby they have picked up on the way, are traipsing through a verdant, empty countryside on a glorious spring day. They are ostensibly on their way to visit the grave of Pupu, a pig who, as Fu solemnly informs us in a voiceover, was devoured by a nasty wolf while she was innocently contemplating a butterfly. There is no Pupu: she exists only in story that Fu invents to amuse Suzu, the pouting ingenue who is the love of Fu's life and whom she will do anything to protect. When two loutish boys try to pick them up and one dares to lay a hand on Suzu, Fu thrashes them within an inch of their lecherous lives.

With her boyishly cut hair and robust good looks, Fu would seem to be the stronger of the two girls, but she is really Suzu's love slave. When Suzu tires of the baby and casually pushes the buggy down a slope, Fu only looks on, bemused. What Suzu wants, Suzu gets. What Suzu wants, however, is attention, preferably male, and she will do anything to get it. When a powder-blue Cadillac convertible whizzes past her outstretched thumb, she rips open the front of her dress—and brings the car to a screeching halt. The driver, a golf pro with big ego and expanding middle, proves to be another lech. Once again Fu rises to the occasion, doing apparently lethal damage to his thick skull. But as the girls are about to drive off in triumph in the Caddie, he attacks them with his Big Bertha, grimly determined to drive their brains to the eighteenth green. Just as he is about to tee off on Fu, a round hole blossoms on his forehead. The girls see, in the open trunk of the Caddie, a grinning kid holding a smoking gun. Trunkman to the rescue!

Meanwhile, another, leaner, middle-aged man is doing bench presses in what looks to be a well-appointed bachelor pad. But, as is so often the case in *Pupu*, appearances are deceiving. The pad is a backyard tent and the bachelor, Kishima (Hayato Kunimura), has a nagging wife and a young daughter. Yet another one of Suzu's past lovers, he receives a picture postcard of her holding the baby, with a message implying that she is on her way to collect. Panicked, Kishima contacts a former hitman (Yoshio Harada) he once employed. This time, however, he wants to do the job himself, with the hitman's gun. There are further complications, including a husky transvestite and her lover, who are desperately searching for the baby Suzu discarded, but the climax centers on a showdown between Kishima and his sweetly smiling extortioner.

Mood is everything in a film like this. If Watanabe had ladled on the symbolism and pumped up the tension, *Pupu* would have sunk under the weight of its own pretensions. If he had signaled his superiority to the flimsy material with nudges and winks, it would have dissolved into the ether. Instead, he takes a deadpan approach that milks the gags without trampling on them, and undercuts our expectations without completely betraying them. The movie begins as an offbeat love story with a lift and ends as one. Suzu, that obscure object of desire, may not care about anyone but the girl in the mirror, but by the end we understand Fu's obsession with her. She seems to float through life ever carefree, ever available, ever just out reach. Like the rainbow the girls see at the beginning of the movie, she draws more earthbound spirits on towards a garden of earthly delights. But the road is littered with corpses.

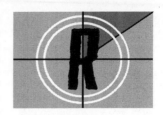

Radio no Jikan *
Welcome Back, Mr. McDonald (1998)

Written and directed by Koki Mitani. Cinematography by Kenji Takama. Produced by Fuji TV and Toho. With Toshiaki Karasawa, Kyoka Suzuki, Masahiko Nishimura, Keiko Toda. (103 mins.)

When I first read publicity material for Koki Mitani's first feature film, *Radio no Jikan* (Welcome Back, Mr. McDonald) describing it as a "situation comedy" (*shichueshon komedi*) I wondered if the film could possibly be the real thing; sit-coms, in the true sense of the word, are nowhere to be found on Japanese television. Perhaps the PR flack was simply using another Janglish expression whose relation to the English original was, at best, approximate.

Radio no Jikan however, is the real thing, with a clever premise, flawless structure, crackling performances and laugh-out-loud gag lines. Based on a play written by Mitani and first performed by his Tokyo Sunshine Boys theater troupe, the film is obviously, even blatantly, stagy. The action is largely limited to one set—a studio in a Tokyo radio station—and the actors are projecting to the second balcony.

But Mitani, who has written numerous plays and TV scripts since launching the Tokyo Sunshine Boys while a student at Nihon University in 1983, knows exactly what he is doing. His actors are not trying and failing, to play Just Folks, but succeeding, hilariously, in impersonating show-business types ostensibly putting on a radio drama, but depending on their place in the pecking order, engaged in ego-tripping or ego-stroking. Nearly everyone is on nearly all of the time, exuding charm one moment, venom the next. It's all quite theatrical, quite inventive, and in its own knockabout way, quite convincing. The movie rattles and roars along in a way reminiscent that masterpiece of show-biz screwball comedy, *The Twentieth Century* (minus the silken glamour of Carol Lombard and the screaming egomania of John Barrymore). While being, in style and manner, closer to Hollywood than even the comedies of Juzo Itami, *Radio no Jikan* dissects the inner workings of Japanese social relations with a finer scalpel than almost any film in recent memory.

The story might be described as Mitani's parody revenge against all the forces that conspire to make a scriptwriter's life miserable. As a promotional stunt, a Tokyo radio station is planning to air a live performance of a drama by the winner of amateur scriptwriting contest: a mousy, achingly naive housewife (Kyoka Suzuki). As first it's like a dream; an important producer (Masahiko Nishimura) calling her *sensei* (professor), big stars rehearsing her dialogue. Then the nightmare begins. The actress playing the female lead (Keiko Toda) decides that she doesn't like her character's name, Ritsuko. Too stodgy, she says. Change it to Mary Jane! And why not give her a sexy job like trial lawyer while you're at it? Desperate to make his star happy, the producer agrees to these outrageous demands, and from that all else follows.

Now that the main character is a foreigner, the setting has to be changed from Atami to New York and all the other characters have to become Americans. Even after the show goes on the air, the star and the rest of the cast keep coming up with bright ideas. Why not juice up the story by adding the Mafia and machine guns? Why not change the setting again, to Chicago? Why not make Mary Jane's lover a pilot? Why not indeed?

Soon, the housewife's heartfelt melodrama about the unraveling of a marriage has becomes an action-adventure story complete with a bursting dam and a plane soaring off into space. Meanwhile, the clock is ticking away, the producer is tearing his hair, and the housewife, watching her play being carelessly trashed, is quietly building to an explosion.

First-time director Mitani has polished his actors to a rare perfection of pace and timing, and together with cinematographer Kenji Takama, has filmed his script with a seamless dynamism that energizes what could have been static scenes. Given their low budgets and murderous production schedules, most Japanese films by new directors cannot escape technical hiccups, from muddy sound to murky lighting, but *Radio no Jikan* is a vibrant exception.

Perhaps Mitani sets up his gag lines a little too slickly and ties up his plot ends a little too neatly—he is, after all, a fan of that master of comic contrivance, Neil Simon—but he also knows how to intelligently entertain. Even America, sitcom glut or no, might some day take notice.

Rakuyo

The Setting Sun (1992)

Written and directed by Akira Tomono. Produced by Nikkatsu and Toei. With Diane Lane, Donald Sutherland, Masaya Kato, Yuen Biao. (150 mins.)

Roger Ebert once proposed what he described as "a useful rule of thumb about movie advertisements which have a row of little boxes across the bottom, each one showing the face of a different international star and the name of a character." Called the Box Rule, it states, simply: "Automatically avoid such films." What, then, is one to do about *Rakuyo*, a Box Rule movie without the boxes? Complain about deceptive advertising?

Perhaps propose a corollary rule for Japanese movies: the Delusions of Grandeur rule. In general, the more money a Japanese producer spends and the bigger his international ambitions, the more awful his movie is going to be. Exhibit A is *Ten to Chi to*, a 1990 epic that cost five billion yen to make, featured three thousand Canadian college students as sixteenth-century samurai, and had all the excitement of a marching band routine.

Rakuyo is another five-billion-yen would-be blockbuster, made to celebrate the Nikkatsu studio's eightieth anniversary. Internationalization is provided by Diane Lane playing a slithery Chinese cabaret singer, Donald Sutherland in a cameo as a corrupt British businessman, and Hong Kong action star Yuen Biao as a Shanghai opium dealer. They are only a few of the many characters in a tangled drama of international intrigue, set in pre-war Manchuria and Shanghai. (The cast page in the program lists twenty-six more actors, all with their own boxes.)

But the star with the biggest box should be former fashion model Masaya Kato, who plays an undercover agent for the Japanese Imperial Army. Kato belongs on the screen the way the young Elvis Presley belonged on the screen: he's got the smoldering good looks, the macho presence, the suggestion of boyish vulnerability. But instead of acting, Kato poses. Some of his poses are striking, but in the way *manga* drawings can be striking, without being the least bit believable.

Perhaps we shouldn't expect much more; like most Box Rule movies, *Rakuyo* is driven not by character—but by plot—one that is almost absurdly complex; first-time scriptwriter and director Akira Tomono evidently felt that a Big Movie must have a Big Story with a Big Theme and subplots that proliferate like kudzu.

His hero is Tatsuma Kaya (Kato), a cashiered officer who returns to Manchuria after a three-year absence to serve the Imperial Army as a fund-raiser of sorts. To supply the army with the money it needs to conquer the country and make it a Japanese colony, Kaya rips off a Manchurian bank and sells scarce salt to Manchurians in the countryside at extortionate prices.

The plot thickens with the appearance of an old flame, a Chinese cabaret singer named Renko

(Lane). She has become the leader of a gang of thieves (they were about to relieve Kaya of his ill-gotten gains) and greets him in flawless American English. (The singer who dubs her cabaret numbers, however, is unmistakably Japanese.)

Before we have recovered from these developments, Kaya and Renko are plunged into an underworld of ruthless opium dealers, corrupt Japanese officials, and desperate Chinese revolutionaries. Kaya doesn't enter this world voluntarily—an army officer threatens to bomb Renko's hideout if he does not deal opium for the greater glory of the Empire—but once in it, he does what a man's gotta to do, including fight his chief rival, a Shanghai mobster (Yuen Biao) with a deadly command of the martial arts. Renko stands by her man throughout, even though his dirty dealings are helping to destroy her people.

Tomono's ostensible message is that drugs, imperialism and war are all bad, bad, bad. But his dashing hero gives the lie to these fine sentiments. Until the end, he has few, if any, qualms about aiding the Japanese war machine and he is so stylish in his trenchcoats, so unflappably cool as he makes another score for his country, that we start to wonder: aren't we really being invited to wax nostalgic about the days when men were men and Japan was the master of Manchukuo?

That question, more than the predictable suspense, the hokey melodrama and the amateurishly staged action, stayed with me as I left *Rakuyo*.

Rampo

The Mystery of Rampo (1994)

Version 1: **Screenplay and direction by** Rintaro Mayuzumi. (93 mins.) Version 2: **Directed by** Kazuyoshi Okuyama. **Screenplay by** Yuhei Enoki. (97 min.) **Produced by** the Rampo Production Committee. **With** Naoto Takenaka, Michiko Hada, Masahiro Motoki, Mikijiro Hira.

It could be argued, cynically, that the two versions of *Rampo* (The Mystery of Rampo) in the theaters are nothing but a cleverly engineered ploy to sell more tickets. After all, if you want judge for yourself which is better—the original by director Rintaro Mayuzumi or the remake by producer Kazuyoshi Okuyama—you gotta see 'em both.

Okuyama cheerfully admits to "playing dirty" to make his *Rampo* a success, resorting to such gimmicks as a splashy celebrity-party scene, subliminal visual and audio messages, and spraying theaters with a special *Rampo* perfume. But he also has a valid point: the Japanese film industry is headed down a gentle, ever downward slope to oblivion. Somebody, somehow, has to do it better.

Following unsuccessful negotiations with Mayuzumi over reshoots, Okuyama decided to remake nearly seventy percent of *Rampo* himself and let the audience decide who had the better side of the argument. He did not play fair, however; Mayuzumi's version is in fewer, smaller venues and scheduled for a shorter run. It is not, however, a horrible botch. A director for NHK Enterprises, Mayuzumi does a competent job of establishing his characters and moving the story forward. His hero is Edogawa Rampo (Naoto Takenaka), a writer who became popular in the 1920s for stories of psychological suspense that recalled those of his namesake, Edgar Allan Poe. Instead of a straightforward bio, the movie is a fictionalized voyage into Rampo's life and imagination that explores the ever-shifting boundary between the two.

After Rampo's short story "Osei Tojo" (The Entrance of Osei) is rejected by the censors, his editor (Teruyuki Kagawa), brings him a newspaper clipping about an incident eerily similar to the murder depicted in the story. The wife of an antique dealer (Michiko Hada) discovered her husband dead in her *nagamochi*—a large, oblong hope chest. He had been playing hide-and-seek with their children, and when he hopped inside and the latch fell shut, he suffocated. A rumor spreads that his wife had found him, barely alive—and closed the lid again.

At the funeral, a spying Rampo immediately falls for the wife, Shizuko. Despite her grief, she exudes a languid sensuousness and an intoxicating air of danger. She also happens to be lovely in kimono.

Inspired, he begins writing a sequel. Osei, in disgrace, becomes the mistress of a depraved count (Mikijiro Hira). A dashing young detective, Kogoro Akechi (Masahiro Motoki) trails her to the count's seaside estate to learn whether she murdered her husband.

While feverishly writing this tale, Rampo frantically pursues Shizuko. In his own mind he becomes Akechi and Shizuko, Osei. As he approaches the end of his story and the goal of his quest, his two worlds begin to merge, to horrifying effect.

Mayuzumi carefully demarks the shifts between Rampo's waking consciousness and writerly fantasies, while keeping the focus on his infatuation with Shizuko. He presents the Akechi-Osei story, rather literally, as Rampo's imaginative working out of his real-life obsessions. There is little, either visually or erotically, that would be out of place in an NHK drama. Towards the end, Mayuzumi ups the emotional voltage with skillful crosscutting, but his climax feels *déja vu*. We've been there before, in bodice-ripping romances if nowhere else.

Okuyama, however, wanted a film that would blow audiences away and become a big, attention-getting smash. He has achieved both aims. His version may not be as delicately attuned to psychological nuance as Mayuzumi's—his faster, flashier editing undermines the first director's rhythms—but Okuyama's conception of the story is more vivid, sensual, universal. He takes us, with dazzling displays of imagery, into his hero's creative and emotional chaos, until we feel it becoming our own.

In hyping the film, Okuyama falls into excess, some of it wretched. One example is the party scene, with its crowd of celebrities in period dress, including an anachronistically crooning drag queen. And yet he manages to bring the scene off. As Rampo struggles unsuccessfully to address the chattering guests supposedly assembled in his honor, the party becomes a metaphor for the real world to which he can never belong. The sight of all those famous faces turned so charmingly and resolutely away from him intensify his feeling of alienation and strangeness. If Okuyama had used a crowd of authentically costumed anonymous extras he would not have achieved the same unsettling effect.

Other attempts to punch up the film do not work as well. A voyeuristic scene involving Akechi, Osei and the Count is less sensual than exhausting. It has a certain fascination, nonetheless. I'd heard of face painting, but this was the first time I'd ever seen a face literally painting—a back.

Too many mainstream Japanese filmmakers are caught in a time warp, trying to recapture today's mass audience with Golden Age methods. In *Rampo* Okuyama has demonstrated that at least one Japanese movie can explode on the screen with the same visual excitement and storytelling energy that film fans have come to expect from Hollywood. His *Rampo* may not usher in another Golden Age, but it has the feel of the future.

Rasen no Sobyo
Rough Sketch of a Spiral (1991)

Directed by Yasufumi Kojima. Produced by Buzz Company. With Yoshikazu Yano, Hiroaki Hirano, Takashi Kiyao, Tadashi Hase, Saeko. (103 mins.)

Rasen no Sobyo (Rough Sketch of a Spiral) is the first theatrical documentary about gay life in Japan. That alone makes it newsworthy. But its sympathetically clear-eyed, carefully detailed treatment of its subject makes it worth watching as well.

The film grew out of a student project of director Yasufumi Kojima. With the encouragement of his teacher at the Japan Film School, Shohei Imamura, Kojima decided to expand a thirty-minute short about a gay couple into a full-length documentary. Unfortunately, he had trouble finding cooperative subjects. The gay men he approached in Tokyo were reluctant to appear in his film using their real names.

Then he met Yoshikazu Yano, a young store clerk, and Hiroaki Hirano, a high school teacher. Both were active in the Osaka gay community and, more importantly, were willing to allow Kojima's camera into their lives. But even after a year of filming his two subjects and their circle, Kojima felt he had failed to capture the reality of their lives. "I was trying to portray them as flawless heroes," he later wrote. "I was looking for aspects of their world that wouldn't make them subject to prejudice." His subjects, not liking what they saw either, withdrew their consent from the project.

Rather than give up, Kojima spent a year discussing the film with Yano and the others and finally persuaded them to continue. "We'll reveal everything," they told Kojima. "All you have to do is film it." They were as good as their word. Three years after starting his project Kojima had a film he could be satisfied with. It delves into his subjects' feelings about their sexuality and the prejudice they encounter in expressing it. It also shows them as people, not talking heads, and captures moments of drama that may be unrelated to the film's ostensible subject, but give it more value as a human document.

Rasen begins like a student attempt to imitate a "daring" TV special, with grainy long shots of men strolling in the Shinjuku Nichome gay district, cruising at a porno theater, and having sex at a beach. Although Kojima may have filmed these images to establish his theme, they have a voyeuristic feel and reinforce images he is trying to change.

Kojima's focus soon shifts to Osaka and here he is on surer ground. His heroes, if you will, are Yano and his roommate, Takashi Kiyao. Beginning the film as a bagger at a local supermarket, Yano is engagingly outspoken about his lifestyle. We believe him when he tells an off-camera interviewer that he's "never felt any regrets about being gay."

Yano also has an ambition that opens up the film: he wants to write and produce a play that examines society's attitudes toward homosexuality. Quitting his job, he recruits his roommate and members of the Osaka gay community for his cast and crew. One cast members is Tadashi Hase, a sixty-one-year-old poet with a ready laugh, who tells an interviewer that, unlike many gay men of his generation, he refused to marry for appearances sake. "Because I had been born as a gay man, I had to live as one," he says.

Another is Hiroaki Hirano, a teacher at an evening high school who tells his students that he is gay, an openness that does not sit well with some of his fellow teachers. Yet another is Saeko, a dancer at a local gay bar. The subject of Kojima's student documentary, he is the most flamboyant of Yano's cast, but is also among the straightest talkers. "I don't consider myself a woman and I don't think about trying to become one," he says.

None of these attitudes may be new to those acquainted with gay life in Western countries, but it is unusual for Japanese gays to be so frank on camera. *Rasen* is an indication that they are finally gaining the confidence to challenge their society's prejudices and norms.

Kojima also records his subjects' arguments, holiday-making and daily routines. His work with this material is less than perfect. The synchronization of sound and image is occasionally poor and the editing is often rough. The film is clearly an apprentice work, but one by a caring and dedicated apprentice.

Kojima says he gave *Rasen no Sobyo* its unusual title because it symbolizes the gay dilemma: "Unlike heterosexual men, who can head straight for the object of their desire, gay men have to circle around and around searching for love." The title also expresses Kojima's accomplishment: via a circuitous route, his film takes us into the heart of the Japanese gay experience.

Rex: Kyoryu Monogatari

Rex (1993)

Directed by Haruki Kadokawa. Screenplay by Haruki Kadokawa and Shoichi Maruyama. Produced by the Rex Production Committee. With Yumi Adachi, Tsunehiko Watase, Shinobu Otake. (106 mins.)

Rex: Kyoryu Monogatari is super-producer Haruki Kadoakwa's latest attempt to manufacture a blockbuster. This time, he has bet his corporate bankroll on a cute dinosaur, the creation of Carlo Ranbardi of *Alien* and *E.T.* fame. The film's subject matter, release date, and promotional strategy seem designed to ride the tailwind of the *Jurassic Park* boom. Kadokawa has given the millions of Japanese moviegoers who are now dinosaur-mad an entertainment just for them. And they can see this twenty-million-dollar companion to Steven Spielberg's sixty-million-dollar epic right now, without subtitles, while the hype for the Japanese release of *Jurassic Park* builds to incredible heights. How can it miss?

The real target audience for *Rex*, however, is not dinosaur fans per se, but the girls who find Hello Kitty adorable. The movie essentially transposes the aesthetic of Hello Kitty and *shojo manga* (girls' comic books) to the screen, together with a big dollop of phony mysticism, drippy sentimentality, lame

humor, and blatant sexism. The film's inspiration may be Spielberg, but the execution is pure Kadokawa: i.e., schlock that has all the subtlety of a sock to the jaw (or rather a cotton candy to the face).

Rex's heroine is Chie (Yumi Adachi), the ten-year-old daughter of paleontologist Akiyoshi Tateno (Tsunehiko Watase). Living in a storybook farmhouse in a rural Hokkaido paradise, together with cute farm animals and a gentle, understanding father, Chie would seem to have it all.

But this beautiful child with the big eyes is not happy. Her mother (Shinobu Otake), a famous geneticist, has left her family to work in New York. Now, Chie refuses to go to school and speaks only to her animal friends and her father. Why, she wonders, does her mother hate her so? Oh cruel world, that has such selfish career women in it!

Chie is distracted from her troubles by an expedition to find a dinosaur egg. Guided by a wise old Ainu, Chie, her father, and two researchers journey to a remote cave and, after a thrilling slide down an icy passageway, they find themselves in a mysterious grotto. In the center, suspended in a pyramid-shaped crystal, is the egg. But when Dr. Tateno and one of his assistants try to examine it, the ground starts to shake and the grotto to collapse around them. The Ainu urges them to escape while he calms the angry spirits they have aroused.

After this slam-bang beginning, with its references to the Indiana Jones films and Toshimaen water slides, we get a long-winded pseudoscientific explanation about how the "natural refrigeration" of the cave has kept the egg in perfect condition and how modern genetics can hatch it.

But the skill of Chie's mother, who has flown in from New York, and the other researchers prove inadequate to the task. It is Chie, blowing a plaintive tune on a pipe given to her by the old Ainu, who succeeds in bringing Rex out of his shell. The newly born Tyrannosaurus Rex looks like a baby E.T. in dino drag and behaves like an infant chimpanzee. Chie teaches it to eat human food, do tricks, and even use a potty.

Rex, the mugging little scamp, will have Hello Kitty fans sighing "*kawaii*" (cute). Other, less sentimental types, may wonder when Rex will stop simpering and start snapping. He doesn't, of course. Instead, he grows to simpering childhood while becoming the object of a media feeding frenzy. Soon his adorable face is everywhere. One of Dr. Tateno's colleagues decides to steal this scaly gold mine for his own nefarious purposes. The rest of the film concerns the struggle to save Chie's darling from his evil clutches and, not incidentally, reunite her warring parents.

The baddies, who look like Blues Brother clones, chase Chie and Rex through the Hokkaido countryside in scenes inspired by *Home Alone* and *E.T.* But *Rex* soon declines into insipid whimsy that makes its models look like towering works of cinematic art. Kadokawa may be shamelessly ripping off Spielberg, but he is also doing him a favor. After seeing this puerile fantasy, we can better appreciate the difficulty of his accomplishment. While appealing the widest possible audience in *E.T.*, he managed to create moments of awe and delight for anyone who loves the art of film. Kadokawa, one the other hand, has created the strongest possible argument for the recycling of waste celluloid.

Rikyu *
(1989)

Directed by Hiroshi Teshigahara. **Screenplay by** Hiroshi Teshigahara and Gempei Akasegawa. **Produced by** Teshigahara Production, Shochiku Eizo, Itochu, and Hakuhodo. **With** Rentaro Mikuni, Tsutomu Yamazaki. (135 mins.)

Can a movie be too beautiful? *Rikyu*, the first film in seventeen years by director Hiroshi Teshigahara, is so visually stunning that the story at times fades into the background. What the actors are saying seems less interesting than what they are holding or wearing. With its lavish use of period tea implements and costumes (the latter designed by Emi Wada of *Ran* fame), it is the cinematic equivalent of an impeccably designed coffee-table book.

It is also a splendid advertisement for traditional Japanese culture. This, given the director and subject matter, is no accident. The third *iemoto* (head master) of the Sogetsu school of flower arranging and an accomplished potter and landscape gardener, Teshigahara is a modern renaissance man, a spiritual descendant of the film's hero, Sen no Rikyu, who personified the cultural efflorescence of the Momoyama period (1568–1600).

This is not to say that Teshigahara has made a gorgeous shell. The script by Teshigahara and Naoki Prize–winning author Gempei Akasegawa is solid if arcane (the program notes contain a glossary for those with a shaky command of medieval Japanese) and the two leads—Rentaro Mikuni as tea master Sen no Rikyu and Tsutomu Yamazaki as warlord Toyotomi Hideyoshi—are perfectly cast. But, like *Kagemusha*, a period film by another veteran Japanese director who returned to the screen after a long absence, *Rikyu* has a static feel, as though Teshigahara had lived with it for years, perfecting

each shot in his mind, while slowly losing track of its narrative pulse.

When the film begins, Rikyu is already a respected tea master, flower arranger, and arbiter of taste at a time when tea ceremony was another excuse for conspicuous consumption by the rich and powerful. One of the worst offenders is Toyotomi Hideyoshi. After succeeding Oda Nobunaga (the country's de facto ruler) in 1582, Hideyoshi indulged his love of display to the hilt. In 1587 he threw a tea party for the people of Osaka and Kyoto that lasted ten days. Oddly enough, Hideyoshi chose Rikyu, who had served under Nobunaga and favored classical austerity, as his tea master. Not so oddly—to refuse Hideyoshi was to court disaster—Rikyu agreed to help the warlord stage his extravaganzas. He also advanced his own artistic agenda, so successfully that his influence is felt to this day. The uneasy relationship between these two strong personalities and their inevitable conflicts form the core of the film.

The nature of this relationship is illustrated early on. Hideyoshi, dressed in all his finery, goes to meet Rikyu at his tea house. When he swaggers into the garden, however, he is in for a surprise: the morning glories that lined the path have all been cut. Crawling through the tea house's tiny doorway, he sees, right in front of his nose, one perfect morning glory. Rikyu says nothing, but his message is clear: less is more.

Rikyu is, however, more than the simple tale of the all-knowing master humbling the know-it-all pupil. Hideyoshi admires Rikyu's genius ("You can change the world with just one hand," he tells him), but tries to manipulate it for his own ends.

Tsutomu Yamazaki's Hideyoshi is a willful but dangerous child: a buffoon one moment, a tyrant the next. Bursting with comic energy, he rattles about the castle like a sixteenth-century Groucho Marx, but when he hears that a visiting tea master wants to return to his lord in Odawara—Hideyoshi's archenemy—he boots his bewildered guest off the veranda in a paroxysm of rage.

Rentaro Mikuni's Rikyu is Hideyoshi's opposite: a genius who practices his art quietly and simply, with an absence of artistic ego and temperament. His movements exude a knowledge that go beyond mere mastery of technique. When he takes a tea cup into his big peasant hands, he seems to be communing with it, absorbing its essence. Mikuni is totally convincing as the man who was not only his generation's preeminent master of tea, but its leading artistic innovator. Rikyu, however, is also an unwilling pawn in a complex political game. Mikuni expresses his fears, doubts, and hard-headed defiance while confirming our belief in his greatness. This is seamless acting and a definitive performance.

Rikyu, one Japanese critic said, should be seen twice: once for its beauty and again for its acting. In any case, it should not be missed.

Ring 2
(1999)

Directed by Hideo Nakata. Screenplay by Hiroshi Takahashi. Executive production by Masato Hara. Produced by Ring 2 Production Committee, Asmik Ace Entertainment, and Oz. With Nanako Matsushima, Hiroyuki Sanada, Miki Nakatani, Rikiya Otaka, Hitomi Sato, Kyoko Fukuda, Fumiyo Kobinata, Kenjiro Ishimaru, Yurei Yanagi. (95 mins).

Last February a double bill of linked psycho-horror films—*Ring* and *Rasen* (Spiral)—became the movie event of the new year for the loose-socks set. Based on novels by horrormeister Koji Suzuki, the films had a premise seemingly sprung directly from the teenage mind—a video that kills anyone who watches it.

A TV journalist named Reiko Asakawa (Nanako Matsushima) investigates the deaths of the first victims—appropriately enough, a pair of teenage girls —and finds herself swept up in a mystery that may take on the appurtenances of modern technology, but has its roots in ancient beliefs about vengeful spirits. A murdered girl named Sadako, who was tossed down a well on Oshima three decades ago turns out to be the culprit, but even after her body is retrieved the tape continues to do its deadly work.

Reiko's ex husband (Hiroyuki Sanada), a college professor who helps her analyze the tape's ghostly images and haul Sadako's body to the surface, dies in agony. Then, to her horror, she discovers that her young son Yoichi has seen the tape as well. At the end of the film she driving off with him in a mad rush to save his life—how she doesn't quite know.

This, clearly, is a set-up for a sequel and a sequel is what we now have in *Ring 2*. The director is again Hideo Nakata, while Nanako Matsushima is back as Reiko Asakawa and Hiroyuki Sanada, as her ex (dead but still back), but like most sequels, *Ring 2* is less about tying up loose narrative ends than scoring again at the box office. The film itself is *déja vu* all over again.

As it opens an autopsy reveals, incredibly, that Sadako was alive until the last year or two of her stay in the well. Also, her spirit is still as wrathful as ever. Among those under its malevolent spell are Mai Takano (Miki Nakatani), the professor's lover, who wants to solve the mystery and end her nightmare of a life, Reiko's son Yoichi (Rikiya Otaka), who survived the tape, but has become a channel for Sadako's rage, and Masami Kurahashi (Hitomi Sato), a classmate of one of the tape's victims, whose reason has been unhinged by what she saw.

As before, left-brained types serve as convenient victims, including a shrink (Fumiyo Kobinata) who in unlocking the secret's of Masami's mind is swept into its black depths, a police detective (Kenjiro Ishimaru) who tries to solve the puzzle of Sadako's death, but is baffled by forces beyond any human law, and a TV assistant director (Yurei Yanagi) who obtains a copy of the tape, to his everlasting regret.

Nakata ties these various narrative strands together with efficiency, if not much originality, but can't disguise the staleness of the material. We've been through this particular *obake yashiki* (haunted house) one too many times.

Romance *
Some Kinda Love (1996)

Screenplay and direction by Shun'ichi Nagasaki. Produced by Office Shiro. With Koji Tamaoki, Lasalle Ishii, Kaori Mizushima. (94 mins.)

Youth, most would agree, is wonderful: free, adventurous, and generous. Youth, as most parents have noticed, can also be willful, capricious, and selfish. Parents can tolerate the negatives because they know (wistfully hope?) their children will outgrow them. Sometimes, they do not; not willingly at any rate. But as these Peter Pans turn thirty, it becomes hard to keep the inner child (or brat) alive. Responsibility, ambition, and experience push them, like it or not, toward adulthood. Some resist, self-destructively, and their inner child becomes a monster.

The difficult transition to adulthood is the theme of Shunichi Nagasaki's *Romance*. The title is both ironic and nostalgic. Romance is what the film's characters long for, briefly gasp, and finally lose. It symbolizes vanishing youth and its fugitive dreams that they try so futilely to preserve.

Working with a small cast and a low budget, he has fashioned a film that, with its neatly plotted structure, restrained camerawork and naturalistic acting, is clearly the product of a mature talent. At the same time, the forty-year-old Nagasaki has brought a youthful energy and passion to his study of aging Peter Pans. Though he sees his characters with uncommon clarity, he is less a detached cinematic observer than a participant in their drama.

The story is of two college friends who have gone their separate ways, with Shibata (Koji Tamaoki) becoming a high-living real estate developer, Anzai (Lasalle Ishii), a low-ranking city bureaucrat. Shibata is a tall, lean extrovert, who regards his housing tracts as projections of his ego, while Anzai is a short, pudgy introvert, who spends his spare time writing a novel he wants no one to read.

In Shibata's presence, however, Anzai reverts to his college self: playful, funny and boyish. Shibata, meanwhile, can't help manipulating his old friend—he wants the city to choose his company's site for a housing development—but he also has a genuine affection for Anzai. When he is with him, he shows a human side that, as a businessman, he habitually suppresses.

One night at a bar, they met Kiriko (Kaori Mizushima), a bright-eyed beauty in a red dress who is a far freer spirit than either of them. After calling Shibata's wife to tell her that she wants to "borrow" her husband for the night, she leads Shibata and Anzai on an UFO-spotting expedition. Stretched out on a rooftop, watching the sky for flying saucers, they become kids again and let the cares of the adult world slip away.

They do not remain kids forever. Shibata and Kiriko become lovers and Shibata's wife, who was also Anzai's college chum, becomes suspicious. Determined to keep the good times rolling, Shibata, Kiriko, and Anzai spend the weekend at Shibata's country house. There they enjoy an idyll that includes a nighttime drive across the countryside in Shibata's car, with a giddy Kiriko at the wheel, and another UFO-spotting session. But Anzai, the most adult of the three, cannot hide his uneasiness. Who is Kiriko and what does she want? What is Shibata, who is wheeling and dealing on his cell phone even as they play, really after?

Romance resembles *The Great Gatsby*, with the object of desire forever elusive and ruin waiting at the end of the bright, glittering road. Also, like Fitzgerald the novelist, Nagasaki the screenwriter is prone to the elegaically sentimental, but more than compensates with a sure grasp of his characters' idiom and milieu.

Anzai, Shibata, and Kiriko come to know each other, not through the usual bald declarations of movie dialogue, but everyday conversational ploys that conceal as much as they reveal. They sound, in other words, much like people we know. While striving for their dream of the perfect moment and the perfect union, they remain, in important ways, strangers to each other. A movie about the impossibility of turning back time also makes a telling statement about the difficulty of communication in modern Japan. In signaling to spacemen, Nagasaki's carefree trio are waving, desperately, to each other.

Roningai
(1990)

Directed by Kazuko Kuroki. Screenplay Kazuo Kasahara. Produced by Hiroyuki Yamada Right Vision, Shochiku, and NTV. With Yoshio Harada, Shin Katsu, Renji Ishibashi, Kanako Higuchi, Kunie Tanaka. (118 mins.)

Kazuko Kuroki's *Roningai* commemorates the sixtieth anniversary of the death of Shozo Makino, the "father of Japanese cinema." It was Makino, in fact, who directed the first, silent version of this prototypical samurai drama in 1928. In 1957 his son, Masahiro Makino, helmed a black-and-white remake. After that, there were ten abortive attempts to bring *Roningai* to the screen again. Kuroki's is the eleventh, and successful, try. Aided by the eighty-two-year old Makino, who appears in the credits as supervisor, Kuroki recreates the energy, flair and humor of the great *jidaigeki* (period dramas) of the past. His film, however, is an homage, not a breakthrough. It revives the conventions of the genre, but doesn't transcend them.

The story centers on a ragged crew of *ronin* (masterless samurai) who first meet at the Maruta, a low-class Edo roadhouse. When a longhaired stranger (Yoshio Harada) tries to leave without paying, he is confronted by the burly, bearded *ronin* (Shin Katsu) who is the Maruta's *yojimbo* (bouncer). The two men continue their discussion outside, followed by a curious crowd. As they are trading insults and working up the courage to draw their swords, a tall, lanky samurai (Renji Ishibashi) strolls by, calls them both fools, and casually tosses two gold coins on the ground. The antagonists simultaneously make a grab for them—and realize that their benefactor is right.

In this scene, Kuroki sketches the characters of his principals and the outlines of their hard-scrabble world with an economy and wit that sets the mood for the rest of film. *Roningai* has a flamboyance typical of so many *jidaigeki*, while taking a belly-to-the-ground view of Edo life and human nature.

Although the three heroes soon become boon drinking companions, they find themselves rivals for the hand of Oshin (Kanako Higuchi), the most beautiful of the prostitutes who make the Maruta their headquarters. The first in her affections is Aramaki Gennai, the longhaired *ronin*, who has returned after a three-year separation and soon takes up residence in her houseboat. Danger lurks, however. Prostitutes plying their trade by the river are being slashed by unknown assailants. One night Gennai learns by chance that the killers are samurai of Obata, a local *hatamoto* (shogunal retainer) who is conducting a deadly anti-vice campaign. The *ronin* and Obata's men clash, but their struggle is not a simple contest of good versus evil. Conflicting loyalties muddy the emotional waters and intensify the pathos of the climatic battle.

Kuroki's *Roningai* is an actor's film, full of neat pieces of business. The actor who contributes the most is Shintaro Katsu, the blind swordsman of the *Zatoichi* series, who made few screen appearances in the 1980s. But whatever the reasons for his absence, a lack of energy isn't one of them. At the age of fifty-eight, Katsu still displays his old macho swagger and trademark explosiveness.

Yoshio Harada and Renji Ishibashi also create flamboyantly vivid characters. Harada's Gennai is the ultimate bum hero, who never draws a sober breath throughout the film, but comes through magnificently, if improbably, in a virtuoso display of drunken swordsmanship. As the thin, silent samurai, Ishibashi exudes classic *bushido* cool, while easily being the best real swordsman of the bunch. Playing a warrior turned bird-seller who allies himself with the *ronin*, Kunie Tanaka chews his usual amount of scenery, but his over-the-top style fits in well with the extravagant goings on.

Though not another *Yojimbo*—it lacks Kurosawa's transforming spark of genius—*Roningai* revivifies a dying genre, not by self-parody, which quickly becomes tiresome, but an unabashedly entertaining return to its roots.

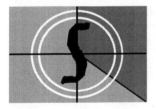

Sada
(1998)

Directed by Nobuhiko Obayashi. **Screenplay by** Yuko Nishizawa. **Produced by** Shochiku and PSC. **With** Hitomi Kuroki, Kippei Shina, Norihei Miki, Bengal, Tsurutaro Kataoka. (132 mins.)

The story of Sada Abe, the former geisha who in 1936 strangled her lover and severed his penis for a keepsake, has inspired several films, most notably Nagisa Oshima's 1976 *Ai no Corrida* (In the Realm of the Senses), whose graphic depictions of sadomasochistic sex made it unreleasable in Japan, though a bowd-

lerized version eventually appeared. Now another director of Oshima's generation, Nobuhiko Obayashi, has filmed the Sada story, with a sharply different approach. Whereas Oshima frontally challenged standards of censorship and taste, Obayashi takes an ironic, distanced, stylized view of his by now familiar material, while giving it a visual gloss reminiscent of MTV in its more artsy moments.

He frames *Sada* as an early Showa-period stage play, complete with a roué narrator and broadly comic staging, as though the actors were performing in a prewar Asakusa variety hall. The object, I suppose, is to place the narrative in its period while commenting on it from the heights of postmodern irony. In certain scenes, this conceit gives what could have been dreary domestic *tsuris* a new, if wacky, spin, as when Sada (Hitomi Kuroki) argues with her mother about her marriage plans and, storming out of the room, sends Mom—and the giant white radish she holding—whirling like the farm house in *The Wizard of Oz*. But the general effect of the archly self-conscious tone is offputting and, at times, offensive. What are we to make of a rape scene, with the victim Sada as a fourteen-year-old girl, played with the gestures of vaudeville farce? Laugh? Admire the director's sophistication? Or wonder, as I did, at his insensitivity?

Give Obayashi credit, though, for making a real attempt to discover the motives for Sada's actions, not simply exploit them for kinky thrills. The story begins with Sada's lonely girlhood in a poor family in downtown Tokyo, but quickly shifts to her fourteenth year and her nightmare introduction to sex by a brute of a college student (Masaku Ikeuchi). She is saved by Okada (Kippei Shina), a medical student who wears creepy dark glasses, but has a warm, consoling touch. She falls in love, but soon after Okada announces that he is leaving for good. His farewell present to Sada is a scalpel, with which he cuts an imaginary heart from his chest, saying it is hers to keep. He is, we learn in a voice-over, a victim of leprosy—a disease then equivalent to a sentence of permanent exile from humanity.

Crushed by this desertion, but unable to forget Okada—or her vision of his bleeding heart—Sada becomes a geisha, a prostitute, and by the age of twenty-nine, the lover of Tachibana (Bengal), a middle-aged angel of mercy who is a member of the Nagoya city council. Tachibana, a fussbudget with a heart of gold, not only rescues Sada from harlotry, but arranges for her to apprentice at the *ryotei* (teahouse) owned by Tatsuzo (Tsurutaro Kataoka), a rake with a smooth manner and an insanely jealous wife. When these meet the attraction is mutual and the progression from hot looks to hot lovemaking as quick as summer lightning. Sada experiences pleasures in Tatsuzo's arms that she had never known from her thousands of faceless johns, but when his wife discovers their affair, finds herself out on the streets.

Tatsuzo, now obsessed, follows her to a nearby inn, where they abandon themselves to days and nights of ecstatic lovemaking. Then Tatsuzo leaves her for three days and Sada nearly goes out of her mind with desire. When he returns, she is determined that he will be hers forever. Feeling he has already tasted all that life has to offer, Tatsuzo allows her to wrap a pink cord around his neck and pull it thrillingly—and then fatally—tighter.

As the fourteen-year-old Sada, Hitomi Kuroki is glaringly wrong; as the mature Sada, unquestionably right. In those eyes glittering with an insatiable desire and a love never consummated or forgotten, we can see dissolution, sadness, and a strange, terrible purity. Over the distracting noise of her director's cinematic games, she gives us the Sada of our imagination—or unquiet dreams.

Sakura
Cherry Tree (1994)

Directed by Seijiro Koyama. Screenplay by Nobuyo Kato. Produced by the Sakura Production Committee, Crest, and Seido Pro. With Saburo Shinoda, Yoshiko Tanaka, Kirin Kiki, Hiromitsu Suzuki. (108 mins.)

"Now that was a Japanese movie," said Donald Richie as we left the screening of *Sakura* (Cherry Tree). And that, I thought, was a perfect one-sentence review. The biopic of a bus conductor who devotes his life to a cherished national symbol, *Sakura* drips with the kind of "typically Japanese" sentiment so dear to the hearts of the mass audience and so hard, say the Japanese themselves, for outsiders to understand. The film is also a showcase of postcard-pretty photography, by-the-book directing, TV-drama overacting and Ministry of Education–approved moral uplift. (The story on which it was based was included in a junior high-school textbook.) It is as quintessentially Japanese as its title.

Those who derive their image of Japanese cinema from the works of Kurosawa and Ozu may find Richie's comment hard to understand. Aren't *Rashomon* and *Tokyo Story* the quintessential Japanese films? But that is like calling *Citizen Kane* the quintessential Hollywood movie. In the Japan of today, as in the Hollywood of the Golden Age, the movies that express the purest essence of the industry do not push the artistic envelope, but the right audience buttons. In the case of *Sakura*, that means making the tears flow. Forget subtlety, forget irony. Have the impossibly dedicated, self-sacrificing hero die a noble death, while the family wails, the music

swells, and the cherry blossoms drift gently to the ground. Ah, the sadness, the transience of life!

Sakura is based on the true story of Ryoji Saito, a bus conductor on the route from Nagoya to Kanazawa. During the building of Mihoro Dam in Gifu Prefecture, Saito (Saburo Shinoda) became interested in two four-hundred-year old cherry trees that construction crews moved to higher ground. Impressed by the life force of these patriarchs, he acquired cherry saplings and began planting them along his route. As the film begins, in 1966, Saito is telling his passengers the story of the rescued cherry trees with enthusiasm, charm, and a satisfied smile. Here is the face a man who has found his *raison d' etre*. Where, I wondered, is the movie?

Saito, however, not only plants the trees, but cares for them, in every spare moment, in all weather. His wife Chikako (Yoshiko Tanaka) worries about him, his older sister Fumi (Kirin Kiki) supports him, and his bus-driver friend Kota (Hiromitsu Suzuki) helps him. Meanwhile, Saito is haunted by the memory of the cherry tree he saw as a child during his mother's funeral procession. He works not only to please his passengers, but to honor her memory. Saito's work attracts the attention of fellow cherry tree enthusiasts and the media; he is awarded honors, interviewed for newspapers and television. But where, I wondered again, is the movie?

As in so many melodramas, the filmmakers answer this question by escalating the conflict between the hero's higher duty and his job and family. Chikako becomes angry at her husband for giving more time to his trees than her and their two children, while endangering his health in the bargain. His boss tells Saito passengers might start thinking that their conductors care more about trees than their work. (Saito, a conscientious sort, cares deeply for both.)

But we really know we are in a Japanese movie when the hero is diagnosed with cancer—that time-tested device for introducing noble suffering into the narrative. This is not contrivance: the real-life Saito also fought a losing battle with cancer. His illness gave him the incentive to link the Pacific and Sea coasts of the Japan with a tunnel of cherry trees along his bus route—a scheme that everyone around him considered mad. Here, at last, is the film's dramatic mainspring. Will Saito realize his dream before the Grim Reaper comes calling?

Saburo Shinoda's Saito is, in his sincerity, purity, and determination, too good for this world. (Not, alas, for the movie.) We see his end coming long before the first symptoms of his illness appear. Playing Chikako, Yoshiko Tanaka has a look of wifely exasperation permanently etched into her features. She is a royal pain. Director Seijiro Koyama tries earnestly to do Saito's story justice, but he is dully predictable as a storyteller and ploddingly pedestrian as a filmmaker. Saito's story needs more poetry and playfulness; in their two thousand or so years as a cultural icons, cherry trees have inspired plenty of both. In April, when Saito's trees are in bloom, I hope that his friends still raise a toast in his honor and, when they are in their cups, shake a few branches for the joy and beauty of it. I'm sure he would have cheered them on.

Sakura no Sono *
The Cherry Orchard (1991)

Directed by Shun Nakahara. **Screenplay by** Hiroaki Jinno. **Produced by** New Century Producers and Suntory. **With** Miho Miyazawa, Hiroko Nakajima, Miho Tsumiki, Yasuyo Shirashima, Yuichi Mikami. (96 mins.)

Sakura no Sono (The Cherry Orchard) sets itself a hard cinematic problem and proceeds to solve it with taste, sensitivity, and wit. The problem is this: make a film focusing on four members of a girls' high school drama club. Set it in and around the clubroom and limit it to the two hours prior to the club's annual performance of Chekhov's "The Cherry Orchard." Keep the presence of boys and adults to a minimum (one chaste kissing scene, one comic teacher-kids chase scene) and make the action as naturalistic as possible (if twenty-two teenage girls are in the same room, show twenty-two of them talking at once). Finally—and most difficult—take the audience inside the lives and hearts of the four main characters and show it the transience of girlhood innocence and the sharp, tender ache of adolescent love.

Scriptwriter Hiroaki Jinno and director Shun Nakahara succeed brilliantly at this task. Their premise resembles that of *American Graffiti* (Jinno has claimed George Lucas's 1973 film as an inspiration) but their approach is utterly different. Whereas *American Graffiti* celebrates the noisy, exuberant exterior of adolescent life, *Sakura no Sono* probes interior longings, desires, and fears. The American film is largely action—adolescence as a series of escapades; the Japanese film, mostly talk—intimate, private, revealing. Though strenuously entertaining, *Graffiti* provides a one-size-fits-all view of boomer youth. *Sakura* is more sparing with its cinematic pleasures, but presents its characters as individuals, not representative types.

The film opens with Kaoru Shiromaru (Miho Miyazawa), a second-year student who is the play's director, alone in the clubroom with her boyfriend. From the room's spaciousness, age, and warm, muted colors we realize that we are in presence of tradition and privilege. We also soon see that the

room is a private, feminine space. When the boyfriend plants a kiss on Shiromaru's neck, a danger signal goes off in her mind (Nakahara underlines it with a perfectly timed close up). She hustles him out just as Yubuko Shimizu (Hiroko Nakajima), a third-year student, walks in.

This seemingly isolated incident (the boyfriend makes only one more brief appearance) resonates throughout the film. It not only establishes a main theme—the girls' awakening to and fear of sexuality—but sets a tone of restraint, furtiveness and intimacy. The boyfriend's absence intensifies our experience of the film's feminine atmosphere, the way the echo of a bell at midnight makes us more aware of the surrounding silence. He also leaves behind a sign of his presence—a pack of cigarettes and a lighter—that Nakahara uses to illuminate the characters and reveal the emotions of his principals.

Nakahara's care in construction—the working of the smallest details into the film's fabric—brings the world of the drama club to vibrant, nuanced life. It is, we see, the one place where the girls can be themselves, free from the pressures of male attention and adult authority. This world is neither innocent nor perfect. Shimizu comes to school wearing a permanent—strictly against school rules. Then Kiko Sugiyama (Miho Tsumiki), the rebel of the group, is seen at a coffee shop smoking a cigarette. Both are called to the teachers' room while the school authorities debate whether to cancel the play because of Sugiyama's misbehavior.

That crisis passes, but another arises: Chiyoko Kurata (Yasuyo Shirashima), a girl who has a major role in the play, contracts a bad case of stage fright. Her best friend, Shimizu, tries to comfort her, but the closeness of their relationship provokes the jealousy of Sugiyama, who is attracted to Shimizu. This may sound like a typical same-sex love triangle comics for girls (the story was based on one), but Nakahara makes us feel the weight these seemingly minor crises have in the girls' lives. It is a virtuoso turn, reminiscent of that master interpreter of youth, Francois Truffaut. As Shimizu, Hiroko Nakajima projects a strong intelligence and precocious sensuality. As Sugiyama, Miho Tsumiki impresses as the most knowing—and thus the saddest—of the film's girls.

Samehada Otoko & Momojiri Onna
Shark Skin Man & Peach Hip Girl (1999)

Written and directed by Katsuhito Ishii. **Produced by** Tohoku Shinsha Film Corporation. **With** Tadanobu Asano, Shie Koinata, Ittoku Kishibe, Susumu Terashima, Kimie Shingyoji, Shingo Tsurumi, Tasuya Gashuin. (107 mins.)

It's official: Quentin Tarantino thinks Katsuhiro Ishii's *Samehada Otoko & Momojiri Musume* is cool. After attending a screening of the film at the Hawaii International Film Festival, Tarentino not only told Ishii how much he liked this weirdly wacky, impeccably stylish chase movie about a hip thief pursued by a gang of cartoon hitmen, but spent several hours schmoozing with the director at a coffee shop. A high compliment indeed from the King of Cinematic Cool.

Deserved? It all depends on your definition of "cool," doesn't it? While bursting with manic energy and burbling with neat comic ideas, this first feature by TV commercial *wunderkind* Ishii is less an *eiga* (movie) than an *eiga gokko* (movie game). For all his movie-geek reputation, Tarantino can deliver emotion as well as attitude. Ishii's *Samehada*, on the other hand, is all postmodern poses that seek only to self-referentially entertain. Having said that, I must admit that, while winking at his *manga*-esque material, Ishii has a true sympathy with it, as well as an undeniable facility for bringing it to the screen. *Samehada* may be a surfacy movie, but it's seldom a dull or annoying one. Given the tendency of films by younger Japanese directors to be one or both, it is a standout for that reason alone.

Samehada's unusual title is derived, logically enough, from the names of its two main characters. Kuro Samehada (Tadanobu Asano) is a thief on the run from a gang he has ripped off—and to which he once belonged. Toshiko Momojiri (Shie Koinata) wants to flee her dull life as a clerk at a seedy provincial hotel and the grasping fingers of her lecherous uncle, who manages the place. These two meet cute when Toshiko, driving to the post office, nearly runs down Samehada, who is fleeing for his life in nothing but his briefs. The next minute he is in the driver's seat, speeding away from his pursuers. This, Toshiko realizes, is the escape she has been looking for.

The gang members bear no resemblance to any real *yakuza* of any known era. The boss (Kishibe Ittoku) is a foppish collector of Oronamin C road signs, while son Mitsuru (Shingo Tsurumi), the gang's heir apparent, dresses in a white jump suit, dyes his hair platinum blonde and moves with the feral quickness and strength of an evil troll on speed. They and the rest of the gang, including Toshiko's sinister older sister Mitsuko (Kimie Shingyoji), are madly determined to find Samehada and recover their loot. The only sane one among them, the lantern-jawed Sawada (Susumu Terajima), is under suspicion as Samehada's best buddy. Meanwhile, the lecherous uncle, whose interest in Toshiko's welfare is not the purest, hires a nerdy hitman named Yamada (Tasuya Gashuin) to bring her back alive, without her new companion.

Ishii, who also wrote the script, stirs plenty of complications into this basic chase scenario, including several sexual torture scenes and a bizarre costume-play interlude, with a flamboyant designer acquaintance of Samehada's orchestrating the festivities. Nonetheless, the movie never quite loses its propulsive force of its first frenetic minutes, which resemble an *anime* in overdrive.

Ishii, who got his professional start making TV commercials for Tohoku Shinsha, has approached his material as an animation character-designer might, paying more attention to his cast's costumery and weaponry than to their performances. The film's highly stylized look, which the English-language program describes as "hyperfashion," gives it a visual gloss that adds to its comic verve, while underscoring the characters' essential traits, from the blazing whites of the manic Mitsuru to the ultrachic blacks of the zero-cool Samehada.

As though jazzed by their flashy fun duds, the cast seems to be having a roaring good time. Even the usually sober-sided Tadanobu Asano, who has seemingly starred in nearly every indie film of note for the past several years, finds it hard to keep a straight face. The film, in fact, might well have drifted off into the giggly ozone were it not for the steadying presence of Susumu Terajima as Sawada, who must make the film's clearest moral choice: go with the gang or save his friend.

The answer is not immediately apparent, but it is also hardly the point of the film. That, Ishii says with every frame, is the visual phantasmagoria he has concocted from his entire *manga*-reading, TV-watching, movie-going experience. No wonder Tarantino considered *Samehada* cool—it is a love letter to pop-culture *otaku* everywhere—and he, as we know, is the biggest *otaku* of all.

Sangatsu no Lion
March Comes In Like A Lion (1992)

Directed by Hitoshi Yamazaki. Screenplay by Hitoshi Yamazaki and Hiroshi Miyazaki. Produced by Uplink. With Yoshiko Yura, Cho Bangho. (118 mins.)

Hitoshi Yazaki's concerns in *Sangatsu no Lion* will be familiar to fans of Jim Jarmusch. Like the director of *Stranger Than Paradise*, Yazaki is fascinated by the significance of the everyday, the mystery of the banal. Not much happens in *Sangatsu*, yet everything happens.

A young prostitute (Yoshiko Yura) and her amnesiac brother (Cho Bangho) live together in a dilapidated apartment. The brother, Haruo, who has lost his memory in a motorcycle accident, and the sister, who calls herself Ice because of her constant craving for "ice candy" (popsicles), lead a seemingly dull and purposeless existence . The brother exists only in the eternal present, groping vaguely for clues to his lost identity. He is content to sit for hours watching workers tear down a building, a slaphappy grin on his face. (The workers, meanwhile, take him for a simpleton.) The sister, who wears the same flirty miniskirt and red high heels through most of the film, spends her days lugging a gaily painted styrofoam cooler about Tokyo or sucking on popsicles in her apartment. She is, in short, something of a space cadet.

Like Jarmusch, Yazaki knows his characters' bizarre world intimately and accepts it without fuss—and soon, so do we. Yet his vision of that world differs greatly that from his American counterpart. Though some scenes in *Sangatsu* have a whimsical humor, Jarmusch's dry hipster wit is not part of Yazaki's repertoire.

Sangatsu has a big theme: incest. Ice wants to be her brother's lover. Happily for her, her brother is too far gone to notice the unnaturalness of such a desire. Why is she so set on poor Haruo? As the montage of family photos at the beginning of the film makes clear, Ice and her brother were close as children. By becoming her brother's lover she hopes to regain that closeness and state of childish grace. She also believes that love, in all its manifestations, is good. Perhaps it can also work wonders—and bring her brother's memory back. She is playing a dangerous game, however: if her brother returns to the land of the normal, she will lose her innocent paradise, and possibly his love as well.

The hot, guilty tension we might be expect in such a situation is largely absent; *Sangatsu* is less a searing emotional drama than a poignant love fantasy. There are times when all of us long for love without complications—and in Ice's case that longing is, temporarily, satisfied. As long as her brother remains a grinning blank, she can live out her dream of eternal innocence. When her brother recovers enough to find a job tearing down buildings (the workers took a liking to him), she feels threatened.

Here, ordinarily, we would expect the beginning of conflict and verbal sparring. Neither Ice nor her brother are particularly articulate, however. What are they really feeling and thinking? What is the film really trying to say? Yazaki gives us symbolic clues: breaking mirrors denote the fragility of personality; tumbling buildings, the inevitability of change. He also gives us moments of emotional revelation that burst on the characters with a mute, irresistible force. More than a storyteller, Yazaki is a poet who is at times gently lyrical, at times willfully obscure.

His indirection can be irritating, but he skilfully uses the symbolic gesture to draw us into the film, to make us think more deeply about the characters and their dilemma. *Sangatsu* is a movie full of reverberations, some of which we only hear if we are listening attentively. Still, I couldn't help being bothered by its incest-is-all-right subtext. As Haruo gradually awakens and realizes who his roommate is, his feelings toward her becomes more complex: paradise is lost. Even so, their relationship endures; love, even of the forbidden kind, conquers all. Then what, I had to wonder, is going to become of the happy couple's baby? Can love also conquer genes?

Score

(1996)

Directed by Atsushi Muroga. **Screenplay by** Atsushi Muroga and Toshimichi Okawa. **Produced by** Team Okuyama. **With** Hitoshi Ozawa, Shu Ehara. (88 mins.)

Japanese audiences love action, with *Terminator 2*, *Cliffhanger*, *Die Hard 3*, and *Speed* all becoming monster hits in Japan. Meanwhile, relatively few younger Japanese directors are making films in the action genre. Even the ones who do put action scenes into their films often stage them jokily or clumsily. This, in business books, is called not meeting your customers' needs. Seeing an opportunity, producer Kazuyoshi Okuyama decied to make a film with thirty-one-year-old director Atsushi Muroga, whose sole credits were four straight-to-video action pics. Okuyama gave Muroga thirty million yen and a cast of unknowns to shoot an action film called *Score*, about a jewelry store heist gone wrong. Instead of relegating *Score* to the video racks—its natural home—Okuyama's company, Shochiku, has released it in downtown theaters. From the evidence on the screen, the intent was to create another *El Mariachi* or *Reservoir Dogs*: i.e., a little film that makes big critical waves and earns big profits.

The problem is, we've already seen those movies, not to mention dozens of others from Hollywood with as much or more firepower but not as cleverly done. When Muroga's four Japanese jewel thieves (with typical Japanese nicknames like Chance, Tequila, Right, and Peking Duck) retire to an abandoned cement plant outside an unnamed third-world Asian city (actually, Manila) to divide their loot and are violently interrupted by a feral Japanese couple (whose typical Japanese names are TJ and Sara), we get the feeling we've been here before. Then, when the victims in the ensuing gun battle spring back to life like Wile E. Coyote in a Road Runner cartoon, we begin to think we've seen enough. But as imitative and just plain dumb as *Score* may be, Muroga films action sequences that have real impact, and more important to his target audience, are undeniably cool.

This latter talent, which might be described as the ability to make fifteen-year old boys mutter "Wow!" is evident in a climatic chase scene, in which the couple makes off with the jewels in a delivery truck. The leader of the thieves, Chance (Hitoshi Ozawa), leaps onto the moving truck while his partner, Tequila (Shu Ehara), closes in by car. This scene, with Chance battling TJ atop the truck at high speed, may be a cliché, but Muroga keeps the editing rhythms tight, the fight choreography lean and dynamic. It also helps that actors are obviously risking their necks with no assists from the stunt crew or effects department. I shouldn't say too much about the denouement—only that it features a cliffhanging rescue of one thief by his pal whose shotmaking is spine-tingling and smile-provoking in its sheer panache. "Wow," I heard myself muttering. "Wow!"

There is more, including a showdown between the thieves and a longhaired Mr. Big and his jutjawed enforcer, and a climatic confrontation with the Philippine cops. More rounds are fired during the film—three thousand by the producers' count—than the Japanese police and yakuza expend in a decade. Those looking for the sly black humor and clever cinematic sampling of *Reservoir Dogs* had better look elsewhere. This is action straight up, with no excuses or apologies, even for its blatant stealing. Quentin, I think, would dig it.

Season Off
Hors de Saison (1992)

Directed by Shun Nakahara. Screenplay by Sanae Iijima. Produced by Japan Home Video. With Satori Tsuchiya, Kazumi Shiomi. (101 mins.)

Many young Japanese directors get started the way many young directors in the West do, by going out with friends and a Super 8 camera or video camcorder and making movies. Not all young directors follow this path, however. Among them is Shun Nakahara. The director of two of the best recent Japanese films—*Sakura no Sono* (The Cherry Orchard) and *Juninin no Yasashi Nihonjin* (The Gentle Twelve)—Nakahara learned his craft by making porno for Nikkatsu. This experience, he insists, was largely a positive one. "Porno is the best way to learn how make films about human beings," he once told me.

Nakahara, however, felt he had missed out on a key directorial experience of his generation: making a no-budget film on a theme of his own choosing,

with a group of like-minded people. So in February 1991 he sailed off to the island of Shikinejima with a cast and a crew. The result is *Season Off*, a film about the lives and loves of five guests—two couples and a single woman—staying at a resort hotel in the off season. Like Nakahara's two previous features, *Season Off* explores a small, self-enclosed world and unfolds within a tight time frame—in this case, two days. Other directors might chafe under these restrictions; Nakahara thrives on them. He is a natural miniaturist, who delights in capturing the the fleeting gestures, looks, and remarks that reveal character and change lives.

His two couples are a study in contrasts: high-school sweethearts who are on holiday after taking their college exams, and the Fujimuras, a middle-aged couple who married after an eight-year affair, but whose passion has cooled since the wedding ceremony. As the film begins, we see the older couple walking on the beach and speculating about the young lovers ("Youth is wonderful, isn't it," says the husband to his wife, "They look like they're having an affair," says the girl to her boyfriend). Ordinarily, however, these people would have remained in their respective worlds, exchanging only polite smiles in the dining room.

But there is a catalyst present: Ayako (Satori Tsuchiya), who is traveling alone after rejecting her boyfriend's proposal of marriage. She is attractive, approachable, obviously at loose ends. She is, in other words, trouble. When Mr. Fujimura (Kazumi Shiomi), he of the lubricious grin, invites himself over to her table for a nightcap (his wife has conveniently gone to bed), we suspect we are in for a sexual farce.

Nakahara, however, has no intention of revisiting his slap-and-tickle cinematic past. Working from a script by Sanae Iijima, he is attempting something more difficult: to capture the inner realities of two very different relationships confronting two very different crises. His tool for prying the cover of surface "niceness" off his two couples is Ayako; her long, late-night chat with Mr. Fujimura makes his wife furiously jealous. As the other woman in his previous marriage, she knows his habits too well. Later, Mrs. Fujimura has a frolic on the beach with the boy—he has come to her, frustrated, after a sexual rejection from his girlfriend—that causes her husband to steam under the collar as well.

But Ayako, we see, is less a wrecker than a healer. Having brought, however inadvertently, the problems of the two couples out into the open, she tries to set them right. Intelligent, perceptive, sympathetic, she is perhaps too good to be true, yet her conversation with Mrs. Fujimura is deeply revealing. A film that has been serving up small ironies and minor epiphanies now gives us two strangers searching, with total honesty, for answers to important questions in their lives.

Technically, *Season Off* is not Nakahara's best work; the acting is not polished to the usual sheen (the two young actors, especially, impress as stagy and stiff) and the photography is not up to the usual high standard. But it is also the product of an adult sensibility and distinctive talent. In today's Japanese film industry, with its extremes of post-adolescent posturing and tired hack pandering, that is something to be grateful for.

Secret Waltz *
(1996)

Directed by Akira Nobi. Screenplay by Akira Nobi and Hiroshi Saito. Produced by Pony Canyon. With Mitsunori Isaki, Natsuo Ishido, Shin'ichi Tsutsumi, Junji Takada. (105 mins.)

Watching *Secret Waltz*, Akira Nobi's debut feature, I thought it was going to be that familiar Japanese cinematic exercise—an "homage" to a foreign idol, in this case Wong Kar-Wai, that perfectly mimics the externals of the original, while failing to understand its spirit. This feeling, however, lasted only as long as the opening sequence, in which a teenage couple mug a drunken salaryman in front of Shinjuku's Koma Theater and scamper gleefully away in the blurred slow-motion shot that has become a Wong trademark. Instead of a Wong knockoff, however, Nobi has produced a film that, in the inventiveness of its conception and the fractured beauty of its execution, is definitely, brilliantly his own.

Secret Waltz would also seem to resemble the doomed-young-lovers films that young Japanese directors have been turning out in such profusion. Nobi's teenaged pair, however, are a brother and sister wandering parentless and directionless through Tokyo's moral wilderness. Also, though Shinji (Mitsunori Isaki) and Maki (Natsuo Ishido) meet the same kinds of underworld characters, commit the same kinds of existential crimes, make the same kinds of uninhibited love, and encounter the same kinds of deadly violence as their counterparts in such recent films as *Helpless* and *Nihonsei Shonen* (The Boy Made in Japan), *Secret Waltz* rejects their hipper-than-thou posturing or post-adolescent self pity. Though its imagery is at times disturbingly grotesque or kinkily erotic, its underlying mood is, as the title implies, elegiac, romantic, tragic.

Nobi achieves this mood through an ingenious combination of devices. The most striking is the soundtrack, which consists of waltzes and other popular classics of nineteenth-century Western music. The effect may be ironic—the sordidness of the onscreen action set to limpid beauty of Strauss—but Nobi uses the music to underline the essential romanticism of his characters' quests for love, the evanescent beauty of their youth, the pathos of their decline and fall.

The story, which was co-written by Nobi and Hiroshi Saito at the suggestion of Hong Kong action director Tsui Hark, is that by-now familiar fable of feral children becoming mixed up with *yakuza* gangsters and beginning a long descent into the world of violence, sex, and illegal drugs.

One night Maki lures an unsuspecting salaryman (Hitoshi Yamazaki) into an underground parking lot to set him up for a mugging by Shinji. The salaryman, to their surprise, turns out to be a *yakuza* who, together with his confederates, beat the two kids to a pulp. But before they can finish them off, a car door bursts open and a hitman (Shin'ichi Tsutsumi) from a rival gang begins to blow them away. He is badly wounded before he can finish his rescue mission, however. Shinji and Maki hustle him into his car, pile the bodies into the back seat and take the hitman to his hide-out—an apartment that looks as though it has been hit by a typhoon.

While attending to the hitman's wounds and cleaning his apartment. Maki starts to fall in love with him. But when the hitman responds to her advances, he discovers that Maki is not quite the childish, eager-to-please waif she appears. After they make love for the first time, she attacks him with a knife.

Their idyll suffers another disruption when a gangster springs through the window one morning. He is Sato (Junji Takada), a sub-boss whose gang once employed the hitman and wants to bring him back into the fold, together with his new friends.

They decide to accept this offer they cannot refuse. Maki fends off the attentions of the gang's scary-looking, waltz-loving boss of bosses, while Shinji, under the hitman's tutelage, learns the gangster's trade. Then a gang war erupts over drugs, bodies pile up and betrayals multiply. Maki and Shinji are caught in the middle and their private world, which they have nurtured since childhood, begins to crumble.

As Maki and Shinji, Natsuo Ishido and former child star Mitsumori Isaki illuminate that world with professional precision and youthful energy. As the hitman, Shin'ichi Tsutsumi exudes an appropriately murderous chill. But the real star of the film is Nobi's agile, inventive camerawork, which expresses the absurdity and rootlessness of the characters' lives, the desperation and fragility of their affections. Over it all is a waltz, dreaming a dream forever out of reach, spinning everlastingly among the stars.

Seishun Dendekedekedeke
The Rocking Horsemen (1992)

Directed by Nobuhiko Obayashi. Screenplay by Shiro Ishimori. Produced by Galuk Premium, PSC, and Liberty Fox. With Yasufumi Hayashi, Tadanobu Asano, Yoshiyuki Omori, Taketoshi Nagahori. (135 mins.)

From the perspective of the 1990s, Japanese teenagers of the 1960s, especially those in the countryside, led lives of almost exotic simplicity. Television was a new addition to the average home, stereo sets were the toys of a privileged few, and no one had a Nintendo. Hearing a Ventures song for the first times, teens in the boondocks got a shivery thrill from the sound of an electric guitar.

Nobuhiko Obayashi's *Seishun Dendekedekedeke* tries to recapture that thrill in recounting the brief career of a high school rock band in a small Shikoku town. Like *The Commitments*, Alan Parker's 1991 about a fledgling Dublin soul band, *Seishun* is a labor of love that remains faithful to the milieu and music. Based on an autobiographical novel by Sunao Yoshihara, it is also a self-indulgence by a middle-aged director who longs to revist to the days of his personal and professional youth. No matter; Obayashi made me enjoy most of the journey. *Seishun*'s humor, spontaneity and honesty are absolutely right for its subject matter. It rumbles along engagingly to the end, like the *ereki* (electric guitar) music it celebrates.

The hero and narrator is Chikura Fujihara (Yasufumi Hayashi), who begins the film as an ordinary junior high-school student, circa 1965. One day during his spring vacation, while sawing away absentmindedly at his violin, he hears a startling new sound coming out of his radio: "Pipeline" by the Ventures. He decides to drop Beethoven and start a rock band.

But in a small Shikoku town in the mid-sixties, Chikura's dream is likely to remain just that. When the band manager in *The Commitments* sends out a call for musicians, dozens of would-be superstars show up. Chikura's first task is find a few kids who have heard the words "rock'n'roll." When he enters high school that April, he heads straight for the clubroom of the Popular Music Circle. There he meets Shirai Seiichi (Tadanobu Asano), a bespectacled boy who is strumming—wonder of wonders!—a real guitar. He is resigning from the club because his seniors are anti-rock. Chikura listens to him play a riff from the Venture's "Driving Guitar" and enlists him on the spot. The two boys quickly recruit the shaven-head son of a temple priest (Yoshiyuki Omori) and the buck-toothed bass drummer of the school's brass band (Taketoshi Nagahori). Now all they need are instruments, a place to practice—and an audience.

Seishun is the story of how The Rocking Horsemen (the new group's name) find all three. Chikaru narrates it from the viewpoint of an older-but-wiser present. From his gently ironic tone we know how it is going to end. The Rocking Horsemen may play their first big gig—a school festival show for their classmates and relatives—but they can't change their destinies. Unlike the band in *The Commitments*, who dream of the big time and then self-destruct, these kids know from the start that their time in the spotlight will be brief. Shirai and Okushita will enter their family businesses and Aida will become a priest. Only Chikaru's future is open-ended; he will go to a university in Tokyo. Though he takes leave of his small town with the aching finality of Richard Dreyfuss in *American Graffiti*, we know that he's not going to reject its values—or become Shikoku's answer to Alice Cooper.

Obayashi's approach to this material is emotionally right, technically wrong-headed. His slice-of-life style brings the Japanese 1960s back to vivid life and persuades us that we are seeing real kids behaving in real ways. But the muddy sound, jerky camerawork, and choppy editing in the opening sequences gave me the impression I was watching a film by amateurs about amateurs. Obayashi's intent may have been to convey the energy and inexperience of youth, but the result is as annoying as an out-of-tune guitar solo. Happily, as the boys put their band together and learn about life and love, the film's look gradually becomes more professional. It even has moments of inspired cleverness, as when Chikura's loopy fantasies become onscreen realities. The Ventures, wherever they might be after their twenty-eighth tour of Japan, would probably be pleased.

Senso to Seishun
War and Youth (1991)

Directed by Tadashi Imai. Screenplay by Katsumoto Saotome. Produced by Kobushi Production, Produce Center, and Senso to Seishun Production Committee. With Yuki Kudo, Hisashi Igawa, Tomoko Naraoka, Keisuke Sano. (110 mins.)

When *Senso to Seishun* (War And Youth) ended and the theater erupted in applause, I knew I was in trouble. It was the kind of applause you hear at political rallies when the speaker has touched on a common wound and said the right healing words. The wound in this case is the Tokyo air raid of March 10, 1945. More than a hundred thousand people died in the conflagration caused by the incendiary bombs dropped from U.S. B-29s. Large sections of the capital were burned to ashes and rubble. The applauders,

I noticed when the lights went up, were old enough to have been survivors of the raid, a wartime holocaust surpassed in Japan only by the atomic bombings of Hiroshima and Nagasaki.

How could I could tell these people, who had identified so strongly with the fictionalized account they had just seen on the screen, that Tadashi Imai's first film in nine years was weakly constructed, indifferently acted, overbearingly didactic, and weepily sentimental? I felt even worse when I learned that director Imai and scriptwriter Katsumoto Saotome were both witnesses to the raid and that 1,449 "citizen producers" from all over Japan had contributed more than two hundred million yen to the film's five hundred million yen production cost. The object was to right a cinematic wrong; the Tokyo air raid had been relatively neglected by Japanese filmmakers, especially younger ones with no memory of the war.

Because those who did remember were quickly passing from the scene, the opportunity for survivors to make a film drawing on their own experiences would soon be lost forever. The primary obstacle was money; a project with uncertain commercial prospects by a seventy-nine-year old director was less than easy to sell. Then one of the film's producers had an idea: enlist the aid of individuals and groups who shared Imai's vision. The response was heartening; the fund-raising campaign far exceeded its goal. The result was Senso to Seishun.

Imai begins his film in the Tokyo shitamachi (old downtown) of the present. A high-school girl (Yuki Kudo) is writing a report about her family's war memories for a school assignment. But her father (Hisashi Igawa) refuses to answer her questions; his memories are too painful to recall. Shortly after, the father's elder sister (Tomoko Naraoka) tries to save a neighborhood child from an oncoming truck and is struck herself. Strangely, she calls the child "Keiko," the name of a baby lost in the Tokyo air raid. When the father hears this and sees his sister in a coma he decides to break his silence.

Unlike recent films about the war by Shohei Imamura and Akira Kurosawa, which take an indirect, symbolic approach to their subjects, Senso to Seishun plunges us into a highly colored wartime melodrama, filmed in black and white. The sister, who is also played by Kudo, falls in love with a teacher (Keisuke Sano) at her brother's school. When the teacher receives a draft notice and decides to run away to Hokkaido rather than serve, the sister is left pregnant with his child and becomes the target of neighborhood abuse.

While realistically conveying the look and mood of wartime Tokyo, Senso to Seishun shamelessly idealizes its war-torn couple. Imai even resurrects chestnuts of the young lovers running ecstatically through tall grass, and the teacher, after a brave but losing battle with the forces of evil, seeing the image of his beloved's smiling face once last time before he expires. This couple is utterly pure-hearted and tragically star-crossed. They are also thundering clichés. Kudo, who starred in Jim Jarmusch's Mystery Train, is more credible as the bubbly schoolgirl than the long-suffering single mother. She looks the latter part in her mompe pants and braids, but Imai's old-fashioned view of her character fits her less comfortably.

When the bombs start falling and the shitamachi streets become a maelstrom of fleeing humanity, Senso to Seishun springs to life. The scenes that follow, filmed in color, have a vividness that makes us forget the hackneyed plot and textbookish explanations that came before. These, we feel, are the hellish moments that Imai himself lived through and wanted to preserve on film. For his fellow survivors, especially, the wait was worth it.

Sentakuki wa Ore ni Makasero
Leave the Washing Machine to Me (1999)

Directed by Tetsuo Shinohara. Screenplay by Shusaku Matsuoka. Produced by Bonobo and Starport. With Michitaka Tsutsui, Yasuko Tomita, Kaoru Kobayashi, Ayano Momose. (102 mins.)

Tetsuo Shinohara makes films about young men living on society's fringes, working at unskilled or semiskilled jobs, be it cutting grass (Kusa no Ue no Shigoto, 1993), raising cabbages (Tsuki to Kyabetsu, 1996), or repairing washing machines (Sentakuki wa Ore ni Makasero)—but their work also puts them in closer touch with their senses, their essential selves. They may be undergoing various crises, but they are leading lives that look, to those of us in the sleep-deprived mainstream, appealingly free of stress. Also, though Shinohara is more interested in probing his protagonists' inner feelings than recording their routines, he convincingly evokes their working worlds on the screen.

In Sentakuki wa Ore ni Makasero, the hero, Kizaki (Michitaka Tsutsui), does more than revive dying machinery—he repairs lives, in the course of a highly eventful week. First, though, he has to get his own in order. He has come to Tokyo from Osaka to make a name as a manga (comic book) artist, but is getting nowhere fast. Meanwhile, he is absorbed in his day job of fixing and selling used appliances for a store in an old Tokyo neighborhood. There is something about an old washing machine, especially, that gets his blood pumping. He knows the quirks of each model the way some people know every Harley ever made.

Not only the gadgets, but many of the people around him are breaking down. First there is Setsuko (Yasuko Tomita), the daughter of the shop's owner and an unemployed radio DJ who is adrift after divorcing her first husband and leaving her job. Though she has little interest in her father's work, his shop offers a needed refuge. She also has a bantering, big sisterly relationship with Kizaki (though he wants to be something more than her little brother). Then one day, she asks him for a date. Flabbergasted, Kizaki accepts.

On the big day, however, he has to play for an amateur baseball team managed by his boss. The game drags on and, by the time he arrives at the meeting place, Setsuko is gone. While waiting, she chanced to meet Okami (Kaoru Kobayashi), a former shop employee who has become a cab driver and degenerate gambler. Nonetheless, Okami was a friendly, familiar face—and she goes with him to have a few rounds for old times sake. While she is renewing her acquaintance with Okami, Kizaki is getting to know Hideko (Ayano Momose), a girl who works at a nearby bakery. She is interested in a way the coy Setsuko is not. Nonetheless, when Kizaki spots Setsuko in a shopping arcade, he runs after her, leaving a puzzled and angry Hideko behind. That night Kizaki and Setsuko end up falling into futon together.

Setsuko is unwilling to go all the way. ("I'm an old-fashioned girl," she announces), but she begins disclose her real feelings in a way that, only a day earlier, would have been impossible. One night soon after, while walking with Hideko, Kizaki spots Setsuko again, this time on a pedestrian bridge—in the embrace of Okami. The path of true love seldom runs smooth, but is it, Kizaki begins to wonder, really true love?

The people of Shinohara's *shitamachi* shopping street may have a human warmth, but they are not Tora-san-like fantasy figures from a nostalgically misremembered past. Instead, he depicts them as the walking wounded, who are searching for a purpose and completeness missing in their lives. Kizaki is one of this number, but has the courage to act on what he feels and believes. When he finally explodes in anger at Setsuko's sexual games or upbraids a fellow Osakan for falling victim to self-pity, he clears the air in much the same way his beloved machines clean clothes.

As played by Michitaka Tsutsui, Kizaki is pleasant to his customers and gentle and shy with the ladies, but he gradually reveals a tougher, smarter, more complex inner self. Though hardly trendy, he is nobody's comic nerd. Meanwhile, Yasuko Tomita, as Setsuko, seems to be reprising the flighty, free-spirited, ultimately irritating heroine in *Tsuki to Kyabetsu*.

But though she may drive poor Kizaki to distraction, Tomita's Setsuko is a type firmly grounded in reality. Watching *Sentakuki*, I wondered whether it would end with the rough edges smoothed over and the loose ends neatly tied up. The film's conclusion, however, is more ambiguous, if upbeat. You can't always get what you want but if you try, sometimes, you get what you need—with a noisy, but fully functional, motor.

Setouchi Moonlight Serenade
Moonlight Serenade (1997)

Directed by Masahiro Shinoda. **Screenplay by** Katsuo Naruse. **Produced by** Shochiku, Office Two One, Fuji Television, and Pony Canyon. **With** Jun Toba, Kyozo Nagatsuka, Shima Iwashita, Hideyuki Sasahara, Sayuri Kawauchi, Hinano Yoshikawa, Shun'ya Nagasawa. (117 mins.)

Masahiro Shinoda has become Japan's James Ivory— a maker of well-researched, beautifully-photographed period pieces that evoke a nostalgia for a lost world. But whereas *Room With a View* and *Howard's End* depict the leisured existence of the Edwardian upper-middle class, the films of Shinoda's Setouchi trilogy, beginning with the 1984 *Setouchi Shonen Yakyudan* (MacArthur's Children), describe the hardscrabble lives of ordinary Japanese during and after World War II. Also, unlike the American-born Ivory, the sixty-five-year old Shinoda is drawing on a personally remembered past.

A Western viewer has little trouble understanding Ivory's fascination with England in the early years of the century; whatever agonies the characters may be enduring, their surroundings look paradisical (save for a lamentable lack of central heating) and their society appears serenely confident. But what about Shinoda's Japan? Poverty is the common lot, the social fabric is rent, and the future is uncertain. Yet present in almost every shot is a longing that all the power and wealth of modern Japan cannot assuage. Shinoda insists that, more than a nostalgist, he is a conservationist trying to capture certain endangered species of the national culture on screen before they disappear forever.

From the evidence of the third film in his trilogy, *Setouchi Moonlight Serenade* one target of Shinoda's cinematic butterfly net is a feeling for family and community that has largely vanished. His five-member family, the Ondas, may be unraveling at the seams, with teenage Koji (Jun Toba) rebelling against the authority of his hardheaded father (Kyozo Nagatsuka), but given the atomization of urban family life today, they look like the Nelsons.

Also, when the Ondas set out on a journey from their home in Awajishima to bury the ashes of the eldest boy—a wartime casualty—the entire neighborhood takes an interest in their doings, particularly their departure in that unheard-of extravagance, a hired car. (This interest is not all positive, however—there is a rumor that the Ondas are setting out to commit family suicide.)

After they board a ship bound for Kyushu via the Seto Inland Sea, they become part of a shipboard community whose members are familiar postwar types: a smooth-talking blackmarket hustler who will do any for a yen, a wild-eyed demobilized soldier who has turned to drugs, a beautiful young woman who intends to sell herself as a geisha to survive, and a nattily dressed middle-aged man who is alone, bereft, and quickly going to pieces. Shinoda also introduces a few offbeat characters, including a traveling benshi (narrator of silent films) and his mute boy assistant.

Despite their differences, the passengers are all in the same literal and figurative boat, drawn together by their losses and the uncertainty of their lot. Also, despite the ravages of the war and the danger from floating mines, they are sailing through a landscape of great natural beauty that has since been destroyed by relentless development.

Though the conflict between Father and Koji is the film's dramatic mainspring, with Mother (Shima Iwashita), younger brother Keita (Hideyuki Sasahara) and younger sister Hideko (Sayuri Kawauchi) standing on the sidelines, the film is full of clichéd subplots. While Koji is avidly seeking formerly forbidden pleasures in a newly democratic Japan, including the company of a pigtailed war orphan (Hinano Yoshikawa), the hustler introduces Father to the joys of foreign liquor, the ex-soldier and would-be geisha fall in love, and the middle-aged man steps off the boat into eternity.

These stories are told with an evident affection, but we have heard them all too often and so, truth be told, has Shinoda. The freshness and immediacy that he might have once brought to them is long gone. Instead, he takes a tired generic approach to his material, right down to the music on the sound track (Glenn Miller's "Moonlight Serenade," for the ten-thousandth time) and the Hollywood movie Father takes Keita to see (Casablanca for the upteenth-zillionth time). While the older actors play to stereotype (Kyozo Nagatsuka being the old-fashioned, admirably upright father, Shima Iwashita, the long-suffering, eternally patient mother), the younger ones latch onto the nearest available attitude, be it pouty rebelliousness (Jun Toda) or theatrically sweaty desperation (Shun'ya Nagasawa).

Shinoda's curatorial intentions are admirable, but his execution shows signs of creative exhaustion. Setouchi Moonlight Serenade may well be the swan song for films on this particular slice of Japan's recent past.

Shall We Dance? *

(1996)

Written and directed by Masayuki Suo. Produced by Daiei, NTV, Hakuhodo, and Nihon Shuppan Hambai. With Koji Yakusho, Naoto Takenaka, Tamiyo Kusakari. (136 mins.)

There are plenty of young Japanese directors who want to make art films that display the daring of their cinematic technique and the brilliance of their vision. Few, however, want to entertain the way a Steven Spielberg can entertain. There is the matter of money. Japanese filmmakers do not have Jurassic Park budgets to work with. But as Masayuki Suo has demonstrated in Fancy Dancer, Shiko Funjatta and, now, Shall We Dance? money isn't everything—attitude and artistry are equally, if not more, important.

Suo is more interested in exploring odd cultural pockets than filming SF fantasies. Also, instead of pounding the audience into submission with high-tech effects, he prefers a more human scale and laid-back pace. But he has a Spielbergian way of injecting his feel-good stories of spiritual discovery and worldly triumph with an unabashed romanticism that is at times affectingly sweet, at times cloyingly sentimental. Suo also surpasses the director of 1941 in his talent for filming even hackneyed comic material with fresh touches that brings it to hilarious life. Finally, both directors have given us cinematic moments that are an uncomplicated joy to be in and leave us glowing as we walk out of the theater. What is wrong with that?

In Shall We Dance? Suo's odd cultural pocket of choice is a dance studio that looks like an architectural leftover from the early 1960s. But to a middle-aged salaryman named Sugiyama (Koji Yakusho), who glimpses the school's dancers through the window every night as he commutes home on the train, it exerts a strange fascination. There is a girl in that window—tall, proud and effortlessly graceful—who is an embodiment of the possibilities that Sugiyama is letting slip away in his humdrum existence. He wants to dance with that girl.

The straightest of straight arrows, who makes a beeline from the office to his suburban home day after day, until his wife urges him to have a bit of after-hours fun to break the routine, Sugiyama does not have dalliance in mind. But he can't get the girl out of his head. One night he finds himself inside the studio, signing up for lessons in the waltz, the rumba, and the cha-cha-cha.

The world of ballroom dancing has been the subject of films before, including Baz Luhrmann's 1992 sleeper hit *Strictly Ballroom*, but Suo is the only Japanese director I know to explore it in a full-length feature. As he shows us with his usual acuteness, in Japan ballroom dancing occupies an uneasy place on the social spectrum between a legitimate cultural pursuit, with associations, contests, ranks, and all the rest, and an *outré* hobby of the weird, the lonely, and the lecherous. There are several examples of the latter types in the studio and Sugiyama beginner's dance class, and Suo uses them to good comic effect, including funny sequences of Sugiyama and his odd-squad classmates botching the basic steps. The funniest is Aoki (Naoto Takenaka), a colleague of Sugiyama's who is a dweebish incompetent in the office, but morphs into a bewigged Latin fireball on the dance floor. A Suo regular, who played the hapless *sumo*-club captain in *Shiko Funjatta*, Takenaka goes hilariously over the top, without letting his clowning overwhelm his lonely-guy character.

The heart of the film, however, is Sugiyama's reawakening to life beyond the desk, the train, and the PC. A rugged hunk of an actor who made his name in TV period- drama roles, Koji Yakusho portrays Sugiyama with a bumbling sincerity that comes straight from the Jimmy Stewart school of aw-shucks comic acting. But he can also affectingly express the inner turmoil of Sugiyama as he struggles to realize his dream, while wrestling with his conscience.

The object of that dream, the girl in the window, is an instructor named Mai (who writes her name, appropriately, with the Chinese character for "dance"). As played by Tamiyo Kusakari, a prima ballerina with a slew of real-life awards, Mai is impeccable on the dance floor, while projecting a steely will and cool sensuality off it. But Suo's camera is too much in love with her statuesque beauty and his script lingers too long on her professional crisis—she fell during a major competition in England and has since lost her desire to dance. (Not surprisingly, after the film's successful release, Suo and Kusakari married to great media fanfare.)

But in his big scenes, most notably Sugiyama's first dance contest, Suo dynamically conveys the glittery glamour and sensual exuberance of his ballroom dancing world, while deftly revealing its human undercurrents of desire, jealousy, ambition, and pride. As a comic filmmaker, he gets the requisite laughs from his world's cheesy, tacky side, but he is at heart a sympathizer, not a caricaturist. By the end we understand Sugiyama's fascination and even Aoki's obsession. Dance, anyone?

Sharaku
(1994)

Directed by Masahiro Shinoda. Screenplay by Hiroko Minagawa. Cinematography by Tatsuo Suzuki. Produced by Seiyu, Tsutaya, and Sakai Sogo Kikaku. With Hiroyuki Sanada, Shima Iwashita, Frankie Sakai, Shiro Sano, Riona Hazuki, Hachijusuke Bando, Shun'ya Nagasawa. (138 mins.)

The sensibility of Masahiro Shinoda's *Sharaku* is more Edo than New Age. Nonetheless, it represents a vigorous attempt to shake free of period-drama conventions and see Edo culture as Edoites themselves saw it. Shinoda has dedicated himself to preserving a Japan rapidly disappearing under a flood of Westernization and modernization; *Sharaku* is his cinematic ark, containing vivid depictions of Edo culture and the people who made and enjoyed it. Its flaws, including a scattershot storyline and unsatisfactory ending, do not destroy its essential value.

Sharaku was the pseudonym of a *ukiyo-e* artist whose first works—portraits of Kabuki actors—appeared in May 1794. Unlike others who had attempted this subject, Sharaku drew the actors realistically, with an element of caricature that verged on the insulting. His woodblock prints were issued by one of the leading *ukiyo-e* publishing houses of the day, and made with an expensive mica dust process to create a glittering dark background. How, his rivals must have asked themselves, did this mystery man from nowhere rate such treatment?

Though strange to contemporary eyes, Sharaku's work had a technical brilliance and psychological insight that somehow conveyed the very soul of his subjects. Then, after ten months of furious activity, during which he created 140 prints, Sharaku disappeared as suddenly as he had emerged. Following a revival of his work by German art critic Julius Kurt in 1910, scholars unearthed every available scrap of information about Sharaku's life and milieu, but no one ever succeeded in learning the truth about his origins, his post *ukiyo-e* career, or even his real name. Theories abound, facts remain few.

The film, a pet project of actor Frankie Sakai for more than three decades, imagines Sharaku (Hiroyuki Sanada) as a bit Kabuki actor who specializes in acrobatic stunts. After injuring his foot, he is thrown out of work and forced to join a troupe of wandering players led by Okan (Shima Iwashita), a former courtesan. When not performing on street corners, he cultivates a talent for drawing. Finally, Tsutaya Juzaburo (Frankie Sakai), a publisher of *ukiyo-e* prints, discovers him painting stage scenery and decides to use him as a pseudonymous replacement for Utamaro (Shiro Sano), the former star of his artistic stable, who has defected to a rival publisher. Tsutaya also uses his Sharaku prints to protest the absurdly strict sumptuary laws of prime minister Matsudaira Sadanobu. Though Sharaku enjoys his initial brush with notoriety, he soon begins to chafe at his straitjacket of anonymity and Tsutaya's increasingly harsh demands. He becomes attracted to a teenage courtesan (Riona Hazuki) who is the latest sexual toy of the filthy-rich Utamaro. Freedom and love begin to look more appealing than art and fame.

In telling this story, Sharaku creates a rounded, richly colored portrait of Edo society, with gorgeous images of Kabuki, street theater, and courtesan life. The cinematography by Tatsuo Suzuki, costumes by Setsu Asakura, and sets by Katsumi Asaba and Senkoku Ikeya are all superb: Edo has never looked better on the screen.

But Sharaku also ambles into thickets of subplot and does not emerge until we are well into film and wondering what we are doing there. Also, while devoting much screen time to minor characters, including prime minister Matsudaira (Hachijusuke Bando) and rival artistic genius Hokusai (Shun'ya Nagasawa), the film fails to bring its love triangle into sharp focus. One problem is a blank performance by film newcomer Hazuki, who plays her young concubine as though she were a Shibuya slacker.

The other two corners of the triangle, however, are strong. Sanada, a former gymnast, flies through his acrobatic routines and fight scenes with athletic vigor and grace. His Sharaku is a street kid whose large talent is accompanied by a fierce, reckless willfulness. Sano, who has cornered the local market on creep roles, plays Utamaro as a man of cold brilliance, whose ego and appetites are almost as great as his art. Though not a member of the triangle, Tsutaya is central to the story and Frankie Sakai, who has written extensively on Sharaku and his period, plays him with splendid ham verve.

The film leaves ends with Sharaku defeated—a mistake. Far better that his ultimate fate remain, like the source of his art, a mystery. Whatever became of him after his ten months of fame, he is with us still, leaping effortlessly over barriers of culture and time.

Shiawase ni Naro ne *
Let's Get Happy (1998)

Written and directed by Akio Murahashi. Produced by KSS and Cinema Haut. With Sho Aikawa, Masumi Sanada, Tsunehiko Watase, Morio Kazama, Seijun Suzuki, Naomasa Musaka, Narimi Arimori, Ryo Amamiya. (115 mins.)

In art, limitations have their uses. What one loses in sweep and scale, one can gain in compression and expression. Thus Picasso's Blue Period. Thus the less-is-more esthetic of much of Japanese art, including the cinematic art of Yasujiro Ozu. Akio Murahashi's Shiawase ni Naro ne is a cleverly conceived and well-executed, if overly long, attempt at genre stretching within a similarly self-locked cage. A veteran TV scriptwriter, Murahashi has made a yakuza movie that plays like Sidney Lumet's Twelve Angry Men: i.e., a drama unfolding in a limited time and space, with the pressure building as the minutes tick by.

One difference between Shiawase and its predecessor is the tone: light, comic, even farcical. But while his yakuza gang may find itself in a ridiculous situation—dragged into a war the day before it is to dissolve—his gangsters are not merely comic grotesques. Posing nobly one moment, calculating cravenly the next, they reveal much about contradictory impulses of real human beings in extreme situations.

The story begins with Kyohei (Sho Aikawa) videotaping the congratulations of his colleagues in the Yamamuro-gumi on his upcoming wedding. He is quitting the gang to marry the sweet, innocent (of gang connections) Chikako (Masumi Sanada) and become a sushi chef. Most of the other gang members, including boss Yamamuro (Tsunehiko Watase) and sub-boss Kiuchi (Morio Kazama), are following him into the straight life. Under pressure from the law and a bad economy, the Yamamuro-gumi plans to disband the next day.

Then comes a TV news flash: the boss of the rival Sasajima-gumi has been knifed to death. They realize with a sickening certainty that one of their number, the absent Hiroshi, made the hit. Soon after, an elderly fixer (Seijun Suzuki) comes calling with an ultimatum from the Sasajima-gumi: either deliver up the head of boss Yamamuro or a hundred million yen in cash by tomorrow morning. What a choice—but what else can they do? Then they hear, from Hiroshi himself, that the Sasajima-gumi is preparing for war. Instead of going gently into the good night, they face the possibility of being hurried into an early grave.

The hot-headed Otaki (Naomasa Musaka), a sub-boss who opposed disbanding, wants to fight. Kiuchi, however, insists that it's better to pay the hundred million than commit group suicide. Yamamuro has the money, locked up in a safe in his office, but his leggy, luscious wife Rie (Narimi Arimori) has the key—and no intention of giving up a long-promised life of leisure. She urges to Yamamuro to run off to Europe. What if they gave a gang war and nobody came? But Yamamuro knows that the reach of his enemies is long. Also, he has his honor to consider. Somehow, though, he can't take the fatal step out the door.

No one can, in fact: the entire plot unfolds inside the Yamamuro-gumi headquarters. This goes against the entire grain of the genre: a *yakuza* movie without the atmospherics of gambling dens, hostess clubs, stretch limos and other gangster-friendly environments is like a Western without wide-open spaces. Murahashi, however, moves deftly from one plot complication to the next, including the unexpected arrival of a gang member (Ryo Amamiya) just released from the slammer, and the sudden appearance of a citizen's group who correctly suspects that the gangsters are up to no good.

Murahashi throws too many narrative balls up in the air and juggles them too long. Still, given all the *yakuza* movies that haven't changed their three-ball acts in decades, *Shiawase* is a welcome change from the genre routine. The cast shines in what is essentially an actor's showcase. Especially good is Morio Kazama's Kiuchi, who projects a strength of character not immediately apparent from his wishy-washy exterior. He gives weight to what otherwise would be a lighter-than-air entertainment.

The most amusing of the cast is Narimi Arimori as Yamamuro's wife. Her hot little vamp with a heart of ice may be a cliché, but she charges *Shiawase* with a sexy verve and a fine, dry comic talent. Her constant, and unexplained, changes of costume, from resplendent kimono to slinky designer gown, are a neat touch worthy of Monty Python—yet another indication of a movie made by a creative mind, not a formula.

Feeling down in these depressing times? *Shiawase ni naro ne!*

Shijushichinin no Shikaku
The Forty-seven Ronin (1994)

Directed by Kon Ichikawa. Produced by Toho, NTV, and Suntory. Screenplay by Kaneo Ikegami, Hiroshi Takeyama, and Kon Ichikawa. With Ken Takakura, Koji Ishizaka, Kiichi Nakai, Rie Miyazawa. (129 mins.)

The *Chushingura* story of forty-seven loyal samurai seeking revenge for the murder of their former master would seem to be a dubious proposition as a major studio film. How many moviegoers today would line up for a paean to feudal loyalty? In these days of downsizing and restructuring, the answer would seem to be, not many. Nonetheless, Toho plunged ahead with *Shijushichinin no Shikaku*, a big-budget *Chushingura* movie made to celebrate the centennial of the birth of film. This version by Kon Ichikawa tries to cut through the encrustations of legend to the complex and not always edifying truth. Slow-paced and unwieldy, the film is nonetheless a sincere and nuanced attempt to set the record straight.

Based on a novel by Shoichiro Ikemiya, *Shijushichinin no Shikaku* presents its principals as individuals dealing with a dilemma not of their making. The leader of the loyal retainers, Kuranosuke Oishi (Ken Takakura), puts his duty to his lord above his own interests, but he realizes the costs of revenge all too clearly. He is a hero who strikes few heroic poses. Takakura, now past sixty, may be too old for the part (his character is supposed to be a forty-five-year-old warrior with young children and a twenty-year-old mistress) but he makes Oishi a man, not a waxworks figure.

The film puts more emphasis on historical reconstruction than imaginative recreation. We never find out exactly why Naganori Asano, the lord of Ako, drew his sword and wounded Kira, lord of Kozuke, a high-ranking shogunate official who was the banquet host for imperial messengers at the shogun's palace. All his retainers in faraway Ako know was that the same day, March 14, 1701, Asano was forced to commit ritual suicide by shogunal authorities, while Kira was allowed to live. Ordinarily both parties would have been held accountable, but Kira is connected to the powerful Uesugi clan and the shogun himself. Asano, on the other hand, is the lord of a minor fief. The decision to order his execution is strictly political, with no personal animosity involved. Asano has a grudge against Kira, but if they give him a chance to publicize it, it might prove embarrassing for all concerned. Also, the shogun is upset—so off with his head, quickly and quietly.

But though Asano has clearly been wronged, not all of his retainers are the stainless heroes of legend. After the clan is dissolved at the order of the shogunate and its three hundred retainers become masterless samurai they dwindle, over the months and years to the final forty-seven. One reason is the maneuvering of Uesugi clan chief retainer Matashiro Irobe (Kiichi Nakai). Knowing that Asano's retainers are plotting revenge, he tries to buy off as many as possible. Meanwhile Oishi, the leader of the retainers, spreads the rumor that Kira was a taker of bribes who became upset when Asano refused to pay up. Thus his insults and Asano's violent reaction.

From this description, it may sound as though *Shijushichinin no Shikaku* is a revisionist retelling, but it is less an exposé than an elegy. Though protagonists on both sides plot and scheme, the overall mood is somber, the conclusion, that there are no winners—only death and ruin for the sake of face. Even the film's one romantic interlude—between Oishi and a bubbly clerk (Rie Miyazawa)s in a writing-brush shop—is shadowed by approaching doom. The clerk sees Oishi as a rock-solid father figure. Oishi, however, is all too aware that the rock is about to dissolve. The finale, with its warriors battling in the snow and blood, is straight slash-and-run *chambara* movie-making. The rousing action is perhaps the second major reason for the story's popularity—one that never goes out of style.

Shikoku ✱
(1999)

Directed by Shun'ichi Nagasaki Screenplay by Takenori Sendo and Kunimitsu Manda.Cinematography by Noboru Shinoda. Executive production by Masato Hara. Produced by Shikoku Production Committee and Asmik Ace Entertainment. With Yui Natsukawa, Michitaka Tsutsui, Chiaki Kuriyama, Toshie Negishi, Ren Osugi, Makoto Sato. (100 mins.)

Shikoku is the smallest of the four main Japanese islands. It is also, according to ancient belief, the place to which dead souls repaired (although the specific location of Hades was the island's southern province of Tosa). Thus "Shikoku" meant "land of the dead," and though today it is written with a different first character (the one for "four" rather than "death") its old identity lingers on, as Shun'ichi Nagasaki's *Shikoku* shows us.

Hinako (Yui Natsukawa) has returned to a remote Shikoku village where she once lived as a child in order to sell the old family home. She has also come to revisit the scenes of her past and, she hopes, discover a way forward into the future. She meets Fumiya (Michitaka Tsutsui), a childhood friend and object of a girlish affection that was never returned because Fumiya then belonged to Hinako's closest friend, Sayori (Chiaki Kuriyama).

Sayori, Fumiya tells her, passed away eleven years ago at the age of sixteen and he has never stopped mourning her. But instead of dying in an accident, as her parents reported, village rumor has it that she was killed by an evil spirit. Hinako thinks this rumor likely: Sayori's family had been shamans for generations and she had once seen Sayori swaying in a shamanistic trance and speaking in the voice of a dead boy.

As the days pass and Hinako and Fumiya grow closer, it also becomes terrifyingly obvious that Sayori has no intention of letting her rival triumph. Investigating Sayori's hauntings, Hinako and Fumiya discover that, though Sayori's father has been incapacitated by illness, her mother is engaged in a bizarre attempt to bring her daughter back from the dead—and is on the point of succeeding.

Based on a novel by Masako Bando, *Shikoku* is the first film in the horror genre for director Nagasaki, a leader of Japan's independent scene in the 1980s, who made a splendid comeback in 1996 with *Romance*. Unlike most horror specialists, who are sadists at heart, Nagasaki is more interested in developing his odd love triangle than reveling in gore. He draws an especially fine performance from Yui Natsukawa as Hinako, who may look as soft as the knit outfits she wears so well, but displays a core of country-bred stubbornness. Working with cinematographer Noboru Shinoda, he creates the right creepy atmosphere, making ample use of the handheld camera to underscore the characters' anxiety at their encounters with the supernatural.

In the climatic scenes, his finely wrought psychological drama threatens to degenerate into the usual *kaidan* (ghost story) trumpery, but Nagasaki maintains emotional credibility to the end. We don't have to believe in the film's cosmology to feel a shudder at a love that kills because it can never die.

Shi no Toge
The Sting of Death (1990)

Written and directed by Kohei Oguri. Produced by Shochiku and Shochiku Dai'ichi Kogyo. With Ittoku Kishibe, Keiko Matsuzaka. (114 mins.)

"Marriage," wrote H.L. Mencken, "is largely talk." By this definition, Bergman's *Scenes from a Marriage*, which is little more than the running conversation of a married couple, who soon become a divorced couple, is the truest film ever made about marriage and its aftermath. Bergman does more than faithfully reproduce the sounds of marital discord, however—he relentlessly strips away the cover of middle-class respectability to reveal the marriage's inner core.

The subject of *Shi no Toge* is also the failure of a marriage, but instead of Bergmanian talk, the warring couple—a struggling writer (Ittoku Kishibe) and his wife (Keiko Matsuzaka)—intone lines of stylized dialogue, punctuated by screams of madness and despair. Director Kohei Oguri is striving for a poetic realism, but the effect he achieves is stasis. The film shows us the husband destroying the marriage with his infidelity and the wife going insane with jealousy, but the scenes are set pieces that stand in isolation. Oguri wants to take us on a tour of an emotional wasteland, but two hours later we're still looking at the same landscape, from the same angle.

Based on Toshio Shimao's 1976 novel, *Shi no Toge* brings the sensibility of the *watakushi shosetsu* (I-novel) too literally to the screen. The best *watakushi shosetsu* give one the feeling of being inside the writer's skin, seeing the world through his eyes. But the rambling, episodic structure typical of the genre does not lend itself easily to film. Instead of reworking the novel's story into a more coherent narrative, Oguri has chosen to go in the opposite direction and reduce the usual apparatus of scene-setting and story-telling to a bare minimum, while focusing on his characters' violent and obsessive emotions.

His warring couple are both individuals and archetypes. We are watching not only two people named Toshio and Miho writhing in their personal hell, but Unfaithful Husband and Jealous Wife, circa 1955, struggling with the general dissolution of traditional values. Oguri lays on the significance of this struggle with a heavy and repetitive hand.

Keiko Matsuzaka plays the wronged wife with intensity and conviction, but after half a dozen rage scenes—all at the same pitch—attention starts to flag. Miho is so insistent on her obsessions, so implacable in her demands, that I began to wish I could slip her divorce papers and the directions to the nearest city hall. As Toshio, Ittoku Kishibe initially seems to be a long-suffering soul, passively enduring his wife's jealous fits. But Kishibe, a former pop star who often plays smarmy, weak-willed types, shows that he too can explode. His air of stoic acceptance makes these eruptions all the more shocking, but, Like Matsuzaka, he repeats them so often, including two suicide attempts, that they begin to verge on self-parody.

There are children in this dismal marriage, played by a boy and a girl recruited in a nationwide audition, but all they are required to do is look sad and waifish. Given the tenor of the film, I expected at least one of them to contract a lingering, fatal illness. Technically, Shi no Toge is superb. The sets and lighting evoke an ethereally lovely Japan that has almost vanished. But the film is the very definition of "depressing." When the husband was poking about a pond, looking for his wife's body, I wanted her to float to the surface to end, not the suspense, but the agony.

Shichinin no Otaku
The Cult Seven (1993)

Directed by Daiki Yamada. **Screenplay by** Nobuyuki Isshiki. **Produced by** Fuji Television Network. **With** Kiyotaka Nambara, Yosuke Eguchi, Tomoko Yamaguchi, Mitsuyoshi Uchimura, Maiko Asano, Shinji Takeda, Toru Masuoka. (100 mins.)

Don't get the wrong idea from Shichinin no Otaku's English title, The Cult Seven. An otaku is not a member of an off-brand religious group, but an obsessed expert in what society considers trivial pursuits. The film's seven otaku, like Kurosawa's seven samurai, band together to defend the weak and defeat the strong. The weak in this case is a Filipina whose baby was snatched by her former husband, a gang boss who is holed up with his cohorts on a small island. A

military otaku (Kiyotaka Nambara) who lives in the same apartment building as the mother decides to rescue the baby.

The story of how he and his fellow otaku carry out their self-appointed mission is closer in spirit to Revenge of the Nerds than The Seven Samurai. Although one of the otaku is a handsome, long-haired computer wizard (Yosuke Eguchi) with a non-otaku stunner of girlfriend (Tomoko Yamaguchi), the others are oddball lonelies who live in fantasy worlds. Their assault on a gang of macho bad guys is the stuff of farce—and that is what director Daiki Yamada (Shonan Bosozoku) and scriptwriter Nobuyuki Isshiki (Byoin e Iko) give us. They also supply pointed insights into the otaku mind and way of life. Their aim, says a program note, was to make "a film that otaku could respect." They did their job almost too well. The dialogue is so loaded with jargon that the film becomes, in places, an entertainment for otaku—i.e., incomprehensible to the uninitiated.

It doesn't take an otaku to get the point, though. When the Sunday soldier and computer wiz, together with a martial artist (Mitsuyoshi Uchimura) who dresses up in superhero costumes, a shy girl (Maiko Asano) who communicates with the world via her ham radio gear, and an idol fanzine publisher (Shinji Takeda) who cruises the streets in a customized "idol-hunter" van, assemble at a ramshackle inn for a strategy session, Yamada sketches their characters and obsessions with quick, humorous strokes.

The wiz's girlfriend, who thought she was going on a weekend lark, immediately has her doubts about this motley crew and they have their doubts about her. "How could you bring an amateur along on a special mission!" complains the soldier to the wiz. But she is to Shichinin no Otaku what Margaret Dumont was to the Marx Brothers comedies—a necessary foil to the madcaps around her.

Their first attempt at rescue ends in failure. When the bad guys corner them, the military and martial arts otaku turn out to be helpless wimps. Rambo has never fired a shot in anger with his "survival game" gun and Jackie Chan has never thrown a punch at a real foe. When Rambo and Jackie regroup at a "survival camp" on the island, they encounter a member of the enemy gang (Toru Masuoka) and discover that he is the long-lost "god" of miniature-model builders—an otaku after their own heart. Hungry for a chance to display his skills, he agrees to join them. The scene of the three of them feverishly working through the night to build a "strategic planning" model of the island's port makes us understand why these guys are otaku and why they can beat the baddies. They may be Peter Pans escaping from reality into their all-absorbing play, but they are also bright and dedicated to getting it right. Though obviously aimed at the school-age fans of stars Mitsuyoshi Uchimura and Kiyotaka Nambara—better known as the Utchan Nanchan comedy duo—the film also has a lesson or two for foreigners who want to know why they are losing the trade war; all they have to do is look at the *otaku*'s intent faces and flying fingers. They are just-in-time quality control personified.

As a film, however, *Shichinin no Otaku* is amateurish. It gets its share of laughs, but the climatic confrontation between the *otaku* and the baddies is clumsily staged. The Marx Brothers had a flawlessly choreographed method to their madness; the makers of *Shichinin no Otaku* resort to recycled Jackie Chan acrobatics. Uchimura gets a good workout, but I would have rather been watching Jackie himself. The real thing is so much better.

Shigatsu Monogatari
April Story (1998)

Written and directed by Shunji Iwai. Cinematography by Noboru Shinoda. Produced by Rockwell Eyes. With Takako Matsu, Rumi, Seiichi Tanabe. (67 mins.)

Whatever one may think of Takako Matsu as a talent, this popular idol with the distinguished pedigree (her father and brother are well-known Kabuki actors) has a glow the camera loves. In a supporting role in last year's *Tokyo Biyori*, she illuminated the screen with a fresh, quicksilver presence that was the essence of ingenue.

Shunji Iwai, who understands the pop-culture sensibility of her TV-raised, *manga*-fed, video-game-addicted generation better than any other director around, made the right choice in casting Matsu as the lead of *Shigatsu Monogatari*. Nonetheless, it's hard to call this mood piece about a college freshman's first steps toward adulthood and love a Matsu vehicle. Iwai, who shot to fame in 1995 with *Love Letter* and scored a mass audience hit in 1996 with *Swallowtail*, is too much the auteur to completely subordinate his persona to that of his star. Few other actresses, however, could make this gratingly over-produced film as bearable. The reason is not so much Matsu's acting skills, as the way she projects the innocence, romanticism, and quietly stubborn determination that are the essence of her character's appeal. It's that glow again.

The season is spring, the place, a suburb of Western Tokyo, and Uzuki Nireno (Takako Matsu) has just started her first semester as a freshman at Musashino University. A country girl from Hokkaido living alone for the first time, she is/both

excited and intimidated by her new surroundings. Asked to introduce herself to her classmates, she covers herself with tongue-tied embarrassment. Despite these and other contretemps, including an unpleasant encounter with a creep at a movie theater, she forges ahead with the business of getting settled: exploring the neighborhood on her new bicycle, browsing at a local bookstore, and making the acquaintance of her neighbor, a pale-faced woman who is big-city sophistication and alienation personified.

She also becomes friends with Saeko (Rumi), a sharp-eyed classmate who grilled her during the self-introduction session, but later asks her to go shopping and join, of all things, a fishing club. Uzuki refuses the first invitation (she has too much unpacking to do) but accepts the second (she can't say no). Soon she is practicing casts in a parking lot and being chatted up by a club senior who wants to teach her more than how to tie a fly. Uzuki, however, is not interested. When she was a high-school student in Hokkaido, she fell hard for an upperclassman (Seiichi Tanabe) who played in a rock band and, after graduation, left for college in Tokyo. Now she is going to his college, living in his neighborhood and patronizing the bookstore where he works. When will she find the courage to say hello?

Iwai, who in his earlier work strove mightily to impress with his technical virtuosity and Gen X cool, tries a different, more traditional tack in *Shigatsu*. For his movie-theater scene, he has even filmed a coy pastiche of a old-time samurai drama, complete with pops on the soundtrack and scratches on the film. Though Iwai has put most his music-video editing tricks back in the box for this film, he still strains to make every frame his own. Together with cinematographer Noboru Shinoda and lighting director Yuki Nakamura, who also collaborated with him on *Love Letter* and *Swallowtail*, Iwai has created the ideal April for his heroine, complete with a dazzling shower of cherry blossoms for her moving-in day, nostalgic golden light for her neighborhood explorations and, at the end, a breathtakingly romantic spring shower. It is charming, this April, but it is also hypergeneric, like those candy-colored Christmases in Hollywood family movies.

In his script, Iwai has abandoned the too-clever plot contrivances of his earlier work. But in honing everything down to the archtypical essentials, he has also lost much of the urgency and intensity has made the best of his work so watchable. Be that as it may, he still has Matsu who, in the rain-soaked climax, lights up Iwai's *shojo manga* (girls' comic) sentiments with that incandescent face and reminds us, for a moment, what it's like to be eighteen and helplessly, gloriously in love. An April story indeed.

Shigure no Ki
A Memory of Late Autumn Rain (1998)

Directed by Shin'ichiro Sawai. Screenplay by Ryoji Ito and Shin'ichiro Sawai. Produced by Central Arts, Fuji TV, and Toei Video. With Sayuri Yoshinaga, Tetsuya Watari. (116 mins.)

In 1997, Yoshimitsu Morita proved that illicit middle-aged love could be sexy at the box office with *Shitsurakuen* (Lost Paradise). Since then there has been a spate of films featuring middle-agers who find love, steamy sex, or a combination thereof outside their marriages. Shin'ichiro Sawai's *Shigure no Ki* would seem to be yet another, but it stars Sayuri Yoshinaga and, as all Sayurists know, Japan's queen of the screen plays by her own rules—some of which were laid down when she was still a schoolgirl acting in *seishun eiga* (youth movies) for Nikkatsu.

In *Shigure* she is reuniting with former Nikkatsu star Tetsuya Watari for the first time in twenty-nine years, since they appeared together in *Ai to Shi no Kiroku* (Memories of Love and Death). The theme this time around: a last chance at love. Based on a best-selling novel by Tsuneko Nakazato, *Shigure* has set that last chance at the age of fifty-six for its hero, a construction company executive named Mibu (Watari) and at forty-eight for its heroine, a teacher of *ikebana* named Tae (Yoshinaga). The year is 1988, when Emperor Showa lay dying and the Japanese economy was at its bubble-era peak. Mibu gets on an elevator and sees Tae, whom he last met twenty years ago. Smitten by this vision in kimono, Mibu wastes no time renewing his acquaintance and pressing his suit, despite the existence of a wife and a grown son.

Tae, a widow who has been leading a quiet life in Kamakura, is taken aback by the sudden appearance of this big, grinning man from her distant past. But something about Mibu's boyish eagerness and sincerity wins her. Soon he is visiting her at her Kamakura home and wangling for permission to stay the night. She grants it—and the sparring of early courtship gives way to passionate love.

A corporate warrior who has dedicated his adult years to paving over Japan for his company and his country, Mibu wants to spend his remaining days doing what he pleases—and that means being with Tae. On a trip to Kyoto with her, he discovers, in a paradisical valley, the ideal site for their dream house. Ever the builder, he begins making plans. There is a catch, however: Mibu has a heart condition that may carry him off at any moment. Will he and Tae be able to live out their desires or will the Grim Reaper come calling first?

Clearly targeted at Yoshinaga's core fans—mainly women of her own generation—*Shigure* is a lushly produced, beautifully photographed throwback to another era, another Japan. Tae is ever-elegant in kimono, while her house, with its exquisite Japanese-style garden, could have been the set for an Ozu film. Meanwhile, the poems that Tae and Mibu quote to each other, the *ikebana* that she produces for her alcove, the temples that she and Mibu visit on their travels, represent Japanese culture at its traditional best. No *Shonen Jump* comics, Glay posters, or trips to Disneyland for these folks! Unfortunately, the film's look is as staid and conservative as the glossy home-decorating magazines it resembles, and its story as predictable as those girl-loses-boy tearjerkers Yoshinaga used to grind out in her teens.

Meanwhile, Watari's performance explains the three-decade gap between appearances with his co-star: this veteran action star is not the most subtle of lovers. At one point he chases Yoshinaga about the room at though she were his opponent in a rugby scrum. After tackling her, he plants a kiss with enough manly force to make one hope she is wearing a mouthpiece to keep her teeth from being dislodged. Watari, I'm afraid, is not going to make anyone forget Leonardo DiCaprio.

Yoshinaga, however, is still undeniably Yoshinaga; i.e., the ideal of Japanese womanhood for a generation. She not only wears the kimono with consummate grace, but behaves with proper matronly deportment and refinement. One cannot easily imagine her grappling in the futon with a *Shitsurakuen*-like abandon and *Shigure* does not show her in such a scene. Traditionalism has its points.

Shigure no Ki does remind us why Yoshinaga has been such a durable star: she projects her trademark sincerity and purity with wholehearted intent. When she sheds tears in memory of a dead lover, she *means* it—and the entire audience sheds them along with her. In short, if you are a Sayurist, you'll probably like *Shigure no Ki*. If you just want to see what the legend is all about, by all means go, but when the girl handing out promotional tissues near the theater entrance shoves a packet in your hand, take it and ask for another. You'll need them.

Shikibu Monogatari
Mt. Aso's Passion (1990)

Written and directed by Kei Kumai. Produced by Seiyu. With Eiji Okuda, Keiko Kishi, Kyoko Kagawa, Mieko Harada. (113 mins.)

The focus of Kei Kumai's latest film, *Shikibu Monogatari*, is Toyoichi Otomo (Eiji Okuda), a young man whose brain has been damaged and spirit has been shattered by an industrial accident. He lives with his mother (Kyoko Kagawa) and wife (Mieko

Harada) in a village in Kumamoto Prefecture, amid the spectacular scenery of Southern Kyushu (including the Mt. Aso mentioned in the English title).

There are usually two directions such a film can take: upward toward a happy ending, with the hero restored, through a combination of love, good genes, and a lucky blow on the head, to his former self (as in *Random Harvest*) or downward, with the hero, after a temporary victory over his condition, succumbing poignantly to his fate (as in *Charly*). Kumai steers a middle course. He veers toward the sentimentality and *deus ex machina* improbability of *Random Harvest*, but rights himself in time to create an oddly compelling drama that unfolds in a seldom-visited corner of Japanese life, where religion thrives like a deformed mushroom, darkly nourished by illusion and desire.

That corner is ruled by Chishu-bo (Keiko Kishi), a Buddhist nun who moves among her frenzied disciples like a queen in procession, bestowing smiles and glances. She is said to be the sixty-eighth descendant of Izumi Shikibu, a Heian-era poet known for her motherly devotion and poetic celebrations of love. Chishu-bo is also believed to be a Buddhist saint, far above ordinary mortals on the spiritual ladder.

Her life intersects with Toyoichi's after a chance encounter. He becomes her disciple and she, his protector. There is nothing unusual about this: saints and madmen have a natural affinity (as Alexander Pope put it, "the worst of madmen is a saint run mad"). But Chishu-bo is also a bored woman with a taste for unusual sexual games. When she plays one with Toyoichi, it leads to an unexpected "miracle"— and eventual disaster.

Kumai adeptly depicts the emotional excesses and intellectual atrophy of Chishu-bo's followers. Their tight little community, with its undercurrents of hysteria, will be recognizable to anyone who has had dealings with sects, Eastern or Western. Kumai is less interested in exposing Chishu-bo as a spiritual charlatan, however, than in exploring the ways that love can save and destroy.

Eiji Okuda, who also starred in Kumai's *Sen no Rikyu*, brings a convincing abandon to his mad scenes. His terror at the drama unfolding inside his head ripples through his body like an earthquake, unstoppable, and uncontrollable. As Chishu-bo, Keiko Kishi is properly Sphinx-like—a robed monument hiding her thoughts behind a stately facade. If anything, she is too much a mask: it is hard to see what lies beneath the surface, other than a creepy sensuality and an iron will. As Toyoishi's mother, Kyoko Kagawa plays Chishu-bo's emotional opposite. An actress who has worked with Ozu, Mizoguchi, and Kurosawa, Kagawa takes a sensitive, restrained approach to a role that could have easily become a

soap-operatic turn. Her natural radiance makes her the most appealing presence in the film.

Despite the excellences of its cast, *Shikibu Monogatari* does not move far enough beyond the boundaries of its narrow world. Like Toyoichi, I found it hard to connect.

Shiko Funjatta *
Sumo Do, Sumo Don't (1992)

Written and directed by Masayuki Suo. Produced by Toho, Daiei, and Cabin. With Masahiro Motoki, Akira Emoto, Naoto Takenaka, Hiromasa Taguchi, Masaaki Takarai, Misa Shimizu, Robert Hoffman. (103 mins.)

Though sumo may be Japan's national sport, its image among young Japanese is, as Masayuki Suo's *Shiko Funjatta* reminds us, very "three K" (*kitsui, kitanai, kiken;* or hard, dirty, and dangerous). One might also add a "D" for *dasai* (uncool).

The film's hero is one of those young Japanese. A senior at a small Christian college and a member of a surfing and skiing club, Shuhei Yamamoto (Masahiro Motoki) is the type of student who has given Japanese universities their "leisure land" reputation. Yamamoto's leisure comes to an end when his seminar teacher (Akira Emoto) tells him that if he wants to graduate—he has never darkened the seminar's classroom door—he will have to join the college sumo club. This is an unusual demand, but the teacher is the coach and the club is in danger of dying. Only one member keeps it going: a skinny loser named Aoki (Naoto Takenaka) who has been a college student for eight years and the clubhouse's sole resident for four years, but has never won a bout. The club, however, needs at least four members if it is to compete in an upcoming tournament. Aoki and the reluctant Yamamoto go on a recruiting drive.

The makers of *Shiko Funjatta*—the title refers to a sumo stamping exercise—have picked an unusual subject. Only a handful of sumo movies have ever been filmed, including a biopic of the popular 1950s grand champion Wakanohana. *Shiko* has a conventional sports comedy plot, however: it's *Major League* in a *mawashi* (sumo belt).

Sumo, as generations of *shokiri* (comic sumo) fans know, has a comic tradition all its own that *Shiko* uses to hilarious effect. The audience I saw it with was letting go with the belly laughs. Not just one or two, but a series of collective explosions that made me wonder whether I was in a Shinjuku theater or a laugh-track recording session. Most of those laughs were for Naoto Takenaka, who plays the hapless Aoki. Short, slight and balding, Takenaka makes an unlikely sumo wrestler, but he happens to be a gifted clown. His attack of stomach cramps during his first big bout is low comedy of the highest order; his sumo, or what passes for it, is an inspired display of total incompetence.

But the main reason the crowds are turning out for *Shiko* is Masahiro Motoki. Once a popular idol singer, who became notorious in 1991 for appearing in a book of semi-nude photos by Kishin Shinoyama that challenged the limits of Japan's pornography laws, Motoki also happens to be well suited for his role. Together with his androgynous good looks, Motoki projects a punkish, puckish charm and smoldering intensity. He not only makes us understand why girls start crowding around the clubhouse to watch practice, but makes us believe Yamamoto can truly become a sumo wrestler, even though he comes to his first tournament with a ring in his ear.

That tournament is also the sumo debut of two other new members; the fat, utterly unathletic Tanaka (Hiromasa Taguchi) and the skinny, boyish Yamamoto (Masaaki Takarai), the hero's younger brother. All four are hopeless in the ring, so much so that they incur the wrath of the winning team and the school alumni who have come to cheer them on. What are these clowns trying to do? Mock the sport? Disgrace their club's illustrious name?

The club, clearly, has nowhere to go but up and up, of course, is where it goes. *Shiko* tells a standard story of gritting through to glory, with the coach's spunky, pure-hearted assistant (Misa Shimizu) serving as the hero's love interest. Suo directs it with a light, whimsical touch while getting us to cheer for the team. Resist Suo's expert manipulation though we may, we end up liking the boys and the sport they play, even if our knowledge of sumo is nil.

I did not, however, care for the film's conception of its token *gaijin* (foreigner), a British exchange student who is recruited for the team. George Smiley (Robert Hoffman) demands to wear pants under his *mawashi* (a bare backside, he says, is not dignified) and refuses to practice more than two hours at a time (overtime is not in his contract, he claims). George, in short, is a compendium of negative stereotypes; a logic-chopping, culturally insensitive jerk, who speaks a stilted Japanese seldom heard outside a textbook. He is not really a bad chap, as we eventually see, but he remains the one sour ingredient in the film's otherwise satisfying sumo stew.

Shindemo Ii *

Original Sin (1992)

Written and directed by Takashi Ishii. Produced by Argo Project and Suntory. With Masatoshi Nagase, Shinobu Otake, Hideo Murota. (117 mins.)

The story of Takashi Ishii's *Shindemo Ii* is that of *The Postman Always Rings Twice*: a young drifter falls for the wife of a middle-aged man and plots the man's murder. In the James M. Cain pulp classic, which has been adapted four times for the screen, most recently in Bob Rafelson's 1981 version, the air is ripe with moral corruption, hot with raw passion. The two lovers, Cora and Frank, not only know they are no good but kind of like it. And, even more shocking for the book's 1930s readers, a corrupt legal system lets them off scot-free. The book is a morality play for cynics that shines a brilliant, mocking light on the dirty little secrets of the American soul.

What about *Shindemo Ii*? It has its own brilliance, of a quite different kind. In his first feature in four years, Takashi Ishii presents a powerful, unsettling tragedy of pure love, not a hard-boiled tale of prurient desire. In fact, all three members of his triangle are pure-hearted types, with nary a leer among them. It is this purity, however, that drives them to extremes, including murder.

From the beginning Ishii creates a dark, charged mood of sensuality and menace, then slowly, inexorably builds to a shattering climax. Though *Shindemo Ii* at times strains credulity—the cuckolded husband has an unerring knack for being in the wrong place at the wrong time—it stays gripping to the end, without resorting to the usual erotic-thriller manipulations.

Makoto Hirano (Masatoshi Nagase) is a drifter who bumps into a thirtysomething woman (Shinobu Otake) in a driving rain. Instantly smitten, he follows her to a tiny real-estate office, where she works as a secretary. He goes in and, after some fumbling about, asks the agent (Hideo Murota)—a bluff, gravel-voiced man—for a job. The agent is willing, but Nami, his secretary and wife, is not so sure. "I don't like his type," she says in the futon that night. "He's too persistent."

How persistent is soon made clear. Now an apprentice real-estate agent, Makoto lures Nami to an empty model home and rapes her on the bare wooden floor, as rain pours through an open window. Instead of seeking help from her husband or the police, Nami begins a passionate affair. The victim who falls for her rapist is a convention of sorts in Japanese films, usually a loathsome one. But Ishii shows us, in a closeup of Makoto's glowing face, exactly why Nami changes her mind. This boy desires her with an urgency and completeness that exists beyond society's norms of good and evil. His is a rare, if dangerous, gift—and she decides to accept it.

But—and here is Ishii departs from Cain—Nami continues to love her husband. He may drink more than is good for him and spend too much time in hostess clubs, but he is, all in all, a decent, caring man. Makoto urges her to decide between them, but she can't. "Why is it wrong to like two people," she wonders out loud. When her husband discovers them together in a hot-springs bath, while on a company trip, he explodes in a drunken rage. Makoto gets another job, as a workman in a metal shop, and tries to forget Nami. She can't forget him, however. One hot summer day, she seeks him out and their affair resumes. This time, however, Makoto is determined not to lose her. He decides that, if she won't leave her husband, he will have eliminate him.

Shinobu Otake expresses Nami's passions and fears with a blazing immediacy and consummate skill. Masatoshi Nagase disturbs with the violence of his mood swings; his Makoto is a bit of a madman and a bit of a saint—and sometimes it's hard to tell which is which. *Shindemo Ii* is not for everyone. I found it by turns shocking, upsetting, and oppressive—and discovered a director who, at the advanced age of forty-six, has finally come into his own.

Shinseiki Evangelion: Gekijoban Shinto Shinsei
Neo Genesis Evangelion (1997)

Written and directed by Hideaki Anno. **Produced by** EVA Production Committee, Project Eva, GAINAX, TV Tokyo, Sega Enterprise, and Toei. (99 mins.)

Much of SF Japanimation is for teenage boys who get off on the cool futuristic gear and hot, big-eyed babes. The better products of the genre go deeper, however; they offer not only adolescent fantasies of super power and super sex, but bold speculations on the uneasy relationship between humanity and its high-tech servants. Will we remain in control of our machines—and our souls—or will we become absorbed in the rising tide of online information?

Now we have Hideaki Anno's *Shinseiki Evangelion: Gekijoban Shito Shinsei*, which throws so much visual and narrative data at its audience, including titles zapping by at almost subliminal speed, that total comprehension is all but impossible. The experience is similar watching a kid play a Final Fantasy video game at warp speed or flipping through a *Shonen Jump* comic in a blur. For teenage SF geeks a pleasantly stimulating sensory, intellectual, and even emotional exercise. For clueless oldies, who still think Road Runner cartoons are the ultimate in animation, a baffling and annoying one-and-a-half hours of *anime* at its most grandiose and pretentious.

Being a Chuck Jones fan, I incline towards the latter view, but I also admit that Anno and his colleagues are onto something. They are not only making state-of-the-art *otaku* entertainment, but creating a new pop-cultural synthesis.

The film begins as a typical dark-future genre exercise. In the year 2015, fourteen-year old Shinji is summoned by his scientist father for a man-to-man talk. Dad wants him, not to get his grades up, but pilot a giant robot called Evangelion against mysterious entities called *shito* (angels) who are threatening the existence of humanity. This threat is not a new one. In the year 2000, the first of the *shito*, called Adam, caused an explosion at the South Pole that flooded the land and darkened the skies with ash. The climatic changes that followed led to the deaths of half the world's population.

Since then, the survivors have battled the *shito* using the giant robots, better known as Evas. In addition to Shinji, the pilot corps includes Asuka, a fiesty redhead who is three-quarters Japanese, one-quarter German, and was raised in the United States; and Rei, a girl with blue-grey hair who is not as human as she looks. Following SF anime convention, they are both faunlike creatures with huge, glittering eyes, buff bodies, and steely wills.

Despite the large cast of characters, decades-spanning story, and a profusion of twenty-first-century jargon, much of it borrowed from early Christian sources, the film is essentially a Power Rangers episode writ large: i.e., super-teens piloting big, powerful machines and saving the world from monsters. We've seen it all before. What we haven't seen, however, is the way the film zaps back and forth through time, slams through narrative shifts and flashes explanatory text, in billboard-sized Chinese characters, at mind-bending speed. It's a hypercharged phantasmagoria that defies easy comprehension, while exerting a hypnotic fascination. Watching, one becomes part of the film's multimedia data stream.

Shinseiki Evangelion is looking forward, toward an integration of all popular media—television, *manga*, movies, and video games—into new forms in which distinctions between real and virtual, viewer and viewed, man and machine, become blurred and finally cease to matter. O Brave New World, that has such animation in it.

Shitsurakuen
Lost Paradise (1997)

Directed by Yoshimitsu Morita. **Screenplay by** Tomomi Tsutsui. **Cinematography by** Hiroshi Takase. **Produced by** Ace Pictures. **With** Koji Yakusho, Hitomi Kuroki, Akira Terao, Kazuko Hoshino. (119 mins.)

First, a confession: though I religiously read the *Nihon Keizai Shimbun*, I ignored the serialization of

Jun'ichi Watanabe's novel *Shitsurakuen* (Lost Paradise) that ran in the morning edition from September 1995 to October 1996 and created a nationwide sensation. So I must have been one of the few in the full-house crowd watching Yoshimitsu Morita's film of the novel who did not know how the affair of its two middle-aged lovers would end.

One reason for the sensation was Watanabe's injection of a device much beloved of pre-modern Japanese drama—love suicide or *shinju*—into a modern urban setting, while making his lovers, not febrile adolescents, but mature, sophisticated adults with professions, families, and despite their various tribulations, futures. As was Yukio Mishima's ritual suicide, Watanabe's choice of endings was at once deliberately shocking and deeply conservative. But instead of recoiling, Japanese moviegoers are sighing at the beauty and sadness of it all, and making Toei's bean counters delirious with joy. Perhaps this shouldn't be surprising. Despite the influence of Hollywood, traditional cultural patterns retain a tenacious hold on the Japanese imagination. Films celebrating the selfless sacrifices of the kamikaze pilots continue to appear and the *Chushingura* story of the forty-seven loyal retainers continues to exert its fascination, though its last two fim adaptations were box-office disappointments

To bring Watanabe's novel credibly to the screen, director Yoshimitsu Morita decided that an emphasis on mood over narrative logic would do the trick—and turned out to be commercially quite correct. But I couldn't quite buy the film's central premise or, to put it another way, bite through its sugared coating to its poisoned core.

To create the desired mood, cinematographer Hiroshi Takase photographed nearly every scene in dim, hazy light and depressing shades of gray and brown. Even when the lovers appear outdoors in broad daylight, the air has a wintry chill. In this antechamber to the tomb called Tokyo, their drift towards death feels natural, inevitable.

Working from a script by Tomomi Tsutsui, Morita carefully sets his lovers at one remove from the trendy, Westernized side of life in today's Japan. True, the man, the fifty-year-old Kuki (Koji Yakusho), was once a hotshot magazine editor, but has since been restructured into a corporate backwater—a contemporary-enough fate. The woman, thirty-eight-year-old Rinko (Hitomi Kuroki), teaches at a culture center and lives alone with her doctor husband—hardly the profile of a tradition-bound Japanese housewife.

Kuki and his office mates, moreover, are paper-shuffling, *shoji*-playing, Chinese-classics-quoting throwbacks, who could have stepped from Kurosawa's *Ikiru*. Also, Rinko teaches that most

Japanese of arts: calligraphy. As one might expect, she is lovely in kimono. By stressing his principals' Japaneseness, Morita is also emphasizing their essential goodness and purity. (He signals the rottenness of the film's one villain, Rinko's horror of a husband, by showing him gorging on cheese and Perrier).

Having placed his lovers in a cultural time-warp, Morita presents them in the throes of an affair more 1990s than 1790s. No traditional agonizing over duties and obligations, just scene after scene of hot lovemaking in soft-focus closeups. At first passive, Rinko becomes possessed, even coming to Kuki's hotel room on the day of her father's funeral. Suspicious, Rinko's husband sets a detective agency on their trail, while Kuki's wife (Kazuko Hoshino) intuitively unmasks her husband's lies. But rather end their affair, Kuki and Rinko decide to give it all up for love—including their lives.

The film has set the stage well for this climax, but Kuki and Rinko's reason for choosing death in a snow country hideaway—that they want to go out in a blaze of passion, rather than let their love wither away into indifference—feels contrived. Middle-aged lovers freed from dead marriages celebrate, they don't self-destruct. I felt like offering Kuki and Rinko, not a poisoned chalice, but two tickets to Bali.

Shizukana Ayashii Gogo ni
In the Silent Suspicious Afternoon (1997)

Written and directed by Makoto Shiina, Kazuhiko Ota, Makoto Wada. **Produced by** Hone Film. **With** Masaaki Hayashi. (71 mins.)

Shizukana Ayashii Gogo ni (In the Silent Suspicious Afternoon) is Makoto Shiina's attempt to revive the anthology film—a genre that has fallen out of favor since its peak in the late 1980s and early 1990s. Unlike the segments of many anthology films, the three parts of *Shizukana* can all stand alone as shorts. Also, though united by the theme of man-in-nature, they are all quite different. One is an animated film with an overlay of nostalgic atmospherics and an underlay of dry humor, one is a nightmarish fantasy of the *Twilight Zone* variety, and one begins as man-and-dog nature idyll, but ends with an excursion into the dream life of its canine hero. The transitions between segments are not jarring, however. All three use a minimum of dialogue (the animation restricts itself to captions) and all three celebrate nature with an intimacy definitely, if not uniquely, Japanese. But theirs is a nature that can be inhumanly uncanny.

The first segment, Kazuhiko Ota's "Suika o Katta" (I Bought a Watermelon), is a black-and-white animated short about a boy's errand in a country town. The time is an indefinite past, the air full of sounds that recall the endless summers of a rural Japanese boyhood. The animation is poky but evocative, the story simple to the point of nonexistence. Based on a *manga* by Hitoshi Sawano, "Suika" draws an amusing contrast between the boy's deadpan sense of purpose (he will get his watermelon!) and the drowsing village inhabitants he encounters (even the train station ticket-taker is nodding off). It also creates an atmosphere that is nostalgically inviting, while being true to the child's sense of the world's essential strangeness.

Makoto Shiina directed the second segment, "Tononada Samehara Kaigan" (The Tononada Samehara Coast), from his own screenplay. Though best known as a nature writer and filmmaker, Shiina also won a Japan Science Fiction Prize in 1990 for his novel *Ado Bado*. In "Tononada," he presents both sides of his creative persona. The segment begins with a comic setup that could have come from a Harold Lloyd film. A nattily mustachioed outdoorsman (Masaaki Hayashi) drives his van onto a sandy wasteland and promptly gets stuck. The harder he tries to extricate himself, the deeper he sinks, until he finds himself buried deep in a rectangular pit and unable to escape. He makes a meal of eggs and rice and waits for help.

It comes the next day in the form of silent crowd of villagers who look like refugees from a Meiji woodblock print. They stare down at him from the lip of the pit and begin building a wooden scaffolding. Finishing, they lower a bucket, but when the man steps into it they motion him away—they want him to fill it with sand—keep filling and keep filling. We are, we see, in a bizarre world reminiscent of Hiroshi Teshigahara's 1964 *Suna no Onna* (Woman of the Dunes). The segment's take on the hero's desperate situation is dryly comic, but final the twist, when it comes, is properly chilling.

In the last segment, Makoto Wada's "Gaku no Ehon" (Gaku's Picture Book) Otosan (Tomosuke Noda) and his dog Gaku are taking a leisurely canoe trip down an unspoiled river. Gaku is fourteen years old and this may be his last journey together with his master. We seem to sit in the canoe for an eternity while Otosan paddles contentedly and Gaku gazes at the wildlife on the river bank. Finally, Otosan sets up camp, man and dog bed down for the night, and we enter the world of Gaku's dreams, both sleeping and waking. Those dreams are both ordinary (a romp through the flowers with a pretty young bitch) and strange (a vision of masked spirits, marching in single file through the forest).

Shizukana Ayashii Gogo ni doesn't escape the unevenness and slightness endemic to the anthology genre, but the segments offer low-key pleasures, as well as a stark object lesson. On that next drive to the beach, I will definitely remember to take those tire chains.

Shizukana Seikatsu
A Quiet Life (1995)

Written and directed by Juzo Itami. Produced by Itami Production. With Atsuro Watabe, Hinako Saeki, Yoshiyuki Omori, Masayuki Imai, Takao Okamura, Nobuko Miyamoto. (121 mins.)

In the 1980s Juzo Itami burst onto the screen with smart, fresh, delightfully funny movies about seldom-explored corners of Japanese life, including the funeral business, *ramen* noodle-making, and tax collecting. Japanese audiences made his first film, *Ososhiki* (The Funeral), a hit and later flocked to the two *Marusa no Onna* (A Taxing Woman) films. By the end of the decade Itami had become a franchise name.

In *Shizukana Seikatsu*, he has taken a new, more coventionally dramatic tack. Based on a book by Nobel Prize–winner Kenzaburo Oe, the film depicts the "quiet life" that a brain-damaged young man and his sister lead when their famous novelist father and housewife mother go to Australia.

In one sense, Itami is the ideal director for this film; he is Oe's high-school friend and brother-in-law. In another sense, however, he is totally wrong. Oe is a man of high seriousness known for his unwillingness to compromise with popular tastes. Despite his didactic fits, Itami is a charmer who tries to give his audience what it wants.

Shizukana Seikatsu gives us Oe as filtered through the sensibility of *Rainman* and *Forrest Gump*. Like Raymond and Forrest, the disabled hero, Iyo (Atsuro Watabe), is a spiritually pure, unusually gifted exemplar, though his talent is writing sweetly melodic tunes in the classical manner (his real-life model, Oe's son Hikari, composed the film's soundtrack). His artist sister, Ma-chan (Hinako Saeki), is dedicated to Iyo, and his mathmatician brother, O-chan (Yoshiyuki Omori), appears only fleetingly, but is a pretty sweet guy too.

`The story tells of Ma-chan and Iyo's awakening to the wider and darker world that lies outside their happy, loving home. The chief awakener is Arai-kun (Masayuki Imai), a health-club instructor who teaches Iyo to swim. Personable and patient, Arai-kun would seem to be the perfect teacher for Iyo— and boyfriend for Ma-chan— but he is living under the shadow of a past that he cannot escape. What Ma-chan and Iyo find out, almost too late, is that shadows can be dangerous.

In exploring Arai-kun's past, Itami shifts the focus from Iyo and Ma-chan, until we are not sure whose movie we are in. He also smoothes over the narrative rough patches, including the occasional murder and rape, with of plenty of warm, human moments between Ma-chan and Iyo and their surrogate family—Iyo's piano teacher (Takao Okamura) and his political activist wife (Nobuko Miyamoto)—but he leaves us wondering what the movie is about. Though he noodles about with several themes, including the difficulty of living clean in a dirty world, his only real aim is to make us leave the theater feeling good.

Watching *Shizukana Seikatsu*, I realized that the Itami of *Ososhiki* and *Tampopo* is no longer with us. The man who is now using his name has made a gentle, glowing, uplifting patchwork of a film that is the cinematic equivalent of New Age music, with the occasional discord. When Yoji Yamada gives up the Tora-san series, we know who to call.

Shonen Jidai *
Takeshi: Childhood Days (1991)

Directed by Masahiro Shinoda. **Screenplay by** Taichi Yamada. **Produced by** Hyogensha. **With** Tetsuya Fujita, Yuji Horioka, Noritake Kohinata, Katsuhisa Yamazaki. (117 mins.)

The time is the summer of 1944. The place is Toyama, a prefecture on the Japan Sea. Shinji, a slight, studious fifth grader, arrives from Tokyo to stay with relatives. This is no ordinary visit: Shinji is an evacuee. To the local boys, clad in ragged clothes and straw sandals, his neat school uniform and leather shoes look outlandish and exotic. He is a messenger—at once ridiculous and wonderful—from a world they know only from flickering images on screens or the pages of books.

Masahiro Shinoda's *Shonen Jidai* begins with this surface clash between city and country, but doesn't dwell on it. Instead, its themes are boyhood friendship and power politics. Shinoda may paint Shinji's new world with a picture-postcard prettiness—his Toyama is a wonderland of spectacular mountains and pines—but he also injects a this-is-the-way-it-was emotional rightness reminiscent of *Stand by Me*.

Like Rob Reiner's film about an end-of-childhood adventure in the American fifties, *Shonen Jidai* centers on a friendship of social opposites. Shinji (Tetsuya Fujita) is a pampered child of the urban middle class who is bright, bookish, and articulate. The boss of his class, Takeshi (Yuji Horioka), is the hardworking son of a fishing and farming family who is sparing with his words, but quick with his hands. A head taller than Shinji, he is a natural leader and something of a bully.

Basing his script on Funio Fujiko A's best-selling comic adapation of *Nagai Michi* (Long Road), a novel by the late Hyozo Kashiwahara, Shinoda creates characters that exist as real individuals and act according to boyhood's real rules. As class boss, Takeshi is ruthless in enforcing his directives, but when Shinji let him handle his battleship medallion and borrow his illustrated storybooks, he becomes the new boy's fast friend.

A class boss also has his pride, however. When Shinji delivers what Takeshi considers a slight—he abandons him to greet a girl from Osaka who is visiting his aunt—he forces his new friend to sing in front of the gang. As these incidents suggest, *Shonen Jidai* focuses on the small crises of a wartime boyhood. Unlike *Stand by Me*, there is no big adventure that will change everyone's lives forever. Instead Shinoda nudges the story along toward Takeshi's inevitable fall, while creating an illusion of utter naturalness. This, I felt, was the way these boys would act if they were away from adult supervision and the camera's eye.

This illusion is shaken, however, when Takeshi's rule is ended by a clever rich boy (Noritake Kohinata) and his overweight ally (Katsuhisa Yamazaki). There is an element of buffoonery in their triumph—Our Gang Comes to Japan— absent from the previous scenes. But the film's core—Shinji's evolving friendship with Takeshi— remains intact. If anything, this crisis injects the story of their friendship with more poignancy.

Though mainly marginal figures, the film's adults include many well-known faces. The worst is Shima Iwashita as Shinji's mother. Babbling inanities about the "good-hearted country folk," she tinkles with insincerity. I liked her better as a gang boss's wife in the *Gokudo no Onnatachi* series. Japan's Joan Crawford has no business trying to be Spring Byington.

Shudan Sasen
Group Transfer (1994)

Directed by Shun'ichi Kajima. **Screenplay by** Hisashi Nozawa. **Produced by** Toei. **With** Kyoko Enami, Masahiko Tsugawa, Atsuo Nakamura, Kyohei Shibata. (108 mins.)

More Japanese workers are learning the hard way that *resutora* (restructuring) is not just another fancy loan word, but an invitation to an early retirement, a posting to Timbuktu, or a pink slip. And sometimes, as Shunichi Kajima's *Shudan Sasen* (Group Transfer) shows, it is a one-way ticket on a corporate group tour to oblivion.

The film's tour members are fifty employees of Taiyo Fudosan, a real-estate company that is paying heavily for its bubble-era excesses and desperately needs to cut costs. The first place to cut, a no-nonsense female lawyer (Kyoko Enami) tells top management, are poor performers with high salaries and expensive benefits. Her proposal: lump fifty of them into a "special sales section," give them an impossible quota, and fire them if they fail to make it. Company vice president Yokoyama (Masahiko Tsugawa), who is the kind of heartless, number-crunching suit we all love to hate, enthusiastically agrees with this plan. He even has names that he wants to put on the list.

To lead this ragtag crowd of timeservers, misfits, and incompetents, Yokoyama chooses Shinoda (Atsuo Nakamura)—a straight-arrow who once objected to Yokohama's misuse of corporate funds and earned the label of troublemaker as a result. Hearing of his old enemy's latest scheme, he first thinks of quitting, but decides to fight instead. He is aided by Takigawa (Kyohei Shibata), a former master of *jiage*—the art of buying small parcels of downtown properties for big developers and jacking up land prices in the process. Now that business in his specialty is dead as the market for gold-flake *sake* (another eighties fad), Takigawa lounges about the office reading sports papers, catching up on his sleep and not giving a damn what anyone thinks. But behind the don't-care exterior lives a warrior's spirit. When Yokoyama exiles him to the "special sales section," he rouses himself for battle.

Shudan wants to be a social satire of the type that Juzo Itami once turned out with such facility. The punchy reggae score by Kazufumi Kodama, the mordant comic persona of Masahiko Tsugawa (an Itami regular), the script with its nuggets of timely information ("the average manager is worth only one-fourth of his paycheck"), are all Itami trademarks. But instead of Itami's brand of wry grotesquery, Kajima serves up corporate melodrama, with comic touches. We come to *Shudan* expecting an inside look at salaryman life—and get it—but after a promising beginning the film becomes a heavily plotted, tediously told struggle between the restructured salarymen and Yokoyama, who is slime in an Italian suit and tie.

This guy not only wants the fifty to fail, he plays dirty to make sure that they do—and quickly degenerates into a cartoon villain. He sexually harasses his female employees, hires *yakuza* to trash condos so the fifty can't sell them, and even sneers at a restructured salaryman's devotion to his cancer-stricken wife. Tsugawa plays this role with his usual brio, but even he cannot make Yokohama credible. As Shinoda, journalist-turned-actor Atsuo Nakamura is a good gray fighter for justice who lacks humor and verve. As

Takigawa, Kyohei Shibata is intense, angry and something of a hustler. His and Tsugawa's characters have more in common than they might imagine.

By the end, Yokohama gets his comeuppance and forty-seven of the original fifty have their triumph (three, seeing the writing on the wall, resign). Yes, it is a familiar number and, if not quite *Chushingura*, *Shudan Sasen* tells the same tale of humiliated men uniting to right a wrong and win back their good name. Some things have changed since the days of Chikamatsu however; evil in this film chats up the company's pretty token *gaijin* in fluent English, listens to Mahler and reads *USA Today*. Insidious things, those foreign influences. Watch and be warned.

Shuraba no Ningengaku
The Anthropology of a Fight Scene (1993)

Directed by Shun'ichi Hajima. Screenplay by Takahiro Okabe and Masahiro Kakefuda. Produced by Tohoku Shinsha, Toei Video, and Toei. With Masanobu Takashima, Hirose Fuse, Yoko Minamino, Shinji Yamashita. (109 mins.)

Modern *yakuza* are hardly romantic heroes. Most are in it strictly for the money and many earn it by exploiting Asian women or selling stimulant drugs. Instead of the gangs' unsavory present, however, *Shuraba no Ningengaku* harkens back to an idealized 1950s, when Japan was emerging from the ruins of war. This, the movie tells us, was a freer, more innocent time, when joining a gang could be a thrilling adventure for a naive but reckless youth.

The youth in question is Heikichi (Masanobu Takashima), whom we first see in 1950 as a *tempura gakusei* (phony student) who is pretending to attend classes to please his mother in the countryside, while delivering ice to put money in his pocket. As played by Takashima, a wide-eyed, burr-headed Japanese Jerry Lewis, Heikichi would seem to be a most unlikely gang recruit. But *Shuraba* is a most improbable movie, in which even a clown can become a wise guy.

While delivering ice to a club, Heikichi becomes embroiled in a street fight between American soldiers and the Ando-gumi, a gang led by Morishima (Hirose Fuse), a beefy sub-boss. The GIs' switch-blades turn out to be no match for Morishima's wooden sword, but before they retire in ignominious defeat, the soldiers administer a thrashing to poor Heikichi. He recovers consciousness in the club to the tender ministrations of a pretty hostess named Junko (Yoko Minamino) and the hearty cheers of the gang. He has found a new love and a new life.

Shuraba comically describes the education of this *yakuza* Candide, but veteran Toei director Shun'ichi

Hajima also wants the film to be an action picture in the traditional slash and swagger mold, suffused with a nostalgia for old-time gangsterism. Imagine Jerry Lewis in a funny gangster movie that expresses a frank longing for the heyday of Sicilian-American thuggery. The story covers eight years in Heikichi's gang career, from his fumbling beginning to his fumbling end. His misadventures include crashing his motorcycle, with Junko aboard, into the gang boss's car, and sleeping with a girl who works at the dance hall of a rival gang. In the former instance, he is let off with a warning from the boss (perhaps because he grovels so sincerely). In the latter, he is grabbed by his enemies and beaten to slush. Fortunately, Morishima rushes to the gang office where Heikichi is being held and frees him with his trusty wooden sword. Heikichi ends up in the hospital, but Junko forgives him and he recovers to bumble on again.

His most serious goof, however, is becoming involved in a beef between a Morishima underling and a sub-boss named Hanagata (Shinji Yamashita). A strutting, sneering dandy who dresses in white and puts out cigarettes on his knuckles, Hanagata is the gangster as cool caricature. But he is a dangerous man to cross, as Heikichi discovers when he threatens him with a gun. Hanagata laughs in his face and ambles over to take the weapon out of his trembling hand. As Heikichi scuttles away, he accidentally fires two bullets, aerating Hanagata. Amazingly, he survives and forgives his would-be assassin.

But Heikichi's luck cannot hold forever; when a businessman who welshed on a loan to the Andogumi is murdered, Heikichi is fingered as the suspect. Although another gang member made the hit, Heikichi, together with Junko, go into hiding. His boss tells him that if he is caught, he must quit the gang and go straight. Not knowing where to turn, Heikichi asks a college friend to find him a hideout. The friend, now a journalist, agrees, but soon realizes that if he turns in his old buddy, he will get the scoop of the year.

In trying to be all things to all audiences, Shuraba ends up being very little indeed. The fight scenes are too brutal to be funny, and too phony to be scary (the soldiers all flip out their switchblades in unison, like dancers in a West Side Story production number). The period cars, clothes, and furnishings are presented for our admiration, like so many mint-condition collectors' items. Instead of sighing with longing for the good old days, I started wondering about prices. I also doubted the macho credentials of movie's yakuza. How could these guys be for real when they let a schnook like Heikichi play gangster with them? The most transparent fake, however, is Heikichi himself. We never see him turn out a hook-

er, do a drug deal, or otherwise engage in actual income-producing yakuza activities. A tempura gakusei at the beginning, he remains forever a tempura yakuza in a tempura yakuza movie.

Sleepy Heads
(1997)

Directed by Yoshifumi Hosoya. Screenplay by Yoshifumi Hosoya, Nick Feyz. Produced by Elephant Studio and Zazu Production. With Eugene Nomura, Toshiya Nagasawa, Takahiro "Engin" Fujita, Sayuri Higuchi Emerson, Nick Feyz. (86 mins.)

Millions of young Japanese go abroad every year in search of sun, fun, and memories to warm them through the long, dull years of struggling through as salarymen or housewives. Many, however, want more than a week in Guam—they yearn to escape their fate at home altogether. Several succeed in living out their dream of freedom abroad, but as Yoshifumi Hosoya's debut feature Sleepy Heads shows, the Japan they left behind is seldom as far away as they think. Even while living in Manhattan, they often find themselves attracted by Japan's familiar comforts, bound by its social strictures. Like expats everywhere, they carry home inside their heads.

Filmed on location by a Japanese and American cast and crew, this comedy about young Japanese expats in New York goes beyond the usual travelogue clichés. Hosoya, who co-wrote the script with Nick Feyz, is a long-time U.S. resident and has based his film on his own experiences of scuffling in the Big Apple. Also, reflecting his film studies at New York University and the School of Visual Arts, Sleepy Heads has an all-American technical sheen.

The obvious point of comparison is Ang Lee, who examined the lives of Taiwanese expats in America in The Wedding Banquet and Pushing Hands. Both directors would rather please audiences than pursue personal agendas and both have become adept at the Hollywood art of screen storytelling. But whereas The Wedding Banquet enlightens with pointed comic observations about the clash between Chinese customs and New World individualism, Sleepy Heads is satisfied with broad, obvious jokes and phoned-in sitcom characterizations.

Hiroshi (Eugene Nomura) is a fledgling singer-songwriter who is trying to make it in New York. Fresh off the bus, he falls in with Kenta (Toshiya Nagasawa), a freeloading martial-arts teacher, and Akira (Takahiro "Engin" Fujita), a deadlock-wearing doper. While Hiroshi pays the rent on their three-man apartment by delivering orders for a Japanese restaurant, Akira is getting high, and Kenta is cadging free meals from the restaurant's woman manager, who has a crush on him. Understandably, Hiroshi is not pleased with this arrangement, but he finds that even Kenta has his uses. After scoring a date with a pretty executive (Sayuri Higuchi Emerson) at JAL's New York office, Hiroshi learns that the show he was planning to take her to is sold out. Desperate, he asks Kenta for help and Kenta, after calling on a well-connected tout for a topless bar (Nick Feyz), comes through with the tickets.

On the day of the big date, disaster strikes. Hiroshi and Kenta discover Akira in the toilet, apparently dead from an overdose. If they call the police, they might be deported as illegal aliens. The tout suggests various disposal methods, such as dissolving Akira in a tub of acid, but they finally decide to cram him into a golf bag and dump him off the Brooklyn Bridge. The boys encounter difficulties in executing this plan. Gangbangers bent on vengeance after being humiliated by Kenta's wooden sword chase them, and a fellow subway passenger who notices Akira's dreadlocks sticking out of the bag calls the cops. Far worse for Hiroshi, however, is a chance encounter with his date, sitting in the BMW of an insufferable yuppie who was Hiroshi's high-school classmate. Dragging a body about the night streets of New York, with barely a cent to his name, Hiroshi begins to think that his classmate's assessment of him as a loser is correct.

Playing Hiroshi, bilingual actor Eugene Nomura displays the same comic gifts and unaffected charm that earned him awards for his work in *Happyaku Two Lap Runners*. As Kenta, Toshiya Nagasawa struts with the Mifune-like swagger that gave a welcome charge to *Sharaku* and *Setouchi Moonlight Serenade*. But in *Sleepy Heads*, these two skim the surface of their roles, mugging for easy laughs.

Sleepy Heads bubbles along entertainingly enough, but though Hosoya certainly knows his New York, he presents it the way expat kids write letters home to their worried parents with cute, comforting fictions that fail to mask unpleasant realities, one being that this foreign interlude is only so much marking time. I felt like telling Hiroshi—and the movie—to get a life.

Somaudo Monogatari *
The Weald (1998)
Directed by Naomi Sento. Produced by Bitters End. (73 mins.)

Naomi Kawase became an instant celebrity in Japan when she won the Camera d'Or prize at the 1997 Cannes Film Festival for her first feature film, *Moe*

no Suzaku. The youngest, at twenty-seven, to ever to receive this prestigious award for new directors, she returned home to find her face in every major newspaper and magazine. In October 1997 a press conference to announce her marriage to *Moe no Suzaku*'s producer Takenori Sento was splashed across the entertainment pages of the nation's daily sport papers, who usually cover independent filmmakers the way they cover semioticians.

A drama about the dissolution of a family and the decline of a way of life in the mountains of Nara Prefecture, *Moe no Suzaku* may have been her first feature, but it was her seventeenth screen credit. She had made sixteen documentary films prior to it, beginning in 1988 while she was a student at the Visual Arts College of Osaka. Several had won prizes at festivals in Japan and had been screened abroad, thrusting her into the forefront of the local documentary scene.

Sento (she now uses her husband's surname) has made a new documentary, *Somaudo Monogatari*, in which she returns to the village of Nishi Yoshino in the mountains of Nara Prefecture—the setting for *Moe no Suzaku*. This time, however, she has come not to tell a story, but to listen as nine elderly villagers tell theirs. Instead of making yet another talking heads documentary on the problems of the aged in rural Japan, she has tried to capture the flavor of her interviewees' lives and the essence of their characters not only through their words, but their environment, their work, and even their faces in extreme closeup, as though she were to trying to read their souls from the lines on their weathered skin.

As in *Moe no Suzaku*, her approach is personal, impressionistic, poetic, and minimalist. There is no narrator telling us everyone's age and occupation, no soundtrack music swelling sentimentally in the background, no designer-clothed reporter looking dutifully solemn as she points a mike at her aged interviewee. Instead, Sento talks with the villagers as a loving, inquisitive and, at times, sassy daughter. They respond in kind, joking and bantering with the woman behind the camera. Slightly tipsy, they dance local folk dances and sing local folk songs, but in their quieter moments they also speak straight from the heart, from the depths of their lives. One man speculates on reincarnation as he cuts trees deep in the Nara woods. Another talks quietly about battling Parkinson's Disease as he bundles twigs. Still another reminisces about a dead son as he uses a chain saw to magically transform a tree stump into an exquisitely patterned wood bowl.

We see seasons changing, bamboo groves swaying in the wind, pine branches glittering in the sunlight. These images are not in the film for their postcard prettiness, but because they help us understand what it means to spend a lifetime in these mountains, living in ways that most city dwellers have long forgotten. Sento may poetically record, but she does not sentimentalize or romanticize her subjects' lives; in the course of the film, we come to see that they did not come by those lined faces from too much time in the tanning salon, but through hard, unremitting toil, in all weathers and seasons.

Often we hear only the voice off-camera as the storyteller continues to silently work. It is as though we were listening to her think. Sometime the words pierce, as when the father of the lost son says that, even many years have passed his son's death, he still cannot bear to look at his photographs, or when another old man, now nearly toothless and bald, remembers a love lost, a life spent unmarried, and after his mother's death, alone.

With patience, sensitivity and art, Sento has again created an evocation of a people and way of life that is strongly individual, intensely felt, entrancingly beautiful. The wisdom of her villagers is also ours, if we are willing to listen.

Sonatine
(1993)

Written and directed by Takeshi Kitano. Produced by Bandai Visual and Shochiku Daiichi Kogyo. With Takeshi Kitano, Aya Kokumai. (94 mins.)

Takeshi Kitano's *Sonatine* tries to prove that a *yakuza* movie can make a statement on the futility and emptiness of the gang life as powerful as that of the *Godfather* films. But the first adjective that sprang to mind as I watched this story of a gangster caught in a war he never wanted was "pretentious."

In *Sonatine* Kitano plays Murakawa, a middle-aged *yakuza* who is tired of the life and wants out. He has a job to do first, however; his boss wants him and his crew to go to Okinawa and help an affiliated gang in a turf war. Murakawa reluctantly agrees, but when he arrives he finds that the rival gang has him outmaneuvered and outgunned. Two of his men are killed in an explosion at their temporary office, then several more take fatal rounds in a gun battle at a local bar. Murakawa and the other survivors retreat to a hide-out in the countryside, where they wait for a chance to counterattack.

The script, which Kitano wrote, has a familiar genre arc, but instead of the usual genre theatrics, he gives us a new version of gangster cool. In one scene Murakawa has his crew lower a hapless mah-jongg parlor owner into the harbor with a construction crane, then watches calmly as the minutes tick by and the twitches of the rope register the drowning

man's death throes. This is not only a ridiculous murder method—the crane could easily be spotted by a passing ship or patrol car—but a sadistic act that made me despise the hero. Kitano evidently wants to establish Murakawa as a tough guy. Then so, I suppose, are boys who seal squirrels inside mason jars.

Kitano does capture the tension, petty protocols and numbing boredom of *yakuza* life (all those hours of killing time in dumpy offices, cheap bars and beach houses in the middle of nowhere). Also, his *yakuza* are often cutups when they aren't being killers—a welcome change from the standard macho stereotypes.

Murakawa is a cutup as well, though his jokes are of the practical variety. While at the hideout on the beach, he sees two of his young underlings shooting a can off each other's heads. He takes their pistol, empties all but one chamber, then makes them play a round of scissors-paper-stone with him. He aims the pistol at the loser's chest, pulls the trigger—and smiles when it doesn't go off. Then he loses and squeezes off a round at his own head. Shaken, the boys wonder if is he is crazy. (They should have counted the bullets in the sand.)

In this scene, as in others, Kitano wants to impress us with Murakawa's contempt for danger and death. But as the stay at the beach stretched to days, then weeks—and it began to feel that long in the theater—I started to see Murakawa less as an existential hero than as a wish-fulfillment for the director, whose TV shows have frequently featured elaborate pranks and violent slapstick, with the general of the Kitano "army" controlling the action and the grunts taking the pratfalls.

Some of the film's comic business is truly funny; Kitano has a wickedly inventive mind. Much of the film, however, is self-indulgent, self-congratulatory, and as the rival gang closes in for the kill and Murakawa prepares to meet his end, self-pitying. Because the plot contains an element of suspense, it wouldn't be fair to reveal too much. There is a sultry Okinawan girl (Aya Kokumai) who likes the off-handed way Murakawa guns down her date-rapist of a boyfriend. (It's love at first shot.) There is also a mysterious stranger in fisherman mufti who knocks off Murakawa's allies and underlings like so many dolls in a shooting gallery (One of the film's conceits is the immobility of the characters in the bang-bang scenes; they shoot at each other as though their instinct of self-preservation had been surgically removed.)

The focus, however, remains on Murakawa—and his grim and, at times, grimly comic obsession with death. I have seldom seen a film in which death is so drained of drama and emotion; Kitano seems to be saying that because his characters' lives have no meaning, their deaths can have no charge. So they go down, one by one, passive victims all. Only Murakawa gets the last laugh and the last bullet. By now, we know how he's going to use it—and give *Sonatine* its long-awaited *coup de grace*.

Sono Otoko, Kyobo ni Tsuki
Violent Cop (1989)

Written and directed by Takeshi Kitano. Produced by Shochiku Fuji. With Takeshi Kitano, Ryu Haku, Sei Hiraizumi, Maiko Kawakami. (103 mins.)

Takeshi Kitano's *Sono Otoko, Kyobo ni Tsuki* (Violent Cop) is a movie for people who don't mind raw violence and plenty of it: nearly every scene has its share of beatings, stabbings, shootings, and slaps upside the face. It is also the first movie directed by Japan's most popular comedian, who plays the tough-guy lead. This, by Hollywood standards, is incongruous. Imagine Woody Allen making his directorial debut with *Dirty Harry* and playing the Clint Eastwood role.

The incongruity disappears, however, if the comedian in question is Kitano, who has often portrayed tough guys in films and televsion, most famously as the brutal POW camp sergeant in Nagisa Oshima's *Merry Christmas, Mr. Lawrence*. He has played the tough guy in real life as well. In 1987 he led a gang of comic disciples in an attack on the editorial offices of *Friday*, a weekly photo magazine, to punish the editors for running candid photos of his then girlfriend. Although Kitano and his gang used only folded umbrellas as weapons and caused no serious injuries, the incident created an uproar and Kitano was forced to absent himself temporarily from the tube in atonement.

In *Sono Otoko* Kitano plays Azuma, a police detective who, like Dirty Harry, is always getting into hot water with his superiors for administering his own brand of rough justice. Because this is Japan, however, it seldom comes out of the barrel of a gun. Instead, his favorite weapons are a backhand to the face or a knee to the groin. The film begins with a gang of teenagers viciously beating an old bum. Catching them at their game, Azuma follows the ringleader home, barges into his room and smacks him silly as he cowers next to his plastic model collection. Azuma is in the wrong—he should have sent the misguided child to the judge for a stern lecture—but unfortunately, nearly everyone in the audience cheers him on.

"I want to avoid spectacular action and make a detective drama that's low-key, but different from all the others," Kitano told the press before beginning production. His "low key" hero may begin the film as a winsome Columbo-like cop, but he cannot carry

out an interrogation (I almost wrote "conversation") without loosening a few teeth. He meets his match in a *yakuza* hitman (Ryu Haku) who enjoys his work, which includes testing the blade of his knife on the knuckles of a punk hanging by his fingers from the roof of a tall building. Before their final confrontation Azuma's colleague and best friend (Sei Hiraizumi) ends up dead when Azuma discovers he is selling speed to the hit-man's boss, and Azuma's younger sister (Maiko Kawakami) falls into the hit-man's clutches, becoming an amphetamine addict. He even loses his job when he accidentally shoots a cop who had been trying to extract the barrel of Azuma's gun from the hitman's esophagus.

Kitano approaches this story as though he were doing over-the-top comedy: everything but the kitchen sink and then the kitchen sink. In this film, however, punches have taken the place of punch lines. There's hardly a joke anywhere, even of the "make my day" variety. This might not matter so much if the punches hit home, but for all the action, there is not much excitement, even of the Dirty Harry sort. Kitano not only lays it on too thick, but too conventionally. When the hitman puts his gun to Azuma's forehead and Azuma's hand creeps towards his knife, we know what's coming: we've seen it coming in a thousand other cop thrillers. Also, too many of the scenes are just one tough guy working over another. A little of this goes a long way, and Kitano give us a movie full of it. His renegade hero becomes a self-destructive loner whose constant violence is more numbing than cathartic. Walking out of the theater I felt as though I'd spent two hours in his interrogation room—sitting on the wrong side of the table.

Sotsugyo Ryoko: Nihon kara Kimashita
Trip to a Strange Kingdom (1993)

Directed by Shusuke Kaneko. Screenplay by Nobuyuki Isshiki. Produced by Toho and Bandai Visual. With Yuji Oda, Takeshi Kaga, Mayu Tsuruta. (98 mins.)

Few of the millions crooning in *karaoke* clubs will ever fill stadiums, but we all have our dreams of stardom, pop or otherwise. *Sotsugyo Ryoko: Nihon kara Kimashita*, a silly but entertaining movie about a young man who becomes a pop idol in a mythical Southeast Asian country, allows us to live out some of them. The situation is similar to that of *Bokura wa Minna Ikiteiru*, another film by *Sotsugyo* scriptwriter Nobuyuki Ishhiki, but instead of four salarymen caught up in a Third World war, one salaryman-to-be stumbles into a Third World time warp.

Yasuo Miki (Yuji Oda) dreams of becoming a pop star like Hideki Saijo (remember the Japanese cover of "YMCA"?). Instead, he is a dweeb who goes through life apologizing for his existence, regards kissing girls as a form of torture, and after four years at a mediocre college, is as innocent of thought as the day he entered. Yasuo is eager and ready to take his place as a cog in the corporate machine, but first he begs his boss-to-be for a last fling before buckling down: a graduation trip to Chitowan, a Southeast Asian country with wonderful ruins that he is crazy to see.

He boss agrees, but when Yasuo arrives in the land of his dreams, he finds that the Chitowanese are mad about old Japanese pop music—the stalls are full of pirated Pink Lady and Seiko Matsuda tapes and the native boatman croon *enka*. Poor Yasuo develops a horrible cases of the runs, however, and, at a critical moment, meets a strange Japanese man with a roll of toilet paper hooked to his belt.

His savior is a promoter named Momoyama (Takeshi Kaga) who is looking for new blood—and asks Yasuo if he would like to try a singing career. Though Yasuo is dubious (what about his archaeological itinerary?) Momoyama is persuasive. Soon, as the appropriately named Ippatsu Taro (One-Shot Taro), he is making his first appearance before the TV cameras. Incredibly, his first number, a disco retread, makes an immediate hit and a star is born.

Sotsugyo wields a broad comic brush. Oda, a pop singer in his own right, plays Yasuo as a grinning, bespectacled buffoon. Also, the Chitowan he conquers is as authentically Southeast Asian as the Bali of a Hope and Crosby road movie. When Ippatsu Taro becomes the national rage (though he can barely carry a tune), an heir to a rubber fortune invites him to his estate and, as they dine under the stars, appears to offers him his sister in marriage. (Given his broken Japanese, it is hard to be sure). The sister is a big fan and, to Taro's lust-befuddled eyes, a vision of exotic delight. He agrees. But then his old girlfriend, Reiko (Mayu Tsuruta), arrives with his parents and begs him to return to Japan. Should he hold his farewell concert and retire to a life as a Chitowanan grandee, or return to the nine-to-nine grind and his role as Reiko's eternally platonic lover? Having seen similar questions posed dozens of times before, we think we know the answer. But *Sotsugyo* surprises us, pleasantly.

Oda milks laughs from Ippatsu's awfulness, while making us like him in all his dweebishness. Kaga does a wonderfully slimy turn as the promoter; he seems to have had plenty of inspiration from real-life models. Mayu Tsuruta's Reiko initially impresses as cultivated, sophisticated, internationalized, and something of a terror in a designer dress. By the end, however, she has begun to resemble a human being.

Sotsugyo Ryoko is a clever entertainment with a satirical bite. Somehow, though, I don't think the soundtrack album will sell.

Spriggan
(1998)

Directed by Hirotsugu Kawasaki. **Screenplay by** Yasutaka Ito and Hirotsugu Kawasaki, **Executive production by** Katsuhiro Otomo. **Produced by** Shogakkan and Bandai Visual, TBS, and Toho. (90 mins.)

Animation has long accounted for a major share of box office in Japan and its producers are discovering that it is eminently exportable as well. One of the avatars of the overseas Japanimation boom is Katsuhiro Otomo, whose 1988 *Akira*, an SF animation set in a nuclear-devastated Tokyo, made *anime otaku* (animation geeks) of legions of foreign fans. Since then Otomo has embarked on several film projects—none, however, quite as ambitious as *Akira*.

In his latest project, *Spriggan*, Otomo incorporates new advances in computer graphics into a hyperkinetic, hyperviolent, hyperbusy SF action-adventure that plays like an episode in the adventures of the young Indy Jones, set in the present instead of the early decades of the century. As viscerally exciting as a video battle game and just about as easy to follow, *Spriggan* is obviously made for export to *anime otaku* abroad, but to this non-*otaku* outlander, it seems that Otomo and director Hirotsugu Kawasaki are recycling and reworking familiar SF *anime* motifs and formulas, not reinventing the genre. Otomo-quality animation, yes, but Steven Spielberg did this kind of thing better.

Based on a *manga* by Hiroshi Takashige and Ryoji Minagawa that ran in *Shonen Sunday* from 1989 to 1996, the story resembles *Raiders of the Lost Ark*: Three members of a secret organization named Arkam are exploring Turkey's Mt. Ararat—the Biblical landing site of Noah's Ark—when they stumble upon what appears to be the Ark itself — and are obliterated, together with three U.S. military satellites, by a massive magnetic force field.

Half a year later, Arkam's number one agent (in organizational jargon, Spriggan), a high-school boy named Yu Ominae, gets a rude shock when he is nearly blown to bits by an explosives-laden classmate. He also receives an unsettling message: "Noah will be your grave." Storming into Arkam's Tokyo office to demand an explanation, Yu find photos of the bodies of the exploration party members, together with another message: "Yu Ominae, your time has come." Yu immediately leaves for Turkey to unearth the mysterious author of these messages, who evidently wants him dead—but why? After leaving the Istanbul airport, he walks into a lethal trap that he escapes by being as buff and tough as Arnold Schwarzenegger in one of his younger robotic incarnations, only far more agile. When he finally arrives at Arkam's camp on Mt. Ararat, after his own people nearly waste him as one of the enemy, he finds out more—and the pieces of the puzzle fall into place.

Arkam, it turns out, has a rival in its race to unlock the Ark's mysteries: a ruthless U.S.-government special assault team, whose members include a murderous block of human granite named Fightman and a fiendishly clever trickster named Little Boy. They are commanded by a pale-faced bionic boy with extraordinary psychic powers, including the ability to freeze attacking enemies dead in their tracks.

Arkam, other the other hand, is devoted to protecting humanity from immense forces sealed in the remains of an ancient supercivilization that had been destroyed in a war with similarly advanced rivals. If those forces are unleashed, mankind will follow its ancestors into oblivion. Naturally, the Americans, the original unleashers of nuclear Armageddon, are greedy for the power, careless of the risk. It's up to Arkam to stop them! The ensuing battle between good and evil features a enormous amount of video-game violence, with a correspondingly high body count. Yu and his fighting companion, a blond Spriggan named Jean-Jacques, account for many of the victims, while remaining virtually indestructible themselves. One reason: they are wearing special battle suits that increase their strength by a power of thirty.

Given that FBI, CIA, and other U.S. government agents, rogue and otherwise, are routinely cast as the bad guys in Hollywood films, I wasn't too surprised by the choice of villains in Spriggan. But I was puzzled by the title, until I did a bit of poking about on the Internet and discovered that it is a name for a grubby-looking and prank-loving variety of English fairy. Not quite the image, one would think, for a stud fighting machine. But given that the film's target otaku audience is more into firepower than fairy lore, perhaps it doesn't matter. Just sit back and enjoy the carnage, guys.

Sukiyaki

(1995)

Directed by Jun'ichi Suzuki. Screenplay by Jun'ichi Suzuki and Tetsuo Osugi. Produced by Film Voice. With Sachiko Hidari, Kamio Kawachi, Yuka Sekiya, Rika Sekiya, Jin Yamaguchi, Kai Shishido, Mieharu. (94 mins.)

I've always wondered what marketing genius decided to give "Ue o Muite Aruko" (I'll Walk With My Head Held High) the title "Sukiyaki" when it was released in the United States in 1963. This song by Kyu Sakamoto is about smiling through tears, not satisfying a craving for beef, but the English title made a loopy kind of sense; it identified the song, unforgettably, as Japanese and helped push it to number one on the American charts (the only Japanese pop song to ever achieve that distinction).

There is a deeper connection between sukiyaki and Sukiyaki, Jun'ichi Suzuki's latest film. Set in Yokohama's Isezaki-cho—the open-air mall near Kannai Station—it depicts the lives of a family that runs a Western-style restaurant called Boston Grill. The matriarch, Hanako (Sachiko Hidari), loves sukiyaki. To her, the bubbling broth, full of nourishing delights waiting to be plucked by eager chopsticks, symbolizes familial warmth and happiness. It's the taste of home.

But home is not what it used to be. Hanako, who suffers from Alzheimer's disease, has become a worry to her son, Ryohei (Kamio Kawachi), and her twin granddaughters, Yuka (Yuka Sekiya) and Rika (Rika Sekiya). She is forever reliving the horror of the war years, or wandering off alone. Yuka tries to help, but she is an epileptic who is afraid to venture far from home. Though Ryohei is determined to care for his mother, he is busy trying, without much success, to run the restaurant. Most of the burden thus falls on Rika, who works at a nearby post office, but spends her evenings and many of her days waiting tables at the restaurant and watching over of Hanako. When will she ever have a life of her own? A dweebish salesman (Jin Yamaguchi), whose father owns a thriving trading company, has an answer to that question, not one she is sure she likes. Then she meets a ship's cook (Kai Shishido) who is wild and rude, but has a wonderful way with a croquette. He offers her something that her salesman admirer does not.

This is traditional family-drama material, but as director Suzuki notes in the program, hardly anyone is making traditional family dramas any more, for either the big or small screen. The genre, with its stress on the mundane and its frequent descents into bathos, strikes many younger Japanese as turgid and dull. Suzuki, who began his career in the Nikkatsu roman porno factory and made his straight feature debut in 1988 with Marilyn ni Aitai (Shiro and Marilyn), is well aware of these pitfalls. Though Sukiyaki is thematically in the family-drama tradition, its approach to the problems of aging is refreshingly free of the usual cant, its mood surprisingly light.

In some ways a throwback, this quietly appealing film also represents an ambitious attempt to point the way forward for the Japanese film industry. What we need, says Suzuki, are more truly independent filmmakers working out of a personal commitment, fewer subcontractors filling holes in a distributor's line-up. I think he has a point. In *Sukiyaki* Tetsuo Osugi's script helps him make it. While resorting to mistaken-identity gags that were a wheeze before the *Patty Duke Show* went into reruns, it tells its story with vigor, charm, and little waste motion.

As the cook, Kai Shishido has the rugged good looks and feral energy of the young Toshiro Mifune. His career should be interesting to watch. As the cook's friend, who takes his place behind the grill and touches Yuka's heart, Mieharu is goofily sincere, winningly restrained. Though relative amateurs, Yuka and Rika Sekiya bring a credibility to the film that trick photography could never equal.

At the end *Sukiyaki* ties all its various strands neatly together. Shall I tell you what is playing on the sound track and what is being planned for dinner? Enough said that the song, dish, and movie make an upbeat, satisfying blend. Enjoy.

Suna no Ue no Robinson
A Sand Castle Model Home Family (1989)

Written and directed by Jun'ichi Suzuki. **Produced by** Big Bang, Ultra Kikaku, and Japan Home Video. **With** Yoko Asaji, Yasuo Daichi, Hitomi Takahashi, Shun'ichi Hashimoto, Takejiro Suzuki, Natsuki Asakawa, Shoichi Ozawa. (105 mins.)

"There are two tragedies in life," said George Bernard Shaw. "One is not to get your heart's desire. The other is to get it." In Japan, the heart's desire of the middle class is a home of one's own. In recent years, however, skyrocketing land prices have forced many to place that desire on hold. *Suna no Ue no Robinson* tells the story of an average family that finds its dream house—to its everlasting regret.

Based on a novel by Ryo Ueno, *Suna* begins as a full-throttle black comedy but gradually decelerates to a TV-drama ending. One problem is the cluttered script. In boiling Ueno's opus down to size, scriptwriter and director Jun'ichi Suzuki retained its *tour d'horizon* of contemporary social issues. In addition to soaring land prices, the movie comments on school bullying, entrance exam-stress, office romances, working mothers, job-hopping salarymen, juvenile crime, and harassing phone calls. Even so, Suzuki films this material a light, humanizing touch. His family never becomes walking headlines and his film never completely loses its comic tone.

The Kido family—Mom (Yoko Asaji), Dad (Yasuo Daichi) and their three kids—are crowded together like so many happy clams in a public housing flat. They want a house (who doesn't?) but as Mom says, "The only way we'll get one is if we win the lottery or if Dad gets run over by a car and we collect the insurance money." There is, however, another way: a real estate developer announces that it is recruiting an "ideal family" to live rent-free for a year in a two-hundred-million-yen model home. There is string attached, however—they must serve as shills for the developer while their ideal home is open to the public.

The Kidos apply, are selected and promptly find snakes in their new Garden of Eden. The young saleswoman (Hitomi Takahashi) who shows the house to customers has the temperament of a drill sergeant, while the customers are snoops, schnorrers, and other undesirables. Also, as "ideals" the Kidos become targets of that most Japanese (and human) of emotions: envy. Dad is demoted to demonstrating kitchen gadgets in a department store, Mom gets nasty anonymous phone calls, elder son Kyohei (Shunichi Hashimoto) is shaken down by a trio of punks for "insurance money," younger son Sota (Takejiro Suzuki) receives a razzing welcome from his classmates after they see his picture in a newspaper ad, and little Yoko (Natsuki Asakawa) is handed a box by a smarmy girl she has never seen before. It contains a dead kitten.

The first part of the film rattles along amusingly enough, but Suzuki wants more than laughs—he wants his happy family to become a problem family. The film's descent into home-drama *Sturm und Drang* is only intermittently interesting, while its assurances that nothing bad will happen to the Kidos are mostly unconvincing. Dad finally quits his job, leaves home, and becomes a bum, but he's a *nice* bum, who stays mostly sober and has whimsical conversations about bumhood with an older bum (Shoichi Ozawa). Not the type, in other words, that one is likely to find sleeping in Shinjuku Station.

Suzuki gets lively performances from his actors, including such well-known names as Hiroyuki Nagato and Kiyoshi Nishikawa in cameo roles. Yasuo Daichi brightens Dad's stolid, Mr. Average persona with his cherubic charm, but Yoko Asaji, as Mom, gives the movie its real spark. Mom has a face that registers every tremor of emotion and a personality that, even when she is most harassed, never loses its bubbly vivacity. The martyred mother look is absent from her repertoire.

Suna no Ue no Robinson ought to be shown to Japan-bashers who think that consumers here could spend away the trade deficit, if they were only given a chance. A glance inside the Kido's rabbit hutch would give them a quick lesson in the realities and limits of the Japanese dream.

Super no Onna
Supermarket Woman (1996)

Written and directed by Juzo Itami. Produced by Itami Production. With Nobuko Miyamoto, Masahiko Tsugawa. (127 mins.)

Juzo Itami is closing in on the ten-billion-yen mark for career theatrical-film rentals. Translated into U.S. dollars, that may not sound like much, but few living Japanese directors can match Itami as a money spinner. Animation wizard Hayao Miyazaki, Tora-san series director Yoji Yamada, and veteran Kon Ichi-kawa are the only other ones who come to mind.

One secret to Itami's success is his ability to package his social comedies as adroitly and consistently as McDonald's packages Big Macs. First there is the thematic hook, which addresses real-life audience interests and concerns, be it death (*Ososhiki*), taxes (the two *Marusa no Onna* films), sex (*Ageman*), violence (*Mimbo no Onna*) or the proper way to make a bowl of *ramen* noodles (*Tampopo*). Second, the Itami take on these themes is always practically informative. A corporate warrior who considers most movies a criminal waste of time can walk out of a Itami film feeling satisfied that he has learned something, if nothing more than how to cheat the taxman. Third, for all his appearance of pushing commercial cinematic limits and tweaking the noses of the powerful, Itami is predictable in a way that many filmgoers find reassuring. They know exactly what they are going to get. Just as in the Tora-san series, certain elements vary little from film to film, be they the main cast members, including Nobuko Miyamoto and Masa-hiko Tsugawa, the punchy score and even the bright, colorful ad posters, drawn in the popular *hetauma* (good-bad) style. Finally, by appearing in ad after ad and interview after interview, Itami has become one of the few directors, Japanese or foreign, whose name and face are known by the non-moviegoing public. Like Alfred Hitchcock and Colonel Sanders, he not only represents his product, but has come to seem bigger than it.

Itami's latest film, *Super no Onna* (Supermarket Woman) is in many ways a standard Itami effort. What could be more down-home than a movie about a housewife who, by applying know-how acquired through countless hours of grocery shopping, boosts a failing neighborhood supermarket to success? Naturally, the housewife is played by Nobuko Miyamoto, with her patented spunk, energy, and toothy, sardonic grin. Once again her male foil is Masahiko Tsugawa, this time as a former elementary-school classmate who is the supermarket's managing director. While playing yet another of his sexy but ineffective males who brings out the mother in women—he's as close as a Japanese actor will ever get to Marcello Mastroianni—Tsugawa out-mugs even his rubber-faced co-star.

As the film begins, Tsugawa's supermarket, the Shojikiya (Honest Store), is being thrashed by a glitzy new discount rival, whose unscrupulous owner aims to take over Tsugawa's supermarket and jack up prices. Meanwhile, Tsugawa is quietly drinking himself into oblivion when he runs across Miyamoto, who has been shopping in his store and does not like what she has found: wilting veggies, unkempt shelves, dirty floors, and clueless staff in food-stained uniforms. There is more, but far from being offended by her diatribe on his store's defects, Tsugawa is fascinated. This woman can help him! So she does, but not before running up against opposition in the form of a yen-squeezing store manager, a crooked master butcher, and the discount store's Mr. Big. As was her lawyer in *Mimbo no Onna*, Miyamoto's housewife is dauntless, fearless, and adept at recruiting the store's employees and customers to the cause of justice and truth—in packaging.

Super no Onna, as Itami said in a comment to the press, is a "fastball" aimed at his core audience. It is also an attempt to come back from the box office disaster of *Shizukana Seikatsu*, Itami's misconceived attempt at serious filmmaking. Does it hit the strike zone? Like his better movies, *Super no Onna* is briskly paced, cleverly constructed and wittily instructive. You will be a smarter shopper when you leave the theater. But those expecting something new from a director who was once the most original in Japanese films will be disappointed. Having abandoned the dangers of experimentation for the more certain delights of big box-office numbers, Itami has become a purveyor of an easily digestible product for the cinematic mass consumer.

Will you be a having an order of fries with that movie, ma'am?

Swallowtail
Swallowtail Butterfly (1996)

Written and directed by Shunji Iwai. Cinematography by Noboru Shinoda. Produced by Uronsha, Pony Canyon, Nippon Herald, Ace Pictures, and Fuji TV. With Chara, Ayumi Ito, Hiroshi Mikami, Atsuro Watabe, Abraham Levin, Yosuke Eguchi. (149 mins.)

Since the success of his debut feature, *Love Letter*, Shunji Iwai has acquired a reputation as a director who may be impeccably hip, but knows hows to fill seats—a golden combination that has translated into media attention and creative freedom.

Iwai has used that freedom to film *Swallowtail*, a fantastic vision of a near-future Tokyo that has become a mecca for yen hunters from around the globe. That was also a fairly accurate description of the city during the bubble years, when Iwai first conceived this project. *Swallowtail*, however, bears little relation to the spate of Asians-in-Japan films released early in the decade, with their view of their Asian heroes as innocent victims of Japanese prejudice and exploitation. Instead it is closer in look and spirit to Ridley Scott's *Blade Runner*, whose moral universe is murky, to say the least.

The matrix of his dark future is a multicultural encampment on the outskirts of Yen Town (i.e., Tokyo) called Aozora (Blue Sky), whose ragtag inhabitants engage in every imaginable hustle, from whoring and contract-killing to puncturing the tires of passing Japanese motorists so they will have to make an unscheduled stop at the encampment's filling station. Among the inhabitants are Glico (rock singer Chara), a Chinese prostitute who has tattooed her chest with a swallowtail butterfly as a way of identifying her otherwise anonymous body, an orphaned teenage girl (Ayumi Ito) whom Glico takes in and dubs Ageha (Caterpillar), and Feihong (Hiroshi Mikami), a street-smart Chinese illegal who is in love with Glico and will do any for a yen.

The story revolves around a cassette tape that Feihong and two other Aozora residents—a cool, calculating Chinese named Ran (Atsuro Watabe) and an easygoing, if excitable Iranian, named Nihat (Abraham Levin)—find in the stomach of a dead Japanese gangster. The tape, they discover, contains computer code for making counterfeit ¥10,000-yen bills. Soon the Aozorians are fooling ATMs and getting rich quick. Feihong uses his ill-gotten gains to start a nightclub, the Yentown, with Glico as the star chanteuse. Before long, Glico is packing them in and attracting the attention of a major record label. Meanwhile, the rightful owners of the tape, a Chinese gang headed by the long-haired Ryou Ryanki (Yosuke Eguchi), are hot on the trail of the thieves.

Together with cinematographer Noboru Shinoda, Iwai has created a phantasmagoric world that is continually splintering into brilliant visual fragments. The aim is to draw us into the characters' turbulent inner lives, to share their synapses as they try to survive on Yentown's margins. The approach resembles that of Oliver Stone's *Natural Born Killers*, though Iwai does not indulge in the overwrought editorializing that made Stone's vision of a media-mad, violence-obsessed America so oppressive. Instead he sees Glico, Ageha, Feihong, and even Ryou Ryanki as admirable in their ambition and spunk. But though Iwai generates considerable visual energy himself, his Yentown lacks the degenerate glamor and dangerous aura of Ridley Scott's Los Angeles in the year 2019. We are too aware that Aozora is a shantytown set in the middle of a bayside wasteland and that the Yentown club is a stage for the film's made-for-MTV musical interludes.

Also, the film's condemnation of a Japan whose yen soils all it touches seems too pat and, in these recessionary times, passé. It is also strange that, after printing all those fake Fukuzuwas, the denizens of Aozora would still be living like funky bohemians, not *nouveau riche*. Finally, the film's mixing of English, Chinese, and Japanese, often in the same sentence, has its charms, but like the movie's childish scams (literally childish: at one point, the Aozorians hire school kids to pass the phony bills) lacks credibility and even comprehensibility. The Japanese dialogue often comes out sounding too fluent for supposed non-natives; the English lines, too garbled for Japanese subtitle non-readers. Is there a dialogue coach in the house?

Synch
(1998)

Written and directed by Masahiro Muramatsu. **Produced by** Small Light Pictures. **With** Nae Yamazaki, Kei Noda, Minoru Mitsuyasu. (85 mins.)

The biggest barrier to anyone hoping to break into filmmaking has always been the expense. One solution is to shoot in 8mm—that time-honored choice of the directorial novice. More and more often, however, novices are opting for video, perhaps the easiest, cheapest way to go. Video, however, has become the No. 2 pencil of the electronic media age: utilitarian, universal, and, let's face it, declassé. How can our novice express her soul-searing ironies about God and Man in the medium that Dad used to record her high school graduation?

But in his psychic fantasy *Synch*, Masahiro Muramatsu uses video's very humbleness to create links between his Gen X characters and his Gen X audience. Muramatsu's graduation project at the Tokyo University of Art and Design, the film has the mood of a wandering, free-associating rap session among age mates. It also offers an unmediated look inside his charmed circle for us outsiders. Most *seishun eiga* (youth movies) are tinged by an idealizing nostalgia, even if their makers are barely out of film school. *Synch*, however, feels as though the twenty-seven-year-old director and his actors are experiencing the emotions of the characters in real time. It's the home movie of a generational *zeitgeist*.

The central premise, however, could have come from the sugar-stimulated brain of a Hollywood scriptwriter penning a sequel to *There's Something About Mary*. Three strangers—an effervescent apprentice hair stylist (Nae Yamazaki), a fashionably goateed biker (Kei Noda), and a chubby bespectacled college student (Minoru Mitsuyasu)—discover that they can read each other's minds. It is, they find, like having a free cell phone—the ultimate Gen X dream. One can well imagine how the above-mentioned scriptwriter would develop this idea, with plenty of sexual complications and gross-out humor. How about a scene of the biker having a soul-baring exchange with the stylist while engaged in a session of rumpy-pumpy with his girlfriend? How about a cut to the student, seething with frustration, listening in? A laff riot, no?

No, Matsumura would say, not really. Instead, he has opted for a faux documentary approach, with the scenes of this threesome's various encounters, both physical and otherwise, dated with titles (the story begins on 11/12/96 and ends on 1/12/97) and presented with maximum poetic spontaneity, minimum structure. Nothing builds, including the romance among the three principals. Strangers when they meet, they keep their distance while pursuing their individual destinies

This is not to say that Matsumura totally downplays the comic potential of his off-beat triangle. In one scene the student, Minoru, is carrying on a conversation with the stylist, Kumi, in the men's room when a pony-tailed stranger walks in and finds him talking to the walls. (The telepathic trio voice their thoughts, with Kumi using the prop of a portable phone and the two men speaking into the air.)

His central interest, however, is the relationships of his Gen X characters, who find beaming brain waves through walls easier than achieving real intimacy. It's obvious from the beginning that the two men have a crush on Kumi—a vision of perky, pouty loveliness in an orange cloth coat—but it also becomes obvious that neither is going to do much about it. After their initial meeting in a field, where they play telepathic games like kids with a new walkie-talkie set, they go their separate ways as if nothing too bizarre has happened.

Emotional connections, however, have been made. When Kumi is left waiting at the station by a forgetful pal, she tries to contact Minoru to vent her anger and disappointment, but he fails to tune in. Later, however, both Minoru and Kumi catch a rambling monologue the biker, Satsuki, delivers to a date. The subtext: he is nervous at the prospect of turning twenty-five and leaving his youth behind. Perhaps to fend off encroaching adulthood, Satsuki buys a new motorbike and breaks up with his old girlfriend. Meanwhile, Minoru interviews for a job and Kumi finally meets her mysterious pal. There is

a sense that a turning point is approaching, when the trio assemble on the beach to celebrate Satsuki's twenty-fifth birthday.

Matsumura, who won a Pia Film Festival Grand Prize in 1997 for *Synch*, employs a rough, fragmented *cinema verité* style that may be intended to enhance his film's credibility, but makes it, in places, hard to watch and follow. In the night scenes, especially, the characters are little more than specks in the murk, muttering over the pounding of the surf. Yet for all its inwardness and idiosyncrasies, *Synch* gets its message across. It doesn't take a mind-reader to understand the blithe emptiness of its characters' lives.

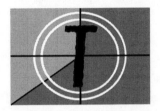

Tada Hitotabi no Hito
The Singing Bamboo (1995)

Written and directed by Tetsu Kato. Produced by JJS Plan Sequence. With Namihiko Omura, Emiko Yamamoto, Sachiko Hidari. (105 mins.)

"Starving artist" has a quaint ring in these days. One imagines Knut Hamsun down to his last few crusts in a frigid garret or Henry Miller cheerfully scrounging meals from American tourists in Paris. Today, their descendants are teaching composition at the local commmunity college.

In *Tada Hitotabi no Hito*, Tetsu Kato updates the starving artist story, focusing on an eccentric musician's journey through a private abyss to salvation. Despite belabored minimalist symbolism (his hero is forever trudging through empty landscapes) and wearisome stylistic affectations (including interminable hand-held camera shots), Kato seems to have seen that abyss himself, in his imagination if nowhere else. This may not be an autobiographical film, but it is a deeply personal and idealistic one. It tells us what is it is to live for one's art, not one's art career.

Namihiko (Namihiko Omura) plays jazz *shakuhachi* (bamboo flute) in clubs. Though he hustles for gigs, he barely earns enough to put Cup Noodle on the table. His girlfriend (Emiko Yamamoto), who lives with him in a grubby walkup, complains about his lack of ambition and drive, while his landlady harasses him for the rent. He receives a reprieve from this dreary existence in an invitation to his older sister's wedding. Back home in the countryside, however, his mother (Sachiko Hidari), younger sister, and an old school friend all ask the same weary question: what are you going to do with your life? He briefly toys with the idea of getting a real job, but has a change of heart at the plant gate. It's got to be art or nothing, he decides.

With little more than his *shakuhachi* and renewed determination, he returns to Tokyo. Abandoned by everyone—his mother has told him to never darken her door again and his girlfriend has flown the coop—he takes to the streets and begins to play his music to the sky, the pavement, and anyone who will listen. A certain self-pity is inherent in such a tale. Ah! The poor suffering artist, says the (presumably) equally suffering film director.

The film also self-consciously strives after archaic romanticism. The hero's instrument, the *shakuhachi*, has the same wandering minstrel associations in Japan as the lute has in West. Playing it soulfully as he drifts down Tokyo streets, his long hair blowing and his wrinkled coat flapping in the wind, Namihiko has an air of pathos that he would not have if he had strummed, say, the banjo.

Though *Tada Hitotabi* could have easily degenerated into etiolated fantasizing, Kato has stripped it bare of cinematic artifice. He used only a brief treatment and had his actors make up their own dialogue as they went along. He also cut his big emotional scenes to the bone. Just as well, because singer-songwriter Omura isn't much of an emoter. He is, however, a strong, dark presence.

What remains is an unsparingly intimate film drenched in the piercing, otherworldly sound of the *shakuhachi* (played by Yukihiko Mitsuka). By forcing his actors, both professional and amateur, to *be* instead of act Kato has brought them closer to us. Namihiko never says or does much that is conventionally revealing, but as we watch him wandering about Tokyo, falling ever deeper into madness and despair, we begin to see him with a directness that most films don't permit. Despite our daily encounters with street people, we often find it hard to imagine how they became what they are—the gap between them and the hurrying crowd is too wide. *Tada Hitotabi* relates the process of disintegration in intimate, unsparing detail, until we understand almost too well.

Namihiko, however, is more than a sifter through trash bags; he is an artist. Having lost everything, including his ego, he finds that he still has his music. As he hits bottom, the pallid noodlings of his earlier career give way to melodies that soar and dip with a wild, careless beauty amidst Tokyo's urban gray-

ness and gloom. He is free and so, for a few moments, are we.

Tadon to Chikuwa ✱
Tadon and Chikuwa (1998)

Directed by Jun Ichikawa. **Screenplay by** Jun Ichikawa with Nobusuke Sato ("Tadon"), and Masashi Nakamura ("Chikuwa"). **Produced by** Gaga Pictures. **With** Koji Yakusho, Jimpachi Nezu, Hiroyuki Sanada, Tomoro Taguchi. (102 mins.)

Of all Japanese directors now working Jun Ichikawa is probably the closest to Yasujiro Ozu in style, spirit, and talent. *Tokyo Kyodai* was a deliberate Ozu homage, while other films, such as *Tokiwaso no Seishun* and *Tokyo Yakyoku*, evoke Ozu in their quiet tone, deliberate pace, humanistic storytelling, and elegant shot-making. Though low-key, his films contain moments of sublime beauty and emotional truth. But because he is working in the 1990s, not the 1950s, Ichikawa has been typed, dismissively, as *jimi* (plain) and eclipsed by directors with flashier styles and trendier concerns.

Ichikawa long chafed under this label and now, in *Tadon to Chikuwa*, he has spectacularly abandoned it. In his films characters often seethe with suppressed emotion, but here they explode. He films these eruptions using surreal computer graphics—not the most Ozuesque of devices. Based on short stories by Makoto Shiina, *Tadon to Chikuwa* is an anthology film with two heroes and two separate story lines that link, improbably but satisfyingly, at the end.

The first story, "Tadon," is that of Kita (Koji Yakusho), a cabby who spends his days listening to the conversations of strangers, but is never allowed to join in. As this former taxi driver knows, after months of tooling about an endless urban maze, while other human beings ignore your existence, your mind begins to play tricks. In an inner monologue that unfolds during an opening montage, Kita begins to wonder where he is moving through the streets—or whether the streets are moving through him.

Then he picks up Anzai (Jimpachi Nezu), a salaryman on the way to an assignation with a young lover at a distant hotel. On the way, Kita begins talking with the air of desperate man whose obsequious smiles might give way at any moment to ferocious snarls. Anzai, thinking only of the delights to come, toys with Kita. When the cabby asks him what he does for a living, Anzai says he makes *tadon* (charcoal balls). Kita goes along with this charade, but inside he is ready to burst. When the explosion comes, Anzai finds himself on a deserted riverbank making "*tadon*" from black slime and wondering if he will survive this cab ride from hell.

The second story, "Chikuwa," features Asami (Hiroyuki Sanada), a minor novelist with a writing block. Sucking on an unlit cigar as though it were a malignant lollipop, he strides irritably into the Tokyo night. Stopping at an *oden* stand, he orders *chikuwa*, which might be described as a fish-paste hot dog. When the stall man says he doesn't have it, Asami takes out what he calls his personal "*chikuwa*," sprays the *oden* with it and, cackling with glee, scampers away.

His next stop is a Japanese-style restaurant whose manager (Tomoro Taguchi) is a fan. Since Asami's last visit, the manager has redecorated the place but to Asami's fevered brain, the new atmosphere is as inviting as an operating room staffed by trolls. Worse, the restaurant is packed with leering, grimacing fools making sneering remarks about him, while the *chikuwa* he orders crawls and slithers on his plate like so many graveyard worms. Suddenly losing his appetite—and upchucking his dinner—he retreats to the men's room, where he makes a horrifying discovery—his "*chikuwa*" is gone! Vowing revenge on his tormentors, he explodes in an orgy of violence that litters the restaurant with bodies and splatter its walls with, not blood, but a rainbow of colors, like a Jackson Pollock action painting. Is this slaughter of innocents really happening, we wonder, or is it, like Anzai's moving feast, a figment of his overheated imagination?

Ichikawa's heroes are familiar types from his other films: lonely guys with sensitive souls who can't adjust to the world around them. Also, his subtle, sure grasp of character is still much in evidence, as is his fine, sharp eye for composition and color. He can make even his comic grotesques come revoltingly alive, while injecting his scenes of stylized mayhem with ironic beauty.

Koji Yakusho turns in a powerful, effective performance as Kita, unraveling with a velocity and force that are all too real. Hiroyuki Sanada's Asami is a less likable type—disintegrating egotists are not high on many sympathy lists— but he conveys his descent to madness with a Dostoyevskian flair. Also, he gets to play with neater, if grosser, effects. Ozu's characters may have logged many hours at the dinner table but none, I believe, ever had a chance to projectile vomit in Technicolor red. Thus does the art of film progress.

Takkyu Onsen
Ping-Pong Hot Springs (1998)

Written and directed by Gen Yamakawa. Produced by NTV, Hakuhodo, and Nihon Shuppan Hanbai. With Kaiko Matsuzaka, Keizo Kanie, Yosuke, So Yamanaka, Senri Sakurai. (110 mins.)

In 1996 Masayuki Suo, a protegé of Juzo Itami, had a surprise smash hit with *Shall We Dance?*, a comedy that about a middle-aged businessman's infatuation with a young dance instructor that became the highest grossing Japanese film ever released in the United States. Gen Yamakawa's second feature, *Takkyu Onsen*, might be described as a Suo film by proxy. Though Suo himself did not become directly involved, Suo's production company, Altamira Pictures, was instrumental in bringing the film to the screen, and Yamakawa served as Suo's assistant director on *Shall We Dance?*

Takkyu, however, lacks the comic energy and emotional charge that make Suo's films so appealing. The film is Suo made nice (or rather nicer), with the oddball characters and feel-good story still intact, but the quirky edges smoothed over. Instead of a hilarious *pas de deux* in the company men's room, we get a heart-warming ping-pong duel in a funky old hot springs.

The film's central figure is, for a change, a woman, but she is, like Suo's male heroes, a decidedly unheroic type—a full-time housewife named Sonoko (Keiko Matsuzaka) whose life has been swallowed by routine, whose identity has become subsumed in her socially defined roles. Meanwhile, the beneficiaries of her incessant labors—her workaholic husband (Keizo Kanie) and flame-haired teenage son (Yosuke)—are barely aware of her existence. Like Suo's hero in *Shall We Dance?* she longs to somehow inject excitement into her dull life, but the usual escapes, including infidelity, don't appeal. She finally decides on a desperate expedient: calling a radio DJ for advice. The DJ, a flippant young woman named Kanae (Riho Makine), tells Sonoko to walk out the door and, soon after, she does, driving the family car to Takkyu Onsen (literally, Dragon Temple Hot Springs).

On the way, she picks up six stranded men who turn out to be the owners of hot springs inns. Takkyu Onsen, she hears them complain, is in dire need of a new gimmick to draw guests. *Karaoke* no longer does the trick—but what next? Arriving at the inn—a rambling old pile where she stayed twenty years ago with her husband—Sonoko tries to enjoy her newfound freedom, but she is still a housewife for whom a messy room is an invitation to battle. Soon, she is making the place spick-and-span, while thinking of ways to help the hot springs thrive again. Then she stumbles across an old ping-pong table and rediscovers an old love. Soon she has recruited Kohei (So Yamanaka), the young master of a rival inn, as a partner, and attracted the friendly attention of Odana,

(Senri Sakurai), a village elder. The hot springs, she tells them, was once a table-tennis (*takkyu*) mecca—why not make it one again?

But while Sonoko and her local allies are organizing a table-tennis tournament and giving the hot springs new characters for its name—allowing Dragon Temple to be read as Table Tennis instead—a subplot is brewing around Kanae and Kohei. Kanei, it turns out, is an innkeeper's daughter who left Takkyu Onsen and broke off a budding romance with Kohei to pursue fame and fortune as a DJ in the big city. Will Kanae and Kohei rekindle their old love? Will Sonoko and her new-found friends make their tournament a success? Will her rock-headed husband wake up and smell the coffee?

We see the answers, like a fat lob, coming from a long way off. The film's formula, like the volley contest that provides its climax, is more entertaining for participants than for paying spectators. The next time out, Yamakawa and company should try a box-office slam from a new angle.

Tekken

Metallic Boxer (1991)

Written and directed by Junji Sakamoto. Produced by Arato Genjiro Jimusho. With Bunta Sugawara, Takeshi Owa, Karen Kirishima. (128 mins.)

In *Raging Bull* Martin Scorese discarded the sappy melodrama endemic to the boxing genre and replaced it with a gritty naturalism derived from early postwar boxing broadcasts and news photos. He was obsessive and heavy-handed, grinding our faces in the hero's primitive emotions—and he brought us closer to the intoxicating thrill and brutal pain of boxing than any other director in the history of film.

In *Tekken* (Metallic Boxer), Junji Sakamoto hardly takes us inside the ring at all. Instead, he creates a pugilistic fantasy that seems to have sprung full-blown from a boy's comic. *Tekken* does not lack for action—enough blows are landed with tooth-rattling impact to satisfy most martial-arts fans—but it is closer in spirit to *Dragonball Z* than *Raging Bull*.

An ex-boxer (Bunta Sugawara) decides to sell the small lumber company he runs and and devote himself entirely to his boxing gym. His midlife career shift, however, is prompted more by sentiment than sense. Financially, the gym is on the ropes. Then he meets a reform-school alumnus (Takeshi Owa) who can demolish a rental-car agency with his bare fists. The ex-boxer become the kid's manager and together they start the long climb to the top.

Sakamoto, however, is not making another *Rocky*. He cuts the training-through-pain sequences to the bare minimum. The kid is a natural who obliterates his early opponents with almost ridiculous ease. (This is not hard to believe: Takeshi Owa, who plays the kid, became the Japanese middleweight champ in 1988.) Then, just before the big championship bout, the kid argues with his manager, tears off in his sports car and smashes into the rear end of a truck. His girlfriend (Karen Kirishima) survives, but his right hand is crushed in the wreck. His career, it would seem, is ended, but his real struggle has just begun.

Here *Tekken* heads off the genre trail into comic-book country, while presenting its absurdities with a straight face. It wants us to believe that a local veterinarian could design a prosthesis for the kid's ruined hand and start him on the comeback trail. The kid's new fist has a cyborgian look and power, but what, I wondered, are referees going to say when they learn he's got more in his glove than flesh and bone?

Instead of stepping into the ring, however, the kid squares off against a bizarre martial-arts club dedicated to cleansing the town of the weak and unfit, including boxers with damaged hands. From the moment the club members make their first appearance, looking like sinister cult converts in their white shirts and dark slacks, we know exactly where the film is heading: a big, climatic showdown.

Takeshi Owa has the right look and attitude for the boxer hero. When he puts a fist through a rental car counter, it's easy to believe that he makes his living with it. But out of the ring, Owa's acting is strictly from Palookaville. As the manager, Bunta Sugawara does not makes us forget Owa's deficiencies. He tries to humanize his character with lame comic schtick (one is his fear of dogs, even pooches who look like Lassie's cousin), but next to Owa, a for-real boxing pro, Sugawara comes across as a clownish amateur. Why, we ask, should this hardnosed kid respect this bumbling middle-aged man? Rather than supply the answers, Sakamoto performs radical surgery on the early, crucial establishing scenes: the boxer and manager seem to be celebrating their first victory before they are properly introduced.

Tekken is Sakamoto's second feature film. His first, the 1989 *Dotsuitarunen* (Knock Out) was another boxing movie starring Owa that won several awards and got Sakamoto the nod from executive producer Genjiro Arato to make a big-budget followup. With its story of a boxer making a comeback he knows might kill him, *Dotsuitarunen*, had a endearing vitality and genuine pathos, but *Tekken* is the product of a directorial ego run wild. The jumbling of shots that defy explanation, the jump cuts that kill continuity, and the general goofiness of the proceedings reminded me of John Simon's comment on the misuse of the artistic imagination: "It's very easy to be imaginative if you are incorrect: if you tie your necktie around your knee instead of around your neck, you are imaginative, but you are imaginative in an imbecile way."

Tekken comes out slugging and trips over that blasted necktie.

Tenkawa Densetsu Satsujin Jiken
The Noh Mask Murders (1991)

Directed by Kon Ichikawa. Screenplay by Kurishitei, Shin'ya Hidaka, and Shin'ichi Kabuki. Produced by Tenkawa Densetsu Satsujin Jiken Production Committee. With Takaaki Enoki, Takeshi Kusaka, Naomi Zaizen, Shota Yamaguchi, Keiko Kishi. (109 mins.)

The classic mystery, with its who-done-it puzzle and clever sleuth, still has its fans, but in the 1990s, as Hollywood filmmakers strive for new levels of violence, the dead dowagers in the library have largely disappeared from big screens, though they can still be found on small ones. Not yet in Japan, however. The latest film by Kon Ichikawa is such a mystery. Titled *Tenkawa Densetsu Satsujin Jiken* and produced by Haruki Kadokawa, it could have been scripted by Dame Agatha Christie herself, with assistance from a master of Noh. In fact, Ichikawa, who also co-wrote the script, is a devoted Christie fan who has taken "Kurishitei" (in Chinese characters) as his pen name.

The director of a popular series of mysteries starring Koji Ishizaka, as well as classics like *Burma no Tategoto* (The Burmese Harp, 1956) and *Sasameyuki* (The Makioka Sisters, 1983), Ichikawa hypes the classic formula with razor-tight editing, flashy crosscutting, and lavishly staged Noh performances. The film is a fast-paced puzzler that bogs down only toward the end. Instead of the literally explosive climaxes we have come to expect from Hollywood, *Tenkawa* supplies logorrheic explanations.

The story revolves around a Noh troupe headed by Kazunori Minakami (Takeshi Kusaka), an imperious and willful old man. The time has come for him to choose a successor, but he cannot decide between his granddaughter (Naomi Zaizen) and grandson (Shota Yamaguchi). Then a businessman drops dead near Shinjuku Station and the old man's *choro*, or right-hand man, is found draped over a tree branch near Tenkawa Village in Nara Prefecture. In the former case, the only clue is an bell charm from the Tenkawa Shrine. In the latter, the prime suspect is Mitsuhiko Asami (Takaaki Enoki), a freelance writer who was the last person seen talking to the *choro* before his death.

Asami, however, has an alibi in a mysterious older woman (Keiko Kishi) who had helped him out of

trouble with the police once before. He also takes a professional interest in the case: the son of an elite police bureaucrat, he has a cop's curiosity running in his veins. Snooping about, he unearths connections between the bell charm, his benefactor, and the Noh troupe. Another murder, this time on the Noh stage, sends him back to Tenkawa Village and puts him on the trail of the culprit.

The puzzle, as well as the relationships among the large cast of characters, are more complex than I have outlined here, but Ichikawa keeps the narrative lines untangled, the pace brisk, and the tension high. A technically impressive, youthfully agile performance from this seventy-five-year-old director. Ichikawa also drawn strong performances from his largely veteran cast, but his real discovery is Enoki, who displays a talent for light comedy as Asami.

Tenkawa doesn't escape the weaknesses endemic to the genre: the puzzle takes precedence over the people, and the plot is impossibly contrived. Even so, it provides fascinating behind-the-scenes peeks into the tightly knit world of Noh and the tangled web of Japanese family politics. Maybe someday Ichikawa will give us Miss Marple in a kimono.

Tenshi no Harawata: Akai Senko
Entrails of an Angel: Red Flashback (1994)

Written and directed by Takashi Ishii. Produced by Video Champ, King Record, and TV Tokyo. With Maiko Kawakami, Jimpachi Nezu. (88 mins.)

Takashi Ishii's characters are not romance-novel heroes translated to the screen or sexually unawakened adolescents, but adults who live out their sexuality to its limits, sometimes with deadly results. Like Brian De Palma, he can be accused of exploiting his women and overusing gore, but in the 1992 *Shindemo Ii* and the 1993 *Nude no Yoru* he proved that he can be stylish without being manipulative, intense without being pushy, intelligent without being pretentious. Though his theme is always the same—life, love, and death in the modern urban jungle—he never tires of finding new facets. As an explorer of the erotic, Ishii is an usually knowledgeable guide who, after his many expeditions, still stands in awe of his subject.

Ishii's *Tenshi no Harawata: Akai Senko* is an erotic thriller without the raw emotional charge of *Shindemo Ii* or the David Lynchian strangeness of *Nude no Yoru*. Instead it journeys to the fine line between acts and crimes of passion—and beyond. The sixth in the *Tenshi no Harawata* series, *Akai Senko* occasionally falls into standard genre attitudes, but it keeps the heat and tension high until the end. Porn taken to another level? Perhaps, but then so was *Dressed to Kill*.

As in all the series installments, the heroine is a young woman named Nami (Maiko Kawakami); the hero, a middle-aged man named Muraki (Jimpachi Nezu). They meet while Nami is taking still photos at the filming of a porno video. Watching the on-camera rape of a high-school girl by an older man, Nami recalls a similar incident from her own past. When Muraki, an editor visiting the set, sees that she can't control her emotions, he offers his assistance. Nami flees—Muraki reminds her of her assailant—but she can't forget him.

She tries to find comfort in the arms of a lesbian bar mama, but when she learns that the mama is playing the field, she drinks herself into a stupor and wakes up the next day naked in a love hotel. With no memory of what happened between bar and bed, she panics—who was her partner? She discovers him, a blood-soaked corpse, on the floor. Horrified, she runs from the hotel. The next day, she tells Muraki the whole story and shows him a video that the victim had shot at the scene of his death. Was she the one who did it?

I won't say more, only that the story has many twists and a few surprises. Perhaps, Ishii, like De Palma, has been taking lessons in suspense from the master, Alfred Hitchcock. In any event, he has timed his shocks well, especially the one that ends the film. Some are clichés—including the never-say-die-victim—but Ishii make most of them work. He succeeds, I think, because he is more interested in his characters than his plot points. We see, not just bodies in heat, but a complex interplay of desire and doubt, erotic passion and murderous rage.

Ishii's current Nami, Maiko Kawakami, may project the cutsey cuteness of a *baradoru* (variety idol) on one of the lamer game shows, but she can portray the adult woman beneath Nami's girlish exterior, who is at once frightened and bold, emotionally scarred and sexually confused. Through her eyes, we can see the lingering horror of rape, the shock of finding oneself a possible murderer, with no memory of the crime. She spends too much time in a quivering-jelly state, but hardly by choice. Ishii subjects Nami's system to so many jolts, alcoholic, and otherwise, it's a wonder she doesn't collapse entirely. As Muraki, Jimpachi Nezu presents himself as beacon of maturity and strength in Nami's frightening world, but other forces are also at work beneath his placid surface. He plays his hand well, almost too well, never flinching as blood flows on the TV screen.

Unlike many Japanese erotic thrillers, *Akai Senko* does not treat rape as a big sexual thrill for both parties, but many of its images are neither pleasant nor PC. They are strong enough, however, to hold us in

fascinated horror. Ishii doesn't pitch that horror as high as DePalma did in *Body Double*, another blood-soaked exploration of passion gone wrong. His violent ones don't want to kill Nami, just love her in their own way—till death do they part.

Ten to Chi to

Heaven and Earth (1990)

Directed by Haruki Kadokawa. Screenplay by Toshio Kamada. Produced by Ten to Chi to Production Committee. With Takaaki Enoki, Tsunehiko Watase, Atsuko Asano, Masahiko Tsugawa. (119 mins.)

Japanese can sell cars and VCRs and computer chips abroad, goes the constant lament, but why not films? What's the solution? In *Ten to Chi to*, Haruki Kadokawa has gone the Cecil B. de Mille route with spectacle that cost the earth—his budget of five billion yen set a new record for Japanese films—and was filmed with a cast of thousands, many of them recruited from the University of Calgary student body.

His subject is suitably epic: the rivalry between Takeda Shingen and Uesugi Kenshin, two Warring States–period (1482–1558) warlords whose deeds and personalities still have a strong hold on the Japanese imagination. *Ten to Chi to*, is less reminiscent of de Mille's sword-and-sandal films, with their cavalier attitude toward fact, than *Midway*, the 1976 Japanese-American co-production that told the story of the World War II sea battle with numbing literalness. I knew I was in trouble when the camera tracked down a row of Uesugi's generals as the name and title of each one flashed on the screen. I felt as though I were being given a pop quiz in Japanese medieval history and hadn't done my homework.

The fim's biggest historical event is the Battle of Kawanakajima, a 1561 clash between the forces of Takeda Shingen and Uesugi Kenshin that required fifty days, a thousand horses, and three thousand extras to film. The battle, not the names that appear on the marquee, is the movie's real attraction. The plot—all that boring stuff you have to sit through until the action starts—revolves around the character of Uesugi Kenshin (Takaaki Enoki). At the beginning of the film, he is Nagao Kagetora, the younger brother of the lord of Echigo Province, in present-day Niigata Prefecture. At the urging of his generals, including loyal mentor Usami Tadayuki (Tsunehiko Watase), he confronts his weak-spirited brother, who is leading the province to ruin, and kills him in a duel. He also falls in love with Tadayuki's daughter, Nomi (Atsuko Asano). But he soon faces a threat to his power. Takeda Harunobu (Masahiko Tsugawa), the lord of nearby Kai Province, in present-day Yamanashi Prefecture, dreams of entering Kyoto at the head of a conquering army. First, however, he has to deal with his neighbor to the north, the "Tiger of Echigo."

The clash of these two personalities—Kagetora, torn by regret over the killing of his brother, and Harunobu, driven by his vision of ultimate power—has rich dramatic potential, as countless novelists, scriptwriters, and playwrights have already discovered, but Kadokawa presents his story as a series of set pieces that highlight the historical record. It's the tableau approach to filmmaking. Ten to Chi to painstakingly details the decision-making process for every strategic move, while obscuring the faces of its decison-makers with the formal masks of samurai etiquette. As Harunobu (later Shingen), Mashiko Tsugawa seems to spend most of the film seated rigidly on his general's stool. When he finally mounts his horse for his climactic fight with Kenshin, it comes as something of a shock, as though a Boy's Festival doll had suddenly come to life.

There is action galore in the final thirty minutes. Kadokawa gives his battle sweep (as when Kenshin's black-clad cavalry cut through Shingen's red-clad foot soldiers like a giant knife) and color (as dozens of black and red lances thrust and parry), together with a snappy rhythm and clear-cut form. These, however, are the virtues of a good marching band routine. For all its banging and crashing, the battle feels tame. Kadokawa shows us the splendor of war, but little of its pain and terror. This is not all to the bad: with body parts flying like smashed watermelons in so many Hollywood films, it's almost a relief to see a female warrior, shot off her horse by Kenshin's gun, fall unmarked by a bullet-hole or drop of blood. But somehow, I don't think it will play in Peoria.

Todokazu no Machi de
Northern Song (1998)

Written, directed, and produced by Koichi Onishi. Cinematography by Toru Akiyama. Music by Masaru Watanabe. With Koichi Onishi, Akiko Ono. (119 mins.)

Koichi Onishi's second feature, Todokazu no Machi de is a late show film that truly has to be seen late, when the rational gates of the daytime mind are down and the uneasy wanderings of the nighttime mind begin. The mental clock of its hero—played by Onishi himself—is permanently stopped at three in the morning. While chained uncomfortably to the past, he longs desperately for a new dawn.

Shot in 16mm black and white, the film resembles a waking dream that is somehow pregnant with meaning, even as it annoys with its banalities. Its careful stylization, designed to evoke a timeless, borderless northern landscape of the spirit, may verge on the precious and the hackneyed—the hero is forever shuffling alone, collar turned up, down dark alleyways or along deserted beaches—but it evokes his troubled soul and draws us into its darkest places.

Based on Onishi's own experiences, Todokazu is an "I-novel" brought to the screen. The hero is a directorial doppelganger named Koichi (Onishi) who has quit his job, separated from his girlfriend in Tokyo, and returned to the family house in Sapporo. There he is alone and at loose ends. Going on thirty, with no family or profession, he is at a crossroads, but does not know which way to turn. He visits the grave of his father and telephones his ex-girlfriend, only to hear her predict, in a sultry voice edged with contempt, that tomorrow he will meet a girl in an orange coat.

Annoyed, he hangs up, but soon after walks into an old hangout and finds a new girl, Yumiko (Akiko Ono), working as a bartender. He is soon distracted by the arrival of a wandering accordion player who bears an uncanny resemblance to his late father. The next day, he returns to the bar and discovers, to his embarrassment, that Yumiko is alone. When she asks to sit next to him, he mumbles his assent, but is too occupied with his own angst to respond to her advances.

Undeterred, she begins to tell him the story of her life. After spending the early years of her childhood in Portugal, she returned to Japan, but was orphaned when her parents were killed in a traffic accident. An aunt in Tokyo raised her, but has since died, leaving Yumiko with no other family. She broke up with her boyfriend and is now living alone in the town she claims to like best in all the world. She is, however, also looking for something to define her life and give it meaning. That night she goes with Koichi to his house of ghosts.

There they continue to talk as they did at the bar: plainly and honestly. Describing his still-strong attachment to his old girlfriend, Koichi begins to open his heart to this new woman with the sad eyes and flashing smile. From the emaciated loner of indeterminate age, locked in a private world of memory and regret, he begins to look like a young man still capable of falling in love and imagining a future. Finally, he confronts the ghost that has haunted him the most deeply and persistently—his father.

In telling this story, Onishi positions his camera at a discreet middle distance and keeps it there. He uses Masaru Watanabe's score—mainly eclectic selections of soulful guitar and piano music— create the appropriately introspective mood, but in the critical scenes he turns off the sound entirely. This unadorned approach, combined with the shadows and mists of Toru Akiyama's black-and-white photography and the retro look of Yutaka Fujikawa's sets, lifts *Todokazu* out of the roil of present-day life to a quieter, starker realm where the usual defenses dissolve and emotional truths emerge. One truth: playing Koichi, Onishi is not the most likable of actors. In his opening scenes, he is too mannered, too tense, too self-importantly the soul in anguish. Then, as Koichi's masks fall away, that soul begins to express itself freely and powerfully. But it needs the cover of the night.

Tokiwaso no Seishun *
Tokiwa: The Manga Apartment (1996)

Directed by Jun Ichikawa. **Screenplay by** Jun Ichikawa and Hideyuki Suzuki. **Produced by** Culture Publicize. **With** Masatoshi Motoki. (97 mins.)

What kid in the *manga*-loving country of Japan has not thought, at one time or another, about becoming a cartoonist? To be paid and celebrated for doing what every classroom doodler gets scolded for? What bliss! And, as Jun Ichikawa's *Tokiwaso no Seishun* shows us with the director's usual attention to detail and nuance, what an illusion.

Based on a true story (or rather a selection of true incidents), *Tokiwaso* tells how a group of young *manga* artists, several of whom are now patriarchs of the *manga* world, came to live together in a Tokyo rooming house and seek their fortunes in the hardscrabble early days of the *manga* industry. When we first meet them, in the mid-1950s, the original nucleus of the group, Osamu Tezuka, is already an in-demand *manga sensei*. The "god of *manga*," Tezuka had redefined the form with his pioneering story *manga*, including the serial *Jungle Taitei* (Jungle Emperor) that may have been the inspiration for Disney's *The Lion King* (or may not have been, if you believe the denials of Disney publicists). The film's focus, however, is Hiro Terada (Masatoshi Motoki), a cartoonist who becomes Tokiwaso's de facto leader after Tezuka's departure to greener fields. Though a steadying presence to his younger colleagues, Terada is, like the other residents of Tokiwaso, a struggler, who must make the rounds of publishers to receive the judgments of editorial panjandrums on his work.

To *manga* aficionados, the film will be a fascinating look at the beginnings of some highly successful careers, including those of Hiroshi Fujimoto and Motoo Abiko, who created dozens of popular series under the collective pen name Funio Fujiko; Shotaro Ishinomori, who blazed new trails with his best-selling *manga* introduction to the Japanese economy; and Funio Akatsuka, whose *Osomatsu-kun* serial became one of the biggest *manga* sensations of the 1960s.

Ichikawa has painstakingly recreated the look and atmosphere of the place and period, aided by the wonderfully evocative black-and-white photographs of Takenori Tanuma. Often subjects of movie bios complain about inaccuracies and distortions. Former Tokiwaso residents have publicly praised Ichikawa's knack for getting it right. *Tokiwaso*, however, is not only a celebration of a special moment in *manga* history, but an examination of the dynamics of success and failure, friendship and rivalry. The film does not glamorize its heroes. Instead, it draws a group portrait that depicts their loneliness and frustrations, as well as their camaraderie and joys. Its story is a mosaic of significant moments— some gently funny, some starkly revealing. Its heroes (and one heroine, the touchingly earnest Eiko Mizuno), are young, determined, and ferociously ambitious *manga* geeks. They are also poor, unknown, and working in a disreputable profession. Their four-and-a-half mat rooms must serve as living quarters, studio, and social hall. Though Terada and his colleagues occasionally play a game of baseball or fight improvised *sumo* bouts, they have little money or time for more expensive forms of recreation. Given their monkish existence, romance is almost out of the question. Instead, almost all of their waking hours are devoted to drawing, selling, and talking *manga*.

From the perspective of today, when the fashionable urban young regard ski trips, foreign vacations, and designer clothes as their birthright, this life must seem almost masochistically grim. And when we watch Terada draw his baseball *manga* with loving care, only to stoically endure painful slights from editors (one tells him bluntly that his gentle-spirited stories are too old-fashioned), we understand its sadness as well. If the film has a fault, it is that paints its story a shade too dark. It captures the hardships of being young cartoonists together uncommonly well, but it seems to miss some of the wickedly childish fun. I'm glad the forty-seven-year-old Ichikawa made this film. I only wish he'd had a nineteen-year-old *manga* artist as a technical consultant to tell him, once in a while, to lighten up.

Tokyo Biyori *
Tokyo Fair Weather (1997)

Directed by Naoto Takenaka. **Screenplay by** Ryo Iwamatsu. **Produced by** Fuji TV and Burning Production. **With** Naoto Takenaka, Miho Nakayama, Takako Matsu. (121 mins.)

The failing marriage is a common enough movie theme, the happy marriage is not. There is, as any glinty-eyed producer will tell you, not a lot of box office in domestic bliss. Naoto Takenaka must have known that when he became enthralled with *Yoko*, a book by photographer Nobuyoshi Araki about his wife, who had died of cancer in 1990. He decided to make a movie about their marriage anyway, commercial considerations be damned. Titled *Tokyo Biyori*, his film has become a standing-room-only hit. One reason, perhaps, is that though definitely happy, his onscreen marriage not, thankfully, blissful (two hours of two people cooing sweet nothings would have been unbearable).

His principals may not resemble anyone we know—it would be hard to find another turbulent spirit quite like Yoko—but their feelings for each other, from playful rapture to unconcealed exasperation, ring true. Also, though the film may go gooey in places—there is too much of Yoko running in slo mo with an ecstatic expression plastered on her face— it mostly gets it right, including the intimate details of a relationship that outsiders seldom see. By the end we understand why the film's Araki doppleganger, a struggling freelance photographer named Shimazu (Naoto Takenaka), remained so devoted to a woman who would try the patience of saint and why Yoko (Miho Nakayama) always returned to him after her wanderings, mental and physical.

Told almost entirely in flashback, the story begins after Shimazu quits his job at an ad agency to spend his days wandering about Tokyo taking photos. To pay the rent, wife Yoko works as a clerk at a travel agency. But this family pillar, we soon see, is what the polite used to call high-strung, what the impolite would today label a flake. When Shimazu invites former colleagues to their apartment for dinner and Yoko mistakes the name of an earnest young editor (Takako Matsu), her *faux pas* reduces her to a querulous wreck. She and Shimazu have a shouting match and the party becomes a shambles.

Then, after a dinner-table spat with Shimazu, Yoko disappears. When Shimazu inquires at the travel agency, her boss tells him she has taken a leave of absence to care for Shimazu's injuries in a fictional traffic accident. After three days, he walks in the door to find a boy playing in the living room and Yoko bustling about, acting as though nothing had happened. The boy, who calls Yoko *obaasan* (grandmother), lives in the same building. Yoko has taken him in much as she might a stray kitten. She plays strange games with the boy, trying to dress him, despite his protests, in girl's clothes. One night Shimazu find the boy's mother outside his building; the boy has not come home and she is worried. Shimazu finds Yoko in a nearby park, abjectly pleading with the boy—

now in a dress and begging to go home—to stay with her. He interrupts this psychodrama, but there is more to come.

If this sounds like a latterday version of *A Woman Under the Influence*, the John Cassavetes film about a housewife's descent into madness, it is not. Yoko never slips over the border from eccentricity to psychosis. And despite the aggravations and provocations, Shimazu never falls out of sympathy with her. The marriage survives the loss of her job and her brief encounter with a handsome admirer (Tadanobu Asano). Finally, Shimazu takes her to the countryside *ryokan* (traditional inn) where they spent their honeymoon. There they rediscover their delight in each other's company. For them, "meant for each other" is not a cliché, but an inescapable reality.

In *Tokyo Biyori*, Takenaka largely abandons the pawky humor of *Muno no Hito* and *119*, while retaining his affection for out-of-the-way corners that time has forgot and the gentleness of spirit that made his earlier films such a pleasure. His Shimazu is less a clone of Araki, who is best known for his raw, shocking depictions of female nudity, than a brother to other Takenaka characters who, whatever their foibles, have a kindly, even worshipful, affection for the women in their lives. Shimazu's marriage to Yoko is portrayed as virtually sexless— in the entire film there is not a single bed scene or even hot look. The perfect couple in Takenaka's world is the artist and model: he passionately dreaming his ideal in his work, she glorying in his reverence and love, with the camera in between, creating the necessary distance.

Tokyo Fist *
(1995)

Written and directed by Shin'ya Tsukamoto. Music by Chu Ishikawa. Produced by Kaiju Theater. With Shin'ya Tsukamoto, Kaori Fujii, Koji Tsukamoto. (87 mins.)

If there is such a thing as a born filmmaker, Shin'ya Tsukamoto is it. By the age of nineteen, when most film students of his generation were sitting in classrooms, his work had been screened at an NTV-sponsored film festival, featured three times on the TBS network, and shown in a portable theater at various sites around Tokyo.

His first film, the 1989 *Tetsuo* (Tetsuo: The Iron Man), was an ultraviolent, ultraerotic fantasy about a man who transforms into a metallic monster. Using thousands of cuts, many flashing by like images out of a bad speed trip, Tsukamoto created a world of chaotic, primal impulse that may have looked surreal and grotesquely funny (the morphed Tetsuo resembled an ambulant metal junk pile), but had a raw emotional punch. No one had distilled the extremes of freakout violence and lust on the screen with such obsessive detail and unbridled directness. Though his vision may have verged on camp, Tsukamoto took us inside the very cells of his hero's rage. *Tetsuo II: Body Hammer* was more of the same, in color, but the rush of images was less migraine-inducing and the story, about a mild-mannered salaryman who morphs into a low-tech Terminator after his young son and wife are kidnapped by a gang of shaven-headed punks, was easier to understand. I felt that with a keener eye for the box-office main chance, Tsukamoto might morph himself into a Japanese James Cameron.

In *Tokyo Fist*, Tsukamoto gives further evidence that he is reaching out for a wider audience, while continuing to work out his obsessions. Once again we have shots of Tokyo office buildings, high-rises and freeways in all their totalitarian splendor, juxtaposed with shots of factory furnaces, industrial scrap-piles and dark forests of freeway pylons in all their hellish glory, while in the background, Chu Ishikawa's score pounds away with its spiky, hypnotic rhythms.

Having set a familiar stage, Tsukamoto tells a story of a love triangle that stirs the base passions of its principals in exotically violent ways. Yoshiharu (Shin'ya Tsukamoto) is a nerdy salaryman living contentedly with his willowy girlfriend Hizuru (Kaori Fujii) in a Tokyo high-rise. One day, their lives are invaded by Yoshiharu's high-school classmate, a boxer named Kojima (Koji Tsukamoto, the director's younger brother). Attracted by Kojima's smoky aura, repelled by Yoshiharu's insane jealousy, Hizuru moves into the boxer's run-down rooming house. Enraged by what he considers to be Kojima and Hizuru's betrayal, Yoshiharu begins to train at Kojima's boxing gym. Gradually, the flabby wimp transforms himself into a mean fighting machine. A showdown of apocalyptic proportions is in the making.

As in Tsukamoto's other films, the storyline is pulp-simple, the forces driving the characters, elemental. His way of telling his story, however, is anything but primitive. Again working with a minimal budget, Tsukamoto creates a fanatically complex, maniacally insistent visual mosaic. If his film descends into the most wretched of violent excess, with gouts of blood spraying skyward and faces dissolving into masses of bruised flesh, its sincerity is so naked, its fantasies so vivid, and its artistry so original that we have to grin with admiration (even while wincing at the overload).

In *Tokyo Fist*, however, he also constructs, for the first time, characters of more than primary colors. Kaori Fujii's Hizuru is not a passive pawn in a macho sexual game, but a strong-willed type who, through the tattoo artist's needle and her own experiments in body piercing, explores the erotic ecstasy of pain. Sharing the men's fascination with violence, she begins to inflict it herself. The film's most intriguing character, she is, in some ways, its most frightening. But it is Tsukamoto, as Yoshiharu, who stands at the center of *Tokyo Fist*. Compared with the mugging nerds Tomoro Taguchi portrays in the Tetsuo films, Tsukamoto is less comic, more ferociously sincere. His fiery-eyed little salaryman burns with a high, wild, ultimately absurd flame, while exposing the inner machinery of the mad, bad, perversely likable talent that is Tsukamoto himself.

Tokyo Kyodai *

Tokyo Siblings (1995)

Directed by Jun Ichikawa. **Screenplay by** Yoshihiro Fujita, Hideyuki Suzuki, and Toshiro Inomata. **Produced by** Right Vision. **With** Naoto Inogata, Urara Awata, Toru Tezuka. (92 mins.)

The line between directorial homage and theft can be a fine one. On which side is Jun Ichikawa's *Tokyo Kyodai* (Tokyo Siblings)? It is clearly intended as a homage to the films of Yasujiro Ozu, right down to the simple but evocative title; Ichikawa admits as much in a program interview. Once again we are in a well-ordered middle-class world, with the clock stopped around 1955. And once again, we sense an intelligent, sensitive, disciplined directorial hand shaping that world.

His people seem all too ordinary in the dailyness of their round and the banality of their concerns. Nothing, except the inevitable wedding or funeral, ever happens. But somehow their story holds and absorbs us. In a word, gesture, or glance, we see emotional landscapes unfolding, and realize that beneath the outer calm of their lives they are struggling with the same crises of change and separation that we all face, sooner or later. By the end, we know them as well as we do our friends, our relatives, ourselves. Little has been explained, everything has been revealed.

The siblings of the title are an orphaned brother and sister who live together in their parent's traditional Japanese-style house. A clerk in a used bookstore, Ken'ichi (Naoto Inogata) is in his early twenties, but has the settled air of a middle-aged man. Even his sweaters have the look of Ozu cast-member hand-me-downs. Though barely out of high school, younger sister Yoko (Urara Awata) dutifully plays the wife in this relationship, ironing her brother's shirts, pouring his beer, and daily preparing the cold garnished tofu that was also his father's favorite food.

Though Ken'ichi and Yoko resemble each other both temperamentally and even physically, they are not made for each other so much as playing their assigned roles. It is as though, having lost their parents, they feel compelled to recreate their lives. Ken'ichi is not faking it; he takes his responsibility as his sister's keeper seriously. Despite the pleas of his girlfriend, a clerk at the bookstore, he refuses marry until his sister becomes a legal adult. Unable to wait, the girlfriend quits her job and marries another man.

But though Yoko looks to be the picture of the well-brought up young miss—she dishes out the rice as though she were performing tea ceremony—she is uneasy in her role; she wants to live. When Ken'ichi brings home a loutish amateur photographer (Toru Tezuka) who occasionally stops by the developing shop where Yoko works, she sees a way out. She begin sleeping with him and spending more and more time away from home. Ken'ichi, sensing that his well-ordered world is crumbling, becomes anxious, desperate. What can he do to bring his sister back?

Working from a script by three young writers, two of whom produced a half-hour TV drama that became the inspiration for *Tokyo Kyodai*, Ichikawa has tried to reproduce Ozu's style—on the set he jokingly told his crew that he wanted a certain "percentage of Ozu" in each shot. But *Tokyo Kyodai* is less an Ozu replica than an Ichikawa original—and that is quite good indeed. Ichikawa brings the same fine pictorial sense to his filmmaking so evident in his TV commercial work; nearly every shot is perfectly composed, beautifully photographed.

But he does more than take pretty pictures of his Tokyo time-pocket; he injects it with an organic, individual life. Though we know that there is something unreal about Ken'ichi and Yoko's world—they live like caretakers in a museum, without so much as a Walkman to indicate the presence of late twentieth-century Japan—we come to accept it, and as we come to understand its fragility, appreciate it.

That world must end, of course. In chronicling its demise, Ichikawa creates a mood of elegiac sadness reminiscent of *Byoin de Shinu to Iu Koto*, his 1993 film about terminal cancer patients. With artistry and conviction, he paints the preciousness and beauty of his siblings' lives. Though a work in a minor key, *Tokyo Kyodai* offers further proof that Jun Ichikawa is a major talent.

Tokyo no Kyujitsu
Tokyo Holiday (1991)

Directed by Naoki Nagao. **Screenplay by** Kang Zhenhua, Naoki Nagao. **Produced by** Tohoku Shinsha. **With** Eddie Constantine, Dick Rude, Sonserai Lee, John Dreszer, Kaori Kawakami, Hiroshi Mikami. (96 mins.)

Why are movies by younger Japanese directors taking flight of reality? Even films by under-forty directors that deal with the theme of the Asian influx into Japan, such as *World Apartment Horror* and *I Love Nippon*, reject conventional narrative structures and a committed stance (or, depending on one's political orientation, leftist pieties). Instead, their attitude is ironic, their approach cartoonishly surreal.

Tokyo no Kyujitsu, TV commercial director Naoki Nagao's feature debut, wants to impress us first of all, with the brilliance of its images, not its story, a trifle about a quest for a mysterious drug called Tokyo Holiday. But unlike many of the young directors who have come from outside the film industry, Nagao has a thorough command of film vocabulary and strikingly original ways of using it, even when the dialogue descends to shopping-bag sentiments and the plot develops a bad case of the sillies. Also, he has daringly made most of the main characters foreigners, hired real actors, not local *gaijin* amateurs to portray them, and given them lines that sound like real English. (The translator or rewriter, if there was one, is uncredited.)

Eddie Constantine (*Alphaville*) plays Mr. Light, a lonely, ailing tycoon who has come half way around the world to find physical and spiritual rebirth in Tokyo Holiday. Dick Rude (*Straight To Hell, Sid and Nancy*) plays Elvis, the punk rocker who drives Mr. Light's motor home (!) and serves as his man-of-all-work. Elvis's slinky Chinese girlfriend (Sonserai Lee) and Mr. Light's slimy Colombian rival (John Dreszer) are present as Third World spice. Though all of them are desperately searching for Tokyo Holiday, none of them have ever seen it, let alone tried it. Then Mr. Light and Elvis encounter Nasha (Kaori Kawakami), a rocker who has just been fired from her band and is being pursued by Tokyo Holiday's love-struck, loony inventor (Hiroshi Mikami).

This is the Grail myth in yet another cinematic guise, but Mr. Light is less Indiana Jones than Aldous Huxley in his magic-mushroom period. He is also a poet and philosopher, whose cosmic insights may sound deep to fans of Shonentai and Kyoko Koizumi, for whom scriptwriter Kang Zhenhua has written songs, but are in fact trite New Ageisms. When Nasha tells Mr. Light she is worried the stars might someday disappear from the sky—the expanding universe and all that—he replies that "if you close your eyes, you can still see them." And hear, I might add, the hum of the void between the ears.

With his battered mug and hollow voice, Constantine is an ideal end-of-the-tether man, and Rude, with his screw-you snarl, is an amusing punk. *Tokyo Holiday*, however, is less an actor's than a director's show. Nagao grabs our attention with clever images, including the final closeup of Nasha's pompadour, rising up like a red-dyed Gibraltar. His most memorable, however, are those of Tokyo itself, the film's real star. Nagao's city is that of a just-off-the-plane foreigner, who still sees the Statue of Liberty atop a Kichijoji love hotel as laughably bizarre (What kitsch!) and moves through Shinjuku's neon forests in a wide-eyed daze (I guess I'm not in Kansas!). This view of Tokyo is right for the film, most of whose characters, after all, are *gaijin* (even Nasha speaks English and has an androgynously international look). Also, it corresponds to the Tokyo that we see more and more often in our mind's eye, the Tokyo of the internationalized night.

Nagao's Tokyo, however, is also an impossibly empty place. When Elvis chases Nasha on his bike down a deserted Nakamise-dori in Akasaka, we feel we are in Fantasyland. If we were to glimpse an Israeli selling framed photos of James Dean, we would feel more at home. But a real foreigner on a real quest would be a different movie, wouldn't it?

Tokyo Skin *
(1996)

Directed by Yukinari Hanawa. **Screenplay by** Yukinari Hanawa and Xiu Jian. **Produced by** Only Hearts. **With** Xiu Jian, Mika Takahashi, Yukio Yamato, Ali Ahmed. (92 mins.)

In the early nineties, Japanese films about Asians in Japan tended to idealize them as innocent victims and view them from the outside in. Now, a more complex and sophisticated view is starting to emerge. One indication is Yukinari Hanawa's debut feature, *Tokyo Skin*. Though its view of Asians struggling to survive in Tokyo may verge on the cartoonish, it lives up to its title by getting deep inside the skins of its characters, particularly its Chinese hustler hero.

Played by Xiu Jian, a long-time Tokyo resident and in-demand actor, Zhou will do anything for a yen, from fencing stolen goods to forging passports. But after five years in Tokyo, he is still a scrambler and outsider who is not getting any younger or closer to his dream. Riding on Yamanote Line around and around the city center, he silently quotes Confucius: "Everyone wants riches and power, but they are hard to come by. No one wants poverty and misery, but they are hard to avoid."

Zhou has had his share of both, but finds Tokyo—this city of fabled riches and power—a frustrating enigma. Are the Japanese happy? Are they suffering? Looking at the sphinx-like faces of the commuters on the train, he sees no answers. All he knows is that he wants to penetrate the mystery of this city and build a place in it for himself. He find a key in Kyoko (Mika Takahashi), a Japanese woman who is searching for her Chinese boyfriend and comes to Zhou for help. He hustles Kyoko—who looks like a mousy prey for big city hawks—the way he hustles everyone, with a blitz of manipulative charm. Kyoko, however, is an unexpectedly hard sell and Shu finds himself falling for her. When he spills out his frustration, rage, and dreams to her, the barrier between these two lonely people crumbles and they become lovers. Zhou discovers a new woman in Kyoko: sensuous, affectionate, sympathetic. Then he learns, to his horror, that he may the one who has been manipulated.

Though the focus of *Tokyo Skin*, this love story is just one of the film's several narrative strands. There is also an eccentric Japanese artist (Yukio Yamato) who returns to his native land an alien after ten years in New York, and a young Pakistani (Ali Ahmed) from a wealthy family who comes to Tokyo naively seeking adventure but is quickly stripped of everything he owns. Like Zhou, both are searching for love and both run up against walls of Japanese indifference, but their stories are essentially comic relief. The artist's inamorata is an elaborately bored SM club habitué who regards his demonstations of affection as an annoyance. The Pakistani's heart-throb is a convenience store clerk who gives him free cakes as a way of getting rid of him.

The intent is to create a Tokyo version of Spike Lee's *Do The Right Thing*, but Hanawa, who worked as an assistant director for Shun Nakahara and Kaizo Hayashi, does not have Lee's talent for blending his film's comic and dramatic elements. The acting, particularly by the supporting players, is amateurish; the veerings from slapstick to soliloquy jarringly wide. Even so, Xiu Jian is not playing at being a stranger in a strange land, but is Zhou totally, from his eloquent Mandarin thoughts to his stumbling spoken Japanese. His performance has something to say to all of us who carry *gaijin* cards, whether we sell BMWs to Japanese businessmen in Aoyama, or ship used Toyotas to Vietnam. We may not quote Confucius to ourselves on the train, but we've all butted our head against Zhou's wall. *Tokyo Skin* may not be the right thing, but it's the real thing.

Tokyo Yakyoku *
Tokyo Lullaby (1997)

Directed by Jun Ichikawa. **Screenplay by** Shinsuke Sato. **Produced by** Eisei Gekijo and Kindai Eiga Kyokai. **With** Kyozo Nagatsuka, Mitsuko Baisho, Kaori Momoi, Takaya Kamikawa. (87 mins.)

Stories of middle-aged romance have been producing hit after hit at the Japanese box office. Following the smash success of *The Bridges of Madison County* came Masayuki Suo's *Shall We Dance?* and Yoshimitsu Morita's *Shitsurakuen* (Paradise Lost), both of which filled theaters with over-forty filmgoers. Now Jun Ichikawa has filmed yet another set of middle-aged lovers in *Tokyo Yakyoku*.

Ichikawa, however, can hardly be accused of cashing in. He has self-deprecatingly described *Tokyo Yakyoku* as *jimi* (plain, quiet)—an adjective he has often bestowed on his other work—and he is not far off the mark. A film that describes the persistence of desire and the difficulty of its fulfillment, *Tokyo Yakyoku* tells its story more by stolen glances than fervent speeches, in a style characterized by an economy of means and suffused with an austere beauty.

It would seem that Ichikawa, a successful director of TV commercials, is rejecting the glitter of his day job for the stoic delights of uncompromising artistry. But though Ichikawa may be accused of prettifying the urban landscapes of *Tokyo Yakyoku*—his dawns are invariably rosy, with nary a trace of the usual dirty brown haze—he rejects the pose of self-important auteurism. Instead, his approach resembles that of a self-effacing documentarian patiently waiting to capture the fugitive moments that reveal, amidst the mundane flow of his character's lives, the drama of their innermost desires. Ichikawa may shape his material with the deliberate stylization of an Ozu, but he never forces it. His films persuade because they breathe with a rhythm that is quietly, naturally, exhilaratingly alive.

Tokyo Yakyoku's hero is Hamanaka (Kyozo Nagatsuka), a middle-aged man who appears, disheveled and subdued, in the Tokyo *shitamachi* (old downtown) after years of wandering. With some embarrassment, but little fuss, he returns to his wife (Mitsuko Baisho) and resumes his job at his father's electrical appliance store in the town's *shotengai* (shopping street). Everyone in the *shotengai* community knows that, years ago, Hamanaka was in love with Tami (Kaori Momoi), who ran the coffee shop across the street from the appliance store. But Tami jilted him for another man and Hamanaka never recovered. He married, had a child and otherwise tried to build a semblance of a life, but one day suddenly disappeared.

Now, he is back and slowly picking up the pieces. He junks the store's dust-covered stock and sells game software to crowds of schoolkids. He achieves a rapproachment with his wife, though the fires of their marriage—if they ever burned at all—have long since cooled. The problem is Tami. His feelings for her still exist and so, he knows, do her feelings for him, but the eyes of the *shotengai* are watching, the weight of the years is pressing. Day after day, they exchange glances across the street that separates

their stores, send signals across the chasm that separates their lives. One night, they cross over.

An actress who has been know to mistake self-indulgence for honesty, Kaori Momoi plays Tami with a characteristic naturalness but uncharacteristic restraint, submerging her star ego in her less-than-glamorous character. Meanwhile, Kyozo Nagatsuka may not look like a computer game salesman—he is too much the severe samurai in his looks and bearing—but he exudes an individuality and intensity that his years have only deepened. No wonder the women were willing to wait for him for so long.

As befitting the film's title, Ichikawa does not pound out his theme so much as delicately insinuate it. He adds counterpoint in the form of a young writer (Takaya Kamikawa) who becomes fascinated with Tami and Hamanaka's story—and while developing a crush on Hamanaka's wife—and an assistant of Hamanaka's who marries a Chinese waitress at Tami's coffee shop, and in doing so sorely disappoints a quiet young woman who clerks at a used bookstore. In skillfully blending these subplots into the main body of his film, Ichikawa creates patterns whose logic and purpose may seem hidden, but are anything but random. His lullaby has the sound of life.

Tomie *

[1999]

Written and directed by Ataru Oikawa. **Produced by** Daiei and Art Port. **Cinematography by** Kazuhiro Suzuki. **With** Miho Kanno, Tomoro Taguchi, Mami Nakamura, Kota Kusano. (95 mins.)

Horror movies are, for me, like heavy metal songs—with a few notable exceptions (*Night of the Living Dead*, *The Shining*) they run together in my brain. Hollywood horrormeisters often hit the same cinematic power chords to hold the attention of their target audience—slack-jawed teenagers—racheting up the volume when that attention starts to wander.

In Japan, horror is also a declassé genre, but several talented younger filmmakers' approach to their scary material is less formulaic and bombastic. Rather than bludgeon the audience, they would rather ask "what if" questions that have their roots in Japanese folklore, but touch contemporary psychic cords in ways fresh, clever, and frightening

Ataru Oikawa's third feature, *Tomie*, has a simple-but-brilliant premise: a murder victim who won't stay dead. Police investigating the killing of a teenaged girl named Tomie Kawakami (Miho Kanno) learn that, in the months since her death, four of her classmates have killed themselves and six more, as well as one teacher, have gone insane. Then they discover that another Tomie Kawakami was murdered three years ago in Gifu Prefecture. Searching unsolved murder files, they find other dead Tomie Kawakamis, going back to the beginning of the Meiji Period (1868-1912). What is going on here?

A detective (Tomoro Taguchi) on the case tracks a classmate of Tomie's named Tsukiko (Mami Nakamura) to Tokyo, where she is attending a photography school and being treated by a psychiatrist (Kinuko Horaguchi) for insomnia and amnesia—she lost three months out of her life that coincide with the murder. Did a traffic accident cause the amnesia (as her mother told her), or was it something else? Why does she have visions of herself bathed in blood?

Meanwhile, next door to the apartment where Tsukiko lives with her lover Yoichi, a furtive young man (Kota Kusano) who works as a short-order cook is tenderly raising what seems to be a baby in a cardboard box. The cries of this creature, however, are not quite human. In a matter of weeks, it grows into a young woman with a sugary voice and a devilish temperament. Her face? We never see it. The young man is obsessed with her, though she teases and tortures him. One day she leaves him, writhing in excruciating pain, to venture into the world. She finds a job as a waitress at Yoichi's restaurant. Her name? Tomie Kawakami.

Tomie, it turns out, is not content to wait for her next murderer to come along. Others have to die first, including the restaurant manager and a big-haired classmate of Tsukiko's. Tomie's real target, however, is Tsukiko. How, she laments, could her old classmate have forgotten her? Weren't they once friends?

Based on a horror *manga* by Junji Ito, *Tomie* takes the risk of portraying its title character as a pretty (if orange-eyed) teenage girl, minus the usual jack-in-box trickery of the genre. Imagine Freddy Krueger, in medium close-up, having a long, intimate chat with a trussed-up victim prior to dicing her. Tomie, however, is played by Miho Kanno, who has become the queen of horror since her debut in Shimako Sato's 1995 *Eko Eko Azaraku*. Though suitably creepy, she gives Tomie dimensions that the usual horror-movie monster could never imagine. Tomie's envy of Tsukiko—her former friend is entering the country of adulthood where she can never follow—has a genuine, if goosebump-inducing, pathos.

As Tsukiko, Mami Nakamura initially impresses as a big-eyed victim-in-waiting, but in battling Tomie she projects a stubborn will to live reminiscent of her breakout performance as a sexually abused teenager in Genjiro Arato's *Father Fucker*. In the key confrontation scene between the two antagonists, most actresses would run standard fear and panic riffs. Nakamura, however, smolders with an anger and disgust that makes her more than Tomie's equal. Finally,

the photography by Kazuhiro Suzuki, makeup by Pierre Suda, and score by Hiroshi Nimi creates the right skin-crawling atmosphere.

In Hollywood, horror is a ghetto most directors with big ambitions try to avoid. In Japan, it is becoming a genre that attracts rising talents, who are producing strong, original films with a mass-audience appeal. Stephen King, move over—the next Japanese invasion is about to begin.

Tsuge Yoshiharu World: Gensenkan Shujin *
Gensenkan Inn (1993)

Written and directed by Teruo Ishii. **Produced by** Kinocita Eiga. **With** Shiro Sano, Akio Yokoyama, Chika Nakagami, Kaoru Mizuki, Nana Okuda. (98 mins.)

Japanese comics are often stereotyped as exploitations of sex and violence. They actually are far more various. The *manga* of Yoshiharu Tsuge present an individual, eccentric vision at once strange and familiar, disturbing and funny. They take us into a dreamworld that engages our senses and imagination, but remains, finally, elusive. Tsuge's work inspired Naoto Takenaka's 1990 *Muno no Hito*, a film about a failed *manga* artist who sells rocks by a river bank. Now Teruo Ishii has made *Tsuge Yoshiharu World: Gensenkan Shujin*, a four-segment anthology, all scripted and directed by Ishii. Once a director of Ken Takakura *yakuza* movies at Toei, Ishii is returning to the screen for the first time in fourteen years.

Tsube (Shiro Sano) is a struggling *manga* artist who resembles the young Tsuge. But though narrated by Tsube as autobiography, the film passes into the territory of fantasy. The first segment is the slightest and funniest. After renting a ramshackle house in the countryside, Tsube becomes acquainted with Ri (Akio Yokoyama), a man who can talk to birds. One day, without warning, Ri moves into Tsube's place with his slatternly wife (Chika Nakagami) and his two dirty kids. The wife, who is as cracked as her husband; walks into Tsube's garden every day and snatches his cucumbers off the vine, while glaring at him in brazen defiance. Puzzled, Tsube does nothing. He doesn't even react when the kids begin to gorge on his dinner like starved animals—and the mother joins in. The climax comes when the wife is taking a bath in an oil drum and the husband offers to show Tsube how long she can hold her breath under water. When she passes out, the husband and Tsube rescue her from the drum—and Tsube falls with his face between the unconsciousness woman's thighs. Tsube's slip might well have been Freudian.

In "Akai Hana" (Red Flower) Tsube is walking to the river to fish when he encounters a boy sexually harassing a girl selling tea at a roadside shop. Instead of scolding the boy. Tsube ends up following him to what the boy says is a good fishing spot, where red flowers are growing wild on the banks. The boy then circles back and discovers the girl, wading in the stream. She hikes up her robe, squats in the water and, as the boy looks on in amazement, red flowers emerge, one after another, from between her legs. He experiences a mystery and power he had never known existed. He has also been cured of looking up girls' skirts.

The third and title segment plunges us into the eerie, twilight world of the Japanese ghost story. Tsube arrives in a town whose buildings look like stone mausoleums, whose inhabitants are grotesquely wrinkled old women, and whose skies are gloomy and gray. The women excitedly tell him that he is a double for the master of a local inn—the Gensenkan. One of them, the mistress of a candy store, tells him the story of how the master came to live there. In a flashback, the master, who is indeed a ringer for Tsube, stops at the Gensenkan and is greeted by the inn's ancient maid and its voluptuous mistress (Kaoru Mizuki). The mistress, however, has a tick that twists her face and renders her all but speechless.

When the new guest goes to the bath he sees the mistress, unclothed, praying fervently at a shrine blazing with candles. The scene that follows promises more cleverly metaphorical erotic humor, but ends with a graphic attempt at rape. Escaping from her attacker, the mistress crawls to a steamed up mirror and writes "heya de" ("in my room") on it with her finger. The progression from rape to lovemaking to love is common enough in Japanese films. Ishii films it as inevitable, if not quite desirable. We see violence, but we also recognize a mutual desire. Wearers of social masks who live outside normal society, these two are meant for each other.

The final segment is set in 1959. Tsube, together with a writer friend (Mayo Kawasaki) and the writer's waitress girlfriend (Nana Okuda) decide to start a city magazine, and fail to get it off the ground. Disappointed, the writer returns to his wife in Chofu, and the girlfriend and Tsube begin a life together as platonic roommates. Tsube wants something more, but the girl can't forget the writer. Finally, they go off in search of him. Ishii tells the story of this romantic triangle with a gentle humor and warm nostalgia for a vanished bohemia.

At the end, the film's cast leave their seats in a tiny theater and come up on stage to applaud their characters' creator. Tsuge seems to be pleased with their work. I know I was—and I hope we hear more from Ishii before another fourteen years elapse.

Tsuki yori Kaeru *

Return from the Moon (1994)

Written and directed by Hiroaki Jinno. Produced by Cine Quanon. With Yuko Takahashi, Koichiro Mitsuda. (84 mins.)

Ever since Star Wars, the science-fiction genre has been associated with high-tech effects and stratospheric budgets. But as Hiroaki Jinno's Tsuki yori Kaeru reminds us, sci-fi was once the refuge of the no-budget filmmaker with a message, an attitude, or a pressing need to pay the rent. There was Jean-Luc Godard, with his dark and finally silly vision of a computerized future in Alphaville. There was also Ed Wood, with his plates masquerading as flying saucers in Plan Nine from Outer Space.

Jinno tries to take the Godardian high road in his black-and-white feature debut, but his vision is less ponderously dark than wryly blank. His Japan of the year 2039 is like an architectural drawing for a new condo development: bland, characterless, and underpopulated. But the Japanese who inhabit this future world still have many of the same problems as their counterparts in 1994. By traveling into the near future, Jinno makes some apt comic observations on the present. His lapses into Godardian silliness in his ultraviolent finale do not spoil the minimalist pleasures of his film. It's an instant classic for cultists who like their SF intellectualizing light, dry, and cool.

The setting for Jinno's future world is Ranjuku, a sprawling development that was built for a space-colony simulation. Now that the colonists have presumably orbited into the great beyond, the only inhabitants of Ranjuku (which translates as "Orchid House") are the kanrinin (estate managers) who kill time placing endless games of mah-jongg, wandering about the grounds, or in the case of one obsessed kanrinin, digging a hole in the ground. One day, while patrolling Ranjuku, a kanrinin named Miruko (Yuko Takahashi) encounters Kagero (Koichiro Mitsuda), a stranger who claims he has just returned from the moon. He has come to Ranjuku, he tells her, to practice his profession: counselor.

Kagero is soon advising an endless stream of clients on their personal problems, with Miruko serving as his receptionist. The clients come from near and far, attracted by Kagero's reputation as a caring, sympathetic healer (it helps that he has the spacey manner and pleasantly melodious voice of a DJ on an FM easy-listening station). Despite his popularity Kagero remains a mysterious, vaguely troubling figure. Perhaps this man from the moon has a problem of his own that he isn't telling us about?

In making Tsuki yori Kaeru, Jinno spent next to nothing on sets, makeup, and special effects. His only concession to sci-fi movie convention is a man in a space suit who makes a brief, if memorable, appearance at the end. But by the clever use of camera work and sound effects he creates a convincing Utopia that is seductively peaceful though essentially sterile (even the constant hum of machinery is less ominous than lulling). Ranjuku is his satire on present-day Japan, where long decades of peace, prosperity, and administrative guidance have built a society with little want, conflict, or creative energy.

Representatives of this society, the *kanrinin* and clients are mostly pleasant nonentities who speak a clearly enunciated, oddly schoolbookish Japanese (this is a good movie for intermediate Japanese students; you can understand most of the dialogue). As played by Yuko Takahashi, Miruko is an exception to the colorless rule: a bracingly acerbic presence who, alone among the film's characters, is defiantly "normal." She is also the lone skeptic, who realizes that Kagero's guru act is not what it seems.

Koichiro Mitsuda's man from the moon has the appropriate round face and ambiguous manner, by turns comforting and unsettling. When, halfway through the film, he appears with corporate logos tattooed on his face—a way, he explains, of earning extra cash—it makes sense. Why not use that big empty space as a billboard? Among the other odd characters are a young *kanrinin* who becomes obsessed with going to the moon and a mystery man who plans to build a weather satellite for collecting data on the environmental blight that has destroyed the ozone layer and spoiled the water.

But the characters are less interesting than the questions Kagero asks with such quiet persistence in his counseling office. What is your first memory? What do you want to do with the rest of your life? Basic and banal, they turn us toward thoughts about what existence really means and what really matters. *Tsuki*, however, is less interested in providing pat answers than in prodding us out of our complacency. At the end, by introducing bloodshed into its bloodless paradise, it veers toward B-movie melodrama, but not, thankfully, very far. The dead, like their cityscapes, are quietly stark and drained of energy or emotion. There is no horror—they were never that alive to begin with, and now they look so peaceful, as the machinery clanks and grinds.

Tsuki to Kyabetsu
One More Time, One More Chance (1996)

Directed by Tetsuo Shinohara. Screenplay by Tetsuo Shinohara and Azuki Mashiba. Produced by Seiyu and Ace Pictures. With Masayoshi Yamazaki, Masumi Sanada. (100 mins.)

There is a subgenre in Japanese films that I call the Virginal Young Woman In A Long Dress movie. One example is the 1989 *Kitchen* by Yoshimitsu Morita, about a lonely young woman who, having lost her last living relative, a beloved grandmother, finds a new family in the form of a male acquaintance and his transvestite "mother." Another is Tomoyuki Furumaya's 1995 *Kono Mado wa Kimi no Mono*, about a summer romance in the Yamanashi wine country between a ripe-but-unpluckable young woman and a silent-but-seething young man. The latest addition is Tetsuo Shinohara's *Tsuki to Kyabetsu*, whose heroine pursues a fading pop star to his country retreat and becomes his nuisance, muse, and obsession. She is, however, more than just another starry-eyed fan, and not in a way that we might expect.

What these films have in common is a celebration of feminine purity and innocence— the heroines are typically nineteen-going-on-twelve—and a chasteness that would have warmed the puritan heart of Will Hays. In situations that, in Hollywood, would cry out for an obligatory sex scene, the lovers sublimate by playing house in a consumerist fantasy apartment (*Kitchen*), slurping watermelons in a romantic old farmhouse (*Kono Mado wa Kimi no Mono*) or dancing and making pop ballads together in the hero's country house (*Tsuki to Kyabetsu*).

Such reticence is not altogether unpleasant—I have seen enough soft-focus grappling in movie sex-scenes to last a lifetime—but the smug self-congratulation in these films annoys and the *faux naiveté* cloys (or inspires a rude urge to hoot). Nonetheless, there is a large, mainly female, audience for these zipless romances, whose heroines keep a tight rein over the story's sexual dynamics. The men in these films are, necessarily, Ken-doll figures, whose sexuality is tamed, if not totally suppressed.

In *Tsuki* that man is Hanabi (Masayoshi Yamazaki) or "Fireworks," a pop star who once commanded a large following, but has since retired to a remote schoolhouse-turned-retreat to contemplate his navel and mourn the death of his creativity. One day, while parked in a Tokyo bayside wasteland, he spies a pale young woman (Masumi Sanada) in a long white dress leaping artlessly among the weeds. She is a dancer on her way to a recital, who has been stranded in this wilderness without bus fare. She also happens to be his ardent fan. Annoyed by her enthusiasm, Hanabi shoves a wad of bills in her hand and speeds off.

That night at the schoolhouse, he has an unexpected visitor—the dancer, who has come to return the money and, as she soon confesses, become his assistant. Hanabi rejects her with an unfeeling abruptness, but the sincerity of her desire to please touches him. There is something different about her, something he can't quite put his finger on. He relents and is soon making music on his baby grand, while she dances, always in her white dress, always with one eye on the ripening moon. Her name is Hibana—a "Spark" to his "Fireworks." They fall in love but, unknown to Hanabi, she is living with a secret that threatens to drive them apart.

Tetsuo Shinohara films the Gumma countryside with same limpid sensuousness that made his prize-winning *Kusa no Ue no Shigoto* (Work on the Grass, 1993) such a joy to watch. We can not only see the wind blowing through the grass in the golden light of a summer dusk, but feel its warmth and smell its fragrance. His style is well suited to his elemental ying-yang story, whose ethereal heroine communes with the moon and whose earthly hero raises cabbages (the literal translation of the Japanese title of the film is "Moon and Cabbages"). But though the story, which Shinohara wrote with Azuki Mashiba, has an opposites-attract appeal, *Tsuki* degenerates into a slick exercise in teen-audience manipulation and merchandising. When Hibana's secret is revealed, we are reminded that we are watching a film for adolescents who think the sub-Billy-Joel balladeering of real-life pop star Yamazaki is profound, and after the show will rush to buy the CD on sale in the lobby. I, however, left the screening room vowing to hereafter watch only films in which the heroine's dress comes above her knees.

Tsuma wa Filipina
My Wife Is Filipina (1994)

Directed by Yasunori Terada. Produced by Mampukuji Cinema. (100 mins.)

Documentary filmmakers commonly spend years getting close to their subjects. Unless they know them intimately, they cannot expect to capture the moments that illuminate their lives. But documentarians rarely turn their cameras on their own families. Why should they? To record the progress of Junior's growth and Dad's grant application?

Yasunori Terada, however, found a theme in his private life that he felt would justify a film: his marriage to a Filipina. When Terada began the project that would become *Tsuma wa Filipina*, he was a student at the Japan Film School and engaged to marry a twenty-seven-year-old Filipino bar hostess. Terada's family, particularly his businessman father, opposed the marriage, which had been prompted by the bride-to-be's pregnancy. Terada, who had, in his own words, been "jilted by three Filipina" and become engaged to a fourth, had an obvious personal interest in relationships between Japanese men and Filipino

women and the way those relationships are viewed by Japanese society.

He also saw the thematic potential in his own situation. "The child [in Teresa's womb] symbolizes the present state of affairs [between our two countries]," he wrote in his project proposal. "[By filming] our marriage and the birth of our child, I plan to highlight the current relationship between Japan and the Philippines." He succeeded beyond his expectations. His graduation project—the first part of *Tsuma*—won the Grand Prize in the Documentary Division of the Second Film Festival of International Cinema Students and the second part was awarded the Newcomer's Prize presented by the Japan Film Directors Association.

Made on a shoestring, *Tsuma* has the look of a learn-as-you-go student production. In scenes shot in a Manila go-go bar blurry figures wander about in the gloom. The first meeting between Teresa and Terada's father—one of the film's dramatic high points—is shot mostly out of focus. But for all its technical blips, *Tsuma* captures the characters of its two principals and presents their dilemmas with an honesty that charms as well as enlightens.

It is not, as Terada found, easy to put one's family on public display. Terada's father flatly refused to cooperate, and though his mother and sister agreed to appear on camera, they are obviously ill at ease. In explaining why she first opposed the marriage, and later, why she has not invited Teresa to her own wedding, Terada's sister Sanae churns up a blizzard of verbal chaff, while flinging occasional darts at her brother for putting her on the spot. But Terada gently persists until Sanae tells the truth: she thought that Teresa was using her pregnancy to trap her brother into marriage. She also feels that inviting Teresa to her wedding without first introducing her to her relatives would be putting the social cart before the horse.

Watching these scenes, we sense the rightness of Terada's choice of subject; he can make Sanae move beyond the usual banalities and evasions because they are brother and sister and are talking about issues that concern them both. Sanae may be an unwilling representative of Terada's family and, by extension, Japanese society, but after traveling to the Philippines for her brother's wedding, she begins to relax and reveal more of her true self. When she confesses her suspicions of Teresa's motives to Teresa herself and bursts into tears, the moment has an emotional impact that few professional actors could equal.

Nonetheless, the stars of the film remain Teresa and Terada. In depicting his marriage, Terada remains remarkably—some might say coldly—detached. How many husbands would invite a camera crew to record his marital spats and pillow talk?

Terada, however, is not entirely comfortable with his dual role. It was, he later wrote, "very hard to act naturally before the cameras." He finally impresses as likable, unpretentious man who genuinely loves his wife and is trying, in the best way he knows, to tell his family's story.

Teresa's is a story worth telling. A "water trade" worker from the age of eighteen, a former drug user who still suffers from flashbacks, she is a woman of experience—not all of it pleasant. But beneath a sometimes hard exterior is an unquestionable strength, intelligence, and vitality. When she laughingly crows over purchase of a plot of land near Manila, offering tufts of grass to the camera as "presents," we see a Philippine Scarlet O'Hara, clawing her way out of poverty with grit and determination. When she imitates the speech of the stereotypical Japanese female, in all its grating submissiveness and cloying sweetness, we hear a critique of Japanese society that is unfair, but frankly amusing.

Terada skillfully shapes his film (and, in a sense, his life) to illustrate its main themes and heighten its dramatic impact. There is no pat conclusion, no happy ending. At the end, Terada and Teresa are still united, still struggling, still uncertain of the future. In them we may see people we know. We may, if we look closely enough, even see ourselves.

Tsuri Baka Nisshi Special
Free and Easy Special (1994)

Directed by Azuma Morisaki. **Screenplay by** Yoji Yamada, Toshio Sekine. **Produced by** Shochiku. **With** Toshiyuki Nishida, Eri Ishida, Rentaro Mikuni, Yasuko Tomita, Kei Tani, Taishu Kase, Ko Nishimura. (106 mins.)

If movies are celluloid dreams and filmmakers are the dreamers, then much of Hollywood would seem to suffering from a collective nightmare. But fulfillments of our fondest wishes also find their way onto the screen. One example is the *Tsuri Baka Nisshi* (Free and Easy) series. The hero, Hama-chan (Toshiyuki Nishida), is a fanatic fisherman who puts his hobby ahead of his job as a salesman for a construction company. He is also a devoted family man, who dotes on his zaftig wife Michiko (Eri Ishida), and his cute infant son, Koitaro.

This behavior is totally contrary to the ethos that requires corporate warriors to devote nearly every waking hour to the company. Hama-chan, however, not only rebels against this ethos, but is rewarded for being the nail that sticks up. The stressed-out company president (Rentaro Mikuni) considers Hama-chan his fishing master and his happy family the wellspring of the life force. Su-chan, as he is known

around the Hamazaki household, may rank higher than Hama-chan on the company food chain, but he considers himself Hama-chan's disciple in the art of living. Talk about wish-fulfillment!

Beginning with the first *Tsuri* film, which appeared in 1989 on a double bill with a Tora-san installment, this formula has proven popular, so much so that the sixth installment is being released independently, during the summer season. Though titled *Tsuri Baka Nisshi Special*, it is really more of the same. Once again Hama-chan and Su-chan are reeling in the big ones as the credits roll. The focus, however, quickly shifts to a sub-plot involving the marriageable daughter (Yasuko Tomita) of Hama-chan's section manager (Kei Tani) and the shy son (Taishu Kase) of a Ginza jewelry-store owner (Ko Nishimura). The son is smitten with the daughter, whom he stares at on the train day after day, but he cannot work up the courage to say hello. So he hires a detective agency to run a background check and discovers that his father and Su-chan are old school chums. Sooner than you can say *omedeto* (congratulations), an *omiai* (meeting for the purpose of arranging marriage) is in the works, with Su-chan serving as the go-between.

Then the company loses a bid for an important contract, with Su-chan the unwitting guilty party, and an old boyfriend makes a sudden appearance, upsetting Su-chan's wedding plans. After both catastrophes, Su-chan shows up drunk at Hama-chan's house to seek consolation for his loss of face. The second time, he finds Michiko alone. What happens next threatens to destroy Su-chan and Hama-chan's friendship and provides the narrative and comic fuel to carry the film to its conclusion.

Director Morisaki does a workmanlike job of setting up the gags, but the film's inspiration is in the popular *manga* by Juzo Yamasaki on which it is based, and much of its cinematic heart in the script co-written by Yoji Yamada and Toshio Sekine. The writer and director of the Tora-san series, Yamada has cast Hama-chan as the same sort of lovable loser as Shibamata's most famous peddler. Also, he has injected the earthy humor and folksy atmosphere that are Tora-san trademarks. The series is not Tora-san redux, however. Hama-chan may, Tora-like, screw up and goof off, but he also has what Tora-san has long been studiously avoiding: a wife, a kid, and a nine-to-five job. On the other hand, he lacks Tora-san's *giri-ninjo* chivalric ethic; instead of fulfilling self-imposed duties to all and sundry (especially attractive women), he would rather go fishing.

Toshiyuki Nishida's Hama-chan is a slob clown who has a sage's (or idiot's) lack of awe for the powers that be. Despite Nishida's incurable scenery chewing—in his big scenes he works facial muscles I never knew existed—he makes Hama-chan an appealing sort, at once laughable and admirable. An actor of genuine talent and accomplishment, Rentaro Mikuni is wasted in this formulaic fluff, but he also seems to be enjoying himself immensely. He goes beyond the blustering company president stereotype to portray Su-chan as pathetic in his loneliness, funny in his eagerness to please his fishing *sensei*.

The *Tsuri Baka Nisshi* series pokes fun at corporate hierarchies through its role reversal comedy, but its real message is that the Japanese company can be a humane place to work, as long as the president likes to unwind and soak a line. Though the nation's corporate drones may find comfort and laughs in Hama-chan's antics, few will be tempted to follow his footsteps. They know how the real Hama-chans of the world end up: as Tora-sans. But we can all dream.

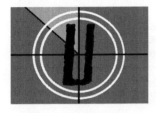

Umi Sora Sango no Iitsutae
The Legend of the Sea, Sky, and Coral (1992)

Directed by Makoto Shiina. **Screenplay by** Makoto Shiina and Yasuhiko Sawada. **Cinematography by** Masao Nakamura. **Produced by** Hone Film. **With** Kimiko Amari, Yoko Honno. (110 mins.)

Ryukyu islanders hold some of the same fascination for Japanese filmmkers that Native Americans do for their Hollywood counterparts. Makoto Shiina's *Umi Sora Sango no Iitsutae* explains why. Like the Sioux of Kevin Costner's *Dances With Wolves*, the natives of Ishigaki Island are good people living the good life in a soon-to-be spoiled natural paradise. (Shiina show us developers buying up the land and bulldozers tearing it to bits.) Although they are hardly "primitives"—they watch NHK and play with Game Boys—they live in closer contact with nature and their native gods than do most Tokyoites, while their culture is exotically different from the national mainstream. Even their dialect is all but incomprehensible to most Japanese. (When they speak it in the film, Shiina thoughtfully provides subtitles).

Like Costner in *Wolves*, Shiina is a sympathetic outsider who portrays his Ryukyu characters in the best possible light, with his two non-native principals—a girl and her mother—soon converting to the local way of life. Here, however, the analogy starts to break down. Rather than create a larger-than-life drama on a broad canvas, Shiina takes typical TV drama situations, with their potential for bathos, and deflates them to everyday proportions. He prefers natural sound (no studio looping) and natural acting (islanders play several of the key roles and many of the minor ones). The real stars are not the professionals who play the girl and her mother, but the islanders, their island, and the sea that surrounds it.

With cinematographer Masao Nakamura, Shiina captures stunning images of this island and sea. A shot of a young fisherman diving thirty meters to spear a squid captures a moment of daring and grace in an underwater world of ethereal beauty. It is moments like that, more than the film's clichéd plot, make us understand the islanders and why Shiina admires them.

How many times have we seen the story of the new girl in town, whose "foreign" (in this case, Tokyo) ways make her a target of scorn for the neighborhood boys? How many times have we seen that girl learn to love her new home and strike up a friendship with one of those boys? And how many times have we seen her take a tearful leave of her by-now-beloved companions?

Too many times? Perhaps. Shiina even serves up a subplot about kids lost on a desert island. We know how that one is going to turn out as well. But he also gives his cinematic chestnuts real flavor. When the boats leave to search for the lost children, the mothers of the boy and the girl sit side by side on a log and talk. In a TV drama, the tears would soon be flowing. In *Umi*, however, the two women, who have known each other from childhood, keep up a stoic front. This, we feel, is the way they would actually behave.

In striving for realism, however, Shiina turns the emotional volume so low that it barely registers. The girl (Yoko Honno), a shy, quiet type, doesn't put up much of a fight when Mom drags her off to the island or when the boys tease her. Realistic perhaps, but a snore. Originally, Shiina conceived this character as a deaf-mute. Thankfully, he gaveher a voice, or she might have vanished from the screen altogether.

Fortunately, the islanders, particularly a wizened old fisherman who teaches his grandson the ways of the sea and a bronzed young fisherman who becomes the object of the mother's romantic interest, are very much present on the screen, as is the sea, the sky, and the breathtakingly lovely coral.

Umihozuki
The Breath (1996)

Directed by Kaizo Hayashi. **Screenplay by** Juro Kara. **Produced by** For Life Record and Pony Canyon. **With** Juro Kara, Haruko Wanibuchi, Shigeo Harada, Tang Na, Ni Shujun. (138 mins.)

When Howard Hawks was directing *The Big Sleep* he sent a telegram to scriptwriter Raymond Chandler, asking who had murdered the chauffeur. Chandler, who had become thoroughly confused by the tangled storyline himself, wrote a one-sentence reply: "I don't know."

That puzzlement would not be an unreasonable reaction to Kaizo Hayashi's *Umihozuki*. Based on a novel and play by Juro Kara, *Umihozuki* would seem belong to the long line of films about antihero detectives, from Philip Marlowe to Columbo and Popeye Doyle. There is definitely a lot of Columbo in Hayashi's hero, a P.I.-turned-junkie named Haida (Juro Kara). Short, squat, and pushing fifty, he is not a candidate for Boy Toy of the Month. Columbo-like, he wears a rumpled trenchcoat, walks with a waddle, and never packs a gun. He even has a Columbo-like gimmick: he carries a clear tube container for *kanten*—a jellylike sweet— and uses it as a telescope to peer into the heart of his case.

That is where the resemblance ends. Whereas Columbo is a winner who only happens to look like a loser, Haida is a former star P.I. who has spent the past several years in a drug-induced haze. As the film begins, he is in a rehab center, feebly mouthing the words to the center's Druggie Creed: "I only have myself. I am not someone else. Somewhere there is an unknown Me. I ask the Higher Power to help me find him."

That search is the theme of the movie. Yes, there is a case—a Japanese college student who went missing five years ago in Taiwan. A police detective (Haruko Wanibuchi) who respected Haida's work in his clean-and-sober days offers it to him, and Haida boards a plane to Taipei. This case, however, is less the mainspring of the plot than a metaphor for exploring life's mysteries, including the greatest mystery of all: death.

That exploration violates nearly every genre convention. There are no bodies, gun fights, or car chases. Instead, early in the film, Haida is collecting trash by the riverside in a cleanup organized by the center. Shaky from going cold turkey, he passes out, falls into the water, and drifts downstream, until he bumps into something that look disconcertingly like a corpse. He comes to and discovers the still-breathing body of Sakatani (Shigeo Harada), a down-and-

outer who has apparently attempted suicide. After spending the night at the center, Sakatani disappears, but not before telling his savior that he owes him one—and wishes he that he didn't.

These fateful meetings recur throughout the film. Once in Taiwan, Haida places an ad for an assistant and the young woman (Tang Na) who answers it happens to know the missing student. Unable to speak a word of Chinese (he communicates by writing on a white slate) Haida decides call her by the student's name: Mariko. Not long afterwards, he runs into Sakatani, who is now an expatriate in Taiwan, living on the wrong side of the law. He has an assistant of his own—a slinky, sexy type (Ni Shujun) who seems to want Haida dead.

Hayashi and Kara, a playwright and actor who is a central figure in Japan's avant-garde theater scene, withhold the genre pleasures of tension and climax. Instead they strive for epiphanies that, in another film, might have only inspired laughs. Haida, for example, has an odd habit of pratfalling into bodies of water. In addition to the above mentioned river, he slips into a full bathtub in his hotel, is thrown from a ship into the ocean by a Taiwanese associate of Sakatani's, and, together with his assistant, leaps from a rock to explore the sea where Mariko was last seen swimming. These dunks, however, are not comic turns but baptisms that lead Haida to the ultimate end of his search: a confrontation with mortality. The sea shells that Mariko wore as earrings—the *umihozuki* of the title—become symbols of that confrontation. They are, after all, the bones of the creatures that once lived in them. As he grasps for one on the ocean bottom, Haida watches it transform into a grinning skull.

Hayashi, whose previous credits including the winkingly meretricious Mike Hama series, subordinates his own cinematic personality to Kara's script. This is not always to the benefit of the film; Kara's vision is at times willfully obscure, finally bleak. Imagine a Japanese Bergman producing a Columbo episode, with the Grim Reaper as the guest villain.

Unagi *
The Eel (1997)

Directed by Shohei Imamura. **Screenplay by** Shohei Imamura, Motofumi Tomikawa, and Daisuke Tengan; **Produced by** KSS, Eisei Gekijo, and Groove Corporation. **With** Koji Yakusho, Misa Shimizu, Mitsuko Baisho. (117 mins.)

Shohei Imamura is among the most internationally celebrated of living Japanese directors and in recent years among the most silent. Slowed by illness, occupied with the running of his film school, Imamura allowed seven years to lapse between the 1989 *Kuroi Ame* (Black Rain), a drama about the postwar lives of a family of Hiroshima bomb victims, and his latest film, *Unagi*.

The second Imamura film to win the Palme d'Or at the Cannes festival (*Narayama Bushiko* [The Ballad of Narayama] was the first, in 1984), *Unagi* tells the story of ex-con Takuro Yamashita (Koji Yakusho), who has been paroled after serving a sentence for murder. Eight years ago he stabbed his wife to death after discovering her with a lover. Once an ordinary man leading an ordinary life, he has been transformed by this trauma into an eccentric loner who distrusts humanity, particularly the female half of it, and can communicate only with an eel that he kept as a pet in his cell.

Released into the care of his former teacher, who is now a priest at a rural Buddhist temple, Yamashita takes up a new occupation—barber—and sets up shop outside of town, by the shores of a lake. Though off the beaten path, his shop soon attracts the locals, including a laborer who takes him eel fishing (Yamashita throws his catch back into the lake) and a construction worker who wants to use Yamashita's revolving barber pole to attract UFOs (none, unfortunately, arrive).

Yamashita's most fateful encounter is with Keiko (Misa Shimizu), a young woman he finds unconscious in the weeds by the lake. She had tried to commit suicide by taking an overdose of sleeping pills. When she recovers, Keiko announces that she doesn't want to return home to Tokyo. The priest's wife (Mitsuko Baisho) suggests that she work in Yamashita's shop as his assistant. At first opposed to the idea (Keiko reminds him of his dead wife) Yamashita at last agrees. Slowly, he begins to open up to her and the possibility of trust in another human being.

Unagi's populist strain—its delight in low humor, its tolerance for human foibles and its preference for the warmly emotional over the coldly rational—recalls the films of Yoji Yamada, especially the forty-sixth installment of the Tora-san series, in which Tora falls for a pretty barber, and the 1977 *Kokufuku no Kiroi Hankachi* (The Yellow Handkerchief), which also depicts an ex-con's discovery of love's redeeming power. But while Yamada is a cinematic socialist, who celebrates the commonality of his characters' humanity (even his outsider hero, Tora-san, never strays too far from the family fold) Imamura is a cinematic anarchist, who rejects middle-class morality and explores the unruly impulses of the loins and the heart, including the impulse to kill.

In showing the cheating wife in bed with another man, while the cuckolded husband watches from the bedroom window, Imamura is almost pornographically frank. The scene, however, explains Yamashita's subsequent crime with a persuasiveness that more than justified its excess. We see what Yamashita sees from inside his skin. Koji Yakusho, a veteran stage actor who rose to stardom in Masayuki Suo's *Shall We Dance?*, and Misa Shimizu, who won international acclaim for her work in Takehiro Nakajima's *Okoge*, delicately build the foundations of the film's central relationship, while vividly expressing their characters' wounded human core.

In a pre-Cannes press conference, Imamura said that "more than winning a prize, I want to show that Japanese films are still alive and well." In *Unagi*, he has succeeded.

Unlucky Monkey *
(1998)

Written and directed by Sabu. **Produced by** Shochiku. **With** Shin'ichi Tsutsumi, Hiroshi Shimizu, Akira Yamamoto, Ren Osugi, Ikko Suzuki. (106 mins.)

Was Sabu Buster Keaton in a previous incarnation? Like the deadpan master of silent comedy, this actor-turned-director (*Dangan Runner*, *Postman Blues*) builds narrative machinery into his films that, once set in motion by a mistake or misunderstanding, develops a giddy, headlong momentum, according to a crazily logical design. But whereas Keaton's cinematic machines moved in a clean arc, at an increasing rate of speed, Sabu's have tended to start fast, but later sputter and slow, with plot complications serving as brakes.

Also, Sabu's chases are not only—or even primarily—for laughs. In a way more reminiscent of Quentin Tarantino, he puntuates his absurdities with outbursts of violence and comments on them from the heights of cineaste irony. Sabu, however, is more sincere and single-minded.

His third film, *Unlucky Monkey* (Unlucky Monkey) is his most ingeniously constructed yet. Like his two previous films, it features a long, breathless chase sequence, this time of a bank-robber named Yamazaki (Shin'ichi Tsutsumi) being pursued by the bank's rent-a-cops. Carrying a bag full of cash that has literally dropped into his arms from the sky, Yamazaki eludes his pursuers, but not before a knife he is holding accidentally plunges into a young beautician. Now a possible murderer as well as a thief, he desperately searches for a sanctuary—and finds it in the unlikely form of a citizen's group protesting pollution from a local factory. Through yet another strange twist of fate, he becomes the group's spokesman.

Meanwhile, on a parallel narrative plane, two

yakuza, Kamada (Hiroshi Shimizu) and Matsuda (Akira Yamamoto), are conferring in their gang headquarters with Tachibana (Ren Osugi), a high-ranking honcho in a rival gang. With their boss in the slammer on a drug charge, they are at loose ends and ready to listen to Tachibana's proposal for a new overseas joint venture. Then a third gang member, a drunken practical joker named Kaneda (Ikko Suzuki), bursts in the door wearing Yamazaki's discarded ski mask and, by a freak accident, Tachibana ends up dead. Now the boys have a body to dispose of and an entire gang of angry yakuza to deal with.

Faced with a life-and-death dilemma resembling Yamazaki's, they find their lives becoming entangled with his in ways that may seem madly improbable, but in the context of the film's other goings-on, make an odd sort of sense. The title, we see, ought to be plural. Like Sabu's other heroes, Yamazaki and his three gangster acquaintances are playthings of circumstance who refuse (or are simply too harassed) to play along. Driven by greed, living in fear, they are, not Tarantinoesque icons of cool or Keatonesque masters of slapstick, but creations uniquely Sabu.

A veteran character-actor, Sabu is adept at drawing layered, individualized performances from his players. Shinichi Tsutsumi's Yamazaki is possessed of that most unlikely accessory for a postmodern cinematic hero—a tormenting conscience—while Ikko Suzuki's Kaneda boils with a rage that feels like the genuine, borderline psychotic article.

The plot is, like those in Sabu's other films, an absurdist contraption whose characters become the butts of cosmic jokes. After three outings, those jokes would seem to be wearing thin, but Unlucky Monkey is bolder in conception and tighter in execution than its predecessors. Like a standup comedian wood-shedding his act, Sabu is using the same bits, but giving them a different spin—and getting more laughs—each time out. Yes, he overworks coincidence and, yes, he stretches credibility to the breaking point (especially in a return-from-the-dead scene whose returnee must be a yogi), but the dynamism, inventiveness, and goofball conviction carry us through. One wonders, though, if its director will ever make a movie in which the hero doesn't have to be a marathoner to survive.

Untama Giru ✳

(1989)

Written and directed by Go Takamine. Produced by Parco. With Kaoru Kobayashi, Chikako Aoyama, Yoshiko Hazama, Susumu Taira, Eiko Miyamoto, John Sayles. (120 mins.)

Okinawa—as Go Takamine's Untama Giru makes abundantly clear—is in Japan but not of it. With their own culture, language, and history, Okinawans remain stubbornly resistant to assimilation. They are an undissolved lump in the "homogeneous" Japanese mass. In 1969, however, they were a bitterly divided people. Some called for independence, some for reversion to Japan, and still others for continued rule by the U.S. military. It is against this backdrop of factional infighting that Untama Giru unfolds, but Takamine, an Okinawan native, is less interested in local politics than the ever-shifting border between dream and reality.

In Takamine's Okinawa the native gods still live and magic is an everyday event. At the sugar refinery where the title hero works, a pony-tailed tree sprite strolls out of the woods for a daily lump of sugar, while the refinery owner's voluptuous mistress spends her days puffing languorously on a hookah, or lying in a pen, metamorphosed into a fat, pink pig. Takamine treats this material with a welcome matter-of-factness. Instead of trivializing it with whimsy or weighing it down with metaphor, he goes straight to the heart of the island's mystery and ultimate tragedy.

The story is based on an Okinawan version of the Robin Hood legend. Giru (Kaoru Kobayashi) works at the refinery, and on his break time, dreams of making love to Mare (Chikako Aoyama), the owner's mistress. He gets his wish one night when he goes with Mare to Untama Forest—an enchanted wood the local people are afraid to enter. Unluckily for Giru, Uto-basan (Yoshiko Hazama), an ally of the owner who has the power to read dreams, discovers his secret passion. When she tells the owner, Nishihara-oyakata (Susumu Taira), he becomes furious and vows to kill Giru with the lance he conceals in his cane. There is only one problem: Nishihara is blind.

He is not without cunning, however. After setting fire to his own warehouse, he accuses Giru of arson. Giru escapes to Untama Forest, where he obtains magic powers from Kijimura (Eiko Miyamoto)—the tree sprite with the sweet tooth—and embarks on a life of crime: robbing from U.S. Army bases and Japanese companies to help the villagers who are fighting for Okinawan independence.

Although set in 1969, the film takes place in a dreamy timeless present, its pace an endless summer crawl. The local barber may wear a set of smile buttons— the latest fad—but he and his cronies are ever ready to burst into song about the adventures of the local hero, Untama Giru.

Takamine uses the down-home atmosphere to not only add humor and charm, but make the supernatural natural. In Giru's village no one blinks at an old woman who reads dreams or a young man who floats through the air. They are both part of the magical reality that everyone takes for granted and always has. Like Gabriel Garcia Marquez, Takamine seems to not only have imagined that reality, but lived it. He is not recording his own dream life so much as the inner life of a time, place, and culture that has long been under severe pressure from the world outside.

In *Untama Giru*, that pressure takes the grotesque form of Kamajisa (director and screenwriter John Sayles), the American commandant of the island who lusts after the blood of Mare the pig. The scene of Kamajisa (which means "grumpy" in Okinawan) receiving a transfusion of Mare's blood fits in well with the rest of proceedings, but as satire is obvious and crude. As Giru, Kobayashi has the requisite heroic handsomeness, but lacks Robin Hood-like panache. Perhaps the Okinawan countryside is not the right place to look for it. Many of the other actors are amateurs playing themselves with an admirable naturalness. The only irritant is singer Jun Togawa, who gives a woozy, flaky performance as Giru's sister. When she started crooning in her quavery Betty Boop voice I felt the need for an armrest volume control.

Be that as it may, *Untama Giru* gives a glimpse of a world seldom seen on JTB travel posters, but all the more attractive for its elusiveness. At the end of the film, Takamine suggests its death. We can only hope that he is wrong and that Giru and his companions live on.

Waga Ai no Uta: Taki Rentaro Monogatari
Bloom In the Moonlight (1993)

Directed by Shin'ichiro Sawaii. Screenplay by Shin'ichiro Sawaii and Akira Miyazaki. Produced by Toei and Nippon Television Network. With Toru Kazama, Isako Washio, Ryo Amamiya, Miki Fujitani. (125 mins.)

Shin'ichiro Sawai's *Waga Ai no Uta: Taki Rentaro Monogatari* is what the Japan film industry considers a prestige production. With its elaborate period sets, "Great Moments" storyline and hagiographic treatment of its subject, it has the flavor of a thirties

Hollywood biopic. Rentaro Taki was a composer and pianist who died of tuberculosis in 1903 at the age of twenty-three. During his brief career, however, he composed songs that are still known today by every Japanese.

Waga Ai tells his story with a dogged literalness, punctuated by frequent musical intervals, minor subplots, and brief appearances by period celebrities. It even supplies subtitles so that the audience knows exactly which "Great Moment" it is watching. Pitched at a female audience in the mood for an old-fashioned tear-jerker, the movie contains plenty of old-fashioned moral uplift. Its Taki is a hero who sacrifices his youth, health, and life for the greater glory of the nation. Japan, he proclaims, has to "catch up with Europe" in the field of music. This resolve is touching, but one imagines stern-faced teachers herding students into the theater to hear real Japanese music and learn about real Japanese values.

Waga Ai begins with the fifteen-year-old Taki (Toru Kazama) entering the Tokyo School of Music as its youngest student. A bumpkin from Oita Prefecture, Taki marvels at his first grand piano and his first foreign teacher. Though a rank beginner, he makes such rapid progress that he excites the envy of the bluff, good-hearted Suzuki (Ryo Amamiya) and a pretty but impeccably proper Yuki (Isako Washio). Both students, however, come to love Taki for his talent, dedication, and pureness of heart.

Taking a hint in eccentricity from Tom Hulce's performance as Mozart in *Amadeus*, Kazama plays Taki as a dweeb who walks with a stiff-backed lope and speaks with unfailing politeness, as though he were chatting with the Crown Prince at a garden party. In an ordinary high school, with its ordinary complement of louts, he would have quickly become the class paperwad target. The real-life Taki was a whiz at tennis and a traditional Japanese card game called *hyakunin isshu*. He was also a fashion-plate who, while in Germany, impressed the natives by sporting the latest styles. *Waga Ai*, however, prefers to see him as a saintly victim who grows through suffering.

While recuperating at a hot springs from a physical collapse brought on by overwork, Taki meets a young maid, Fumi (Miki Fujitani), who becomes infatuated with him. Oblivious, he does not reciprocate. In need of money, her father sells her as a concubine to a rich Tokyo merchant and, after a last, tearful meeting, she disappears from his life. He is oblivious to Yuki as well, even when she volunteers to give up her scholarship so that he can go to Germany in her place. Taki manfully tells her that he will win the next one and urges her not to miss this once-in-a-lifetime chance.

He gets the scholarship, but when he finally meets Yuki again, in a palatial country home, she is desperate; a concert is approaching and she is unprepared. Taki helps her practice her piece, and after working day and night, she regains her confidence. In gratitude, she embraces Taki and he responds in a way he could not with Fumi. But a spray of tubercular blood ends their romantic dream.

Whatever its defects, *Waga Ai* supplies more classical music on the sound track that almost any film since *Amadeus*. Though most of the pieces are warhorses, to the ears of Meiji-era Japanese they must have sounded dazzlingly new. The film succeeds in capturing some of that astonishment and delight.

Taki's own compositions also fall into the familiar category, especially for older Japanese. Even for a first-time listener, they evoke a simpler time and reflect the sincerity and charm of Taki's personality. *Waga Ai no Uta* may not live on in the annals of Japanese film history, but the music and the man will be us a good while longer,

Ware ni Utsu Yoi Ari
Ready to Shoot (1990)

Directed by Koji Wakamatsu. Screenplay by Eiji Marunouchi. Produced by Shochiku. With Lu Xiuling, Yoshio Harada, Kaori Momoi, Keizo Kanie. (106 mins.)

In *The Big Chill* Lawrence Kasdan gave us a bleak and surfacy view of sixties activist types slipping uneasily into middle age. Though the movie wasn't all that good, it spawned a catchphrase—"the Big Chill generation"—and gave Tom Berenger, Glenn Close, William Hurt, Jeff Goldblum, and Kevin Kline a boost toward stardom. In Koji Wakamatsu's *Ware ni Utsu Yoi Ari*, the heroes are also aging radicals who feel guilty about not living up to their old ideals and make one more try at recapturing the past.

But whereas *The Big Chill* was made by a boomer for boomers and came along at a time when its target audience was ready for the film's inward-looking mood, *Ware ni Utsu Yoi Ari* is a movie in search of a audience. It wants to address Japan's own Big Chill generation, but knowing that that generation is past its moviegoing prime, it carefully explains its characters' midlife crisis to the kids who are actually going to be watching. One scene even shows two of its middle-aged heroes regaling a group of young women with tales about the good old days. It also gives them a heavy dose of action to hold their attention. It's *The Big Chill* for the 1990s all right, but it's also *Columbo Comes to Kabukicho*.

The owner of a funky bar in the Kabukicho entertainment district of Tokyo (Yoshio Harada), is about to hold a party to mark the closing of his place after twenty years in business. Among his guests are old friends from his radical student days, including a former lover (Kaori Momoi). But while he is preparing for the big event, a young woman (Lu Xiuling) bursts in the door. She is wounded in the arm and says, in halting Japanese, that she is being pursued by *yakuza*. We learn that she is a Vietnamese refugee who entered Japan on a false passport. The *yakuza* are after her because she shot a gang boss and stole a gang home video that contains an incriminating scene. The boss's murder soon comes to the attention of the police, including a detective (Keizo Kanie) who is a Peter Falk ringer. The detective begins his investigation while the *yakuza* continue their pursuit.

The story has holes big enough to drive a Hino truck through. One example: the young woman goes to the Koma Theater in Kabukicho to pick up her passport and hand over a large sum of money. This, on the face of it, is absurd: the theater area has the highest gangster-per-square-meter ratio in Tokyo, making it likely that an unfriendly *yakuza* will spot her. Sure enough, one does, and gives chase. (One of many such scenes: Taiwanese star Lu Xiuling spends so much time outrunning gangsters that she deserves a medal in the Kabukicho Olympics.)

Kanie, as the detective, may have a few Columbo-like mannerisms (he can't get his lighter to light), but he is a convincing cop. He seems to have been on the Kabukicho beat so long, striking terror into the hearts of the local bad guys, that he has become more street than straight. More Harvey Keitel than Peter Falk, in other words. Director Wakamatsu also understands its middle-aged radicals and the place they once called their own—Shinjuku was once his own stamping ground, he tells us in a program note. He photographs its grubby vibrance and lurid glamour—the bamboo forests of neon rising up to the night sky—with an insider's eye.

He has a strong center for the movie in Yoshio Harada. With his unruly locks and ravaged face Harada looks the aging revolutionary who has survived with his ideals bruised, but intact. He makes the film's strained premise—that the bar owner can only salvage his radical conscience by saving a Vietnamese girl from the gangs and the cops— almost work. As his former main squeeze, Kaori Momoi is so laid-back that she is almost out of the movie. Her lazily sensuous style, which was once a challenge to the chipperly sexless norm, comes across as lazy, period.

Even so, I liked *Wari ni Utsu Yoi Ari*. In addition to being an excellent guided tour of a familiar neighborhood (I had the uncanny feeling of knowing exactly where I was in nearly every scene), it was an instructive look back at an era as far removed from the Japan of today as "Blowing In the Wind" is from "Justify My Love."

Watashi o Daite Soshite Kiss Shite

Hug Me, Then Kiss Me (1992)

Directed by Jun'ya Sato. Screenplay by Toshiyuki Tabe, Kasane Aso, and Hiroshi Takahashi. Produced by Toei. With Yoko Minamino, Kaho Minami, Hidekazu Arai. (106 mins.)

"I find it ironic that, at a time when traditions and customs are disappearing and conventional melodrama is becoming harder to make, a new form of drama is being born from an incurable disease called AIDS," writes director Jun'ya Sato in the program notes for his latest film, *Watashi o Daite Soshite Kiss Shite*.

Ironic, indeed. It is also unfortunate that Japan's first film about AIDS is less a new type of drama than a conventional melodrama. Faced with a plague that has inspired extremes of protest and prejudice, Sato resorts to the clichés of the TV tearjerker. Change the heroine's diagnosis to terminal cancer and she could be a character on an agonizingly earnest installment of *Nichiyo Gekijo* (Sunday Theater).

Based on a book by journalist Shoko Ieda, *Watashi o Daite* is not an crass attempt to cash in. It presents badly needed, if baldly presented, information and takes a sympathetic view of its heroine's plight. Also, the very existence of the heroine herself—who contracts the disease from a former boyfriend—challenges the stereotype of AIDS victims as either gays or drug addicts. As the film makes clear, the size of the "at risk" group is growing with alarming speed.

Soon after the opening credits roll, Keiko Aida (Yoko Minamino) learns that she has been exposed to the HIV virus. A travel agency clerk whose biggest problem in life to date has been finding Mr. Right, she is shattered. After testing positive, she plunges into a black despair. A journalist (Kaho Minami) covering the AIDS crisis tries to befriend her, but Keiko rejects her advances. "What do you have to do with me?" she asks. Her reaction is a natural one, especially in a society that treats the HIV-infected as outcastes and regards their condition as shameful. Keiko's response to her plight, however, is disturbing; soon after meeting a rugged-looking businessman named Akira (Hidekazu Arai) in a park she goes to a hotel with him. What can she be thinking?

Because she is a nice Japanese girl, revenge at the male sex is not the answer. The reason for her behavior, the film indicates, is loneliness. A pair of strong male arms will make her feel more like a woman, less like a freak. At first, she resists temptation; then, when she meets Akira a second time, she succumbs. Undeniably, she is attempting murder. The film, however, presents her dangerously selfish action as a natural expression of her weak, dependent, womanly nature. "You don't understand my *onnagokoro*

(woman's heart)," she teases Akira at one point. If he did, he might have left her in the park, walking steadily but swiftly in the opposite direction.

But just as Keiko is a womanly woman, in conventional Japanese movie terms, Akira is a manly man. Though he leaves her after learning the truth, when he meets her again and she tells him that she is three months pregnant with his child, he decides to stand by her. (We can't help wondering whether a negative test for HIV may have made him more inclined to do the right thing). Meanwhile, the journalist has broken down Keiko's reserve and won her trust. Together this threesome faces a momentous decision: Should Keiko have her baby and risk the thirty-percent chance that it might be infected, or abort and avoid the life-shortening strain of childbirth?

To give it credit, *Watashi o Daite* illustrates the yawning gap that exists between our intellectual knowledge and our instinctive fear of AIDS. When Keiko licks the journalist's cut finger, the journalist recoils in horror. The shot of her scrubbing it with manic desperation, while knowing perfectly well that she hasn't been infected, is revealing and instructive.

I wish I could recommend *Watashi o Daite* more strongly. Yoko Minamino, who has appeared in some awful dreck, gives the performance of her career. Even Hidekazu Arai, an ex-boxer who looks as though he would be more comfortable in a ring than on a sound stage, slugs it out with an incompatible part. I can only hope that the first Japanese film about AIDS won't be the last.

Watashitachi ga Suki Datta Koto

When We Were In Love (1997)

Directed by Joji Matsuoka. Screenplay by Hisashi Nozawa. Produced by Amuse, Toei Video, and Digital Media Lab. With Goto Kishitani, Yasufumi Terawaki,, Isako Washio. (105 mins.)

Hollywood date movies are easy enough to figure out. If boy and girl meet cute in the first reel, they will be each other's arms by the last, even if, as in *Ghost*, death do them part. In Japan, however, screen romances long took a different turn, with fate keeping the lovers forever apart, as the audience snuffled into its hankies. Today, however, more Japanese dating movies have Hollywood-inspired story lines and even include scenes shot in the United States and other foreign climes. Also, many of the characters, especially the women, work at groovy *katakana* jobs (*jyanarisuto* [journalist], *dezainaa* [designer]), wear expensive designer clothes and live in classy downtown condos—no hour-and-a-half schleps into the city for these folks!

Though these movies do not follow a rigid formula, certain elements reappear again and again. Christmas motifs are common (understandably so: Christmas Eve is the biggest date night of the year). The lovers usually have a shouting argument in a driving rainstorm. And poured over everything, from beginning to end, is the J-Pop soundtrack, which is used less to subtlety heighten emotion than to intrusively dictate it.

Joji Matsuoka's *Watashitachi ga Suki Datta Koto* is undoubtedly a date movie, but not a typical one. Yes, its stars are all familiar faces to TV-drama fans, and three of the four play thirtysomething *katakana* professionals with bright futures and money in the bank. Yes, they celebrate a warmly soft-focus Christmas together. And yes, they all dress well, eat well, and live well, in a new penthouse condo. But Matsuoka, who directed the 1992 *Kira Kira Hikaru*, one of the first Japanese films to feature a gay man as a main character, takes these hackneyed elements and combines them in entertainingly fresh ways, with a true understanding of the wayward impulses of the heart.

Yoshi (Goto Kishitani), a lighting designer, and Roba (Yasufumi Terawaki), an advertising photographer, are two friends who have just beat out seventy-five other applicants to buy a two-bedroom condo in a new high-rise. While they are drinking in a crowded bar and excitedly discussing the decoration of their urban Shangri La, two women named Aiko (Yui Natsukawa) and Yoko (Isako Washio) join them. Soon, the two men are telling these strangers of their good fortune and inviting them to see their new pad. The next day, hungover from the previous night's celebration, they find they have visitors: Aiko and Yoko, who have since hired a moving truck to haul their stuff to the men's condo. Yoko blithely thanks them for their invitation to move in—an invitation that they do not remember making—and assures them that their stay will be only temporary, "until we find a place of their own."

There is, as it turns out, nothing temporary about this arrangement, but there is a reason for it. Yoko's friend Aiko suffers from disabling panic attacks. Yoko has been caring for her, but she is also working full-time as a hair stylist and is tiring of her burden. The two men, particularly the simple, trusting Roba (his nickname, Japanese for "donkey," is appropriate), strike her as ideal nursemaids. Though initally opposed to this imposition, Yoshi becomes the first to discover Aiko's illness, and soon after, falls in love with her. Meanwhile, without a word to anyone, Roba begins sleeping in Yoko's room. This odd foursome become two loving couples, toasting their mutual good fortune around the dining room table. At New Year's they go to a shrine together to wish for a happy and prosperous future. To fulfill that wish,

they help Aiko realize her long-cherished dream: quit her dead-end job at a cement company and study to become a doctor.

But the women's pasts arrive in the form of Aiko's Philistine mother, who is horrified by her daughter's unconventional lifestyle, and Yoko's rat of a former boyfriend, a married businessman who abandoned her but still can't forget her. They besiege the highrise Shangri La, and though the foursome resist the intrusion, cracks begin to appear in the walls.

The ending is not a downer—the ultimate date movie taboo—but it feels right. The music never drowns out the dialogue, and nary a drop of rain falls. Reasons enough to see *Watashitachi ga Suki Datta Koto* with someone you love.

Wild Life *
[1997]

Directed by Shinji Aoyama. **Screenplay by** Shinji Aoyama, Kumi Sato. **Produced by** Bitters End. **With** Kosuke Toyohara, Ken Mitsuishi, Mickey Curtis, Yuna Natsuo. (102 mins.)

Shinji Aoyama started making 8mm films while a student at Rikkyo University and in 1996 released his first feature, *Helpless*. In less than a year the thirty-two-year old director has filmed two more theatrical features—*Chimpira* (Two Punks) and *Wild Life*—and a video movie, *Waga Mune ni Kyoki Ari* (There's a Weapon in My Chest). In *Wild Life*, as in *Helpless*, the hero is a tall, longhaired outsider, lost in a sea of anomie and mixed up with the *yakuza*, with violent results. But Aoyama's treatment of this familiar material is drier, funnier, stronger.

Despite its cartoonish moments, *Wild Life* is less a genre send-up than a stylized exercise in genre stretching. While delivering a few laughs, a few chills, and a few fresh takes on *yakuza* movie conventions, the film explores broader themes, including the unpredictability of life and the elusiveness of truth. It wants to be an existential black comedy, with a thriller punch.

The title is semi-ironic. The hero, Hiroki Sakai (Kosuke Toyohara), is a *kugishi*—a professional adjuster of the pins in *pachinko* pinball machines—whose life has settled into a dull routine. A phlegmatic, self-deprecating sort, Sakai accepts this existence as a given, until he is roused from his stupor by several blasts from his past.

One is Mizuguchi (Ken Mitsuishi), a thin, nervous man who once managed a game center for Sakai's boss but quit after being robbed and beaten by *yakuza* thugs. Now he is out for revenge and wants Sakai's help in getting it. Another is his boss's daughter, Rie (Yuna Natsuo), grown into sexy, wide-eyed womanhood since he last saw her six years ago. She is eager to renew her acquaintance with Sakai, depite the objections of a nerdish boyfriend. Then, without understanding why, Sakai becomes the target of a *yakuza* boss and his minions, who are convinced that he has a mysterious envelope and, later, an incriminating video tape. Though he tries, sensibly, to stay out of trouble, he is forced into action when his boss, the bearded and pony-tailed Tsumura (Mickey Curtis), is abducted by the *yakuza* and the police refuse to help. But while riding to the rescue, Sakai learns that the good guys, including his boss, have spots on their white hats, and that the truth of this tangled affair is not what is seems.

As Sakai, Kosuke Toyohara is diffident with the ladies and polite to the tough guys, while packing a devastating punch and deadly aim with a full can of beer. His nonchalance is more than a comic pose; it becomes the key to his character. When, at the end, Sakai laughs uproariously at the *yakuza* boss's offer to join his gang, we can laugh with him, understanding not only the joke but why he thinks it so funny.

While Toyohara's performance is unobtrusive, Aoyama's direction is anything but. As in *Helpless*, he often uses one cut per scene and keeps his camera in motion. But whereas in the earlier film some cuts seemed to go interminably, in *Wild Life* Aoyama breaks his story into eight segments (all titled in English, including such familiar borrowings as "Light In August" and "As Time Goes By"), while cutting for conciseness, rhythm, and humor. Some of his effects are ingenious. In an interrogation scene, the camera circles 360 degrees, focusing first on the detective, then on the person he is questioning. In one of the sweeps we see Tsumura, in the next, Sakai, in the next Tsumura again—around and around on a surreal merry-go-round, with the interrogator's questions and the interrogatee's answers matching perfectly. Though his detective gets nowhere, Shinji Aoyama has come a long way indeed.

Winds of God

(1995)

Directed by Yoko Narahashi. **Screenplay by** Masayuki Imai. **Produced by** Shochiku Daiichi Kogyo and KSS. **With** Masayuki Imai, Shota Yamaguchi, Setsuko Ogawa. (97 mins.)

As we approach August 15 and the inevitable outpouring of remembrance over the fiftieth anniversary of Japan's defeat in World War II, Toho, Toei and Shochiku are gearing up to fight their own final battle in the war-movie wars. For the younger generation, however, World War II belongs to not only

another time but another world. The young *tokkotai* (special attack unit) pilots, who flew off to certain death, and today's teenagers, whose only battles are digitalized, would seem to have little in common.

Shochiku's entry in the war-movie sweeps, *Winds of God* is an unusual and ambitious attempt to bridge the generation gap. Based on a play of the same title by Masayuki Imai that director Yoko Narahashi first staged at the Actors Studio in New York in 1993, this film about two *manzai* comedians who find themselves in a *tokkotai* squadron resists standard Japanese war movie pieties. It portrays its *tokkotai* pilots as flesh-and-blood young men in extraordinary circumstances, rather than as heroic "living gods" (the way their Japanese contemporaries were taught to regard them) or death-bent fanatics (the way their American enemies came to see them). *Winds* is antiwar, but in a universal rather than specific sense. Some, longing for the Japanese movie that finally rips the lid off Japan's conduct of the war, will regard this approach as a cop out. But I think Narahashi deserves credit for promoting dialogue between 1945 and 1995 without heavyhanded editorializing or sentimentalizing. War may be the supreme political act, but the men who fight it usually see it in personal terms. Despite the humanistic halos it places around the heads of its *tokkotai* pilots, *Winds* is alive to that fact.

The film begins in present-day Japan. The film's two comedians—Tashiro (Masayuki Imai) and Kinta (Shota Yamaguchi)—play their on-stage roles in real life. Tashiro, or Aniki (Older Brother), as his partner prefers to call him, is fast-talking, quick-thinking and forever spinning from one emotional extreme to another. Kinta, on the other hand, is a clueless plodder who nonetheless burns with an inner fire. He is Innocence to Aniki's Experience. Their routine is full of topical gags, but they are only dimly aware of history the day before yesterday.

When, following a traffic accident, they find themselves in the infirmary of a *tokkotai* squadron, they at first think they are in the slammer and try to get on the good side of the other inmates by performing their routine. But jokes about the PKO only mystify their audience, who believe that two of their pilots, after a near-fatal crash on an aborted mission, are suffering a strange loss of memory. Then, when an air-raid begins, and the comics see bombs exploding on the airfield, they realize that they are in a very different place and time indeed.

The date is August 1, 1945 and Japan, they know, is heading for defeat, but the *tokkotai* pilots keep flying on their one-way missions, regardless. Aniki excoriates them for their stubbornness and stupidity. Can't they see it's hopeless? But Kinta, after meeting the pure-hearted fiancee (Setsuko Ogawa) of the pilot whose body he is inhabiting, starts to admire them, and ends by wanting to join them. Though full of a youthful idealism, the pilots are intensely aware of their approaching fate. One spends the night before his flight desperately trying to break his schoolboy long-jump record (he succeeds and Aniki cheers). Another is a Christian who has been forced to publicly renounce his beliefs, but secretly clings to them. Still another is a former college student who believes the comics' time-traveling story—he studied the transmigration of souls—but is resolved to die anyway. ("It's my fate," he says.)

In their determination to make a war movie with no bad guys, only victims, Narahashi and Imai seem to be dodging the issue of evil, but their approach also has deep cultural roots and reflects historical realities. As Ivan Morris noted in *The Nobility of Failure*, "…far from being fierce, superstitious, jingoistic fanatics…[*tokkotai* recruits tended to be] quiet, serious, and above average in both culture and sensibility." So are the film's pilot heroes.

While drawing crisp, vibrant performances from her actors, particularly Masayuki Imai as Aniki, Narahashi gives them line readings more suited to the stage than screen. The dialogue sounds slightly overprojected, as though the actors are speaking to the balcony rather than each other. Even so, *Winds of God* deserves praise for inviting discussion rather than preaching, offering insights rather than jerking tears. What may be one of the last World War II movies from Japan is also one of the better ones.

Wonderful Life
After Life (1999)

Written and directed by Hirokazu Koreeda. Cinematography by Yutaka Yamazaki. Produced by TV Man Union.With Arata, Erika Oda, Takatoshi Naito, Kyoko Kagawa, Takashi Naito, Susumu Terajima. (118 mins.)

In *Wonderful Life* Hirokawa Koreeda proves again that he is an original talent who can take a well-worn theme—the journey to the Other Side—and re-imagine it with none of the usual clichés. (Though one inspiration is the 1943 Ernst Lubitsch comedy *Heaven Can Wait*.) Set in Limbo, which looks like the campus of a crumbling small college on a perfect fall day, the film depicts the work of guides who help the newly dead select a memory to take with them into eternity. They have three days to accomplish this task, after which they film a video of the selected moment. Some of their charges have no trouble choosing, while others agonize and still others refuse to choose at all.

The genesis of the film lay in Koreeda's own experience as a child watching his grandfather grow senile from Alzheimer's disease. "I remember thinking that people forgot everything when they die," he said. "I now understand how critical memories are to our identity, to a sense of self." Koreeda first explored the relationship between memory and identity in *Without Memory*, a 1994 television documentary about a man with a rare condition that prevents him from forming new memories.

In making *Wonderful Life*, Koreeda also used documentary methods, interviewing nearly five hundred ordinary Japanese, young and old, some of whom later appeared in the film. Also, several of the film's professional actors related their own most cherished moments to the camera. These reminiscences convey an honesty, spontaneity, and humor that rarely comes from a prepared script. A teenage girl says the high point of her life was a ride on Disneyland's Splash Mountain. An old man lovingly recalls a cigarette smoked in the jungle during World War II. An old woman struggles to remember how, as a young girl, she sang and danced in a new red dress.

In assembling these moments into a cinematic montage, Koreeda creates an intimate human reality that has nothing to with New Age wish-fulfillment, everything to do with the essence of who we are and the meaning of where we've been. As his camera reveals, the edges of memory may become corroded by the fictionalizing mists of time, but they can also be a ruthless mirror, plunging his characters into regrets for time wasted, loved denied.

Wonderful Life tells a story of the elderly Mr. Watanabe (Taketoshi Naito), who cannot come to a decision, even after watching dozens of tapes of his humdrum life. He is helped by Mochizuki (Arata), a long-haired young guidewho is unusually solicitous and sympathetic. The reason, we discover, is that, despite appearances, he is of Watanabe's generation—after fifty years of working as a guide, he is still unable to choose his own memory. Meanwhile, Mochizuki's young assistant, Shiori (Erika Oda), who has more than a professional interest in him, is shattered to learn that he has an undying love for another woman—someone he and Watanabe both know.

There is an artifice in this story not present in the unscripted reminiscences, but the disjunction is not great enough to harm the film. Koreeda keeps the tone constant throughout—the feeling that, though still in a familiarly human place, one has left the pettiness and passions of the living world behind to embark on a final journey of self-reflection and self-discovery. The atmosphere is nearer that of a religious retreat than a secular resort, but one created by a sensibility more visual than literary. The final act before departure from this Limbo is not the reading of a sacred text but the viewing of a videotape. One suspects that, for Koreeda at least, this way station to a Higher Ground is Paradise.

World Apartment Horror
(1991)

Directed by Katsuhiro Otomo. Screenplay by Katsuhiro Otomo and Keiko Nobumoto. Produced by Sony Music Entertainment. With Hiroyuki Tanaka, Yuji Nakamura, Weng Huarong. (97 min.)

Tokyo has become a magnet for Asian workers who want a piece of the First World dream. The evidence is at construction sites and factories where Asians are doing the jobs Japanese avoid. It is also in Yushima, Itabashi, Adachi, and Kita wards, where Asian workers and students live in cheap rooming houses in fear of immigration authorities. This influx has stimulated debate between internationalists and xenophobes, changed attitudes (small children don't stare at us outlanders as much as they used to) and even generated new urban legends (the "Bangladeshi rapist"). Now Katsuhiro Otomo has produced a film about the new cultural clash: *World Apartment Horror*.

The setting is a rundown rooming house in Tokyo. The residents include a rotund Pakistani factory worker, a fast-talking Filipino cabaret hustler, a brooding Bangladeshi youth, a straight-arrow Taiwanese student and four Chinese who seem to spend their all their time either cooking or playing mah-jongg. Into this all-male United Nations comes Itta (Hiroyuki Tanaka), a lanky, lantern-jawed *chimpira* (apprentice gangster). He is there to persuade the tenants to leave: a new building is going up on the site and his gang has been hired to clear the way. A predecessor (Yuji Nakamura) was assigned the same task but went mad before he could complete it. Itta soon learns why: the tenants refuse to listen to reason (for one thing, they can barely understand his slangy Japanese). Worse, a mysterious force shows its displeasure with his presence in strange and terrifying ways. The ceiling heaves when he is making love to his tarty girlfriend, geysers of foam erupt from his beer cans, and even his boom box develops a mind of its own. Itta becomes paranoid (those foreigners are out to get him!) and quickly slides over the edge.

Despite the menace of its title, *World Apartment Horror* is more *Ghostbusters* than *Friday the 13th*. Itta is a swaggering, sneering punk who will do anything, including carting off the house's toilet, to accomplish his ends, but is baffled by the tenants' maddeningly passive resistance and boggled by the odd happenings.

As Itta, Hiroyuki Tanaka gives an amusing and winning performance. While laughing at Itta's mus-

cleheaded bullying and dumb terror, we sympathize with the poor sap's desperation and believe that he is salvageable in the end. With the exception of Weng Huarong as an earnest Taiwanese student, all of the foreigners are played by amateurs. The presence of foreign actors, amateur or otherwise, does not usually bode well in a Japanese film, but Otomo has drawn surprisingly good performances from his non-professional cast. One reason is that, for most of the film, they are either silently scuttling about the hallways or speaking broken Japanese. It is only toward the end, when they are required to act in English, that we see them for the amateurs they are.

The veil drops in the film's key scene, when we learn why the strange events are taking place. The reason is a lame one; the acting, appalling. After an hour of lightfooted comedy, *World Apartment Horror* takes a plunge into ham-handed drama. This lapse doesn't completely ruin the film—we like the characters too much by then—but it can't help violating its own mood. Otomo wants us to laugh at his characters' antics, take the silly horror story seriously, and feel a surge of emotion when Itta finally sees the all-Asians-are-brothers light. He wants it all, in other words, but ends up with much less.

An innovative *manga* artist who directed the cult SF-animation hit *Akira*, Otomo deserves praise for tackling a difficult subject in an imaginative and entertaining way. I would have liked to see him dig deeper, however. He never shows us more than the surface of his foreigners' lives or explains why they are living in such a rat trap in the first place. An article in a recent issue of the magazine *Aera* suggests why. Posing as an Asian student, a writer for the magazine went to thirty real-estate agents looking for an apartment and was turned away by all of them. Now that, I thought, might make a movie.

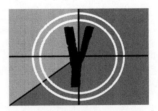

Yaju Shisubeshi: Fukushuhen
The Beast Must Die: Revenge (1997)

Directed by Masato Hironichi. Screenplay by Toshiyuki Morioka. Produced by Daiei. With Kazuya Kimura, Toshiya Nagasawa. (86 mins.)

For a film, the right title can spell the difference between box-office life or death. David O. Selznick wanted to call a thriller about postwar intrigue in Austria's multicultural capital *A Night in Vienna*. But fellow-producer Alexander Korda and scriptwriter Graham Greene held out for the original title: *The Third Man*. It's lucky for us they did.

Likewise enjoying a long shelf is the title of *Yaju Shisubeshi: Fukushuhen*. Based on a best-selling novel by Haruhiko Oyabu, the first *Yaju Shisubeshi* was released in 1959, with Tatsuya Nakadai starring as a graduate student "beast" who plots the perfect crime. Another version was made in 1980, with Yusaku Matsuda playing the lead, this time as a former war photographer who turns to crime in rebellion against Japan's straightjacket society.

The third and latest "beast" is Kazuya Kimura, an actor in the Richard Gere mold who looks more the pretty-boy gigolo than the cold-blooded killer. But Kimura is appropriately affectless playing a man who is a printer by day, a ruthless criminal by night. Watching his cold, dead eyes as he took aim at yet another victim, I couldn't help thinking that his handsome face was the ideal mask for his purpose. Looks may not kill, but they make it easier to get within range.

Directed by Masato Hironichi, from a script by prolific thriller-scenarist Toshiyuki Morioka (*Fudo, Risutora Daimon, Chimpira*), *Yaju* follows the nefarious career of Kunihiko Date (Kimura), the aforementioned printer, who happens upon a cop staking out a druggie's hide-out one rainy night, runs him over with his BMW, clips him with his own gun and drives off, barely breaking a sweat.

Equipped with a shooter and a badge, Date next targets the boss of a gambling den for the Shanghai mafia. On the pretext of a making an arrest, Date handcuffs the boss to his fancy foreign car and proceeds to beat his shiny-domed bodyguard to a pulp. He then walks off with a suitcase full of ten-thousand-yen notes, as casually as though he'd just passed through a supermarket check-out line.

Meanwhile, the police, led by a longhaired detective named Katsu Oki (Toshiya Nagasawa), are hot on the trail of the cop killer. Was it a mob hit, or, wonders the intuitive Oki, was it someone else?

Not satisfied with his new-found fortune, Date plans to rob an armored truck loaded with three hundred million yen in cash. Needing a driver, he recruits a former colleague who has just lost his job and learned that he is dying of cancer. The heist is successful, but the cough-wracked driver begs Date to put him out of his misery and take care of his widow and child. Date obliges. What we have here is the dirtiest of dirty heroes, who will do whatever it takes, including murder, to commit the perfect crime

and thereby escape social ties and economic burdens. His ultimate object is to become a free agent, beyond the bounds of God and man.

This is a monstrous ambition and the man who achieves it is truly a beast who must, of course, die. Nonetheless, Date has a wretched past that makes his crimes more understandable, if not excusable. Also, though capable of the most heinous crimes, he can laugh and joke with his younger sister while taking a stroll on the beach. Finally, he can shoot a gun with consummate skill and tool his Honda motorbike about the urban jungle with panache. The beast, in short, is a cool dude, whose fashionable gear, including replicas of the guns he uses to whack his victims, are being offered to fans in a drawing by distributor Daiei. Step right up!

All this, as well as the shock ending, may alarm and repel the more tender-minded, but *Yaju* also issues a strong, frank appeal to the antisocial loner in all of us. Made on the cheap and bound for the video shelves, with hurried shot-making and choppy editing, the film nonetheless achieves an impact that more carefully crafted genre products often lack. There is an instructive purity in its absolute amorality. This, we see, is not so much a cautionary fable about a human monster as an unapologetic plunge into a male fantasy world.

"Sooner murder an infant in its cradle than nurse unacted desires," wrote William Blake. The makers of *Yaju Shisubeshi* seem to agree.

Yamai wa Ki kara: Byoin e Iko 2
Love Never Dies (1993)

Directed by Yojiro Takita. **Screenplay by** Nobuyuki Isshiki. **Produced by** Fuji Television Network and Melies. **With** Hiroshi Mikami, Hiroyuki Sanada, Kyoko Koizumi, Bengal, Hana Kino. (110 mins.)

Is it possible to make an upbeat movie about terminal cancer? When the producers of *Byoin e Iko* (Let's Go To the Hospital), a 1990 "docu-comedy" about hospital life, first announced that they were going to answer that question in the affirmative, I had my doubts. Was the star, Kyoko Koizumi, going to meet death with the smile that had launched a thousand TV commercials? Were there no corners of Japanese life safe from the cult of the *kawaii* (cute)?

The film they made, *Yamai wa Ki kara: Byoin e Iko 2* is cute all right, but it also has the comic patient's-eye view of illness that made its predecessor such a pleasure to watch. It's said that laughter is the best medicine. *Yamai* may not cure cancer, but it might better educate viewers about the disease—and give them more hope that they can beat it—than the standard three-hankie hospital melodrama.

The film's first lesson—one that we already know from the melodramas, if not from life—is that cancer is no respecter of age. Yuko (Kyoko Koizumi) is a twenty-five-year old beautician who is diagnosed with terminal stomach cancer. What to do? Her hospital, as is often the case in Japan, is a family business; the founder is semi-retired and his two sons have succeeded him. The older son, Ichiro (Hiroyuki Sanada), believes in battling cancer with all the pharmaceutical resources at his command. The younger son, Tamotsu (Hiroshi Mikami), believes in sparing terminal patients therapy that can only prolong their agony. He is building a hospice on the hospital grounds, where they can meet their ends in comfort and dignity.

Not knowing the true nature of her disease, Yuko first tries Ichiro's way, but chemotherapy reduces her to a physical wreck, while her doctor's evasions make her fearful and suspicious. Is she supposed to feel this miserable with a stomach ulcer? She pries out the truth and decides to move into the hospice. Yuko has seemingly chosen "good" passive care, with its doses of soothing morphine, over "bad" aggressive therapy, with its hellish pain, but the choice, the film shows us, is not that simple. Ichiro is a skilled doctor who helps his patients (including his father) win more than their share of battles against cancer.

Also, Tamotsu's patients are not saints, but ordinary mortals who fear death and want to live. A sake-store owner (Bengal) with a passion for women and gambling tries a series of quack cures. A widow (Hana Kino) with a mountain of debts and a nebbish of a son, turns to Christian fundamentalism and tries to convert her fellow patients. They will not go gently into the good night. Neither will Yuko. Recovering from her chemo-induced stupor, she finds she still has a twenty-five-year-old's hopes and desires. She leaves the hospice to pack all the living she can in the three months left her.

Instead of doing the expected—nights of club-hopping or a trip to Bali—She appears in a TV commercial for a life-insurance company and calmly announces that she "won't be alive to celebrate Christmas." The ad draws a huge response and she finds herself famous and rich. She also falls in love with Tamotsu.

Kyoko Koizumi, whose own career as super-idol has been the stuff of fantasy, brings the needed credibility to these scenes. I didn't find it too much of a stretch to believe that her character—a gutsy woman with Koizumi's patented charm—could stir up a nationwide sensation with her confession. Yuko's moment at the top, however, is brief. Takita films her leave-taking with sensitivity, style and the required tear. What a way to go.

Yamato Nadeshiko
Fake Lovers (1998)

Written and directed by Takayoshi Yamaguchi. Produced by Far East Entertainment. With Keiko Sugano, Taiyo Kitakaze, Jiko Uchiyama, Kunitoshi Manda, Masaya Hoshi. (58 mins.)

Takayoshi Yamaguchi made his feature debut in 1993 with Koi no Tasogare (Breakable), a street-level view of Japanese Gen Xers that illuminated its characters with a coolly ironic intelligence, while telling a story of a failing relationship that seemed to come directly from life. It was an impressive performance. I hoped that Koi would lead to bigger and better things for Yamaguchi, but it was not to be. Other young directors grabbed the critical and popular center stage, while he seemed to slip behind the curtain. Now he is back with Yamato Nadeshiko (Fake Lovers), which returns to the themes of Koi, in much the same style and to much the same effect.

The title Yamato Nadeshiko, which the dictionary translates as "a daughter of Japan" and which conjures up an image of traditional Japanese womanhood, is ironic. Though the heroine, Yuka (Keiko Sugano), works desultorily at a Tokyo bar, her real occupation is extracting yen from customers in return for her after-hours companionship. She is, however, no loose-socked cutie living for kicks and designer bags, but a worldly-wise woman who is tiring of the hustle and wants to settle down with a comfortable nest egg.

She decides to tell her three current benefactors that she is biding them sayonara and would appreciate a farewell gift, preferably in large denominations. Afraid, with reason, that this trio may not react to her news with equanimity, she begs an old boyfriend, a roughhewn Tsukiji fishmonger named Takuya (Taiyo Kitakaze), to pose as her latest conquest—and protector. Reluctantly, Takuya agrees. Though knowing every trick in Yuka's well-thumbed book of coquetry and guile, he can't get her out of his system.

This would seem to be an ideal set-up for a sexy romp—She's Gotta Have It in reverse—but Yamaguchi plays against our expectations. Rather than goose his story with lubricious laugh lines and steamy sex scenes, he tells it as a slice of life, with quietly ironic observations that may not be laugh-out-loud funny, but have the resonance of truth. This, Yamaguchi seems to say, is the way a with-it young Japanese woman plays the sexual game in 1996 (when the film was completed). Instead of a retiring, self-sacrificing, eternally pure ideal, Yamaguchi's Yamato Nadeshiko brassily sets out to get what she wants, with no nonsense about love and its various physical and spiritual corollaries. The film's big romantic moment comes when Yuka, in a teasing gesture of friendship, tries to take Takuya by the arm during a walk in the park. Takuya brushes her off with ill-concealed irritation. Who does she take him for—another one of her marks?

The most pathetic of those marks is Aizawa (Kunitoshi Manda), a balding university professor who thinks Yuka is a prize, even after she sashays into his office in a black mini, offhandedly introduces him to her new boyfriend—a scowling Takuya—and coolly demands a thick wad of ten-thousand-yen notes. Not all of her men are such saps, however. When a shaven-headed disco manager named Omura (Jiko Uchiyama) runs into the professor, he steathily extracts ¥200,000 intended for Yuka from his rival's coat. When Takuya comes to claim it, the manager calmly informs him that he is squaring a debt Yuka owes him—and demands the remainder. An abashed Takuya pays. Then there is an actor named Kominami (Mayasa Hoshi) who is staging a one-man show, ostensibly to raise the cash for Yuka's going-away present. But when Yuka and Takuya come to collect, the theater is empty and Kominami is nowhere to be found. When he does finally show his face, at the bar, he is full of smarmy praise for his latest triumph, but has nary a word for his one-time paramour.

Keiko Sugano, who was amusingly caustic as a sister to an irresponsible *manga* artist in *Koi*, does not have the usual equipment for leading ladies in Japanese comedies. Instead of a squeaky, squirmy Miss Bubbles, she is an alto-voiced Miss Average who is more sardonic than sweet, with more ice in her veins than brightness in her eyes. And yet there is something in that thick shock of teased hair, knowing gaze, and slow walk that promises more to her hapless lovers than Miss Bubbles could ever imagine. In movies like this one the girl's gotta have it—and Sugano has it.

But while watching *Yamato Nadeshiko*, I couldn't help wanting more. Scenes that cried out for a comic spin played frustratingly flat. More realistic perhaps, but not as satisfying as early Spike Lee. Yamaguchi may have a pitch-perfect ear for his very Gen X blend of new-found freedoms and old-fashioned avarice, but he is playing slow blues on a tune that calls for more pop and sass.

Yonigeya Hompo 2
Midnight Run 2 (1993)

Directed by Takahito Hara. Screenplay by Takahito Hara, Makoto Masaki, and Yukio Nagasaki. Produced by Towa International. With Masatoshi Nakamura, Miho Takagi, Toshiyuki Hosokawa, Morio Kazama. (100 mins.)

Box-office success is often a matter of timing. If *Yonigeya Hompo*, a black comedy about an agency that helps debtors escape their creditors, had appeared during the bubble economy years it might well have sunk without a trace. When everyone was going to make fortunes on NTT shares, who wanted to reminded about the downside? But the film came out in 1992, when more than a few Japanese were getting dunning letters and looking for a way out. *Yonigeya Hompo* enjoyed a long theatrical run and big success on video. Now, with the line at bankruptcy court showing no signs of shortening, we have *Yonigeya Hompo 2*.

Once again the director is Takahito Hara and the star is the ever-affable Masatoshi Nakamura, but his premise has changed and the plot has thickened. Instead of planning midnight getaways, Masahiko Genji (Masatoshi Nakamura) and his intrepid crew guide debtors to the promised land of personal bankruptcy, beyond the grasp of rapacious creditors. (Appropriately, the name of the agency has been changed, from Midnight Run to Rising Sun.)

Also, instead of the slickly executed slapstick of the first film, the sequel is a fast-paced, tightly plotted drama that remains resolutely dry-eyed, while preserving the spirit and style of its predecessor. Fans worrying about a letdown needn't; if they liked the first film they will probably like the second as well.

In the first scene, a distraught salaryman enters a bank, grabs a female customer (Miho Takagi) and, holding a paper cutter to her throat, demands ¥4,028,562. He then has her fill out a deposit slip in that amount to Toyotomi Finance and hand it to the bewildered teller. "No more debt!" he exclaims with relief. While waiting for the police to arrive, a female hostage hands him a flier from the Rising Sun agency. Later, visiting him in jail, she proposes a solution to his difficulties: personal bankruptcy.

Hara and his collaborators have a flair for the kind of absurdist, topical humor that enlightens and provokes as well as entertains. We may laugh at the film's parade of contemporary grotesques, including the charge-till-you-drop office lady with the nobody-upstairs manner, but we are also learning how to get out of debt—the film is a personal bankruptcy manual. Being in debt is hardly pleasant anywhere, but the Japanese culture of shame can, as *Yonigeya* shows us, make a debtor's life a living hell—and death seem the only escape.

The villains of the film are the *sarakin*—the loan sharks who prey on the credulous and the desperate. The arch-villain is Fukujiro Toyotomi (Toshiyuki Hosokawa), the president and CEO of Toyotomi Finance—he of the slicked hair and funereal voice, who can exude more menace with the flutter of a drooping eyelid than most gangsters can with their entire bodies.

The story centers on one of Toyotomi's victims, a *sarakin* named Shoichi Aratama (Morio Kazama) who is too tenderhearted to put the arm on his customers and who is driven to the wall when Rising Sun escorts one after another through bankruptcy court. Finally Toyotomi, who was once Aratama's employee, agrees to loan his former boss twenty-three million yen on one condition—that he take out a life insurance policy with Toyotomi as the beneficiary. Then Aratama Finance goes belly-up and Aratama finds himself at Rising Sun's door. But even after Aratama declares bankruptcy, Toyotomi refuses to surrender; his specialty is squeezing yen out of bankrupts and Aratama presents the ultimate challenge. If he can break this man, who knows the ins and outs of the business, he can break anybody. Also, he has a personal score to settle with Rising Sun.

In making entertainment from personal misery, *Yonigeya* occasionally goes too far, undercutting the horror of a debtor's suicide with a camera angle that makes the corpse look like a drunk passed out on the kitchen floor. The callousness of this undergraduate black humor can undercut the film itself; how can we care about the characters if the film presents them as caricatures and sniggers at their deaths? Despite its stumbles, *Yonigeya Honpo 2* doesn't self-destruct. Instead it offers well-made comedy with a timely message: bankruptcy isn't scary if everyone does it together. Bad things may happen to good people, but amusing things can also come of bad economies. The *Yonigeya Hompo* series is one of them.

Yukai

The Abduction (1997)

Directed by Takao Okawara. Screenplay by Tadashi Morishita. Cinematography by Daisaku Kimura. Produced by Toho. With Tetsuya Watari, Masatoshi Nagase, Miki Sakai. (109 mins.)

Kidnapping may be a rare crime in the real world, but in Japan it has become a hackneyed device of bad cop-dramas, ranking a not-too-distant second to hostage-taking. Inevitably the victim is a child and inevitably the overwrought mother goes into screaming hysterics when she hears the news, until one longs for a scene of little Taro happily playing Super Mario with his kidnapers, free from overbearing Mom at last.

In a script that won the 1995 Seito Prize, Tadashi Morishita managed to come up with some intriguing variations on the kidnapping theme. First, instead of yet another apple-cheeked Taro, make the victim an executive of a major corporation. Second, instead of the usual cat-and-mouse games, the kidnappers demand that another company executive, an elderly gent whose heavy lifting is limited to hoisting glasses of Suntory Reserve, haul heavy sacks full of ransom money through downtown Tokyo, while the media records every grimace and bead of sweat—until the near-fatal collapse.

Subject two more grandfatherly types to this torture, until the hero, a straight-arrow detective, is seething with rage. "This is no game," he declares. "This is a public execution!" Then, reveal that the three old men are not blameless victims, but responsible for industrial pollution that, twenty-six years ago, poisoned an entire rural community. The cop hero and his young partner, a fiery, impulsive type who learned the art of profiling in the United States, as well as the American way of spouting off to his seniors, are faced with a new dilemma: the good guys and bad guys have exchanged hats. Should they do their duty (*giri*) and arrest the perpetrators, or follow the inclinations of their heart (*ninjo*) and let them get away what is clearly less a scheme of enrichment than a long-delayed protest against injustice?

As the above question indicates, the Takao Okawara film based on this script, *Yukai*, presents new packaging for a traditional Japanese dramatic theme. At first a thriller, it becomes a mystery, and finally a *giri-ninjo* drama. It ends with, not the initially expected bang, but a wrenchingly emotional confrontation between the two principals.

In the film's first act, Okawara and cinematographer Daisaku Kimura create, with the aid of five thousand extras, crowd scenes of a scale seldom seen in recent Japanese films. Watching the media swarm around an aging ransom carrier as he made his agonized way past familiar Tokyo landmarks, I was impressed by not only the impact of this spectacle, but the dedication of the filmmakers, who must have jumped through hundreds of bureaucratic hoops to make it happen.

Playing his first lead role in films in twenty-one years, action-star Tetsuya Watari is true to formula as the stoic detective, but he also reveals the gentle-spirited but angry man under the macho mask. As his Americanized partner, Masatoshi Nagase once again reprises Tom Cruise's more annoying mannerisms, including his high-pitched hysteria. He can also be rawly effective, however, as when he pours out his affection for the senior detective in their final scene.

Japanese independent filmmakers are winning more recognition both at home and abroad, as the triumph of Shohei Imamura's *Unagi* at the 1997 Cannes Film Festival indicates, but the local industry needs to make stronger commercial films if it intends to recapture the mainstream audience. Though hardly the equal of *Die Hard 3* in explosions or *Independence Day* in effects, *Yukai* points the way to future success: a well-constructed script, solid performances, and an ability to cut through swaths of red tape to get the big scenes on the screen. Perhaps one day we'll be able to see half a block of the Ginza blow skyward in a Japanese movie. We can only hope.

Yukie
[1998]

Directed by Hisako Matsui. **Screenplay by** Kaneto Shindo. **Cinematography by** Zensho Sakamoto. **Produced by** Essen Communications. **With** Mitsuko Baisho, Bo Swenson. (93 mins.)

We reviewers ought to have an open mind, even when seeing the umpteenth installment of a series we didn't care for the first time around. That's the ideal. The reality is that we walk into the screening room with prejudices and preconceptions. Alert readers could write the review for us even before the lights go down.

I was hauling my own baggage when I saw *Yukie*, Hisako Matsui's debut feature about a Japanese woman living in Louisiana who discovers she has Alzheimer's disease. First, it came with a seal of approval from the Agency for Cultural Affairs—the kiss of death as far as I am concerned. Second, it was the latest film made by a Japanese director in the United States, with a Japanese star, Mitsuko Baisho in this case. Over the years I've panned such films as regularly as certain of my colleagues sneer at any Hollywood movie with a budget larger than *Pulp Fiction*'s. In trying to leap cultural barriers to film in the United States, Japanese directors often get skewered on stereotypes and their own tin ears for linguistic and cultural nuances. Examples include *Iron Maze*, *Painted Desert*, and *Kyoko*.

Yukie must leap this barrier as well, and because it is set in Baton Rouge, Louisiana—a community whose mores most Japanese know as well as they do those of New Guinea hill tribes—the bar is set even higher. Director Matsui lowered it by basing her film on an Akutagawa Prize–winning novel by Yasuhiko Yoshimeki, who had lived in the place for two years. She also had a script by Kaneto Shindo, the veteran director and scriptwriter whose 1995 *Gogo no Yuigonjo* was a highly-acclaimed film on the problems of aging. Shindo's adaptation keeps the focus properly intimate, while largely avoiding the pat generalizations that so often doom projects of this type. She also has an excellent cinematographer in Zensho Sakamoto, whose muted but vibrant palette gives the

film the right tone of elegiac sadness, without descending to dull solemnity.

Most of all, she has Mitsuko Baisho as Yukie, as a nurse who married a big hunk of Americana named Richard (Bo Swenson) forty-five years ago and came with him to Baton Rouge over her parent's objections. She has since raised two sons and made a home in an alien environment. Unfortunately, Richard's crop-dusting business went into a tail-spin a decade ago, when a partner wrongly blamed him for a poisoning scandal. His reputation in tatters, he is reduced to begging another former Korean War pilot—now a corporate executive—unsuccessfully for a job.

Disaster strikes again when Yukie is diagnosed with Alzheimer's. Richard is convinced that if he can only reopen his case and restore his good name, Yukie will get better and they will have their old life back. But his sons, his daughter-in-law, and even Yukie know better. In the end, he has to acknowledge the truth—that he is saying goodbye to the love of his life.

Baisho plays her role almost entirely in English, with hardly a false note anywhere. Her Yukie is a simple woman who loves her husband, her sons and, despite the racism she has encountered over the years, their country, while being intensely aware of what she is losing. Baisho portrays the gamut of Yukie's emotions, including her affection for her rock-headed, madly devoted man, with no straining for effect. Every look and gesture seems to flow from the character's innermost nature, while registering the progress of her disease. As Richard, Bo Swenson can't quite keep up with his co-star—he is too stolid, plodding, and painfully earnest—but the current running between him and Baisho is genuinely strong. Matsui has less luck with her supporting actors, several of whom are thuddingly obvious amateurs. Also, she does not entirely avoid the squirm factor inherent in her theme. Everyone is so goshdarn noble and selfless—even Richard's quest for vindication stems from his desire for Yukie's recovery—that one begins to long for a few anti-role-models.

Yukie, however, has Mitsuko Baisho and that is enough. One last confession: I've had a big crush on Ms. Baisho for at least two decades—another piece of baggage I carried into the theater, I suppose. Now that she's performed so superbly in a role a dozen years older than her real age, couldn't we see her at least once more in one a dozen years younger? Life isn't fair.

Yume
Dreams [1990]

Written and directed by Akira Kurosawa. **Produced by** Kurosawa Production. **With** Mitsunori Izaki, Chishu Ryu,

Akira Terao, Mitsuko Baisho, Mieko Harada, Martin Scorcese. (120 mins.)

Many directors have an autobiographical streak—Federico Fellini is one example that springs to mind—but perhaps only Akira Kurosawa could have put his dreams on the screen. One reason is industry clout. Kurosawa has climbed from the valley of his middle years, when he despaired of ever making another film, to the sunny uplands of an old age bathed in universal acclaim, as evidenced by his Special Academy Award in 1989. More importantly, his fans, whose ranks include such directorial luminaries as Steven Spielberg, Francis Ford Coppola, and Martin Scorcese, are willing to underwrite and support his talent. Spielberg "presents" and Scorcese stars in *Yume*, Kurosawa's twenty-eighth feature film.

Yume is what its title implies: Kurosawa has filmed eight of his dreams. In the first the Kurosawa character is a five-year old boy (Mitsunori Izaki) watching a wedding procession of human-looking foxes. In the last he is a middle-aged man (Akira Terao) listening to a 103-year-old village patriarch (Chishu Ryu) expound on the good life. Although each of the dreams stands alone, Kurosawa imposes a thematic progression and stylistic unity. *Dreams* is a masterfully guided tour of his nocturnal mind.

Though a movie staple, dreams seldom provide the basis for an entire film, save for fantasies such as *The Wizard of Oz* and *Alice in Wonderland*, which don't really count. Audiences will accept a certain amount of onscreen dreaming as a peep behind a character's psychic curtain (*Wild Strawberries*) or a farcical romp (*The Secret Life of Walter Mitty*), but few directors have been so bold as to test their patience with a two-hour dream sequence. Kurosawa, however, directly and matter-of-factly puts us into his dreamworld. (His only framing device is the title "I dreamed this dream" against a black background.) It is a world at once personal and universal. Although his dreams are those of a Japanese man born in the early years of the century—of Hina Festival dolls come to life and dead comrades returned from lost World War II battles—they have a chills-up-the-spine familiarity.

In dreams we find ourselves stripped of our psychic armor, acting out our innermost fears and desires. (No one is an ironist in their sleep.) Kurosawa replicates the rhythms, language, and atmosphere of those nighttime dramas. I am thinking in particular of the third dream, in which a party of mountain climbers struggle back to base camp in a blinding snow storm. They are trudging forward with the slow, drunken movements of exhaustion. Because this is a dream, Kurosawa prolongs their agony for

what seems an eternity, until we are trudging along with them and feeling the leader's helplessness and terror as his companions sink, one by one, into the snow. The scene is reminiscent of the final battle in *Kagemusha*, in which Kurosawa used the fallen horses to create a slow-motion ballet of death. The effect is stronger in *Yume* because Kurosawa is compelling us to relive a familiar nighttime terror.

In his two films of the 1980s—*Kagemusha* and *Ran*—Kurosawa worked on a epic scale with an energy that seemed amazing for a man in his seventies. But for all their dazzling imagery, the films felt somehow impersonal and remote, as though he were trying to build monuments to his career. In *Yume* he is no longer making grandiose statements, but ranging freely over the course of his inner life and summing it up with unsurpassed insight and beauty. I am reminded of Hokusai, who styled himself "the old man mad about painting" and continued to paint furiously and brilliantly until his death at the age of eighty-nine. If *Yume* is any indication, Kurosawa also has much more to give us in the coming decade.

Yumeji
(1991)

Directed by Seijun Suzuki. Screenplay by Yozo Tanaka. Produced by Arato Genjiro Jimusho. With Kenji Sawada, Masumi Miyazaki, Yoshio Harada. (128 mins.)

Seijun Suzuki has long been a cinematic destructionist. More than two decades ago he told *Cinema 69* magazine that "making things is not what counts. The power that destroys them is... I just don't like construction. I look down on it actually. Everyone says that it's better to sleep. That way you can do what you want."

His latest film, *Yumeji*, puts that philosophy on screen. Though ostensibly based on the life of painter and poet Yumeji Takehisa (1884–1934), it is a 128-minute dream sequence, a voyage to the center of the artist's imaginative world. Takehisa, a representative artist of the Taisho period (1912–26) who painted delicately emaciated women in a manner reminiscent of Aubrey Beardsley, was condemned by his conservative family for his choice of occupation and had several intense, if unhappy, love affairs. But it is Takehisa's inner life, not his biography, that Suzuki wishes to explore. It is, as one might expect from this director, a whimsically chaotic and luxuriantly sensual exploration that makes no attempt at realism, psychological or otherwise. "You should look at this film as you would a book of photographs," says the program. It is good advice; Yumeji's images are its message.

The first is among the most striking and significant. Takehisa (Kenji Sawada) sees a woman in a gorgeous red kimono at a garden party. Fascinated, he tries to draw closer, but his view is blocked by guests tossing paper balloons in the air. None seem to notice what is so blindingly apparent to him; that the woman has her back turned and is standing high up in the branches of a tree. The film depicts his quest to paint this "faceless" woman. But though Takehisa is haunted by her beauty and mystery, he is also pursued by a strange dream, in which he duels with a man in a frock coat, whose face is also hidden, and who draws a final, fatal bead on him just before he wakes up, screaming.

But is Takehisa really awake or in the midst of a newer, stranger dream? He travels to Kanazawa to meet his lover, Hikono (Masumi Miyazaki), but instead encounters Tomoyo, a woman whose husband, Wakiya (Yoshio Harada), has been murdered by a wild, sickle-wielding man named, appropriately, Onimatsu (literally, Devil Pine). Onimatsu had found Wakiya in bed with his wife and killed them both. But Wakiya, sporting a blond wig, emerges from the lake where Onimatsu had dumped his body. An enraged Onimatsu resumes the chase just as Takehisa begins an affair with Tomoyo. From here, as Alice once said, things get curiouser and curiouser. Little of the ensuing romantic roundelay has any relation to the facts of Takehisa's life. He did travel to Kanazawa with Hikono in the summer of 1917, but it is almost certain that the couple did not encounter a blond ghost.

It is also almost certain that Takehisa had little in common with the character portrayed by Kenji Sawada. A former glam-rock singer who went by the stage name Julie, Sawada would seem to an appropriate choice to play a Taisho decadent. But his portrayal is more Sawada than Takehisa, more sex-obsessed superstar than beauty-haunted artist. Sawada brings a needed playfulness and charm to the role, however. The same could be said of Yoshio Harada, who plays Tomoyo's "ghost" husband. A Japanese Lee Marvin, Harada has a ravaged face and a hip, macho persona equally suited to action or comedy. In Yumeji he plays funny—too much so. It's all nonsense anyway, he seems to say, so why bother? Perhaps the wig put him in this don't-care mood.

And should we care? It's not easy. Suzuki wants to mesmerize with his images, both beautiful and bizarre. Our connection with his characters is secondary. Although Yumeji bears Suzuki's flamboyant signature, what is he trying to say? The answer is, quite deliberately, as elusive as a dream.

Yume no Ginga
Labyrinth of Dreams (1997)

Written and directed by Sogo Ishii. Cinematography by Norimichi Kasamatsu. Music by Hiroyuki Onogawa. Produced by KSS. With Rena Komine, Tadanobu Asano. (90 mins.)

Who said that watching a movie is dreaming with your eyes open? Ironically, movies that are merely dreamy quickly become soporific. Sogo Ishii's Yume no Ginga takes us into a dreamworld, but one that absorbs rather than lulls. In the end, though it replicates the atmosphere of a troubled dream, it lacks the emotional charge that makes us wake in a cold sweat.

One creator of that atmosphere is Rena Komine, a teenaged actress who, with her big staring eyes and expression of solemn innocence, seems to have no definite age and belong to no definite era. Ishii has likened her to Hideko Takamine, but though she has the right look for the film's 1950s milieu, she does not self-consciously try to imitate 1950s attitudes. Even so, her performance as a bus conductress who falls in love with her potential murderer is effortlessly authentic.

Ishii has shot Yume in black-and-white, that most dreamlike of mediums. Working with cinematographer Norimichi Kasamatsu, he has created a silver-toned world that is lovely and austere, nostalgically distant and mysteriously present. To ground his dream in real-world emotions, he tells a story that James M. Cain might have written as a sordidly thrilling pulp fiction. The aforementioned bus conductress, Tomiko Tomonari (Rena Komine), has what most young women of her day would consider a ideal job. But though she may be wearing a spiffy uniform and holding a position of authority of a kind once reserved for men, she is bored with the routine and looking for something new. What, she can't quite say.

Then, one day, that something appears in Tatsuo Niitaka (Tadanobu Asano), a new driver. Forbiddingly silent and remote, Niitaka nonetheless exerts a strange attraction over the women in the bus company. There a danger in that attraction, as Tomiko is well aware. Her best friend, a bus conductress in another town, was once engaged to Niitaka and was killed in an accident while he was driving. Just before the accident, Tomiko received a letter from her friend in which she alluded her own death—at the hands of her fiancee. Also, she has heard rumors of a bus driver who seduces his conductresses and then cold-bloodedly murders them. She is convinced that this driver is Niitaka. But rather than expose this fiend, she falls, quite deliberately, under his spell. This, she tells herself, is the big adventure she has long been looking for. She will embark on it, even though it may kill her.

In telling this story, Ishii drains its pulp charge. In the opening credits, he tells us the outcome of Tomiko's adventure: one dark and stormy night, Niitaka, with Tomiko aboard, drives his bus into the path of an oncoming train. The real mystery, he implies, is not whether Niitaka will cause her death, but why Tomiko chooses to become his victim. While exploring that mystery, which is based on a short story published in 1934 by Kyusaku Yumeno, Ishii does not try to solve it. Instead, he amplifies its ambiguities in the pursuit of inner truths. He creates his dreamscape by slowing the pace, muting the feeling tones, and lowering the sexual temperature, until we feel we are watching, not a man and a woman entrapped in a mutually fatal attraction, but two performers in a hieratic ritual, advancing to their foreordained ends. Hiroyuki Onogawa's thrumming ambient music contributes to the hypnotic, ominous atmosphere.

But though Ishii leads us into his dream, he can't quite make us believe it. One problem is the performance of Tadanobu Asano as the driver. The heartthrob of the independent film scene, Asano has the right hooded-eye look for an affectless killer, but he is essentially a physical actor, who can convey menace in a single, explosive gesture. Held to little more than a few significant glances, he seems disembodied, as though he were phoning in his performance from another dimension. His Niitaka drives to his death asleep at the wheel, as Tomiko dreams on, alone.

Yume no Onna
Yearning (1993)

Directed by Tamasaburo Bando. Screenplay by Motoki Yoshimura. Cinematography by Mutsuo Naganuma. Production design by Takeo Kimura. Produced by Shochiku, Asahi Shimbun, Oji Paper, and Asahi National Broadcasting. With Sayuri Yoshinaga, Kirin Kiki, Sumie Kataoka. (98 mins.)

Last year Tamasaburo Bando had a popular success with his first film, Gekashitsu. Only fifty minutes long, its story of a Meiji matron's forbidden passion for a dashing young doctor was the stuff of nineteenth-century romance. Bando filmed it as a soft-focus, slow-motion, hypercharged dream.

His second film, Yume no Onna, is another romance of the Meiji period (1868–1912). Taken

from a shimpa play that was in turn based on a 1903 novel by Kafu Nagai, Yume tells the familiar story of a woman blessed with beauty but thwarted in love and life by an unkind fate. Once the mistress of a rich merchant, Kaede (Sayuri Yoshinaga) was cast out after his death and forced to give her young daughter to strangers. As the film begins, she is a courtesan in a red-light district that fronts Tokyo Bay.

Kaede would seem to be one of the elite in the Oyawata bordello: she wears the finest kimonos, enjoys the service of a faithful attendant (Kirin Kiki), and is the object of a young drug wholesaler's mad passion. In modern Japan, she could be a Ginza hostess in control of her bank account and her life. In the film's Meiji Japan, however, she is a beautiful victim, crushed by obligations to those around her. She must not only pay off her debt to the bordello, but support her aged parents and younger sister. When she hears from an old servant (Sumie Kataoka) that her daughter's foster parents are mistreating her, she acquires another burden—crushing guilt. She has the servant reclaim the child and extends her term at the Oyawata so she can raise it. Her disappointed lover begs her to leave and live with him "if only for a month." When she refuses, he hangs himself.

A renowned Kabuki onnagata (player of female roles), Bando has appeared as Kaede many times on stage. In telling her story, he removes it from the sordid reality of the everyday to a dreamworld full of refined pathos and beauty. That, of course, is also the approach of traditional Japanese drama—and Yume no Onna has the smell of the shimpa stage about it. The bordello is quite obviously a set, and Sayuri Yoshinaga, who made her first movie in 1959, is quite obviously a mature woman playing young. The convention of Japanese theater is that these things do not matter. The reality of film is that they do.

Nonetheless, Yume no Onna has visual allure and inner coherence. The velvety tones of Mutsuo Naganuma's black-and-white photography and the exquisite authenticity of Takeo Kimura's period sets evoke a world at once vividly present and achingly past. Also, Bando understands the period and the characters: he makes us believe that, in some essential way, he is Kaede. (He might have taken Yoshinaga's role if he thought he could get away with it.)

Forever ascribing her misfortunes to fate, Kaede would seem to be its passive slave, but she also possesses a Scarlet O'Hara-like spunkiness. Drifting in a haze of alcoholic despair after the death of her wholesaler, she quickly recovers when her old servant gives her a talking to. "You've got your daughter to care for and your whole life ahead of you," she says. Kaede enthusiastically agrees—and strides forth to meet a customer. She will work harder than ever to give her child a good life! This, as it turns out, is an another fated meeting—the customer is a rich businessman who takes an immediate liking to Kaede, despite her "vampire" reputation, and rescues her and her dependents from debt and penury.

Several years later, Kaede meets her former attendant at the Oyawata and her new replacement there, a girl with the pale beauty and quiet grace of a Kannon statue. The two Kaedes—one a matron who runs a small store in Tsukiji and the other a whore whose father is a poor carpenter—reach an immediate understanding under the romantic light of a gas lamp and a full moon. In their distaste for the men who have bought their bodies ("I have never liked any of them," the first Kaede confesses), their struggles to survive, and their hopes for the future, we see the love, pride, and stubborn ambition that gives their lives meaning. We imagine Kaede, after many more trials, living with her daughter, selling cigarettes from a tiny booth and thinking that it was all worth it. Happy at last.

Yuri

(1996)

Written and directed by Yuji Sakamoto. Produced by Pony Canyon, Max Japan, and Euro. With Maki Sakai, Masatoshi Nagase, Omid Moradi, Issei Ishida. (102 mins.)

Judging from recent Japanese films, Japan would seem to be in a down, despairing mood as it nears the end of the millennium, with old values discredited and no new ones arising to take their place. Younger directors have frequently expressed this end-of-the-tether feeling in the form of fantastic allegory. They yearn for an innocence and purity that they find only in the young, the psychic, and the mad.

Yet another is Yuri, the debut feature of twenty-nine-year-old TV drama scenarist and playwright Yuji Sakamoto. The title is a reference to Yuri Gagarin, the Russian cosmonaut who was the first man in space and who, in the context of the film, becomes a symbol of abstraction from the messy living world to a sphere of pure, dead nothingness. The film itself has nothing do with space travel, a lot to do with the inner travails of the spacey. It describes the pilgrimage of Nami (Maki Sakai), a young woman who offhandedly shoots her lover (Masatoshi Nagase) in an "experiment" bred of boredom and spends the rest of the movie lugging him about in an old refrigerator. For Nietzche, the devaluation of all values was a sobering prospect: abandoning God and

His laws, one contemplated the abyss. For Nami, who floats through life with the value-free innocence of a soap bubble, death is an inconvenience. When an Iranian janitor (Omid Moradi) helps her carry the fridge down a flight of stairs shortly after the shooting, she complains that she is missing a favorite television program.

Sakamoto depicts Nami not as a cold-hearted flake, but as a lovably eccentric free spirit who embarks, fridge in tow, on a journey to the sea, to which she intends to commit her lover's remains. (She is soon calling him "Yuri" because he has made the ultimate trip to the Great Beyond. The name is also a pun on yurei or "ghost.") There is nothing furtive about this journey. Rather, Sakamoto presents it as a fantastic adventure, during which Nami finds find love, meaning, and closure in her own elfish way. In addition to the Iranian, who performs magic tricks and delivers pearls of wisdom in broken English ("Accident is beautiful"), Nami finds a traveling companion in Masayuki (Issei Ishida), a slim, delicately handsome youth who more than matches her in feyness. But though he spends much of the movie sucking on a big green toothbrush and vamping with moist mascara'ed eyes, Masayuki is hot for Nami in the normal male way. When a wacky policeman tells him that Nami is really a robot and gives him a remote control for pushing her buttons, so to speak, he immediately hits the one for seduction—and watches glumly as Nami sashays past him, indifferent.

Bits of foolery like this keep Yuri from succumbing to its own preciousness, but the film's popularity derives, I suspect, from its stylishly photographed and scored romantic fantasy, in which three dishy men compete for the heroine's affections (I'd better not mention the third, or the movie will seem even quirkier on the page than it is on the screen). Nami and the winner of this contest kiss in a driving rainstorm, walk together down an empty railroad track, frolic in the waves and sit side-by-side on the beach staring out at the water—date-movie clichés dressed up in postmodern garb. At certain points, the story stops dead as we are treated to ready-for-MTV video clips, with soulful English-language vocals provided by folkie Janis Ian.

While being a slickly produced entertainment for teenage sensitivos, Yuri offers a vision of narcissistic Peter Pans who play childish games with death and regard a fridge with a body inside as a kind of metaphysical toy. In their world the barriers between fantasy and reality, thought and deed have been obliterated. It's a world that Shoko Asahara, the cult leader who disposed of a few bodies of his own, would find familiar.

Zankyo
Remains of Chivalry (1999)

Directed by Ikuo Sekimoto. Screenplay by Yoshiyuki Kuroda, Ichiro Otsu. Produced by The Zankyo Production Committee. With Masahiro Takashima, Masaya Kato, Yuki Amami, Takeshi Kitano, Hiroki Matsukata, Kaori Takahashi. (111 mins.)

Toei's *yakuza* movies have come to resemble Mike Tyson's boxing career—stretches in the box-office slammer, followed by yet another comeback. But like Iron Mike, they can't shake their old habits and soon the cell doors are clanging shut again.

What's the problem? Toei believes in getting back to the genre basics, but the world has moved on since the days when Ken Takakura, Koji Tsuruta, and Junko Fujii were bestriding the Japanese movie business like so many tattooed colossi. Not only are the stars and the studio system that supported the genre gone, but the formulas that were once so thrilling to audiences have grown stale.

The latest example of Toei's blast-from-the-past approach is Ikuo Sekimoto's *Zankyo*—a "Best Of" boxed collection of *yakuza*-movie clichés. An assistant director under *yakuza* specialists Tai Kato, Norifumi Suzuki, and Sadao Nakajima before making his first contribution to the genre with *Sukeban Taiman Shobu* in 1974, Sekimoto is the directorial equivalent of the graying lounge singer trying, and failing, to channel Frank Sinatra. Sorry guy, but the original was better.

Zankyo is a *ninkyo eiga*—a genre subcategory of films usually set in the late nineteenth to early twentieth centuries: a time once recent enough to be personally familiar, yet remote enough to allow room for fictional license. While plumping for real (i.e., feudal) Japanese values, *ninkyo eiga* are the *yakuza* version of the Robin Hood tales, with only a passing resemblance to the dirty deeds of real-life gangsters.

Zankyo's Robin Hood is Tatsugoro Iwaki (Masahiro Takashima) who begins the film as a young Kyoto brawler, circa 1937. In the opening scene he defeats a rival, the slithery Toyama (Masaya Kato) in a fight to the death, but instead of driving a knife through his rival's black heart he lets him live— a big mistake, as it turns out.

Fast forward three years. Iwaki is now a guest of the Hamanaka Gang in Kyushu. Striding alone into a den of rival gangsters who have been encroaching on Hamanaka turf, he subdues them with his sword, thereby repaying a debt of gratitude to the Hamanaka boss.

His next fateful encounter occurs at a card game. A beautiful dealer (Yuki Amami) exposes three cheats and incurs their wrath. Iwaki springs to her aid, and after skewering one cheat and sending the other two packing, learns that one of the survivors (Takeshi Kitano) had murdered her father. The dealer has been pursuing him ever since with a relentless determination, symbolized by the dragon tattoo on her lovely back. Though tempted by her formidable charms, Iwaki resists them—yet another mistake, if I may say so.

Hit the button to 1942. Iwaki returns to Kyoto, where he assembles a band of brothers and begins to stake out his own turf. His fledgling Iwaki-gumi, however, soon runs afoul of a gang run by his enemy, Toyama. Before the two rivals can settle old scores, a senior boss (Hiroki Matsukata) calls for a truce: Japan is at war and needs the help every able-bodied gangster. Soon Iwaki, Toyama and their men are hauling war materials for the army. But Toyama is still burning to revenge himself on Iwaki—he can never forgive the man who spared his life.

There is much more. Iwaki falls in love with the pure-hearted Chiyoko (Kaori Takahashi), saves a young Korean from Toyama thugs, and survives a Toyama plot to frame him as a thief of army supplies. Finally the war ends and Iwaki is swept up in the chaos of postwar society. While battling nefarious Korean gangsters, fending off Toyama hitmen, and taking care of his *kobun*, Iwaki rises steadily in the Kyoto gang world. But before he can reach the top, he must first prevail in a final confrontation with Toyama. Naturally Iwaki faces his rival—and all his minions—alone.

Director Sekimoto has hailed Masahiro Takashima as the next Ken Takakura. As Iwaki he is suitably big, buff, and close-cropped, but for all his stoic posing, he is only a Takakura stand-in. Sekimoto does a competent job of choreographing his generic set-pieces, including Iwaki's swordplay heroics, but he also gives his actors license to chew the scenery, with ludicrous results. One scene, in which the Korean gangsters expire, grimacing and clawing the air, made my companion laugh so hard he nearly gagged on his mint.

Instead of *Zankyo*, this latest lame attempt to revive Toei's signature genre ought to be titled *Zannen* (Regret)—a disappointment that will probably do for the studio's bottom line what Iron Mike's latest flake-out has done for his career. Tyson needs a new attitude, Toei needs a new idea. Don't hold your breath waiting.

Zenshin Shosetsuka *
A Dedicated Life (1994)

Directed by Kazuo Hara. Produced by Shisso Pro. (157 mins.)

Good documentarians should have something of the pit bull and the saint about them. They need tenacity to uncover stories buried beneath layers of half-truths and lies. Dedication to a higher ideal also helps; the material rewards are seldom adequate for the months and years of searching for the revelatory words and images that make their films come alive.

By this standard Kazuo Hara is an exemplary documentarian indeed. In a career that began in 1972 with Sayonara CP, a film that probed the lives of the physically disabled, Hara has sought out subjects that the mainstream media consider either too difficult or dangerous. His best known film is the 1986 Yuki Yukite Shingun (The Emperor's Naked Army Marches On), which depicts a former soldier's quest for the truth about the Japanese army's deeds in New Guinea. The film's criticism of the Emperor system and its sensational revelation of cannibalism made it a cause célèbre in Japan, while its artistry earned it the Caligari Prize for documentary film-making at the Berlin Film Festival.

In Zenshin Shosetsuka, Hara once again focuses on an extraordinary individual who challenged society's conventions. Born in 1926 in Kurume, Fukuoka Prefecture and raised on a small island near Kyushu, Mitsuharu Inoue became a popular and critically acclaimed writer whose Chi no Mure (Multitudes of the Earth, 1963) was nominated for an Akutagawa Prize. But Hara was attracted to Inoue less because of his work—he had only read one of Inoue's novels prior to meeting him at a lecture in 1986—than his charismatic personality and artistic concerns. "I am a pushover for people [like Inoue] who are skillful agitators," he later wrote. "Two phrases of his captivated me: 'changing relationships' and 'truth and fiction.' They are also the core interests of Shisso Pro, my production company."

Zenshin is accordingly less a literary analysis than a personal exploration of its subject, in all his variety and duplicity. For Inoue, we see, was not only a revered sensei (master), surrounded by disciples who hung on his every word, but as interviews with students, friends and family members make clear, an incorrigible womanizer and liar, who revised his own past as though it were the rough draft of a novel.

The dramatic core of the film, however, is Inoue's battle with cancer during the two years recorded on the screen, from December 1989 to January 1992. Hara did not even know that Inoue was suffering from cancer when he decided to make Zenshin, but he confronts the disease squarely, even going into the operating room to film the extraction of half of Inoue's liver. There is nothing exploitative about Hara's approach; he may probe his interviewees to the limit and take his camera into places where many would hesitate to go, but he makes us feel that, through it all, he is on his subject's side.

Meanwhile Inoue keeps on writing, teaching, and socializing, while battling his disease with everything from modern cancer drugs to quack remedies. But alone with his wife on his return home from liver surgery, he frankly acknowledges that his time may be short.

The film also revisits the events in Inoue's past that shaped the novelist and man, and examines how Inoue reshaped that past to suit his own ends. Appearing on NHK, Inoue recalls how his father—a highly regarded pottery painter—neglected to meet the deadline for submitting applications to the elite junior high schools that Inoue, with his excellent grades, could have entered. "I never forgave him for that," Inoue says, his voice trembling with resentment. Later in the film, however, his younger sister reveals that Inoue failed the entrance exams and that, sailing with him on the boat back to the island after hearing the news, his grandmother feared that he might jump overboard.

Talking about his first love, a Korean girl, Inoue says that she dropped out of the local junior high to work in Nagoya, but later resurfaced at the island's Korean brothel. When Inoue, then fifteen, went to the brothel to see her, he was accosted by and lost his virginity to a thirty-year-old whore. As he left, the other residents bade him a jeering farewell. One of them, he saw as he hurried away, was the girl he had loved.

The story, Hara's interviewees agree, is a complete fiction, and that is how Hara films it, with actors and soft-focus black and white photography. Watching it, we realize that Inoue was creating a necessary myth that both justified his failure at love and elevated it to art. "I knew him a long time and I came to realize that Inoue had truths he couldn't tell anyone," said Jakucho Setouchi, a writer and Buddhist nun who first met him in 1968. "Sometimes, I felt that he had to lie to protect those truths." Now, the lies are no longer needed, but, as Zenshin Shosetsuka shows us so brilliantly, the artist and his art still remain.

Zipangu

(1990)

Directed by Kaizo Hayashi. **Screenplay by** Kaizo Hayashi and Noriyuki Kurita. **Cinematography by** Masatake Tamura. **Produced by** Tokyo Broadcasting System and Ekuze. **With** Masahiro Takashima, Narumi Yasuda, Xiu Jian, Haruko Wanibuchi, Yukio Yamato, Shiro Sano. (119 mins.)

Zipangu is an Edo-period *Raiders of the Lost Ark*. Like Steven Spielberg, director Kaizo Hayashi not only wants to breathe new life into old pulp, but use it to send his audience on a roller-coaster ride. Spielberg puts us in the front seat and sends us roaring through two hours of visual and narrative loop-the-loops. With Hayashi, however, we are never allowed to forget we are on a fantasy ride. Spielberg wants to get our pulses pounding; Hayashi would rather have us admire his imaginative flights.

Some of those flights are indeed amazing. No one but this thirty-three-year-old wunderkind could have dreamed up certain of his images. But the emptiness of the story—the feeling that the images are all we are going to get—gives even the best of his scenes a soap-bubble fragility. I knew I was seeing something, but after the lights went up I had a hard time remembering what it was.

The films begins as a take-off on the classic Miyamoto Musashi story. The hero, Jigoku-goku-raku-maru (Masahiro Takashima), is a renegade samurai with a price on his head. One of the would-be collectors is Teppo Oyuri (Narumi Yasuda), a pretty young bounty hunter who is a dead shot with a pearl-handled revolver. (Her name translates as Pistol Lily). But before she can draw a bead, the hero is attacked by crowd of sword-wielding reward seekers. This sequence, with the hero slashing his way through dozens of opponents without breaking a sweat, is a triumph of choreography that establishes the film's over-the-top tone. Like Spielberg in *Raiders*, Hayashi starts with a climax, then spends the rest of the movie trying to stay the frentic pace.

As the hero, Masahiro Takashima has the swagger, athleticism, and looks of a boys-comic hero. That is also where he seems to have gotten his conception of the role. True, he doesn't need much more than two

dimensions for this film, but he is so blithely fearless, so effortlessly triumphant that I began to root for the bad guys to put the fear of God in him. He nearly meets his match, however, in Teppo Oyuri. She is a little firebrand who falls for the hero only he after bests her in battle and tries to save her life. Narumi Yasuda plays this Karen Allen role to the hilt, but is so much the tomboy (her Dutch-boy hairstyle underscores this trait, just as freckles do in Hollywood films) that when she finally decides that she likes the hero, it as though she's found a pal, not a lover.

When the hero discovers a mysterious golden sword in an ancient burial mound, he unwittingly awakens a warrior (Xiu Jian) who has been sleeping a thousand years. His body half-covered with a blue tattoo but little else, the warrior tears off like a steroid-charged sprinter after the fabled sword and his long-lost love: the Queen of Zipangu—the Land of Gold. Here *Zipangu* takes a leap from samurai-swashbuckler parody to pure fantasy. The change allows Hayashi, together with production designer Takeo Kimura and cinematographer Masatake Tamura, to indulge his love of gorgeous visuals to the fullest. In scenes shot inside the King's palace, the gold of the palace interior and the pastels of the Queen's gown have a distracting vividness. At such moments I wanted to turn off the sound—and the dumb story—and just watch.

But when Jigoku-gokuraku-maru is battling Zipangu kings who look like animated *haniwa* (burial mound figures), the movies descends to the level of the live-action kids' shows that feature costumed heroes and evil robots. Why, I wondered, is this beauty being wasted on this junk? But an affection for the pulp of his film-going and TV-watching childhood seems central to Hayashi's sensibility. Having seen two of his films—*Zipangu* is his third feature—I can sense the size of his talent, but also its limitations. He may have made his *Raiders*, but not his *E.T.* I am not suggesting that he Japanize yet another Spielberg megahit, only that he step outside the film library and take his imagination on a trip deeper than the pop culture detritus of his youth. Who was the kid watching the junk? What were his dreams? His fears? I'm sure the answers would be interesting—if Hayashi remembers.

Index

English Title Finding List

Since the reviews in this book are alphabetized according to their Japanese titles, this finding list is provided for readers who only know a film by its English title. The English title is given first, followed by the Japanese title. Films with the same title in both languages are not listed.

A

Aa, Spring · *Aa, Haru*
The Abduction · *Yukai*
Adrenaline Drive · *Adrenaline Drive*
After Life · *Wonderful Life*
After the Wind Has Gone · *Kaze no Katami*
A-Ge-Man: Tales of a Golden Geisha · *Ageman*
All About Love, Tokyo · *Ai ni Tsuite, Tokyo*
The Anthropology of a Fight Scene · *Shuraba no Ningengaku*
April Story · *Shigatsu Monogatari*
Asian Beat: I Love Nippon · *Asian Beat Nihon-hen: I Love Nippon*
Asian Blue · *Asian Blue: Ukishima Maru Saikon*
August in the Water · *Mizu no Naka no Hachigatsu*

B

Bakayaro! 2 · *Bakayaro! 2: Shiawase ni Naritai*
Bayside Shakedown · *Odoru Daisosasen*
The Beast Must Die: Revenge · *Yaju Shisubeshi: Fukushuhen*
Begging for Love · *Ai o Kou Hito*
Beijing Watermelon · *Pekinteki Suika*
The Bird People in China · *Chugoku no Tojin*
Black Angel, Vol. 1 · *Kuro no Tenshi, Vol. 1*
Bloom in the Moonlight · *Waga Ai no Uta: Taki Rentaro Monogatari*
Blue Fish · *Aoi Sakana*
Body and Soul · *Karada mo Kokoro mo*
The Boy Made in Japan · *Nihonsei Shonen*
Bounce · *Bounce Ko Gals*
Boys, Be Ambitious · *Kishiwada Shonen Gurentai*

Breakable · *Koi no Tasogare*
The Breath · *Umihozuki*
Buddies · *A Un*

C

The Cherry Orchard · *Sakura no Sono*
Circus Boys · *Nijuseiki Shonen Dokuhon*
A Class to Remember · *Gakko*
Congratulations! Condolences · *Ohigaramo Yoku Goshusho-sama*
The Cult Seven · *Shichinin no Otaku*

D

de Chirico's Landscape · *Kiriko no Fukei*
Deborah, the Rival · *Deborah ga Rival*
A Dedicated Life · *Zenshin Shosetsuka*
Deep River · *Fukai Kawa*
Defiled Maria · *Kegareta Maria*
The Dimension Travelers · *Nazo no Tenkosei*
Dr. Akagi · *Kanzo Sensei*
Dog Race · *Inu, Hashiru*
Down the Drain · *Hadashi no Picnic*
Dreams · *Yume*
Dreams of Russia · *Oroshiyakoku Suimutan*
Dying at the Hospital · *Byoin de Shinu to Iu Koto*

E

The Echoes of Folkloric Traditions · *Dozoku no Ranjo*

The Eel · *Unagi*
800 Two Lap Runners · *Happyaku Two Lap Runners*
End of Our Own Real · *Asu Naki Machikado*
Entrails of an Angel: Red Flashback · *Tenshi no Harawata: Akai Senko*
Eternal Monument · *Himeyuri no To*

F

Fag Hag · *Okoge*
Fake Lovers · *Yamato Nadeshiko*
The Fire Within · *Onibi*
Fireworks · *Hana-Bi*
Fishing from the Treetops · *Ki no Ue no Sogyo*
The Forty-seven Ronin · *Shijushichinin no Shikaku*
Free and Easy Special · *Tsuri Baka Nisshi Special*
The Friends · *Natsu no Niwa*

G

Gamera 3: Awakening of the Demon-God Iris · *Gamera 3: Jashin Irisu Kakusei*
Games Teachers Play · *The Chugaku Kyoshi*
Gang Wives: Decision · *Gokudo no Onnatachi: Kejime*
The Geisha House · *Omocha*
Gensenkan Inn · *Tsuge Yoshiharu World: Gensenkan Shujin*
The Gentle Art of Japanese Extortion · *Mimbo no Onna*
The Gentle Twelve · *Juninin no Yasashii Nihonjin*
Getting Any? *Minna Yatteru ka?*
Ghost at a Drinking Joint · *Izakaya Yurei*
Ghost in the Shell · *Kokaku Kidotai*
The Girl of the Silence · *Father Fucker*
Give It All · *Gambatte Ikimasshoi*
Goodbye for Tomorrow · *Ashita*
The Grave and Divorce · *Ohaka to Rikon*
Greetings · *Goaisatsu*
Group Transfer · *Shudan Sasen*

H

Happy-Go-Lucky · *Natsu Jikan no Otonatachi*
Hard-Head Fool · *Bo no Kanashimi*
Heaven and Earth · *Ten to Chi to*
High School Teacher · *Koko Kyoshi*
Hong Kong Nightclub · *Hong Kong Daiyasokai: Touch & Maggie*
Hors de Saison · *Season Off*
House of the Sleeping Beauties · *Nemureru Bijo*
Hug Me, Then Kiss Me · *Watashi o Daite Soshite Kiss Shite*

I

I Can't Study · *Boku wa Benkyo ga Dekinai*
I Don't Have a Grave · *Ohaka ga Nai*
I Find Myself Getting Smaller and Smaller · *Oinaru Gakusei*
I Want to Hear the Wind's Song · *Kaze no Uta ga Kikitai*
In the Silent Suspicious Afternoon · *Shizukana Ayashii Gogo ni*
Invincible Handicapped · *Muteki no Handicap*

K

Kiki's Delivery Service · *Majo no Takkyubin*
Kikujiro · *Kikujiro no Natsu*

L

Labyrinth of Dreams · *Yume no Ginga*
Last Christmas · *Mirai no Omoide: Last Christmas*
The Last Dance · *Daibyonin*
Last Friends · *Kike, Wadatsumi no Koe*
A Last Note · *Gogo no Yuigonjo*
The Learning Circle · *Gakko 2*
Leave the Washing Machine to Me · *Sentakuki wa Ore ni Makasero*
The Legend of the Sea, Sky, and Coral · *Umi Sora Sango no Iitsutae*
Let's Get Happy · *Shiawase ni Naro ne*
Let's Go to the Diet! · *Kokkai e Ikko*
Let's Go to the Hospital · *Byoin e Iko*
Like Grains of Sand · *Nagisa no Sindbad*
Lost Paradise · *Shitsurakuen*
Love Never Dies · *Yamai wa Ki kara: Byoin e Iko 2*
Luminous Moss · *Hikarigoke*

M

Maborosi · *Maboroshi no Hikari*
Madadayo: Not Yet · *Madadayo*
The Man Who Caught the Rainbow · *Niji o Tsukamu Otoko*
The Man Who Killed the Don · *Don o Totta Otoko*
The Man with Two Hearts · *Otokotachi no Kaita E*
Many Happy Returns · *Kyoso no Tanjo*
March Comes in Like a Lion · *Sangatsu no Lion*
Marks · *Marks no Yama*
A Memory of Late Autumn Rain · *Shigure no Koi*
The Meridian in the Mist · *Kiri no Shigosen*
Metallic Boxer · *Tekken*
Midnight Run 2 · *Yonigeya Hompo 2*
Midnight Run 3 · *Daiyonige: Yonigeya Hompo 3*
Moonlight Serenade · *Setouchi Moonlight Serenade*
The Motorcycle Girl · *Autobike Shojo*
Mt. Aso's Passion · *Shikibu Monogatari*

Tokiwa: The Manga Apartment · *Tokiwaso no Seishun*

Tokyo Deluxe · *Heisei Musekinin Ikka Tokyo Deluxe*

Tokyo Fair Weather · *Tokyo Biyori*

Tokyo Holiday · *Tokyo no Kyujitsu*

Tokyo Lullaby · *Tokyo Yakyoku*

Tokyo Siblings · *Tokyo Kyodai*

A Touch of Fever · *Hatachi no Binetsu*

Tough Guys · *Gorotsuki*

Traffic Jam · *Jutai*

Trip to a Strange Kingdom · *Sotsugyo Ryoko: Nihon kara Kimashita*

The Tropical People · *Nettai Rakuen Club*

Turning Point · *Onna Zakari*

Twentieth-Century Nostalgia · *Nijuseiki Nostagia*

Twinkle · *Kira Kira Hikaru*

2 X 2 · *Avec Mon Mari*

U

Uneasy Encounters · *Kowagaru Hitobito*

V

Village of Dreams · *E no Naka no Boku no Mura*

Violent Cop · *Sono Otoko, Kyobo ni Tsuki*

W

War and Youth · *Senso to Seishun*

Watcher in the Ceiling · *Edogawa Rampo Gekijo: Yaneura no Samposha*

We Are Not Alone · *Bokura wa Minna Ikiteiru*

The Weald · *Somaudo Monogatari*

Welcome Back, Mr. McDonald · *Radio no Jikan*

When We Were in Love · *Watashitachi ga Suki Datta Koto*

Whisper of the Heart · *Mimi o Sumaseba*

Will to Live · *Ikitai*

Wind-Up Type · *Nejishiki*

Winter Camellia · *Kantsubaki*

Wizard of Darkness · *Eko Eko Azaraku*

Wizard of Darkness 2: Birth of the Wizard · *Eko Eko Azaraku 2: Birth of the Wizard*

Woman of the Police Protection Program · *Marutai no Onna*

Work on the Grass · *Kusa no Ue no Shigoto*

Y

Yearning · *Yume no Onna*

Directors Finding List

The following list is alphabetical by director, with the films of each director reviewed in this book listed after the director's name.

Ishii, Teruo · *Nejishiki; Tsuge Yoshiharu World: Gensenkan Shujin*

Ishikawa, Jun · *Ki no Ue no Sogyo*

Isomura, Itsumichi · *Gambatte Ikimasshoi*

Itami, Juzo · *Ageman; Daibyonin; Marutai no Onna; Mimbo no Onna; Super no Onna*

Ito, Hidehiro · *Otokotachi no Kaita E*

Ito, Shun · *Pride: Ummei no Toki*

Iwai, Shunji · *Love Letter; Picnic; Shigatsu Monogatari; Swallowtail*

Iwamatsu, Ryo · *Bakayaro 2!: Shiawase ni Naritai; Ohaka to Rikon*

Izumi, Seiji · *Nagare Ita Shichinin; Ohigaramo Yoku Goshusho-sama*

Izutsu, Kazuyuki · *Kishiwada Shonen Gurentai; Nodo Jiman*

Jinno, Hiroaki · *Tsuki kara Kaeru*

Jissoji, Akio · *Edogawa Rampo Gekijo: Yaneura no Samposha*

Kadokawa, Haruki · *Rex: Kyoryu Monogatari; Ten to Chi to*

Kajima, Shun'ichi · *Shudan Sasen*

Kaneko, Shusuke · *F; Gamera 3: Jashin Irisu Kakusei; Mainichi ga Natsuyasumi; Sotsugyo Ryoko: Nihon kara Kimashita*

Kato, Tetsu · *Tada Hitotabi no Hito*

Kawasaki, Hirotsuki · *Spriggan*

Kitano, Takeshi · *Ano Natsu, Ichiban Shizukana Umi; Hana-Bi; Kids Return; Kikujiro no Natsu; Minna Yatteru ka?; Sonatine; Sono Otoko, Kyobo ni Tsuki*

Kiuchi, Kazuhiro · *Kyohansha*

Kobayashi, Masahiro · *Closing Time*

Kogami, Shoji · *Boku ga Byoki ni Natta Wake*

Koike, Masato · *Menda Sakae: Gokuchu no Sei*

Koike, Takashi · *Oinaru Gakusei*

Kojima, Yasufumi · *Rasen no Sobyo*

Kokami, Shoji · *Aozora ni Ichiban Chikai Basho*

Kon, Satoshi · *Perfect Blue*

Konaka, Kazuya · *Nazo no Tenkosei*

Kondo, Yoshifumi · *Mimi o Sumaseba*

Koreeda, Hirokazu · *Maboroshi no Hikari; Wonderful Life*

Koyama, Seijiro · *Gekko no Natsu; Himeyuri no To; Mitabi no Kaikyo; Sakura*

Kumai, Kei · *Ai Suru; Fukai Kawa; Hikarigoke; Shikibu Monogatari*

Kumakiri, Kazuyoshi · *Kichiku Daienkai*

Kumashiro, Tatsumi · *Bo no Kanashimi*

Kuroki, Kazuko · *Roningai*

Kurosawa, Akira · *Hachigatsu no Rhapsody; Madadayo; Yume*

Kurosawa, Kiyoshi · *Cure; Door 3*

Kurotsuchi, Mitsuo · *Jutai*

Maeda, Kenji · *Dozoku no Ranjo*

Makiya, Tsutomu · *Pineapple Tours*

Masuda, Toshio · *Doten*

Matsui, Hisako · *Yukie*

Matsuoka, Joji · *Kira Kira Hikaru; Watashitachi ga Suki Datta Koto*

Matsushima, Tetsuya · *Level*

Matsuura, Masako · *Deborah ga Rival; Hitodenashi no Koi*

Matsuyama, Zenzo · *Niji no Hashi*

Mayuzumi, Rintaro · *Rampo*

Miike, Takashi · *Chugoku no Tojin; Gokudo Kuro Shakai Rainy Dog*

Mitani, Koki · *Radio no Jikan*

Mitsuno, Michio · *Hero Interview*

Miyazaki, Hayao · *Kurenai no Buta; Majo no Takkyubin; Mononoke Hime*

Mochizuki, Rokuro · *Onibi*

Momoi, Kaori · *Goaisatsu*

Mori, Tatsuya · *A*

Morimoto, Koji · *Memories*

Morisaki, Azuma · *Tsuri Baka Nisshi Special*

Morita, Yoshimitsu · *Haru; Keiho Daisanjukyujo; Mirai no Omoide: Last Christmas; Shitsurakuen*

Motohiro, Katsuyuki · *Odoru Daisosasen*

Murahashi, Akio · *Shiawase ni Naro ne*

Murakami, Ryu · *Kyoko*

Muramatsu, Masahiro · *Synch*

Muroga, Atsushi · *Score*

Nagao, Naoki · *Tokyo no Kyujitsu*

Nagasaki, Shin'ichi · *Nurse Call; Romance; Shikoku*

Nakagawa, Yosuke · *Aoi Sakana*

Nakahara, Shun · *Coquille; Juninin no Yasashii Nihonjin; Lie, Lie, Lie; Season Off; Sakura no Sono*

Nakajima, Sadao · *Don o Totta Otoko; Gokudo no Onnatachi: Kejime*

Nakajima, Takehiro · *Okoge*

Nakajima, Tetsuya · *Beautiful Sunday; Natsu Jikan no Otonatachi*

Nakata, Hideo · *Ring 2*

Nakata, Toichi · *Osaka Story*

Narahashi, Yoko · *Winds of God*

Narita, Yusuku · *Bakayaro 2!: Shiawase ni Naritai*

Negishi, Kichitaro · *Chibusa; Kizuna*

Ngai, Lee Chi · *Fuyajo*

Nishikawa, Katsumi · *Ippai no Kakesoba*

Nobi, Akira · *Secret Waltz*

Obayashi, Nobuhiko · *Ashita; Kaze no Uta ga Kikitai; Mizu no Tabibito: Samurai Kids; Onna Zakari; Pekinteki Suika; Sada; Seishun Dendekedekedeke*

Ochiai, Masayuki · *Parasite Eve*

Subject Guide

The following list is organized by theme or content.

Afterlife

Ashita; Futari; Izakaya Yurei; Love Letter; Wonderful Life; Mirai no Omoide Last Christmas; Ohaka ga Nai; Poppoya

Anthologies

Bakayaro 2!: Shiawase ni Naritai; Boku ga Byoki ni Natta Wake; Goaisatsu; Kowagaru Hitobito; Shizukana Ayashi Gogo ni

Aged, problems of

Daiyukai: Rainbow Kids; Bokuto Kidan; Goaisatsu; Gogo no Yuigonjo; Hachigatsu no Rhapsody; Ikitai; James no Yama; Madadayo; Nemureru Bijo; Somaudo Monogatari; Yukie

Animation

Black Jack; Heisei Tanuki Gassen Pompoko; Kokaku Kidotai; Kurenai no Buta; Majo no Takkyubin; Memories; Mimi o Sumaseba; Mononoke Hime; Omoide Poro Poro; Perfect Blue; Shinseiki Evangelion: Gekijoban Shinto Shinsei; Spriggan

Biopics

Rikyu; Waga Ai no Uta: Taki Rentaro Monogatari

Buddy Flicks

A Un; Hanabi; Inu, Hashiru

Childhood

E no Naka no Boku no Mura; Gakko no Kaidan; Ie Nakiko; Kikujiro no Natsu; Mizu no Tabibito; Natsu no Niwa; Ohikkoshi; Omoide Poroporo; Shonen Jidai; Umi Sora Sango no Iitsutae; The Chugaku Kyoshi

Comedy, social satire

Ageman; Bakayaro 2!: Shiawase ni Naritai; Beautiful

Sunday; Billiken; Boku ga Byoki ni Natta Wake; Bokura wa Minna Ikiteiru; Byoin e Iko; Daiyonige: Yonigeya Hompo 3; Heisei Musekinin Ikka Tokyo Deluxe; Ikinai; Inu, Hashiru; Jutai; Kokkai e Iko; Kyoso no Tanjo; Marutai no Onna; Mimbo no Onna; Minna Yatteru ka; Shudan Sasen; Super no Onna; Yamai wa Ki Kara: Byoin e Iko 2; Yonigeya Hompo 2

Comedy, mainstream

119; Daiyukai: Rainbow Kids; East Meets West; Himitsu no Hanazono; Hong Kong Daiyasokai: Touch & Maggie; Izakaya Yurei; Juninin no Yasashi Nihonjin; Lie, Lie, Lie; Menkyo ga Nai!; Nettai Rakuen Club; Niji o Tsukamu Otoko; Nodo Jiman; Odoru Daisosasen; Ohaka ga Nai; Radio no Jikan; Shiawase ni Naro ne; Shichinin no Otaku; Shiko Funjatta; Sotsugyo Ryoko: Nihon kara Kimashita; Takkyu Onsen; Tsuri Baka Nisshi Special

Cop drama

Hanabi; Marks no Yama; Odoru Daisosasen; Onna Keiji Riko: Seibo no Fukaki Fuchi; Yukai

Delinquent youth

Bounce Ko Gals; Nihonsei Shonen; Endless Waltz; Junk Food; Kids Return; Kishiwa Shonen Gurentai; Love & Pop; Secret Waltz

Disabled

Ano Natsu, Ichiban Shizuka na Umi; Kaze no Uta o Kikitai; Muteki no Handicap; Shikibu Monogatari

Documentary

A; Dozoku no Ranjo; Menda Sakae: Gokuchu no Sei; Muteki no Handicap; Somaudo Monogatari; Zenshin Shosetsuka

New Wave

Adrenaline Drive; Dangan Runner; Nihonsei Shonen; Far East Babies; Hadashi no Picnic; Helpless; Kegareta Maria; Keiko Desukedo; Kichiku Daienkai; Kusa no Ue no Shigoto; Love & Pop; Sangatsu no Lion; Mizu no Naka no Hachigatsu; Picnic; Porno Star; Postman Blues; Pupu no Monogatari; Samehada Otoko & Momojiri Onna; Synch; Tada Hitotabi no Hito; Tokyo Kyujitsu; Tokyo Fist; Umihozuki; Unlucky Monkey; Wild Life; Yuri

Osaka

Billiken; Kishiwada Shonen Gurentai; Osaka Monogatari

Parent-child relations

Ai o Kou Hito; Autobike Shojo, Crepe; Father Fucker; Mainichi ga Natsuyasumi; Musuko; Poppoya

Period films (to 1868)

Gohime; Kaze no Katami; Misty; Mononoke Hime; Niji no Hashi; Onnagoroshi Abura Jigoku; Oroshiyakoku Suimutan; Rikyu; Roningai; Sharaku; Shijushichinin no Shikaku; Ten to Chi to; Zipangu

Period films (after 1868)

An Un; Bokuto Kidan; Doten; E no Naka no Boku no Mura; Gekashitsu; Hitodenashi no Koi; James no Yama; Nijuseiki Shonen Dokuhon; Omocha; Sada; Shi no Toge; Tokiwaso no Seishun; Yume no Onna; Yumeji

Post-adolescent crisis

Gorotsuki; Hatachi no Binetsu; Helpless; Kichiku Daienkai; Romance; Koi no Tasogare; Tokiwaso no Seishun

Problem films

Ai Suru, Alice Sanctuary; Bounce Ko Gals; Father Fucker; Focus; Gakko; Gakko 2; The Chugaku Kyoshi

Relationship films

Chibusa; Avec Mon Mari; 2/Duo; Endless Waltz; Karada mo Kokoro mo; Kegareta Maria; Okaeri; Romance; Season Off; Shi no Toge; Koi no Tasogare; Tokyo Biyori; Tokyo Yakyoku; Watashitachi ga Suki Datta Koto; Yamato Nadeshiko

Religious themes

Kyoso no Tanjo; Shikibu Monogatari; Shinseiki Evangelion

Salaryman and OL

Aozora ni Ichiban Chikai Basho; Ohigaramo Yoku Goshuso-sama; Shall We Dance?; Shudan Sasen; Tsuri Baka Nisshi Special

Sports

Gambatte Ikimasshoi; Shiko Funjatta; Shall We Dance?; Takkyu Onsen; Tekken; Tokyo Fist

Supernatural

Eko Eko Azaraku; Eko Eko Azaraku 2; Futari; Izakaya Yurei; Kiriko no Fukei; Night Head; Winds of God; Poppoya

Surrealism on the screen

Tsuge Yoshiharu World: Gensenkan Shujin; Nejishiki; Nemuru Otoko; Tokyo Kyujitsu; Untama Giru; World Apartment Horror; Yume; Yumeji

Teen Films

Alice Sanctuary; Boku wa Benkyo ga Dekinai; Bounce Ko Gals; Deborah ga Rival; Eko Eko Azaraku; Eko Eko Azaraku 2: Birth of the Wizard; Far East Babies; Gambatte Ikimasshoi; Happyaku Two Lap Runners; Kids Return; Kishiwada Shonen Gurentai; Kono Mado wa Kimi no Mono; Mimi o Sumaseba; Nagisa no Sindbad; Nazo no Tenkosei; Nijuseiki Nostalgia; Sakura no Sono; Seishun Dendekedekedeke

Woman power

Ageman; Avec Mon Mari; Bounce Ko Gals; Eko Eko Azaraku; Eko Eko Azaraku 2: Birth of the Wizard; Gokudo no Onnatachi; Gambatte Ikimasshoi; Gonin 2; Love & Pop; Majo no Takkyubin; Marutai no Onna; Mimbo no Onna; Mononoke Hime; Onna Zakari; Shikibu Monogatari; Super no Onna; Yamato Nadeshiko; Yume no Onna

World War II and aftermath

Asian Blue: Ukishima Maru Saikon; Gekka no Natsu; Hachigatsu no Rhapsody; Hikarigoke; Himeyuri no To; Kanzo Sensei; Kike, Wadatsumi no Koe; Mitabi no Kaikyo; Natsu no Niwa; Pride: Ummei no Toki; Rakuyo; Senso to Seishun; Setouchi Moonlight Serenade; Shonen Jidai; Winds of God

Yakuza

Adrenaline Drive; Aoi Sakana; Bo no Kanashimi; Dangan Runner; Don o Totta Otoko; Gokudo Kuro Shakai Rainy Dog; Gokudo no Onnatachi; Gonin; Gonin 2; Gorotsuki; Kamikaze Taxi; Kantsubaki; Keisho Sakazuki; Kids Return; Kishiwada Shonen Gurentai; Kizuna; Kuro no Tenshi, Vol. 1; Level; Mimbo no Onna; Nobody; Nude no Yoru; Onibi; Otokotachi no Kaita E; Porno Star; Postman Blues; Samehada Otoko & Momojiri Onna; Score; Secret Waltz; Shiawase ni Naro ne; Sonatine; Sono Otoko Kyobo ni Tsuki; Unlucky Monkey; Wild Life; Yaju Shisubeshi: Fukushuhen; Zankyo